The History of the County of Bruce and of the Minor Municipalities Therein, Province of Ontario, Canada

County Council of Bruce for 1905-6 and Officers.

THE HISTOR.

OF THE

County of Bruce

AND OF THE MINOR MUNICIPALITIES THEREIN,

Province of Ontario, Canada

BY

NORMAN ROBERTSON

Treasurer of the County of Bruce
Secretary Bruce County
Historical Society

TORONTO
WILLIAM BRIGGS
1906

AUTHOR'S INTRODUCTION.

As the numbers became reduced of those who had entered the county of Bruce as its first settlers, a desire prevailed that, ere it was too late, an attempt be made to gather from their lips the story of the pioneer days; as this, with an accurate narrative of the early evolution of Bruce, must be obtained, if ever, before those who had been the active participants had passed away. In the preface to the Atlas of the County, published by H. Belden & Co., in 1880, is to be found the first effort made in this direction. This Atlas, however, was an expensive volume, and is in the possession of but few, and the historical sketch contained therein is but little known. In 1896 the County Council offered a prize of $50 for the best paper on the history of the county. In response to this, two papers were submitted, one written by John McNabb, the other by the author of this volume. Both of these papers were considered to possess such merit that the Council offered to give to each of the writers the prize offered, provided that two additional chapters be written—one on the Schools of Bruce, and the other on the Militia and Volunteers of the County. These two chapters were supplied by the writer. After paying the promised reward, the County Council let matters rest, taking no steps to publish the manuscripts submitted. From the foregoing it may be seen that a knowledge of any historical facts relating to the county has been largely confined to the recollections of the oldest inhabitants, and to them only.

The two historical sketches above referred to were prepared along different lines. Mr. McNabb wrote largely of the history of the several minor municipalities. The other sketch was a continuous historical narrative of the county as a whole. Perceiving that each form possessed merits the other had not, and thinking that a larger work combining these two forms would cover every historical feature

iii

necessary to be recorded, the writer suggested to Mr. McNabb a compilation of the two narratives. Nothing, however, was done to carry out the suggestion. After thinking it over for two or three years, the author resolved to start *de novo* and write a History of the County of Bruce along the line spoken of above. Putting both of the above papers aside, work in the way of gathering necessary material was commenced. It was not long before the author became aware that he had not commenced a day too soon. Death was very busy among the old pioneers, and in a short time he would have been too late. During the past eight years scores of old settlers have been personally interviewed; those who are no longer residents of the county have been corresponded with; the records of the county offices at Walkerton and Goderich have been searched, and also those of many of the minor municipalities. Various Government Departments at Ottawa and Toronto have, on application, supplied documents full of interesting historical facts. The libraries of Parliament have also furnished a quota of information. Files of old newspapers have been closely scanned, and no stone has been left unturned to secure material for a full and accurate history of the county and of the minor municipalities therein.

The first eleven chapters of this work refer to the county at large. Then follow twenty-seven chapters, each of which deals with a separate minor municipality. This method may have resulted in some repetition, but only where for the sake of the narrative it has been unavoidable, which, under the circumstances, the reader is asked to excuse.

The author has met with the greatest kindness and willingness to oblige from every one from whom information has been sought. He desires to tender his most hearty thanks to all those who have so aided him. Especially would he mention the late **Thomas Adair;** W. R. Brown and Henry Smith, of the Crown Lands Department; W. S. Gould, County Clerk of Bruce; W. M. Dack, Registrar, and George A. McKay, Deputy Registrar of the County; the late Fred Lamorandiere, Indian interpreter, and the several county newspapers, from the columns of which many items have been culled. **His** thanks are also markedly due to James Warren, C.E., who generously permitted his large map of the county to be used for the purpose of obtaining the plates from which the sixteen maps of the townships contained herein are printed.

The expense of publishing a volume such as this is greater than is generally imagined. To help over this obstacle the County Council of Bruce, in a broad-minded, liberal spirit, granted one thousand dollars to the Bruce County Historical Society—under whose auspices this volume is issued—to assist in publishing it, on the understanding that the sum granted be refunded out of the first sales of the book. In connection with this grant a committee, consisting of A. W. Robb, William McDonald and W. J. Henry, was appointed by the County Council for consulting purposes.

In writing this History the author has done so with a conscientious desire to avoid writing simply for effect. His effort has been to give a truthful historical narrative, lightened up with such local coloring as was available from the individual incidents and experiences of the pioneers. These personal experiences are fittingly narrated in a history of the county, for when the early settlers pass away there will be no one left to tell at first-hand the tales of the backwoods life of the pioneers of Bruce. While conscious of many defects in literary style, the author sends this volume forth with hopeful anticipation of a kindly reception from all those whose home is in, or whose home memories are associated with, the county of Bruce.

NORMAN ROBERTSON.

WALKERTON, ONT.

CONTENTS.

CONTENTS

APPENDICES.

ILLUSTRATIONS.

HISTORY OF THE COUNTY OF BRUCE.

CHAPTER I.

THE SURRENDER OF THE INDIAN TITLE.

"To the lands in this Province acquired by conquest, the British Crown has invariably waived its right until what the Crown has been pleased to recognize as the Indian title has been extinguished by a treaty of surrender."
—*Mr. Justice Gwynne.*

DURING the period which has elapsed since the red man of this continent came first in contact with his pale-faced brother, he has experienced at the hands of the latter a process whose general trend has been toward the extinction of his race and the spoliation of his territories. To-day we find that his numbers are largely reduced, and his lands, both forest and prairie, have passed from his possession. At times it has been the bloody hand of war that snatched from the Indians their ancestral inheritance. At others this process of divestment was as effectively, but more peacefully, accomplished while sitting in conference at the council fire, smoking the pipe of peace with white men sent to treat with them; there, yielding to plausible and beguiling arguments, the simple-minded Indians have by treaty surrendered their territories for a comparative trifle. Four centuries ago, from the Atlantic to the Pacific, this continent formed the hunting ground of large numbers of Indian tribes. To-day, owing to the causes above recited, supplemented by the ravages of disease and "firewater," the Indians have been dispossessed of their lands, while their reduced numbers find ample accommodation and provision in the reservations that have been set apart for them by the governments of Canada and the United States. The British Government in its dealings with the Indians has always manifested a liberal and honorable spirit, as well as a fair regard for their treaty rights. The result of this has been that Canada has known no merciless and bloody Indian wars, and the Indians who live under the British flag, although diminished in numbers,

1

have made fair progress in the path of civilization, entertaining
meanwhile friendly feelings toward the whites

Our knowledge of the Indian tribes who have resided in the territory now comprised in the county of Bruce and adjacent thereto
commences with the advent of the French explorers and the Jesuit
missionaries in the early part of the seventeenth century. At that
time a branch of the great Algonquin family of Indians inhabited
the Manitoulin Islands, with scattered bands to be found in what
is now known as the Saugeen peninsula; these bore the tribal name
of the Ottawas To the south and east there dwelt the Tobacco
nation, or Wyandottes, whose territories extended from the Blue
Hills, near Nottawasaga Bay, to the mouth of the Menesetung, or
Maitland River Yet further east dwelt the Hurons, in the district
north of Lake Simcoe, a tribe whose memory is perpetuated by the
broad lake which bears their name, but who as a nation were almost
exterminated by their inveterate foes, the Iroquois. This nation,
after their victory over the Hurons, proceeded to occupy all the
lands in the peninsula between Lake Ontario and Lake Huron.
How the Iroquois were in turn dispossessed by the Ojibways,[1] or
Chippawas, is here given, in the form of a condensed extract, from
a book written by one of that nation [2]

"The Ojibways, who, prior to the extirpation of the Hurons and
Wyandottes, dwelt in the Lake Superior country, annually sent
some of their number to trade with the French at Quebec or Montreal. A party of these were waylaid and killed by the Iroquois.
Threats of reprisals were treated by the latter with scorn. After
a second party had been similarly attacked and slain, a council of
the nation was held, resulting in some of their chiefs being sent to
confer with the Iroquois. The meeting was held at Saugeen, and
resulted in the Iroquois agreeing to pay a bale of furs for each
man that had been killed, and in addition granted permission to
the Ojibways to pass peaceably on trading trips to Montreal. This
treaty held good for three years, when bands of Iroquois waylaid
simultaneously several parties of Ojibways, returning from a trading
journey. This happened in the fall of the year, too late in the
season to commence warlike operations; so the war decided upon

[1] "Ojibway" is the correct name of this tribe, but "Chippawa" is that
most generally used It is of this tribe that Longfellow writes in
"Hiawatha"

[2] "The Traditional History of the Ojibway Nation." By George Copway,
or Kah-ge-ga-gah-bowh, Chief of the Ojibway nation Published in 1850.
See also "History of the Ojibway Indians," by Rev Peter Jones, for statements substantiating Copway's account

was put off until the following spring In the meantime, runners
were sent to the various allies of the nation, dwelling in the region
between the west end of Lake Erie and the head-waters of the
Mississippi, to join them in the coming war. In the month of May
following, the combined forces gathered in two parties, one at Lake
St. Clair and the other at Sault Ste. Marie, seven hundred canoes
being there assembled. This latter party divided into two bands
One advanced on the enemy by way of the Ottawa valley, while the
other proceeded to Penetanguishene. The Lake St. Clair division
at the same time came up the east coast of Lake Huron to the
mouth of the Saugeen River, where a fierce battle was fought with
the Iroquois, who ultimately gave way and fled before the savage
onslaught of the Ojibways"

Further details of the conflict carried on between these two
Indian nations would be foreign to our subject. Suffice it to say,
that the Ojibways succeeded, after several fiercely fought battles,
in driving the Iroquois south of Lake Ontario, and retained possession of the territories obtained by their victories until surrendered
by treaty to the Crown
The treaty by which the Indian title was surrendered to that
tract of land comprising the original county of Bruce, viz, the
townships of Saugeen, Arran, Bruce, Elderslie, Kincardine, Greenock,
Brant, Huron, Kinloss, Culross and Carrick, was concluded by Sir
Francis Bond Head, at Manitowaning, on August 9th, 1836, the
consideration given to the treating tribes being "twelve hundred
and fifty pounds per annum, as long as grass grows or water runs."
The treaty itself is such an interesting document that it is here
given in full·

" My CHILDREN :—
 "Seventy snow seasons have now passed away since we met in
Council at the crooked place (Niagara), at which time and place
your Great Father, the King, and the Indians of North America
tied their hands together by the wampum of friendship
 "Since that period various circumstances have occurred to
separate from your Great Father many of his red children, and as
an unavoidable increase of white population, as well as the progress
of cultivation, have had the natural effect of impoverishing your
hunting grounds it has become necessary that new arrangements
should be entered into for the putpose of protecting you from the
encroachments of the whites.
 "In all parts of the world farmers seek for uncultivated land as
eagerly as you, my red children, hunt in your forest for game If
you would cultivate your land it would then be considered your own

property, in the same way as your dogs are considered among your-selves to belong to those who have reared them; but uncultivated land is like wild animals, and your Great Father, who has hitherto protected you, has now great difficulty in securing it for you from the whites, who are hunting to cultivate it.

"Under these circumstances, I have been obliged to consider what is best to be done for the red children of the forest, and I now tell you my thoughts.

"It appears that these islands on which we are now assembled in Council are, as well as all those on the north shore of Lake Huron, alike claimed by the English, the Ottawas and the Chippewas

"I consider that from their facilities and from their being sur-rounded by innumerable fishing islands, they might be made a most desirable place of residence for many Indians who wish to be civil-ized, as well as to be totally separated from the whites; and I now tell you that your Great Father will withdraw his claim to these islands and allow them to be applied for that purpose

"Are you, therefore, the Ottawas and Chippewas, willing to relinquish your respective claims to these Islands and make them the property (under your Great Father's control) for all Indians whom he shall allow to reside on them: if so, affix your marks to this my proposal.

> " F. B Head.
> " J. B Assekinack.
> " Mokommunish (totem).[1]
> " Tawackuck.
> " Kimewen (totem).
> " Kitchemokomon (totem).
> " Pesiatawick (totem)
> " Paimausegai (totem).
> " Nainawmuttebe (totem).
> " Mosuneko (totem).
> " Kewuckance (totem).
> " Shawenauseway (totem).
> " Espaniole (totem)
> " Snake (totem).
> " Pautunseway (totem).
> " Paimauqumestcam (totem).
> " Wagemauquin (totem).

"Manitowaning, 9th August, 1836."

[1] *Totem* Some natural object, usually an animal with which the mem-bers of a clan or family connect themselves. Thus, among the Algonquin Indians, the name Bear, Wolf, Tortoise, Deer or Rabbit serves to designate each of a number of clans into which the race is divided A man belonging to such a clan being himself actually spoken of as a Bear, a Wolf, etc, and the figure of these animals indicate the clan in the native picture writing." (*Ency. Dictionary.*)

" To the Saukings:

" My Children,

" You have heard the proposal I have just made to the Chippewas and Ottawas, by which it has been agreed between them and your Great Father that these Islands (Manitoulin), on which we are now assembled, should be made, in Council, the property (under your Great Father's control) of all Indians whom he shall allow to reside on them.

" I now propose to you that you should surrender to your Great Father the Sauking (Saugeen) Territory[1] you at present occupy, and that you shall repair either to this Island or to that part of your territory which lies on the North of Owen Sound, upon which proper houses shall be built for you, and proper assistance to enable you to become civilized and to cultivate land, which your Great Father engages forever to protect for you from the encroachments of the whites.

" Are you, therefore, the Sauking Indians, willing to accede to this arrangement; if so, affix your marks to this my proposal.

" Manitowaning, 9th August, 1836.

" Witness:

" T. G. Anderson, S.I.A.
" Joseph Stinson, Genl. Supt. of
   Wesleyan Missions.
" Adam Elliott.
" James Evans.
" F. L. Ingall, Lieut. 15th Regt.,
   Commanding Detacht.
" Talfourd W. Field, Distrt.
   Agent."

" F. B. Head.
" Metiewabe (totem).
" Alexander (totem)
   Kaquta Bunevairear.
" Kowcisawis (totem).
" Mettawanash (totem).

The Indians who after the Manitowaning treaty located permanently on the Bruce peninsula were largely of the Ojibway tribe, incorporated with whom were some Pottawatamies, Tawas, and a few stragglers from other tribes.

By a " Royal Deed of Declaration," dated 29th June, 1847, it is provided for these—" That the said Ojibway Indians and their posterity for ever, shall possess and enjoy and at all times hereafter continue to possess and enjoy the said above tract of land (the Bruce peninsula), or the proceeds of the sale thereof—for the use and bene-

[1] " The hunting grounds in those days belonging to the Saugeen and Newash Indians, extended from Meaford to the Maitland River, and included all the watershed to the Caledon Mountains, as well as the Indian Peninsula." So says Fred. Lamorandiere, Chief Interpreter at Cape Crocker, an authority elsewhere quoted.

fit of the said Ojibway Indians and their posterity." As a result
of the provisions of this deed, when the lands in the peninsula ultimately came into the market, the sale was under the control of the
Indian Department, the proceeds of the sales being funded and the
interest thereon paid to the Indians, instead of a fixed annuity, as
it otherwise would have been, according to the generality of Indian
treaties. In many ways the settlers who took up lands in the peninsula would have preferred that the lands had been sold by the Crown
Lands Department, as were the other lands in the county of Bruce.
The method adopted has, however, been a source of benefit, to those
wards of the government, the Indians interested. All the lands
in the peninsula and adjacent islands, being those mentioned in
the deed above referred to, have gradually been surrendered to
the Crown, with the exception of the Indian reserves. Of these
reserves there is one at the mouth of the Saugeen River, one at
Chief's Point on Lake Huron, one at Cape Croker on the Georgian
Bay, and a reserve for hunting purposes in the township of St.
Edmunds The process of surrender has been effected under various treaties, which will be briefly referred to.

The first land to be surrendered was that part of the "Half-mile
Strip" now included in the townships of Arran and Derby. This
was on September 2nd. 1851 It was made for the purpose of
obtaining a direct road, which the government agreed to open,
between the Saugeen and the Newash (Owen Sound) reservations.
The negotiations for the ceding of this small strip took a long time,
four years or so Long after the surrender the Indians complained
of not receiving satisfactory compensation for the lands sold, inasmuch as a direct road was not opened until 1866

The next, and by far the largest surrender made of lands, was
that of the Saugeen peninsula, effected by a treaty bearing date
October 12th. 1854 [1] This was negotiated by Laurence Oliphant, a
man whose reputation as an author is widely and well known, who
at that time was Secretary to Lord Elgin, the Governor-General,
and also Superintendent-General of Indian Affairs Assisting him
on this occasion were James Ross, M P P , of Belleville; Charles
Rankin. P L S . of Owen Sound and Alexander McNabb, Crown
Lands Agent, of Southampton The negotiations were conducted
in the church of the Saugeen band of Indians. As an inducement
to the Indians to make the surrender, Mr. Oliphant offered, " That

[1] See Appendix A for a copy of this treaty

the lands when surveyed should be sold by auction, and that separate titles to farm lots should be granted to the Indians within their own reserves " The non-fulfilment of this last clause was a cause of complaint for many years by the Indians This was not the only trouble and dispute over this treaty. A more serious one arose regarding the boundary between the Saugeen Reserve and the village of Southampton. The Indians claimed that "Copway's Road" was the boundary agreed upon, while the treaty describes it as "a straight line running due north from the river Saugeen," starting at a given point. This disagreement, the result of a misunderstanding, issued as follows: The survey of the town-plot of Southampton, north of the river, was commenced early in May, 1855, Charles Rankin, P.L.S., having the contract therefor. He sent on a party under Mr. George Gould,[1] who had no difficulty with the Indians until the survey entered on the lands lying north of the Copway Road, the wording of the treaty warranting the survey of these lands. The Indians, thinking otherwise, manifested opposition. The stakes and posts set up to mark the survey were removed and threats were freely uttered Mr. Gould, of course, stopped the survey, and the matter was reported to the Government. The Indians meanwhile called a council, which appointed a deputation consisting of four chiefs, to be accompanied by the Rev C Van Dusen, a minister of the Methodist Church, to wait upon the Governor-General, to lay their version of the dispute before him. On the arrival of the deputation at Quebec, they were informed by Lord Bury, at that time Superintendent-General of Indian Affairs, that they must first obtain a letter from their local superintendent, Capt T. G. Anderson (who resided at Cobourg), before they could see and interview His Excellency The deputation, not having such a letter, failed to obtain a hearing, and returned home much disappointed. Throughout the tribe feeling ran high at the insult— for so they interpreted the reception given their chiefs in Quebec. The more hot-headed were for donning their war paint and proceeding to extremes. Mr. Fredk. Lamorandiere, Indian Secretary at Cape Croker, has furnished the writer with a description of the conference by which an amicable settlement was arrived at, which is here given in his own words, as follows: "Without loss of time Lord Bury came to Owen Sound (June, 1855) with a staff of officers, and cited the Saugeen Indian chiefs to appear before him there,

[1]Afterwards, and for many years, clerk of the county of Bruce

sending a special courier to personally deliver the message. The chiefs, however, not being in good humor, flatly refused. A second message more conciliatory in tone was dispatched, but to no effect. At last, after long parleying, it was agreed that each party come half way, to the 'Flood-wood Crossing,' as the place was then called, now Allenford, where a regular Pow-wow was held in full Indian style, commencing with a feast. After this was disposed of, Capt. T. G. Anderson,[1] the Indian Superintendent of the District, an old, wily Indian trader, who knew the Indian character and the means to please them, conducted the proceedings by dancing the pow-wow in a circle around the Council-fire. A lot of young braves followed. Immediately after this exhibition the conference began, that led to the 'pipe of peace' being smoked by everyone, by which good feeling and friendship were restored where a few days before discord reigned supreme." The conference dissolved upon Lord Bury promising the Indians that justice should be done and their grievances redressed.[2] On this they consented that the surveyors might proceed and complete the surveys.

The Colpoy's Bay Reserve of six thousand acres was surrendered to the Crown, August 16th, 1861. This surrender affects the county of Bruce, however, only as regards that part of the town-plot of Wiarton, lying toward the south-east, the rest of the reserve being now included within the county of Grey.

The Saugeen Fishing Islands, along with those lying adjacent to Cape Hurd, were surrendered October 7th and 15th, 1885. This, with the later surrender of the large islands at the entrance to Colpoy's Bay, has placed in the hands of the Crown all lands not included in the reservations, and extinguished the "Indian title" thereto. One more treaty of surrender, and that but a small one, has to be recorded. It is as follows: The interests of the public required the making into public highways of two trails or roads lying within the Saugeen Reserve. One was that which connects the village of Southampton with what is known as the Owen Sound Road. The other, going north, is called the French Bay Road. These required road allowances were surrendered September 30th, 1899.

[1] Capt. Thos. G. Anderson was connected with the Indian Department for over forty years, retiring on a pension in 1858 In the War of 1812-13 he specially distinguished himself. An interesting account of his life is to be found in "Papers and Records," Vol. VI, of the Ontario Historical Society.

[2] See Appendix B.

As it may interest some of my readers to know the present condition of the Indians residing in the reservations within the county of Bruce, a Schedule (see Appendix C) has been compiled by the author from Government Reports, for the year ending the 30th June, 1900. It shows a highly satisfactory state of affairs, complimentary to all who have worked for the uplifting and civilization of our native tribes on these reservations.

CHAPTER II.

THE QUEEN'S BUSH.

Extract from a Report of a Committee of the Executive Council, Dated February 26th, 1842, and approved by His Excellency the Governor-General two days later:

"William H Peterson with a petition from the inhabitants of a tract of land called the 'Queen's Bush,' in the District of Wellington, praying to have it surveyed.

"The Committee recommend that the tract of land above mentioned be forthwith surveyed, and that a plan of survey be submitted for approval of your Excellency-in-Council The charges for survey will be against the Clergy Reserve Fund "

MEMORY has an odd way at times of retaining a recollection of that which is unimportant, whilst the relatively important things too often are forgotten. To some such peculiarity of memory the writer must attribute his recollection of a school Geography, in use some fifty years ago—which even then must have been almost obsolete—in which was a map of Upper Canada, showing its divisions into Districts Besides the Districts, the map also showed a large blank tract, which was designated " Indian Territory," roughly bounded, as far as memory recalls, by the Home District on the east, the Huron District on the south, and Lake Huron on the west and north respectively This " Territory " is that tract of land mentioned in the preceding chapter as ceded to the Crown by the treaty executed at Manitowaning. Shortly thereafter it came to be known as the " Queen's Bush," a title given, no doubt, to distinguish it from the lands belonging to the Canada Company, the German Company, and others that had obtained large blocks of land from the Crown, holding them largely for speculative purposes.

Filed away among the records of the Crown Lands Department are several petitions presented in 1847-8, similar in effect to the one referred to in the above headnote, the constant demand being for the opening up of lands suitable for settlement.

At that period Canada was being favored with a large wave of immigration, landing a yearly increasing number of immigrants upon her shores. There were but 25,375 immigrants in 1845, but 1847 saw this figure increased to 89,440. The population of Upper Canada, which in 1842 was 486,055, rose to 723,332 in 1848, and to 952,004 in 1852, an increase of nearly one hundred per cent. in ten years, which in a large measure was due to immigration.

The demand for lands for settlement resulting from such a rapid increase in population was responded to by the Executive, and plans were made for the opening up and settlement of the "Queen's Bush." On the 19th April, 1847, an Order-in-Council was passed, "To open up the waste lands of the Crown in the Huron District, by the survey of a double concession of lots on a line from the northerly angle of the township of Mornington, to the north-east angle of the township of Wawanosh. Also a single concession along the rear boundary line of the townships of Wawanosh and Ashfield,[1] and one along the shore of Lake Huron, northerly from Ashfield." This to be all in one survey.

The Hon D B. Papineau, Commissioner of Crown Lands, followed up this order, on May 8th, 1847, by directing Alex. Wilkinson, P L S., to make the foregoing survey, with the proviso, that "the extent of the survey along the lake shore is to be limited by the demand for lands."

Mr. Wilkinson promptly proceeded to undertake the work allotted to him. Taking a party of twelve men and the needed supplies, he started for the Bush At Goderich he endeavored to engage a man sufficiently acquainted with the locality to act as guide, so as to reach the north-east angle of Wawanosh, the point where he purposed to commence the survey So completely was the Bush a *terra incognita* that he could not obtain anyone who possessed the required knowledge. In his report Mr. Wilkinson says, "I was forced to find the place myself from the best information obtainable from the settlers in Wawanosh, which was but little, as none of them had ever been back that far" Following the course of the river Maitland, the surveying party at length reached their destination. After running the Wawanosh road south-easterly to the townships of Mornington and Maryborough, Mr. Wilkinson retraced his steps to his original starting point; thence reopening and reblazing the line to Lake Huron,[2] at the same time planting

[1] This "single concession" became Con 1 in the townships of Kinloss and Huron

[2] This line formed the rear of the townships of Ashfield and Wawanosh, these two townships having been surveyed several years prior to this

the posts along the north side of the line, marking out the farm
lots in what are now the first concessions of the townships of Kinloss
and Huron, which farm lots, therefore, can claim the honor of
being the first surveyed farm lands in the county of Bruce.   Mr.
Wilkinson was not, however, the first surveyor to work in the county.
Mr. Charles Rankin preceded him, having in 1846 run the line
from Owen Sound to the mouth of the Saugeen River, that constituted the southern boundary of the Indian Reserve.[1]

The demand for new lands in the summer of 1847 must have
been considerable, for on September 21st of that year, further
instructions were issued to Mr. Wilkinson, in which he was directed
to " survey the eastern shore of Lake Huron northerly from the
township of Ashfield to the extent of two townships.   From thence
to make an angular survey of the shore to the mouth of the Saugeen
river, and a survey of the river for about ten miles."

An examination of a map of the county of Bruce will show
that the lots surveyed by Mr. Wilkinson, which extend from the
south-east corner of Kinloss to the lake, thence northward along
the shore line, are in form narrower and longer than are to be
found elsewhere in the county in farms of equal size.   The reason
assigned for this is, such a shape of lot would result in the settlers
dwelling closer together.   They would, therefore, be able the more
readily to render each other assistance in case any trouble with the
Indians should occur, a contingency that fortunately has never
arisen.

In the winter following the completion of the above-mentioned
surveys, Mr Wilkinson furnished the Crown Lands Department
with an outline map, by which he showed how the unsurveyed part
of the " Queen's Bush " might be desirably blocked out into townships · The uniqueness of this document makes it an exceedingly
interesting one.   The fact of it having been drafted at that time
indicates that the question of a suitable division into townships of
the last of the wild lands in the western part of Upper Canada
belonging to the Crown was being considered.   Although the projected surveys suggested by Mr. Wilkinson were but partially carried out, his plan no doubt formed the basis for the one ultimately

---

[1]Whether Mr. Rankin at the same time surveyed the "Half-Mile Strip"
or not, the writer cannot say.   It is indicated in a draft map of the proposed new townships in Bruce, made in 1848, but the land was not ceded
to the Crown until 1851

adopted, which divided the tract into seventeen townships. Eleven of these comprise those townships in Bruce south of the Indian Reserve; the other six are Turnberry, Howick, Morris and Grey, in the county of Huron, and Elma and Wallace, in the county of Perth. The exact date when the plan of the final surveys was decided upon cannot be given, but it is a safe surmise to say that it must have been some time during the spring or early summer of 1848.

To attract the attention of prospective settlers to the district about to be surveyed, the Government decided to open up a coloniza- tion road from the county of Simcoe to the mouth of the Penetan- gore River on Lake Huron, and to offer as a free grant to actual settlers a fifty acre farm lot on one of the two concessions north or south of this road. This decision was formulated by an Order- in-Council passed August 26th, 1848.[1]

On the day the order was passed, A. P. Brough, P.L.S.,[2] received instructions to survey the western part of the road, from where the village of Durham now stands, to the lake; also to make a cursory survey of the reserve for a town plot at the mouth of the Penetangore River.

Mr. Brough had among those who formed his surveying party some men who ultimately became settlers in the county and assisted in its development in a prominent manner. Latham B. Hamlin, his principal assistant, years afterward became the County Engineer,[3]

[1]See Appendix D for copy of this Order, and note the conditions therein given attached to the offer of a free grant.

[2]Allan Park Brough, P.L S, surveyed not only the Durham Road, but also the Elora Road, from the north-west corner of Carrick to its southerly terminus in the township of Maryborough, the town plot of Kincardine, the township of Brant, and was proceeding with the survey of the township of Bruce when he died His name is preserved in the name of "Allan Park," bestowed on a village on the Durham line in the township of Bentinck.

[3]Latham B. Hamlin, after ceasing to be County Engineer of Bruce (see Chapter VII.) was engaged in the construction of the Intercolonial Rail- way, and afterwards in that of the Canadian Pacific Railway in British Columbia. While in the west he accumulated some means, but unfortu- nately lost them. Advanced in years as he was, he went to the Klondike, hoping to be fortunate enough to retrieve his fortunes. He and a partner took up a claim on Hunker Creek, a small tributary of the Klondike, some thirty miles from Dawson. The two men were caught out in a severe snow- storm and were badly frozen before they succeeded in returning to their cabin. The Mounted Police found the partner dead, and Mr. Hamlin with his arms and legs frozen almost up to his body. They brought him to Daw- son, where he died within a few days after reaching there This sad occur- rence happened in the month of February or March in the year 1898

and superintended the construction of the system of county gravel
roads   Another was Peter Smith, a pioneer settler of Saugeen
Township   Others were John Caskanette and Joseph Chartrand,
of Greenock, who survived to see the county of Bruce attain its
jubilee.

The report of this survey submitted by Mr. Brough is a lengthy
one   Many details in it are interesting, and will be referred to in
the chapters relating to the minor municipalities through which
the survey ran. Having been supplied with the required astronomi-
cal bearings, Mr. Brough projected his lines accordingly. Starting
at Penetangore (now Kincardine), the party pushed their way
through the unbroken forest that then covered the lands comprising
the townships of Kincardine and Kinloss, until they reached the
large tract of swamp subsequently known as the Greenock Swamp,
of which Mr Brough says in his report: " Previous to deciding
upon the route for the Durham Road in the township of Greenock,
I explored the country some eight or ten miles in extent and found
it to be almost continuous swamp, the extent of which was not fully.
ascertained , but it may in general terms be said to embrace a belt
of country some ten or twelve miles in length by four in width, and
contains more than 25,000 acres. This immense swamp lies on the
west side of the Au-shuskisibbi, or Muddy River.[1] On the east side
of Otter Lake (in the township of Kinloss) a small neck of hard
land protrudes itself into the swamp; of this I took advantage to
carry forward the Durham Road into the township of Greenock, as
it is the only piece of land in a range of several miles that is practicable for a line of road " The taking of this route through the
swamp brought the line of road so far south, that the survey pro-

---

[1]This stream bears so many names that it will not be out of place to
refer to them here   On the map of the county of Bruce, published by James
Warren, P.L S , the river is called the " Yokasippi," which is a corruption
of the Indian word " Ah-ta-yahko-sibbi," which means " The Drowned Lands
River "   At the junction of this stream with the Saugeen, the Indians
call it the " Mekenakoncesibbi," or " Small Mud Turtle River " The " Mud
River " is what the early settlers called it , but it is probably more frequently called the " Teeswater " to day than by any other of its numerous
names   As to the origin of the name " Mud River," the following incident
is given   The late Peter Smith, of Saugeen, was flagman in Brough's surveying party   He used to relate that, during the progress of the survey,
when he reached the river he somehow fell into it, and was thoroughly
bemired in its oozy bed   As he floundered out upon firm ground Brough
came up and said, " What name shall we give this river?" Smith, looking.
down on his mud-covered garments, said, " You had better call it Mud
River " Being apt and descriptive of part of the stream, the name stuck
for many years

ceeded on what would have been the "South Line," if the first projection had been followed out. It also resulted in bringing the line of road distant but the width of a concession from the southerly boundary of the township. In consequence the survey of free grant farm lots was limited to one concession on each side of the Durham Road throughout Greenock. The deviation necessitated by the foregoing circumstances no doubt influenced Mr. Brough to drop the survey at this point and proceed to Durham, and from there to survey the road westward, through the townships of Bentinck and Brant. These details have been given as an explanation of the jog of a mile and a quarter which occurs in the Durham line at the boundary of the townships of Brant and Greenock, where was laid out the Greenock town-plot to connect the roads running east and west with each other. This town-plot failed to respond to the early expectations, never developing into even the semblance of a centre of population. It ultimately was surveyed into farm lots.[1]

The surveys made by A. Wilkinson and A P. Brough, extended in long lines through several townships, attained the object sought, namely, that of opening up the "Queen's Bush." It was upon these surveys that the first permanent settlers in search of farm lands located, the initial settlements being on the lake shore at or near Kincardine, in the summer of 1848. Others who came into the county in the fall of the same year located on the Durham Line in the same vicinity. The spring of 1849 added to these and also witnessed many of the "free grants" in Brant being settled upon.

The town-plot of Penetangore (Kincardine) was laid out toward the close of 1849, and with it the survey assigned to Mr. Brough was completed.

Up to the last-mentioned date no township in the county of Bruce had been surveyed into farm lots; this was a work commenced in the ensuing year. The following is the order in which the various subsequent government surveys were made. In 1850, Brant and Kincardine Townships were surveyed. In the winter following, the Elora Road from the Greenock town-plot southwards was laid out.

[1]An Order-in-Council, dated April 7th, 1852, abolished the Greenock town-plot. Although not in the market the lands therein were largely squatted upon. As a matter of speculation the lands were purchased from the Crown by James Webster, of Guelph, and Dr. Hamilton, of Goderich, who succeeded in having the actual settlement clause waived, but on condition that they satisfy the claims of the squatters. They held the lands, still mostly bush, until 1862, when John S. and James Tolton purchased the greater part of the block.

A survey was made in 1851 of the townships of Arran, Elderslie, Huron, Saugeen, the west part of Bruce, and the town-plot of Southampton; in 1852, the east part of the township of Bruce and the townships of Carrick, Culross, Kinloss, and Greenock; in 1855, the townships of Amabel and Albemarle and town-plot of Alma; in 1856, the townships of Eastnor and Lindsay, the town-plot of Wiarton and the village of Paisley; in 1857, the township of St. Edmunds; in 1875, the six hundred acres reserve forming the southerly part of Southampton town-plot, and in 1899 and 1900 the Fishing Islands, completing the last of the Crown surveys of any moment.

CHAPTER III.

THE PIONEERS.

1831—1849.

In attempting to give a narration of such incidents regarding the pioneers of the county of Bruce as the author has succeeded in gathering, the reader is asked to bear in mind the fact that they who have a right to be so entitled should properly be referred to under several widely divergent classes. Of these the first were the early fur traders, to be followed by explorers, Indian missionaries and the hardy fishermen, who were profitably engaged in their calling at the Fishing Islands years before a surveyor had even entered this part of the province. The work of these venturesome men was largely past when the pioneers who formed the vanguard of progress and civilization entered the "Queen's Bush," and made the first permanent settlements in the county. This latter class of pioneers were the men who cleared the forest, opened up roads, established schools, formed the various municipalities within the county and started the wheels of its many industries; men characterized by an enthusiasm, fortitude and industry that made them the peers of any that ever made a clearing and a settlement in a Canadian forest.

Ruins of what evidently were forts erected by fur traders are to be seen at Cape Croker, Stokes Bay, Red Bay and Southampton. Many are the surmises about these ruined forts. Of what nationality were they who erected them, and when and why abandoned? To these and kindred questions no certain reply can be given. Some assert that they were Hudson Bay Company forts, but satisfactory proof that such was the case has not been met with by the writer. Canada was not ceded by the French to Great Britain until 1763. Before that date it is incredible to think that the Hudson Bay Company's factors were venturesome enough to erect trading posts on French territory. If erected since that date, surely these forts would have been known and referred to in the records of the War of 1812, when vessels of both the English and American navies sailed on Lake Huron. These and other reasons, such as the finding of small relics of apparently French origin near the sites of these

17

ruins, lead to the supposition that the forts were erected by French traders. Lacking positive evidence, any view, however, is only conjecture.

The following facts about the early fur traders at Saugeen were given by Joseph Longe, sen., to Joseph Normandin, an old voyageur, who as a boy lived at Goderich at the time of its settlement, but who removed to Penetanguishene in 1837, and then to Killarney. Normandin's age is uncertain, except that he was born prior to 1820. He related these incidents to Fred. Lamorandiere, the Indian interpreter at Cape Croker, to whom the author is indebted for them, and which are here given in a form but slightly changed from the recital as received.

"One Pierre Piché, in the year 1818, came from Lower Canada to Mackinaw to take part in the adventures and profits of the fur trade. He engaged with one Dr. Mitchell, of the military post of Michilimackinaw, as it was then called. (The Indian name of that island was "Mishi Mikinac," meaning a "great turtle.") Having heard of the richness of the Saugeen country in furs he went there to establish a trading post. It was on the flat, on the south side of the Saugeen River, that he built for himself a house and store, and completed the establishment by taking to himself a wife from the tribe of Indians residing in that vicinity. He received his supply of goods for trading through Dr. Mitchell, and afterwards from his sons George and Andrew. The Mitchells resided first at Mackinaw, but when that was ceded to the United States, they moved to Drummond Island, and when that, too, became American territory, to Penetanguishene Piché was a man of great strength and bravery, and on account of these qualities he succeeded in obtaining and keeping control of the best part of the fur trade in the vicinity of Saugeen. He had many competitors, however, who obtained their supplies from W S. Gooding, of Goderich, Joseph Longe, sen.,[1] who supplied these facts, being one of them. On Piché's death, about 1828, his business was taken up by Edward Sayers; he in turn was succeeded by Achille Cadotte and Registe Loranger; the latter had been a clerk in Mitchell's store at Penetanguishene. He came to the Saugeen trading post with his bride, Adelaide Lamorandiere, remaining there until the breaking out of

[1]Joseph Longe, sen., died about 1858 or 1859, and was said to have attained the age of nearly a century. A number of his descendants reside at Southampton

the rebellion in 1837. The competition to purchase furs was keen, and many were the ' *ruses de guerre* ' used by the traders to get ahead of a competitor; consequently men good for a long, fast tramp through the woods to visit the various Indian camps were in demand. Among those so employed were A M McGregor (afterward Capt. Achille Cadotte), Louis and Sam Thibeau, Thader Lamorandiere and Joseph Longe, jun."

Besides the traders mentioned by Mr. Lamorandiere in the above narrative, there were others who came later into the field, and were well known by many settlers in Bruce These men made Goderich their headquarters, from which point they visited, either by boat in summer or by dog-train in winter, the various Indian camps in Bruce or on the Manitoulin Island, returning with large quantities of furs, maple sugar, and other products of the forest and lake Among the last of these traders were Hugh Johnston, of Goderich, and William Rastall, who finally settled at Kincardine For a number of years after taking up his residence at Kincardine, Mr. Rastall each fall visited the Indians at Saugeen, returning before the ice broke up in the spring, bringing his purchases with him, packed on toboggans drawn by dogs. In trading with the Indians traders made a practice of paying them the price asked for their commodities, without any beating down, payment was always in goods, but the trader took care that the price he received for his goods was proportionate to that asked for the furs he had purchased.

Of those who were merely explorers, the first to be mentioned is Capt H. W. Bayfield, R.N., who made a hydrographic survey of Lake Huron and its shores in 1822. His chart of the same has been in use by navigators of the lake to the present day An examination of this chart shows the changes which have taken place in the names of places as well as in the spelling, as for example, " Saugeen " we there find spelled " Saugink," and Tobermory bears the name of Collins' Harbor.

In 1844 the Government sent out a party to explore the Saugeen River, at the head of which was Col Casimir S. Gzowski, at that time holding a position in the Department of Public Works Accompanying him were Mr James Webster, of Fergus, afterwards Registrar of the county of Wellington, and Mr. Thomas Young, Crown Lands Agent at Arthur Going north, probably by way of the Garafraxa Road, until they reached the Saugeen River, they followed its course in a canoe, making notes as they journeyed.

From these notes Mr. A. Wilkinson marked the course of the river
in a wonderfully accurate manner, in the sketch map of the
" Queen's Bush " referred to in the preceding chapter.   The author
has searched both at Ottawa and Toronto in various governmental
departments in an endeavor to obtain a copy of Col. Gzowski's
report, but unsuccessfully, much to his regret, as it must have contained a description of part of the county of Bruce as seen for the
first time by a white man

It was in 1848 that the first geological survey was made of that
part of the province in which the county of Bruce lies.   The survey
party engaged in this work seem only to have coasted along the lake
shore front of the county, without extending their researches beyond.
A letter received by the author from Dr. Bell, Director of the Geological Survey of Canada, given in a footnote,[1] covers all that is
necessary to record about this, or the subsequent survey made by
himself of the geological features of the county.

In 1834 the Rev. Thomas Hurlburt,[2] of the Wesleyan Methodist
Church, was appointed to commence a mission among the Indians
residing at the mouth of the Saugeen.   During the six previous
years Mr. Hurlburt had labored as a missionary at the .Indian

[1]" Geological Survey of Canada,
"Robert Bell, M D , D.Sc. (Cantab), LL D., F.R S I S O ,
"Acting Deputy Head and Director,
"Ottawa, September 15th, 1904.
" Dear Sir,—In reply to your question I beg to say that the eastern
shore of Lake Huron was not surveyed or examined by Sir W. E. Logan
himself, but by the assistant provincial geologist, Mr. Alexander Murray,
in 1848.   His delineation of the geological boundaries in the county of
Bruce was only tentative, and on my examination of that county in 1863 I
established these boundaries much more accurately, and as they are now
represented on our geological maps. The contours of these boundaries are
of some geologic interest, as showing what must be the general geological
structure under the waters of the eastern part of Lake Huron, which is
important in connection with anticlinals and the occurrence of petroleum in
south-western Ontario.   The corrected geology of the county of Bruce is
described very briefly by Sir William Logan in the ' Geology of Canada,
1863 '
" Yours truly,
" ROBERT BELL,
" Acting Director.
" In Mr. Murray's report for 1848 (published in 1849) he does not mention ' county of Bruce,' but speaks of Pt. Douglas, Maitland River, ' Saugeen '
River, Cape Hurd, etc."

[2]Rev. Mr. Hurlburt's ministerial activities extended from 1828 to 1872.
The greater part of his work during this period was among the Indians.
His death occurred April 14th, 1873. Mrs Hurlburt was a daughter of the
Rev Ezra Adams, and was an aunt of Mrs. (Rev.) D. A. Moir, late of
Walkerton, and was also related to J. H. Adams, banker, of Hanover.

Reserve at Muncey, in the township of Caradoc, obtaining there a training that stood him in good stead in opening the mission at Saugeen As an assistant Mr. Hurlburt had a native Indian local preacher named David Sawyer[1] Their outfit consisted of a few necessary household and farming utensils, with such provisions as were requisite, all placed in a cart, to which were yoked an ox and a cow. With this novel team they made their way through a hundred miles of bush to Goderich, the rest of their journey being made in a sail boat, while the cattle were driven along the beach to Saugeen. The missionaries met with encouraging success in their work, and in 1835 reported a congregation of fifty-nine members. Mr. Hurlburt's stay at Saugeen extended over three years. While there he had a son born to him, who without doubt was the first white child born in Bruce. This mission prospered in its work, and the great majority of the band are at this day members, or adherents, of the Methodist Church. The following are the names of the missionaries, successors to Mr. Hurlburt, who during the first thirty years of the mission labored in this field: Rev. Gilbert Miller (1838), Wm. Herkimer (1839-40 and 1850), Thomas Williams (1840), George Copway (1843-5), J. K. Williston (1846-9, 1856-1862), James Hutchinson (1851-2), Peter Jacobs (1853-5).

The earliest attempt to develop the natural resources of the county of Bruce is to be credited to Capt. Alexander MacGregor, of Goderich,[2] who in 1831, when sailing among the group of islands now known as the Fishing Islands, discovered that the locality was teeming with fish. He soon established himself on one of the islands and commenced to gather in the harvest of its adjacent waters. Capt. MacGregor's greatest difficulty in taking advantage of this source of wealth of nature's providing, was to dispose of the immense quantities of fish that could be secured, as the number seemed unlimited. Some time about 1834, when in Detroit, Capt. Mac-Gregor entered into a satisfactory contract with an American com-

---

[1]David Sawyer, born in 1811, was the eldest son of the Head Chief of the Credit, or Mississagua band of Indians. He was converted to Christianity from paganism when about fourteen years of age, and was appointed a local preacher in 1829. In 1849 the Indians of Saugeen and Newash asked him to reside among them, to act as their agent in transacting business with the government, and become one of their band, which he did His name appears as one of the chiefs who signed the treaty of October 13th, 1854, surrendering the Bruce Peninsula to the Crown.

[2]Father of Capt. A. Murray MacGregor, whose name appears elsewhere in this history

pany, to catch and deliver in storehouses a quantity of fish of not less than three thousand barrels annually, the company at the same time agreeing to take as many more as he could secure. The price to be paid was one dollar per barrel, the company undertaking to clean, cure and pack all fish so delivered. The fish caught were principally white fish and herring, the catches of which were generally made by a seine, and were so large as almost to surpass belief. The process of securing the fish was conducted in a manner somewhat as follows. A man to watch for the approach of a shoal of fish would be stationed on a tree so situated that he might obtain a good outlook over the nearer part of the lake. The shoal when sighted seemed like a bright cloud moving rapidly through the water. The announcement of its approach filled each member of the camp of fishermen with a spirit of excitement and energetic activity. The large row-boat, the stern piled high with the seine, which for hours had been lying idly awaiting a sudden call like this, was then hurriedly manned. Under the lusty strokes of its crew it sped rapidly forward, guided by signals from the man on the outlook, the net was quickly dropped so as to encircle the shoal. The hauling of the net to shore then began. When the fish commenced to feel the pressure from the narrowing of the net, the scene was one long to be remembered. There in a small area were entrapped thousands and thousands of fish, sufficient possibly to fill five hundred to a thousand barrels [1] The water in that circumscribed space seemed to be fairly alive as the fish in their efforts to escape rushed madly about, causing its agitated surface to glitter with the sheen of their silvery sides. All their efforts were futile; the seine was drawn closer to shore, and soon the fish were thrown out on the beach, this process being accomplished by a man standing bare-legged in the midst of the net-imprisoned fish, scoop in hand, who soon transferred them from their native element to land, where they formed a splendent mass, flapping and gasping life away. At times the catch was so large that the landing of the fish was extended over three days, so that none be lost through inability of the curers to handle so many. At other times, when the supply of barrels, or salt was running low, the net was opened to let a portion of the catch escape.

The establishing of such an extensive fishing business required

[1] In those early days and for some time after, before these waters had been over-fished, catches as large as these were not unfrequent.

the erection of permanent buildings for the storage of supplies, for the barrels of salted fish, and for the residence of the number of men engaged in the enterprise. As Capt MacGregor had the bus.-ness running upon a most satisfactory financial basis, he erected on Main Station Island a substantial stone building, measuring 57 x 18 feet externally, whose massive walls, now in partial ruin, evidence the character of the masonry of those days. An effort has been made by some writers to associate these ruins with the presence of the French in this part of the province in the seventeenth century. The arguments urged in support of this view may apply to the remains of the forts mentioned in the first part of this chapter, but as regards the ruins on Main Station Island, the writer has the word of Capt. A Murray MacGregor, that he, as a boy, visited the Island shortly after the buildings had been erected by his father, Capt Alexander MacGregor. The author also has conversed with several persons who remember when the roof on the building was extant. Statements such as these, definite 'and clear, must assure the reader that these ruined walls are the remains of the first permanent building erected in the county of Bruce, and that to Capt. Alexander MacGregor belongs the credit of having erected them.[1]

The financial success met with by Capt MacGregor in his contract with the Detroit company was so great that a feeling of envy was developed among his fellow townsmen, combined with a desire to participate in his fortunate discovery and grasp the profits thereof. This was manifested by certain representations made to the government to the effect that Americans were obtaining an undue advantage by the exclusive contract they had obtained in these fisheries in Canadian waters. As the result of these representations, a lease was granted to a company, conferring to it the sole right of fishing at these islands Among the promoters of the company we find the names of W. S. Gooding, Dr William Dunlop, Dr. Hamilton, and others, of Goderich As a result of the granting of these exclusive privileges, Capt. MacGregor was compelled to give up the fishing industry he had developed and begin work anew elsewhere The

---

[1]The question should be considered settled by what is said in the following extract from the report of Alex Murray, Assistant Provincial Geologist, when referring to his survey of this part of the province in the year 1848, he says "With the exception of a building which was raised some years ago by a fishing company at Gaheto, or Fishing Islands, there is not a single dwelling on any part of the coast all the way (from the Saugeen River) to Cape Hurd"

search for fishing grounds equally as good was, however, in vain. He first tried the vicinity of Tobermory, then Cape Croker. With the latter place his name will be forever associated in the local appellation bestowed of " MacGregor's Harbor." Finally he tried the fisheries in the neighborhood of the Manitoulin Islands. But none of these proved as remunerative as his first discovery. This pioneer of the fishing industries of the county of Bruce lies buried near the mouth of the White Fish River, a stream that flows into the North Channel, Manitoulin Islands

The " Niagara Fishing Company " was the name borne by the company above referred to. For some reason it did not meet with the same success as had rewarded the labors of Capt. MacGregor, so in 1848, having found a purchaser in the persons of Capt. John Spence and Capt. Wm. Kennedy, of Southampton, the company disposed of its property and privileges for the sum of eight or nine hundred pounds These two men jointly carried on the fisheries at the Islands for several years, until Capt. Kennedy was called away, in 1852, to engage in a polar expedition.

The first permanent settlers to take up land in the county of Bruce did so in the year 1848.) Less than a dozen locations were made in the whole county in that the first year of actual settlement. They who then became settlers well deserve the name of pioneers. Miles and miles of forest lay between them and the most ordinary comforts of civilized life; over these long and weary miles every pound of the necessary supplies of food had to be carried until, after months of hard labor and much privation, these stout-hearted men had brought their land into a condition to produce something on which they could subsist while the work of underbrushing, chopping, logging and clearing the land went on. To fully appreciate what these and most of our pioneers have endured, it would be necessary to call upon your imagination and picture yourself in their place. Let us try to follow one of these stalwart men as he leaves some outpost of civilized life and starts out into the bush, in search of a location on which he may settle, clear a few acres of land, erect a shanty, and thereby establish a squatter's claim to the lot of his choice. Before he starts he carefully prepares the pack he has to carry. This contains a supply of provisions, a few necessary cooking and eating utensils, a blanket, an axe, and possibly an auger and a chisel; some, in addition to these necessaries, took also a gun After a weary tramp through the woods along a surveyor's " blaze,"

Photographed by H. G. Tucker

RUINS OF THE BUILDING ON MAIN STATION ISLAND

a spot that seems somewhat near the ideal he is looking for is reached. 'The land, he notes, is covered with heavy hardwood timber, a safe indication that the ground on which it grows is good; the soil, exposed where some ancient monarch of the forest had stood, but now fallen and uprooted, seems all that could be desired, and a spring flowing clear and cool fairly captivates him. Here his search ceases. After securing his provisions in the hollow of some tree, so they may be safe from rain or the depredations of wild animals, he proceeds to do some underbrushing, and erect a shack or shanty, which has to be made of timber of such a size that he unaided can lift it into place. Cutting the logs into suitable lengths and notching each one for the corners, he erects after much hard work his shanty. A narrow opening is made for a doorway; planks split from cedar logs are made into a door. The chinks between the logs are filled with splints and stuffed with moss or clay. The roof is covered with elm bark. His bed of hemlock boughs is placed in one of the corners. The table is made by driving four crotched sticks into the earthen floor, on which rest, supported by cross-pieces, a couple of split or hewed planks. With a block of wood for a seat, his furniture is complete. The cooking, if it is summer, is carried on out of doors, gipsy fashion, what is done is of the simplest—flour mixed with water and a little salt is made into bannocks or scones, which are baked in a frying pan. These and a cup of tea are the common articles of his fare. Dwelling in such a structure, for the word "house" is hardly applicable to it, the hardy backwoodsman proceeds with the work of making a clearing, persevering thereat until want of provisions compels him to go back to the settlement for a fresh supply. Only those who have experienced it know the intense feeling of loneliness that oppresses the solitary backwoodsman, dwelling alone in the bush—no one to speak to, or ask for the most trivial assistance, the sound of a human voice is longed for, but vainly. Inanimate nature in the forest gives forth sounds in the minor key, both soft and soothing; the ringing sound of the axe as it makes the white chips fly is cheery; the rush and crash of some giant of the forest as it falls before the blows of the woodsman is exciting, yet these voices of the backwoods fail to dispel the sense of loneliness which is one of the most trying experiences of pioneer life. Individual instances of hardships endured and of difficulties overcome by pioneers will be given in relating the settlement of various localities within the county. Therefore, without further ado for the present, we will pass on to consider the disputed topic, to whom belongs the distinction of being the first pioneer settler in the county.

Kincardine and Southampton are the only localities in the county to claim that the initial settlement of Bruce was made within their borders   As to which had precedence we leave the reader to judge, after a consideration of the most reliable data that the author has been able to collate

Shortly after the opening of navigation in 1848, Capt. Murray MacGregor conveyed from Goderich in his sailing vessel, and landed at the mouth of the Penetangore River, the two pioneer settlers of that locality, with their effects. These two men were William Withers, an Englishman, and his brother-in-law, Allan Cameron.[1] On a spot a little south of where the Kincardine railway station now stands, these two men erected a small log house, which for a year or two did duty as a tavern, kept by Cameron; subsequently it was used as a store by John Keyworth, and as such may be remembered by many who traded in Kincardine during the "fifties." Foreseeing the demand that there would be for lumber as soon as settlers commenced to take up land, Mr. Withers commenced the construction of a mill-dam, which he placed across the river about where it touches the east side of Huron Terrace Street,[2] in the town plot of Kincardine   Here he erected a frame saw mill, at the raising of which assistance was rendered by Indians and the few settlers who had taken up land in the vicinity   Mr. A P. Brough, in his report of survey, refers to this mill as "a substantial, well-framed building, which was in full operation in the summer of 1849." When Mr. Withers erected his mill and dam he neglected to secure permission from the Crown to do so; this oversight resulted unfortunately for himself, he being forced, at a considerable loss, to remove his newly erected mill from the site where first erected to one on his farm (lot 3, con. 2, S.D R, Kincardine), just outside the townplot, the exact date of his doing so the author being unable to find out[3]   Mr. Withers had further difficulty in regard to

---

[1] Owing to his dark complexion his name was generally prefixed by the early settlers with the distinguishing title of "Black," or "The Black Prince."

[2] At what is marked in original plan of the town as "Mill Block No. 1."

[3] In the Crown Lands Department records is a copy of a letter to J. Clark, C L, agent at Goderich, dated 14th February, 1850, to the following effect . "You will also warn the person who contemplates purchasing Mr. Withers' interest in the Mill-site, that when open for sale the unauthorized occupation of the land will confer no rights to pre-emption"

cutting timber on Crown lands. The lands in Penetangore and vicinity were not offered for sale by the Crown until August, 1851, so that any timber cut by him prior to that date was cut on Crown lands,[1] and subject to Crown dues, which the Crown Lands Agent at Goderich was told (Dec. 14th, 1848) to take steps to collect or have the timber seized.

The first settlement at Southampton was made by Capt. John Spence and Capt William Kennedy. The former of these was a native of the Orkney Islands; the latter was a well educated half-breed. Both of these men had been in the employ of the Hudson's Bay Company, from which service they had retired in 1847 and taken up their residence at Kingston Learning of the profitableness of the Lake Huron fisheries and of the opportunities for trading in furs, in the spring of 1848 they left Kingston westward bound, for the purpose of investigating for themselves as to the truth of what they had heard; travelling *via* Toronto and Lake Simcoe, at Rama they purchased a canoe from the Indians, in which they journeyed down the Severn River to the Georgian Bay and thereon to Owen Sound, from this point they travelled on foot by the Indian trail to the mouth of the Saugeen River, arriving there in June, 1848 Satisfied with the location and their prospects there, they returned to Owen Sound to obtain supplies; with these they loaded their canoe and in it proceeded to follow the coast line until the head of Colpoy's Bay was reached. Being old Hudson's Bay Company voyageurs, the necessary portage to Boat Lake was expeditiously made, the sail down Rankin and Sauble Rivers safely accomplished, and 'it took but a short time to paddle over the waters of Lake Huron to the Saugeen. Close to its mouth they pitched their tent and in it resided all that summer. Before winter set in they erected a log house, which served Capt Spence and family as a residence for many years. The stay of Capt Kennedy in Southampton extended over only some four years. In 1852, at the request of Lady Franklin, he went out in charge of a party in search of her husband, Sir John Franklin, the Arctic discoverer and navigator. In 1850 Capt. Spence brought his wife to his new home at South-

[1]Extract from letter of the Commissioner of Crown Lands to H Clark, C.L , agent at Goderich, dated September 29th, 1848   "I take this opportunity of informing you that the road leading to Lake Huron, through the new townships in the north of the Huron District, will not be carried through this year, and it is not the intention of the Government to offer for sale at present the Crown Lands in that section of the province "

ampton, where they continued to reside until the death of Capt.
Spence on October 13th, 1904. Mrs. Spence, surviving her husband, is to-day one of the oldest living of the early female settlers of
the county of Bruce   ,   ,

Early in the fall of 1848 John C. Digman, a German by birth,
settled in Kincardine Township, on lot 3, first concession north of
the Durham Road, he being the pioneer settler on the free grant
lands   The date of his settlement shows that he must have acted
promptly after the issuing of the offer of the Crown. How long
Mr. Digman resided on the lot he located the writer is not able to
say, certainly long enough to have the Crown patent issued to him,
the date of which is December 4th, 1851. Some time after that he
returned to the county of Waterloo, from whence he originally came.

The next settler on the Durham Road was John Beatty, a young
Scotchman. He was accompanied by his sister, Miss Beatty, who is
entitled to the distinction of being, in all probability, the first
woman to undertake the hardships of the bush in the county of
Bruce. The facts here related concerning Mr. and Miss Beatty have
been supplied by Major William Daniel, who, when he settled in
Kincardine Township in October, 1848 (on lot 23, con. 1, N.D.R.),
found that they were his nearest neighbors. The Beattys had come
on foot from Owen Sound, each carrying a pack. Their route had
been by the Indian trail (known later as the "Gimby trail") to
the mouth of the Saugeen, thence by the beach to Kincardine. They
pitched their tent towards the rear of lot 14, con. 1, S.D.R., on
the bank of the creek, it being the attraction that decided them to
locate there. "When the stock of provisions in our two camps
were almost exhausted," the Major goes on to relate, "I shared my
last loaf with them and started for my father's home in Waterloo
for further supplies, expecting to find my neighbors on my return.
Beatty had arranged with a man who was going to Goderich for
the purchase of a supply of flour. The man to whom the commission was entrusted made other use of the money, consequently no
flour was forthcoming. As winter was at hand, the outlook for the
Beattys was alarming. Feeling discouraged and disheartened, they
decided to forsake bush life and return to Owen Sound. A young
man named Dick Eaton, who was employed by Wm. Withers as ox
teamster, accompanied them on their journey, which was over the
same route they had so laboriously travelled not many weeks previously. The weather was cold; through the streams to which they

came they waded, carrying Miss Beatty, except at the Saugeen, over
which they were ferried by Indians in a canoe. Eaton unfortunately
cut his foot with an axe, and had to be left in charge of the Indians."

During the summer of 1848 the small settlement at Kincardine
was increased by the incoming of some dozen other settlers, who
took up land either at the town plot, on the free grants, or on the
lake shore to the north of the town. Among these were Donald,
Alexander and John McCaskill, James and Alexander Munroe,
Anthony Copp, Alex. McKay, George McLeod, Wm. Dowell and
Patrick Downie. The last-mentioned opened a tavern on the site
of the Rightmeyer Salt Block. During the fall of this year a
steamer laden with supplies for the Bruce Mines was burnt somewhere out in the lake. The wreckage from it, consisting of flour
and provisions, drifted ashore, and proved a perfect godsend to those
early pioneers, who that winter had to purchase from their slender
means all their supplies in Goderich, added to which was the time
and labor of bringing these over the intervening thirty-six miles,
absolutely devoid of anything that might be called a road for most
of the distance.

Early in the year 1849 settlers in increased numbers took up
lands in the vicinity of Kincardine, of whom quite a number survive. One of these is Elijah Miller. The 6th February of that
year is the day when he, then but a boy, first saw Kincardine. He,
with his father, mother, uncle and aunt, were driven over the ice
from Goderich by Capt. Thomas Dancey. To him it seemed that
nothing was to be seen but woods everywhere. The clearings that
had been made were so small and scattered that the forest appeared
to have lost nothing of its unbroken vastness   Mr. Miller, sen.,
settled on lot 12, con. 1, N.D R. That winter he made a small
clearing and thereon raised a small crop the following summer.

Capt. Duncan Rowan is another "forty-niner," who when alive
was ever ready to speak of pioneer days. He reached Kincardine
on February 18th, 1849, accompanied by his brother John and his
sister, afterwards Mrs. McLeod.[1] They put up for the night at
Patrick Downie's. There they learned of Stoney Island, three miles
farther north, as a place where small vessels might find a haven.
This, to one possessing the instincts and training of a sailor, was

---

[1]The mother of Angus McLeod, one of Canada's noted professional
bicyclists. His mile with flying start in 1 minute 46 and a fraction of
seconds still stands as a record on Canadian tracks.

attractive, in addition, good farming land was to be had in the
adjacent Lake Range, already surveyed Appreciating these advantages the party decided that on some of these farm lots they would
settle. Next day they yoked their oxen and journeyed on to the
spot that they had decided upon Before long they had erected
near the beach, a log house, the site of which can be identified by the
ruins of the chimney It was a familiar sight to all who passed
up and down on the Beach Road in the "fifties"

In the roll of the early pioneers of the county the names of
those who settled in the township of Huron must not be forgotten,
the date of their settlement being as early as many of those already
referred to The survey of the first concession and the Lake Range
in that township in 1847, as mentioned in a previous chapter,
had prepared the way for those desirous of taking up land. An
exactness as to date of settlement is possible respecting the township
of Huron not to be had so authoritively in the case of other townships, as it is based upon a report made by E R. Jones, P.L.S, who
after completing the survey of that part of the township untouched
by A. Wilkinson, made a list of all settlers on the Lake Range,
giving the date of settlement and extent of improvements made up
to the date of his report, Sept 11th, 1851 From this report we
learn that in October, 1848, Louis Lizars settled on lots 47 and 48,
Lake Range, and was followed in the May of 1849 by Abraham
Holmes, Wm Blair, Peter Wanamaker, James Donnelly and David
Walden The fall of the same year added to the number of settlers
in the persons of Joseph and Christopher R Barker, John Emmer-
ton, Thomas and Elisha Barnes The foregoing names and dates
are beyond dispute, but it is said that Louis Bellemore, a French-
Canadian, was the first to locate in Huron, and the summer of 1848
is given as the time when he "squatted" on lot 19, beside Pine
River, where he made some improvements and kept a tavern. In
the following spring he sold his squatter's rights to David Walden
and moved to lot 36, and at the time of E R. Jones' report, he had
made a clearing thereon of thirteen acres in extent.[1] Among the
foregoing names that of (Capt) Abraham Holmes deserves more
than a passing mention He owned and sailed a dug-out canoe of

[1]Bellemore at one time had been in the employ of the Hudson's Bay Company, and had married the daughter of an Indian chief. The sign of the
tavern which he kept had painted thereon, in rather rude artistic style, a bottle
and a glass, with the motto, "A French Tavern"

unusual size, having a carrying capacity of five barrels of flour in addition to its crew of two men, who, using oars and sails, brought many a settler with their effects from Goderich to Penetangore. For several years this vessel sailed regularly on this route.

Other pioneers took up land in Huron in 1849, besides those on the lake shore. The first concession received its first settlers in October of that year, who located near what is now Lochalsh, Duncan McRae, Finlay McLennan and Alex. McRae, with their families, coming in at that time. One cannot but admire the courage of these men and women in taking up land miles back from the lake, in the midst of the bush. If severe hardships fell to the lot of those who had the advantage of water transit to reach their base of supplies, how much more severe must have been the hardships endured by these families. It is pleasing to be able to record that "Big" Duncan McRae is still living, and has passed his jubilee on the same farm lot.

The rapidity with which the county of Bruce was settled may be largely attributed to the offer made by the government of a free grant, to actual settlers, of a fifty acre farm lot[1] on either of the first two concessions north or south of the Durham Road. This was accompanied with the promise that this road would be cleared and opened up by the Government. The third concessions were at first intended to be held for sale to those who had obtained a grant. This intention was not, however, adhered to. The prospect of purchasing additional land had the effect of inducing many to locate on the second concessions, doing so under the condition that they were to open up the road between the second and third concessions unaided by the government; and until this was satisfactorily done they could not obtain the patent to their grant.

The notice that the "free grants" were open for location was made in August, 1848, and renewed in June, 1849. The mode of taking up these grants and the conditions attached before a patent from the Crown thereto could be obtained, are given in Appendices D and E, but will here be related in a more detailed manner.

A personal application[2] to the Crown Lands Agent at Durham,

---

[1] 806 lots in all were so offered in the townships in the county of Bruce.

[2] The applicants were so numerous in the summer of 1849 and 1850 that they could with difficulty find accommodation in Durham, and were glad to keep anywhere, as long as they had a roof over their heads.

the late Mr. George Jackson,[1] was necessary. Mr. Jackson gave to
each applicant a list consisting of certain lots not taken up. These
lists did not contain many lots, and were drawn out as far as possible with a view of preventing two men inspecting and selecting
the same lands. Mr. Jackson also planned to have people of a con-
genial type settle in close proximity; in this he was assisted by
those whom he had acting in the sense of sub-agents, from whom
the land-seekers were instructed to receive directions as to the
locality of the lots on their lists. In Kincardine Township Allan
Cameron and Thomas Harris so acted, and in Brant Thomas Adair
and William Johnston—who received his sobriquet of "King Johnston" in consequence from the hands of Mr. Jackson, a title that
clung to him for life. The applicant started off from Durham with
the list in his pocket and in his pack a supply of provisions sufficient to last until his return to the clearings. Striking out along
the Durham Line, which at the first was only a blazed path through
the woods, after a good four hours' tramp he would reach the
Saugeen River just west of the county line,[2] at Buck's Crossing,
where the village of Hanover now stands. If the water were
low he could wade across the river, otherwise he had to follow up
the stream in a northerly direction for about a mile to where the
mill-dam was afterwards erected. There a jam of driftwood had
formed, over which he crossed. This jam continued to be thus used
until the government had constructed a bridge on the line of the Durham Road, in the fall of 1850. The land-seeker now entered upon a
weary march pursuing his search for a suitable lot, sleeping at
nights in the open when distant from any settler's shanty, or meet-

---

[1]George Jackson, although residing at Durham, was closely connected
with the early days of Bruce and Walkerton. His name was also well-
known to all settlers along the length of the Durham Road The few condensed particulars of his life here given are, therefore, quite in order.
George Jackson was born at Hutton, Yorkshire, England, in December,
1809. He came to Canada in 1844 The appointment of Crown Land Agent
(see Appendix E) for the Free Grants in Bruce and Grey was conferred
upon him in August, 1848 He was elected member of parliament in 1854
for the county of Grey, being the first representative from that county.
With the exception of two parliaments, he continued to represent that constituency until 1882 Mr. Jackson exercised discretion and judgment in
allotting settlers their free grants in Bruce, and was much respected and
admired by both friends and opponents He died March 6th, 1885.

[2]This part of the Durham line was chopped, but not logged, during the
summer of 1849

ALLAN CAMERON   p. 26   WM. WITHERS   p. 26
The two pioneer settlers in the County of Bruce

GEORGE JACKSON   p. 32   LATHAM B. HAMLIN   p. 31
Crown Land Agent for the " Free Grants "

ing with a warm and kindly hospitality if he were so fortunate as to reach one. At last, having made his selection, he returned to Durham, to have it registered to him. From one to three month's grace were allowed before he commenced to fulfil the conditions and make the improvements required by the Crown. These stipulated continuous settlement, the clearing of twelve acres in not less than four years, and the erection of a dwelling house of at least 18 x 24 feet in dimensions. These terms complied with, a patent to the land was granted by the Crown. Conditions so easy were in many cases performed long before the four years' limit of time expired, as is instanced in Kincardine Township, where to settlers on the " free grants " patents to the number of a dozen or more were issued in the year 1851. It is possible, however, that politics were at the bottom of this early issue of patents, as in those days a voter was liable to be called upon to produce his title deeds when he tendered his vote for a member of parliament; and it has been asserted, by parties who should know, that only those men who were known *to vote right* received their patents early.

The first notice of the opening of the " free grants " was issued by Crown Land Agent George Jackson, as already stated, in August, 1848. This action on his part seems to have been premature, as we find that the Commissioner of Crown Lands wrote to him under date of October 12th, 1848, notifying him, " That neither location tickets can issue, nor sales be confirmed, until the surveys are completed and the Department be in a position to make records." This was followed, June 13th, 1849, by another letter instructing him to make returns of locations on the Durham Road " in the township of Brant, the surveys of which are completed," in order that location tickets may be issued. Also, " That to comply with the statute passed at last session (12 Vic., chap. 31., sec. 4.), to suspend for the present the sale on the third Ranges of the 150 acres adjoining the free grants of 50 acres." The notice of the opening of the " free grants " seems to have been renewed on the receipt of this last letter. During the interval a number of squatters had settled upon the free grant lots, and seem to have succeeded in having their names entered as locatees in anticipation of the Departmental regulations. The first were those in Kincardine Township, already referred to. Early in the spring of 1849 intending settlers com-

3

menced to flow into <u>Brant</u>. The first to do so was Joseph L. Lamont,[1] Thomas Weir and John Brown. This was early in May, 1849. On presenting themselves at Mr. Jackson's office he told them that as they were the first prospectors they might select any lots they thought best. They spent three days in the bush engaged in making their selections. Returning to Mr. Jackson to register the lots chosen, they met Thomas Jasper and Abraham Buck, who formed the second contingent of would-be settlers, preparing to leave and do as they had done, select a farm lot in the bush. These two did not go as far into the woods as the first party had done, Mr. Jasper selecting lands but a short distance west of the county line, while Buck took up a lot just east of it His name is associated with what is now the village of Hanover, the locality at first bearing the name of " Buck's Crossing," and, after the erection of the bridge, as " Buck's Bridge." The next party of prospectors to enter Brant consisted of William Johnston, Charles Nelles and James Purdy. These men followed almost immediately those already mentioned, the date when their lots[2] were allotted to them being May 22nd, 1849. Purdy did enough work on his lots that spring to ensure his claim, then returned to the settlements, where he died during the summer. His lots were taken up for a second time that fall by George Neely. William Johnston spent the summer clearing land and erecting a fair-sized shanty for his family, which he brought into the bush in the following November. As all pretensions to a road or tract through the woods ceased at Buck's Crossing, he constructed a good-sized raft of logs at the jam on the Saugeen already referred to, on which he placed his wife, two daughters[3] and two of his sons, Andrew and Samuel. Jos. L. Lamont and Geo Weir were also on the raft, to act as crew. The number of persons, with its cargo of household effects and farm implements, made the raft unwieldy, resulting in its being stranded in one of the rapids that it attempted to pass

[1]Mr Lamont must share the honor of being the pioneer of Brant with his wife, *née* Elizabeth Jasper, who was the first white woman to enter the township, although not the first to enter to reside there permanently (that honor belongs to Mrs. James Bacon). While still Miss Jasper she paid her father a visit, while he was engaged in making a clearing on his lot, and to do so had to cross the Saugeen on ox-back.

[2]Johnston, in his own name and that of his sons, took up lots 5, 6 and 7, on both concessions, north and south of the Durham Road. Nelles, in like manner, took up lots 1 and 2, concession 1, S.D.R , and Purdy, lots 1 and 2, concession 1, N.D R.

[3]Who were subsequently married to William Walker and William C. Moffatt, respectively.

through. As soon as their position was realized, the two men set to work and put together the waggon that formed part of the cargo; on this the women folks were drawn to the shore. The raft so lightened now floated, and was successfully navigated down the river as far as Silver Creek. There it was met by Mr. Johnston and his sons, Abraham, David, William and Robert, who had walked through the bush driving the cattle. Some Indians were camping near by; these Mr. Johnston engaged to go up the river in a canoe and fetch the women folks and Mr. Lamont, who had remained with them. From Silver Creek to Johnston's Corners[1] the axe had frequently to be used to make the way at all possible. Mrs. Johnston and some of the children were the guests that night at James Bacon's, his family having moved in shortly before. To Mrs. Bacon is due the honor of being the first white woman to take up her residence in Brant.

About the time Wm. Johnston took up the free grant lots he afterwards settled upon, another prospecting party, six in number, entered Brant. In this party were Thomas Adair, Kenneth Kemp and Adam Clement. The latter quickly made his selection (which were lots 51, 52, 53, con. 1, N.D.R., and 53, 54, con. 1, S.D.R.), not considering it worth while to push on any great distance into the bush. Mr. Adair prospected further and was influenced in his choice of lots (43 to 46, con. 2, N.D.R.) on the "North line" by the expectation of purchasing more land across the road in the third concession. On registering his location (June 3rd, 1849) he found but sixteen lots had been taken up in Brant. Mr. Adair, accompanied by his brother John, returned to make a clearing on their lots in the following September. Being expert woodsmen, they soon had a comfortable shanty erected, in which they resided until the snow came, when they returned to their families near Peterborough to complete arrangements to bring them to their new home in the woods of Bruce. The journey was long and toilsome. The sleighs on which their effects were packed could be brought no further than Buck's Crossing; from that point everything had to be shouldered and carried through the snow over the weary miles that lay between them and their shanty. Their mother was an invalid;

[1]"Johnston's Corners" is the name that will always be given to the corner at which Mr. Johnston located. He there, in 1854, erected a tavern, subsequently burnt down. His son, Nathaniel, born June, 1850, was the first white child born in Brant. Mr. Johnston's death took place September 22nd, 1870.

it was therefore necessary to improvise a sedan chair, on which she was carried over what was but a footpath in the deep snow. But slow progress could be made, and half a day was occupied in reaching the small but hospitable shanty of Adam Clement, in which sixteen persons were accommodated that night. Next morning the journey was completed, and they reached their own shanty, two miles further back in the woods

The number of settlers who came into Brant in 1849 the writer is not able to state. Among them were the following, in addition to those elsewhere mentioned: Archibald, Alexander and Moses Stewart, John Lundy, Thomas Todd, Joseph L. Lamont, John Brown, William and Johnston Smith, William Jasper, Edward Boulton, Patrick Godfrey, Richard Everett, and others.

In the year 1849 lands were also taken up in Greenock, where the village of Riversdale now stands, by two French-Canadians, Joseph Chartrand and John Caskanette. These men were in the employ of A. P. Brough, P.L S , during the survey of the Durham Road, the township of Brant and the Elora Road. The exact date of their settling on the lots they selected is uncertain. The author has conversed with them on the subject, but found their recollections lacking in definiteness. Goderich was their base of supplies, a point more than fifty miles distant.

A tragic incident marked the early days of the settlement of the Durham Road, too often repeated in varying details during the clearing away of the forest here and in other parts of the province. Thomas Jasper, as is stated in a previous paragraph, was in the second company of prospectors that entered Brant. He then took up lot 65, con. 1, N D.R., as well as other lots for various members of his family. Previous to entering the bush he had resided at Durham, or Bentinck, as it was known in those days. It was in June, 1849, when, accompanied by his sons, Thomas and Charles, he commenced making his clearing. Satisfactory progress was being made. One morning in the following month the father and his two sons started out to do some chopping before breakfast. The young men were engaged in felling a tree, and the father, not far off, was cutting some underbrush, a small knoll hiding him from their sight. From the sound of his axe they knew that he was close at hand; they therefore called out to him to look out, when the tree they were chopping was almost ready to fall, repeating it a little later on, which warnings he answered to. The tree felled, the young men

as they started for their shanty to get breakfast called out to the
father to come along. Receiving no reply they felt alarmed. A
search was made, which revealed the shocking sight of his dead body
held under a wide-spreading branch of the tree they had just cut
down. He had been struck and killed instantly, the first of many
a pioneer in Bruce to meet death as he wrought at making a home
for himself in the woods. His body lies buried not far from where
he died.

In closing this chapter on the pioneers, the author wishes it to
be borne in mind that the names mentioned are of those who came
into Bruce prior to the year 1850, who came so early in the history of the county that not even one township within its boundaries
had been surveyed into farm lots. Thousands followed in their
footsteps, of whom many will be referred to when the history of the
various municipalities is taken up, as their pioneers. The author
does not underestimate what labor and hardships these later ones
have experienced. But he does bespeak a special word of appreciation for the pioneers of 1848 and 1849, men who entered a trackless forest, and who then and there laid the foundation of the
county's development and prosperity.

> " When the hill of toil was steepest,
>   When the forest-frown was deepest,
>   Poor, but young, you hastened here ;
>   Came where solid hope was cheapest—
>   Came—a pioneer.
>   Made the western jungles view
>   Civilization's charms ,
>   Grasped a home for yours and you
>   From the lean tree-arms.
>   Toil had never cause to doubt you—
>   Progress' path you helped to clear;
>   But to-day forgets about you,
>   And the world rides on without you—
>   Sleep, old pioneer ! "
>   —Will Carleton

CHAPTER IV.

THE INFANT COUNTY.
1850—1856.

THAT there was a time when the " County of Bruce" was an unknown designation is a statement to be readily admitted. To fix the date when as a corporate municipality it came into existence and first bore its present title is what this chapter will endeavor to set forth, as well as to narrate the beginnings of its municipal life.

The facts so far presented to the reader have largely anteceded the existence of the municipality of and even the name of the county of Bruce, which was bestowed, as we shall see, some time after the inflow of settlers had well set in. Prior to this, as related in a previous chapter, the appellation of the " Queen's Bush " was commonly applied to the unsettled lands lying north of the Huron District, the larger portion of which ultimately comprised the county of Bruce. This same territory is described more formally in an Act of Parliament[1] that provides for the administration of justice therein as, " That portion of the province lying to the northward of the District of Huron, bounded on the north by Lake Huron and the Georgian Bay, which is not included in either of the Districts of Wellington or Simcoe, (which) is declared, for all purposes of and connected with the administration of justice, civil and criminal, to form part of the District of Huron."

An effort was early made (the particulars of which are given[2] in a foot-note) to have this territory formed into a county with Owen

---

[1] 9 Vic., Chap. 47, passed May 23rd, 1846.

[2] Copy of notice appearing in *The Canada Gazette*, August 26th, 1848 : " Notice is hereby given, that application will be made to the Legislature, at the next sitting of Provincial Parliament, by the inhabitants of the townships of St. Vincent, Euphrasia, Collingwood, Osprey and Artemesia, in the Simcoe District, and of the townships of Sydenham, Derby, Holland, Sullivan, Glenelg, Bentinck, Normanby, Egremont, Proton and Melancthon, in the Wellington District, for an Act to be passed to form these townships into a county, *including the unsurveyed lands west of the said townships and extending to Lake Huron and the Indian Territory and Islands contiguous thereto,* and that the town of Sydenham, on the Owen Sound, be the county town of said county."

Sound as the county town, the agitation for which, however, proved abortive.

James Bruce, Earl of Elgin and Kincardine, was Governor-General of Canada at the time the "Queen's Bush" was surveyed. It was out of compliment to him that his family name was bestowed upon the new county, which was brought into existence by authority of an Act of Parliament,[1] passed May 30th, 1849, dividing the district of Huron into three counties, Huron, Perth and Bruce. This Act defines the boundaries of each of the new counties, and goes on to say: "The counties remaining nevertheless united until the union be dissolved, so soon as it shall appear by the census that any junior county contains a population of fifteen thousand, on order of the Governor-in-Council and upon petition of two-thirds of the Reeves." *The County Division Substitution Act,* passed at the same session of Parliament, to abolish the old territorial district divisions within the province,[2] names the townships that were to comprise the county of Bruce as follows: The townships of Arran, Brant, Bruce, Carrick, Culross, Elderslie, Greenock, Huron, Kincardine, Kinloss and Saugeen While "All the peninsular tract of land, lying to the north-ward of the townships of Derby, Arran and Saugeen and between Lake Huron and the Georgian Bay and known as the Indian Reserve, shall be annexed to, and form part of, the county of Waterloo."[3, 4] These two last-mentioned Acts of Parliament came into force on the 1st January, 1850, which date is, therefore, the birthday of the county of Bruce, for under the terms of these Acts of Parliament it on that day became a municipality, although only the junior one of the united counties of Huron, Perth and Bruce.

With the abolishing of district divisions within the province, and contemporaneous with the advent of Bruce among the municipalities thereof, came also a change in the mode of municipal government.

[1]12 Vic., Chap. 96

[2]Prior to this and kindred Acts coming into force, the districts within the province, comprised the limits of the respective shrievalties within which Courts of Assize, etc., were held, each district, subsequent to January 1st, 1842, being a corporate muncipality. The counties comprised the political divisions for parliamentary representation, and the limits wherein registration of titles to property were made, there being a registrar for each county.

[3]The county of Waterloo in 1849 comprised the same territory, and was conterminate with the District of Wellington, extending from the Georgian Bay, in the north, to the township of Wilmot as its southerly limit.

[4]The Saugeen Peninsula became a part of the county of Bruce by 14 and 15 Vic, Chap 5, passed August 2nd, 1851

The earliest form of local government that existed in Upper Canada was that administered by the Quarter Sessions, held in the several district towns, the members of which were the justices of the peace within the district. This body possessed, besides judicial powers, administrative, and to some extent legislative functions. This system of local government continued in force until 1842, when district municipal councils were established,[1] the members of which represented the several townships in the district and were elected by the ratepayers. The district council performed the work now undertaken by county, township and village councils, levying taxes for local improvements and school purposes. Annual township meetings were held, at which the freeholders and householders elected the following officers: a clerk-treasurer, assessor, collector, overseer of highways and pound-keeper. These officials, before the passing of the District Councils Act, acted under the direction of the Quarter Sessions. There were also two township wardens; these acted "as a Corporation to represent the whole inhabitants of the township" in any action at law, but had no legislative powers or functions.

The change indicated in the mode of municipal government, spoken of in a preceding paragraph, affected the county of Bruce when on Monday, January 28th, 1850, the first session of the Council of the united counties of Huron, Perth and Bruce was held at Goderich, when Dr. Wm. Chalk, the Reeve of Tuckersmith, was elected warden, and Alfred W Otter appointed county clerk. Among the members of the Council then and there assembled was Thomas Johnson, who sat as reeve for the municipality of the "United townships of Ashfield and Wawanosh, in the county of Huron, and all the townships in the county of Bruce,"[2] which municipal union had been brought about by a by-law of the Huron District Council, passed at a special meeting held October 2nd, 1849, called to make the necessary preparatory arrangements for the new order of muni-

[1] The first meeting of the Huron District Council, it being the council that had charge of the territory afterwards comprised in the county of Bruce, then but the "Queen's Bush," was held February 8th, 1842. The first warden was Dr. William Dunlop, M P P., and Daniel Lizars, the first municipal clerk for the district.

[2] This enormous stretch of country, so formed into one municipality, had its Township Council composed, in 1850, of Thomas Johnston, reeve, and Councillors John Hawkins, William Graham, Jeremiah Flynn and John King. The clerk and treasurer was Michael Healy. In 1851 Charles Girvin was reeve, and John Strachan, clerk-treasurer. Not one of those here mentioned was a resident of the county of Bruce. The author has been told that the settlers in Bruce sent Allan Cameron to this meeting of the Council as their representative, this being unauthorized by either statute or by-law. His claims as a representative were not recognized.

cipal government required by the Acts of Parliament just passed.
The idea of forming a municipality by a union of townships in two
different counties was a blunder, productive of trouble that was not
smoothed out until a couple of years had passed. It is not difficult
to surmise why the District Council formed the union of townships
indicated in the foregoing lengthy title. The Municipal Corporation Act of 1849[1] provided that townships having less than one hundred resident freeholders or householders were to be attached to
some adjacent township in the *same* county. As the required number were not to be found in the whole of the county of Bruce, the
District Council thought that it was acting within the limits of its
authority in attaching the whole county of Bruce to the two adjacent
townships of Ashfield and Wawanosh.[2] The settlers in Bruce thought
otherwise, and after obtaining legal advice they repudiated the
by-law forming them into a municipality conjunctly with the townships of Ashfield and Wawanosh, and refused to pay taxes either
to the township or the county. This position was maintained until
the separation from the two townships in Huron was effected, after
a nominal union which had lasted for the years 1850 and 1851.
The attitude of the settlers in Bruce in refusing to pay taxes was
sustained, and it was not till 1852 that taxes for township purposes
were first collected in the county of Bruce, and 1853, when the first
levy for county rates was paid An assessment of the county was
attempted in 1850, but only Kincardine and Huron Townships were
included therein; Brant, where, as we have seen in a preceding
chapter, a small settlement was commenced in 1849, was not assessed.
The statistics[3] obtained by this assessment are most interesting,
revealing the actual progress made by the settlers during their first
year in the bush, and are given in a foot-note

[1] 12 Vic. Chap. 81.
[2] The recurrence of similar mistakes was obviated by a change made by
Parliament in the following August, 13 and 14 Vic., Chap. 64, Sec. 8.
[3] STATISTICS FROM THE ASSESSMENT OF 1850.

	Tp Kincardine	Tp Huron	Total
Population	262	114	376
Acres under crop	11	42	53
Wheat, in bushels.... . . .	30	175	205
Barley, "		20	20
Oats, "	20 .	20	40
Corn, "	.	56	56
Potatoes "	180	305	485
Buckwheat, "	.	20	20
Turnips, "	375		375
Maple sugar, in lbs	30	450	480

The above townships are the only townships mentioned in this assessment roll
Brant and Saugeen should have been included, but were not.

Although, owing to the above mentioned blunder of the Huron
District Council, an enforced collection of taxes could not be legally
made in the townships within the county of Bruce, the settlers were
not content to escape the burden of taxation, the penalty being loss
of municipal rights and privileges. A petition was therefore presented to the Council of the United Counties in December, 1850, asking that the townships in Bruce be separated from Ashfield and
Wawanosh and formed into a separate municipality. This the council declined to do that year, owing to legal technicalities. The
petition was, however, complied with in 1851.

At the first session of the united counties council in 1852 there
was present Francis Walker, who sought to sit as reeve for the township of Kincardine and the remaining townships within the county
of Bruce. He was not, however, permitted to take his seat, owing
to some irregularity which had occurred regarding his election, the
nature of which the author has not been able to trace, beyond that
a protest as to his right to hold the office was entered. That the
vacancy might be filled, the Council directed the warden to issue a
warrant for a fresh election at Kincardine, and " that Mr. Francis
Walker be returning officer." The result of this election was that
William Rastall was elected reeve. To him belongs the honor of
being the first representative from Bruce to sit at the County Council.
The date when he took his seat as such was May 3rd, 1852.

The municipality of which Mr. Rastall was the head comprised
all the townships in the county of Bruce, Kincardine being the
senior township This municipal union lasted during the years
1852-3. The Council thereof for the year 1852 consisted of Wm.
Rastall, reeve, and councillors, Rev Wm. Fraser, Francis Walker,
Wm. Blair and Thos. Harris. The meetings of Council were always
held in Kincardine. The clerk was Christopher R. Barker, to whom
was deputed the duty of appointing pathmasters, it being impossible
for the Council to have a personal knowledge of the best available
men living throughout a territory as large as the eleven townships
lying within the municipality, so Mr. Barker travelled the length
and breadth of the county to make the necessary appointments.

The Council for 1853 differed but little, as regards its members,
from that of the preceding year, excepting that the Rev. William
Fraser held the position of reeve of the municipality,[1] while C. R.

[1]Francis Walker was elected deputy reeve in 1853, but did not sit in the
County Council, as that body considered his certificate of election irregular,
owing to the roll not being certified to as a true copy of the names of the
householders and freeholders in the united townships

Barker remained as the clerk-treasurer. In a footnote[1] are to be found the names of the assessors and collectors for the years 1852-3 and of the taxes collected in the latter year.

Without exception the members of the Council of "The United Townships in the County of Bruce," as given in the preceding paragraph, resided in either Kincardine or Huron Townships. The councillors being all from one section of the county, it is easy to perceive how the actions of the Council might be biased by local interests. The incident about to be related proved that in some instances, at least, this was the case.

Those who settled at Kincardine and in the immediate vicinity were from the first strongly impressed with the desirability of having a harbor constructed at that point (in accordance with the plan suggested in the original survey of the town-plot), which would permit vessels to load or unload safely in any weather. This sentiment was, of course, from local interests, one in which the individual members of the Townships Council participated. Blinded by a strong

---

[1] NAMES OF THE ASSESSORS AND COLLECTORS OF THE UNITED TOWNSHIPS FOR THE YEARS 1852 AND 1853, AND OF THE LEVY FOR TAXES FOR THE LATTER YEAR

Township		Assessor	Collector	Total Taxes Levied in 1853.
Kincardine,	1852 ..	Wm Daniel	... Wm Daniel	
"	1853 ...	. Geo Ryckman .	....Wm Daniel .	£405 12 5½
Bruce,	1852 ...	. Hector Lamont .	Wm Daniel.	
"	1853	John Guest	.M McLennan .	28 6 1
Kinloss,	1852 .	John Guest	John Guest	
"	1853	Geo. Ryckman	..Wm Daniel. ..	14 0 9½
Huron,	1852.	John Hunter .	... Wm. Daniel	
"	1853.. ..	Hugh Teskey . .	John Hunter . ..	55 10 1½
Brant,	1852	John Guest	John Guest ...	
"	1853	Geo. Ryckman . .	Wm Daniel . . .	117 8 2
Carrick,	1852	Nil	Nil.	
. "	1853....	Geo. Ryckman.... .	Wm Daniel..	2 9 9
Greenock,	1852.......John Guest		John Guest .	
"	1853....	Geo Ryckman	Wm Daniel... ...	33 17 2½
Saugeen,	1852....	M. McLennan ..	M. McLennan	
"	1853	John Guest . .	.J T Conaway . ..	115 3 4
Arran,	1852	Nil.	Nil ..	
"	1853 ...... John Guest . .		J. T. Conaway ..	55 6 9
Eldershe,	1852-3	Nil. ..	Nil .	
Culross,	1852-3	Nil	Nil . ..	

£827 14 8

1852 was the first year that taxes were paid in the county of Bruce, and then only on account of local rates. The above shows the first levy in which county rates were included. The available figures are very conflicting, but the above is believed to be correct. Of the total about £500 was for local requirements, £19 for reduction of county debt, £42 payment on Maitland River bridge, £15 lunatic asylum tax, £55 on account of railway debentures

desire to accomplish this local improvement, it was but a step to
believe that the county at large would also derive therefrom benefits
sufficient to warrant the passing of a by-law, under the " Consolidated Municipal Loan Fund Act," to raise the required funds for
the construction of a harbor. On steps being taken to obtain the
concurrence of the ratepayers to this, a storm of indignation was
raised in all the townships outside of the two that supplied the quota
of councillors This feeling of indignation was accentuated by dis-
approval of the action of Reeve Rastall in voting in support of a
by-law, passed October 20th, 1852, by the Council of the United
Counties, to take stock to the extent of £125,000 in the Buffalo,
Brantford and Lake Huron Railway.[1]

The proposed Kincardine harbor by-law was to be considered
and voted upon by the ratepayers on May 28th, 1853, at the village
of Penetangore (Kincardine).[2] A great rally was organized in the
outside townships to vote the project down. The voters from the
north reached Kincardine by sailing vessels, Capt. D. Rowan, in
command of the *Emily,* and Capt. John Spence, in the schooner
Sea Gull, bringing large contingents. From Brant there started
a procession that comprised most of the resident freeholders
of the township, and which gathered in numbers until Kinloss was
reached; by that time it numbered fully four hundred within its
long strung out ranks. At the head rode Joseph Walker, mounted
on the one solitary horse of the settlement. The rest trudged
sturdily along on foot, one of their number carrying a banner, on
which was painted the motto, " *Brant, No Taxation, No Surrender,*"
the lettering of which was the handiwork of Mr. Malcolm McLean,
the present postmaster of Walkerton. At Johnston's Corners Mr.
John Eckford and others addressed the gathering, and united action
was decided upon, one item of which was to the effect that not a
penny was to be spent for food or drink in Kincardine, and thus
show in a marked manner, as well as by their votes, the sentiments
they cherished regarding this scheme, which originated, so, they
vociferously asserted, in a desire to tax the county at large for the
benefit of Kincardine. This proposal was actually carried out by

---

[1]The necessity of railway communication was a felt want in the western part of the province at that time, and the enterprise shown by the
County Council is to be commended. The taking of this amount of stock
enabled the road to be extended to Goderich. True, it was a half-dozen years
after this before the rails were laid to the lake, but for the succeeding
fifteen years this railway was the main outlet for travel to and from the
western part of the county of Bruce.

[2]See procedure of such a meeting, given in 16 Vic, Chap 22, Sec. 5 and 6.

many, who brought with them food and whiskey sufficient to last during their stay, and who also, when night came, slept under the juniper bushes on the lake shore rather than ask for shelter in some house in the village. The preliminary meeting, as well as the voting, was held at "Paddy" Walker's tavern. During the proceedings the Roll of Brant was surreptitiously purloined and buried in the sand near the beach. Any action after the disappearance of this Roll would have been irregular, so Messrs. Wm. Gunn, Valentine, Conaway, Benson and Hilker served a protest, and demanded that all proceedings in regard to the by-law be stopped, which, under the circumstances, had to be complied with. The excitement, which all day had been at fever heat, was much augmented by stirring speeches and an abundant supply of whiskey. In such an atmosphere fights started very easily. These at last became so general that it seemed at one time as if the many fights would merge into a general riot. To prevent this Reeve Fraser had some twenty-two special constables sworn in, who succeeded in maintaining the peace and in dispersing the excited throng to their homes.

Thus Kincardine's first effort to secure the construction of a harbor collapsed; nevertheless, there remained implanted in the breasts of many throughout the county a resentful feeling against that village, cherished for years afterward.

One effect of the foregoing incident was to develop a desire for a dissolution of the municipal union of townships. In pursuance of this, petitions were presented to the Council of the United Counties, at its several sessions in the year 1853, for the erection of several minor municipalities within the county of Bruce. At the September session of that year it was decided to carry out the expressed wish of so many ratepayers in Bruce, and there was passed, September 21st, 1853, a general by-law[1] changing the municipal conformation of the county, and erecting six minor municipalities therein. This took effect on the 1st January, 1854. The following list gives the names of the six municipalities so formed and of the reeves thereof for the year 1854:

United townships of Kincardine, Bruce and Kinloss ....William Rastall, Reeve.
Township of Huron .... John Hunter, "
United townships of Brant and Carrick . ... Joseph Walker, "
  "   "   . Greenock and Culross........ ... George Cromar, "
Township of Saugeen.................. ....Alexander McNabb, "
United townships of Arran and Elderslie .... Richard Berford, "

[1]As this by-law is the authority for the separate municipal existence of the townships named therein, it is given in full in Appendix F.

The dissolving of the union of all the townships in the county and forming thereof six municipalities was a measure much appreciated by the ratepayers. A large increase in the number of settlers was required, however, ere each township could enter upon a separate career as an independent municipality. The first to do so was Kinloss, which in 1855 was detached from Kincardine and Bruce. The following year (1856) witnessed the severance of the union of Kincardine and Bruce Townships, of Brant and Carrick, of Greenock and Culross, as well as of Arran and Eldershe. It was in this last mentioned year that for the first time each of the several townships comprised in the original county of Bruce sent a representative to attend the Council of the united counties of Huron and Bruce, there being but these two counties in the union at that time, Perth having separated therefrom on January 1st, 1853. In doing so Perth assumed two-fifths of the liabilities of the originally united counties.

Among the many municipal alterations which occurred during these changeful years, the uniting of the township of Amabel to that of Arran should not be overlooked. This union was accomplished December 18th, 1856, when the United Counties Council passed a by-law to that effect. Amabel was the first of the newly surveyed townships in the Indian Peninsula to come into possession of municipal privileges and responsibilities.

By this time the population of Bruce had so increased as to warrant an application being made to have abrogated the union of the counties of Huron and Bruce This was acceded to and Parliament passed an Act on May 16th, 1856,[1] authorizing the formation of the provisional County Council of Bruce, the preliminary step towards a separation from Huron At this time it was hoped that a few months would see the separation completed, but local jealousies as to where the county town was to be, intervened to prevent a consummation so desirable. The story of the ten years' struggle for the county-town is reserved for another chapter.

The tabulated statement of the equalized assessment of the several municipalities within the county, as given in Appendix M, indicates the growth, as well as the relative development, of each township during the days when Bruce was but an "infant county."

[1] 19 Vic., Chap 19.

CHAPTER V.

THE SETTLEMENT OF THE COUNTY.
1850—1856.

THE most marked characteristic of the settlement of the county of Bruce was the rapidity with which it was accomplished, combined with the vigorous life of its development, which were phenomenal in the history of this province. The short space of thirty years, commencing with 1850, wrought changes that were marvellous. During that period the vast primeval forest that spread over the county largely disappeared before the axe of the settler; instead of "Nature's solitude" were to be found cultivated farms, active centres of commerce and manufacturing industries. The trackless bush vanished as the county became covered with a network of gravel roads. To these avenues of traffic were added four lines of railway that entered the county during those years of pronounced development, thus bringing the markets of the world to the doors of its farmers and manufacturers. To have emerged from nature's wilderness and to have attained a population of 65,000 and an assessed value of over $25,000,000 in the space of but three decades, is the proud boast of the county of Bruce, evidencing abundantly the richness of its natural resources, as well as the energetic type of its early settlers.

Prior to 1850 not a township within the county had been surveyed into farm lots. What had been done by the Crown in the way of preparing for the inflow of settlers that subsequently poured into the county, is related in Chapter II. of this history.

The enterprising men who had settled at Penetangore and vicinity early perceived the advantages, as well as the necessity, of having the rich lands in the township of Kincardine surveyed for settlement, for only the Lake Shore and Durham Road Ranges were at the time we speak of laid out into farm lots. They therefore raised by subscription, limited as their means were, an amount sufficient to send Allan Cameron as their representative to urge upon the government an immediate survey of the block of land comprised in concessions four to twelve of that township. The representations made were well received, and in July, 1850, J. W. Bridgland, P.L.S, with a staff of assistants, landed at Penetangore and completed the required surveys during the course of that summer.

While J. W. Bridgland was at work in Kincardine Township, A. P. Brough, having completed the survey of the " free grants," commenced the survey of the township of Brant, north of the Durham Road Ranges. These two surveyors were the only ones at work in Bruce during 1850. In the fall of that year Mr. Brough, having completed the survey of Brant, proceeded, as already mentioned, to lay out the Elora Road from Greenock town-plot as far as the township of Maryborough, thus preparing another route whereby the county could be entered and by which its inhabitants could take their produce to market.

The number of settlers that came into the county in 1850 was largely in excess of the preceding year. As these settled principally on " free grant " lands, it is but fair to assume that the advantageous character of the offer made by the Crown was becoming widely known and realized. The greater portion of these settlers found farms to their satisfaction in either Brant or Kincardine, while a few passed into Kinloss, which in 1850 received its first inhabitants, who settled in the vicinity of " the Black Horse," among them being Joel Eli Stauffer, Thomas Hodgins, Thomas Smith, John and William Shelton and others. A fair number of settlers located on the Lake Ranges in Huron and Kincardine, largely attracted by the advantage offered of water communication, which gave ready access from the first. Arran received its first settler in this year in the person of Henry Boyle, a squatter who located on his lot in advance of the survey of the township

The reader may have noticed that to Greenock Township (in which a portion of the free grant lands lay) a quota of settlers has not been assigned. An explanation of this is made clear by the following extract from a letter received by Mr. George Jackson, C. L. Agent, from the Department: " August 15th, 1850. *Re* Tp. Greenock. As the survey is not fully completed, and as there is no intention of opening the road through the township at present, it is desirable that no locations should be made this season." These instructions were not countermanded until the following April.

Action was taken by the government early in the summer of 1850 to fulfil the promise made to open the Durham Road. Under instructions received from the Department, Mr. Jackson, on June

28th, 1850, issued notices asking for tenders for the making of the road through the township of Brant, the work to be commenced on or before July 10th and to be completed by the 1st October following. That the reader may have an idea of what was considered the requisites of an ordinary bush-road, and what was called for in the specifications, a copy of the same is given in a foot-note.[1] This piece of work was let in eleven sections. The names of the respective contractors are as follows, commencing at lot 1 and thence eastward to Bentinck: Wm. Johnston, Richard Guinn, Johnston Smith, Jos. Walker, Ed. Bolton, Wm. Bottrel, Thos. Todd, Adam Clement, Ephm. Fursman, Jas. McCartney and Jas. Gaffney. The prices paid under the different contracts varied from £23 to £25 per mile for chopping and logging, and for causewaying, 7s. 6d. to 10s. per rod. The contract for the two bridges over the Saugeen was let for £277 10s. to Joseph Walker, who had assisting him in the construction thereof John McLean, Wm. McIntosh, Archd. Fraser and ("Big") Sam Colwell, of Kincardine Township. The total cost to the government of opening the road through Brant was £665 4s. 9d. The contractors were all paid during the month of November, evidencing that the time limit in the contracts must have been fairly adhered to. The details here given may seem somewhat too minute, the excuse therefor being that these were the first road contracts let in the county of Bruce.

That the reader may have an idea of what travelling meant in the county of Bruce in the year 1850, in a footnote[2] is given the reminiscences of a tramp made in that year from Hanover to Kin-

---

[1]The contracts called for the performance of the following work : " The whole extent (of the road) to be chopped a width of 66 feet. All trees 8 inches and under in diameter to be cut close to the ground. The whole of the timber on the allowance for road to be cut into logging lengths, these together with all the brushwood and rubbish found thereon to be piled on each side of the road, so as, that the same shall be fit for burning, and so that a clear space of 45 feet shall be left in the centre of the allowance for the road. Timber may be felled into the woods on each side, but not into the clearings. In swamps and other places where causewaying is required the whole of the timber to be cut close to the ground a width of 20 feet in the centre of the road allowance. The causewaying to be made of sound, straight logs laid even, close together, and at right angles to said road, and each log to be 16 feet in length. All bridges of 15 feet span and under to be included under the head of causewaying, and without extra charge."

[2]NOTES OF TRAMP MADE IN 1850, BY M. C. SCHOFIELD, P.L.S.

" Desirous to see the beautiful country being surveyed in Bruce, as also to descend the highly applauded Saugeen River, I accompanied men of A. P. Brough's surveying party to what was then called the "First Crossing,"

cardine, thence to Southampton and Owen Sound, by M. C. Schofield, P.L.S.

Early in 1851 the government, realizing the necessity of taking steps to prepare for the large number of would-be settlers who desired to buy bush farms and make a home for themselves in the new county of Bruce, issued instructions for the survey into farm lots of the townships of Arran, Elderslie, Saugeen and the residue of the townships of Bruce and Huron that lay back of the Lake Ranges Arran was so surveyed by Mr. George Gould for Charles Rankin, P.L.S., Elderslie by G. McPhilips, P.L.S., Saugeen by Alex. Vidal, P L S.,[1] Huron by E. R Jones, P.L.S., and Bruce by A P. Brough, P.L.S. These surveys were all completed during the summer of 1851, except that of Bruce, the survey of which was brought to an abrupt termination owing to Mr. Brough having contracted a fatal illness during its progress, causing the work to be stopped at the sideline between lots 10 and 11.[2] In addition to the

now the town of Hanover   Here Jos. Walker, with a party, were throwing the first bridge across the river. There I embarked with the men, carrying supplies to their camp, at the present town of Walkerton, on a raft. The anticipated pleasure of a sail down the river, in many places wide and deep, was greatly marred or lessened by a continuous heavy rain, causing us to appreciate a warm, dry camp and a hearty supper.

"Early next morning I started for Penetangore, 27 miles distant, reaching it that evening rather fatigued With the exception of five miles of dense forest, where I had blazed trees for my guide, the road was being cleared by various contractors.

"At Mud River I became impatient, waiting for the Frenchwoman to come and ferry me across—in response to my repeated shouts—which was her custom I therefore disrobed and was fording the river when she came to the bank where her boat was

"After remaining a couple of days at the real comfortable hotel, kept by the late Allan Cameron, I started to walk to the present village of Southampton There were two houses there then. Owing to a severe storm the previous day (which completely closed the outlet of the river at Kincardine) the sandy beach was in fine condition for pedestrianism. But there were miles of various sized boulders upon which it was most difficult to walk, or step from one to the next , still worse, I found miles of pebbles or gravel, about as laborious to walk on as hard peas.

"At Baie De Dore was an Indian in camp whom I could not persuade, for money or brandy, to ferry me to the opposite point, thus saving me four miles' travel around through water a foot or more deep. Further on were three or four more Indian families, camped for fishing. In one of the wigwams I took a short refreshing sleep, and finally reached my destination after the most fatiguing day's labor of my life

"The following morning, with a young Scotch lass from my own neighborhood for a pilot, we started on the Indian trail for Owen Sound, about twenty-five miles, arriving quite early in the day, tired out"

[1]The late Hon. Senator Vidal

[2]When the serious nature of Mr. Brough's illness became apparent his assistant, Latham B. Hamlin, started for the clearings to obtain help to

township surveys, a survey of the town-plot of Southampton was also ordered, and was carried out by R F. Lynn, P.L.S. Judging from the large area he laid out into town lots, this officer must have had an exaggerated idea regarding the possibilities of what was then expected to be the county town of the new county.

Besides ordering the surveys of these five townships the government decided to establish an agency for the sale of Crown lands within the county (see Appendix G for copy of Order-in-Council relating to this), and on the 19th May, 1851, Mr. Alexander McNabb was gazetted as Crown Lands Agent for Bruce, with Southampton designated as his place of residence. This position Mr. McNabb held until his death, which occurred May 1st, 1882.[1] The above appointment was followed by a notice in the *Gazette,* June 27th, 1851 (see Appendices G and H), offering for sale lands in the townships of Brant and Kincardine and the villages of Penetangore and Southampton, "on and after the 5th August next," on application to Mr. McNabb. These were the first lands offered *for sale* in the county of Bruce. All of them were known as "school lands," the price of which at first was 12s. 6d. per acre [2] Arriving at Southampton in August, Mr McNabb opened his office for the sale of the lands so offered by the Crown. He also, shortly afterward visited Penetangore for the convenience of would-be purchasers there

take the sick man to where he could obtain medical treatment. At Stoney Island he met Capt Murdoch McLeod, who informed him that there was not a sailing vessel in the vicinity, but offered the use of a small row-boat he had ' In this the Captain rowed to Inverhuron (known at that time as the Little Sauble River), reaching there just as the men of the party arrived from camp, carrying the invalid on a stretcher. Without loss of time he was placed in the boat and taken to Penetangore. Medical assistance not being available, once more the sick man was placed in the boat. Captain McLeod and another, taking turn about, rowed the long distance to Goderich, where, at Rattenbury's Hotel, this veteran surveyor of Bruce died a day or so afterward.

[1]Mr. Alexander McNabb was born in Lower Canada at The Cedars, Soulanges County, October 7th, 1809 In his early life he was employed by Colonel By, during the construction of the Rideau Canal. At the time of his appointment to be Crown Lands Agent for Bruce, he held the position of bookkeeper for the Crown Lands Department. The thirty-one years of his connection with the county of Bruce were marked by a conscientious attention to the duties of his office. Many difficult disputes regarding squatters' rights came before him, as well as attempts made by speculators to avoid the "actual settlement" required by statute, which Mr McNabb settled strictly on their merits. His son, John M. McNabb, now residing in the old homestead at Southampton, is the possessor of a wonderful fund of reminiscences of the early days of the county of Bruce

[2]See Appendix O.

The summer and fall of 1851 witnessed a busy scene along the western end of the Durham Road, arising from the carrying out of the contracts[1] let by the Government to chop and log the road from the lake eastward as far as Riversdale; from that point to the Greenock town-plot the contracts let were only for bridging and causewaying. Those whose contract was located at a distance from the lake had special obstacles to overcome, arising from the difficulty of obtaining necessary supplies. It is related regarding one of the contractor's camps, situated near a small clearing planted with potatoes, but left by the owner to take care of itself during his absence at the settlements, that on his return, instead of finding his expected winter's supply of potatoes ready to be gathered, found instead his field stripped. The necessities of the men in camp having led them to appropriate and consume his total crop, for which lawless action amends were made by paying the settler a fair price for what had been taken. Meat for the men reached the camps in rather a novel way. " Paddy " Walker, who had a camp of his own to provide for, would drive a beast out to one of the camps in Greenock, there slaughter it, and divide up the meat with the other camps as he returned to his own in Kincardine, receiving remuneration enough to recoup him for his trouble. The various contracts above referred to were completed before winter set in, the total cost to the government for the same being £1,004, exclusive of what was paid toward opening a road through the town-plot of Penetangore, which, however, was not completed until 1856.

To enable settlers to reach the township of Elderslie, the survey of which was in progress that summer (1851), Mr. Jackson asked for tenders (July 14th, 1851) for the opening of what he termed the " Durham and Southampton Road," through the township of Brant   This line of road commenced at " Rosewell's Corners," on the north side of the Durham Road, between lots 15 and 16, thence along the side-line to the concession line between the fourth and fifth concessions, thence west to the front of concession " B," and along that, the present Elora Road, to the town-line of Elderslie.

[1]The following are the names of the various contractors, commencing at Lot 1, Kincardine, thence eastward : Wm. Sutton, Robert Stewart, Wm. Millar, Robert Brown, Andrew Horn, Francis Walker, Wm. Armstrong, John Moffatt, James Thorn and Samuel Colwell in Kincardine. In Kinloss : Samuel Colwell, J. Eli Stauffer, John Smith and Martin Meredith.   In Greenock : John Sherridan, David Smith, Luke Chatreau, John McLean For the bridge at Riversdale : Arch Stewart and William McIntosh, and Hans Hawthorne for causewaying and culverts east of Riversdale.

The work of chopping, logging and opening up was completed that same season.[1]

The work done in the way of opening up roads up to the end of 1851 throughout the county may be summed up by stating, that the Durham Road was cleared from the county-line, west to the lake, excepting a break extending from lot 1, Brant, to the Teeswater River, causewayed in all swampy places, and all streams spanned by substantial bridges, with similar work done on the road through Brant from the Durham Line to the boundary of Elderslie.

Prior to the opening of the above-mentioned roads all settlements made in the county were at points situated on its borders (excepting the case of Messrs. Orchard and Rowe, presently to be related) that were fairly accessible, as well as comparatively convenient to places from which supplies could be procured, such as Goderich and Durham, water carriage being obtained from the former by the lake, and from the latter by the Saugeen, which was utilized to float rafts bearing settlers and their effects as far as where Walkerton now stands.[2] A notable extension of this means of travel occurred in

[1]The following are the names of those who had contracts for opening up this road. Commencing at the Durham Road: Joseph Bacon, George Briggs, Arch. Stewart, James Wilson, James Bacon, Hugh Young, Samuel T. Rowe and Simon Orchard. An explanation for the detour this road made in its way from the Durham to the Elora Roads is given in the chapter on "The Township of Brant."

[2]Regarding the navigation of the Saugeen, the following incidents may be noted : One adventuresome Irishman, named McMullen, who had resided on the Garafraxa Road, being desirous of living near Lake Huron, built at Durham, in October, 1849, a small scow, in which, with his wife, two small children and their few effects, he sailed down the river in safety to Southampton, and thence to the vicinity of Penetangore, where he settled. In 1851, a man living near Hanover, named Shupe, built a scow, and with the assistance of William Summers, sailed down the Saugeen to its mouth, and thence by lake to Goderich, where he purchased six or eight barrels of flour, with which he loaded his craft, and returned by the same route. Coming up the river was a laborious work, the rapids having to be surmounted by towing and poling ; one man wading in the water with a rope over his shoulders, while the other assisted by pushing with a long pole. The following item appeared in the columns of the Paisley Advocate, in its issue of April 28th, 1876, and vividly refers to this subject of the navigation of the Saugeen : "When the first steam sawmill, built in this county, was to be erected at Southampton, about twenty-five years ago, it became a question how the large boiler could be brought to its destination, as there was no road through the county. The boiler was conveyed to Hanover, if we remember rightly, and there left by the side of the Saugeen to wait the turning up of some genius who would invent some method of taking it further. It was at last decided to make an ironclad of it and float it down the river. All the openings were tightly plugged, and with levers and handspikes the huge boiler was started, rolling at a rapid rate down the steep bank into the deep river at the foot. The boiler, being very heavy, and

April, 1851, when a settlement was made in the very heart of the
county by Simon Orchard and his family.   Arriving at Walkerton
by way of the Durham Road, Mr. Orchard constructed a raft on
which he placed his family and belongings.   Shoving off, the raft,
with its venturesome passengers, floated down the rapid stream,
whose banks at that time were covered by a dense, unbroken forest.
Night found them at the junction of the Saugeen and Teeswater
Rivers.   Here Mr. Orchard pitched his camp for the night.   On
examining the locality in the morning he was so well satisfied with
it that he determined to locate there.   Using the boards of his raft
for building material he soon erected a temporary shanty.   Mr.
Vidal and his party of surveyors made their appearance on the spot
a day or so afterwards, and with their kindly assistance a log building was put up.   On May 9th, three weeks after Mr. Orchard's
arrival, he was joined by his friend, S T Rowe.   These two families
formed the embryo settlement which later developed into the village
of Paisley   This settlement in the centre of the county was not
long without neighbors.   David Lyons and Thomas Hembroff in
the fall of 1851 took up lands at what afterward was known as
Lockerby, some two miles distant from Paisley.   They were not
joined by their families, however, until the following spring.

On the withdrawal of the restriction regarding settlement on the
"free grants" in Greenock in April, 1851, a number of settlers
poured into that township, and speedily the last of the "free grants"
that were at all desirable to settle upon were taken up.   Among those
who settled in Greenock at this time were. Adam Ritchie, sen., and

going down with great force, it at once disappeared with a tremendous
splash. The experiment was voted a failure at the very commencement, and
the costly concern was supposed to be lost, but while the disappointed
navigators looked on with blank faces where their craft had disappeared, it
came slowly to the surface, raising its black shape high above the water.
The boiler, which had started on its way north without waiting for any one
to take command, was at once captured, and a dry cedar log lashed to each
side, oars were rigged, and away went the strangest craft that ever navigated
the Saugeen   The boiler was safely taken to Southampton, passing Paisley
on the way down with a flag flying, and the heads of the great rivets showing like the scales of some huge sea monster. It was not unusual in those
days for settlers to come down on rafts from far up the river, sometimes
bringing their whole outfit on one crib   On one occasion, early in the morning, a commodious raft passed where this village now is. On one end was a
cow with her calf ; on the other, along with considerable baggage, was a
cooking stove, in which was a good fire, and while the enterprising settler
was attending to the navigation of his vessel, the good wife was busy at the
stove getting breakfast ready   The smoke, which streamed from the elevated
pipe, gave the moving raft the appearance of a rustic steamer in motion."

his sons, John B., Sterling and William D, also Hans, Thomas and Samuel Hawthorne, Alexander, Samuel and William Cunningham, Henry, James, Robert, William and George Pinkerton. Settlers also located in Arran about the same time, the most prominent of whom was George Gould and Richard Berford, who took up farm lots afterwards surveyed into the villages of Invermay and Tara. .About the same time several settlers squatted upon the unsurveyed lands in Carrick, near the boundary of Brant The names of these were John Hogg, Andrew Hutton, Louis Fournier and Oliver Toronjeau.

When the determination of some would-be settler became fixed to go into the backwoods and take up a bush-farm in the county of Bruce, the question how to reach the eligible lands there opened for settlement was a most serious one. The completion of the two roads mentioned in a preceding paragraph, supplemented by similar work to be referred to hereafter, performed in 1852 and subsequently, solved the problem in a measure. The difficulties and hardships that individual settlers surmounted prior to the opening of these roads, have been outlined in various parts of this history Those who settled in Kincardine and Huron Townships made use of the lake; in winter they entered the county by driving along its shore on the ice, or if they came during the season of navigation, they did so by sailing vessel The two first settlers, Allan Cameron and William Withers, entered the county in this way, having been brought to the mouth of the Penetangore River by Capt. Murray MacGregor on his schooner, *The Fly*. Capt. MacGregor about this time was engaged largely in sailing to and from the Bruce Mines, but as opportunity offered carried many a settler and his belongings to Penetangore or Southampton. The first vessels to engage regularly in sailing from Goderich to county of Bruce ports date back to 1849, and were limited in that year to two small craft, one of which was a dug-out canoe, of unusual dimensions for that description of craft, commanded by Abraham Holmes (referred to in the chapter on the township of Huron). The other was a two-masted open sailboat, called the *Wing and Wing*, sailed by Capt. Soper. These two vessels were sufficient for all the traffic of that year. Many a settler in Bruce has kindly recollections of Capt. Duncan Rowan and of his estimable wife, who frequently sailed with him during his long career as a lake captain. In Chapter III. Capt. Rowan's early advent into Bruce is related In 1850 he laid aside the woodman's

axe to navigate the waters of Lake Huron. In that and the following year he had command of a small schooner called the *Mary Ann.*
In the years 1852 to 1855 he sailed the *Emily*, leaving that vessel
in 1856 to take charge of the *Ploughboy*, the first steamer to sail
regularly on the route from Detroit and Windsor to Southampton.
Another lake captain who as a man and as a sailor has the esteem
of all who know him, is Capt. Murdoch McLeod. He commenced
to engage in the trade along the lake about the same time as Capt.
Rowan   Capt. McLeod's first vessel on this route was the *High-
lander*, which he sailed in the years 1850-51. In 1852-53 he commanded the *Waterwitch*, and in 1854, and for several years after,
the *Mountaineer.* William Rastall had a vessel built in the winter
of 1851-52, at Kincardine, which bore the name of the *Forest;* Capt.
John Murray was in charge of her until sold to Capt. John Spence
in 1854, who during the two previous seasons had sailed the *Sea Gull.*
Another vessel on this route in 1853-54 was the *Fairy*, commanded
by Capt. Edward Marlton, of Goderich. Of these vessels, many were
but open boats, in some cases not nearly as staunch as those in common use to-day by the fishermen on the lake. The names of the
various vessels engaged in the lake traffic and of their captains have
been given in what may seem a somewhat detailed manner. As an
excuse for this, the reader is asked to remember that hundreds of
settlers found their way into the county of Bruce by their instru-
mentality. Of these, those who survive and read the foregoing will
note with pleasure the name of the vessel and of the captain that
brought them safely over the waters of Lake Huron to their destination; and they will recall the voyage and the novelty of a prolonged
sail in a small, over-ladened craft, accentuated by incidents of
danger,[1] for in those days there were no harbors of refuge or light-

---

[1]The following episode, written by Mrs. John Reekie, late of Kincardine
Township, details vividly the dangers and hardships referred to   After
relating the particulars of the journey from Glengarry with her father
(Archibald Sinclair, of Sinclair Corners, township of Bruce) and the rest
of the family to Goderich, Mrs Reekie goes on to say : " The only available
transport for the rest of the journey was an open boat   In this we embarked
after waiting a few days for favorable winds. There were eighteen passengers in all. We left port about 8 p.m. The night was dark and the lake
rather rough   In about an hour or two the wind rose to such a gale that
it was considered too great a risk to attempt to round Pine Point.   The
boat was accordingly headed for shore at a place called 18-Mile Creek—the
only place where it was said a landing could be effected with safety   It was
a perilous run, but it had to be made ; and as we went plunging through
the foaming breakers the boldest held his breath, as it seemed that every
plunge might be the last. When we struck the beach our little craft went to

houses to guide or warn. Such early voyagers can recall the unpleas-antness, especially to women and children, of being landed on the beach amid the breakers as they rolled in and broke in foam on the sandy shore, for pier or wharf existed not, and of how many an article of freight or of personal effects was wet and possibly ruined by water in being transferred from the vessel to land

In April, 1851, the control of the postal system of the province was transferred from the British to the Canadian Government; as a result there was an extension of postal privileges in which Bruce participated. That summer a post-office was established at Kincardine and another at Southampton.[1] The postmasters of these two offices were David MacKendrick and Robert Reid, respectively. Prior to the establishment of these offices all mail matter for Bruce had to be obtained at either Goderich, Owen Sound or Bentinck (Durham).[2]

Parliament was dissolved November 6th, 1851. At the election which followed, the Hon. Wm. Cayley, who had previously repre-

pieces, and it was with no little difficulty that the women and children were rescued. How thankful we were, though wet and dripping, to find our-selves once more on solid land. The night was bitterly cold, and there was no shelter nor habitation to be seen Only a narrow beach, with high clay banks on one side and the raging waters on the other. The sailors told us that above the bank was a clearing, with a house about half a mile away. We climbed the bank, and after wandering around in the dark for a while we discovered what we took to be the house on the opposite side of a deep ravine. Down into this we went, crawled across the creek on a log, and up the other side The occupants of the shanty lost no time in making us as comfortable as possible under the circumstances ; two of the men being left to guard what was saved of the cargo and luggage on the beach Some of the neighboring settlers, who learned of the disaster, kindly offered to relieve them, bidding them go and get shelter and rest, with the result that several articles of value disappeared in their absence. The next morning men, women and children started on foot to reach Kincardine, as there was nothing else to be done, there being nothing but a footpath We made ten miles that day. There could not well be a more weary lot of children than we were when we arrived at Bellemore's tavern at Pine River that night, where we found accommodation so limited that we children, with the girls of the house, had to sleep on the straw in the barn, none too well covered for the cold night. Our party had not proceeded far along the shore next morning when we were met by a boat that had been despatched to our assistance by some of the men who had walked through to Kincardine the night before, in which we reached our destination, thankful to be done with travel either by land or water."

[1]This post-office at first, and until about 1890, was known as "Saugeen."

[2]The mail service to these three places at the time the first settlers came into Bruce was as follows · Goderich received a mail from London twice a week, conveyed by coach or horseback ; from Preston thrice a week, con-veyed by coach Bentinck received a mail from Guelph once a week, con-veyed on horseback. Owen Sound received a mail from Guelph once a week, conveyed on horseback ; from Barrie once a week, conveyed likewise.

sented Huron and Bruce, was defeated by the Hon. Malcolm Cameron, who, as a member of the Hincks-Morin Government, held the position of President of the Council.

Before passing on to narrate the incidents of the following year, attention might be drawn to two events relating to the town of Kincardine, where in 1851 the first school in the county was established, and the establishing in the same year of the first settled pastorate of any denomination in the county, that of the Rev. Thomas Crews, of the Wesleyan Methodist Church, whose congregation was organized with a membership of forty. Rev. Mr. Crews was in charge of the congregation at Kincardine for the years 1851-2.

The winter of 1851-52 was unusually severe; it was also noted by an excessive snowfall. The combination of these has caused its dark days to be well remembered by isolated settlers who had not laid in a large store of the necessities of life, as the difficulties of replenishing were under the circumstances almost insurmountable.

With the opening of the spring of 1852, five parties of surveyors were sent into the county by the government. Of these, one in charge of J. D. Daniels, P.L.S., was allotted the survey of the township of Carrick; to G. McPhilips, P.L.S., was allotted the survey of the township of Culross; to E. R. Jones, P.L.S., the survey of that part of the township of Kinloss not divided into farm lots by the early surveys of A. Wilkinson and A. P. Brough, referred to in Chapter II.; to C. Millar, P.L.S., was allotted the survey of the eastern part of the township of Bruce; and to Robt. Walsh, P.L.S., the residue of the township of Greenock.

The work of opening up the Owen Sound Post Road, as it was called, was busily prosecuted during the summer of 1852. The contracts for the same were let by A. McNabb, Crown Lands Agent. This road extended from Southampton to Owen Sound, via Burgoyne and Invermay. Part of the required work thereon was the construction of the first bridge erected over the Saugeen, north of Walkerton,[1] Thomas Lee[2] and Thomas Godfrey being the contractors.

---

[1]Mr. McNabb on leaving Toronto to assume his new duties at Southampton was supplied with $6,000 by the Government to be disbursed in the opening up of roads. On rendering a statement of contracts entered into, that for the bridge over the Saugeen was disallowed, the Crown Lands Department claiming it to be unauthorized, as the grant had been made for roads and roads only. Until this bit of red-tape could be got round the money to meet this obligation was raised on the joint personal note of Mr. McNabb and the Hon. Malcolm Cameron. (See also Appendix O.)

[2]Thomas Lee filled the position of postmaster at Southampton from 1857 until his death, February 20th, 1901.

The site was at Henry Boyles', lot 21, concession "A," Arran. The contract for opening this road through the township of Arran was secured by George Gould[1] for nearly the whole way. The author has only been able to surmise the reasons why this road was opened up years before the more direct one, which is known as the Northern Gravel Road, and which, as far as he has been able to find out, the government had engaged with the Indians to open when they made the surrender (in September, 1851) of the "Half-mile Strip."[2] The following are the surmises offered: First, the funds at the disposal of the Crown Lands Department for the purposes of road-making being very limited compared to the demands thereon, every penny had to be prudently and economically spent, and as there was along the northern boundary of Arran a long stretch of swampy land through which it would be difficult and expensive to construct a road, very much more so than to open the road decided upon; and also, by starting the Owen Sound Road at Burgoyne, a point on the Elora Road, instead of at Southampton, the erection of one bridge over the Saugeen would answer both the roads, and so the cost of a second bridge be avoided. These considerations probably led to the road by the longer route being decided upon And, as a further consideration, the opening of a road through the centre of the township of Arran instead of along its northern boundary, would expedite its early settlement, as well as being a convenience to a larger number of settlers, although, be it remembered,[3] the Indian Department were offering for sale the lots on the Half-mile Strip at the same time

Up to the time under consideration no road had been constructed which permitted communication between the townships in the north and those in the south excepting that through Brant, mentioned in a previous paragraph, and this only to the extent of about nine miles To remedy this, Simon Orchard undertook (November, 1851), on payment of £12 10s., to open up "a sleigh track" from

[1]George Gould's name is closely identified with Arran. He had been engaged in its survey, under Charles Rankin, and he was among the first to take up land in the township. He was the first postmaster of "Arran," now Invermay. He also filled the office of township clerk for several years, until he resigned in 1861 to assume the duties of county clerk.

[2]In October, 1865, the Government paid into the hands of the treasurer of the United Counties the sum of $4,000, to be expended in the opening up of this road and to build Denny's bridge.

[3]See Appendix I.

the vicinity of Paisley as far as Lachlan ("Lochbuie") McLean's tavern, standing where is now the village of Port Elgin; from there the beach afforded a road to Southampton [1]

The expression just used, "a sleigh track," recalls the primitive conveyances used in those early days throughout the county. Summer or winter the only conveyance the early settler used was a sleigh, alike in winter's snow or summer's mud. A waggon would have been bumped or racked to pieces among the stumps and trees, or have sunk inextricably into unknown depths of muck or mud in the tracks cut through the woods, or possibly only cleared of underbrush, which did duty for roads, these being utterly devoid of every requisite that is considered necessary in a good road The sleighs were the handiwork of the settler alone Rough looking though we might call one of them, he no doubt looked with pride upon it. The runners and frame-work he had hewed with much labor out of suitable wood, selected on account of possessing the requisite curve, and had put it together with wooden pins and wedges, his only tools an auger and an axe With such a primitive conveyance, which always had an axe stuck in a slot in the side bar, drawn by a yoke of oxen, he could travel through the bush with no fears of "a break down." The "jumper" also was much in use, especially in summer, on account of its lightness. It was even more primitive in its con· struction than the sleigh already described, as its runners were made from ash saplings, which had been flattened a short distance from one of the ends so as to be readily bent into the shape of a runner, The "jumper" frequently lacked a pole, this to enable it readily to twist about trees and stumps.

Of the many disadvantages endured by the early settlers, that of being compelled to go long distances to have their grain ground into flour was one of the most serious. The mills at Goderich and Port Albert in the early "fifties" ground many a bushel of wheat grown in Bruce, access being readily had by means of the lake to these distant mills. Those living in the rear of the county had to take their grain to Bentinck or Inglis' Falls for a similar purpose. As a makeshift, hand-mills were sometimes used. One of these, in the possession of Angus H. McKay, of Tiverton, is in a good state of preser-.

[1]It is said that after Orchard got through to his objective point that on returning, he could not find his way back over the supposed track that he had made, and had to come back through the woods by another path. Said, no doubt, in fun to illustrate how difficult it was to find the track

vation; being a curiosity in these days of roller mills, a description of it may not be amiss. This mill was brought from the county of Oxford by Hector McKay (of lot 1, con. 10, tp. Kincardine), father of the present owner, when he took up his land. An examination of the two stones that compose the mill leads one to suppose that the nether stone was originally intended for a grind-stone, but not possessing the required "grit," was adapted to a mill-stone. The upper stone is of limestone, which has been shaped so as to fit the lower one. The stones and the principle of this hand-mill are a copy of the large ones of a grist-mill, excepting that instead of regular grooves being cut on the face of the stones they have been simply roughened and indented. The upper stone shows a socket used for the insertion of a handle. The present owner relates how, after the evening meal had been disposed of, the mill would be placed on the table; one end of the handle, which was a long one, would be inserted in the socket in the stone and the other adjusted to a socket in a beam overhead, and then the mill would be run by the boys, grinding the porridge-meal for next day; or perhaps it would be used by some of the neighbors, who had brought over some grain to grind.

Major Wm. Daniel, of the Durham Line, Kincardine Township, describes the difficulties of the settlers in regard to getting their grain ground as follows: "Our only mill was an old spice-mill owned by Jacob Latschaw, driven by hand. I took half a bushel of corn there once to grind, but the work was so slow and hard that I did not attempt it a second time. We could not send a team with a grist to the mill in summer because the roads were so bad, consequently we had to wait until winter to have gristing done. Sometimes the snow was deep and the track but little better than a footpath, for settlers and teams were but few through Greenock. Consequently one beast only could utilize the single track to advantage, and in order to do this we would drive an ox single by taking a short piece of timber, cut a notch in the centre to set on its neck; into this single yoke was inserted the bow; then by a trace-chain or rope fastened to each end of the yoke we could hitch it to a light narrow 'jumper,' that would bear two or three bags of wheat. A number of us would start together, for company's sake, forming a sort of caravan of these single ox sleighs."

Disadvantages such as those referred to in the two preceding paragraphs called for redress. George Jackson, who had ever the interests of the settleis at heart, appreciating to the full the need of a grist-mill in the western part of the county especially, issued notices in the summer of 1850, calling a meeting of the settlers at Penetangore. This meeting, held opposite William Rastall's store, appointed as chairman Mr. C. R. Barker, while Joseph Barker, his brother, acted as secretary. A hundred settlers or more were present. The topic discussed was the securing of a mill-site and the erection of a mill, Mr. Jackson being the principal speaker. What results were achieved by this meeting the writer has not been able to find out. Municipal aid was granted toward the erection of a grist-mill somewhat later than this, as we find that in the levy of 1853 there appears the sum of £38 for a "mill-site." This was the first municipal bonus granted in Bruce to encourage any industry, and the author regrets that fuller particulars are not available. It was early in 1852 when William Sutton built a small log building for a mill at Kincardine (in the hollow that still bears his name), in which he placed the necessary machinery for milling purposes, and started that summer the first grist-mill in the county. The next grist-mill to be operated was that at Walkerton, erected by Joseph Walker, which was started in November, 1853. In the following year the Rev. Wm. Fraser built a mill at Lorne. These three mills were sufficient at first to supply the requirements of the southern part of the county. The northern townships had to wait for equal privileges until 1855, when Shantz's mill[1] at Mill Creek, Saugeen, was in operation. Wm. Reekie in 1855 built a grist-mill at Armow, which place was then known as "Reekie's Mills." Valentine's Mill at Paisley was running in the same year, and the one at Lockerby shortly after. At Invermay, Luke Gardiner commenced to run a grist-mill in 1857. Other mills on the Teeswater River were also in operation prior to the last given date at Pinkerton and elsewhere.

The prevailing rule that marked the settlement of the county of Bruce was that, in respect to nationality, previous occupations, and other characteristics, the original settlers of the county were fairly mixed up. Men Canadian born took up land alongside of other nationalities; experienced backwoodsmen settled alongside of

[1]So great was the run upon Shantz's mill that settlers had to wait over a month for their grists, although the mill was kept running night and day. One of the millers, a German, in order to gain on the arrears of work, determined to run on Sunday; but good old Deacon Sinclair used to tell with a chuckle how the mill showed its moral superiority over the miller by stopping punctually at 12 o'clock on Saturday night. Soft wheat had formed a dough and stopped the stones.

those that were town-bred; men who had been merchants, or who had followed some profession, settled beside trained farmers. This aggregation was to the good of all, and the succeeding generation has manifested its benefits in the energy and intelligence they possess. But in September, 1852, a marked exception to this practice took place, when what was known as the " Lewis Settlement " was made in the centre of Huron Township. This settlement comprised 109 families, all from the Isle of Lewis, Scotland. Coming into the backwoods ignorant of the country, of the requirements of pioneer life, and also of farming, for the majority of the men were by occupation fishermen or shepherds, and handicapped by being able only to speak Gaelic, these settlers were placed at a marked disadvantage, which it took a number of years to overcome, as it ultimately was. The surveyors were hardly out of the township of Carrick (1853) before settlers began to pour in. Of these a very large percentage were of German origin, who formed a second group within the county of people of one nationality. These settlers possessed the advantage of being practical farmers; the majority having come from the county of Waterloo, were accustomed to Canadian ways of farming . Many of them were possessed of means, this, combined with the natural industry and economical habits characteristic of their nationality, enabled them from the first to do well. Possessed of such advantages, these German settlers forged ahead and founded one of the most progressive settlements made throughout the whole county.

The government, on July 30th, 1852, made a change in the price charged for farm lands in the county of Bruce that was very acceptable to settlers. The price for school lands was at the first 12s 6d. and Crown lands 10s. per acre. At the date given the price was reduced to 10s. and 7s. 6d. per acre respectively. This reduction in price is said to have been made at the instance of the Hon. Malcolm Cameron, the newly elected member for the constituency in which Bruce lay.[1] On the same date the government offered for settlement and sale all the school lands in the county.[2]

The census of the province, taken in 1852,[3] shows that all the townships within the county had received a number of settlers with the exception of the townships of Carrick and Culross. With the

[1]See Appendix J.
[2]See Appendix J.
[3]The particulars of this census are to be found in Appendix L.

increase of population the government established a mail route from Durham, extending west as far as Kincardine. On this route two post-offices in Bruce were established,[1] bearing the names of "Brant" and "Greenock." John Shennan received the appointment of post-master at Brant, a name retained until September 23rd, 1857, when the name of Walkerton was given to it. The name of Greenock is still borne by the post-office, although the village is known as Enniskillen. The officer who received the position of postmaster there was J. B. Ritchie.[2]

In closing the narrative of the events of the year 1852, it may be noted that it marked the completion of the survey of the residue of Crown lands in the county into farm lots; the last survey consisted of that part of the township of Greenock not included in the Durham Line" free grants."

Previous to the organization of the Bureau of Agriculture in 1852, the annual grants made by Parliament for roads and bridges in Canada were expended under the direction of the Crown Lands Department. On September 14th, 1853, the Minister of Agriculture submitted to the Governor-in-Council a scheme, which was adopted, recommending the opening of two roads which affected the

---

[1]The first post-office established in the county of Bruce, in nearly every case, bore the name of the township in which they were located. Thus, the settlers in the township of Brant obtained their mail at "Brant P.O.," and in like manner those in Greenock at "Greenock P.O." The same rule applying to Kinloss, Kincardine, Bruce, Saugeen and Arran, where the first post-office established bore the name of the township. The townships of Elderslie and Huron are the only exceptions to the rule among the townships settled prior to 1853.

[2]Mr. J. B. Ritchie supplies the following particulars regarding the Greenock post-office. After stating that he held the office of postmaster for sixteen years from the establishment of the office, he goes on to say: "Cowan Keys (of Huron Township) was the first mail-carrier. His route was from Durham to Kincardine, a distance of 45 miles, which he traversed on foot once a week, each way. There were no horses here in those days, and even if there had been, it would have been utterly impracticable for them to get along the road, owing to its being so rough. The mail was contained in a small bag, like a schoolboy's satchel, hung by straps over the carrier's shoulders. How glad the settlers were to see the mail-carrier coming, bringing news from friends, wives and sweethearts; it made the saying true, "Absence makes the heart grow weary." Cowan brought the first mail to Greenock post-office on October 9th, 1852, and continued the weekly routine for a year or so, when the route was divided, after which Cowan brought the mail from Kincardine as far only as Greenock. There he was met by old Mr. Hunter, of Durham, with the mail of his route. Matters went on in this way for some years, until, finally, the mail was made a daily one to and from Walkerton and Kincardine."

DONALD SINCLAIR

p. 125

GEORGE GOULD

p. 93

JOHN GILLIES

p. 97

ALEX. McNABB
Crown Land Agent

p. 51

county of Bruce. The construction of these roads was entrusted to the supervision of David Gibson, P.L.S., of whom a government report speaks as "a surveyor and civil engineer of high standing and long experience in forest surveys and in the construction of roads and bridges and other public works, which he has brought to bear most favorably in the performance of the duties devolved upon him."[1] The appointment of Mr. Gibson as Superintendent of Colonization Roads bears date of September 14th, 1853. He is here referred to at length, as his connection with the county of Bruce, in the opening of government roads extended over a period of eight or ten years. As chief assistant Mr. Gibson had Wm. Lyons, P.L.S.

The scheme referred to in the preceding paragraph, which proposed the making of the two roads known as (1) the Elora and (2) the Woolwich and Huron (or "Wawanosh") Roads, was supplemented and enlarged as follows: (3) The completion of the Durham Road across Greenock and Kincardine to the village of Penetangore, chiefly cross-logging the swamps and reducing inequalities of the surface; (4) a road connecting the Elora and Sydenham Roads along the town-line between Elderslie and Brant and eastward in Grey, thirty miles in all; (5) a road in Co. Wellington with same object as (4); (6) a road along the southerly boundary of the townships of Carrick, Culross and Kinloss, uniting the Elora and Wawanosh Roads; (7) a road in Co. Wellington with the same object as (6); (8) a road south from Lucknow to the lands of the Canada Company; (9) a road between the townships of Carrick and Culross and southward a total distance of twenty miles; (10) a road connecting Southampton and Sydenham, north of Derby and Arran (about fourteen and a half miles of this road were previously opened by Mr. A. McNabb, leaving seven miles to be made); (11) a good winter road from Southampton to Goderich along such a route as may be most useful and practicable, forty-five miles.[2]

Mr. Gibson seems to have let the contracts for making a number of the foregoing roads without loss of time, and good progress was

[1] David Gibson took an active part in the Rebellion of 1837. As one of its leaders he was indicted for high treason. In the Provisional Government set up by William Lyon Mackenzie at Navy Island, Mr. Gibson held the position of comptroller.

[2] Probably this "Lake Shore Road" was included in response to a petition of the County Council, made in January, 1853.

made in their construction, as may be noted in the footnote[1] referring thereto.

To provide for the payment of such extensive works as the fore-going comprehensive scheme of roads indicate, the government was authorized by Parliament (see footnote)[2] to reserve from the pro-ceeds of sales of School and Crown lands in any county a percentage, which was to be used to form a fund for public improvements within the county.

Among the incidents of 1853 to be noted is the commencement

[1]Extracts from report made to Parliament, dated 30th September, 1854, re Colonization Roads, by the Department of Agriculture (the figures here given in the margin correspond with those in the scheme as proposed) ·

" (1) He [Mr. Gibson] has surveyed the line for the Elora and South-ampton Road, which is now all under contract, and will be opened and fit for travel 1st January next

" (2) The Woolwich-Huron Road is also let and will be passable by the same time

" (3) The improvements required to complete the Durham Road are in progress, and will also be finished by the New Year, with the exception of that portion which lies in the town-plot of Penetangore, which is not required at present, as there is a parallel road already opened at a short distance to the north "   [This, no doubt, refers to the road opened by William Sutton through his property]

" (4 and 10) These roads will also then be completed

" (11) Road from Southampton to Goderich. Mr. Gibson has let the open-ing of this road across the townships of Saugeen, Bruce, Kincardine, Huron and part of Ashfield, to meet the road formerly cut by the Government under the superintendency of Wm Hawkins, P L S. It is to be made a good winter road by bridging the streams, crosswaying the swamps and cut-ting out and removing the fallen timber and underwood less than 8 inches in diameter at chopping height, from a space in the middle of the road allow-ance 44 feet in breadth, leaving the heavy growing timber for the present.

" These new roads to be opened by January, 1855.   The sum of £2,000 was placed to Mr Gibson's credit, of which, on September 1st, 1854, he had paid out £1,492 1/6   Some of the payments were as follows :   For work in Carrick, to Joseph Bacon, £330   For work in Brant to S. Orchard, £9 4/2, and to Wm Johnston, £50   For work in Elderslie, to J. Lundy, £50   To S. T. Rowe, £50.   To D Currie, £12 10/   To P. J Benson, £150   For work in Saugeen, William Cunningham, £25   To D McMcNeill, £15   To J Camp-bell, £70   For work on Durham Road, to E Stauffer, £25.   To M. Mc-Leod, £20 "

[2]Extract from " Public Lands Act," 16 Vic , Chap. 159, Section 14 Assented to June 14th, 1853   " It shall be lawful for the Governor-in-Coun-cil to reserve out of the proceeds of the School Lands in any county a sum not exceeding one-fourth of such proceeds, as a fund for public improvements within the county, to be expended under the direction of the Governor-in-Council   And also to reserve out of the proceeds of unappropriated Crown Lands in any county a sum not exceeding one-fifth, as a fund for public improvements within the county as above"   To be expended under con-ditions to above   " Provided always, that not exceeding 6% on the amount collected, including surveys, shall be charged for sale and management of lands forming the Common School Fund, arising out of the 1,000,000 acres of land set apart in the Huron Tract." (See also Appendix O.)

of the settlement of the township of Carrick. Among the first to
settle there, subsequent to those previously mentioned, who had
squatted on unsurveyed lands in 1851, were Robert Young, Joseph
Grey, Thomas Liscoe, James and Andrew Dunbar, who took up
land on the Elora Road in the vicinity of Mildmay in November of
1853, while Peter Emal and a few others of German extraction
settled in the vicinity of Deemerton about the same time It was
in this year, also, that the original boundaries of Arran were enlarged
by the addition of the "Half-mile strip," made by proclamation
December 3rd, 1853. The lots in this "strip" were offered for sale
nearly a year and a half previous (see Appendix I), the agent
for the sale being John McLean at Guelph.

Two post-offices were opened in Arran this year—"Arran," now
Invermay, and "West Arran," now Burgoyne The township of
Bruce also was fortunate in having a post-office established bearing
the name of "Bruce," and was situated at what became known as
Sinclair's Corners, Peter Sinclair being the first postmaster Huron
Township was similarly favored; "Pine River" post-office was
opened this year with J. W. Gamble as first postmaster

The first port of Customs within the county was established in
1853, the honor coming to Southampton, which was known as the
Port of Saugeen, Mr. J. McLean being the first revenue officer, who
was succeeded by W. Keith.

The "Big" Land Sale, as it is commonly called, at which the
residue of Crown and school lands in the county were offered for
sale (see Appendix K for copy of advertisement), was the great
event in the county during the year 1854 The date of this sale
was September 27th. The lands then offered for sale had been surveyed into farm lots in some cases for several years, and in many
cases had been squatted upon by enterprising pioneers. To make
good their claim as squatters and retain their rights to the land
settled upon it was necessary to have their names entered as purchasers, make a first payment, and obtain a license of occupation.
On the day named in the advertisement these settlers and other
intending purchasers appeared at Southampton two or three thousand strong Those who are alive and tell of the crowd and excitement of the week or more they remained in the village relate many
amusing incidents.

The limited accommodation of the village could not begin to
give house room to the throng, and hundreds slept in sheds, others

under the first stories of such buildings as stood on posts, and many
had to put up with such resting-places as could be found among the
cedar and juniper bushes near the beach. The sole baker in the
village was Hugh McLaren, sen (now of Port Elgin). The demand
on him for bread was so great that he had to work night and day;
at the same time his shop door was kept closed so as to keep an
unmanageable crowd out, but as soon as a baking was completed,
loaves were handed out through a window to his hungry customers,
whose struggles to secure some of the baking was so great that no
time to make change was allowed, and a "York shilling," or a
"quarter," as the case might be, was paid gladly by those of the
mob who were fortunate enough to get to the window ere the supply
of loaves, hot and steaming from the oven, was exhausted. Among
the many gathered at Southampton were a large number of Highland Scotchmen, many of whom spoke English imperfectly   In
some way, not clearly made known to the writer, a temporary race
feud became manifest.   One evening, when whiskey was flowing
freely, and after several fights had started between the Highlanders
and others, one fiery Celt mounted a stump and shouted in his mother
tongue, "Anyone who cannot speak the Gaelic, hit him." The natural
clannish feeling of the Highlanders drew them together and bound
by a common language they presented such a solid front that many
that night who had never been known to utter a word of Gaelic were
only too glad to use any smattering of it they may have heard and
remembered, and so escape a thrashing

The following extract from J. M. McNabb's paper on the history
of the county throws further light on this exciting sale: " The Crown
Lands Agent stood at the window of his office and the money was
handed up to him   So quickly did the bank bills roll in that he
did not have time to count them, but threw them into a large clothes
basket, and when the basket was full put a cloth over it. In two
days upwards of $50,000 in cash was thus taken in and $8,000 in
drafts. The strain on the agent was so great after some days that
he was completely prostrated, and Doctor Haynes would not allow
him to do any more business for a week or so. In fact, if he had
not taken the physician's advice his life would have been in danger.
It may be added that two gentlemen volunteered to assist the agent,
but they also succumbed to the strain and gave up "

Why the government should have so long delayed opening up
for sale the lands referred to in the foregoing paragraphs it is

now hard to say, most probably it was departmental inertia, from which it was roused by a motion passed at the June session of the Counties Council to the following effect: " That as there are now a great number of settlers located within the several townships of Greenock, Culross, Carrick, Bruce and Kinloss in the county of Bruce, and many of these are laboring under the greatest disadvantages for the want of roads, etc., in consequence of the lands within the said townships not being opened for sale by the government, thus depriving the settlers therein from any chance of receiving any benefit from the reserve fund of 2s 6d per acre, intended for opening roads, and also as many of the settlers who have squatted upon the lands within the said townships are endeavoring by unjust means to obtain and hold possession of more land than is allowed by the recent Land Act to each settler, and thus preventing many other good and active settlers from obtaining land, and so materially retarding the progress and improvement of the said townships and the wealth and influence of these united counties, that the warden be instructed by this Council to represent the matter to the Governor-in-Council and petition him to have the lands within the said townships opened for sale at the earliest possible period "

If the chief event in Bruce in the year 1854 was the " Big " Land Sale, hardly second to it was the surrender by the Indians of their lands in the peninsula, the details of which transaction are given in Chapter I. of this book. Coupled in importance with this was the division of the county in this year into six separate municipalities, referred to in the previous chapter.

A general election was held in the summer of 1854, resulting in the return as member of Parliament for Huron and Bruce of the Hon William Cayley, who defeated Thomas McQueen, editor of *The Huron Signal,* a man who through his newspaper exerted a great influence in many parts of the county.[1]

[1]The returns for this election give an idea of how few settlers in Bruce had the required qualifications to enable them to cast their vote The returns are as follows

Township.	Cayley.	McQueen	Total
Huron			
Kincardine, Bruce and Kinloss . .	22	43 -	65
Greenock	1	9	10
Brant and Carrick	31	8	39
Saugeen	2	10	12
Arran and Eldershe . .			
	56	70	126

The years 1854 and 1855 were marked by a widespread prosperity throughout Canada, in which the county of Bruce shared to
some extent.   Several causes lay at the bottom of the prevailing
good times   Railway construction was proceeding extensively,
involving the outlay of immense sums of money to the contractors,
but ultimately to be diffused throughout the length and breadth of
the country   Then the American Reciprocity Treaty came into
operation March 16th, 1855, opening up new channels for our commerce   In addition to the foregoing, all kinds of farm products
advanced materially in price   during these years,[1] owing to the
Crimean War   This flood of prosperity to the country, while it
brought some brightness into the hard lot of the backwoods settler,
interfered with the carrying out of contracts with the government
which some of them had taken, to open up or improve roads   Mr.
David Gibson, in his report anent colonization roads in this district,
says: "Little progress had been made in 1854 owing to the scarcity
and high prices of labor and provisions, succeeding a time, when the
contracts were made, of moderation in both.   The difficulties of the
contractors increased in 1855, during which labor and the necessities of life attained prices quite unprecedented in this section of
country   Some of the contractors found themselves compelled to
suspend operations and relinquish their contracts"   Further on in
his report of work accomplished during 1855, Mr. Gibson says:
"That the Elora and Saugeen Road may now be travelled between
these places, and that with few exceptions the whole works originally intended to be executed upon it are now completed.   But to
make this a good summer road a considerable expenditure will yet
be necessary in levelling, cross-waying and draining"   Of the Durham Road, Mr Gibson says in the same report·   "All contracts
finished, except that in town-plot of Kincardine, where the excavation of a hill and some bridging remain to be finished"   Of the
Southampton and Goderich Road   "This road is now open for
travel over its whole extent, except a portion of the contract of Cowan
Keys in Huron.   This obstruction is, however, obviated by a small
portion of the Wawanosh Road adjoining the lake being opened, by
which the public get to the lake shore which it follows to Kincardine   There is also an obstruction at the point where the line
crosses the river Penetangore, over which a bridge has not yet been

[1]Wheat was sold in 1853 on the Toronto market at 4s (80c) per
bushel, advancing in 1854 to 9s 8d ($1 94), and in 1855 to 11s 9d. ($2 35),
a price never attained since

built." In a foot-note[1] is to be found the expenditure on colonization roads affecting the county of Bruce up to December 31st, 1855.

The above extracts from Mr Gibson's report give a more flattering account of what the roads in Bruce were like than would be concurred in by the general public of that day. The author remembers a remark he heard in the fall of 1856 regarding the Durham Road, " There is only one mud-hole on the road, but it extends from Walkerton to Kincardine."

The United Counties Council of 1855 were determined to have good roads, and here are given extracts from the minutes of each session held that year Some of the expressions used exhibited a breezy freshness unusual in County Council proceedings, and all show a determination to agitate until what was wanted was obtained. They also cast a light upon the difficulties undergone in going to and from market, owing to the state the roads were in even as late as that year, and indeed for long after.

Item 53, January session, reads: "This Council cannot refrain from expressing regret that the road from Goderich to Saugeen *is yet impassable even for sleighs,* although a grant of two thousand pounds was given by government "

Item 51, June session, reads: " That this Council is led to believe that Mr Gibson is only authorized to cut the underwood and make a sleigh track on the mail line of road between Saugeen and Goderich, making no provision for the opening up of the road to the full width That a petition be sent to the Bureau of Agriculture, praying that it may be chopped this season to full width, so that the track may be kept dry and not form one vast mud-hole, or at least allow the stumps and roots to rot in order that said road may at some future time be turnpiked "

At the December session a special committee was appointed to report on a scheme for gravel roads for the united counties, in which

[1]Statement of expenditure on colonization roads, paid up to 31st December, 1855, in county of Bruce.

	£	s	d
Elora and Saugeen Road	5,001	18	7
Durham Road	937	11	1
Sydenham and Southampton Road . .	1,108	7	0
Southampton and Goderich Road	2,226	3	10
Carrick and Culross Road	200	0	0
Elderslie and Brant Road	927	10	0
Wawanosh Road	25	0	0
Proportion of Expenditure for Management	724	0	0
	£11,150	10	6

Bruce was to benefit by a gravel road from Goderich to Saugeen, and another from Kincardine to Hanover. The following is an extract from the committee's report:

"We only ask the public to look into the counties of Perth and Middlesex and ask their neighbors how they like their gravel roads, as a speculation how do they find them pay? What do they think of the counties of Huron and Bruce for allowing themselves to continue enveloped in mud, literally locked up for three months in the year, unable to proceed with their legitimate vocations and urgent business by the deplorable state of the so-called roads! What a cruel mockery to call such sloughs roads! The mere idea of them and what we have suffered in them during past months and years makes our blood run cold. How long are we to suffer such a state of things, how long allow a cloak of apathy, a narrow-minded and selfish policy, to chain us in the mud? Hard indeed would it be to suffer such and not have power to improve our state. Still harder is it to have to endure such grievances and know and feel that nothing save a well-directed, thoroughly-understood action is required to place us in a state of comparative comfort, and in a position to hold up our head amongst neighboring counties, free from the foul imputation of being styled 'Mud Turtles.'"

The foregoing report, in as far as the county of Huron was concerned, resulted in a system of gravel roads, but the proposal for the gravelling of roads in Bruce was allowed to fall through.

It was in 1855 that the first Division Court within the county was established. Its limits were co-extensive with all the municipalities therein Christopher R. Barker held the office of clerk of this court, his office being at Kincardine Before the erecting of other Division Courts in the county an immense amount of business came before it, as many as seven hundred cases being heard at one sitting, which would be extended so as to occupy three days. The holding of the court broke in upon the sameness of life in the bush, and numbers used to be found in attendance whose only reason for being present arose from the craving for a break in the monotony, for some excitement, mild though it may seem, the craving being the result of living the isolated life of a backwoodsman. The most numerous cases in the early courts were suits entered for the collections of promissory notes given in payment for the "Brockville Air-tight Cooking Stove." This was the first of many articles which large numbers of the farmers of Bruce had been induced to purchase, and gave their notes for, under the specious arguments of travelling agents and under the promise of long credit. These stove men were followed in later years by agents for fanning mills, sewing machines, organs, agricultural implements, etc., down to the present day, in a procession that seems to have no end

The advent of the cooking stove, just referred to, into the log-shanties, marked an advance in prosperity. The settler purchased one because he felt that he was getting on his feet financially, and therefore he would lighten the good wife's labors, and at the same time add to the comfort of their home. Previously the household cooking equipment consisted of a much-used frying pan, a cast-iron pot with legs, a tea kettle and a bake kettle, called by some a Dutch oven. This latter not being a familiar article to the present generation, its appearance and uses may as well be described. In shape it was a shallow, flat-bottomed pot, ten to fourteen inches in diameter, standing about five to six inches high, the lid, like the body of the pot, was of cast-iron, and fitted closely. In this vessel meat, bread, or anything else that now would be cooked in an oven, was placed; the lid was then set on and covered over with hot ashes and coals, the heat having to be calculated with judicious care, despite which the food would often be burnt. All cooking was done at the open fire-place; the fire on the hearth not only did the cooking, but furnished all the heat, and in many a shanty all the light they could afford.

On July 1st, 1856, the law regarding the election of members to the Legislative Council of Canada came into force; prior to that date the government appointed the members of the Upper Chamber. The new law directed that they be elected and retain office for a term of eight years. Twelve districts were contested in the fall of 1856, one of these being the Saugeen District, which consisted of the counties of Bruce, Grey and the north part of Simcoe. The candidates were Messrs James Patton, John McMurrich and James Beatty, the former of whom was elected after an exciting contest.

The government, in addition to the expenditure made for colonization roads in Bruce in 1855-6, commenced to spend money on various harbors along the lake shore.[1] It was in the former of these

[1]The Commissioner of Public Works, in his report made in 1855, says regarding Lake Huron: '' Along the entire side of the Canada coast of this vast lake the mariner is wholly unaided by either lights or bouys, with the exception of the solitary light at Goderich '' The report goes on to recommend that lights be placed at Chantry Island, White Fish Island, and the Isle of Coves Also that a pier 500 feet in length be constructed at Chantry Island

yeais that Kincardine received its first help from the government
toward its harbor. A breakwater was constructed at a point 150
yards north-west of the end of the present pier; this breakwater
was, however, washed away a few months afterwards in a severe
storm; its remains are yet to be traced on the bed of the lake at the
spot mentioned above. Encouraged possibly by the hope of harbors
of safety and the promise of light-houses at Pine Point and Chantry
Island, the lake ports in 1856, and from that time onwards until the
opening of the W G & B Railway, were served by steamboats, the
Ploughboy being the first. She ran between Detroit and Southampton, and was commanded by Captain Duncan Rowan. The wharf
accommodation along the coast was very meagre, there being only
two in the county, one at Southampton and the other at Stoney
Island, while at Kincardine there was none. From the latter port
a large scow used to be rowed out to the steamer if the weather were
fine to take off freight and passengers; if it were at all rough, they
were landed at Stoney Island, to the great indignation of the Kincardine people, who openly charged Captain Rowan with being too
partial to Stoney Island because of his property there.

The survey of the peninsula was in progress during the years
1855-6, being conducted in Amabel and Albemarle by Geo. Gould,
for Chas Rankin, P.L.S, and in the three northern townships by
J. S. Dennis, P L.S, and H C. Boulton, P L.S The Indian
Department offered for sale at auction at Owen Sound, on September 2nd, 1856, those lands lying in Amabel, Albemarle and in Southampton north of the river. Prices then paid for the village lots
were in some instances so high that on second thought the purchasers forfeited their deposit Many speculators purchased quantities of farm lands, as there was no immediate settlement clause
in the conditions of sale; this tended to retard immediate settlement of this part of the county The year 1856 marked the close,
of the settlement of that part of the county of Bruce as originally
laid out, that is, of all of the county south of the township of Amabel.
True, the Greenock swamp was still held by the Crown, and maybe
a few undesirable farm lots elsewhere, but with this year land-seekers
had to search for land in the Indian peninsula or elsewhere outside
of the county. The peninsula is not even yet all taken up, and owing
to the rocky nature of large sections of it, it will be many years
before this is accomplished, although it may eventually be done by
selling these unarable lands in blocks to be made use of as sheep
farms.

Before closing that part of this history relating to the settlement of the county of Bruce, it is but fitting to write a few words regarding other things than the mere incidents of settlement and development. At length the time came when it could be said that the county was settled, that the land was all taken up, but the question naturally arises, From whence came these thousands of settlers, thrown together as neighbors and fellow-citizens? How have they been fitted by previous training for the work of opening up the bush, so that it may be made to feel the throb of civilization? In an earlier part of this chapter an effort was made to show that, with two exceptions, the settlement of the county was about as mixed as it could well be. The census taken in 1861 gives a reliable basis on which to form an opinion as to the place of birth and of the religious denomination of these early settlers. The five years intervening between the close of this chapter and the taking of the census witnessed, it is true, an increase in population within the county, but no material change in the character of its inhabitants. From the census of 1861 we glean the following statistics as to place of birth of the people: Of Canadian birth, 59 per cent (of course this included many young children born in the county); of Scotch birth, 19 per cent, of Irish, 11 per cent, of English, 5 per cent.; of German, 4 per cent, from the United States, 1 per cent, and all others, 1 per cent. In their religious tendencies, 44 per cent were Presbyterians, 18 per cent. belonged to the Church of England, 16 per cent. were Methodists, 12 per cent. Catholics, 4 per cent Baptists, and 2 per cent. were Lutherans, while there were 4 per cent. scattered among a number of other denominations. Of these settlers a marked characteristic was that so many were young couples commencing life together in the bush. It was youth that was needed to face and endure the hardships of those early days, falling to the lot of both husband and wife, and with brave hearts the youth of the country responded and sought out and made homes for themselves in the backwoods.

Probably the most marked characteristic of these early settlers was the whole-hearted hospitality to be met with in every locality. The names of some households are still spoken of by "the old timers" as standing out pre-eminently for the many instances of help rendered, often at the cost of self-privation and inconvenience suffered. Not a township but could give the names of such, and the author feels diffident about mentioning any, for many others, equally worthy, would be certain to be overlooked. Where all were poor it was felt that mutual assistance, when possible, must be rendered, so the meagre supplies of the necessities of life were cheerfully shared, implements were loaned, day labor was exchanged, and logging-bees, raising-bees, etc , were exceedingly common; hired help could not be obtained even if the money to pay for it were available, which it was not, so mutual co-operation was forced upon these backwoodsmen, even if the natural good-heartedness which prompted to helpfulness did not exist

The dwellings of the settlers were largely of two classes   There was the low, flat-roofed shanty, covered with "scoops," or bark, with its "notch and saddle" corners and single-pane windows, the chinks between its bark-covered logs being filled with cedar splints and clay; its one door, a home-made one, had ever the latch-string hanging outside in a hospitably inviting manner.   Then there were the more pretentious and larger one storey and attic buildings, of hewed logs and shingled roof, with square, "dove-tailed" corners, which have not yet entirely disappeared, but are still to be seen on all of our concession lines   These latter buildings were warm and far from uncomfortable   The windows were of a fair size, there was a back as well as a front door; while partitions divided the interior into several rooms   Whatever there was in the way of a barn or stable was very primitive , the winter's wind could blow through the chinks between its logs, and any cattle therein had but little shelter. But few cattle had even this pretence for shelter; they had to live during the winter in the bush on the browse provided by the tender twigs of trees, felled by their owners for that purpose   One feature marked the outside of each house, and that was a grind-stone, used for sharpening the axe.   This was roughly rigged up alongside the house, and if you happened along when the good-man was not in the bush, you would see the axe leaning against it.   Not far off was a plough, strongly made so as to be able to tear up the roots lying buried in the newly cleared land   Beside it was the harrow,[1] or "drag," as it was sometimes called, made from the crotch of a tree, looking like a huge letter "V", its teeth had been forged by the nearest blacksmith, who also had hammered out the heavy hoe that leaned against the house, made heavy enough to cut the small roots of the stumps around which the expected winter's supply of potatoes had

[1] The top of a small tree, called a "brush-harrow," was in use to cover turnip and other small seeds

been planted. And what potatoes grew in that black mould! and how sweet they did taste with salt and butter, even though the latter did often have a flavor of leeks, which were common enough in the woods where the cows sought pasture

One of the most marked changes to be noticed betwixt the farm of the present day and that of the period of which this chapter relates is the complete revolution which has taken place in regard to the beasts of burden on the farm At the time the bush was opened up the slow, patient and enduring ox was of far more service than the more delicately organized horse could have been. This fact was recognized to such an extent that a team of horses in the possession of a farmer during the days of the early settlement was almost unknown When the author arrived at Kincardine in 1856 there were only three teams of horses in the village, and he cannot recall any farmer in the vicinity who at that date owned, or worked, a team of horses

The pioneer who takes up prairie land in the far West is enabled to obtain a harvest, in return for his labor, during the very first year of his settlement. Very different was the lot of those who took up a bush farm in the heavy timbered land of the county of Bruce The process of clearing was a slow one; to chop, log and burn five or six acres was a fair season's work for the man who had no capital This work had to be accomplished before the ground could be ploughed and planted, while in the long interval between the felling of the first tree and the reaping of his first harvest, the family had to be sustained. To do this rigid economy and self-denial were essential; the majority of the settlers possessed but scanty means, and to keep " the wolf from the door " taxed these to the uttermost. Those who prior to entering the " Queen's Bush " had had some experience on a bush farm, through being the sons of Canadian farmers in the older settlements, possessed a great advantage over those to whom everything in the bush was a novelty. The former were able to wring much out of the forest to help them along financially. They could make ox yokes and ox bows for their less skilled neighbors. They were able, where cedar was convenient, to manufacture shingles for sale in the settlement, working long and late with frow (or shaving-horse) and draw-knife to earn the moderate price paid for such in this country of much wood Others had among their effects a whip-saw, and they, with the help of a companion, would by manual labor cut lumber in those localities destitute of saw-mills Where

there were saw-mills, hemlock and pine logs were in demand to a
small extent   The supply, however, was so abundant that the price
obtained was unremunerative.   Others again, who had a little capital,
made potash   This, however, was an industry which does not seem
to have flourished to any great extent among the farmers of Bruce.[1]
It demanded an initial outlay that few were prepared to make, but
some help in this line did come to the needy settler who wished to
realize something on his wood ashes when, in 1858, P. & N McInnes,
opened a pot and pearl ashery at Kincardine, to be followed two
years later by one at Tiverton.   The poor bush-whackers were only
too glad to get some ready money by selling the ashes that were to
be found wherever a brush heap or log pile had been burned.   The
price paid was only 2d a bushel, yet the supply was ample.   At the
time the ashery was first established settlers of too poor means to
either own or hire a yolk of oxen would carry ashes on their backs
in a two-bushel bag for several miles to obtain the small sum of 4d.
Can anything emphasize more forcibly than such incidents the destitution of the pioneers?   But then, as now, the man with his eyes
open, possessing energy and forethought, found means of providing
some comfort for his family that others not so favorably endowed
could not   One luxury all might have was maple sugar and maple
syrup   No farm but had growing on it an abundance of sugar
maples, and the demand for sugar kettles in the early spring was
very satisfactory to the village store-keeper.   Game was plentiful.
The creeks, especially those tributary to the Saugeen, were full of
trout   Partridges were not uncommon, while deer were plentiful.
Many a settler has been able to stock his larder with venison, the
result of a fortunate shot at a deer that had come at early dawn to
feed on his growing grain   The species of game which existed in
greatest numbers, but which has entirely disappeared, even as the

---

[1]The author recollects that his father had at his store, for sale, during
" the fifties," half a dozen pot-ash kettles which were after a time duly
sold, but the demand was not sufficient to warrant the stock being
renewed
There was great difficulty in unloading from the small sailing vessels
such a large, heavy mass of iron as a pot-ash kettle, where there were
no wharves on which to deliver them, and the small boats which landed
ordinary freight not being of strong enough construction to undertake
such an exacting task   Captain Rowan used to tell with some gusto how
he got over the difficulty by gently placing the big kettle into the water
and then getting into it himself and paddling to shore   Without doubt
the first instance of sailing in an iron vessel on Lake Huron

buffalo on the Western prairie, was the wild pigeon.[1] Those who have not seen the flocks of pigeons that flew over this county, from their " rookery " in Grey, cannot imagine the number of birds so congregated, thousands and thousands, stretching out in a flock possibly half a mile long, so close together as to cast a shadow, and the whirr of their wings being like the loud hum of machinery. The flocks in general flew low, so low that many instances are on record of people knocking them down with a stick as they flew by. It was useless to fire a shot at the flock as they came toward you, as the shot glanced off the thick shield of feathers which covered their breasts. The sportsman—probably pot-hunter would, be the correct designation—would wait until the flock was a little more than abreast of him before pulling the trigger. As flocks in many cases followed one after another over the same route, there was no difficulty in posting ones self to advantage, and in a short time fill the game bag. Pigeon pie was a common dish in those days, and found in many of the settler's houses, where it was much appreciated, for animal food was a rare article among them.

This chapter cannot be more appropriately concluded than by quoting an old pioneer poem, written by Mr. David Martin, of Beverly Township, county of Wentworth, a good many years ago, entitled:

THE AULD NICK IN THE DOOR

In the rough old times,
In the tough old times,
  Of twenty years agone,
There was nae a clock in the settlement
  To tell how the time went on,
But we kenned very well when the day began,
  And we kenned very well when 'twas o'er,
And our dinner-bell was the gude wife's shout,
  When the sun reached the nick in the door

---

[1]About the last notice the author has met with regarding wild pigeons in large numbers is the following extract from the *Paisley Advocate* of April 28th, 1876:
" The immense flocks of pigeons which have been flying over various parts of the country in an undecided way for the last week or two have gathered in the township of Amabel, in countless numbers, and have begun building. The nests are in thousands, and many eggs lie on the ground owing to the breaking down of branches. The place is visited by scores of persons who are shooting the pigeons, and all the shot in Owen Sound and Southampton seems to have been fired away as a telegram has been received in Paisley asking for a supply "

Cash, we had none, we were all alike,
    But we whacked awa' at the trees,
And when summer came, ah, then we had
    The splores at the logging bees;
The affairs o' the kirk, the affairs o' the state,
    We seldom did review,
But we talked and sang o' our native lands,
    And fair we whiles got fou

Now fields are cleared, and every stump
    Has vanished from the ground;
And now the ladies, bless them all,
    Are hoopit round and round
Now every house one time-piece has,
    And some have even more,
And youngsters laugh at their mother's clock—
    The guid auld nick in the door.

And now we blether politics,
    And knowing folk are we,
And some oppose and some support
    The present ministry,
But who is bought, and who is sold,
    And wherefore, why and how,
We know as well as A, B, C,
    O, what a difference now

CHAPTER VI.

THE COUNTY-TOWN CONTEST YEARS.
1857—1866.

THE events recorded in this chapter may lack the picturesqueness of events associated with pioneer life, or those attendant upon
a life in the bush, but they in their own way have had a marked
influence in the evolution of the county of Bruce. The settling of the
county-town question and the construction of an extensive system of
gravel roads, the marked features of the decade recorded in this
chapter, did much to consolidate and develop the county.

The necessary legislation having in view the separation of the
united counties of Huron and Bruce was passed in May, 1856. In
January following the reeves who were to compose the provisional
municipal council of the county of Bruce were elected, but owing to
the long fight over the county-town question and consequent delay
in erection of the county buildings, ten years elapsed before the
separation from the county of Huron was completed. In the interim
each county carried on all improvements for roads and bridges
separately.

The provisional County Council of Bruce was organized in the
manner described in the following extract from its Minutes:

" PEACOCK'S HOTEL, SOUTHAMPTON,
"March 19th, 1857.

" The Reeves and Deputy Reeves of the several Townships in the
County met this day, pursuant to the warrant under the hand and
seal of the High Sheriff of the United Counties of Huron and Bruce,
for the several purposes for which Provisional Municipal Councils
are by law erected David McKendrick, Esq , Reeve of the Township of Kincardine, who was appointed chairman by the said warrant, having taken the chair, the following gentlemen took their
seats, viz., Alexander McNabb, Reeve, Saugeen; William Riddell,
Reeve, Arran; George Cromar, Reeve, Greenock; Malcolm McLennan,[1] Reeve, Huron; William Hall, Reeve, Brant; John Findlay,

[1] Secretary *pro tem* for this meeting.

Deputy Reeve, Brant; Joseph Walker, Deputy Reeve, Brant, Peter B Brown, Reeve, Culross; John Purvis, Reeve, Kinloss, Peter Mc-Vicar, Reeve, Carrick, John Gillies, Reeve, Elderslie; Alexander McKinnon, Reeve, Bruce "

The deputy reeve of Kincardine, Nichol McIntyre, was not present at the first meeting of the Council. Of the two deputy reeves present from Brant only one, Joseph Walker, was permitted to sit.

The first meeting elected George Cromar as provisional warden. The Council then adjourned to meet two days later at Waterson's Hotel, Walkerton. At this meeting the Council, after appointing William C. Bruce as county clerk, proceeded to select a fit and proper place to recommend to the Governor-General as the one to be mentioned in his proclamation as the county town of Bruce

The places voted on and the votes taken were as follows: ·

Greenock Town Plot, 6: *vs.* Teeswater, 6.—Warden gave casting vote for Greenock Town Plot.

Greenock Town Plot, 6: *vs.* Riversdale, 6.—Warden gave casting vote for Greenock Town Plot

Greenock Town Plot, 1: *vs.* Walkerton, 11.

Walkerton, 8· *vs.* Southampton, 4.

Walkerton, 10: *vs.* Inverhuron, 2.

Walkerton, 9: *vs.* Paisley, 3.

Walkerton, 7. *vs* Penetangore, 5

On the Governor-in-Council being informed of the result of the voting above mentioned, he by proclamation, issued 15th June, 1857, appointed Walkerton as the county town of Bruce. This action, seemingly decisive in favor of Walkerton, was not to be acquiesced in by the supporters of the claims made by other villages for the possession of this coveted honor So, when on July 8th the provisional County Council sat again, and on the introduction of a by-law to raise $24,000 by debentures to erect county buildings, it was moved in amendment, " That whereas a great and grievous dissatisfaction exists on the part of the ratepayers generally throughout the greater part of the county as to the action taken by the reeves at the last meeting of the provisional County Council of this county with regard to the county town. It is moved, therefore, that no by-law be at present published for raising money to erect county buildings at Walkerton " This amendment carried by a vote of 8 to 4.

The next move in the game for the county town developed at a succeeding meeting of the Council, held July 22nd, at "Kinnard's Hotel, Penetangore," when William Rastall moved, seconded by John Purvis, "That it is expedient to divide the county of Bruce and to form two counties thereof, the southern portion to be called the 'county of Bruce,' and to consist of the following townships, viz., Kincardine, Huron, Brant, Kinloss, Culross, South Greenock and Carrick, with Penetangore or Riversdale for county town; the northern portion to be called the 'county of Wallace,' and to consist of the following townships, viz, Bruce, Arran, Amabel, Lindsay, Saugeen, Eldershe, Albemarle, Eastnor, St Edmunds and that part of Greenock north of the line between Brant and Eldershe, with Southampton for the county town." The amendment to the above motion is very pungent in its expression It is as follows "That it is only a few weeks since the united counties of Huron and Bruce have been separated by Royal Proclamation; it is as uncalled for, impudent and illegal to ask a second separation and divide the infant county of Bruce as it would be contemptible in the eyes of the community." The motion carried and an advertisement of application for legislation to the above effect appeared in the *Gazette.* At the same session a motion passed authorizing a by-law to be published to raise $32,000 to erect county buildings at Penetangore and Southampton, and to take steps to have a Bill passed by the Legislature to confirm the steps taken by the provisional Council.

At the October meeting the action relating to the division of the county and issue of the debentures was revoked, and the following motion passed, "That a special Act be applied for by this Council at the next meeting of the Legislature for the purpose of empowering the Governor-General to reconsider the proclaiming of a county town for the county of Bruce, and empowering him to proclaim either Penetangore, Riversdale, Walkerton, Paisley, or Southampton, after each of the above-named places has been allowed to present their several claims, to be named as the county town of Bruce, the same as if no proclamation had ever been issued" Yet this motion was not allowed to stand, and the warden at the first meeting in the following year was instructed to withdraw the notice of application; so after all the shifts and turns made during the year Walkerton at the end of 1857 still held possession of the title of county town, empty and barren though it might be. The vacillating course pursued by the provisional County Council throughout the year shows what adepts at "log rolling" and "wire pulling" existed in those days.

✓   To have a railway enter the county and connect it with outside markets was a hope long cherished by the citizens of Bruce, but many years slipped by before the hope materialized and became a reality. That the railway did not come sooner was not from want of effort on the part of Bruce. In 1857 a proposal was being considered to build a line, to be known as the North Western Railroad, from Guelph to some point on the Durham Road Sanford Fleming, C.E., was at the back of it The provisional County Council thought so well of the proposition that it was prepared to vote £100,-000 towards it, and had the Legislature pass an Act[1] to authorize the county to take stock in the railroad company to that extent. For some reason unknown to the author this railway was never gone on with, and the memory of a name is all that remains of it.

Another proposal was before the county in 1857, one to spend £100,000 in making gravel roads. This scheme had as abortive a termination as that which characterized the North-Western Railway. A special meeting of the United Counties Council was held 30th December, 1857, to consider a by-law to issue debentures for £100,000 for the above-mentioned purpose. It was read a first time and directed to be published The Council adjourned to meet at Rowe's Hotel, Paisley, at the expiration of the proper time for advertizing the by-law; but without further comment, as far as the minutes of the Council show, the matter here dropped Not a word of explanation is given why this was so

With the advent of the year 1858 the first village municipality within the county came into existence Kincardine village had a census taken during 1857 which showed that it possessed a population of 837, and was therefore entitled to commence a separate municipal career as a village, which it did 1st January, 1858, and forever dropped its double name of Penetangore Southampton likewise attained the position of a municipality in the same year, being created a village by Act of Parliament,[2] assented to 24th July, 1858. Among the townships during the same year there was one municipal change to be recorded. To quote the words of the by-law, " The newly laid out township of Albemarle " was on the 1st January united for municipal purposes to Arran and Amabel

During 1858 the struggle for the county town was as bitter and intense as in the preceding year As the result of a petition of the

[1] 20 Vic. Chap 78
[2] 22 Vic Chap 42

County Council, Parliament passed on August 16th an Act[1] voiding the appointment of Walkerton as county town, and directing that the selection shall be left with the Governor-in-Council, and providing that each place shall present its claims to the Governor-in-Council before the 1st of October That the decision given shall be final, and that the provisional Council shall before action be taken pass a valid by-law providing the necessary supplies.

In December the Council passed a by-law to raise $24,000 for the erection of the necessary county buildings, but owing to some informality this by-law was declared invalid Plans and specifications had been advertised for[2] and were examined at this session, but nothing definite was done to forward the erection of the buildings

With the opening of the railway to Goderich on June 28th, 1858, ✓ and the establishment of a daily mail to Kincardine,[3] the inhabitants of the latter place felt themselves to be no longer outside of the great world. The Toronto daily papers were only a day old when received, and a delay like that was promptness itself compared to the past record. Other parts of the county were not favored so highly as Kincardine, and waited for years for a daily mail

The office of treasurer for the county of Bruce during the first year of the provisional County Council was filled by George Brown, treasurer of the united counties His office was at Goderich, which proved somewhat inconvenient, so the provisional County Council at its first meeting in 1858 appointed the warden of the previous year, George Cromar, as county treasurer. This appointment bears date April 14th, 1858 The office of warden for the year 1858 was filled by John Purvis, reeve of the township of Kinloss

The summer of 1858 was one long to be remembered in this part of the Province of Ontario on account of the long and severe drought If the recollection of the writer is correct no rain fell between June 23rd and August 11th in that year The result was an utter failure of the crops. The harvest of 1858 was in many cases hardly worth

[1]22 Vic Chap III

[2]There is in the office of the county clerk a plan drawn up in response to this advertisement, superscribed as follows· " Plan of The Court-House and Jail,—*Kinloss*, C. W. By William Thomas & Sons, Architects, Toronto and Hamilton Dec 21st, 1858 " This is the only trace that the author has met with that " Kinloss " was in the race for the county town, though possibly the fact of the warden's post-office address being " Kinloss " may have led the architects to suppose the county town was there.

[3]This mail service was carried on horseback from Goderich

gathering. This to numbers of industrious settlers meant nothing less than starvation; they had but a few years previously taken up their lands; what little means they had at first sufficed only to sustain them until enough land had been cleared to raise their first crop; with no reserve accumulated it was a dreadful outlook for them, no crops and no money. Is it to be wondered at that the year from the harvest time of 1858 to that of 1859 will be remembered in this county by those who resided here then as "starvation year"

The feature of the year 1859 which stands out as the most prominent is the distress arising from the failure of the harvest in the preceding year. The direful prospect that stared many of the people of Bruce was realized by the County Council, which at its first meeting, held on February 4th and 5th, appointed a special committee to report on the destitution then prevailing and to suggest what measures should be adopted to relieve it The report made by this committee is to be found printed as Appendix P, which is worthy of a careful perusal. The result of the report was the passing of a by-law to raise by means of debentures the sum of eight thousand five hundred pounds currency, " for providing means to relieve the destitution, existing and increasing, in the county of Bruce, and to supply a sufficiency of seed grain and provisions for the inhabitants, prior to the ensuing harvest." Such a by-law to be legal required to be confirmed by Act of Parliament, which was done.[1] The debentures were very considerately cashed at par by the government, so saving the county any discount or delay The money so raised was paid over to the minor municipalities as required as soon as its Council had passed a valid by-law undertaking to issue debentures, payable in ten years, for a sum equal to the amount received from the county, and also binding the local municipality to expend the amount so received in improving roads, thus giving employment to those in . need The proportion of money allocated to the different municipalities varied according to the amount of distress therein. The particulars of this distribution are as follows: To Arran £2,500, Brant £2,000, Bruce £5,400, Carrick £2,000, Culross £2,700, Elderslie, £3,600, Greenock £2,700, Huron £4,400, Kincardine £5,400, Kinloss £2,700, Kincardine village £600 That the reader may form an idea of the manner in which the funds so placed in the hands of the minor municipalities was used to relieve the widespread needs, some

[1] 22 Vic Chap 7. Passed March 26th, 1859

extracts taken from the regulations adopted by the Council of the township of Bruce are here given; these may be accepted as a sample of the general practice in other municipalities, all of which purchased seed grain and flour for distribution as needed   The extract is as follows: " That not more than five bushels of seed grain be issued to any one ratepayer until all are served, when if a balance remains it shall be rateably distributed among such as were not fully supplied. That the seed be sold at an advance of one shilling and three pence per bushel over cost price, and that in all cases when the same is paid for in road work this sum shall be deducted from the face of the note. That ratepayers entitled to receive seed grain, who have not performed work, shall be entitled to receive an allowance of breadstuffs not exceeding fifteen pounds per head, for the present, and this after signing a declaration setting forth the nature of the case and that relief was required "

The author here gives some extracts from the Bruce Township Council minutes of June 13th, 1859, which forcibly illustrate the prevailing distress. " That disclaiming any desire on the part of this Council to interfere with matters beyond their jurisdiction, the members of the Council would beg most respectfully to draw the attention of Mr. Gibson (Supt. of Colonization Roads) to the sufferings endured by many of those performing work on the Goderich and Saugeen Road for want of food, and request him if convenient to open a credit with some party or parties for the supply of breadstuffs until the jobs are completed." Again, " That the corn meal ordered for the relief of destitution be deposited with Mr. Macfarlane, at Port Bruce, to be given out as usual on road certificates, except in extreme cases, when he will take notes, payable in work or money, for the amount advanced   That, as a general rule, regard be strictly had to the circumstances of parties requiring meal, the preference being given to weak families, it being expected that families consisting of two or more able-bodied young men will shift for themselves without calling upon the Council."

Besides the relief furnished by the prompt action of the provisional County Council, contributions came in from outside points, among them some from Scotland   The Grand Trunk Railway aided materially, considerably reducing its freight rates 50 per cent on grain and provisions sent on to the municipalities. The steamer *Islander*, running from Goderich to Southampton throughout the spring and summer of 1859, was heavily laden every trip with pro-

visions[1] and seed grain The writer remembers seeing numbers of
country people waiting on the Kincardine pier for the arrival of
the steamer, so as to obtain without delay their allotment of breadstuffs and seed grain. After much suffering the crisis was successfully tided over, with a good harvest in 1859 hope returned to the
despondent and distressed inhabitants of the county, and an era
of prosperity commenced which has not since been materially checked.

The by-law, passed in September, 1858, to provide funds for
the erection of the county buildings having been declared invalid,
another one was submitted to the ratepayers to be voted upon March
7th and 8th, 1859, to raise £6,000 for this purpose, which was carried; but on being submitted to the Attorney-General, West, was
disallowed, owing to some informality On the 8th and 9th of July
following, the ratepayers once more voted that the required debentures be issued Everything was as it should be on this occasion,
and the by-law directing the issue of the debentures was passed by
the County Council July 19th. These debentures were made payable
in twenty years. As they could only be used for the special purpose
of paying for the erecting of the county buildings, it was many a
day before they were required One for $400 was sold in Septem-
ber, 1860, possibly to pay for the plans of the proposed buildings;
the remainder of the issue remained unused until 1863. John
Gillies was warden in that year, as he was strongly opposed to the
way county town matters were going, a mandamus had to be applied
for before he would sign the remainder of the issue, which were
finally disposed of in December, 1865

Mr N. Hammond received in 1859 the appointment of registrar
of the county of Bruce, the office to be at Southampton, awaiting
the final decision of where the county town was to be located. The
provisional County Council on hearing of this appointment petitioned
the Governor-General that the registry office remain in Goderich,
a request that was not acceded to. As an account of Mr. Hammond's
was presented to the Counties Council for payment of rent from 9th
July, 1859, it is probable, therefore, that this is the date on and
from which the county of Bruce has had a separate registry office.

Mariners on Lake Huron rejoiced over the completion, in 1859,
of the lighthouses at Point Clark (Pine Point) and at Chantry
Island. John Brown, of Thorold, had the contract of erecting these

[1]Provisions were not only scarce, but high-priced as well Flour sold
at $10 a barrel at many places

two substantial buildings, which in that year first sent their rays over the stormy waters of Lake Huron to guide the sailor on his course

In the early summer of 1859 an incident took place that created quite a talk throughout the southern part of the county, although the centre of disturbance most of the time was just over the county line in Bentinck. A mile and a quarter east of Hanover, on the Durham line, lived a family by the name of Campbell, in whose veins must have run the blood of those Highlanders whose joy it was to make raids and forays on the lowlands. Certain it is that in many ways they set law at defiance and terrorized the neighborhood on both sides of the county line With them were associated some young fellows, several brothers named Baillie, Andrew McFarlane, and Wm. McMahon. In 1858 a span of horses belonging to McFarlane were found at Vesta and seized for debt, removed by the Division Court bailiff, J Benson, and placed in the stables of a Walkerton Hotel. McFarlane and the Campbells were determined to retake the horses, even if the seizure had been under authority of the court. So they broke into the stables one night and decamped with the horses This was followed by an order to arrest from Judge Cooper George Simpson and Caleb Huyck were the constables to whom the warrant was given to execute. Word of the coming of the constables had reached the ears of the Campbell gang, so when the constables were crossing the bridge at Hanover they surrounded them Every one of the gang was well supplied with fire-arms. The warrant was ordered to be produced and was immediately torn up, but there being a full sense of humor in the Campbells, they ordered Huyck to eat up the torn fragments. A sorry meal it was to partake of, but it was a case of eat or be shot. A meal of paper is not one to be rapidly finished, and Huyck, like many a greedy boy when he has a chance at a pile of cakes, pocketed a part of his fare, and these parts of the torn and dismembered warrant were afterwards pasted together and produced at the trial of Colin Campbell at Goderich Such an open defiance of law startled the community, and the necessity for vigorous and prompt measures was felt. Judge Cooper directed that a posse of constables be collected, sufficient in number to enforce the execution of the warrant. The writer remembers seeing a waggon starting for Walkerton from Kincardine filled with constables, each one with a rifle or shot gun The posse of constables on arriving at

Campbell's[1] surrounded the building and demanded the surrender
of all in the house, seven men in all.   The reply was a prompt
refusal, with a warning that if they did not leave the premises they
must take the consequences.   Defiantly the seven armed men stood
at the windows, pointing their guns at any who came too near.   Mr.
Jamieson, the magistrate in charge, endeavored to point out the
uselessness of resisting the law, but his reasoning had no weight
with the Campbells, or McMahon, who was very wild.   Some excited
constables set fire to the house, but the wiser and more sober-minded
knew that they neither had authority to do so, or yet to be the first
to open fire upon these defiers of the law; but a second time the
flames were started, and this time the Campbells, to save being burnt
to death, were forced to make a break for liberty.   They came out of
the building holding their rifles at full cock ready to fire if touched.
The great bulk of the constables thought it best to be out of the way,
and sought shelter behind the house, leaving a number, too few,
however, to attempt the task of arresting the gang as they rushed
down the side-line to the woods for shelter.   Colin Campbell and
another of the gang, William McMahon, while on the run were shot
in the back with a charge of buck-shot.   Being unable to obtain
proper attention in the woods, Campbell gave himself up and was
tried at Goderich at the next Assize, and sentenced to a term in the
penitentiary.   The family years after moved to Manitoulin Island
and purchased the property of Jos Walker, the founder of the county
town, then lately deceased   A law suit was entered by Campbell
against those who had taken part in the burning of his house, which
was tried at Owen Sound, the defendants winning their case.

Although a decade had elapsed since the government had commenced the opening up of the main roads in Bruce, the work was
far from being completed in 1859.   David Gibson, in his report of
the work of that year, says " In April contracts were let to the
extent of $6,000 for making the Saugeen and Goderich Road ' a sum-
mer road '   At that time much privation and distress were reported
to prevail along the line of road.   To give employment to as many
of the needy settlers as possible, the work was let in sections of five-
eighths of a mile each.   In this way a great many were enabled to
make a little money and relieve themselves of the severe pressure
upon them.   Most of the contracts have been completed   The whole

[1]June 8th, 1859

of the road lying in the county of Bruce has now been cleared of timber to the width of 44 feet and chopped to the width of 66 feet. A considerable amount of causewaying has been laid, as well as extensive ditching on both sides of the road, and the stumps on the space between the ditches grubbed and removed " Reading between the lines of the foregoing extract, it is not difficult to imagine what this road, and many others in Bruce, as well, were like, even after ten years or more of settlement.

A shipwreck, that would have been notable in the history of Canada, nearly occurred (July 3rd, 1859) on the rocky cliffs which form the coast line along the north end of the Bruce peninsula The steamer *Ploughboy,* having on board an excursion party consisting of several members of the ministry and a number of members of the House of Parliament, was on a trip to Sault Ste Marie. During a severe gale an accident happened to some of the machinery, rendering the vessel perfectly helpless, so that she drifted at the mercy of the wind and waves. As they neared the precipitous rocks hope was almost given up. As a last resort the anchor with full length of cable was let out, but owing to the depth of water it did not catch until the steamer was within about fifty yards of the perpendicular cliff, when it held firmly The scenes on board, as described after they had all reached a place of safety, had some comical features The prospect of immediate death made every one feel the desirability of holding some religious service, but there was not a soul on board who had any pretensions to be able to conduct any sort of a meeting but a political one, or to possessing any of the qualifications looked for in a leader of a religious meeting It was therefore forced on the Speaker of the House, Sir Harry Smith, to read the prayers for those in peril on the sea While the steamer remained in this perilous position in the midst of the boiling surf, the lives of all on board depending upon the stability of the cable, Duncan McLean, first mate on the steamer (a brother-in-law of Capt. Duncan Rowan, of Kincardine) got a few of the crew to volunteer to row with him through the stormy waters to Owen Sound, which venturesome trip, for such a small boat in such a gale, was successfully accomplished, and help for the endangered vessel and its crew of passengers was promptly forwarded

The position of warden for the county was held in 1859 by John Valentine, reeve of Greenock. Owing to the extent of the distress which prevailed in that year, the issue and sale of debentures to

meet it, and also the county building debenture by-law being twice
submitted to the ratepayers, Mr. Valentine's duties were more than
usually onerous His successor, Mr. John Bruce, reeve of Brant, tne
warden for 1860, had much less arduous duties to occupy him during
his term of office.

The year 1860 was comparatively uneventful as far as the county
of Bruce was concerned. A bountiful harvest blessed the year, the
sale of which brought into the hands of many a poor farmer of
Bruce more money than he had ever been the possessor of since he
had entered the bush.

The county town question still dragged its weary way along without coming any nearer a final decision In 1858 the question had
been referred to the Governor-General, who was then asked to select
a place. That year and the following passed without a place being
named The reason for delay is revealed by the purport of a letter
written on the 31st May by the Provincial Secretary, in which he
asks, " That the County Council give an opinion as to the most desirable place to name as county town, as owing to the contradictory
statements of different municipalities, laid before His Excellency
the Governor-General, it was difficult to arrive at a decision " The
County Council by a majority of two carried a motion to the effect
that His Excellency the Governor-General should select either one
of the two villages, Kincardine or Walkerton, the reason assigned
being that each of these were located on the Durham Road. On the
8th November the Governor-General[1] for the second time proclaimed
Walkerton as the county town. The December session of the County
Council, after most exciting discussions, selected plans for the county
buildings, but took no steps as to finding a site therefor, leaving
that question to be settled by its successors

The cause of higher education in the county took a marked step
in 1860 when the grammar school at Kincardine, the first in the
county, was established Southampton made an effort at the same
time to obtain a similar school, but failed to secure the consent of
the County Council to this request.

The year 1861 saw a change in the county officers. W. C. Bruce,
who had acted as provisional clerk from the first, resigned his office
at the beginning of this year He was succeeded by the late George

[1]Sir W F. Williams was, at the above date, the administrator of the
Government, and the proclamation bears his signature.

Gould,[1] who filled the position until his resignation in December, 1895. During this long term of office the unvarying kindliness of heart and manner so characteristic of Mr Gould, combined with his willingness to oblige, made him the most popular of public officers During the summer of this year Mr George Cromar, the provisional county treasurer, died. Mr. Cromar entered upon the duties of this office in 1858. During his absence in Scotland in the following year an issue of debentures had to be signed by the county treasurer. It was therefore necessary to appoint someone to do so in his absence. Thomas Corrigan was under these circumstances made treasurer until Mr Cromar's return, when the latter gentleman was re-appointed On Mr Cromar's death Mr. Corrigan received the appointment to the office so vacated, the date being August 16th, 1861. In this year Mr John Purvis once more filled the warden's chair, it being the second time the honor was conferred upon him

The general census taken in 1861 shows what strides the county of Bruce took in its infant days By this census we learn that during the nine years intervening between it and the preceding one, the population of the county increased from 2,837 to 27,499, almost ten fold, whilst the assessment in the same period increased from $147,196 to $3,997,187, an increase of over twenty-seven fold

This year witnessed another determined fight for the county town in the provisional County Council. No time was lost in commencing hostilities, as we find at the first meeting of the year a motion was passed to petition Parliament to avoid the proclamation naming Walkerton the county town and to divide the county into two counties, the dividing line to be the town line of Brant and Eldershe, the 17th and 18th concessions of Greenock and the 7th and 8th con-

---

[1]George Gould was born at Enniskillen, Ireland, November 5th, 1820 When nine years of age he came with his parents to Canada, and resided at Toronto for some time. His father and grandfather both were soldiers, the former holding a commission in the 86th Regiment Mr Gould received his education at Nashville, Tennessee. The southern climate not agreeing with him, he returned to Canada in 1845, and pursued the profession of surveyor He assisted in the survey of five townships in the county of Grey, and also of Arran, Amabel, and Albemarle, in Bruce He was one of the first to take up land in Arran, the location being where Invermay now is He filled the position of county clerk of Bruce from 1861 until shortly before his death, which occurred in February, 1896 His son, William S Gould, succeeded to his office He married on January 19th, 1855, Elizabeth Snowden, of Owen Sound Their family consisted of four sons and two daughters Mr Gould's name is frequently mentioned in this history, he having filled many prominent positions In private life he was most popular and highly esteemed

cessions of Bruce. The south part was to be called the county of
Bruce and the north the county of Saugeen, with Kincardine and
Southampton as the respective county towns. This action of the
County Council was met by Joseph Walker, Walkerton's champion,
obtaining a *mandamus nisi* asking the Council to show cause why
the erection of the county buildings should not be proceeded with
at Walkerton The council defended the suit and ultimately won .
the case, but experienced considerable difficulty in recovering their
costs. The loss of this lawsuit did not discourage Joseph Walker,
whatever effect it may have had upon his friends, he still showed
fight, and commenced without delay another suit This time he
sought to obtain a mandamus directing that the county buildings
debentures be sold, and also directing that the funds so obtained
be used for the purpose specified in the debenture by-law The
County Council defended this suit also, and again came out victor
in this contest in the courts, so that the year closed with the county
town' dispute being as unsettled as ever

The harvest of 1861 was much below an average one. This fact
was used as the basis of a petition forwarded by the County Council
to the Governor-in-Council, " To remit the accumulated interest up
to the end of the year, and to extend the term for payment of purchase money of the public lands in the county of Bruce " The
Crown Lands Department having given notice that payment must
be made About the same time (March 6th, 1861) an order rescinding
the Land Improvement Fund[1] was issued by the Governor-in-Council.
The payments received from this fund by the various local municipalities had enabled much work to be done in the way of opening
up township roads. Possibly on account of the action of the government, the United Counties Council passed a by-law to expend $2,050
during this year on the roads in Bruce This was the first grant of
a comprehensive nature known to the county, though not the last
by any means

The sole change among the municipalities of the county during
the year 1861 was the advent of the united townships of Amabel and
Albemarle as a separate municipality, the union of these two townships with Arran having been dissolved by by-law of the United
Counties Council, passed in September previous The first reeve of
this new municipality was the Rev. Ludwick Kribs, a Congregational minister who had labored faithfully and successfully among

'See Appendix O.

the Indians as a missionary for a number of years, and finally took up land at Colpoy's Bay and settled thereon.

The provisional County Council for the year 1862, over which J. T. Conaway presided as warden, followed the practice of the preceding councils in tackling the county town question in a vigorous manner, but only to leave it unsolved as previous councils had done. A special committee appointed to consider the matter reported in favor of applying for a Bill at the next session of Parliament to divide the county of Bruce into two counties, to be called Bruce and Wallace, of which the county towns were to be Kincardine and Southampton respectively. The assent of the municipal electors to this proposition was to be obtained by a vote of the same. A Bill[1] to this effect passed two readings of the House in 1863, but for some reason unknown to the author it did not obtain a third

If the County Council of 1862 could not settle the apparently interminable county town question they at least originated a scheme of the utmost importance to the county, namely, the comprehensive system of gravel roads, which, although not approved of when voted upon by the ratepayers in the following year, was, when again submitted in 1865, carried by a substantial vote. When we remember the necessity of good markets and a ready access thereto, we wonder that the proposition did not carry at once, for good roads and safe harbors were absolutely necessary for the development of the county in the days when railways were unknown in Bruce, for then farmers when marketing their grain had to team it to some lake port, from whence it would be shipped by sailing vessel, or else to some station on a line of railway, such as Guelph, Seaforth or Clinton. What this meant to a farmer in the back townships may easily be imagined. Owing to the wretched condition of the roads in the fall of the year, he had to wait until the sleighing was good before he could seek a market. Then, having loaded his sleigh over night, he would make an early start and be miles on his way before it was daylight If the price of grain was satisfactory and the sleighing good, it would not be long before he found himself in what seemed a long drawn out procession, so numerous were the grain-laden sleighs. The streets of our lake-port villages were a busy scene in those days, when sometimes 10,000 bushels of wheat would be marketed in one day. To save such long hauls, and that a market might be brought nearer to the doors of the farmers of Bruce, the County Council advertized in

[1]Bill No. 292, 2nd Sess, 7th Parlt, 26 Vic, 1863

the Toronto daily papers during the summer of 1862, offering to
bonus any railway entering the county. The harvest of this year
was secured under most unfavorable conditions; many a farmer found
his wheat sprouted in the ear as it stood in the stook. Such grain,
of course, was sold at prices that were a disappointment to those who
were only getting upon their feet financially, after the hard times
attending their settlement upon bush farms and clearing the same.

At Baie de Dore two villages had developed into business centres,
known as Port Bruce and Malta, which largely supplied the township of Bruce with all the merchandise required. On July 4th, 1862,
in some unrecorded manner a fire started, and fanned by a high
wind completely wiped out these two villages, only a few houses being
left The loss was so complete that the people seemed to have beco.re
disheartened and moved away with anything they might have saved,
instead of rebuilding The result was that Underwood started up
and obtained the trade that previously had gone to Port Bruce and
Malta, and nothing now remains of these two villages beyond a
name and the outlines of the stone foundations of some of the buildings now mostly hidden by a dense growth of cedar.

In February, 1862, the last bounty paid by the county treasurer
for "wolf scalps" ($6.00 each) seems to have been paid, the
recipients being Dr. Garner and H Sperien, but whether the animals
were killed in Huron or Bruce is not very clear. Wolves were not
common after settlers came in, yet it was less than four years previous to the above date that a Mrs Sullivan obtained a grant from
the United Counties Council on account of her husband having "lost
his life from the effects of a desperate encounter with a wolf. We
recommend," the motion of Council goes on to say, "that the sum
of $60 be granted, as we consider that the destruction of the animal
was a public benefit," a sentiment in which all might join.

In its early days Bruce had rarely, if ever, been favored by a
visit from any of the leaders in Canadian politics So when it was
announced that the Hon Geo. Brown was to speak in the Saugeen
District in the interests of Mr John McMurrich in the bye-election
for representation in the Legislative Council,[1] the enthusiasm of

---

[1]The Hon. James Patton, representing the Saugeen District in the
Upper House of our Legislature, had been offered a seat in the McDonald-
Sicotte Ministry, as Solicitor-General, West He was now seeking re-election that he might assume office, but met with a defeat, Mr. McMurrich
being elected by a majority of 769 The date of this election was May
1st, 1862.

Mr. McMurrich's supporters was unbounded. Ten days before the day of voting Mr Brown was at Kincardine and spoke at a meeting held in the town hall, a much smaller building than the present one, and on that day it was crowded to its full capacity This was the only opportunity the author ever had of listening to a speech by Mr. Brown, and he would willingly record the purport of it if his memory of what was said was more vivid and retentive.

In the year 1863 several incidents occurred worthy of record in a history of the county At the general election for the Legislative Assembly, held in June, James Dickson was again returned as the representative for Huron and Bruce It was in the same year that the village of Lucknow, having attained growth sufficient to make it desirous to assume the regulation of its own improvements, asked to be erected into a police village, which request the United Counties Council, at its December session, complied with It also was in 1863 that a change was made in the mode of remunerating township treasurers for their services Previously, one item to be found in the county estimates was that of the township treasurers' commission, which was a percentage of 2 1-2 per cent. Since 1863 these officers have been paid a fixed sum as a salary by their own municipality.

The by-law to issue $300,000 worth of debentures for the purpose of constructing gravel roads was voted upon by the ratepayers March 31st, 1863. The by-law carried, but by so narrow a majority that although the United Counties Council passed the by-law in April, it thought best to reconsider its action, and at its June session repealed the by-law, consequently no debentures were issued.

The business of the provisional County Council for 1863 was presided over by John Gillies [1] Of its four sessions the author has only

[1] John Gillies was a native of the parish of Kilcalomnell, Argyleshire While still in his teens he left Scotland, in company with two brothers, to seek his fortune in Canada, landing in August, 1852 Shortly after he settled upon a farm in Elderslie, of which township he was reeve from 1857 to 1873, both years inclusive; he was also warden of the county for the years 1863, 1869, 1870, 1871 and 1872 In politics he was a Liberal He successfully contested the North Riding of Bruce, for the House of Commons, with Colonel A Sproat, in 1872 In 1874 he was re-elected by acclamation In 1878 he and Colonel Sproat once more were candidates seeking to be the representative of this constituency, Mr Gillies again being successful, this time by a majority of 156 votes In 1882 he was defeated by Alex McNeill. The following year he contested the same riding for the Ontario Legislature, his opponent being James Rowand, and was elected by a majority of 120 votes. In 1888 Mr. Gillies was appointed police magistrate at Sault Ste Marie. His death occurred December 10th, 1889.

5

been able to obtain the minutes of those of the session held on October 16th and 17th   One motion then passed shows what action had been taken during the early part of the year in regard to the county town.   The motion referred to reads: "That whereas at the last meeting of the provisional Council of the county of Bruce held at Port Elgin, it was agreed by this Council that any place which should obtain a majority of votes was to be the county town for the county of Bruce   And whereas Pinkerton obtained such majority, therefore be it resolved that this Council take the necessary steps to have the county buildings erected at Pinkerton with the least possible delay." The motion was lost on a vote of 6 for, 14 against   At this same meeting of the Council, and after a number of motions had been proposed to settle the vexed question, a surprising proposition, considering that it came from two representatives who lived in Kincardine, was proposed   It was moved by William Sutton and seconded by John McLay, "That whereas this Council have shown by their votes on several occasions their inability to settle the county town at Pinkerton, Southampton, Kincardine or Paisley, therefore it is desirable under the circumstances that the Council should at once go on with the erection of the county buildings at Walkerton," etc. The change of the two votes from being opponents of Walkerton to supporters of it gave the necessary majority in its favor, and there was promptly passed a by-law appointing a committee to purchase the necessary site for the buildings, to advertise for tenders, to let contracts, and directing the treasurer to pay orders issued by the committee.

One would almost expect the foregoing to be the conclusion of this long fought out question, but not so.   The provisional County Council of the following year upset the whole matter at its first meeting.   After electing James Brocklebank as warden for 1864, it proceeded to consider the report presented by the Building Committee, which, slightly abbreviated, reads as follows: "At the last meeting of your honorable body, held 22nd December, 1863, your committee reported: That they had purchased and paid for a suitable site from George Jackson, whereon to erect the county buildings, for the sum of $600.   That David Murray, of Guelph, had been appointed architect.   That your committee had advertized for tenders   That the contract had been given to John Elliot, of Brantford, for the sum of $21,136.95.   That your committee had been prevented from carrying out the instructions of the Council, owing to the warden's refusal to sign the contract, with other particulars. Which report your honorable body adopted. Your Council at said meeting, owing to the warden's continued refusal to sign the contract or vacate his seat, appointed John McLay chairman, and by resolution instructed him in behalf of the Council to sign the contract, which was done in open Council. That Mr. Elliot refuses to go on with the erection of the county buildings till the contract is signed by the warden." The committee appointed to consider this report commend Mr. Gillies, the ex-warden, for refusing to sign the contract. Both reports had eleven votes for and against. The minutes do not say so, but the warden must have given his casting vote against the Building Committee report, as it was dropped, and the Council petitioned Parliament to pass an Act repealing all Acts having reference to the county town question, and empower the ratepayers to choose by vote which of two places, Kincardine or Paisley, be the county town of Bruce. The Legislature acquiesced and passed[1] "An Act to void the proclamation declaring Walkerton the county town of the county of Bruce, and to enable the municipal electors of the said county to select a county town." This Act did not limit places to be voted upon, as requested, but inserted a clause which resulted in the end sought for being as far off as ever, in that the place selected must "receive the assent of the majority of all persons entitled to vote at such election." The election was held on September 20th, 1864, with the following result· Paisley, 1,652; Kincardine, 1,403; Walkerton, 1,110; Southampton, 78; Invermay, 1; Riversdale, 1. Such a futile result, none of the places named having obtained a plurality of votes, made the majority of the Council desperate and resulted in a motion being passed to petition Parliament " to abolish the provisional County Council and remodel the tract of country comprising the counties of Grey, Bruce, Huron, Perth and Wellington and its division into counties of compact form and size, in order to avoid the clashing of opposite interests which inevitably exist when counties are of irregular form and unwieldy extent." The result of the contract for the buildings not being gone on with was the payment to the contractor and architect of $500 and $300 respectively for compensation An effort to effect some kind of a compromise by way of giving good roads and improved harbors to Kincardine and Southampton in lieu of these villages waiving their claims to the county town in favor of Paisley or

[1]27-28 Vic. Chap. 77.

Walkerton did not carry, but it may have had some weight when the gravel roads by-law was submitted in the following year.

Two railway propositions were laid before the people of Bruce in 1864. One by F Shanly, C.E, which was to construct a road running north from the main line of the Grand Trunk Railway at Guelph and known as the " Wellington, Grey and Bruce Railway." This had Southampton named as the point where it was to reach Lake Huron The other projected railway was known as the " Stratford and Huron Railway," which had Kincardine named as its lake terminus Both roads were sanctioned by Act of Parliament this year. The names of several Bruce reeves appear in the list of each of these companies so seeking incorporation, incidentally showing how anxiously looked for was the advent of a railway, wherever it might be laid to, so long as it entered the county of Bruce. These projects were considered by the County Council which, without committing itself to either, offered a bonus of $400,000, to be paid on the completion of the railway.

Thomas Corrigan, who had held the position of county treasurer since August, 1861, resigned in May, 1864. Alexander Sproat was appointed his successor. Another change in county officials was that of the registrarship The appointment of Mr. N. Hammond to this office was cancelled early in the year by the government, and Mr John McLay, reeve of Huron Township, was appointed to it. Mr Hammond refused to surrender the books Ultimately Mr. McLay forcibly obtained possession of the same, but the inconvenience to the public was great while the contention lasted, which was settled by the courts, but not until 1868 [1] A change in the member for the Saugeen division in the Legislative Council occurred this year, D. L Macpherson obtaining the seat, which he held until his death thirty-three years later. Mr Snyder, of Owen Sound, was the other candidate in this election

The year 1865 is a memorable one in the history of the county of Bruce, witnessing as it did the passing of the gravel roads by-law by a vote of the ratepayers, the conclusion of the battle for the county town, and the final settlement of that troublesome question.

James Brocklebank was in 1865 again elected to fill the warden's chair The first meeting for that year of the provisional County Council was held in Kincardine. After some desultory voting about the

---

[1] In the Provincial estimates for 1871 is this item, " To reimburse John McLay for costs incurred by him in re Hammond, $1,097.46."

county town, which did not further matters in any way, the following motion carried, " That a committee of five be balloted for to draft a petition to the Legislature praying for the passage of an Act declaring Paisley the county town of Bruce, in accordance with the majority of ratepayers, when given at the poll held for that purpose." After the above motion was carried, a committee was appointed to select a site for the county buildings at Paisley This committee selected a site which was to have cost $300. They also arranged with Mr Elliott, the contractor, to erect the buildings in Paisley at an advance of $5,000 over his contract price for their erection at Walkerton. The report made by this committee, when presented at the next meeting of the County Council, was not adopted, an amendment being carried to the following effect, " That steps be immediately taken for the erection of the county buildings at Walkerton, and that the warden do sign the contract for the same " This motion was followed by another, which is here given in full, as it is the last motion that carried, although not the last motion voted upon in the Council regarding this long, vexatious and wearisome dispute that had lasted eight years, trying the patience of the ratepayers and making them almost despair of a settlement. The motion reads: " Moved by Wm. Sutton, seconded by Paul Ross, That the warden petition the Legislature in behalf of this Council for a bill to repeal all past Acts having reference to the county town of Bruce, and to pass a Bill appointing Walkerton the county town of Bruce in accordance with the action of this Council " The vote as taken was—yeas 13, nays 10 One of the results of the above decision was the entering of a suit against the county to compel the Council to erect the county buildings at Paisley, the plaintiffs being John Valentine, John Gillies, John McMillan, J. B Shepman, Samuel T Rowe, Simon and Thomas Orchard Parliament acceded to the petition of the Council and passed an Act, assented to 15th September, 1865,[1] which declared Walkerton the county town, also legalizing the by-law appointing the Building Committee, and directing all legal proceedings against the Council in the matter to be stayed, and directing the Council to pay all costs of such proceedings. The costs incurred by the plaintiffs, $593 00, were duly paid December 4th, 1865, and the county town question became a thing of the past

At the June session, 1865, of the United Counties Council the Road and Bridge Committee of Bruce brought in a report recom-

'29 Vic. Chap 66

mending a scheme of gravel roads, also the spending of $16,000 on improving other roads, as well as the spending of $22,000 on improving the following harbors: $10,000 at Kincardine; $3,000 at Inverhuron, $3,000 at Port Elgin and $6,000 at Southampton; and that debentures for $220,000 be issued to pay for the same. A by-law to the above effect was voted upon September 21st and 22nd, 1865, and carried by a majority of 738. The by-law was then passed at a special meeting of the United Counties Council held for that purpose October 5th, 1865, at which session a committee was appointed to carry out the scheme   L. B. Hamlin was appointed engineer, and he immediately got out the necessary profile plans, and at the December meeting of the Council fifty-eight tenders were received. The work of constructing the gravel roads and building a bridge at Paisley was let in eight contracts, at a total of $167,397. Extras for about $36,500 were subsequently allowed. The total cost of the gravel road scheme was $199,704 75. The work at the harbors was let in the following year.

It was thought that a separation of the two counties could be effected at the end of the year 1865, and an arrangement was made adjusting the accounts between the two counties, the principal item being the assuming by the county of Huron of $253,000 and by the county of Bruce of $55,000 of the united counties' indebtedness to the Municipal Loan Fund. The Governor-General was also petitioned to dissolve the union by proclamation   This was not complied with just then, owing to the incomplete state of the gaol and court house, and so the union lasted until the end of the following year.

About this time, the days of the American Civil War, this country was flooded with American silver coins, owing to the depreciation of the United States currency.   For a time this foreign coinage passed at par, but the bulk of it at length became so great that bank bills were to a large extent put out of circulation.   Merchants made their remittances to the wholesale houses at Toronto or Montreal in silver, hundreds or thousands of dollars at a time.   It was not until a discount of 20 per cent was put upon it that the influx was stopped. The people of this county, in common with others, lost heavily thereby.   Among the entries in the county treasurer's books at this time is to be found the item, " Discount on American silver."

The agitation for a railway into the county continued in 1865, the route suggested being different from either of those herein mentioned when relating the incidents of the preceding year.   This time

COURT HOUSE AND GAOL, WALKERTON

p. 103

the route proposed was to start from some point on the Northern Railroad, to pass through the village of Durham and the southern townships of Bruce and find a lake port at Kincardine In support of this scheme the County Council petitioned the Governor-General to bonus such a line of railway

The raid made by the Fenians in 1866 called to arms the volunteers of Bruce, who promptly responded and assembled at Goderich, where an attack was looked for The features of this marshalling of our volunteers is dwelt upon fully in another chapter in this book, devoted to "Militia and Volunteers."

During this year good progress was made in completing the contracts for gravelling the leading roads and on work at the harbors at Kincardine, Inverhuron and Southampton. The weather was not favorable for this work, resulting in many contracts not being completed until the following year. The assuming as county roads of "the public highways known as the Goderich and Saugeen Road, Durham, Elora, Kinloss, Culross and Northern Roads," was one of the most marked acts in 1866 of the United Counties Council that affected the county of Bruce.

James Brocklebank, for a third term, held the position as warden of the county in 1866, and presided over the last of the provisional County Councils, which, compared with its predecessors, had a tranquil term of office No question of moment arose and its sessions were largely taken up with considering reports of the Building Committee. This committee made an earnest effort to get the county buildings advanced enough to be accepted by the Board of Prison Inspectors before the meeting of the June session of the council. This could not be accomplished, and it was not until November 1st that the committee reported the gaol and court house as complete. The cost of these buildings was greater than expected when the contracts were let, and it was found necessary to pass a by-law to raise $20,000 to pay for the completion of them. Being so late in the year, the dissolving of the union of the counties was postponed until the end of the year, thereby saving trouble in closing up the joint accounts of the two counties.

CHAPTER VII.

FULL DEVELOPMENT ATTAINED.
1867—1881.

THE year 1867 is a noted one in the history of the county of Bruce, as it is the year which marks its entrance into the ranks of those counties within the province that had attained the dignity of being a separate municipality. The union of the counties of Huron and Bruce was dissolved by a proclamation of the Governor-General, the dissolution taking place December 31st, 1866, so that New Year's Day, 1867, witnessed a marked change in the municipal status of this county

It might not be amiss at this point to concisely recall the various forms of municipal government Bruce as a county had known The first attempt to constitute a municipality was abortive, it being the union of all of the county of Bruce with the united townships of Wawanosh and Ashfield, as directed by the District Council of Huron in 1849, a union not contemplated or sustained by statute. This so-called union ended after a duration of two years on December 31st, 1851 As a separate municipality this territory was first known as "the united townships in the county of Bruce" This endured only for two years, 1852 and 1853; then (January 1st, 1854) came the division of the county into separate local municipalities, consisting of one or more townships, each of which sent a representative to the United Counties Council of Huron and Bruce This continued during the years 1854-5-6. The next change in the form of municipal life commenced in 1857, when the provisional County Council was created and lived—the centre of a storm which raged over the county town question—until its existence terminated December 31st, 1866. The next era in the municipal life of the county commenced when the reeves[1] of the various minor municipalities, twenty-three in number, assembled on January 22nd, 1867, and organized as the County Council of the county of Bruce.

[1]The election which had resulted in the returning of these gentlemen as reeves was the first election at which reeves were elected by the direct vote of the ratepayers Prior to 1867, the Council of each local municipality chose its reeve, as now the County Council chooses its warden

The fact of being a separate county required the appointment
of certain officials, either by the government or by the County Council
The following list gives the names of all who were appointed to
office in 1867, most of whom continued in office for many years after.
J. J. Kingsmill,[1] County Judge, William Sutton, Sheriff; D W.
Ross, County Attorney and Clerk of the Peace; William Gunn,[2]
Clerk of the County Court, John McLay, Registrar, James Brockle-
bank, Warden; Alex. Sproat, County Treasurer; George Gould,
County Clerk; Alexander Shaw, County Solicitor; Latham B. Ham-
lin, County Engineer; Wm. Oldright, M D., Gaol Surgeon; Samuel
Roether, Gaoler, William Richardson, Caretaker of County Build-
ings; James Benson, Inspector of Weights and Measures.

The separation of the counties of Huron and Bruce antedated
the Confederation of the Dominion of Canada by six months
Shortly after the latter was accomplished, a general election was
held   Bruce had been divided for representation purposes into two
ridings. The following was the result of the election then held for
the House of Commons. In North Bruce Lieut -Col Alex Sproat

[1]John Juchereau Kingsmill, M A , D.C.L , held the position of Judge
within the county of Bruce for twenty-five years, retiring toward the end
of 1891. During this long term of office he retained the respect and confidence both of the Bar and the general public He was born in the city
of Quebec, May 21st, 1829, and was of Irish descent, being a son of
Col. Wm Kingsmill He studied at Upper Canada College, Toronto
University, and Trinity College He commenced the practice of law at
Guelph in 1853 After retiring from the bench he became a partner in
the law firm of Kingsmill, Saunders & Torrance, Toronto   Judge Kingsmill was married four times He was a prominent member of the Church
of England His death occurred while at sea on a voyage to Genoa, Italy,
February, 1900

[2]William Gunn was born, May, 1816, near Glasgow When twenty
years of age he came to Canada, residing first at Prescott, from whence,
in 1838, he removed to Kingston In both places he was in the employ
of large shipping firms In 1848 he went to Napanee and opened up a
general store ; moving from there, he came to Kincardine in 1852, and
for a short time had a store there Once more he moved, this time to
Inverhuron, and for fourteen years conducted a general store there, acting
also as postmaster. He was Local Superintendent of Schools in West
Bruce from 1853 to 1858 inclusive   In 1859 he was elected reeve of
the township of Bruce   He acted as census commissioner in Bruce
County when the census was taken in 1861, and when the county of
Bruce was separated from Huron he received the appointment of deputy
clerk of the Crown and of the Surrogate Court, which office he held until
his death   In 1889 Mr Gunn was appointed by the Dominion Government to visit Scotland and Holland to inquire into and report on the
herring fishing industry He married Susan Douglas, daughter of George
Douglas, of Kingston. His death occurred 13th November, 1894   He was
survived by but one son, William, who has held for many years a position
in the employ of the Government at Kingston

was returned, and in South Bruce, Francis Hurdon, the unsuccessful candidates being respectively Dr Robert Douglass and Wm. Rastall. To the Provincial House of Assembly, Donald Sinclair was returned by acclamation for North Bruce, while in South Bruce Hon Edward Blake was the successful candidate, defeating James Brocklebank, the warden

The successful opening of the salt industry at Goderich this year induced the County Council to offer a bonus of $1,000 to any one who would sink, within the county of Bruce, an artesian well to the depth of 1,000 feet in search of salt, the bonus to be divided if more than one well were sunk. This led to wells being sunk at Kincardine, Southampton and Port Elgin. In the following year salt was reached at Kincardine at a depth less than a thousand feet, but the wells sunk in the other two places failed to yield salt. The base of the Onondaga formation, in which salt is to be found, comes to the surface at the mouth of the Saugeen River, so the attempt to obtain salt at the two latter places was an ill advised one, but it has been partially recompensed by the obtaining of a flow of excellent mineral water that now enjoys a widespread patronage. The Kincardine company which sunk the well there received $600 as its share of the bonus, and the Southampton company $400.

On the 20th October, 1867, the Commercial Bank, in which the county account was kept, failed. At this time the county treasurer held $12,000 of the bills of the bank, part of which was intended to pay $7,000 of coupons falling due on the first of the following month. As the county was consequently very awkwardly placed, the county treasurer at once started for Toronto to do all that was possible to protect the credit of the county. On arriving there he found financial circles very much excited over the failure, so much so that it was at first impossible to raise any money, although he offered to put up $10,000 of Commercial Bank bills as security for a $6,000 loan. The Honorable D. L Macpherson, Senator for the Saugeen Division, came nobly to the rescue of this part of his constituency, and offered, "rather than see the credit of the county of Bruce in the least depreciated, to advance the requisite acount." Fortunately the crisis was tided over, and that, too, without accepting the honorable gentleman's liberal offer.

The year 1868 may be given as that when railway matters commenced to take a deep hold of public attention in Bruce In the previous year a delegation had addressed the County Council in the interests of a line from Toronto. It was 1868, however, when matters were urgently brought before not only the Council, but the general public as well. Of the several railway schemes discussed throughout the county about this time interest settled chiefly upon the merits or demerits of two propositions, namely, that of the Toronto, Grey and Bruce Railroad and that of the Wellington, Grey and Bruce Railroad. The first mentioned was to be a narrow gauge road, and Kincardine was the lake port it aimed to reach. The other company, generally referred to at that time as "the wide gauge," in contradistinction to the other, sought to pass from the south-eastern corner of the county to Southampton, and was backed by all the influence that Hamilton could bring to bear, to secure the promised bonus offered by the county. Adam Brown, Thomas White and William McGivern, of Hamilton, were its most prominent advocates and speakers in support of its claims for approval. The other company strove just as hard, with Toronto at its back, and with John Gordon and George Laidlaw of Toronto to speak of its advantages at the various public meetings called to consider railway matters. In no political election ever held in Bruce has excitement run higher than it did in this railway contest. Walkerton, with the eastern and northern townships, favored the "wide gauge," as the route proposed was very favorable to them. On the other hand Kincardine and the townships along the southern boundary favored the "narrow gauge," its proposed route suiting them best. It was urged in favor of the "narrow gauge" that, as it was an independent road, Bruce would be under no railroad monopoly, whereas the wide gauge was to be leased, equipped and run as a branch of the Great Western Railroad, recently amalgamated with the Grand Trunk Railway. But the "wide gauge" people pointed out that freight shipped on it would not require transhipment on reaching Toronto, the gauge being a standard one, and cars could go from Bruce direct to any market. But many felt bitterly against the Grand Trunk Railway since its amalgamation with the Great Western Railroad because of a serious advance in freight rates. Before amalgamation the rate from Guelph to Montreal was $45 per car and 13 cents on each bushel of wheat. After the roads were amalgamated the rate was raised to $60 per car and 21 cents per bushel for wheat, rates that were justly stated to be extortionate. Many other arguments on both sides were used, but the above constituted the groundwork of nearly all of them, besides indicating how opinions might be biased.

Waiting for the construction of a railway was a tedious matter. To bridge over the interval, and obtain cheaper freight communica-

tion to Walkerton than was paid for teaming goods all the way from
Guelph, the distance being over sixty miles, some of the enterprising
citizens of the former place purchased at this time a traction engine,
to be used to haul freight from and to Kincardine. Unfortunately
the amount of success they met with was not equal to the enterprise
shown   Their lack of success arose from want of bridges substantial enough to carry such a heavy engine; besides this, the grades at
some of the hills were found to be too steep to enable a profitable
load to be hauled up them.

The completion of the gravel road contracts resulted in many
claims for extras, these in many cases were excessive and were contested, with the result that the county had at one time to defend
six suits of this description.

When settlers purchased their bush-lots from the Crown at the
" big " land sale in 1854, or earlier, as the case might be, one of the
conditions of the sale was that payment for the same was to be made
in ten annual instalments. In cases of ill health, poor crops, bush
fires, or other misfortunes, the settler found himself unable to carry
out this condition, the consequence was an accumulation of arrears
and interest that amounted in many instances to a considerable sum.
To such unfortunates there came, as the knell of doom, the announcement made by the Commissioner of Crown Lands on October 23rd,
1868, that it was the intention to enforce payment on all arrears
not paid by March 2nd, 1869 [1] Thoroughly alarmed, the settlers
hastened to take steps to protect their farms by making payment of
all claims held by the Crown against their lands.   Many had to
mortgage their farms to do this, a step which in some cases resulted
in seeing them pass out of their hands. Many years passed before
the county was relieved of the burden of mortgage indebtedness
assumed at this time

There rests one foul blot on the history of the year 1868, as far
as Bruce is concerned   During the month of February a man
named Stephen Neubecker, returning from Seaforth with the proceeds of a load of grain he had sold, was assaulted and killed and
his money taken   John Haag was convicted of the crime and hung
on December 15th, the only man who ever suffered capital punish-
ment in the history of the county.

[1] An extension of time for payment of lands purchased from the
Crown had previously been granted, possibly in response to a petition
forwarded to the Governor-in-Council by the United Counties Council of
Huron and Bruce in 1862, asking that the time of payment be extended
for five years, because of a partial failure of the crops that year.

Before passing on to the events of the next year it might be well to note that what are now two of the most flourishing towns within the county, Chesley and Wiarton, commenced to take form in 1868, this being the year in which the former was surveyed, as well as the date of the opening of a post office at Wiarton. It also was the year when Bruce was first connected with the outside world by electric telegraph.

The various proposed railway schemes tantalizingly brought before the people of Bruce during a dozen years previous were in 1869 brought to a head, after a number of excited meetings, ably addressed by good speakers, had been held in towns, villages and district school-houses, until everybody was well aware of the advantages to be gained by the entrance of the Toronto (narrow gauge) line or of the Hamilton (wide gauge) line The County Council, at a special meeting held in September, decided to submit a by-law to the ratepayers to aid the Wellington,. Grey and Bruce Railway by " a free grant or donation of debentures by way of a bonus, to the extent of $250,000," upon the terms that " the said company do extend and carry the line of railway through the county of Bruce from the south-east boundary thereof, at or near Clifford, to the waters of Lake Huron at Southampton; the said line to be complete and ready for traffic to Southampton within three years of the passing of this by-law." The vote was taken on November 2nd. 2,911 voted in favor of the by-law and 2,626 against it, the by-law being carried by a majority of 285 [1] Kincardine Town was charged with

[1] STATEMENT SHOWING THE VOTE CAST ON BY-LAW 35 TO GRANT A BONUS OF $250,000 TO THE WELLINGTON, GREY AND BRUCE RAILWAY.
TAKEN NOVEMBER 2ND, 1869.

	For By-law.	Against By-law	Majority for.	Majority against
Amabel and Albemarle	194	13	181	
Arran	383	11	372	
Brant	509	107	402	
Bruce	151	166		15
Culross	50	372		322
Carrick	492	58	434	
Elderslie	401	33	368	.
Greenock	400	19	381	
Huron	1	579		578
Kincardine Village		265		265
Kincardine Township	32	500		468
Kinloss	7	466		459
Saugeen	· 243	33	210	
Southampton	48	4	44	.
	2911	2626	2392	2107
	2626		2107	
Majority for By-law	285		285	

casting many illegal votes, the feeling there being very strongly in
favor of the "narrow gauge." This charge the reeve had to
acknowledge as true at the next meeting of the County Council. As
soon as the result of the voting was known, a long procession was
gotten up at Walkerton to escort the speakers and advocates of the
by-law, present from a distance, on their drive back to Guelph, a
photograph of which, taken just before starting, is here given. At
Mildmay they were halted, to be feasted and congratulated, a pleasing feature again repeated at Harriston. It was many a long day
before the county settled down and forgot the bitter words spoken,
and all the attendant unpleasantness of this intense contest.
Although the by-law carried by a majority of votes throughout the
county as a whole, the municipalities of Culross, Kinloss, Huron
and Kincardine Township and Village recorded a heavy vote against
it, and in the following year an effort was made by these localities
to get the County Council to memorialize Parliament to pass an Act
exempting these municipalities from being taxed for the same, but
were not successful In addition to this, some private individuals
went so far as to apply to the courts to quash the by-law, but with
like unsuccess.

The expenditure made by the county in the construction of
gravel roads, bridges and harbors far exceeded the original scheme
as voted upon in 1865, consequently it was found necessary to make
a further issue of debentures to pay for the same. Debentures to
the extent of $20,000 were so issued in 1867; again in 1868 and 1869
debentures for a similar amount and purpose were sold, bringing
the amount so raised to a total of $280,000 spent within four years
for the purpose of improving the means of communication within
the county, so that the produce of the fertile fields of Bruce might
reach outside markets more expeditiously and cheaply than in the
past.

When the county buildings were first occupied the office of the
Registrar of Deeds was within the court house. This arrangement
not meeting with the approval of the inspector, in 1869 the separate
building now in use was built at a cost of $5,360, but it was not
until November, 1870, that it became occupied, the fittings having
been long delayed

The cessation of payments by the government on account of the
Land Improvement Fund for five or six years led to an agitation for
the resuming of such payments, to which the government in 1869
yielded so far as to appoint a committee of the House to report on

PROCESSION FORMED ON DURHAM STREET, WALKERTON, NOVEMBER, 1869, TO CELEBRATE THE PASSING OF THE RAILWAY BY-LAW

p. 110

the facts (see Appendix O). A number of prominent men from Bruce appeared before this committee and gave evidence, among whom were Donald Sinclair, M.P.P., John Gillies, M P., John Eckford, Samuel Rowe, Henry Brown, James Rae, Thomas Adair, James Somerville and Alex McNabb, Crown Lands Agent. The report of the committee showed that the government was wrong in withholding payment, and, yielding to the justice of the claim, commenced in 1871, and regularly since, to make payment on this account. The amount involved was so large that to neglect seeking to obtain it would have been gross culpability. How large an amount may be imagined from the figures furnished to the author by the treasurer of Greenock, which show that the aggregate amount he received to the end of 1901 was $11,947.13. Other townships would show proportionately large receipts, making a total of something like $200,000. Up to the end of 1859 this fund paid for the colonization road work conducted by David Gibson, referred to in a preceding chapter. The fund collected from January 1st, 1860, to March 6th, 1861 (the date of the order stopping payment), was made in 1864-5 to township treasurers, and so also all payments made in and since 1871.

The townships in the Indian Peninsula had during the "sixties" been quietly filling up with settlers. As a result we find, with the advent of 1870, Eastnor becoming one of the municipalities within the county, being united to Albemarle for municipal purposes The union of the latter named township with Amabel had been dissolved the preceding summer by a by-law of the County Council.

In the southerly range of townships a series of meetings were held in 1870 in the interests of the narrow gauge railway, with the intent of getting the ratepayers to consent to a sectional bonus being granted, to enable that road to be pushed on to Kincardine from Teeswater. At these meetings the leading men of Kinloss and Lucknow held out for the road to pass through the village of Lucknow The railway authorities were just as determined that if the road were to be constructed it should take the straightest line practicable from Teeswater to Kincardine. As neither party would change its views no progress was made, and the railway to this day never got beyond Teeswater.

The year 1870 is to be noted as the year when the county was first invaded by the potato bug, and also of the first use of reaping machines by any of our farmers.

The expenditure of the county being very large and burdensome it was felt by many that the expense of maintaining and keeping in repair the newly-made general roads throughout the county was one that should be assumed by the municipalities in which these roads were situated, the work to be performed by statute labor. Yielding to this sentiment, the County Council in June, 1870, repealed the by-law by which these roads had been assumed by the county. As a result of this action, his duties being greatly minimized thereby, the county engineer, Mr. Latham B Hamlin, handed in his resignation   Six months' experience satisfied the County Council that a mistake had been made, and in January, 1871, the roads were again assumed by the county, and Cyrus Carroll was appointed county engineer.[1]

A census of the Dominion was taken in 1871, which gave the population of the county of Bruce as 48,575, an increase of 21,016 (equivalent to 76 per cent.) during the decade that had elapsed since the previous census of 1861. The assessment of the county during the same period had increased from $3,997,187 to $8,398,651, or something over 110 per cent.   Both of these classes of figures give satisfactory evidence of the rapid, and at the same time substantial, development of Bruce in that period

In the spring of 1871 a general election for the Provincial House of Assembly was held.   In the north riding of Bruce, Donald Sinclair was returned by acclamation   In South Bruce the contest was between Mr Edward Blake, who had sat for this riding during the preceding term, and Alex. Sproat, the representative of North Bruce in the House of Commons, dual representation at that time being permitted   The election was carried by Mr Blake, who had a large majority of votes   In December, 1871, the John Sandfield Macdonald Government was defeated.   Mr. Blake was then called upon to form a cabinet   His undertaking to do so once more brought him before the electors of South Bruce, when he was elected by acclamation, January 5th, 1872

During 1871 the Wellington, Grey and Bruce Railway made rapid progress, but fearing that it could not be constructed to Southampton in time to claim the full amount of bonus, the President had a special meeting of the County Council held, at which he offered, if

---

[1]Mr Carroll retained the county engineership until the end of 1877, the year in which the county finally handed over the leading roads to the municipalities in which they were located

the Council would extend the time for twelve months for the construction of the last section of the road, that is, from Paisley to Southampton, the company would hand over to the county all the bonus it might receive from the government under an Act just passed The Council held back and nothing was done. At the June session of Council the railway company withdrew its offer, an action that awakened a good deal of ill feeling against it. The company, having further favors to ask, at length agreed to give to the county one-half of what it might receive from the government[1] on account of that part of its road lying within the county. There was nothing said, however, about extending the time within which the road was to be completed. An Act of Parliament[2] passed that year gave the company permission to construct a branch to Kincardine from some point on the main line, and also sanctioned a sectional levy to pay for bonusing such an extension. The result of this legislation was another conflict between the broad gauge and the narrow gauge railway companies as to which was to secure a bonus from the southwestern municipalities for extending their road to Kincardine. Each company this year pressed on the work of construction, the narrow gauge from the village of Arthur, to which it had been completed, while the broad gauge advertized in November for contractors to tender for the construction of the road from Palmerston to Lucknow, following up which, with the usual ceremonies, the first sod of the Southern Extension Railway was turned at Listowel, December 16th. In the contest for the bonus, once more the W G and B. Railway was successful over its opponent, and we find that when, in February, 1872, a by-law was submitted to the ratepayers of the townships of Kinloss, Huron and Kincardine, granting $51,000 to the W. G. and B. Railway on condition that the road was extended to the lake at Kincardine, it was carried. By the conditions of this by-law these three townships were to raise such an amount by a sectional levy annually as was required to pay the debentures and coupons that were issued in the name of the county for the $51,000 so bonused. The railway company, besides this, received from the village of Kincardine an additional bonus of $8,000 and from the county $20,000. This latter amount was in reality the surrender of the share of the government bonus which the company had arranged, as mentioned above, to hand over to the county.

[1] $23,000 of cancelled debentures comprised the refund made
[2] 34 Vic. Chap 37.

Work on the main line of the W. G. and B. Railway was vigorously prosecuted during the season of 1871   As soon as spring opened parties of engineers were engaged in laying out the route; during the summer contractors were at work at several portions of the road, with the result that on November 30th of that year the first locomotive steamed into the county town

The Dominion Government, after much solicitation, decided this year to make an extensive harbor of refuge at Chantry Island, the contract for which was secured by Messrs. Reed and Walker, of Kincardine.

For the first four years after Bruce was set apart as a separate county the county town existed only as a part of the township of Brant. Walkerton had not up to this date even sought incorporation as a village, although it had population sufficient to claim such, but its ambitious inhabitants desired that it should rank as a town from the first   To accomplish this (the population being only 995) it was necessary to have an Act of Parliament passed.   This was done, and on February 15th, 1871, Walkerton became a municipality, and without ever having been classed as a village municipality, took rank as a town

The summer of 1871 was marked by a heavy frost on the 30th June, and also as being a very dry one; in consequence of this there were large bush fires, accompanied by the burning of many barns and farm houses in different parts of the county.

The year 1872 witnessed several political elections within the county.   As already mentioned, on January 5th the Hon. Edward Blake was returned by acclamation for South Bruce on seeking re-election when he became a Cabinet Minister.   On the passing of the Act doing away with dual representation he resigned, and in September R. M. Wells and James Brocklebank contested the riding, the result of the election being the return of Mr. Wells by a majority of 146.   At the general election for the House of Commons, held in August, Hon. Edward Blake was returned for South Bruce, his opponent being Mr. Francis Hurdon, the late member, who retired from the contest subsequent to his nomination.   In North Bruce, at the same election, John Gillies defeated the late member, Col. Alex. Sproat, by a narrow majority of 22.

In other chapters of this history are to be found two events belonging to 1872, the presenting of a stand of colors to the 32nd Bruce Battalion of volunteers, and the formation of an increased number of High School districts   But the most noted feature of the year was the completion of the railway to Southampton, the date of which auspicious event was December 7th, being the time agreed upon when the bonus was given.   The county at large has benefited and prospered greatly through having railway communications with out-side markets, far more so than can be calculated, and its inhabitants can look back with thankfulness to the enterprise of the people of a generation ago, who assumed so large a burden of debt for the pur-pose of bonusing this initial line of railway, which, with others since constructed, enabled the markets of the province and the world at large to be reached by our farmers and manufacturers at all seasons of the year.   The bonuses to the Southern Extension Railway having been granted this year, work was commenced on it at both ends, June 10th being given as the date when the contractors commenced at Kincardine.   The northern part of the county could not but cast curious eyes on the more favored inhabitants of the county dwelling south of them in regard to railways, and naturally commenced to agitate for a branch line which was to run from Paisley to Colpoy's Bay, but were unsuccessful in their efforts.   Ten years were to pass before their desire materialized, and they entered into railway communication with the rest of the world.

Settlers had in small numbers previous to this entered the two extreme northerly townships, Lindsay and St Edmunds, and this year these two townships were united for municipal purposes with Albemarle and Eastnor.

The harvest of 1872 was an excellent one, as is shown by the shipments of wheat made from various points within the county during the fall of that year and the early part of 1873. The figures are as follows:

Kincardine	225,000 bushels	Mildmay	37,000	bushels.
Port Elgin	197,000 "	Southampton	24,000	"
Walkerton	195,000 "	Pinkerton	8,000	"
Paisley	100,000 "			
Inverhuron	60,000 "		846,000	bushels.

The above was calculated to have yielded an average price to the farmer of $1.15 per bushel, representing $972,900.   This large amount received from one description of its crops shows very clearly how rapidly the county was growing in wealth.

In March, 1873, the Ontario Legislature passed an Act[1] whereby

'36 Vic Chap. 47.

a distribution of surplus and refund of indebtedness of Municipal
Loan Fund Debts was directed and authorized. According to the
schedule attached to the Act there was to be distributed among the
local municipalities within the county of Bruce $116,379.40   The
Act contained a clause permitting amounts to be changed if errors
or omissions had been found in the original calculations   As regards
Bruce, this clause must have been made use of to a considerable
extent, as the total payments made to the townships and villages
amounted to $142,659 55.   The first payments were received in 1874
and the final ones in 1877.[1]

For years there had been more or less grumbling, in certain
sections of the county, over alleged advantages that other sections
had obtained when the scheme of gravel roads was adopted, and also
from the route taken by the railway; the gravel roads and railway
alike being wholly or in part constructed by the county at large.   To
see what there was in these murmurs of discontent, the County Council
at its first meeting in 1873 passed a motion asking Judge Kingsmill
to investigate the alleged grievances and report thereon.   The report
was made and presented at the June session and discussed, and also
again at the December session, but resulted in no action being taken;
the expenditure proposed, to construct certain roads so that all
might share alike, was more than the heavily taxed ratepayers would
have stood, so the matter, after much debate. was allowed to drop

The necessary preliminary steps required for incorporation were
taken in 1873 by the three villages of Port Elgin, Paisley and Lucknow   In regard to the latter village a difficulty arose owing to its
lying partly in the county of Huron   It was not until the following
summer that the part lying in Huron was annexed to Bruce, when
the latter county assumed the amount of debt apportioned to the
village of Lucknow of the total indebtedness of the county of Huron,
the amount being $1,200.

[1]Total refunded in 1874. $71,281 14   Total refunded in 1875, $52,918 36.
Total refunded in 1876, $13,029 14   Total refunded in 1877, $5,430 91   In all,
$142,659 55, distributed as follows   Albemarle, Eastnor, Lindsay and St.
Edmunds, $1,951 65; Amabel, $5,238 44, Arran, $10,975 79; Brant, $14,642 52;
Bruce, $10,464 44; Carrick, $15,122 29, Culross, $11,186 76, Elderslie,
$8,330 40, Greenock, $8,788 11, Huron, $11,970 47, Kincardine Township,
$12,194 83; Kinloss, $9,108 38; Saugeen, $5,246 81; Kincardine Village,
$5,567 02; Lucknow, $1,128 93; Paisley, $2,844 62; Port Elgin, $2,195.20;
Southampton, $2,463 54; Walkerton, $3,239 35   The division was on the
basis of population as shown by the census of 1871. The amount allocated
to Bruce was about $2 93 per head

Alex. Sproat, who had filled the office of county treasurer since May 19th, 1864, handed in his resignation at the December session of the County Council, which was accepted, to take effect at the end of the year. His successor, James G. Cooper, was at the same time appointed, his duties to commence January 1st, 1874 Mr. Cooper had worked as assistant to Mr. Sproat for a number of years, and was fully conversant with the office and its duties

The inhabitants of the Indian Peninsula, who in 1872 had been scheming to get a branch line of railway from Paisley, in 1873 first learnt of the proposition of the Lake Erie and Stratford Railway to push its line through to Colpoy's Bay, the Grand Trunk Railway being at the back of the project.

The railway to Kincardine was completed in the fall of 1873, but owing to the W. G. and B Railway Company being financially straitened, owing to the government not paying the promised bonus, it was not handed over by the contractors, but was run by them for a year.

In the ministry formed by Hon Alex. Mackenzie in November, 1873, the Hon. Edward Blake took office, and once more he had to appear before the electors of South Bruce seeking their suffrages. He was returned unopposed December 4th. Mr. Mackenzie not feeling confident of his majority in the House, Parliament was dissolved January 2nd, 1874, a general election being held that month. On this occasion Hon Mr Blake was opposed by Mr Robert Baird, of Kincardine The contest was a keen one, in which Mr. Blake was returned by a majority of 321 In North Bruce John Gillies was returned by acclamation.

The peaceful, law-abiding inhabitants of the county were surprised and shocked in the spring of the year when they learned that its borders had once more been stained by the crime of murder, which deplorable event occurred March 17th, 1873, in the vicinity of Baie du Dore. One George Price was the victim. A trivial matter originated a dispute between two families that led to blows, which, later on, when whiskey had been freely partaken of, resulted in an assault being made in which Price was killed. James Johnston was convicted of the crime and received a death sentence, which was commuted to life imprisonment. Four others implicated in the case received sentences varying from six months to three years' imprisonment

That the reader may be enabled to have some idea of what were the products of the county in the early " seventies," and the proportion of each, there is here given a statement of shipments from Walkerton station from 1st September, 1873, to 20th July, 1874:

Wheat, 160,000 bushels. Oats, 6,500 bushels. Barley, 24,500 bushels. Peas, 5,200 bushels. Flour, 5,300 barrels. Oatmeal, 500 barrels. Eggs, 2,100 barrels. Dressed hogs, 25 cars. Lumber, 202 cars. Lath, 6 cars Bark, 4 cars. Potatoes, 20 cars. Butter, 6 cars.

The above, no doubt, fairly shows what Bruce at that time produced for export. Compared with to-day, when stock, dairy products and manufactures generally form a large percentage of exports, the change is very marked.

Two years after the advent of the Wellington, Grey and Bruce Railway into the county the Toronto, Grey and Bruce Railway reached Teeswater, it being opened to that point on the 16th November, 1874. It was hoped that the road would be extended to the lake shortly afterward, but these hopes have not been realized. In the period when operated by the parent company such an extension could not be made on financial grounds; since it passed into the hands of the Canadian Pacific Railway, the reason for not pushing on to a lake port is said to be an understanding that existed between the two great railway companies not to encroach upon the territory of the other; this understanding has lapsed, and hopes are bright for a further extension of this railway within the county. The Southern Extension Railway was after long delay taken over by the W. G. and B Railway, and from 17th December, 1874, it has been operated by that company or its successor, the Grand Trunk Railway

The preliminary steps towards erecting the village of Teeswater into a separate municipality having been taken, the County Council in June, 1874, passed the necessary by-law whereby Teeswater became an incorporated village on the 1st January following.

The time was certain to come when Bruce would cease to be looked upon as a locality to which settlers might go in search of a home, and change to one from which emigration to new settlements might be expected. The latter period was certainly reached when a meeting was held at Southampton April 16th, 1875, the object of which was set forth in the following motion, which was duly carried thereat: "That from the experience we have had as settlers in the county of Bruce, we believe the system of settling by the formation of a colony is attended by less hardships and privations than many of us endured in the early settlement of this county; that being anxious to plant a colony in the province of Manitoba from the county of Bruce, immediate steps be taken to further this project, and that a suitable location be made as speedily as possible." At this meeting " The Bruce Mutual Colonization Company was organized, and James Stirton was appointed to select a proper location in Manitoba. The movement so started proved to be the prelude to a large emigration, which has not ceased, of the most energetic and enterprising of each generation, as it appeared, until the western prairie land seems to teem with those who are proud to say that they come from the county of Bruce.

A general election for the House of Assembly was held January, 1875. R. M. Wells, the member for South Bruce in the previous House, ran again and was elected. He was opposed by D. W. Ross, who resigned his office as Clerk of the Peace so that he could qualify for nomination. It was an unfortunate move for him, as he lost both the election and his office Mr. Thomas Dixon received the appointment[1] to the vacant office and has held it since In North Bruce at this election Donald Sinclair was opposed by a namesake, Dr. A. C. Sinclair. The contest resulted in favor of the former.

Hon. Edward Blake, who had accepted a seat without a portfolio in the Mackenzie Ministry on its formation, shortly afterward withdrew therefrom, but was again persuaded to accept office, and on May 19th, 1875, was made Minister of Justice, and so again had to appear before the electors of South Bruce The nomination was held on June 2nd, when he was returned by acclamation. This was the sixth occasion that Mr. Blake was returned by South Bruce within five years, either to the House of Commons or to the House of Assembly

From the time the gaol was built, the county held that the government should refund the cost of alterations made in the construction of the building insisted on by the Inspector of Prisons after the original plans had been passed by him, and for the carrying out of which contracts were let. Other counties besides Bruce were pressing similar claims, with the result that the Legislature passed an Act[2] authorizing a refund of $6,000, which was the amount of the county's claim. Some discussion arose as to what would be a proper mode to dispose of this sum. On first learning of the passing of the Act the County Council resolved to distribute the amount among the various local municipalities of the county according to assessment, but in the interval which elapsed before the money was paid over

[1]March, 1875.
[2]37 Vic. Chap. 31. Passed March 24th, 1874.

it was made apparent that increased accommodation was required for county offices, so in January, 1876, a committee was appointed to see to the erection of a new building, which was to be paid for out of the refund.[1] This building, that in which the County Council now meets, was erected that year, and was first occupied and used as a place of meeting by the County Council at the following December session The dwelling of the caretaker of the county buildings was erected the same year. This building was built by Wm. Richardson, caretaker, on the county grounds at Walkerton at an outlay of $1,300 In 1884 an agreement was made with him by which he was to occupy the house as long as he held the oce offife of caretaker, when it was to revert to the county, he to receive in full consideration the sum of $1,000. This reversion took place on Mr. Richardson's death in May, 1888.

In January, 1876, the southern part of the county had another railway route opened to its borders, namely, the London, Huron and Bruce Railway, which connected with the Southern Extension Railway at Wingham This line has proved of great advantage to those within the county who are doing business in the south-western part of the province or in the western states The town of Kincardine gave a bonus of $3,000 to this railway, although it did not directly enter the town or come within many miles of doing so.

The County Council of 1876 vacillated about the county retaining control of the gravel roads. The January session repealed the by-law by which they were assumed, but at the June session re-assumed them. However, in 1877 the Council finally handed them over to the local municipalities in which they were situated.

A petition bearing over two thousand signatures was presented to the County Council at the December session of 1876, asking that body to appoint a day on which a vote should be taken whether there should be enforced the provisions of the " Temperance Act of 1864," commonly known as the " Dunkin Act." The Council, at the session held in June following, fixed September 18th, 1877, as the required date. The vote then given showed a majority of 1,142, of a total vote of 6,352, in favor of the Act coming into force in the county, which it did May 1st, 1878 In Bruce the Act had but a short life, it being found to have inherent defects that made it unworkable, and

---

[1] The refund paid for this building, which cost approximately $4 600, and also for an extension to the gaoler's residence, built that year, costing about $1,400.

ALEX SHAW, K.C.

p. 123

WILLIAM GUNN

p 105

J J KINGSMILL

p .05

HENRY CARGILL

p 136

consequently failed[1] in the end sought, and was therefore repealed
as far as this county was concerned. The ratepayers voted, by a
majority of 1,347, to that effect when the question was again submitted to them January 21st, 1879   The Act ceased to be in force
in Bruce from 1st May following.

At the opening of the Northern Exhibition, held October, 1877,
the county town was honored by a visit from Lieut.-Governor D. A.
Macdonald, who had consented to come and open the Exhibition. He
was greeted by a large concourse, despite most unfavorable weather.

Agitation for more railways was in the air during 1877, Wiarton
still hoping to obtain a line from Stratford, and Walkerton to get
a line from Mount Forest, to connect with the T G. and B Railway.
Owing to financial inability this railway company could promise
nothing towards the construction of the proposed extension, but
offered to run and keep in repair the line if built   The year ended
with the question still under discussion whether or no the municipalities to be benefited would advance the needed amount, some
$250,000

The harvest of 1876 was a poor one, so much so that many
farmers did not find their crop of wheat sufficient to supply the
needs of their families. As a natural consequence, the following
year was one of marked business depression. Bruce was not alone
in this experience, as we find, arising from various other causes, such
was almost world-wide in extent. Although the harvest of 1877
proved to be an excellent one in Bruce, it could not remove the commercial depression that was so far reaching.

About 1877, or a year or two earlier, the author has not been

---

[1]The following extract, from the *Bruce Herald*, of June 7th, 1878, reflects
the condition of affairs pretty generally throughout the county regarding
the enforcement of the Dunkin Act :
" There has, so far as we have been able to learn, been nothing done
in this section of the county to enforce the Dunkin Act   If the present
state of affairs is allowed to continue, we should say that the passage
of that Act has been a positive injury to the community. There is now
no liquor law in force in the county and the liquor dealers have everything their own way. This is a serious evil, and the temperance organizations are mainly responsible for it   Had it for a moment been supposed
that they were not prepared to have the Act put in force there would
have been fewer votes cast for it than there was   The temperance organizations, in agitating for the passage of the Act, have assumed a responsibility
which they cannot get rid of. It was not to produce a worse state of
things that outside support was given them, and if they were not prepared
to carry the Act into effect, it would have been far better to have allowed
matters to remain as they were. The Dunkin Act has been productive of
nothing but evil so far."

able to obtain the exact date, the organization or order known as
X "The Grange" was introduced into the county of Bruce, which was
some two or three years after the Dominion Grange was formed.
Its membership was confined to those engaged in agriculture. Many
lodges were opened within the county, the total of which must have
numbered nearly one hundred, judging from the only data the author
has been able to obtain, which gave twenty-two subordinate lodges
in what was known as the Lucknow Division. The aim of the Grange
was to advance the interest of the farmer. One of the means of
doing so was by an effort to bring its members, the farmers and the
manufacturer, into closer relations, and to do away with all middle-
men as far as possible   Another aim was to draw the farmer out
of his isolation, so that by an interchange of ideas and by united
action to strive to promote common interests. In carrying out these
objects the Dominion Grange purchased and conducted "The
People's Salt Co." at Kincardine.   There was also established a
so-called wholesale warehouse at Toronto which filled orders for
goods as sent in by the various lodges on the requisition of its various members. This practice of sending away for articles of common
home consumption, to the loss of the local storekeeper and mechanic,
produced strongly antagonistic feelings against the Grange by those
who suffered a loss of business as a result of the above-mentioned
practice. The Grange reached its fullest measure of activity in
Bruce during the early "eighties," but it fell off rapidly, and it is
doubtful if there are more than three or four active lodges in the
county in 1905. The reader must bear in mind that "The Grange"
was not in any sense a political movement; it differed in this particular from the later movement, in the "nineties," known as that of
"The Patrons of Industry," referred to in the succeeding chapter.

It is not the object of this history to refer to events outside of the
county except as they may have affected it. The political campaign
of 1878 was such an event   It was, from a·Dominion standpoint,
pivotal in character, for in that year the election contest was over
the "National Policy" question as laid down by the leader of the
Conservative party, Sir John A. Macdonald, and which was enthusiastically sustained by the country at the polls. There is no doubt
that the fall of the Liberal government arose from its unwillingness
to take any action having in view the amelioration of the commercial
depression referred to in the preceding paragraph, holding fixedly
to the theory that anything the government might attempt in that

line would exert as much influence as "a fly on a wheel," as the Finance Minister expressed it, a phrase remembered for many a year. The election was fiercely contested in both ridings of Bruce. Hon Edward Blake at first declined to accept the nomination, but on pressure being brought to bear, and the party leaders in the riding guaranteeing his election without a personal canvass on his part, he consented to run. The Conservative candidate was Alexander Shaw, county solicitor [1] Both sides worked with a determination to win When the votes were counted Mr. Blake, so often the choice of South Bruce, was found to be in a minority of 75. In North Bruce the suffrages of the electors were sought by John Gillies and Col A. Sproat, who again, and for the last time, contested this riding, which resulted in Mr. Gillies being returned by a majority of 156.

For a number of years there had been constant complaint, at the time the County Council struck the annual levy, regarding unequal assessment among the various municipalities To enable justice being done to all, the County Council in July, 1878, appointed James Rowand, of Saugeen, and M L McKinnon, of Tiverton, to make a valuation of the assessable real property in the county. They commenced their duties shortly after the date of their appointment, but were unable to complete their report so that it might be used as a basis for equalizing the assessment of 1879, but that of 1880 and the nine following years was so based Their work was satisfactory to the County Council, and it seems to have been the means of settling a long-standing grievance The total assessment of the county was raised $922,906 by the report.

In response to a petition of the County Council the House of Assembly passed an Act[2] to enable the county of Bruce to assume the railway debt of the municipalities that had bonused the Southern Extension and T. H. G. and B Railways. The next step should have

---

[1]Alexander Shaw, K C, was born in the township of Ramsay, January 13th, 1833, and received his education in the town of Perth, where he also studied law. He came to Bruce in 1858, and settled at Kincardine, where he married Anna, daughter of Peter Robertson, merchant, and has had a family of five sons and two daughters. When Walkerton became the county town he moved there and was appointed county solicitor in 1867, which office he has retained since. At the general election in 1878 he defeated the Hon Edward Blake in the contest in South Bruce, but in 1882 failed to be re-elected. In 1890 he ran as an Independent for Centre Bruce, being opposed by W. M. Dack, who carried this election Mr Shaw stands at the head of the Bar in Bruce, and by many years is the oldest practising lawyer in the county.

[2]41 Vic. Chap. 31.

been the submitting to the ratepayers of a by-law for their consent
to the county assuming this indebtedness, but on second thoughts
the County Council decided to take no further action, consequently
the Act became inoperative and the local municipalities obtained no
relief.

The eastern part of the county had the subject of railways
brought before it continuously throughout 1878. Walkerton was
anxious to obtain a competing line of road, and succeeded in having
the Saugeen Valley Railway scheme launched, the company being
incorporated in 1878 by Act of Parliament,[1] John McLay, Registrar,
and Dr A. Eby, Editor of the *Telescope,* both of Walkerton, were
appointed president and secretary when the company was organized.[2]
Stock-books were opened and a fair amount of stock subscribed
Surveys were also made to show that the route proposed presented
no special engineering difficulties. Public dinners and speeches, having in view the exciting of public interest, were given and seemed to
attain their object, but through some mismanagement the scheme,
after being before the public for a number of years, ceased at last
even to be spoken of. The other railway scheme was that of the
Stratford and Lake Huron Railway, from Listowel to Wiarton.
Bonus by-laws were submitted to the ratepayers of Brant, Elderslie,
Arran, Albemarle and Amabel in the fall of 1878 and carried. In
Carrick and Eastnor similar by-laws were defeated. The bonuses
granted by Bruce municipalities to this railway are given in a footnote.[3]

December, 1878, is the date when Tiverton, the smallest of the
village municipalities within the county was incorporated. The next
village to seek incorporation was Chesley, which in this respect was
just a year behind Tiverton, but nevertheless has forged ahead of
it and every other of the newer villages in the county, Wiarton alone
excepted.

The year 1879 was rather uneventful as far as the county as a
whole was concerned. The harvest was an excellent one. To aid in
securing it self-binding reapers were used for the first time, Duncan

[1] 41 Vic Chap. 52.

[2] The first sod for the proposed road was turned at Walkerton, March
1st, 1880, by the President and Mr J P. Johnston.

[3] The following are the bonuses granted to the Stratford and Lake
Huron Railway by the several municipalities named: Brant, $20,000;
Elderslie, $35,000; Chesley, $10,000, Arran and Tara, $45,000; Amabel and
Wiarton, $45,000, Albemarle, $10,000; Total, $165,000.

and Archibald Kippen, of Bruce, and C Thede, of Saugeen, being credited as being the introducers of these machines into the county.

A general election for the House of Assembly came off June 5th, 1879, in which R. M. Wells secured a majority over Robert Baird in the south riding, while in the north riding, Donald Sinclair was again returned, his opponent on this occasion being J. W S Biggar.

Tara, the youngest of the village municipalities in Bruce, became incorporated by by-law in June, 1880. Wiarton preceded Tara by a few months, securing incorporation by a special Act of Parliament [1] The town plot being partly in the county of Grey and partly in Bruce, this special Act was asked for so as to prevent any difficulty such as Lucknow, similarly situated, had experienced On becoming annexed to Bruce county it assumed the amount of debt apportioned to the village of Wiarton of the indebtedness of the county of Grey, the amount being $400, which was paid in one instalment [2]

For a length of time reports had been circulated that the county was not receiving from the Registrar of Deeds the correct refund of fees payable to it. Urged on by some individuals who entertained most bitter feelings toward Mr. McLay, the County Council at length, in December, 1879, took action. The matter came before the courts, and as a result of a suit the county, in 1880, recovered $2,496.16. The County Council in December of that year followed this up by forwarding a petition to the Lieutenant-Governor, asking for the removal from office of Mr. McLay. No response was made to this until September, 1881, when A E. Irving, Q C , was commissioned to report upon the complaints made against the Registrar. The commission sat in the following November and took a large amount of evidence. The result of the investigation was that on December 19th, 1882, the government dismissed Mr. McLay. For some time the office was in charge of the Deputy-Registrar, Charles Astley. On March 14th, 1883, Donald Sinclair,[3] late member for North Bruce, received the appointment, and held the office till his death in 1900.

[1] 43 Vic. Chap 46

[2] See County of Bruce By-law No 173

[3] Donald Sinclair was born in the Island of Islay, Scotland, in July, 1829 He immigrated to Canada with his parents in 1851, who settled the following year in Arran Mr Sinclair came to Bruce in 1853 and followed the profession of a schoolteacher here, and also later in the vicinity of Toronto From 1858 he was permanently a resident of Bruce. In 1863 he was elected deputy reeve of Arran In 1869 Mr Sinclair moved to Paisley and carried on a general store. In the general election of 1867 he was elected as member of the House of Assembly, by acclamation, for

The census of the Dominion taken in 1881 showed the population of the county of Bruce (see Appendix L) at the highest recorded point, the number being 65,218, certainly a wonderful development in population during the thirty-three years which had elapsed since the first settler entered the county. To enable the reader to form an idea of the material wealth of the county of Bruce at this time, there is given in a footnote[1] the equalized assessment of the several local municipalities for the year 1881, these figures have changed but little since then, except in the case of some of the towns.

Early in December, 1881, the contractors had the rails· of the Stratford and Lake Huron Railway laid to Wiarton, but traffic to

the riding of North Bruce This seat he held until 1883, when he was appointed Registrar of Deeds for the county of Bruce. In April, 1871, he married Isabella, daughter of Thomas Adair, and had a family of two sons and three daughters. In politics he was a Liberal In religious belief he was a Baptist. Mr Sinclair possessed a character for upright-ness and integrity, ever having the courage to uphold his convictions. His death occurred November 19th, 1900, at Toronto, where he had gone to obtain medical advice. He was buried at Southampton.

[1]EQUALIZED ASSESSMENT SCHEDULE FOR 1881, AS PASSED BY COUNTY COUNCIL OF BRUCE

Albemarle	$156,238
Amabel	726,858
Arran	1,843,490
Brant	2,618,302
Bruce	2,137,520
Carrick	2,316,270
Culross	1,765,720
Eastnor, L. & St Ed	181,047
Eldershe	1,755,765
Greenock	1,582,680
Huron	2,145,990
Kincardine	2,213,640
Kinloss	1,380,170
Saugeen	1,169,465
Total of Townships	**$21,993,155**
Chesley	$176,440
Lucknow	299,750
Paisley	310,530
Port Elgin	422,097
Southampton	159,225
Tara	105,820
Teeswater	210,100
Tiverton	117,480
Kincardine Town	851,620
Walkerton	722,205
Wiarton	70,481
Total of Towns and Villages	**3,445,748**
Total Assessment of the County of Bruce	**$25,438,903**

that point was not opened officially until 1st August of the following year. This line of railway has been one of the most profitable
in the county, as over it is carried a large part of the commerce of
the peninsula

In recording the completion of the above-mentioned railway, the
author brings this chapter to a close, as the title of it, " Full Development Attained," at last had become an accomplished fact. This
statement might be qualified by saying that what further development
has taken place since has been along lines which were then in existence

CHAPTER VIII.

THRIVING AND PROGRESSING.
1882—1906.

THE title given to this chapter is one by which the author would desire to indicate that the period of rapid, lusty development within the county of Bruce, which had been one of its marked characteristics, closed with the final years referred to in the previous chapter. The era when the increase of the county's wealth and population and of the development of its resources took place by leaps and bounds, could not be enduring and continuous; the change to a less rapid advancement must come, and the author would place the date thereof, approximately, at the close of the third decade of the county's history. High water mark for a long time to come, as regards population, is to be found in the census of 1881.

The Redistribution Act passed in 1882 by the Dominion Parliament gave Bruce three members in the House of Commons. In the election which followed the passing of this Act, North Bruce returned Alex. McNeill, his opponent being John Gillies, the late member. In East Bruce the late member also failed in being re-elected, R. M. Wells being successful in this contest against Alex. Shaw. The riding of West Bruce was contested by James Somerville and J. H. Scott, in which contest the former was returned. R. M. Wells had to resign his seat in the Ontario House of Assembly to qualify for nomination in the above election. This necessitated a by-election in South Bruce. The Liberals nominated H. P. O'Connor, a lawyer of Walkerton, and the Conservatives, J. C. Eckford, a leading farmer of Brant. This election resulted in Mr. O'Connor's favor.

The last change in the number of minor municipalities within the county which occurred for the next twenty years took place in June, 1882, when the united townships of Lindsay and St. Edmunds were separated from Eastnor and established as a separate corporation on and from January 1st, 1883.

In 1883 a change took place in regard to the wardenship. During the twenty-six previous years this honorable position was frequently

128

conferred year after year upon the same person, so that only nine names occur during that period among the list of wardens. Commencing with 1883, the honor and the duties of the office have been passed around, and no one since then has held the office for more than a single year, as will be seen by consulting Appendix Q, which shows that altogether thirty-two individuals have attained to the wardenship, commencing with the first County Council, that of 1857. Of these, it is interesting to note, about one-third, having plumed their wings in the County Council, have sought a loftier flight, and have stood for parliamentary honors.

A general election for the Ontario House of Assembly took place February 27th, 1883. In South Bruce H. P. O'Connor was returned by acclamation. The contest in North Bruce was between John Gillies and James Rowand. The former was elected by a majority of 120 votes

The burning question before the people of Bruce for the greater part of 1884 was the "Scott Act," the name by which the Canada Temperance Act of 1878 was commonly known The campaign commenced early in the year with the obtaining of the signatures of 3,790 ratepayers to a requisition praying that the Act be submitted to the electors to be voted upon. During the summer public meetings were held in many localities to discuss the features of the Act. Speakers from outside places were obtained by both parties to stump the country and present their views either for or against the temperance question in general and the Act in particular. Literature was freely circulated, and every means used to enlighten the electors upon the question on which they were called upon to vote on 30th October of that year. The vote cast gave a majority of 1,321 in favor of carrying out the provisions of the Act in the county of Bruce.

Seven times have the electors of Bruce been called upon to express their attitude on the temperance question. What that has been may be seen by a study of Appendix R, which shows the number of votes cast for and against prohibition on each of these occasions. The inference the author draws from a comparison of the various votings is that there is a strong sentiment within the county for sobriety, but which sentiment is not vigorous enough to see that temperance legislation is enforced. As a result of this lack of moral fibre neither the "Dunkin Act" or the "Scott Act" were enforced as they might have been. In addition to this, respect for law was lowered, per-

6

jury was commonly practised when those who violated the Act were prosecuted, and drinking habits were in no sense changed. The result of this evading of law, of this moral abasement, was a revulsion of feeling as to prohibition enactments, so that both in 1879 and 1888, when the next occasion of voting occurred, large majorities were given against the continued enforcement of temperance legislation in Bruce.

At this point it might not be amiss to refer to the great change which has occurred in regard to the drinking customs of the people since the settlement of the county. Then whiskey was so low in price that its cost was not considered,[1] the price being twenty-five cents to thirty cents a gallon. So universal was the use of whiskey that no social gathering would have been considered complete without it. It was passed around as a necessary and expected thing at every logging bee, in every harvest field, and wherever any strenuous effort was to be put forth. It was looked upon as the elixir of life, to be drunk in winter to warm one up, and in summer to preserve from being overcome by the heat[2] Such being the habits of the people, taverns were everywhere. In confirmation of this it may be stated that during the sixties there were on the Durham Road, between Walkerton and Kincardine, no less than thirteen taverns, and other

---

[1] It is related of one of the first settlers at Hanover, who had hung out a shingle to indicate that his shanty was a tavern, finding he could not spend time waiting for chance customers to call at the bar, he, when working in the bush, left a pail filled with whiskey and a tin cup for any one to help themselves, and a box to put their money in. The cost of what might be drunk being so small it was not worth while considering it, even if it were not paid for.

[2] The following account of an hotelkeeper at Goderich, presented for payment to the United Counties Council of Huron and Bruce, January session, 1852, would be considered unique at the present day, especially when it is considered who contracted the indebtedness It also throws a strong light on the then prevailing drinking customs :

The Board of Education   Dr.
To J. Rattenbury.

1850			s.	d.
Dec.	9	To 3 Glasses of hot brandy	1	6
	9	4 Dinners, including beer	6	0
	9	2 Bottles of brandy	6	3
	10	4 Lunches 7½	2	6
	10	2 Bottles porter, 1s. 6d.	3	0
	10	2 Glasses brandy, 1 hot do, 2 lunches.........	2	4½
			£1 1	7½

Payment of the above was refused by the Council.

leading roads would have shown a correspondingly large number. At the time of writing (1905) the thirteen taverns have dwindled down to four. It had been asserted that the reason taverns were so close together on the leading roads in the early days was because then people did not dress as warmly as now. Then a fur coat was rarely seen. Warm knitted underwear was almost unknown. A knitted sash wound around the waist and a muffler round the throat were the only additions made to the ordinary dress of a man by way of preparation for a long, cold drive, consequently the drive consisted of a number of haltings at the different taverns to get warmed. Now, wrapped in warm furs, long drives are only broken when necessary to water the horses. The manufacture of liquor was carried on then as never since. To-day the only manufacturers in this line of business within the county are three brewers of lager beer. Forty years ago whiskey distilleries were flourishing in several villages in the county; now there is not one. When the author reached Kincardine in 1856 he found a distillery and a brewery there, to which another brewery was added in the following year. In time all of these closed up, and it is years since liquor has been manufactured at Kincardine. The following figures as to the number of licenses issued tell most forcibly the rapid change regarding the use of liquor in Bruce. In 1874 there were issued within the county 180 tavern and 20 shop licenses. In 1902 the number stood at 80 and 4, respectively.[1] The finding of excitement in other ways, the different view taken of one who becomes intoxicated, and the general elevation of the standard of what a man is expected to live up to has, in addition to what churches and temperance organizations have done, produced in the county of Bruce a generation of men who are of temperate, sober habits.

During the summer of 1884 the subject of a re-arrangement of the counties of Bruce, Huron, Perth, Wellington and Grey was much spoken of, the idea being the creation of a new county. This matter had been before the public for twenty years, and was now discussed with some vehemence, especially by those towns or villages which cherished any hope of being made a county seat, the ground for such proposed change being that the construction of railways had changed the lines of travel and centres of business since the days

[1]There are three townships in Bruce (Elderslie, Lindsay and St. Edmunds) in which no liquor licenses are issued, and three townships (Arran, Kincardine and Saugeen) in which only one license is issued.

when the counties were laid out and county towns selected. A deputation from Harriston, which waited on the government regarding this matter, were informed that it was under consideration. The question was also discussed in the Bruce County Council, but there and elsewhere the agitation resulted in nothing, Wiarton and Kincardine being probably the only localities in Bruce that considered they might derive any benefit from a re-arrangement of the county.

The county of Bruce was deeply stirred, especially at those eight points where volunteer companies existed, when on May 11th Lieut.-Col. Cooper received orders to muster the 32nd Battalion for active service in the North-West, to aid in suppressing the Riel Rebellion. This matter has been mentioned in the chapter on "Militia and Volunteers," but is here referred to as one of the historical features of the county during the year 1885 It would be hard to overestimate the excitement felt at that time. A week was put in by each company drilling, after which the various units of the battalion assembled at Southampton. So enthusiastic were many of the volunteers to respond to the call of their country, that good positions were thrown up by many. One man belonging to the Paisley company, earning a salary of $75 a month, gave it up to accept 50 cents a day as a private in the ranks Another, Dr. Ben. Jeffries, of Texas, gave up a lucrative medical practice there and returned to Canada that he might go with his company to the front. Many other examples occurred of self-sacrifice springing from full-hearted patriotism; the above are sufficient, however, to show the spirit felt by our volunteers. At Walkerton it was estimated that 4,500 people assembled at the station to see the boys off. This seems to have been the acme of enthusiasm, although every other point was deeply stirred.

In November, 1885, gravel road debentures amounting to $191,000 matured Mr. Cooper, the county treasurer, reported that only $175,405 of sinking funds were on hand to pay these debentures He also informed the County Council that the sinking funds raised to pay these debentures had been encroached upon by excess of expenditure, in years gone by, over amount of rates levied. The County Council accepted this explanation, and proceeded to issue debentures to the extent of $20,000 to make up the deficit These debentures were made payable in ten years and bore six per cent. interest. They were sold at a premium, netting the county $22,256.75.

Farmers' Institutes have been the means of diffusing a great deal of information and of developing a higher type of farming in

Bruce, as well as elsewhere throughout the province The first step towards the starting of such was in 1885, when the Provincial Commissioner of Agriculture sent a circular to the various county councils asking for a grant of $25 to supplement one of like amount made by the government, to establish a Farmers' Institute in each electoral district. The County Council of Bruce promptly acquiesced. Two years elapsed before the several Institutes in Bruce, then just organized, applied for the grant.

In October of 1885 the appointment was made of a permanent junior county judge, the position being conferred upon William Barrett, at that time a practising barrister at Walkerton. He had for several years prior to this acted as junior judge, as occasion required, but without a fixed appointment or salary. On the retirement of Judge Kingsmill, towards the latter part of 1891, Mr. Barrett was appointed senior judge, the position of junior judge being conferred upon A. B. Klein in 1893.

Owing to a partial failure of the crops in the northern part of the county in 1884, a certain amount of distress and destitution was felt by many of the poorer settlers in that sparsely settled portion of the county On this being known, joint commissioners were appointed by the government and the warden in the following year, as is mentioned in the chapter on the " Indian Peninsula," to take such steps as might be deemed necessary for the relief of the needy settlers.

The supporters of the Canada Temperance Act within the county during 1886 and 1887 made repeated efforts to have the County Council pass a resolution affirming that it was expedient to have a salaried police magistrate appointed, to have the provisions of the Act enforced. When such action was taken by the County Council, under Statute (48 Vic, chap. 17), the Lieutenant-Governor might at once make such appointment Each application of the supporters of the Act was unsuccessful, there being in the County Council a majority adverse to the Act, and also others who thought that if the Act was not enforced and convictions obtained it was not for lack of effective judicial machinery, but for want of evidence, which, owing to the peculiar vagaries of public opinion, was difficult to obtain The temperance people had good grounds for endeavoring to have a police magistrate appointed, difficulty being experienced in getting a justice of the peace willing to receive an information against any alleged violators of the provisions of the Act This, in a measure, arose because magistrates who had performed their duty were[1] on several occasions made to suffer therefor. The necessity of the initiative being taken by the County Council, as above, was overcome when in 1887 the Legislature passed an Act[2] empowering the Lieut.-Governor to appoint police magistrates with salary at his discretion. Under the provisions of this last-mentioned Act, Richard Vanstone, a barrister, residing at Kincardine, was gazetted, June 4th, 1887, as police magistrate for the county of Bruce, at an annual salary of $1,000 and expenses, to hold office as long as the Temperance Act remained in force. For almost two years Mr. Vanstone impartially tried all cases of infringement of the Act, and they were numerous.

In 1886 another railway to enter Bruce obtained a charter[3] under the title of the "Georgian Bay and Lake Huron Railway." The eastern terminus was to be at Meaford, while its western one was to be either Port Elgin or Southampton. Unfortunately the charter lapsed before anything was done in the way of construction.

The excitement marking a general election for the House of Assembly closed the year 1886, the voting being on December 28th, with the result that J. W. S. Biggar was elected in North Bruce, W. M. Dack in Centre Bruce, and H. P. O'Connor in South Bruce. This was the first time Bruce sent three representatives to the Legislature, the additional one being granted by the Franchise Act of 1885.

The county at large was startled, when, about the last days of February, 1887, it became known that James G. Cooper, the county treasurer, was a defaulter and had fled the country. A special audit was made by W. F. Munro, accountant, of Toronto, extending over the period from the 1st January, 1870, to the time Mr. Cooper left. To fully take up this matter would fill many pages of this history. To those who wish to become acquainted with the facts the author would refer them to the report of Mr. Munro and also to that of A. B. Klein, which are given in full in the printed copies of the

[1] No unprejudiced person, at the time, had any doubt as to the origin of the fire that consumed the barn of Wm. Daniel, J P., or of the two fires Joseph Barker, J.P., experienced, one of his office, and another of his stables; or of the shots fired at his daughters one night when nearing their home.

[2] 50 Vic. Chap 11.

[3] The floating of this railway scheme was, in all probability, a political scheme to catch votes, in view of the election to be held later on in that year.

minutes of the County Council of the April and June session, 1887, and to by-laws No. 232 and 233 discharging from all claims the sureties of J. G. Cooper and Alexander Sproat. The books of the office show that the loss sustained by the county was $25,701.69. To this might be added the cost of the investigations and the loss of interest. At the special meeting of the County Council held in April, Norman Robertson was appointed county treasurer, which office he has held up to the present time.

Among the incidents of 1887 worth recording, and alluded to in a preceding paragraph, was the organizing of a Farmers' Institute in each of the three electoral divisions of the county.[1] These Institutes have fully carried out the purposes aimed at, the promoting of scientific farming and the disseminating of information in regard to agriculture. Their worth has been recognized by the County Council making annually a grant to each Institute. The large membership they have is a very encouraging feature, showing a desire on the part of the farmers of Bruce to possess a knowledge of the latest and best methods of farming.

The possibility of having the Canadian Pacific Railway continued through to Lake Huron engaged the attention of the various municipalities in the southern part of the county during 1887. One route proposed was to continue the railway from Teeswater to Kincardine; another was to be along the route proposed by the Saugeen Valley Railway, from Mount Forest to Inverhuron, via Walkerton, Cargill and Glammis Towards this latter scheme the member for East Bruce, Mr. Cargill, succeeded in having put in the estimates for this year a grant of $3,200 per mile for the twenty-four miles from Mount Forest to Walkerton. For the other scheme Kincardine town was willing to grant a bonus of $30,000. Capitalists, however, could not be interested sufficiently in either proposition, consequently both fell through

The Dominion Parliament was dissolved January 15th, 1887, followed by an election, which took place February 22nd following. In North Bruce, Alexander McNeill was again returned, his opponent being Dr. Bonnar, of Chesley. In West Bruce Hon. Edward Blake was elected, J. H. Scott having contested the riding against him.

---

[1] In 1896 a fourth Farmers' Institute was organized, for that part of the county north of Hepworth, to be known as the "North Bruce Farmers' Institute". What remained of the North Riding had an Institute known as that of "West Bruce."

As Mr. Blake was also returned for West Durham he resigned his seat for West Bruce, and James Rowand, of Saugeen, was elected by acclamation. In East Bruce the two candidates were Henry Cargill[1] and R. M. Wells. In this contest the former was successful, but as he was the nominal postmaster at Cargill, he had to resign. In the by-election that followed he was again returned, this time defeating R. E. Truax.

Early in March, 1888, a vote of the ratepayers throughout the county was taken in response to a petition that the " Scott Act " be repealed. The vote (see Appendix R) was decisively against the Act remaining in force in Bruce.

The valuation of the county, as fixed in 1878-9 for equalized assessment purposes, continued for ten years as the basis on which to calculate the levy of county rates. This period having nearly elapsed, a fresh valuation was decided upon. The men selected by the County Council to do this work were James Brocklebank, of Brant, and H. T. Potts, of Arran; both being practical farmers, they were well qualified to judge correctly the value of farm lands, and at the same time were men of wide municipal experience. The work of valuating was commenced in 1888, and at the June session of 1889 the report was presented to the County Council and adopted. The township of Kinloss, however, thought it had not been equitably assessed, and entered an appeal, which was sustained by Judge Kingsmill, who ordered a reduction of the Kinloss assessment to the extent of $82,366.

The last of the outstanding debentures of the large issue of $250,000, given as a bonus to the Wellington, Grey and Bruce Railway, matured December 6th, 1889, and were promptly paid as presented. The effect on the finances of the county on being relieved

---

[1]Henry Cargill was born, August 13th, 1838, in the township of Nassagaweya. His father and mother were natives of the county of Antrim, Ireland. He was fortunate in having had the advantage of a course at Queen's College, Kingston. While still a young man he entered into the lumber business in his native county of Halton. In 1879 he came to reside in Bruce. Having succeeded in purchasing a large portion of the Greenock swamp, he was enabled to develop its almost untouched resources, and built up a large lumber industry, and ultimately became the wealthiest man in the county The village that bears his name owes its existence to him. He was reeve of Greenock for three years, and represented East Bruce in the House of Commons almost continuously from 1887 until his sudden death, which occurred at Ottawa, October 1st, 1903. He was married in 1864 to Miss Margaret Davidson, of Halton, and had a family of four children A staunch Conservative in politics, yet possessing the esteem of his political opponents. He was a man of the most kindly disposition, and a member of the Presbyterian Church.

of such a large debt was very marked, the county rate being reduced to about one-half of what it had been

In 1890 the County Council surprised itself and the constituency at large by accomplishing its legislative duties for the whole year in two sessions, an achievement never attempted before or since; no complaint, either, was ever made that any one suffered from delay in legislation, or from a dearth of it

A general election was held June 5th, 1890, for the Ontario House of Assembly The result of this election was that in North Bruce, John George (Con.) was elected, his opponent being David Porter (Lib.).[1] In Centre Bruce, W. M. Dack (Lib.) was returned, this riding being contested by Alex. Shaw (Equal Rights). In South Bruce the two candidates were H. P. O'Connor (Lib.) and Dr. John S. Tennant (Con.), the former of whom was successful.

The year 1891 was not in any way eventful to the county of Bruce in its entirety, the general elections for the Dominion House, held March 5th, being the only event to record. In the riding of North Bruce, Alex McNeill defeated Dr. Bonnar. This election was petitioned against unsuccessfully. In West Bruce, James Rowand was re-elected, his opponent being Hugh Morrison, of Lucknow. East Bruce returned R. E. Truax, who had a majority of 114 over the old member, Henry Cargill, but was unseated at the election trial which followed a protest. At the by-election that followed, the positions were reversed, Mr. Cargill carrying the constituency.

On November 29th, 1891, an old servant of the county, Samuel Roether, died, the ' vacancy caused by his death resulting in a scramble for the position. It seems that the gaolership has anomalous features: the sheriff appoints the official, the government confirms the appointment, while the County Council fixes the salary and pays the greater part of it. The first appointment made by Sheriff Sutton was Geo. A. Henry, of Port Elgin, of which appointment the government did not approve; neither did it of H. B. McKay, of Walkerton, the sheriff's second appointment, political interests and influences being the cause of the delay in filling the post The man the politicians at first wished to have made gaoler the sheriff refused to consider. The upshot of the controversy, which became intense, was evidently a determination to change the sheriff. In the summer of 1892 Æmilius Irving, Q.C., was directed by the government to hold

---

[1]In a by-election held March 9th, 1891, the situation was reversed, and Mr. Porter obtained the seat and represented the riding until his death.

an investigation in the matter of some charges made against Mr. Sutton in his official capacity. On the receipt of the report of this investigation, in which some of the charges were sustained, Mr. Sutton was asked to resign. This he would not do, so he was dismissed, and on November 5th, 1892, Frederick S. O'Connor (a brother of the member for South Bruce) was gazetted as sheriff of the county, and a week later the office of gaoler was given to Donald McKechnie, on the recommendation of the new sheriff. Nothing but the highest commendation can be uttered of these two appointees, who proved capable and well qualified for their respective posts.

The question of having established a House of Refuge for the county (a matter which will be referred to more fully later on) was much talked about in 1892, and at the municipal elections held in January, 1893, a vote of the ratepayers was taken, which proved to be adverse to the proposition. The rural municipalities, with one exception, opposed it, while the urban municipalities, with two exceptions, were in favor of having such an institution.

The County Council of 1893 proved to be one of the most liberal the county had known in the matter of making grants for roads and bridges. The grants made that year totalled well over $20,000, resulting in several large iron bridges being constructed over the Saugeen and other streams

Grasshoppers were so numerous in the summer of 1893 as to be a scourge in some parts of the county, especially towards the south-western part of it, gardens and meadows especially suffering therefrom. It is stated that these pests developed a taste for binder-twine, and sheaves in the harvest fields had, by the row, their binding devoured, and had to be rebound by hand.

David Porter, M P.P. for North Bruce, died August 7th, 1893. An election to fill the vacancy so caused resulted in the return of D. McNaughton, the reeve of the township of Bruce. The political atmosphere of the county, from several causes, was much stirred during 1893. The Premier, Sir. John S. D. Thompson, and some of his colleagues, visited the county and addressed large meetings. As a set-off to this the leader of the Opposition, the Hon. Wilfrid Laurier, and some of his lieutenants, followed the same course, and enlightened the electors of Bruce on political measures from their point of view. Most of the meetings were held during the month of September. Another element in the political atmosphere was a new party known as the Patrons of Industry, a party or society which to some extent has by many been associated with the Grange movement. This is an error, the ends sought by these two societies being entirely different. In the preceding chapter an outline of the objects of the Grange Society is to be found, which shows that what the Grange strove after was the advancement of the material interests of the farmers. The Ontario Association of the Patrons of Industry was organized at London, September 22nd, 1891, with aims avowedly political.[1] There were thirteen planks in the platform of the society, as then laid down, most of which were largely along the lines of securing improved legislation, of rigid economy in the public service, and of purity in the administration of government. It was not long after the above date before the order had lodges established in Bruce, which increased in number to eighty-five, or thereabout. The first representative of the order sent to Parliament from Bruce was D McNaughton, elected as member for North Bruce in the by-election for that riding in 1893, as mentioned above. At the general election for the Ontario House of Assembly in 1894, a Patron candidate was nominated in each of the three ridings in Bruce: D. McNaughton in North Bruce (elected), John S. McDonald in Centre Bruce (elected), and William Valens in South Bruce (defeated), R. E. Truax being the successful candidate in this riding. At the next general election for the Dominion House of Commons, held in 1896, Patron candidates were nominated, but, as herein stated in the events of that year, only one, John Tolmie, was elected. As a political party the Patrons of Industry have lost much of their influence, but the effect they have had, in Bruce at least, has been to lead electors to break away from mere party lines and think and vote in an independent manner, instead of being but a cog in a political machine.

The municipal elections for 1894 were held on New Year's Day. Concurrent with them there was cast a vote in all municipalities throughout the province on " The Prohibition Plebiscite Act," which in Bruce brought out the largest vote the temperance question there polled, the particulars of which are to be found in Appendix R.

The year 1894 marked the first failure of a private bank within the county, the firm being that of H. A. Allen, of Port Elgin. In

[1]Some organizers added, as an inducement to establish a lodge, a clause authorizing an arrangement being made with some merchant to sell goods at an advance of 10 per cent on cost price to members of the Order, but this was outside of the Constitution of the Order. At Paisley, Dobbington, Chesley, Walkerton, and possibly elsewhere also, such an arrangement was made with a storekeeper, which, proving unprofitable to the latter, did not last long.

the following year J. C. Graham, a private banker of Tiverton, also failed. Other failures of this description, which may as well be grouped together, were those of F. X. Messner, of Formosa, in 1897, and that of the Carrick Banking Co., of Mildmay, in 1898. Those who suffered most by these various failures were farmers who, to obtain a higher rate of interest, had deposited with them their savings Of late years the number of private banks within the county has materially decreased, they having been absorbed by chartered banks on the latter establishing an agency in the towns and villages where they were in business.

Those who make a note of the condition of the weather had in 1895 many unusual items to record. During the first week of February, at Walkerton, the thermometer dropped so low that the mercury froze and during four days remained below zero. The last week of April and the first in May were marked by summer-like weather. As a result the trees were in full leaf by May 7th. This unseasonable heat was followed on May 12th by a hard frost, so severe that not only were the fruit trees injured, but also many forest trees, beeches especially, were in many cases either killed or permanently injured, the result of all the freshly opened leaves being frozen and falling off. The spring and summer of 1895 were unusually dry. The grain crops did not suffer for want of rain to such an extent as did the hay crop, which was such a complete failure that, to meet the needs of stock owners, large quantities of hay had to be imported into the county This baled hay found a ready sale at $18.00 a ton, and in some cases even more was paid. Chopped straw mixed with grain was largely used to feed stock, but even straw was so scarce that $11.00 a ton was paid for it. The exigencies of the season made farmers try various methods of feeding stock, and in doing so they learned the lesson that stock could be carried over until spring, and even do fairly well, on other fodder than what had in the past been principally relied on, namely, hay and roots. So the drought was not without some measure of benefit, although the lesson was a hard one, and felt by all classes of the community.

With the payment, in 1895, of the $20,000 worth of debentures issued ten years previously, the county became free of debt. In Supplement T there is given a complete list of the various issues of debentures of the county of Bruce The total, $709,000, is a large sum. Still none can say but that the ends sought,—while incurring large obligations,—were for the good of the community at large

Mr. George Gould, who had performed the duties of county clerk since 1861, felt compelled by failing health to tender his resignation in December, 1895. With much regret the County Council accepted Mr. Gould's resignation, and appointed his son, Wm. S. Gould, to fill the vacancy, which post he has held unto the present time.

The House of Commons having been dissolved in the spring of 1896, a general election was held June 23rd. The Patrons of Industry had candidates in the North, East and West ridings of Bruce, they being respectively, H. T. Potts, James Tolton, and John Tolmie. The latter alone was returned, the other two ridings returning A. McNeill and Henry Cargill, who had sat for these constituencies in the preceding parliament.

The southern part of the county had, in the winter and spring of 1896, presented to them for the first time the proposition of an electric railway. Mr. E. A. C. Pew, a railway promoter, came into the county and held public meetings at Walkerton, Kincardine and other points. The scheme he proposed was on a large scale and obligingly comprehensive, the various terminal points being Port Perry at the east, Goderich at the west, Meaford at the north, while radial lines were to connect all points in the intervening country that would subscribe to a fund for getting surveys made and a Bill passed through the House of Commons. Mr. Pew found little difficulty in having his proposition taken up by the business portion of the community, a provisional Board of Directors appointed, and funds raised sufficient to enable initial steps being taken. In April, 1896, the House of Commons passed a Bill,[1] but not without a good deal of opposition, incorporating this the "Huron and Ontario Railway Coy." The charter, so obtained, has been extended and offered to any capitalists who would construct the road, but so far without success. Such a line of electric road will surely be constructed some day, and will be found a great convenience to the public.

Lieut.-Col. A. E. Belcher, reeve of Southampton in 1896, had for some time been impressed with the necessity of taking steps towards collecting historical data about the settlement of the county, before all the pioneers had passed away. After several attempts, he brought the County Council to his way of thinking, and at the January session a motion was passed, offering a prize

[1] 59 Vic. Chap 20

of $50 for the best historical sketch of the county, to be submitted at the next session. In response, two papers were handed in, one written by J. M. McNabb, of Southampton, and the other by the writer; both papers were considered so deserving of a prize that each received the full amount offered.

The increase in the number of reeves and deputy reeves and consequently in the size of County Councils throughout the province, arising from the increase of population, gave cause for much discussion as to the advisability of reducing the number of county councillors.   As early as 1884 the Provincial Secretary sent to the various municipal councils within the province, a list of questions, requesting answers which would express their opinion on this matter.   The question was a difficult one to settle, and no action seems to have resulted until ten years later, when the Legislative Assembly then asked for "a return showing the population of each county and district, and the municipalities therein."   This was followed in 1896 by an Act[1] "to reduce the number of county councillors."   By this act a county was to be divided for County Council purposes into divisions; each division to be entitled to two representatives, the number of these divisions was to be based upon the population of the county.   Commissioners appointed by the Lieut.-Governor-in-Council decided the limits of the divisions, and in doing so endeavored to have them as nearly equal as possible in regard to population.   The commissioners so appointed met at Walkerton June 29th, 1896.   After hearing and considering the evidence offered, they divided the county of Bruce into nine divisions, thereby reducing the size of the County Council, which under the old system had forty-four members, but under the new would have only eighteen.   The report made by the commissioners is given in full in Appendix U.   The views held by the forty-four reeves and deputy reeves who, under the new order of things, would no longer be *ex-officio* members of the County Council of Bruce, may be best recorded in the words of the warden (the late J. H. Elliot, of Chesley), in his final official report to the Council at its last session, held in December, 1896.   "I cannot help feeling that this sitting of the County Council is memorable from the fact that it marks the end of a long-established system and the introduction of an experimental one.   We have hitherto assembled as chosen representatives of twenty-six municipalities of the county of Bruce,

[1] 59 Vic Chap 52

and our ranks have swelled in the course of time to the high water mark of forty-four members, but the hand of revolution has been laid upon our system and has shattered its foundation and substituted for it an elective system by districts, created and delimited by judicial commissioners.   Our county is now divided into nine districts, and two representatives will be elected by the people next January for each of these districts instead of an assembly of forty-four.   The next County Council will number only eighteen.   Instead of men who are here because they are associated with local council boards, there will be men who will be elected by the direct vote of the people.   These changes may or may not be an improvement.   The new system is an experiment which should receive a fair trial before we condemn or commend it, but this much at least is certain, that we will not hereafter know as much about each other as heretofore.   One of the pleasant features of our meetings has been the friendly intercourse which we have had with members from every part of the county, and the larger the representation the wider that intercourse of thought and opinion has been, the wider has been the circle of our county acquaintance.   That hereafter this is to be narrowed down brings to our mind the pleasant memories of the past, and regret that the future has not in store for our successors such opportunities as we have hitherto enjoyed. I am pleased to be able to say for this little parliament of the county of Bruce what cannot be said of the great Dominion Parliament of this Canada of ours.   We leave a clean slate, no debt behind us for our successors to grapple with, though we have taken this county of ours from the forest to what it is to-day, and we leave many monuments behind us of the work we have done, those fine steel bridges all over the county and the many other improvements we have made.   And how did we do all this work ?   By direct taxation, which in my opinion is the proper source from which all public money should come.   The County Council is dead; long live the County Council!"

The councillors could not separate for the last time without having a bit of fun over being put out of office, so when all the sessional work was over the following bogus motion was brought forward : "Moved by James Shouldice, seconded by Henry McKay, 'That as the death of the County Council is at hand, and as we desire that everything be done decently and in order, we would therefore recommend that the following be named as chief mourners, viz,

Messrs: Lieut.-Col. Belcher, Robert Johnston, and Henry McKay, and that the following be engraved on the tablet to be erected—

> " ' *Sacred to the memory of the County Council of the County of Bruce.'*
>
> " ' Peaceful may thy slumbers be,
> From cares and labor thou art free ,
> By action of the Government
> Into oblivion thou art sent.
>
> " ' Thou stalwart, gallant forty-four,
> Your services are required no more ,
> Eighteen men shall be elected
> To do the work you were expected.
>
> " ' But should the change not work, as is suspected,
> Old boys, you may be re-elected
> To fill your places as before,
> Thou gallant, stalwart forty-four ' "

After a laugh at the above, the members joined hands, feelingly sang " Auld Lang Syne," and then parting, the little parliament of Bruce County became a thing of history.

The County Council of 1897, reduced in numbers so as to seem but a petty body of legislators compared to its predecessors, although retaining all the authority they had possessed, tackled the House of Refuge question in earnest, and passed a motion directing that the wishes of the ratepayers be obtained by a plebiscite vote, to be taken at the time of the next municipal elections,[1] in January, 1898.

The initial move towards securing a House of Refuge for aged and enfeebled indigents within the county, dates back to the December session of 1881 of the County Council, when Edward Leslie (of Kincardine) and Wm. Bradley (of Greenock) moved : " That the County Clerk obtain information as to the cost and maintenance of the lately established Poor House of the county of Wellington ; at the same time the two reeves of Carrick (Wm. Dickison and James Johnston) moved that reports be obtained from the various local municipalities in Bruce as to the amount spent by them annually in support of indigents.   Following these motions a committee was appointed to consider the matter, which at the

---

[1] In 1893—The majority against establishing a House of Refuge was 2,378   Total votes polled, 8,880   In 1898—The majority in favor of establishing a House of Refuge was 2,477.   Total votes polled, 7,996.

next session reported in favor of the establishment of a House of Refuge. There was not, however, enough enthusiasm felt to urge on the question ; so it lay in abeyance until 1888, when the matter was again brought to the front, Dr. De Witt H. Martyn (of Kincardine) and Dr. W. S. Scott (of Southampton) being the movers therein, at the January session of that year of the County Council. The committee then appointed chose Lieut.-Col. J. H. Scott as its chairman From that time on until he laid the corner-stone of the House of Refuge ten years later Col. Scott labored assiduously and untiringly in the interests of this most humane and charitable object The voluminous tabulated reports made by him in 1888, 1892, and 1897, to the County Council, and the sheets of information prepared by him for the ratepayers on the two occasions when a vote was taken on this question, namely, in 1893 and 1898, deserve more than a passing word of commendation. This fact was recognized when there was conferred upon him the honor of laying the foundation stone of the building, June 24th, 1898.

The inquiry as to the cost of maintaining indigents by the local municipalities showed that in 1881 nineteen municipalities (all that then reported) had spent $2,508.43 in granting such relief. In 1887 all townships and villages furnished reports, the total of expenditure was $3,946 34, while in 1890 it had risen to $4,393 66. These amounts are much in excess of the net expenditure of the House of Refuge at present, showing that even from the low level of economy the ratepayers did wisely when, in 1898, they voted to establish this charitable institution, while those who voted from humane motives have seen in the comfort and content of the old folks residing at the House of Refuge their fullest anticipations realized. The inquiries made of the local municipalities revealed one uncommendable practice, namely, that of foisting, if possible, the poor on neighboring municipalities. This practice was candidly confessed by the village clerk of one of the smallest of our villages in his reply to the questions propounded. His report reads as follows: " In. 1885 this municipality had one indigent, which cost only $2, because we shipped him off. In 1886 one indigent cost $10; we shipped him, too. In 1887 we had also one indigent, who was brought here, and was too far gone for shipping purposes He died on our hands, and cost $124."

The vote of the ratepayers, given 3rd January, 1898, on the House of Refuge question, was so pronounced in favor of having one established that the County Council, without loss of time, took the preliminary step of advertising for a suitable site for the building, and met again in March to decide on the offers made. These numbered over fifty and from all parts of the county. A process of weeding out had to be undertaken The decision finally arrived at was that only farms in close proximity to the towns of Kincardine, Port Elgin and Walkerton would be considered.[1] The County Council then decided that it, as a committee of the whole, should visit and examine the various sites offered. Port Elgin was first visited and what it had to offer considered. The next day the councillors drove to Kincardine and inspected the sites there offered. At a meeting held in that town the County Council decided to continue its journey to Stratford and see the House of Refuge lately built there by the county of Perth, it having been reported to be the one which for size, arrangement and cost would most probably be suitable for Bruce. The visit to Stratford was not ill judged; many members of the Council were largely in the dark regarding the requirements of the building and of the regulations of an up-to-date House of Refuge. There they had an object lesson, and one that pleased them so well that on its return to Walkerton the Council instructed the architect[2] of the building they had so admired to make plans and specifications for a building along similar lines, but to embody whatever improvements experience showed could be made, and large enough to accommodate 125 inmates. It was no easy matter to settle where the building was to be erected. Each of the four towns set a high value upon having the institution in its vicinity, so that it was not until the forty-sixth ballot was cast by the County Council that Walkerton obtained the much coveted honor. The lands there secured for a site are very suitable, having an area of sixty-two and a half acres, between forty and fifty acres of which are profitably cultivated. The amount paid for the land was $3,821. Having decided where to build, and also having settled on the plan, tenders were advertised for and considered at a meeting of the County Council held in May. The tender of Messrs. Cawsey and Young (of Stratford) for all the work was accepted, the price being $16,440. The building was completed in December, and received its first

[1]This was afterwards amended and the neighborhood of Paisley was also included

[2]The late Harry J Powell, of Stratford

inmates in the first week of January, 1900 In a footnote[1] are given the particulars of the actual cost of this fine building and equipment. The following were the officers appointed to look after the House of Refuge and its inmates: Keeper, Joseph M White; Matron, Mrs. Joseph M. White; Inspector, Wm. S. Gould. After a year's experience it was decided that the inspector's duties could be undertaken by the keeper, which arrangement is still in force. The average annual net cost of the House of Refuge for the five years, 1900-04, has been $3,036.25. Now that the agitation as to the advisability of having a comfortable home for infirm or aged indigents is settled, and also the controversy where it should be located has calmed down, there exists a feeling throughout the community that all through a wise course has been followed, and nothing but commendation is extended towards the men who carried the issues to a successful termination.

The same spirit which led to the establishment of a House of Refuge for the indigents of the county led also to the establishment of the Children's Aid Society of the County of Bruce. This was organized at a meeting held at Walkerton November 21st, 1898, and was incorporated by order of Council passed in the following month. The object of this society is to improve the condition of all neglected and dependent children within the county. This is done by providing homes for the homeless, by securing better treatment for those neglected by their parents, and in assisting really needy families in caring for their little ones. Over fifty cases have been dealt with by the society, which has been very fortunate in securing comfortable homes for its wards. Funds for this work are obtained from mem-

[1]COST OF HOUSE OF REFUGE.

Total preliminary expenses, cost of taking vote, etc .		$1,727 89
Total cost of land and buildings and sewer	$23,843 84	
Total cost of furnishing and equipment. . .	2,613 32	
Total cost of granolithic walk	141 04	
	$26,598 20	
Less Provincial Grant	4,000 00	
		22,598 20
		$24,326 09
Less premium on sale of Debentures		1,160 00
Total net outlay		. $23,166 09

The payments as above were made from the sale of debentures, the issue being for $20,000 The balance was paid out of the current revenue of the county

bership fees and voluntary contributions. The late Miss Janet Chisholm, of Brant, left a legacy to the society amounting to $50.00, and the late W. J. Moore, a farmer living near Walkerton, bequeathed to it half his estate, which will amount to seven or eight thousand dollars. This last bequest has not as yet, at the time of writing this history, come into the possession of the society, as it is subject to an annuity payable to Mr. Moore's widow for life. A. Shaw, K.C., has been the president of the society since its inception, and has given a great deal of time and attention, without any remuneration whatever, to the various cases which have been considered and provided for. The office of secretary has been filled by E. J. Rowland and Joseph Morgan.

On March 1st, 1898, a general election for the Legislative Assembly was held, at which the candidates for the several ridings in the county were: In North Bruce, C. M. Bowman (Lib.), who was elected by a majority of 265 over D. M. Jermyn (Con.); in Centre Bruce, A. Malcolm (Lib.) obtained a majority of 234 over John S. McDonald (Patron), the late member, while in South Bruce, R. E Truax was re-elected by acclamation.

In September of the last-mentioned year the electors were again asked to cast their ballots; this time it was to vote on the Provincial Prohibition Plebiscite The particulars of this vote are to be found in Appendix R

This section of Ontario suffered during three successive summers from an invasion of forest tent-caterpillars. The last of these years was 1899 These pests, on account of their numbers, proved very destructive, maples, basswoods, as well as other trees and shrubs being stripped of every vestige of foliage; this process repeated three years in succession resulted in the death of many trees. In towns and villages the citizens struggled to save their shade trees from the caterpillars. In this effort they were successful, as the large mat-like clusters in which the caterpillars frequently assembled, enabled a wholesale destruction to be accomplished in short order. The number of these pests was almost incredible. In confirmation and illustration of the statement it is on record in the Walkerton newspapers that a train due there from the north was, near Cargill, brought to a standstill by the caterpillars; the crushed bodies, countless in number, over which the driving wheels of the engine had passed, formed a greasy paste that prevented them gripping the rails, and so the train slowed down until at last it stopped.

A desire, often expressed and deeply felt, that there should be a gathering of the pioneers and old settlers of the county at last became an accomplished fact on 28th July, 1899, at Port Elgin, when in response to an invitation of a committee of its citizens, the pioneers of Bruce and their descendants gathered from all parts of the county, and so had an opportunity of talking over the old days when they entered the bush to make for themselves homes where the tall trees stood. The concourse on that occasion numbered between two and three thousand. About an hour before noon a procession was formed, headed by the brass band of the village. After the band an old familiar ox-team and outfit, driven by R. H. Murray, of Amabel, led the way. On the sleigh, so drawn, were sheaves of grain, the thrashing of which, by flails, was gone on with as the procession wended its way to Lake View Park, where, after a substantial meal, a number of old-timers were called upon to address the assembly and recount their recollections of the days of the early settlements in Bruce. But possibly the most enjoyed feature of the assemblage was the meeting of old-time acquaintances, separated for years, who there met and enjoyed a good old chat of the days when their heads were not grey, but when life was young, and of the hardships they encountered in the bush, now things to be laughed at. The gathering was a success, so much so that it has become one of annual occurrence, much appreciated and largely attended. The citizens of Port Elgin who do so much to maintain the enthusiasm of these annual gatherings deserve a great deal of commendation from those who cherish a warm feeling for the days of the early settlement of Bruce and wish to see its memories preserved.

It is highly probable that the same current of sentiment which prompted the meeting of the pioneers of the county, mentioned in the last paragraph, was also the cause which led to the "Bruce Old Boys' Reunion" that so successfully materialized July 23rd to August 4th, 1900. The inception of this much-enjoyed gathering is credited to some of the sons of the county residing at Toronto. Prominent among them in the originating and working out of this happy idea were the following: James H. Spence, W. A Skeans, John R. Shaw, Geo. H. Kilmer, Walter O'Hara, besides others whose names the author is unable to furnish. The carrying to a successful conclusion of this reunion involved an immense amount of work, the largest part of which fell upon the shoulders of Arthur Collins, of Walkerton, the Secretary of the Executive Committee. First a list of absent

Bruce boys, with their place of residence, had to be compiled. Then the railway companies had to be enlightened as to the advantage it would be to them to offer reduced rates. This secured, circulars inviting all the absentees to the reunion had to be mailed, the number of which exceeded eighteen hundred. The fundamental idea of the originators was to have a gathering of the widely scattered Bruce boys from north, south, east and west. In the past, whenever any of these had returned to revisit the scenes of their youth, they found that they only met of their old comrades those who had remained at home, while those who had wandered away—like themselves, being only occasionally at their old home—were not seen. "If only all the old boys could be back at home together, how much more pleasant it would be," was the thought that urged the promoters on to make the efforts which resulted so successfully. The first steps were taken in February, and by the end of May the invitation circulars were issued announcing special rates on all the railways east of the Mississippi and north of the Ohio rivers. These circulars were sent by the secretary to all known addresses of Bruce boys living between New York and Vancouver. It must be acknowledged that the county town and its sons living at Toronto took the lead in this enterprise. When the 23rd of July came, the Toronto contingent left that city on a special train engaged to take them to Walkerton. They brought with them the full band of the 48th Highlanders, which headed the procession that marched from the railway station to the town hall, where the mayor extended a greeting to all. The welcome the old boys met with from their native town and county must have reached the fullest expectations of any of them   Those whose homes were in other parts of the county received just as cordial a greeting as did those whose destination was Walkerton. All expressed enthusiastically their feelings at the success of the reunion. About seven hundred took advantage of this opportunity to view old scenes and to renew old friendships. Since then there have been, almost annually, excursions from Toronto of the Old Boys of Bruce. These seem to be growing larger from year to year, e g , in 1904 the train that left Toronto consisted of thirteen coaches, filled with "Old Boys" anxious to visit once more their native county. The "Association of Bruce Old Boys" at Toronto has done much to keep alive a feeling of pride and loyalty for the native county of its members, and also a fraternal feeling among those of its offspring who have "swarmed" off from its borders.

The Indian Peninsula had high hopes, in 1900 and 1901, of a railway being constructed through its entire length from Tobermory to Wiarton, when the Ontario House of Assembly incorporated[1] "The Manitoulin and North Shore Railway." This line was to connect Meaford with Tobermory, from whence it was intended that a ferry should convey freight and passenger cars to the Manitoulin Island; from thence, by means of a bridge at Little Current, the line would be continued to Sault Ste. Marie   The promise of government aid to help in the construction of the road was granted; this, with the appearance of surveyors to locate the route of the railway, gave the assurance that the road would certainly be pushed to completion. But since the departure of the surveyors but little has been heard regarding this railway. It has been said that the proposed road was nothing more than a political bait, with which it was expected to catch votes at the next provincial election in the various constituencies through which it was to pass.

Over ten years having elapsed since the county was valuated for the purpose of an equalized assessment, the County Council in June, 1900, appointed valuators to make a fresh valuation   On this occasion four men were appointed: two, L. T. Bland and H. T. Potts, were to value the property situated in the several townships, and two, Edward Kilmer and J. B. Campbell, to value the property in the several towns and incorporated villages in the county. Their reports were received at the June session of the following year   These showed many changes, which made a reduction of $139,040 from the equalized assessment of real property of the preceding year. The total assessment of the county of real property, as returned by the valuators, was $25,378,972.

A general election for the Dominion House of Commons was held November 7th, 1900, resulting in the return, in West Bruce, of John Tolmie (Lib.), his opponent being John George (Con.). In East Bruce, Henry Cargill (Con.) succeeded in being re-elected, John Coumans (Lib.) being the defeated candidate.   In North Bruce, Alex. McNeill was elected by the narrow majority of one. As might be expected an election trial followed, which resulted in the unseating of Mr. McNeill. At the by-election that followed (March 20th, 1901) James Halliday (Con.) was elected. The Liberal candidate in both of these contests was J. E. Campbell, of Hepworth.

The gathering of the pioneers in 1899 and the reunion of the

[1] See 63 Vic Chap. 115 and 1 Edw VII. Chap 23 .

Bruce Old Boys in 1900 were fittingly followed in 1901 by the founding of the Bruce County Historical Society. The initiative in this action came from the County Council, which, at the January session, 1901, appointed a committee to consider the matter. This committee reported in June, strongly recommending that steps should be taken to organize such a society for the preservation of items relating to the history of the county. This report was adopted by the Council, which at the same time gave a grant of ten dollars to meet any preliminary expenses. Following up the resolution of the Council, a meeting was called at Walkerton at the time of the fall Assizes, as at that time a number of persons from all parts of the county would be at the county town. At this meeting Lieut.-Col. A. E. Belcher was elected president and Norman Robertson, secretary. A constitution was adopted, and application was directed to be made for affiliation with the Ontario Historical Society, which affiliation was obtained. The interest in the society has not been as active as might have been expected, but good work has been done in collecting materials bearing on the history of the county, such as files of newspapers extending from the sixties down, also early maps and plans of the villages as they were first laid out. A most successful banquet was given by the citizens of Walkerton to the society in January, 1902, at which a number of old settlers were present, and gave interesting accounts of the early days. Attempts have on several occasions been made to establish pioneer societies with similar objects to the above   The earliest of these societies was organized at Walkerton, October 7th, 1881, when some twenty or thirty of the early settlers gathered and resolved themselves into "The Bruce Pioneer Society." Most of those then present have joined the great majority, among them being Adam Clement and Hugh Todd, of Brant, C. R. Barker, of Kincardine, and Wm. Gunn, of Walkerton   The author has not been able to find any account of further meetings of this society. A society bearing the same name was organized at Port Elgin in 1900 which has shown enviable vitality. To it may be given much praise for the annual pioneers' gathering and picnic at Port Elgin.

The census taken April 1st, 1901, was a disappointment, as it showed that during the preceding decade the population had declined to the extent of 5,583. Emigration is the explanation to be given. The old folks remain at home, while thousands of the young men and women have gone to the North-West or to the cities. Then again, farms are now much larger than formerly, and owing to the use of labor-saving machinery the large farm requires no more help than the small one did. In earlier days there were hundreds of fifty-acre farms and very few over one hundred acres. To-day farms of two or three hundred acres or more are common, while the smaller fifty-acre farms are almost unknown The changed conditions of farming largely account for this and also the decrease in population. Farmers have grown rich and have added farm to farm, and those who have sold out have sought other localities where, with a moderate amount of capital, they too may become rich.

The sudden death of F. S. O'Connor, the sheriff of the county, on August 16th, 1901, caused a vacancy in the sheriffalty. After a short delay the government appointed C. V. Parke, of Wiarton, to the office, which position he has continued to fill.

Two separate lines of railway to run through Bruce were incorporated in 1902. One, The Huron and Bruce Railway Co.,[1] was to connect Wiarton and Goderich, the line to touch at the various lake shore ports between Goderich and Southampton. The other company bore the name of The Huron, Bruce and Grey Electric Railway Co.,[2] which name was changed in the following year to The Ontario West Shore Electric Railway Co. It is intended to be part of a scheme of electric railways radiating from Goderich. One arm of this road is planned to extend to Wiarton and another, via Lucknow, to Walkerton. Up to the time of writing, however, nothing has been accomplished in the way of construction of either of these proposed railways.

The offer made by the Ontario Government of a grant, under certain conditions, to aid in the improvement of public highways[3] (out of a fund of one million dollars set apart for that purpose) was much discussed in 1902 throughout the county, especially so in the Indian Peninsula, where the lack of even moderately good roads is so fully realized. A visit of the Provincial Commissioner of Highways to Wiarton and the vicinity materially increased the interest regarding this matter felt in that part of the county. Mr. R. E. Moore, of Lion's Head, and B. B. Miller, of Wiarton, were prominent in striving to get the public interest aroused regarding this subject, addressing meetings held to consider the proposal made by the government. A study of the conditions attached showed that to obtain the county's share of the grant, amounting to $45,000, an

[1] 2 Edw. VII Chap 77
[2] 2 Edw VII. Chap 78 and 3 Edw. VII. Chap 98
[3] 1 Edw. VII Chap 32.

expenditure of $90,000 would be required, and as about one-third of the grant would have to be expended in the peninsula—which was a ratio of expenditure disproportionate to the amount of county rates paid by the peninsula municipalities—the County Council declined to act in the matter, and the question is still in abeyance. As the offer made by the Government remains open until the 1st January, 1909, it is possible some action may yet be taken.

A general election for the Ontario House of Assembly was held May 29th, 1902, which resulted in the re-election of C. M. Bowman and R. E. Truax for the ridings of North and South Bruce respectively, the defeated candidates being D. M. Jermyn, of Wiarton, and Dr. R. E. Clapp, of Mildmay In Centre Bruce the election was keenly contested by Major Hugh Clark (Con.) and Dr. M. Stewart (Lib), the former being returned. The majority was only five. A protest followed, which brought about another election (held February 26th, 1903), when Major Clark was returned by an increased majority

"The Liquor Act, 1902,"[1] passed by the House of Assembly, subject to being sustained by a majority of the electors of the province, was intended to prohibit the sale of liquor within the province except by licensed druggists under certain restrictions. This Act was submitted to the electors to be voted upon on December 4th, 1902. This balloting was known as the "Referendum Vote." The vote cast in Bruce gave the largest majority the temperance party ever obtained, in the county, for particulars of which the reader will please consult Appendix R.

"The Representation Act" passed by the Dominion Parliament in 1903 reduced the number of representatives from Bruce in the House of Commons from three to two, the ridings to be known as North and South Bruce. As this Act did not come into force until the then existing Parliament dissolved, the by-election, held February 16th, 1904, following the sudden death of Henry Cargill, was for the old riding of East Bruce. In this election the two candidates were J. J. Donnelly (Con.) and A. W. Robb (Lib.), the former carrying the election.

Situated on the Durham Road, partly in Bruce and partly in Grey, the village of Hanover had developed since it was known as "Buck's Bridge" until it had a population sufficient to entitle it to become incorporated But the necessary steps were delayed People asked why. If any answer were given, the delay was assigned to

[1] 2 Edw VII Chap 33

politicians who feared that the new municipality would unite with
Bruce, on account of the proximity of its county town, which was
only six miles distant, and its vote at parliamentary elections in
South Grey would thus be lost. Be that as it may, the matter at
length came before the County Council in December, 1898, when a
petition was presented praying to have the preliminary steps for
incorporation proceeded with. In January, 1899, a by-law was
passed by the County Council granting incorporation, and that that
part lying in the township of Brant be annexed to the county of
Grey. The County Council of Grey, however, failed to take action
to complete the annexation. This gave the inhabitants on the Brant
side of the village time to consider the matter, with the result that
they concluded they preferred to remain in Brant, so they obtained a
repeal of the by-law. The Bentinck part of the village obtained
incorporation, and then in 1903 obtained an Act[1] attaching their
neighbors in Brant *nolens volens* to their village. This is the only
occasion wherein the county of Bruce has lost any of its territory to
its neighbors.

A pleasing incident to relate are the particulars relating to the
establishment of the Bruce County General Hospital, the opening
of which institution supplied the last link required to place Bruce
on a par, as far as regards providing for the suffering or needy, with
any county in the province. This institution owes its establishment
to a bequest of the late William John Moore, of the township of
Brant, who died March 13th, 1899, and bequeathed one-half of his
estate (which amounted to about $15,500, subject to an annuity
payable to his widow), "To aid in the erection and endowment of
a hospital, at the town of Walkerton, for the sick and injured of
the county of Bruce, provided sufficient funds were otherwise raised
to purchase and erect a suitable building and furniture for the said
hospital" Thomas Dixon and Wm. M. Shaw were the executors of
the estate. To obtain the bequest and apply it for the purpose
intended, "The County of Bruce General Hospital Trust at Walkerton" was incorporated June 8th, 1900. An effort was made in the
same year to get the County Council to assume the liability of paying
to Mrs Moore that proportion of her annuity corresponding to the
amount of the hospital bequest, which sum would thus be set free
and be available for the prosecution of the work. The Council of
that year declined to take any action, but a new Council, that of
1902, considered the matter more liberally and agreed to the proposi-

[1] 3 Edw VII Chap 56

tion. The necessary legislation to confirm this action was obtained without delay. Subscriptions also were secured in sufficient amount to warrant the letting of a contract for the building, which was commenced during the summer of 1902 Among the larger contributions received by the Board of Trustees were the following. From the town of Walkerton, $2,000; county of Bruce, $1,500; Henry Cargill, $1,000; David Morrison, $500, and also a great number of others from $100 down. The hospital was erected and equipped practically free of debt, which is said to be the first time in the history of the province such a thing has been accomplished Much credit for this is due to the assistance rendered the Board of Trustees by the Women's Hospital Aid Association throughout the county. It was a happy idea when the trustees requested the ladies of Walkerton to see what could be done by them to assist in raising funds to meet the needs of the hospital. The preliminary meeting was held January 10th, 1903, when it was decided to organize a Women's Hospital Aid Society for the county, with branches in each village and as many townships as possible. That this movement might be one of the women of the county for the support of a county benevolent institution, and that no ground for supposing the hospital was to be a local affair, the meeting to organize the Women's County Hospital Aid Society was called to meet at Paisley in February, 1903. Mrs. Norman Robertson, of Walkerton, filled the chair at this meeting, at which were delegates present from Tara, Chesley, Southampton, Port Elgin, Paisley, Walkerton, and elsewhere. Mrs. Henry Cargill was elected president, Mrs. Thomas Dixon, secretary-treasurer, and also all the other officers. A constitution, which had been previously prepared, was considered and adopted The society thus organized has performed work that has been most gratifying to the hospital trustees. The following extract from their treasurer's report of June 1st, 1904, is short and concise, but it tells of much earnest effort and work. He says: "During the last eight months the ladies have contributed $2,139 73 to the hospital funds." Truly an amount the ladies may well be proud of. The first patient was received at the hospital September 27th, 1903. The total cost of charter, site, buildings and equipment was $16,645.52. The first lady superintendent, Miss Barbara Campbell, it is gratifying to state, is a native of the county. During her *régime* of a year and a half the institution was well started on its career of usefulness.

The winter of 1903-4 was one of almost unprecedented severity. Sleighing commenced November 18th and continued until April

18th following. The storms were severe, blocking both roads and the railways for days at a time. The snowfall was so deep that work in the woods was stopped in consequence. The difficulty of getting firewood raised its price exorbitantly. This severe winter was followed by a cool summer, frost being experienced each month of the year.

The general elections for the Dominion House of Commons was held November 3rd, 1904. This was the first election under the new "Representation Act," by which Bruce was only to return two members. Much uncertainty as to the result was felt on account of the changes in the ridings In North Bruce L. T. Bland (Conservative) and J. E. Campbell (Liberal) were nominated; the former headed the poll by 107 majority In South Bruce the Liberal party nominee, P. H. McKenzie, carried the election by a majority of 150 over the late member, J. J. Donnelly.

In the fall of 1904 a party of surveyors were engaged in surveying the route for a branch of the Canadian Pacific Railway from Flesherton to Teeswater or Lucknow, *via* Walkerton The following year they went over the ground again. This gave occasion to high hopes being entertained of a railway entering the county from the east. In 1906 these hopes materialized by the commencement of construction operations The company promise that the line will be open for traffic to Walkerton (the temporary terminus) by the summer of 1907.

Southampton, on the 1st January, 1905, attained the status of a town, the fourth in the county. The first mayor elected was Lieut.-Col. A. E. Belcher, a gentleman who has always had the interests of the town at heart, and has been associated with it for half a century.

The general election for the House of Assembly, which resulted in the overthrow of the Ross Government, took place January 25th, 1905 At this election the following gentlemen asked for the suffrages of the electors of this county: In North Bruce, C. M Bowman and John George; in Centre Bruce, Hugh Clark and Andrew Malcolm, and in South Bruce, Dr. R. E. Clapp and R. E. Truax. The first named of each of the above candidates was the one who was elected.

The bridge over the Saugeen River near Burgoyne, known as McCalder's Bridge, during the spring of 1905 was pronounced unfit for traffic. At its June session the County Council concluded that true economy required the erection of a steel bridge at this point. This it was found involved an outlay of $9,000 or $10,000. To meet this it was resolved to issue debentures for that amount. That the by-law might have its required reading at the end of three months, the County Council held a special session in October at Chesley. This was the first time this village has been thus honored by the County Council. The meeting there was decided upon out of compliment to the warden, William McDonald, Chesley being his place of residence.

As the author closes his work on this History in the latter part of October, 1906, the narrative of events for the year is necessarily incomplete. The ranks of the politicians have lately been depleted by the death of the member for the House of Commons for North Bruce, L. T. Bland, who, after a long illness, died August 19th. In the by-election John Tolmie represented the Liberal party and Abram McLellan the Conservative, the former being the successful candidate.

Chesley, the most vigorous of the village municipalities in the county, found during the course of the summer that its population warranted the making of an application for its being proclaimed a town. The application was granted, and on October 1st the municipality was raised to the status of a town, the youngest of five in the county. All will rejoice at the growth of the urban municipalities of Bruce; the only regret is that our rural municipalities do not at the same time maintain the number of their population.

With this chapter the history of the county of Bruce as a whole, during the fifty-eight years following the entrance of the first settler, is concluded. In other chapters will be taken up the history of the various local municipalities, in which an effort will be made to supply local coloring more appropriate there than in the wider outlook of the whole county. The years covered in the first eight chapters of this work have witnessed many changes. The solitude of an unbroken forest has given place to the earnest life of a prosperous community possessing every environment conducive to happiness, and surrounded with every evidence of advanced civilization. But the strong, earnest men who came into the county at first and helped to make it what it is, are finding their ranks thinning out, and those remaining are grey-haired and bent; but they have sent out a race worthy of their sires. Besides those who remain in their native county, Bruce can claim children who were nourished on her fertile soil, but now are scattered from the Atlantic to the Pacific. Wherever these have roamed we find that they retain a loving loyalty for Bruce, with its glorious woods, its fertile fields and its grand broad lake. And well they may, for truly it was a noble heritage that the early pioneers hewed out of the bush. All honor to their memory.

CHAPTER IX.

'SCHOOLS AND EDUCATION.

1851—1906.

SETTLERS had resided within the county of Bruce some three years before the largest community therein felt the necessity of establishing a school. When this time came it was after the School Act, 13 and 14 Vic, chap. 9, introducing much that proved to be an advance on previous methods, had come into force, which it did on July 24th, 1850. The initial step taken in the cause of education within the county of Bruce was the appointment of a local superintendent by the Council of the united counties of Huron, Perth and Bruce. School District No. 3 in the united counties comprised the six northerly townships in the county of Huron and all of the county of Bruce. Mr. John Nairn was the gentleman who received the appointment of superintendent for this district, the date of which was December 30th, 1850. At that time there was not a single school in the whole of the county of Bruce, but during the year 1851 a commencement was made by the establishing of one at Kincardine, located in the vicinity of the present railway station, the first teacher being Mrs. Jane Nairn. The following are the particulars concerning it as given in the "Statistical School Report of 1851," of the Department of Education, and are the only reliable ones available:

Pupils on roll, 66; boys, 31; girls, 35. Number of teachers, 1; certificate, second class; salary paid teacher,[1] $145.80 (without board) per annum; length of time school was kept open during the year, six months. The school-house was a rented frame building, containing one room. Amount of legislative grant, $72.90; amount of other receipts, $12.00; total receipts, $84.90. From such a small beginning has arisen the extended and efficient system of public schools within the county.

At this period of school history in Canada West a certain amount of latitude was permitted in regard to what textbooks might be used in teaching, as uniformity was not provided for; those most commonly in use were the Irish National Readers and Arithmetic,

[1] The amounts are here given in dollars and cents, for the convenience of the reader, instead of in Halifax currency, as they appear in the report.

Lennie's Grammar, Morse's Geography, and a spelling-book published in Canada.

The following year witnessed an increase within the county of educational privileges and also in the number of pupils. The Superintendent of Schools reports for the year 1852 three schoolhouses, all log buildings Two of these were built during the year.[1] These three schools were located, respectively, at Kincardine, Southampton and Walkerton.

In January, 1852, a redistribution was made by the United Counties Council of the districts to be supervised by the local superintendents of education, and all of the counties of Huron and Bruce were then formed into one district. Mr William Rath received the appointment of superintendent thereof. He was a painstaking officer, but he found the work so heavy, on account of the extent of territory in his district, that he resigned the position at the end of the year. It was in this year that the first levy of a municipal equivalent to the legislative grant to public schools was made in the county of Bruce. The amount so raised was $214.67.

On Mr. Rath's resignation Mr. William Gunn was appointed local superintendent of education for the whole of the county of Bruce, and performed the duties of his office over this large area during 1853 and the following year. In 1855 the county was divided for educational purposes into three districts, and two other gentlemen were appointed along with Mr Gunn as local superintendents of education, at a salary of $5 00 per school. The details of this division of the county are as follows:

The Western District comprised the townships of Huron, Kincardine, Bruce and Kinloss. The local superintendent was Mr. Wm Gunn

The Northern District comprised the townships of Saugeen,

'SCHOOL STATISTICS

	1852	1853	1854
Population of school age . . .	321	367	438
Attendance of pupils	183	199	321
Number of Schools, log buildings	3	3	4
Number of Schools, frame buildings	0	0	1
Total number of Schools	3	3	5

Mr Gunn, in his report for 1853, says · " Only three schoolhouses in the county at first sight seems disproportionate to the population, now over 10,000 It must be remembered, however, that the county may be said to be entirely destitute of roads, for, with the exception of the Durham and Elora roads, of sectional roads we have not a mile."

Arran and Elderslie. The local superintendent was Rev. James Hutchison, who was a missionary of the Methodist Church to the Indians on the Saugeen Reserve.

The Eastern District comprised the townships of Brant, Carrick, Culross and Greenock The local superintendent was Mr. John Eckford

Mr. Gunn retained his office until the end of 1858, excepting during the early part of 1857, when Mr. Matthew McKendrick held the office

Rev. Mr. Hutchison held office only during the year 1855. He was succeeded by the Rev James H McNaughton, who held the office during the years 1856, 1857 and 1858.

Mr. John Eckford held office for sixteen and a half years, that is, until the office of local superintendent of education was abolished by statute in 1871, and the office of inspector of public schools instituted instead. Mr. Eckford was a most efficient officer, and the reports of the School Committee of each succeeding County Council refer in most complimentary terms to his work as superintendent of schools.

The cost of erecting school buildings was one that many settlers felt was almost beyond their powers, but the desire to have their children educated constrained them to take action, so we find that they contributed willingly of their time and also of their means, as far as they were able, in the erection and completion of schoolhouses; while in most instances the sites for rural schools were freely and generously given by some settler.

It would not be satisfactory to pass over the early days of educational matters in the county with little more than a bare recital of statistics It is, therefore, with pleasure that the writer is able here to insert an unfinished fragment of a paper written by the late Mr Wm. Gunn on this subject. It is to be regretted that it ends so abruptly. It is as follows:

" EDUCATIONAL MATTERS IN THE EARLY SETTLEMENT OF THE COUNTY OF BRUCE.

" The first local Superintendent of Schools in Bruce was the late Mr. Wm. Rath, of the County of Huron, local Superintendent of that County.[1] Finding it impossible to attend to the duties of

[1] Mr. Gunn is in error here in thinking that Mr. Rath was the first Superintendent of Schools. He was the second —Author

7

the office extending over such a wide range of country, he resigned the Superintendency for Bruce in December, 1852, and in January, 1853, without his knowledge or consent, Mr. Gunn, now of Walkerton, was appointed local Superintendent for the County of Bruce. There were at that time only three schools in the whole County, one. at Kincardine, one at Southampton, and one in Walkerton. These had to be visited twice a year, and the only mode of locomotion was on foot, the road often for long distances being indicated simply by the surveyor's blaze, very few miles of roads having been opened in the County. The traveller in those days, in addition to a few necessary articles of toilet, found it very convenient to carry a moderate supply of crackers and cheese in his wallet slung over his shoulders, of which he could partake at noon by the side of some clear creek or spring. The settlers, however, were hospitable in the highest degree, and readily shared their humble meal with the traveller when he happened to come along at meal-time. The quality of the potatoes was always good, the salt excellent, and there was always bread and tea to be had, but fresh meat was a rarity for several years.

"In 1853 and 1854 considerable progress was made. Settlers were coming in freely and the population of the County rapidly increasing, the erection of school-houses was not neglected. The people, as a rule, did wonderfully considering their circumstances, and large were the demands made upon their muscles and purses in moving into this then wilderness country and making a beginning in clearing the forest and erecting places to dwell in.

" The school sections in the whole County were laid out about 1853 by the local Superintendents, the Municipal Clerk, Mr. C. R. Barker, and the Councils of the Townships, as these came into existence,[1] and so well was this done that very few changes were found necessary afterwards.

" For several years the whole County had only one Reeve or representative in the United Counties Council of Huron and Bruce. This was the Reeve of Kincardine Township, but as the population and settlement increased, Reeves multiplied, and our voice became stronger at the Council Board. To the credit of the Reeves of the County of Huron it must be said that they were always most fair and considerate in all municipal action toward the pioneer settlers of Bruce.

" In 1854, as schools began to multiply outside of the triangle formed by Kincardine, Walkerton and Southampton (and as the absence of roads in many places enhanced the difficulty and fatigue

[1]Excepting Kincardine, there were no township councils until 1854. —Author.

of travelling on foot), Mr. Gunn got the County Council to divide
the County into three districts, East, North and West. The late
Mr. Eckford, of Dunkeld, was appointed local Superintendent of
the Eastern District, composed of Brant, Carrick, Culross and
Greenock; Rev. J. H. McNaughton of the Northern District, composed of Arran, Elderslie and Saugeen, Mr. Gunn retaining in the
Western District Bruce, Huron, Kincardine and Kinloss. These
gentlemen's duties commenced in 1855

"In 1856 considerable progress had been made in the erection
of school-houses ready for opening in 1857. The Legislative grant
had increased to $1,325.00, being an increase over 1855 of $1,053.00.
The apportionment of Townships is not given in the Chief Superintendent's Report. The Rate Bill in the County amounted to
$603.50. The total expenditure for schools, $8,872 40 The total
number of children attending school in 1856 was 1819, being an
increase over 1855 of 985. The number of teachers in 1856 was 19,
of whom 12 were males and 7 were females. The highest salary
was $500 (paid by Kincardine) and the lowest $200 Of the 18
school-houses open in 1856, 5 were of stone, 2 of brick and 11
were of logs. Of those schools, 8 were opened and closed with
prayer, in 10 of them the Bible and New Testament were used.
Ten or twelve new school-houses were finished in 1856, ready for
use in 1857.

" From this time on the progress made in all matters educational
was very great and very satisfactory, culminating in the ample school
accommodation and the thorough equipment for educational purposes of the present day, with a numerous staff of thoroughly
trained teachers of the highest attainments. The old dark, dismal log
school-house has everywhere given place to comfortable, commodious
buildings, well lighted, well ventilated and well furnished.

" Perhaps no new settlement in Canada was ever more highly
favored than the County of Bruce in the class of men composing
the pioneers of the County. The early School Trustees and municipal Councillors of the County were men of generous minds and
liberal ideas, many of them being men of excellent educational
standing[1] They laid the foundations broad and deep, as circumstances would permit, of the educational system which now reflects
so much credit on the County of Bruce, the youngest county in
Ontario

[1]This remark of Mr Gunn's no doubt was correct in the great majority
of cases, but some Boards of Trustees did not come up to this standard,
for in his report for 1856 he says : " He had sometimes to transact business with a School Board in Gaelic, as none of the Board were able to
speak English "—Author.

"In his report to the Chief Superintendent for 1852 Mr. Rath says: 'Speaking generally of the County of Bruce, I must do so in the highest praise of the efforts of the people in favor of the estab- lishment of schools. Their exertions in this respect will bear favor- able comparison with older counties, and this, too, in the very infancy of their settlement, and while many of them have had pri- vations and hardships of no ordinary character to endure and diffi- culties of no ordinary character to encounter.'

"At a later date, in 1856, Mr. Eckford in his report says: 'Much has been done; in nearly every section progress has been made. When I consider, however, that the settlers have in general exhausted their funds in the purchase and improvement of lands, and in sup- porting their families before they obtained an adequate return from the soil, and also that the municipal and school taxes are heavy, that the home market is nearly closed, with no outlet for surplus produce, I feel that it would be injudicious to urge them to further exertion. In the face of all this, however, the increase would have been doubled but for the want of suitable teachers.'

"Rev. J. H. McNaughton reports six schools in Arran, all opened for the first time in 1856, and Elderslie one school.

"In his report for 1856 Mr. Gunn says: 'The want of a better supply of efficient teachers is very greatly felt throughout this county We find it impossible to meet the demand and to a great extent the standard of qualifications, although meeting the present requirements of the law, which is lamentably low, Steady young men who intend following the profession of teaching, having matrimony in contemplation, or married men with small families, would find in these new settlements very favorable inducements to remove hither. I would particularly mention the facilities which exist for acquiring a little property, and the satisfaction of possessing a permanent home at a trifling outlay, without in any way interfering with their professional vocations. Such persons may with safety be recom- mended at least to visit this County.

"'In the early years of the settlement of the County, in conse- quence of the tender age of the majority of the children of the pioneers, female teachers were in great demand, their services being generally preferred, and their success in teaching most satisfactory; but it was very generally found that just as soon as an efficient female teacher with her three or four years' experience was becoming of great usefulness in her profession, some keen-eyed young pioneer, on matrimony intent, came along, and without consulting the school authorities, carried her off to adorn his shanty in the bush, leaving

her place to be filled by some young and inexperienced member of
the sex.' "

It is much to be regretted that Mr. Gunn's paper ends at this
point. If he wrote more, the subsequent pages of his manuscript have
been lost—a loss from an historical point of view not easily to be
computed, as no one was better qualified than he to write on this
subject.

It will be in place here to give a list of the local superintendents
of education and inspectors of public schools in the county of Bruce
down to the present day.

In the foregoing, the names of the local superintendents to the
end of 1858 have been given for all the districts, and it has also been
stated that Mr. Eckford remained in charge of the Eastern District
until June, 1871. To this district there were added the townships
of Elderslie and Saugeen for the years 1864 and 1871 inclusive,
excepting that for the year 1868 only, Saugeen was united with Arran
in a separate district, as is related later on.

The Western District was under the charge of the Rev. Walter
Inglis as local superintendent for the years 1859, 1860 and 1861.
and of the Rev. Wm. Fraser, who held the office for the years 1862
to 1867, inclusive For part of 1868 the Rev. A. McKay was local
superintendent, and on his resigning during the year, Dr. De Witt H.
Martyn was appointed, and filled the office until the end of 1869,
being succeeded in 1870 by the Rev. John Ferguson. In January,
1871, the township of Bruce was set apart as a separate district, over
which the Rev. J. Anderson acted as local superintendent, while
Dr. D A McCrimmon filled the same office over the remaining part
of the Western District. On the establishment of a grammar school
at Kincardine, in the year 1860, Mr. Alexander Shaw was appointed
local superintendent for the village. How long after 1860 he retained
the office is not very clear from any available records.

The Northern District was under the local superintendency of
the Rev. K. McLennan in 1859 and 1860, of F H. L. Staunton in
1861, and of Dr. W. S. Scott in 1862. In 1863 this district was
split up, and for that year only a separate school district was formed
of the townships of Saugeen and Elderslie, the Rev. Mr. Waters being
local superintendent, but for the next eight years these two townships were united to Mr. Eckford's district. For the year 1863 the
townships of Arran, Amabel and Albemarle were formed into a

school district, the local superintendent being Dr. E. Hawksworth, who held the office for both 1863 and 1864. In 1865 Mr. William Bull was appointed local superintendent for the townships of Amabel and Albemarle, which position he held until the abolishing of the office in June, 1871. During the last six months of Mr. Bull's duties, Eastnor was included in his district. In 1865 the township of Arran was set apart as a separate district, and Dr. E. Hawksworth placed over it as local superintendent. He died during the year and was succeeded by Dr. W. S Francis, who held the office until the end of 1867. In 1868, Arran and Saugeen were formed into a separate district, over which the Rev. A Tolmie presided as local superintendent. Arran in 1869 again became a separate district, and Dr. W. S Francis was once more the local superintendent. He was succeeded in 1870 by the Rev. R. S. Cooper, who remained in office until June, 1871.

On the 15th of February, 1871, the Legislature passed an Act[1] which abolished the office of local superintendent of education and provided instead inspectors of public schools. The County Council, at the following June session, divided the county into two districts, Eastern and Western, and appointed Richard V. Langdon as inspector over the Eastern District and Benjamin Freer over the Western District, at salaries of $5.00 per school and $2.00 additional for expenses   The number of schools in the county at this time was slightly over 130 in all   Mr Langdon held office for two years and a half, when (December 11th, 1873) Mr. W. S. Clendening was appointed. He was succeeded by Mr. John McCool, April 1st, 1906. Mr. Freer held office until the January session of the County Council in 1877. He was succeeded by Mr. Alexander Campbell, who held office until April, 1902, when Mr. W. I. Chisholm was appointed as inspector of public schools for West Bruce.

At the June session, 1861, of the United Counties Council it was decided that a Board of Public Instruction for examination of teachers, etc., be established in Bruce. This decision was carried out, and the Rev. R. C Moffatt was the first appointed secretary.

The first detailed school statistics of common schools in the county of Bruce that the author has met with are those for the year 1855. They are here given, and to indicate the process of development, those for 1863 are given in part also:

[1]34 Vic Chap 33

	FOR THE YEAR 1855					FOR THE YEAR 1863.	
	School Buildings			School Population	Atten-dance	School Buildings Total No	Atten-dance
	Frame.	Log	Total.				
Tp. of Albemarle .						1	
" Amabel . ..	.		..	.		1	14
" Arran .	.			50		11	350
" Brant ...	1	3	4	520	161	11	430
" Bruce		.	—	50	..	12	357
" Carrick }	.			519		{ 14	511
" Culross }						{ 8	213
" Elderslie	.			50	.	10	196
" Greenock..		2	2	298	119	8	241
" Huron ..		1	1	234	56	8	235
" Kincardine .	1	3	4	540	271	9	466
" Kinloss ..	.	1	1	236	29	9	319
" Saugeen ...	1	2	3	290	198	6	256
Totals .			15	2,787	834	108	3,588

Number of school buildings erected during the year 1855 . .. 8
    " free school " " " " " 7
    " partly free schools " " " " 5
    " schools at 25c rate bill per month . 2

Teachers—1 first-class, 7 second-class. 4 third-class, 3 unqualified

The following extracts from the reports of the local superintendents of education will serve to give an idea of educational matters subsequent to the date referred to in Mr. Gunn's paper and prior to the appointment of inspectors In 1857 Superintendent McNaughton reports that "The township of Elderslie has done admirably in the way of school building during the past year. Although the newest of the three townships under my charge, it is now the first with regard to school-houses. This may be attributed in a great measure to the wisdom of the Township Council in offering a certain sum of money to each section on condition that the school-house would be erected within the year. The result is that there is not now a single section without a school-house."

Rev Mr. Fraser, local superintendent of the Western District, writes, May, 1867. "In a number of our schools pleasing progress is being made in book-keeping, mensuration, algebra and geometry, so that the advanced state of the schools will soon force all the third-class teachers to retire "

Mr. J. Eckford says, in June, 1867: " It affords me much pleasure to be able to state that the schools under my supervision are, with few exceptions, in a prosperous condition. This is to a great extent to be attributed to the teachers, who, both in scholarship and in the art of instruction, are generally very superior to their predecessors of some years ago.   The school attendance over my entire district is becoming very large, partly from the increase of population, and also because the children are coming out better and attending more regularly.   One section has a senior and a junior school, and in another the master has the services of an assistant."

Rev. J. Ferguson reports, December, 1870, as follows: "Considering the newness and remoteness of a good many school sections, the ill-judged selection of trustees in many cases, the employment of poorly qualified, because cheap, teachers, and the inability of some sections to build and equip good schools and otherwise to hold out inducements to both teachers and scholars, there are yet many encouraging features connected with schools in this new county. Some of the school-houses are first-class and a considerable number of the teachers are an honor to their profession."

"The Common and Grammar School Act of 1871" marked the beginning of important changes in both of those classes of schools. All common schools became free public schools, and every child from seven to thirteen years of age, inclusive, was declared to have the legal right of attending some public school   The assessment and collection of public school rates was by these acts transferred from the trustees to the municipalities.   County inspectors with larger powers and duties were substituted for local superintendents.   In place of "County Boards of Public Instruction," "County Boards of Examiners" were established for the examination and licensing of teachers, and county grammar schools became high schools   It might appear as if these changes were of name only; this would be an incorrect view, for with the changed name the scope, regulations and duties of each were also changed and enlarged   In 1877, by further legislation, the Education Department was empowered to arrange with trustees for "constituting one or more of the public schools to be the county model school for the preliminary training of public school teachers."   The above legislative changes in educational matters remain practically in force to the present day

The standing of education in our public schools under the present system of inspectorate may be best referred to by extracts from some of the annual reports of the inspectors, as follows:

R. V. Langdon, inspector of public schools for East Bruce, in January, 1872, reports that under the School Act, two examinations of candidates for teachers' certificates had been held and out of ninety-six applicants, only thirty-two obtained certificates. "It is thought," he goes on to say, "by some that the failure of so many candidates is owing to the introduction of new subjects, but this is not the case, as the majority of failures were in the subjects of spelling, reading, writing, arithmetic and English grammar."

W. S. Clendening, inspector of public schools for East Bruce, in June, 1877, reports the total expenditure in his district in 1874 to have been $46,400, and in 1876, $56,400. That the number of school-houses in 1874 were 73, and in 1876 there were 82. Of this latter number, 19 were brick, 11 were stone, 42 were frame, and 10 were log buildings. Also that in 1874 there were 7,624 pupils on the school registers, and in 1876 there were 8,432. This latter number of pupils were taught by 90 teachers; of these 18 held second-class certificates, 68 third-class certificates, and 4 held permits.

A. Campbell, inspector of public schools for West Bruce, in December, 1877, reports 88 schools in his district (not including the town of Kincardine), and says: "Progress has been made during the year, although the schools taken as a whole are far from being as efficient as I should like to see them," and further on says, "Reading and spelling, which may be considered among the most important subjects of the programme of studies, were taught in a wretched manner in a large majority of the schools; indeed, I may say that they were almost entirely neglected. For instance, I may mention the fact that out of forty-eight candidates for admission to the Kincardine high school who came up from different parts of the county at the July examinations, only five passed, and nearly all the rejected candidates failed in spelling."

In 1885 Inspector W. S. Clendening says, after speaking of the number who had passed the entrance examination, and the high standing of some of the schools in his Inspectorate: "This record is strong evidence that the schools of East Bruce are quite abreast of the times and doing a work of which they need not feel ashamed" In the same year Inspector A. Campbell, in West Bruce, expresses his satisfaction at the progress that was made during the year.

The opportunity to obtain a good elementary education has from the first been the privilege of pupils attending the public schools of Bruce. This statement applies more especially to the last quarter of a century, as a result of the higher standard of teaching then demanded. The educational possibilities of the early days were much enlarged when advanced classes were established in many schools in response to a much-felt need, existing in districts lacking high school privileges. The Legislature gave an impetus to this movement when, in 1891, a grant (to be supplemented by the County Council) was made to such public schools as conduct a "leaving examination" A change in the regulations regarding such was made in 1896, by authorizing the establishment of "continuation classes," the Legislative grant—and the county equivalent thereto—being $100, $50, $25, or $15, according to grade. The number of such classes in the various grades in the county in 1905 was 3, 1, 4 and 6, respectively. That good work is done in these continuation classes is evidenced by the fact that a Chesley schoolboy[1] captured a scholarship at the 1903 departmental examinations, standing fourth among the pupils of the whole province then examined. This is the first time in the history of departmental examinations that a scholarship has fallen to any public school scholar. All honor to the boy from Bruce.

This chapter has woven into it much of mere facts which, although interesting, may to some form somewhat dry reading, so laying aside for the time being school law, inspectors, schools and classes, we shall, for the purpose of brightening up the chapter, let some of the scholars who have studied in our schools step to the front and speak for themselves That this might be vividly done, a teacher who possesses a deep appreciation of humor, and who has taught many years in the county, was asked by the author to furnish some reminiscenses of the school-room, who, consenting, has supplied the following, for which the reader will no doubt be as grateful as the author.

"HUMOR IN THE SCHOOL-ROOM.

"The following may be given as a few of the amusing answers actually given by school boys and girls of Bruce, some of them culled from examination papers, others given orally:

"'From what animal do we get beef?' asked the teacher of a primary class. 'The butcher,' was the ready answer of one of the little ones.

"'Into how many parts is the day divided?' 'Three, breakfast, dinner and supper.'

"A teacher giving a lesson on the proper use of the words 'bring'

[1]R C. Halliday, son of Robert Halliday. The value of the scholarship was $50 in cash and free tuition in Toronto University for four years, amounting to $195 in all

and 'fetch,' asked this question: 'If the cows were in a field and I wanted the dog to go after them, what would I be likely to say to the dog?' 'Sic 'em!' said the boy.

"Here are some of the answers given to the question: 'How do you know that the earth is round?' 'The earth is round, because if it wasn't you'd fall off when you came to the end.' Another still more original was, 'The earth rolls round the sun; a square thing can't roll, therefore the earth must be round.'

"Another answer as to the shape of the earth: 'The earth is round like an orange, flat at both ends. When it was first made it was round like a ball, but it has been spinning so fast for such a long time that it has wore flat at the two ends'

"'What is the capital of a country?' 'Where the jail is.' 'What is a republic?' 'A place where they all elect themselves'

"Here are some rather astonishing historical facts:

"'John did not want to sign the Charta, but the barns said he had to, all the same.'

"'Mary Queen of Scots married the Dolphin of France before she was beheaded.'

"'Charles I. met his doom without a flinch'

"'Who appoints the Governor of Canada?' 'The Pope,' said one. 'Mr. Cargill,' said another.

"'It was very difficult for William Lyon MacKenzie to escape to the United States, because 1,000 lbs. was put on his head.'

"'The British searched American ships for deserters. The Americans looked so like themselves that they could not tell which to arrest.'

"'What is a mummy?' asked the teacher 'A cured man,' replied a boy. 'Cured of what?' queried the teacher 'Not that kind of cured, cured so he'd keep,' was the answer. Another answer: 'A stuffed man.'

"'The foe was sullenly firing.' 'Why sullenly?' 'Because they'd just been licked,' said a boy, who doubtless could easily imagine their feelings.

"The question, 'Give in your own words this quotation from "The Brook," "I linger by my shingly bars," elicited the following from one of the girls, 'I stay about the old frame hotel'

"'What is the difference between "discover" and "invent"?' 'Discover is to find something that was there all the time Invent is to find something that never was there before.'

"'What is the masculine gender of witch?' 'Bachelor.' 'What is the feminine gender of bachelor?' 'Widow.' 'The masculine of duchess?' 'Dutchman.' 'The feminine of monk?' 'Monkey.' 'For what do these letters stand: "B.A"?' 'Before Adam,' 'Begin Again,' 'Bachelor of Adversity.' '"D.D." stands for "Dry Dock."'

"In a school in Kinloss was a little boy who would persist in saying 'have went.' The teacher kept him in one night and said, 'Now, while I am out of the room you may write "have gone" fifty times.' When the teacher came back he looked at the boy's paper, and there was, 'Have gone fifty times.' On the other side was written, 'I have went home.'"

In 1877 two model schools were established, one at Walkerton and the other at Kincardine In his report of that year, Mr. Campbell speaks hopefully of them, and says that there were, in that the opening year, thirteen pupils in attendance at Walkerton and fourteen pupils at Kincardine. Speaking again in 1885, he says: "A great deal of the improvements that have taken place in our schools during the last few years can be traced to the efficiency of our model schools and to the beneficial effects of attendance at teachers' associations." The county can point with pride to these two model schools. The training imparted therein to the future teachers throughout the county has been of the very best, and reflects credit upon the various principals who have been at the head of them since their establishment. There is no doubt that to them is largely due the success which has of late years marked the imparting of instruction in our public schools [1]

The initial step in the way of higher education for the youth of the county of Bruce was the establishment in 1860 of a county grammar school, which was located at Kincardine. This was after several years of agitation, the first petition to the County Council to establish such a school being made in June, 1857 The first Board of Trustees had as its members Rev. K. McLennan, of Paisley; William Gunn, of Inverhuron; and Rev Walter Inglis, Rev. Isaac Middleton, Alex Shaw and Matthew McKendrick, of Kincardine. Its first meeting was on 18th March, 1860. The duties of this Board differed somewhat from High School Boards of the present day. An

[1] Prior to 1877 the Board of Examiners issued third-class certificates, and the Inspector permits to teach, for which it was not required to possess professional training

inspection of the minutes show that committees were appointed to select books, to examine the pupils and grade the classes, and to investigate cases of misconduct. The pupils' fee was fixed at $2.00 quarterly. The first principal, Mr. Albert Andrews, filled the position in a most satisfactory manner for six or seven years. In 1890, S. W. Perry, B A., was appointed principal of this school, and has retained the position since, filling the duties of the position most successfully. For twelve years Kincardine rejoiced in possessing the only grammar school in the county. Considering this circumstance, the County Council felt justified in the years 1870 and 1871 in granting $150 and $100 respectively, as scholarship prizes, an attraction for bright, earnest scholars not now offered at any school in the county. That an idea may be had as to the manner in which these amounts were allocated, the names of the successful competitors for these scholarships at the December, 1871, examination are here given: John Collwell, value $15; Archena McDougall, $10.00; Robert Boal, $8.00; Alexander Baird, $7.00; Sarah Harvey, $5.00. The names of those who carried off the prizes in the June or other examinations the writer has not been able to obtain.

The Act passed by the Provincial Legislature in February, 1871, "to improve the common and grammar schools," gave the County Council extended powers as to the formation of high school districts. Various local municipalities within the county being desirous of taking advantage of privileges now attainable, petitioned the County Council at the January session, 1872, requesting to be established as high school districts The Council complied with these petitions and passed at that session "A by-law to establish five high school districts in the county of Bruce." The places therein named were Kincardine, Walkerton, Paisley, Port Elgin and Southampton. These municipalities were thereby authorized to establish a high school, but it was a privilege that three of the five named municipalities did not avail themselves of, owing, no doubt, to the increase of taxation involved. Kincardine already possessed a high school; of the other four places the ratepayers of Walkerton alone were willing to bear an increase of taxation for the advantages and privilege of possessing a high school in their town. The following comprised the first Board of Walkerton High School Trustees: Messrs. J. J. Kingsmill, John McLay, Alexander Sproat, J. G Cooper, Paul Ross and Alexander Shaw. The first teacher to preside over this school was Arnoldus Miller, B.A. This school, by special permission granted by the Superintendent of Education, was allowed to open without any assistant teacher. It was not long, however, before assistants were secured, one after another, as necessity arose, until the staff of the Walkerton High School became sufficient to entitle it to rank as a collegiate institute, a position that it will, in the near future, no doubt, attain to. Joseph Morgan, M.A., has been principal of this school since 1881.

The high schools at Kincardine and Walkerton remained for many years the only ones in the county, other municipalities being apparently apathetic in the matter of higher education. The first evidence of a move in that direction was when Paisley sent a deputation, in 1886, to wait on the County Council, with the request that that village and neighborhood be set apart as a high school district;[1] but the deputation failed to convince the Council that it was advisable to make any increase in the number of high schools in the county. The following year a similar deputation from Port Elgin was more successful, and despite a strong opposition, a by-law was passed June 10th, 1887, establishing Port Elgin as a high school district. This school was opened in the fall term of 1889 with 75 names on the roll, Mr. J. T. Lillie, B A, being the head master. The attendance rose to 153 in 1891, which figure has not been exceeded since. Mr. Lillie continued to the end of 1904 in the head mastership. The high percentage of the successful pupils of this school who wrote at the departmental examinations speaks well as to his qualifications for the post he held for so many years. Mr. J. C. Clark is the present head master of this school.

The agitation for additional high schools in districts not already provided once more came before the County Council in June, 1891, Paisley and Wiarton being the municipalities applying. Again Paisley failed to obtain the consent of the Council, Wiarton carrying off the coveted privilege, and by by-law passed June 6th, 1891, was established as a high school district, and in the beginning of the following year the school was opened under the head mastership of T. H. Farrell, who was succeeded by Henry De La Mater. For some time the school accommodation was not all that the Department of Education required, but any deficiencies in this respect are now at an end, as the new school building, opened in 1896, is fully abreast

[1]The good people of Paisley then, and again in 1891, as well as the County Council, seem to have forgotten the by-law mentioned in a foregoing paragraph. That made Paisley the centre of a high school district, which by-law is unrepealed.

of all requirements   The next place to obtain a high school was
Chesley. This high school was opened in 1904, R D. McMurchy
being the head master, he being succeeded by Henry Bonis.

The cause of education within the county of Bruce has had an
excellent auxiliary in the free and public libraries scattered throughout its municipalities, in the number of which Bruce is the leading
county in Ontario, having twenty-five in all.[1] Besides these, there
are thirteen rural school libraries, all situated in the West Bruce
inspectorate. The localities where the public libraries are situated,
with the number of volumes on their shelves, are to be found in a
footnote[2]; the figures given are from the report of the Minister of
Education for the year 1903. It is impossible to estimate the educational and intellectual uplift derived by the public having access to
55,000 books of select, pure, good literature   That the opportunities
offered have been made use of the large number of members of the
several libraries testify   Another pleasing feature about the public
libraries in Bruce is that a number of them are situated in purely
rural or semi-rural localities   The first library established in the
county, as far as the writer is aware, was one at Inverhuron in 1856,
which commenced with a total of 39 volumes   From such a modest
beginning has developed the present numerous and well-equipped
library system of the county. The writer was honored by being made
the first librarian of the public library established at Kincardine
(this was in the spring of 1861), he being expected to perform the
duties without any recompense beyond the fact of knowing that he
was helping on a good work. The number of volumes placed in his
charge were under two hundred   This library has grown to be the
largest in the county, and numbers now over 4,500 volumes   Hugh
Black, who was its painstaking librarian for many years, has lately
passed away.

[1]On December 31st, 1903

[2]List of Public and Free Libraries in the county, December 31st, 1903.
Those that are free are marked with an asterisk
Bervie (Vols 1,654); Cargill (Vols 1,932); Chepstowe (Vols 333),
Chesley* (Vols 1,923), Elmwood (Vols 657); Glammis (Vols 446), Hepworth (Vols 1,011); Holyrood* (Vols 2,151), Kincardine (Vols 4 552),
Lion's Head (Vols 1,102), Lucknow* (Vols 3,224); Mildmay (Vols
2,073); Paisley* (Vols 4,232), Pinkerton (Vols. 1,605); Port Elgin (Vols
3,127); Ripley (Vols. 1,727), Riversdale (Vols 923), Southampton (Vols
4 503); Teeswater (Vols. 3,863); Tara* (Vols 2,009); Tiverton (Vols
1,910); Underwood (Vols 2,588); Walkerton (Vols 3,259); Westford*
(Vols 1,423); Wiarton* (Vols. 3,596)   The total number of volumes is
55,823.

In bringing this chapter to a close it might be well to summarize and show what half a century has wrought for the cause of education in the county of Bruce. The first school in the county was opened in the summer of 1851 with sixty-six pupils; fifty years later this solitary centre of learning had developed and multiplied, as is set forth in the figures given in the report of the Minister of Education for the year 1901, which are summarized as follows:

246 Public Schools, with	12,614 pupils	Receipts	$133,707 62
4 High Schools, having .	480 ''	''	15,845 34
2 Model Schools, training	38 ''	'' .	790 00
8 Separate Schools, with	735 ''	''	8,001 56
260 schools.	13,867 pupils	Receipts	$158,344 52

The county of Bruce has no cause to think the money it has spent so freely in the cause of education has been wasted. Her young people have been fitted to enter the battle of life possessing the advantages arising from a sound education. From her schools have graduated many who now fill most prominent positions throughout our wide Dominion, bringing honor to those who have in an enlightened manner encouraged and maintained a high standard of education in their mother county.

CHAPTER X.

THE MILITIA AND VOLUNTEERS OF BRUCE.

1857—1906.

CANADIANS have a well-earned reputation for loyalty; its sincerity, as well as their courage, they have exhibited time and again by taking up arms in defence of their country and their homes. This admirable spirit has not been confined to a few localities, but is widespread. That it has existed in the county of Bruce in a marked degree is something to be proud of. On the several occasions during the last forty years when our land has been threatened with war, invasion or rebellion, its young men have hastened to fill up the ranks of the various volunteer companies which existed, or formed new ones, cheerfully leaving their homes when ordered away to the posts assigned them by the military authorities. Although it has not been the fortune of our volunteers to have endured " the baptism of fire," they have manifested those characteristics which would have enabled them to have given a good account of themselves if called upon to do so. They have realized that in time of peace we should be prepared for war, and since 1861, when for the first time in the history of this county the possibility of war was felt, one generation after another of our young men have voluntarily sought to acquire that knowledge of military drill and discipline which would enable them to effectively aid in the defence of their native land.

The passing of the " Militia Act of 1855 " put the militia of Canada upon an improved basis. This Act divided the militia into two classes, sedentary and active. To the former only of these classes did this Act apply in the county of Bruce, as no companies of active militia were formed while it remained in force. The Act referred to says: " The sedentary militia shall (with some few exceptions) consist of all the male inhabitants of the age of eighteen and under

177

sixty." These were divided into two classes, the service men, of all
over eighteen years of age but under forty, and the reserve, who were
of forty years and upwards. In time of peace no actual service or
drill was required, " but they shall be carefully enrolled," and " the
service men shall also assemble for muster annually, on the Queen's
birthday." The writer's first recollection of the Bruce militia was
the witnessing of one of these musters on the market square,
Kincardine, about the year 1857 or 1858

Shortly after the passing of the Act above referred to, the county
of Bruce was divided, for militia purposes, into three battalion
divisions. This division lasted but a short time, a further division
being made, which is detailed in the following extract from a general
order dated 26th February, 1857. " His Excellency the Governor-
General is pleased to direct that certain changes shall be made in
the limits of the three battalions of the militia of the county of Bruce;
and that three additional battalions shall be formed, to be styled
respectively the Fourth, Fifth and Sixth Battalions of the militia of
the county of Bruce."

The 1st Battalion was under the command of Lieut.-Col. Pryse
Clark, whose commission bears date of February 26th, 1857. He had
been an officer in the British army, and was present at the battle
of Waterloo The next to obtain command of this battalion was
Lieut.-Col. George Jardine. His commission was dated May 6th,
1858 The following were the first to receive commissions as captains
of companies in this battalion: A. Roy, W. Smith, R. Reid, commissioned 10th August, 1857; F H Lynch, N. Hammond,[1] J. T.

---

[1] Lieut Col. Belcher has possession of an historical document which is
of special interest to the old-timers of Southampton This article bears
the heading, " Roll of No 1 Company of the 1st Battalion of Bruce
Militia, for the year 1859 Limits of Company : All that portion of the
town plot of Southampton to the west of the centre of Victoria Street
and the part of the village lying north of the Saugeen River The names
enrolled are as follows · N Hammond, captain, John Eastwood, lieutenant;
Robert Hall, ensign, John Belcher, James Hibbert, Joseph Gilbert, ser-
geants; Richard McInnis, Neil McLeod, Thomas Tallon, Alex. Sproat,
John McNabb, Donald Campbell, William Wallace, James Hogg, George
Hamilton, Alex Angus, Peter Angus, James McCabe, Donald McPherson,
Robert Fury, James Calder, T E Davis, James Kelly, Alex. McIntosh,
James McIntosh, William Much, Samuel Baker, Edward Ferguson, Andrew
Laurie, Thomas Smith, Edward Kennedy, William Chisholm. Alfred Ditton,
James Peacock, James Jack, James George, Thomas Webster, Thomas
Sharp, Thomas Montgomery, John Murray, Alex. Munro, Peter McGregor,
James Fleming, J. D Cathy, James Mason, Duncan Ross, Thomas Adair,
James Orr, Alex Robertson, John Spence, Barth Higgins. John Lee, Wm
Rounding, W S Scott, M D., Joseph Gilbert, Neil Campbell, Barber Fury
Chandler " Of this list of veterans it is known that twelve were alive in
1900, the remainder having gone to their reward.

Conway, T. Godfrey, D. McKinnon, G. Buchart, commissioned 20th October, 1858; P. Smith and T Lee, commissioned 16th December, 1858

The 2nd Battalion was under the command of Lieut -Col John William Linton. His early military experience had been gained in Spain in the so-called Spanish Legion, fighting to uphold the claims of Queen Isabella against Don Carlos.

The 3rd, 4th, 5th and 6th Battalions were commanded respectively by Lieut.-Col. Francis M. Berford, of Tara; Lieut -Col. John Valentine, of Paisley; Lieut -Col. Robert Ross, an old navy officer, who had been a midshipman in Nelson's day, a resident of Kincardine, and Lieut -Col. Joseph Walker, of Walkerton.

The first decade in the history of the county was one undisturbed by any thought of the possibility of war or invasion, and our militia existed simply in the lists of enrolled service men and in the commissions held by those above mentioned, with others whose names and rank have been largely forgotten. That the list of officers was kept filled is evident to the writer by the examination of a couple of old commissions he has met with, one, dated 18th May, 1860, signed by Sir Fenwick Williams, appointing George Gould ensign in the 3rd Battalion, the other, dated 5th December, 1862, signed by Lord Monck, appointing him lieutenant in the same battalion

When the excitement over the *Trent* affair arose, the officers and non-commissioned officers of the militia in some places took advantage of the presence of the drill instructors in our midst, sent by the Imperial Government to drill our volunteers, and formed themselves into classes or companies for drill instruction. The writer, at that time a sergeant in the 5th Battalion, remembers such a class existing in Kincardine and being drilled by Sergt. McGee, of the 63rd Regiment

In 1868 the Militia Act was again amended This was followed by a general order which directed, "That the boundaries of regimental divisions be identical with the electoral divisions into which the Province of Ontario is divided." This general order was dated 19th January, 1869 The above had the result of placing the reserve militia into the regimental divisions of the north riding of Bruce and the south riding of Bruce In the first of these the following commissions were granted on 19th February, 1869: Lieut -Col. Andrew Lindsay, Major John Gillies and Major James Rowand. On 22nd March, 1869, the commissions to the captains of companies were issued. They were to Co. 1, Robt Scott; Co. 2, M. McKinnon; Co. 3, J. H Coulthard; Co. 4, John McIntyre, Co. 5, James Stark; Co. 6, Andrew Freeborn; Co. 7, James Allen. The officer now in command is Lieut.-Col A. E. Belcher, who was gazetted as such September 10th, 1896. In the regimental division of South Bruce the following commissions were granted on 12th February, 1869: Lieut.-Col Joseph Walker, Majors C. R. Barker and Alex. St. L. Mackintosh. In August, 1875, Major Barker was gazetted as lieut.-colonel, and until his death, in 1899, held that position. The commissions to the captains of companies were issued 9th April, 1869. They were to Co. 1, Malcolm McLean; Co. 2, Geo. Harvey; Co. 3, Paul Ross; Co. 4, John Phalen; Co 5, James Johnston; Co. 6, Thos. Bradley; Co. 7, Robert Johnston Having brought the history of the reserve militia down to the present time, we shall close what we have to say of it with this wish, that at no time in the future may the necessity arise for it to assume more arduous duties than have arisen in the past.

The outbreak of civil war in the United States in the year 1861 was followed by complications between that nation and Great Britain, which was generally known as the "Mason and Slidell difficulty," or "Trent affair." For a while it seemed as if the two nations were to be embroiled in war. The possibility of this was enough to kindle the fire of warlike enthusiasm in the breasts of the young men of Canada From end to end of the country companies of volunteers were formed. The credit of taking the initiative in this matter within the county of Bruce belongs to the village of Southampton A company was raised there under Captain Alex Sproat[1] which was authorized by general order dated December 13th, 1861 [2] Kincardine followed a year later and raised a company under Captain Alex.

---

[1] The two subaltern officers of the company were Lieut. J. W. Ridden and Ensign Alex Sinclair

[2] The reason why the village of Southampton had a company of volunteers a year before any other place within the county arose in this wise : The annual muster of the militia on the Queen's Birthday was felt by many in the 1st Battalion Bruce Militia to be a useless proceeding and they refused to turn out Lieut -Col Jardine had such as refused brought before a magistrate, who promptly fined them. To show that no base motives had moved them in refusing to appear at the annual muster, they and others forwarded a petition to the Minister of Militia, requesting that an independent company of Volunteers be organized at Southampton, and offering that if the Government would furnish arms they would provide their own uniforms This the Government held in abeyance, but on the appearance of trouble at the time of the Trent affair the order authorizing the formation of the company was issued. Sergeant Allerdyce of the

Shaw. This company was authorized December 19th, 1862. Paisley followed close after and raised a company under Captain W. C Bruce, authorized January 2nd, 1863. Lucknow next fell into line and raised a company under Captain McDonald. Our rural population was not less enthusiastic, and we find that Kincardine Township raised a company under Captain William Daniel, which was authorized February 6th, 1863.

The writer, who was a corporal in the Kincardine company at the time of its formation, has preserved some memoranda, jotted down at the time, which shows that the roll was signed December 5th, 1862. The officers were elected at a meeting held December 13th. These were Captain Alex. Shaw, Lieutenant J. Brownlee and Ensign Paul D McInnes. The first drill was on December 18th, held in the town hall; afterward the old furniture factory on Broadway was used to drill in. The first drill instructor was Sergeant McLean of the 17th regulars, who finished his term of ten drills on January 2nd, 1863. He was succeeded by Sergeant McGee, of the 63rd regulars, who remained drilling the company for four months, commencing March 12th, 1863. The first drill with rifles was on February 24th. The company was inspected by Brigade-Major Baretto on March 16th The company paraded in full uniform for the first time on July 23rd, 1863. As there were a number of drill instructors provided by the Imperial Government, and a determination was manifested to get the various companies brought up to a thorough state of efficiency at as early a date as possible, there is no doubt that the other companies in the county at that date would have a somewhat similar record to that here given of the Kincardine company

The date of the formation of the other companies of volunteers in the county may as well be given here, although formed at later dates than the above-mentioned companies. These later ones were, as a rule. organized under the excitement of anticipated Fenian raids. The company at Walkerton, under Captain John Chambers, was authorized July 13th, 1866. The company at Tara, under Captain G. W. Drinkwater, was formed and authorized at the same time as the Walkerton company. The company at Mildmay, under Captain John P. Kay, was authorized May 10th, 1872. Teeswater at the same time raised a company, under Captain Archibald Gillies, which

regular army, a man who had seen much active service, was sent to perform the duties of drill instructor The company stood high in point of efficiency and carried off the fourth prize therefor in a competition of all independent companies within this military district.

was authorized June 7th, 1872 In June, 1895, the headquarters
of the Mildmay company was transferred to Wiarton, and a company
was formed in that flourishing town, with Robert Lee Graham as
its captain

As the drill of our citizen soldiers, as a rule, had to be performed
in the evenings, after the ordinary daily avocations of the members
of the corps were over, it was necessary to secure for each company
some large, well-lit hall The difficulty of finding suitable accommodation was felt from the first, and applications for aid were made to
the several local municipalities and to the County Council. In 1862
the village council of Southampton granted $120 for this purpose,
and the County Council granted a like sum, followed by a further
grant of $200 in 1867. Under similar conditions Paisley received
$120 in 1864 and $200 in 1867 from the County Council. The drill
shed at Paisley was erected in an unfortunately chosen situation,
for it became undermined by the river and had to be deserted, what
remained of it being sold in 1875 for $65. In 1868 Tara received
$250 towards its drill shed from the County Council. Four years
later Teeswater also received a grant of a similar amount from the
County Council towards erecting a drill shed for its company of
volunteers formed that year. It was not until 1885 that the Kincardine company obtained any money from the County Council to
aid in providing accommodation for drilling In that year the building formerly used as a place of worship by St. Andrews' congregation
was for sale The government gave a grant of $300; the County
Council then made a grant of $125, and the purchase of the build-
ing was effected. The government subsequently granted $55 towards
making alterations. Since that time the Kincardine volunteers have
had ample accommodation.

At the time of the separation of the counties of Huron and Bruce,
there was a balance of $1,438 22 paid over to Bruce, this amount being
Bruce's share of an unexpended grant to volunteers voted by the
United Counties Council in 1866. It was from this fund that the
aid to the various drill sheds was granted. It had been decided in
1867 that $800 of this money should go towards a drill shed for the
32nd Battalion at Walkerton. In 1869 it was decided to increase
this amount to $1,200. Subsequently an additional $120.80 for
extras was paid, making a total payment by the county of $1,320.80
towards this building The township of Brant also contributed to
the extent of $300 towards its erection. The construction of the

building was gone on with during the summer of 1869, George
Harvey being the contractor and James Benson, architect. Owing
to the granting of large sums by the government for repairs, the
building was maintained in a good state of preservation until sold
in December, 1899, to Henry Clark, who pulled it down five months
afterward to re-erect it in another part of the town as a skating rink.

The companies of volunteers which were first formed in the
county had two or three years to perfect themselves in drill before
they were called upon to leave their homes for active service, the
only change from the monotony of the weekly drill they experienced
being target practice and Queen's birthday parades, which always
wound up with the firing of a *feu de joie*. If the rolls of these old-
time companies were examined, it would reveal the fact that in the
ranks were many men who were prominent in the community, in
fact, its leading citizens. There has been a falling off in this respect
of late years, but only because that in " the piping times of peace "
drilling seems to be too much like " playing soldier," but if necessity
should again arise, the ranks of our volunteers would at once receive
as recruits a large contingent of men who at present say that they
have no time for such things

Saturday, the 2nd of June, 1866, was a day of intense excitement
throughout our land, for on the day previous a large body of Fenians
had invaded Canada, landing at Fort Erie As this news was tele-
graphed over the country, quickly followed by orders to the officers
in command of the various corps to muster the men under their
command and wait for marching orders, the seriousness of the occasion was brought home to all ; but the fact of the existence of a large
number of well-drilled volunteers to take part with the regulars in
repelling the invasion of our land was a source of solid comfort to
many.

There was a great uncertainty regarding the movements of these
armed invaders and of those who purposed to follow their example
as occasion offered Rumors of the massing of men to invade Canada
at many different points were being circulated, and our troops were
forwarded to the most exposed places on our borders. Goderich was
confidently designated as a point where a detachment of Fenians
then in Chicago intended to effect a landing in order to obtain control
of the railway terminus. Acting on the probability of this being
done, the various volunteer companies in Huron and Bruce were
speedily assembled there to repulse any attack. The companies there

assembled were the Goderich artillery and rifle companies, and with them the companies from Seaforth, Southampton, Paisley, Kincardine Village and Kincardine Township. These remained in Goderich for about four weeks, until the alarm had subsided, when they returned to their homes, excepting the Goderich and Southampton rifle companies, which were sent on to Sarnia, or rather Point Edward, where they remained until some time in August, when any danger of further disturbance was past.

A bare relation of the above facts conveys no idea of the excitement existing in those days   The author is fortunate, therefore, in being able to here give some reminiscences of Lieut.-Col A. E. Belcher, at that time drill instructor to the Southampton company, and who was present with his company at Goderich and Point Edward. He says: " Our company was called out and ordered to embark at daylight next morning on the little steamer *Bruce*. There were very few of us who slept any that night   Mothers, wives and friends were on the dock to say good-bye, and I can assure you the women were not the only ones who had wet eyes that morning, for we all expected to face the enemy and the fateful possibilities were felt by all   At Goderich we were billeted at the hotels, our stay there being marked by some stirring incidents.   We had regular drill, fatigue, guard and picket duty.   Quite expecting to have vessel loads of Fenians from Chicago attempt to land at, or near, the harbor, we made preparations accordingly   We had a chain stretched across its entrance, and earthworks for our cannon crowned the top of the hill near Sheriff McDonald's old residence.   One day an alarm was sounded, owing to the sighting in the offing of a vessel carrying the long pennant of a man-of-war, and having the appearance of a gunboat.   The whole force assembled to prepare for what might develop.   We felt assured that we had serious business on hand. Some field works were hurriedly thrown up, the cannon were brought into position, the men placed under whatever cover was available, and all made ready to give a hot reception to the Fenians.   As the vessel drew nearer to the harbor she hoisted the Stars and Stripes, and proved to be a United States gunboat, with General Sherman and other officers of the United States Army on board, out on a cruise.   Of course we were glad the scare terminated as it did, but it afforded talk for the boys for days   In case of a sudden alarm it had been arranged that the town bells were to be rung as well as to have the bugles sounded.   One morning we were so awakened, and orders followed sharply to turn out and fall in on the private parade ground, as the Fenians were landing at Bayfield, some ten or twelve miles away. How well I remember the excitement and confusion, men tumbling out of bed and putting on garments belonging to others, belts put on wrong side up or wrong side out, the bugles sounding the assembly, and sergeants hurrying up the laggards. At last the company was got into shape and we started for the market square on the double, a pace several could not keep up and had to fall out. On our arriving there we found other companies ahead of us and more news of an alarming character from the point named. We formed up, and fifty rounds of ball cartridge were served out to each man. Assisting in this I had an opportunity of noticing how serious were the faces of some of the men. There was a man there named Gregg, who, having a son in our company, had followed us to Goderich, and was on hand at that early hour to cheer and encourage us. He went and bought a cheese and a large box of biscuits, which he distributed among our men. In the rear of our company a body of citizens had lined up, having armed themselves with guns, rifles, or any implement of war they could lay their hands on, so as to take part in the expected scrimmage. The Goderich company headed the march down the Bayfield road to the tune of ' What jolly dogs are we.' We had not gone far when we were halted and found that the alarm had been a false one. Our stay at Point Edward was uneventful, our duty being the guarding of the Grand Trunk Railway station at that important point. From there," the gallant colonel said, in concluding, " we returned home full of glory, honor and pleasant memories."

While the volunteers were at Goderich the United Counties Council there held its June session. This was a fortunate thing for the volunteers, as it forcibly brought home to the members of the Council that it was only at a pecuniary loss and with great self-sacrifice, that these brave fellows had left their various employments and places of business to take up arms when called upon to do so in defence of their country. Realizing this, the Council voted that $10,000 be included in the levy of that year to supplement the government allowance paid the men. This was distributed on the basis of fifty cents a day to the family of each married man and twenty-five cents per day to each single man. The amounts so paid to the different companies from Bruce were as follows: Southampton, $940.25; Paisley, $389.50; Kincardine Village, $288.75; Kincardine Town-

ship, $334 25. In addition to this substantial expression of its feel-
ings, the County Council passed the following resolution: " That
the thanks of this County Council are hereby tendered to the volunteers now in Goderich for so promptly responding to the call for the
defence of our country against unprincipled and unprovoked
aggression, showing themselves ready to maintain the honor of the
British name. We would couple with this our thanks to all the
volunteers throughout the province, especially to those who, under
such trying circumstances for new troops, fought so nobly at Ridge-
way, sympathizing with them in the loss they there sustained "[1]

From the date of their organization until after their return from
Goderich the four volunteer companies in the county which had
been authorized existed as independent companies, but on the 14th
of September, 1866, these, with the two companies formed that summer at Walkerton and Tara, were by general order formed into the
" 32nd Bruce Battalion of Infantry," under the command of Lieut.-
Col Alexander Sproat.[2] The battalion, as such, assembled for the
first time in July, 1868, at Southampton and put in twelve days'
drill They were not under canvas on this occasion; a large temporary building had, however, been put up to accommodate the men.
This first assembly was marked by an unfortunate event which
occurred during a sham fight, in which three companies were under
the command of Col. Sproat and the three others under the com-

---

[1]See Appendix S for list of names of those to whom medals have
been given

[2]Lieut -Col. Alex Sproat was, on his father's side, of Scotch descent.
while his mother was a daughter of a U E Loyalist He was born in
the township of Esquesing in 1835 He graduated from Queen's College at
the age of nineteen, and entered the engineering staff of the Grand Trunk
Railway, then being constructed After the road was completed he commenced business as a provincial land surveyor, first at Elora, and afterward
(1856) at Southampton He filled the position of manager of the Commercial Bank, first at Southampton and then at Walkerton On the
failure of that institution he became manager of the Merchants Bank
in the latter place He was county treasurer from May, 1864, to December,
1873. Mr Sproat had the honor to sit for the riding of North Bruce
in the First Parliament of the Dominion of Canada As the law then
stood a member of the House of Commons might also sit in the Ontario
House of Assembly, so in 1871 Mr Sproat ran for the Ontario Legislature
in South Bruce, but met with a defeat, his opponent being the Hon
Edward Blake He was connected with the Volunteers of Bruce from 1861,
and was Colonel of the 32nd Battalion for some years In 1880 he received
the appointment of Registrar at Prince Albert, in the North-West Territories Being in the midst of the half-breed rising of 1885, he took an
active part in suppressing the same In religion he was a Presbyterian.
He married a daughter of Alex McNabb, Crown Land Agent, who survived
him. His death occurred August 20th, 1890

mand of Major W. C. Bruce. The command to charge was given by
one of the officers. As their opponents did not receive the order to
retire in proper time, but kept on firing with blank cartridge, two
of the men who were advancing at the charge were shot, receiving
powder marks in their faces which they would carry through life.
These men were under the care of the regimental surgeon all that
summer

The ladies of this county have always taken a keen interest in
our volunteers. Shortly after the battalion was organized they took
steps to present it with a handsome set of colors   About $600 was
collected for this purpose, with which the two handsome flags, which
are such a credit to the battalion, were purchased in London, England. The presentation of the colors was a red letter day in the history
of the 32nd Battalion. The ceremony took place at Kincardine, and
the presentation was made by Mrs Sproat in the name of the ladies
of the county of Bruce. The following is the address which was
read on that occasion:

" To the Officers and Soldiers of the 32nd Regiment,—

"I feel much gratified by the circumstances which have led to
this interesting and imposing ceremony now about to be performed,
and it is with much pleasure but great diffidence on my part that
I am here to-day on the part of the ladies of the County of Bruce.

"Soldiers of the 32nd, it has not been your lot to participate
in other than such peaceful campaigns as the one you are now about
to enter upon, but though you have never confronted the enemy, you
have shown in times past that you were prepared, not only to acquire
a knowledge of the military art, but to meet when required the
enemies of your country. The spirit and enthusiasm which on those
times actuated the soldiers sent forth from Bruce, I know, still are
yours   But remember, soldiers, that it is not by valor alone a regiment is distinguished. The allegiance sworn by you all to your
sovereign Lady the Queen, the pride which you have in the glorious
Empire of which we now form no inconsiderable and important a
portion, and the love which you bear to the land of your birth or
adoption will, I am sure, be ever present in your minds as in your
hearts, leading you to maintain the strictest discipline, and ever
to be prepared when called upon to guard the honor and dignity of
the Crown and to support the Laws and Constitution of our country,
to be true to the colors of your Sovereign, and by your sobriety and
good order, obedience and soldierly behavior to uphold, under all

circumstances, the character of the Regiment   In these respects I am confident you will never be found wanting.

" Officers and soldiers of the 32nd, I am now about to place in your hands these colors which are presented to you by the ladies of Bruce   In committing them to your charge, I may well rest assured that should unfortunately occasion arise for the display of your valor in the field, the men of Bruce will maintain their own and their country's honor, and will then be able to place on their colors the records of gallant services well and faithfully performed.

" With the colors I now present you, permit me also to offer the best wishes of the ladies of Bruce for your long-continued happiness and prosperity, and may our God protect you and yours in all times hence

" Dated this 19th June, 1872.

" E. W. SPROAT,
"<i>On behalf of the Ladies of the County of Bruce.</i>"</div>

The " Riel Rebellion " and the Red River expedition of 1870 could not but have an effect upon the volunteers of Bruce. On the decision being arrived at to send a body of troops under the command of Col. Wolseley, a certain number of volunteers were asked for. In the case of the 32nd Battalion the number was three from each company. How readily this was responded to is shown by the fact that ten of the Walkerton company answered to Captain Hunter's call for volunteers. The three of these selected were A. McVicar, Joseph Guinn and Samuel Dandy. A similar spirit was elsewhere manifested, but names cannot be given   All the representatives of the 32nd Battalion assembled at Paisley, from whence they were sent to London to be placed in the battalion of volunteers who formed part of the expedition   The various corps assembled at Collingwood in May, and early in June were taken by steamer to Thunder Bay. The exigencies of the expedition demanded the formation of a " transportation company," which was placed under the command of Thomas Adair, a 32nd Battalion man. He had under him eighty teamsters.[1] The object of this history does not require the following of the expedition any further. It was a bloodless one, and the only

[1]Among these were the following men of Bruce · From the township of Carrick—Jas Clendening, Wm McVicar, Duncan Kerr, Philip Miller, Alfred Hardy; from the township of Arran—D Love; from Culross—James Gilmour, J Gilroy; from Walkerton—F. Burnham, from Southampton—Hutchison Jackson, Donald Robertson, George Smith, J H. Slocombe; from the township of Amabel—Robert McFarlane; from Kincardine—John Kerr

fame was that of good conduct and of trying hardships endured, of which the men from Bruce obtained a good record.

For a number of years after this but little that is worthy of record occurred to mark the history of our volunteers

The following changes have occurred in the headquarters of different companies in the 32nd Bruce Battalion: In 1872, No. 3 Company had its headquarters changed from Kincardine Township to Lucknow, in 1881, No 1 Company had its headquarters changed from Southampton to Port Elgin; in 1883, No. 7 Company had its headquarters changed from Belmore to Mildmay, and again in 1895 to Wiarton.

The battalion went into camp for annual drill in different years at Southampton, Goderich, Windsor, Walkerton and London On nearly every one of these occasions the County Council supplemented the government allowance of pay by a grant,[1] an act which has done much to keep the ranks of the various companies filled with intelligent young men, so that the battalion with its fine band (also encouraged and aided by County Council grants) and its handsome stand of colors has, when in camp, carried off the palm as the best of the rural battalions in the brigade, and has been a credit to the county of Bruce.

The following very complimentary notice of the Bruce battalion appears in the report on the state of the militia by Major-General Luard, for 1881: "This fine battalion marched into camp, eight companies strong, with every commissioned officer and man present. As stores had been issued to supply deficiencies, and as each man had been provided with a linen haversack, they presented a creditable appearance. About 80 per cent. were recruits, but owing to the systematic manner in which the instruction was carried out, progress was noticeable from the commencement. The headquarters staff were encamped in such a position as to enable them to see much of this corps, and I can testify to the strict and honest manner in which the several duties and drills were performed. The only rural battalion with full officers and men in place. In battalion and

---

[1] The liberality of the County Council in bestowing grants to help the Volunteer movement has been very commendable. Besides repeatedly supplementing the pay of the men during attendance at annual drill, the County Council also gave, in 1895, $500 for the purchase of helmets for the battalion, improving its appearance greatly. In 1901 $300 was given to purchase a battalion mess tent, and in 1903 a valuable silver cup was presented, to be competed for annually by the several companies at the rifle ranges.

brigade drill the men moved very steadily; at the field day they acquitted themselves with great credit, not only by marching and general military bearing, but also in the steady and correct manner in which they advanced to attack. Lieut.-Colonel Cooper is zealous and efficient, and ably supported by Major Biggar and his other officers The corps is a credit to the county of Bruce The municipal authorities, like those of Oxford, have been very liberal towards their volunteers, this year supplementing the government pay by twenty-five cents per day to each, or a total of three dollars per man; with such substantial assistance the officers were enabled to bring out full companies Discipline and interior economy good; officers well uniformed. Armories and condition of arms, etc.: No. 1 Co, fair and much improved; 2, not clean; 3, very good; 4, 6, 7 and 8, fair; 5, indifferent" In a note the commander adds, "I noticed Lieut.-Col Cooper's efficiency."

In March, 1885, the rebellion in the North-West broke out.[1] The city battalions were the first called upon to furnish a contingent to suppress it, but as weeks went on it seemed that a larger force was required, and to the credit of the 32nd Bruce Battalion it[2] was ordered (May 11th, 1885) to the scene of conflict. Lieut.-Col. J. G. Cooper was at that time in command To No. 6 Company of Tara, under Captain John Douglass, belongs, on this occasion, the honor of being the first to report themselves ready, awaiting orders The battalion, consisting of 32 officers and 336 non-commissioned officers and men, divided into eight companies, assembled at Southampton on May 18th, and remained there expecting to be forwarded thence by boat to Port Arthur But the need for a larger force at the front had passed and so, after a stay of a fortnight in Southampton, the companies were ordered to return to their homes. Uneventful as this incident was in some respects, it showed, however, once more that the volunteers in the county of Bruce were possessed of the right spirit and could be depended upon to respond to their country's call to duty. The following resolution was

[1] In the first action, that at Duck Lake, which took place in this unfortunate rebellion, the first man slain was an erstwhile Bruce Volunteer, John Morton, at one time major in the 32nd Battalion. He was shot while leading a party of Prince Albert Volunteers Another 32nd Battalion man, Alex McNabb, was severely wounded in the same action. Morton's body lay for two days on the field where he fell, when his old friend, Lieut.-Col. Sproat (32nd Batt.), found the body and took it to his own home to be prepared for burial

[2] The 32nd was the second rural battalion ordered to the front In Chapter VIII. are to be found some other incidents illustrating public feeling over this affair.

passed by the County Council at its June session, 1885, shortly after the above incident: "This Council desire to place on record an acknowledgment of the sacrifices made by the volunteers of the county of Bruce in responding so readily to the recent call on them for service in the North-West, many of the men being compelled to throw up their situations, having since their return been unable to find employment, and all anticipating that their services would be required for some length of time, were put to much expense."

In common with the rest of the Empire, at the commencement of the war in South Africa, a desire was felt among the young men of Bruce to aid in the hour of the Empire's need About a score of our brave young fellows consequently were found in the ranks of various corps in South Africa, and gave a good account of themselves. Some of these were wounded, but only one laid down his life; Gordon Cummings was the name of this young hero, a title he nobly earned during the action in which he was slain The people of Bruce have done well in erecting a monument at Port Elgin, his native place, to commemorate his name and deeds. Lord Aylmer, the Adjutant-General of Canada, presided at the unveiling of the monument, which took place August 28th, 1903.[1]

In looking over a list of those who have held commissions or have been privates among our volunteers, we find the names of those who have been most prominent in the county, 'as members of parliament, judges, reeves, county officials, leading professional men, merchants, farmers and manufacturers; no class but what has contributed a representative. Some of these can claim having seen long service. The one who possibly earned the claim to be the longest associated with our volunteers was the late De W. H. Martyn, M D., surgeon of the battalion, who was a private in the Kincardine company when it was formed in 1862, and remained connected with the battalion until 1898. Captain John Douglass also had a long connection with the battalion, extending over 29 years; he retired in June, 1895. The "Long Service Medal" has been bestowed upon a number who have been connected with the 32nd Battalion; the names of those so honored are to be found in Appendix S

In closing this chapter of interest to the county, it will be fitting

---

[1]The inscription on the monument is as follows: '' In memory of Trooper Gordon Cummings, of Kitchener's Horse, killed at the battle of Nooitgedacht, South Africa, December 13th, 1900, while gallantly attempting to procure ammunition for his column Son of Patrick and Barbara Cummings Born in Saugeen, Dec., 1875 ''

to do so by mentioning the names of those who have had command of the battalion. They are as follows:

Lieut.-Col Alex. Sproat.[1] Commission dated 30th June, 1871.

Lieut.-Col. Jas. G. Cooper. Commission dated 11th February, 1881.

Lieut.-Col. John W. S. Biggar. Commission dated 7th April, 1887.

Lieut.-Col. B. B. Boyd. Commission dated 11th July, 1890.

Lieut.-Col. James H. Scott.[2] Commission dated 24th December, 1891

Lieut.-Col. Adam Weir. Commission dated 24th December, 1899.

Lieut -Col. Hugh Clark Commission dated 15th March, 1906.

The present regimental staff consists of Lieut.-Col Hugh Clark, Major W. J. Douglass; paymaster, Major J. Henderson; quartermaster, G W. Spence; surgeon, H. H. Sinclair; chaplain, Rev. S. F. Robinson   The above named, and also the captains of companies with the subaltern officers of the regiment, possess the full confidence of their men; while officers and men are alike in their desire to live up to the motto of the regiment, " Amor Patriæ."

---

[1]Capt A Sproat, No. 1 Company, received the appointment of Acting Lieutenant-Colonel, September 14th, 1866, and held that position until commissioned Lieutenant-Colonel as above

[2]Lieut -Col Scott was born at Simcoe, Ont., August 6th, 1858. He was educated at Simcoe High School, and called to the Bar in May, 1880. He resided from March, 1881, until the fall of 1902, at Kincardine, when he removed to Walkerton, to practise his profession in partnership with Alex Shaw, K C, the County Solicitor. He entered the active militia on June 11th, 1883, as Lieutenant in the 32nd Bruce Battalion; became Adjutant 15th May, 1885 (the regiment then being concentrated for active service in the North-West); was promoted Major, 13th January, 1888, and attained the command of the corps 24th December, 1891, being at that time the youngest commanding officer in the Canadian force On the expiration of time limit he retired, 24th December, 1899. He holds a first-class R S. I Certificate Politically he is a Conservative. He was one of the vice-presidents of the Young Men's Liberal-Conservative Convention of Ontario, held at Toronto, 1887, and was for a number of years president of the Liberal-Conservative Association of Centre Bruce In 1882 and 1887 he unsuccessfully contested West Bruce for the House of Commons. He was reeve of Kincardine for six years, and from 1888 to 1902, inclusive, was almost continuously a member of the Bruce County Council; ever efficient as a worker, his merits were recognized and he was made warden of the county in 1894 He is actively and prominently identified with many local organizations and fraternal societies. In the Orange and Royal Black Institutions he has been an active worker; is a Past County Master West Bruce, Junior Deputy Grand Master Provincial Grand Orange Lodge Ontario West, and recently was elected Most Worshipful Grand Master of the Grand Black Chapter of British America Col. Scott is a member of the Presbyterian Church. He was married, 1883, to Lizzie M., daughter of late Ald Wm. Stanley, of Toronto They have a family of two sons and a daughter.

CHAPTER XI.

THE INDIAN PENINSULA.

1854—1906.

· THE facts to be related in this chapter may, to some readers, be of a somewhat uninteresting character, but they could not be omitted in a history of the county of Bruce. The particulars here given refer to the throwing open for settlement of the Saugeen Peninsula, the Indian Land Sale, and the subsequent connection and dealings of the Indian Department with those settlers who undertook to settle on and open up the most unpromising part of the county. Only transactions affecting the peninsula as a whole, or at least of more than one municipality therein, will be here mentioned.

In the preceding paragraph the peninsula is referred to as the most unpromising part of the county, in support of which statement the author asks the reader to read the quotations from the reports of the county valuators, as given at the beginning of the chapters following, on each township. Good farming land in the peninsula is the exception, not the rule. Land that at one time had a fair amount of timber on it has been burned over by forest fires, and there now remains nothing but bare rock—square miles in extent in some places—on which a scanty growth of stunted trees is to be seen. What good soil there is, seems to be either in hollows filled by the wash from higher ground; or else land that at one time was a swamp, which having been drained has become excellent land yielding large crops, the township of Eastnor giving the best example of this. Notwithstanding the scarcity of large areas of good arable land, many of the settlers who have remained in the peninsula are to-day very well-to-do, while the stock that cattle buyers bring in large quantities to Wiarton for shipment speaks well of the possibilities of the peninsula as a stock-raising section The main resource of the peninsula in the past has been its timber; how long that will last is a mooted question.

By the treaty made with the Indians at Manitowaning in 1836, as related in Chapter I., the lands in the peninsula were to remain in their possession in perpetuity. On this point (speaking of the

Indians) a clause in the treaty reads as follows: "Proper assistance (shall be) given to enable you to become civilized, and to cultivate land, which your Great Father engages *forever* to protect for
you from the encroachments of the Whites." As the years rolled
by the demand for lands for settlement became imperative, so notwithstanding the above-mentioned agreement, the Indian chiefs
were approached, and after some parleying, consented to the making of another treaty (see Appendix A), which was concluded
October 13th, 1854, by which the Indians surrendered to the Crown,
in trust, all the lands in the peninsula with the exception of special
reservations mentioned, upon the following terms "That the
interest of the principal sum arising out of the sale of our lands be
regularly paid, to ourselves and our children in perpetuity, so long
as there are Indians left to represent our tribe, without diminution,
at half-yearly periods."

At the time of this surrender Lord Bury was Superintendent-
General of Indian Affairs. He seems to have taken measures without much delay to have the lands as above surrendered opened for
sale and settlement. To this effect he issued instructions April
26th, 1855, to Charles Rankin, P.L.S., of Owen Sound, to survey
the townships of Amabel and Keppel, and that part of the present
town plot of Southampton lying north of the Saugeen river. These
surveys Mr Rankin promised to have completed, and the plans prepared by the 1st October following. To accomplish this he had
three separate parties of surveyors at work. In the meantime the
Crown advertised a sale of these lands by auction, to be held at
Owen Sound on October 17th, 1855 Mr. Rankin, for some reason
not known to the author, expected to have been appointed the agent
to conduct this sale [1] The government had another appointee in
view, and on September 12th of that year Wm. R. Bartlett, of
Toronto, was notified that the position was his This was far from
satisfactory to Mr Rankin, and as a result of his displeasure, when
Mr. Bartlett reached Owen Sound he found that there were no plans
forthcoming of the lands advertised for sale; as a consequence, the
sale had to be postponed indefinitely. The heated correspondence
that followed between the Department and Mr Rankin, and the
stormy interview he had with Lord Bury, are to be found recorded
in a government blue book. The upshot of it all was, the plans were

---

[1] As the remuneration was 5 per cent upon all moneys derived from the
sale of the lands, the post was one well worth having.

promised to be supplied by April 30th, 1856, but Mr. Rankin did not get the appointment he desired.

After a delay of nearly a year, the sale of Indian lands was at length held at Owen Sound, the date being Tuesday, 2nd September, 1856. The auctioneer was J. G. Gale, of that town The particulars of the sale are so fully and explicitly given in Mr. Bartlett's official report that it is here given in full:

" TORONTO, NOVEMBER 20TH, 1856.

" *Sir,*—His Excellency the Governor-General having been pleased to entrust to me the conduct and management of the first auction sale of a portion of the Indian Territory in the Saugeen Peninsula, I have the honor to submit with my return all the Books and Maps connected therewith, and a Tabular Statement in detail, showing the result of the sale.

" The two southern townships, Keppel and Amabel, containing about 144,000, were the ones sold. Every lot was put up by the auctioneer, and of the whole number of acres offered, 35,364 were not bid for. They therefore remain over for the next sale

" The Town Plot of Southampton on the north side of the Saugeen River at its entrance to Lake Huron, comprising 38 park lots from 1 to 19 acres, and 279 town lots of about half an acre each, was included in the sale of these two townships, and every lot sold.

" The Town Plots of Oliphant and Wiarton, each containing 1,000 acres, laid out in town and park lots, are both situated in the Township of Amabel. These were not included in my instructions and were not brought forward They also remain for future disposal.

" 10s. 3d. an acre was the average upset price for farm lots and 18s. 6d. an acre the average rate at which they sold.

¹ STATEMENT SHOWING THE RESULT OF THE FIRST AUCTION SALE OF THE SAUGEEN INDIAN LANDS

Number of acres of farm land in the tract   144,000
Acres sold, 109,000 ; acres unsold, 35,000 = 144,000

	Farm Lots.	Park Lots	Town Lots.	Totals.
Total value at upset price.........	£55,823	£4,305	£1,950	£62,078
Total sale price . . .	£100,341	£10,609	£8,382	£119,332
Average upset price per acre . .	10/3	....	. .	. .
Average price per acre for which they sold .	18/6			
Average advance upon the upset price	80%	150%	325%	92%

Total amount sold £119,332
Upset value of unsold land 16;398

£135,730

" The farm lots sold at an average advance of 80 per cent.

" The park lots at an average advance of 150 per cent., and

" The town lots at an average advance of 325 per cent. on the upset prices.

" Some few remaining farm and park lots were also sold on what is termed the Half-mile Indian strip, a portion of which was formerly surrendered to the government by the Indians and sold for their benefit.

" It is to be supposed there will be some defaulters who will not make good their payments, but their number is comparatively small considering the large amount of land sold and instalments paid upon it.

" Assuming that the unsold farm lands sell at a future sale for no more than the upset price, which is a low amount to set them down at, seeing the average advance is 80 per cent. on their upset price, the whole produce of the two townships of Keppel and Amabel (exclusive of the Town Plots of Oliphant and Wiarton) will give for the benefit of the Indians the large sum of £135,730.

" The Au Sable Mill Site, comprising 1,100 acres of land offered at £2,000, sold for £2,390

" The Mill Site near Owen Sound containing 45 acres, put up at £500, sold for £760.

" The amount of the first Instalment of one-third of the purchase money, which has been paid into the Bank by the buyers at this sale, is £34,061 1s 7d. Cy.

" The Caughnawaga Tract, situated very advantageously on the Owen Sound Bay, the surrender of which was only obtained from the Indians during the progress of the late sale, though small, is reported to be good land. Instructions had been forwarded to me, by direction of His Excellency the Governor-General, to offer the same at the first sale, but having got through all the land and closed the auction two days before these Instructions reached me, and the people having nearly all dispersed and returned to their homes, many of whom had been waiting for this land, I felt that I could not in justice to the Department, and without causing much dissatisfaction, carry out that order This tract, will, therefore, remain to be offered at another sale.

" The large tracts of some of the best land in the Peninsula still held as reservation by these Tribes of Indians, and lying as they do upon the borders of the surrendered portions, are considered a great bar to the rapid settlement of those portions already sold. These lands are unoccupied and uncultivated and will probably remain in that state until they are given over to the management of the Department.

" If, therefore, a surrender of these reservations could be obtained, it would tend very much to the benefit of the tribes, and be the means not only of settling the County, but of adding materially to their income.

" Due notice having been given in the principal papers of the Province, the sale was commenced at Owen Sound, and continued for five days in succession. The audience was large and highly respectable, being composed chiefly of the yeomen of the country, and numbered throughout the days of sale upwards of 1,000 persons.

" The greater part of the farm lands were purchased by farmers, many of whom had been waiting more than a year for this opportunity of buying farms for themselves and their sons, and from the opening to the close of the sale the competition was keen and spirited. The greatest good order and good feeling prevailed amongst the buyers throughout the progress of the sale, and all expressed themselves well satisfied with the arrangements of the Department.

" I have the honor to be, sir,

" Your obedient servant,

" W. R. BARTLETT,

" *Agent for the Sale.*"

In Appendix V is given a copy of the advertisement announcing the Indian land sale. The conditions of the sale were: One-third of purchase money to be paid at time of purchase, while no conditions were attached regarding settlement or clearing of the land[1] or erecting of a house, such as were required by the Crown Lands Department of those who purchased in other parts of the county farm lots direct from the Crown. Conditions such as these, or rather the lack of conditions, attracted speculators, and their presence explains the high prices obtained, which, so the author has been informed by one in attendance at the sale, in the case of some farm lots ran up to $30 per acre, while for park lots at Southampton as high as $2,200 was bid. Later on the speculators realized how wild their bids had been and forfeited the one-third purchase money they had paid and threw up their purchases.

A protest from other parts of the county was made regarding the absence of any requirements in the matter of settlement duty, at this sale of Indian lands. Attention having been drawn to the

---

[1]On the lots fronting on the Centre Diagonal and the Saugeen and Sydenham roads, there was an exception as to conditions. In these cases the purchaser had, " within one year after the date of purchase, to cut and remove all the timber from the centre of the road to a depth of ninety feet."

omission, it was not long before a change was made in this respect, assimilating the practice of the Indian Department in this county somewhat to that of the Crown Lands Department. The later conditions are given in a footnote.[1] The author regrets that he is not able to give the date when the revised conditions first came into force

The fact that at first the Indian Land Office was not located anywhere in this district, but at Toronto, was a great inconvenience to settlers, owing to the slow mail service of those days long delays were inevitable in the transaction of business. This unsatisfactory state of affairs lasted until 1878, when the agency at Wiarton was opened. The first person appointed to act as agent there was B. B. Miller, who held the office until 1884, when he was succeeded by Wm. Simpson. In 1901, on the retirement of Mr. Simpson, the position was given to W. J. Ferguson, who still is in charge of the office. Another drawback to a satisfactory relation between the public and the officials was that the Indian Department existed and carried on its business irresponsible to the Government, the Indians and their affairs being a department that had as its head the English War Office, the Governor-General's secretary being *ex-officio* Superintendent-General of Indian Affairs This was changed, however, in 1868, when an Act was passed[2] establishing the Department of Secretary of State, and appointing the holder of that portfolio as the Superintendent-General of Indian Affairs This and subsequent changes have supplied the then much-felt need of a department responsible to Parliament, and that would be willing to listen to petitions asking for some remedy to the unsatisfactory position of affairs which had given rise to so much discontent among the settlers.

That the reader may have some idea of the grounds for the discontent referred to in the last paragraph, the following particulars

---

[1]The amended conditions of purchase, which were in force from an early date, were as follows One-fifth of the money to be paid at the date of sale, the balance to be paid in four equal consecutive yearly instalments bearing interest at 6 per cent. Settlement was required, actual occupation and improvements to commence within six months from the date of sale, and to be continuous for a period of three years previous to the issue of the patent, within which time there should be cleared and fenced at least five acres upon each parcel of land containing one hundred acres A dwelling house not less than 24 x 18 feet was to be erected. Nonfulfilment of any of these conditions might cause cancellation and forfeiture of purchase money Until the patent was issued, it was necessary to obtain from the Land Agent a license to sell wood or timber, but such license did not permit the selling of pine.

[2]31 Vic. Chap 42

are given. The first has reference to undue partiality given to some who bought at the first sale for purely speculative purposes, and is an extract from a speech made by the member for North Bruce in Parliament (session of 1869). Mr Sproat said: Extravagantly high prices were given, but speculators who then had bought three lots at ruinous prices, had been allowed to apply the payment of the one-third of purchase money, made at time of sale upon the three lots, to one of them, for which he got a patent, and then abandoned the other two lots, while actual settlers who had bought only one lot got no equivalent privilege. He believed the one-third of purchase money, required at time of sale, would in most cases represent more than the value of the lot, and he hoped some plan would be adopted to relieve settlers of two-thirds of the price. There were many other grounds of complaint, some of which were set forth in a series of motions passed at a meeting held March 19th, 1872, at which the reeves and prominent men of the district were present. The various motions passed were to the effect: (1) That this meeting petition the Governor-in-Council to appoint a local agent in some central place to transact all business in connection with Indian lands that is at present transacted at Toronto; (2) To make a grant of money for the improvement of the roads in the several municipalities, as an equivalent for taxes lost on lands resumed by the Indian Department; (3) To appoint a commissioner to re-value the unsold lands in the Peninsula with a view of promoting actual settlement of the same; (4) To cause to be re-valued such lands as have been sold at an exorbitant price, or lands of inferior quality on which the whole purchase money has not yet been paid; (5) To appoint a commissioner to confer with the Indian owners of these lands with a view of securing the purchase of the whole Indian Peninsula from them by the government; (6) That all unsold lands in the Peninsula be brought into the market, to be sold to actual settlers only. At the same time a deputation was appointed to visit Ottawa and confer with the government. As a result of the foregoing, the Indian Department announced, shortly after the visit of the deputation, that it would consider cases of special hardships. Liberal concessions were also made, but the author has not been able to learn their exact nature, except that Wm. Bull, clerk of the township of Amabel, was appointed to make a valuation of the lands and report to the government.

The Hon. David Laird, Minister of the Interior, came in the

summer of 1875 to investigate personally the grievances complained
of. He drove through parts of the Peninsula, inspecting the lands
and the circumstances of the settlers, with the result that a re-valuation of the lands was subsequently made, this work being done, so
the author has been told, by a Mr. McKay, who resided at or near
Ottawa. Mr. Laird, on his return to the capital, announced: "That
he had been authorized to grant such measures of relief at once that
shall be just to both the settlers and the Indians interested. That
each settler's case would be dealt with on its own merits, and that
all interest would be remitted up to the end of that year (1875)."
The timber dues were at the same time slightly reduced. In a footnote[1] is given the scale of timber dues in force at the time of Mr.
Laird's visit, which must have been a burden to the settlers.

The re-valuation of lands just mentioned was not to be the final
one. A sense that full justice had not been rendered by the Indian
Lands Department was felt by many a settler, who finding existence
on a farm lot which contained more rock than tillable land a hard
one, readily brooded over any rightful grievance he might have, so
complaints and protests were forthcoming. At length sufficient
pressure was brought to bear to force the government to take action,
which took the form of the appointment of two commissioners, John

[1]Scale of Timber Dues in Force in the Saugeen Peninsula, 11th
February, 1873.

Oak, squared timber, 1,000 cubic feet $30 00
Oak, saw-logs, per 1,000 feet, inch measure 5 00
Red pine, tamarac, elm, beech, ash, maple or hickory, per 1,000 feet,
    cubic measure 16 66
Red pine, tamarac, elm, beech, ash, maple or hickory saw-logs, per
    1,000 feet, inch measure 3 00
White pine, cedar and spruce, per 1,000 cubic feet 15 00
White pine, cedar and spruce saw-logs, per 1,000 feet, inch measure   1 60
Pine Staves, per 1,000, standard 15 00
West India Staves, per 1,000, standard 5 00
Railway ties, tamarac, cedar or pine, per 1,000 ....   3 00
Telegraph poles, per 100 . . ..   8 00
Cedar pickets, per 100 .. . .   3 00
Tamarac knees, lineal measurement, per 1,00 feet 16 66
Shingle bolts, per cord 0 60
Shingle bolts, in advantageous localities 0 70

Cordwood

Hard, per cord 0 30
Hard, per cord, in advantageous localities 0 40
Soft, per cord 0 20
Soft per cord, in advantageous localities 0 25
Hemlock, per 1,000 cubic feet 7 50
Hemlock, 1,000 feet, inch measure 0 80
Hemlock bark, per cord .. . . :......   0 50

Irwin and George Elliott, to make another re-valuation of the lands in the Peninsula. This they did in 1897 and 1898. The result of their report was that the Department made large reductions in favor of the settlers, although in some instances an advance was made in the price at which certain lots were held.

A form of unfair treatment much complained of while it lasted, was the granting to large lumber companies the privilege of cutting timber on lands owned by settlers. The British and Canadian Timber and Lumber Co., of which H. H. Cook, M.P., was manager, was one of such, privileged by license to denude the land to the settlers' loss. In the case of this company, especially, it was decided to energetically protest, so a deputation consisting of Charles Webster, David Dinsmore, Dr. S. Wigle and William Baker proceeded to Ottawa to lay this grievance of the settlers before the government. This was about 1880, Parliament being in session. John Gillies, the representative from North Bruce, unfortunately for the interests of the deputation, sat on the Opposition benches. That their interests might not suffer thereby he asked Alex. Shaw, the member for South Bruce, a supporter of the government, to introduce the deputation. The strength of the opposition to the relief sought, lay in the fact that the license holders were largely government supporters. Mr. VanKoughnet, the head of the Indian Department, stated that it was and always had been the policy and practice of the government to renew these licenses. Mr. Shaw, being in full sympathy with the request of the settlers, finding no headway in their interests was being made, got Sir D. L. Macpherson, the Minister of the Interior, to go with him and argue the question before the Premier, Sir John A. Macdonald. This was successfully done, and the order was finally given to cancel the licenses complained about.

The next grievance under which the Peninsula suffered and for which redress was sought was one not of the individual settler, but of the township municipalities, the complaint being the loss of taxes arising from the cancelling (by the Indian Department) of land sales because of the non-fulfilment of settlement duties. The effect of these cancellations was that the land was resumed by the Crown, and as Crown lands are not liable to be taxed, any arrears of taxes charged against the lands referred to became void and were lost to the municipality. In 1887 the County Council petitioned against the wholesale cancellations lately made. The petition set forth the large sums lost in consequence by the municipalities, which for the yeais 1884-5-6, in the case of Albemarle amounted to over $700, in that of Eastnor to about $850, and in that of the united townships of Lindsay and St. Edmund to over $3,000. The Superintendent-General of Indian Affairs declined to change the practice, the reason assigned being that the Indians interested in the sale of lands in the Peninsula objected to any portion of the sum received from land sales being given to municipalities The Indians were not the only ones to derive pecuniary benefit from the cancelling of land sales, there were some holders of unpatented lots, men whose sense of rectitude and honor was defective, who perceived how the practice of cancellation might be turned to their profit. The process was simple. Means were used to get the Department to cancel their purchase; this freed the land from all claims for taxes; an immediate re-purchase was then made, with the result of a loss of one, two or three years' taxes to the municipality in which their lots lay.

From the day the first settler in the Peninsula sought a place on which to locate, down to the present, the question of roads has been one of much prominence This has been because of the many rocky or swampy tracts existing in that part of the county through which roads had to be made These territorial features have also resulted in the settlers, in many localities, being much scattered. As an offset to these disadvantageous features may be mentioned the ready access to the Peninsula by water, navigation being available to bring settlers and their effects to within a moderate distance of any point at which they chose to settle. There are two main routes for north and south traffic through Albemarle, Eastnor and Lindsay, one on the Georgian Bay side of the Peninsula, the other on the Lake Huron side; the latter of these was the first to be opened. That part of this road passing through Albemarle seems to have been opened gradually during the sixties,[1] and by the autumn of 1870 this road had not only been opened through Eastnor, but had been pushed forward two miles into Lindsay. The work in these two townships was paid for by grants received for the purpose. The author is unable to state the number of grants made by the government towards the opening of roads in the Peninsula with the exception of the two here given; in 1892 the Provincial Legislature made a grant of $1,800 for this purpose, which in 1895 was followed by a grant of $1,000 received from the Dominion Government. The most liberal contributor towards

[1]The by-law authorizing the deviations north of Mar was passed, March 14th, 1866

improving the roads throughout the Peninsula has been the County
Council, which has been most generous in the matter of road grants
to this portion of the county, the total amount of which would run
up into. many thousands of dollars.

A poor harvest and bush fires in 1884 impoverished many a settler
in the four northern townships. To relieve the then existing distress,
a commission was appointed in the following spring. As the report
of this commission, as made to the County Council, covers all the
facts, it is here given in full as follows:

"The Commissioners appointed by the Ontario Government
and the Warden on behalf of the County Council, to relieve the
distress existing in the northern townships, beg to report as follows: That upon being notified of their appointment, and the
amounts granted for said purpose, namely, $700 by the Ontario
Government, and $300 by the County Council, in addition to the
sum of $350 that was granted to the townships of Eastnor, Lind-
say and St Edmund at the January session of this Council, to
be expended upon roads in those municipalities, we proceeded to
Lion's Head, in the township of Eastnor, in company with John
Gillies, M.P.P., and the Warden, Mr. Potts, and attended a meeting
of the settlers called by Mr. Alex. Chisholm, the reeve of that township, which was largely attended by settlers from nearly the whole
of the northern peninsula, and after hearing their statements and
reviewing a list of names of applicants for assistance that had been
prepared by a committee formed there previously for that purpose,
and also consulting with several parties well acquainted with the
matter in hand, a list was prepared giving the names and the amount
of grain to be distributed to each individual, a copy of which is
attached. This the Commissioners found to be a rather difficult task
to perform, and occupied their time fully from 2 o'clock in the afternoon until 2 o'clock the next morning, and it was found upon totalling the list and estimating the cost, that the amount would exceed
the sum granted, and therefore a proportionate reduction had to be
made upon the whole list to bring it within the sum at the disposal
of the Commission. Up to the present time, as near as possible,
giving in round figures, 500 bushels potatoes, 200 bushels barley, 400
bushels oats, 200 bushels peas, 7 tons of flour, and 1,600 pounds of
oatmeal have been purchased, copies of the invoices of which are
also attached to this report. These, together with freight, bags, and
a few incidental expenses, amount to about $1,100, leaving a balance
of $250 still in the hands of the Commissioners. But additional
applications for assistance have been received. It was learned while
the Commission sat at Lion's Head that such would be the case, as
some settlements had not received notice of the meeting called at
Lion's Head. This was unavoidable on account of the shortness of
the time, as the season was already far advanced, and grain had to

be purchased at a distance and brought in, all of which consumed valuable time. The idea of allowing the Commission a small margin for claims likely to come in afterwards was a wise one, as a number of cases of extreme poverty have since been reported and relief granted. The grain supplied has been all distributed. The Commission appointed Mr Chisholm to attend to the distribution at Lion's Head, where it was all distributed, with the exception of a very small amount granted to residents in the township of Albemarle, which was distributed at Wiarton as being more convenient for the residents of Albemarle The parties receiving the supplies have all been required to give an undertaking that they will perform road-work at the rate of 1.00 per day for the amount they have received, with the exception of about ten families who received aid gratuitously, being in indigent circumstances.

"JOHN McIVER,

"Commissioner for Ont. Government.

"A. M. TYSON,

"Commissioner for Co. of Bruce."

The mail service throughout the four northern townships has been none too frequent at any time, so that an early effort to get into touch with the outside world by electric telegraph is not to be wondered at. The prospect of business, however, was not sufficient to warrant the telegraph company to construct a line beyond Colpoy's Bay, where it had an office, although it might be so to operate it. To assist along this much-to-be-desired project the County Council, on the motion of Robert Watt and J. H. Whicher, in January, 1884, voted $150 towards the cost of carrying the electric telegraph to Lion's Head This grant was supplemented from other sources, with the result that in 1887 the telegraph company opened an office for business at Lion's Head Points to the north of "The Head" also wanted to be favored in like manner. In the welfare of his constituents of this locality, Alex. McNeill, the member for North Bruce, got the Toronto Board of Trade to petition the Dominion Government for a grant to carry the telegraph line through to Tobermory, urging the advantage it would be to the shipping interests. What aid was granted the author is not prepared to say, but the line was opened to Tobermory in October, 1887. This office at first and for many years was only open during the season of navigation. The advent of the telephone into the peninsula is due to the enterprise of a single individual, Robert Gillies With some outside assistance he in 1900 or 1901 constructed a line through from Wiarton north as far as Lion's Head, via Mar and Spry Since then he has pushed it forward until now Tobermory can be telephoned to. Much credit is due to Mr. Gillies for what he has done to bring to the Peninsula one of the conveniences of modern life, and it is pleasing to know that he has found the venture a remunerative one.

As mentioned in Chapter VII., the advent of a railway throughout the entire length of the peninsula was confidently expected in 1900-1. These hopes are, for the time being at least, doomed to be disappointed.

In closing this chapter the author would be pleased to write in words prophetic of a glowing future for the Indian Peninsula, but its physical features are such that he cannot conscientiously do so. The men of the north, however, are sturdy and energetic as any that settled in other parts of the county of Bruce. Knowing this, it is difficult to prognosticate what they may accomplish in the development of the Indian Peninsula.

CHAPTER XII.

TOWNSHIP OF AMABEL.[1]

EXTRACT FROM THE REPORT OF COUNTY VALUATORS, 1879.

"Amabel —There is a considerable amount of ordinary land on the south side of this township, the north side is mostly rock, interspersed with lakes and swamps, the east end is wet, sandy land; the west end sandy hills It has a considerable amount of village property. Its average price is $11 58 "

EXTRACT FROM THE REPORT OF COUNTY VALUATORS, 1901.

"This is the most southern township of what is now known as the Bruce Indian Peninsula While there are a number of very good farms in this township, the large majority are the reverse. There is a great deal of rock from the 10th concession north, and thousands of acres are almost valueless, indeed, as you will observe by our figures, that a large number of lots are set down as of no use whatever at present, and no prospective value The northwestern part is sand and considerable of it hilly; it is almost unproductive and has a deserted appearance. A great many of the small habitations being unoccupied, people have existed on these lots so long as the timber lasted, after which they got up and left them We see no bright future for this section.

"There are a few hundred acres about two miles south-west of Wiarton as good as any we have come across in the county The soil of the southern half of the township is fairly good, but a great deal of it is hilly, and roads are hard to make on this account. Amabel is well watered, the Sauble River enters at the south-east and merges with the waters of Lake Huron at the north-west.   There are a number of other small streams that give an abundant supply for stock, etc.

"The rate per acre for this township is $13 26; of this sum the village property amounts to $1 21 per acre "

FOLLOWING the chapter on the Indian Peninsula it seems appropriate, in taking up the history of each municipality in the county separately, to commence with those situated in the Peninsula; which arrangement the author will proceed to carry out, commencing with the most southerly of them, the township of Amabel.

[1] "Amabel "—" Named after Lady Amabel, sister of Lord Bury and wife of Sir Edmund W. Head—Lord Bury seems to have imposed his family names on the peninsula "—" *Nothing but Names.*"

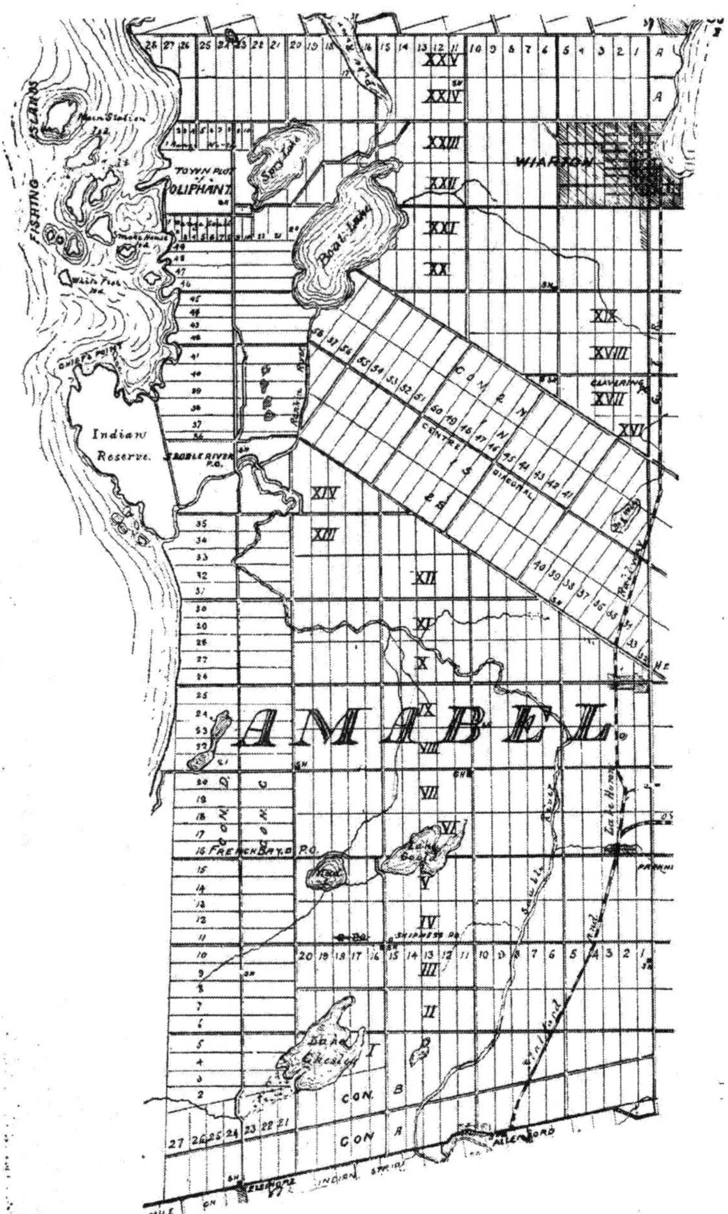

AMABEL
WIARTON
FISHING ISLANDS
TOWN PLOT of OLIPHANT
Boat Lake
Indian Reserve.
CHIEFS POINT
SAUBLE RIVER P.O.
CLAVERING
FRENCH BAY P.O.
CON B
CON A
ALLENFORD
INDIAN STRIP

As stated in the preceding chapter, this township was surveyed in 1855, and the lands therein offered for sale, September 2nd, 1856, by auction at Owen Sound. Unfortunately for the development of the township, large tracts of land were purchased at this sale by speculators, with the result that it was a long time before the effects were overcome of the mistaken policy which had permitted lands to be sold without conditions of actual settlement being attached.

David Forsyth is credited with being the first settler in the township, he having squatted on some land near Elsinore before the Land Sale. The next settler was James Allen,[1] who settled on lots 9 and 10, concession A, in April, 1857. The village of Allenford which developed there preserves the name of its founder. The settlement of the township along the south and south-eastern parts was made as rapidly as could be expected when remembering that large blocks of land were held by speculators. The first to take up land in the vicinity of Colpoy's Bay was William Bull,[2] who settled in the spring of 1857 north of Wiarton, on the boundary line betwixt Amabel and Albemarle. In the fall of the same year he had as a neighbor Alexander Greig, who settled on lot 14, concession 25. As he was one of the first to settle in that part of the township, and as his experience was also that of many who settled in that vicinity, the following narrative, based on a sketch written by himself some years prior to his death, is here given: Alexander Greig was born in Scot-

[1] James Allen came from the north of Ireland in 1832, when a boy six years of age, with his parents, who settled in Peterboro' County In 1850 he moved to the county of Grey and was reeve of the township of Holland for a year or so. As stated above, he settled in Amabel in April, 1857. He took an active part in municipal affairs, filling the office of reeve of the united townships of Amabel and Albemarle for the years 1867, 1868, 1869, and after the separation of the townships was reeve of Amabel from 1870 to 1879, inclusive, and also for the years 1884, 1886, and 1887. The fact that for sixteen years he filled the highest position in the township tells its own tale as to the merits and popularity of Mr. Allen. He died April 4th, 1895, aged 69.

[2] Mr. Bull was a native of Essex, England, where he was born September 17th, 1823. He came to this country in early life and was married at Ottawa, in 1844, to Ann Barward Moving to the county of Perth, he first tried his hand at farming, giving it up to teach school at Mitchell, and later at Owen Sound In the spring of 1857 he settled near Colpoy's Bay, on the twenty-fifth concession of Amabel, the pioneer settler of that part of the township. Mr. Bull was the first clerk and treasurer of Amabel, filling the first-named office for nineteen years, from 1861 to 1879, and the office of treasurer from 1861 to 1867. The Government engaged Mr Bull to make the first revaluation of lands in the peninsula. In 1882 Mr. Bull received the appointment of Indian Agent at Cape Croker, which office he held until the time of his death, which occurred May 17th, 1884

land in 1832 and came out to Canada with his bride in 1857. He was present at the Land Sale held at Owen Sound in September, 1857, and purchased the lands he subsequently occupied, both in Amabel and Albemarle. Going back to Collingwood, where his household effects were, and securing necessary supplies, he and his wife sailed from there by schooner for Colpoy's Bay. Great was his surprise and disappointment to find, on his arrival, that Wiarton existed only in name. Finding a deserted surveyor's shanty, the women of his party were placed therein for shelter. The only settler in the locality was William Bull, but as he was absent when Mr. Greig and party arrived, the place seemed " a lone, vast wilderness." Following the surveyor's blaze they were enabled to locate their lots. That fall they assisted Mr. Bull in taking up his crop of potatoes, which service Mr. Bull reciprocated by assisting them to cut a road through the bush to their lots. Owing to his inexperience as a woodsman, it took four or five weeks to construct their first shanty. Some time in the month of October, Ludwick Spragge and his father came in a boat from Owen Sound to Mr. Bull's to fetch his bride to Owen Sound to be married. Mr. Greig took passage with them, with the purpose of securing a stock of supplies for the winter. The return party consisted of Messrs. Greig, Bull, Andrew Horn and William Patton. An overloaded boat and heavy weather resulted in their being shipwrecked on the Keppel side of Colpoy's Bay, and in losing nearly everything they had purchased   Not to be daunted, and also forced by the necessities of the case, Messrs. Bull and Greig built a boat and started in November on a second trip to Owen Sound. They again met with very severe weather, which severely tested their frail craft and their seamanship, and placed them in danger of a second shipwreck. However, they returned to the bay in safety, and by Christmas were comfortably settled for the winter. A big hemlock stood back of the shanty they had erected, a severe storm which visited them about this time threatened to fling to earth this monarch of the forest, and the household were filled with dread lest it should fall on and crush their dwelling. As soon as the weather calmed we started, said Mr. Greig, to " beaver " the hemlock. It was the first big tree any of us had attempted to cut down, and so we worked all around it just as a beaver would do, until it was about to fall   We were beginning to congratulate ourselves as to the result of our labors, feeling sure it would clear the shanty; but as fate would have it, as it fell it struck a stout sapling, which diverted its

fall so that it struck the roof of our shanty, breaking it in but doing
no damage to the walls. After this accident the house could never
be made comfortable, and we had to build another one. That winter
we made a contract with Hugh and William McKenzie to chop five
acres. The result was a good object lesson in the work of a
backwoodsman. They took us along and showed us how to fell
a tree, how to trim off and pile the brush so as to make it fit for
burning, besides other things every skilled woodsman should know.
The trees then felled were, says Mr. Greig, the first large trees I
ever saw cut down with an axe. By the following midsummer eleven
acres were ready for logging, and in the fall of 1858 Mr. Greig
thrashed with a flail twenty-five bushels of wheat and ground the
same in a coffee mill. The first assessor, T. Roberts, made his rounds
in May, 1859. Mr. Greig's assessment was $200 real, and personal
property *nil.* In 1861 he took thirty bushels of wheat to Owen Sound
by boat, but to his great disappointment there was no market for it
there He could not sell it for either cash or·trade, and had to leave
it at a mill to be ground into flour. The County Council did something that year in opening up the county line, and shortly after a
market for grain was established at Owen Sound About this time
a flour mill was erected by Ludwick Kribs at Colpoy's Bay Unfortunately it lacked a smut machine; as a consequence the flour there
ground was mixed with particles of smut, and the bread made from
it looked as if it were varnished with black lead No ill results,
however, followed the eating of it. It was in the early sixties before
Mr. Greig received cash for any produce grown on his farm, an
experience common to all in the early settlement days. After the
many hardships endured and overcome Mr. Greig passed away, some
forty-five years after he had settled on his bush farm.

The following are the names of those who are credited with
having entered the township in the first year of its settlement: James
Allen, Thomas Knox and John Griffin, in the vicinity of Allenford;
David Forsyth, near Elsinore; James Howe, William Burwash,
William Carson, Isaiah Wilmont, John Murray, Andrew and Angus
McIntosh and James Rushton, near Chesley Lake; William Simpson
and Henry Lewis, at Parkhead; and as neighbors of Alexander Greig,
on the north boundary, William Bull, F. Thompson, Andrew Horne,
William Patton and James Henderson. The early settlers who came
in shortly afterwards were: William White, John and Ed. Loucks,
Andrew Kidd, R. Rutherford, Joseph M. Gunn, R. Webster, Thomas

Ireland, John Aikens, Robert Fraser, Thomas Cascaden, Edward E. Bolton, Thomas Innis, James Montgomery, S. Nelson, S. Burrows, George Wain,[1] Donald McLeod, James Mason, R. Evans, P. Arnott, William Evans, H. Kirkland, E. Blakely, D. Berry, W. Driffel, P. Anderson, Peter Brown, Robert Davis, William Sharp[2] and Thomas Askin. The settlement of Amabel Township has been by no means rapid, as the following census returns show: In 1861 the population was 182, in 1871 it was 1,805, in 1881 the number was 3,046; this rose in 1891 to 3,890, but in 1901 a decrease is shown, the population being only 3,587. The paucity of the population throughout the Indian Peninsula for some years after being open for settlement is evidenced by the fact that at the general election of 1867 the only polling booth north of Arran on the Peninsula was at Parkhead.

For a long time Amabel fared badly in the matter of roads, in fact, it was not until the scheme for a system of gravel roads for the whole county was carried out that the township possessed a good road. In 1865 the road variously known as the North Gravel Road, or the Owen Sound post road, was chopped and cleared. In the same year Denney's bridge was erected. These two improvements gave ready access to Southampton. In the following year this road was gravelled. It seems strange that this important highway should have been delayed so long in being opened. The " B " line, one concession to the north, being cleared earlier, the traffic passed over it westward, by way of the " Gimby Trail," to Southampton A word about the " Gimby Trail,"[3] which was the sole route for east and west travel between Owen Sound and Southampton prior to 1852, and for the settlers along the front of Amabel for many a day. This trail, which at the best had only some underbrushing done to distinguish it from the rest of the forest, struck out from the Saugeen Indian village almost due east, and entered Amabel at the " B " line, then bending towards the south-east and cutting across farm lots, it reached a point a little west of where Elsinore now is, thence along the front

---

[1]George Wain was drowned while crossing the Saugeen River on the ice. He was collector of taxes; his roll went with him into the river, and also the team and its load Weeks after his body and the roll were found. This sad event occurred April, 1864.

[2]First postmaster at Allenford

[3]To make this old Indian trail passable for sleighs, a contract was let in 1855 to a man of the adjoining township of Derby, named Gimby, whose name was bestowed upon the trail. It is said that a wheeled vehicle never passed over it, only sleighs in winter and " jumpers " in summer.

of the "Half-mile Strip" to about lot 35, when the trail passed into Arran Keeping well to the south of the bend of the Sauble and crossing the river at lots 29 and 28, at a point known as " Drift-wood Crossing," the trail again reached the front of the lots on the "Half-mile Strip," and then followed the general course of the present gravel road until the county line was reached. Through the township of Derby the trail followed rather a zig-zag course until near Owen Sound.

The township of Amabel, for municipal purposes, was attached to the township of Arran in December, 1856. This union lasted for four years. In 1861 the townships of Amabel and Albemarle were separated from Arran and formed into a separate municipal corpora-tion.[1] This union was dissolved, after existing for nine years, and as a separate municipal corporation Amabel has existed since 1870. The separation of Amabel and Albemarle from Arran resulted in a long and expensive lawsuit over the proper amount of indebtedness to be assumed by the young municipality just entering into corporate existence. This matter is more fully referred to[2] in the chapter on " Arran." The first Council of the united townships of Amabel and Albemarle was elected January, 1861, and consisted of Ludwick Kribs, James Allen, William Simpson, William Burwash and Edward E. Bolton. Mr. Kribs was chosen reeve, William Bull was appointed clerk and treasurer, R. H. Murray, assessor. The assessment roll for that year contained only 63 names, with an assessment of only $21,600. The development of Amabel is shown by contrasting these figures with the assessment of 1903, which is $676,805. In the same connection the following items from this last-mentioned roll are interesting: Acres of cleared land, 25,397; swamps and waste land, 28,918 acres; woodlands, 6,764 acres. The following are the names of those who have been reeves of Amabel from the first. As reeves of the united townships of Amabel and Albemarle: Ludwick Kribs for 1861, 1862, 1864, 1865 and 1866; James Howe, 1863; James Allen, 1867, 1868, 1869. As reeves of the township of Amabel: James Allen, 1870 to 1879, inclusive, and 1884, 1886 and 1887; David Porter, 1880, 1881, 1882, 1883, 1885; Joseph M. White, 1888, 1889, 1890, 1891; Thomas Askin, 1892, 1893, 1894, 1895; William Beatty, 1896; J. E. Campbell, 1897, 1898; Joseph R. Chambers,

[1]The by-law effecting this being passed by the County Council, Sep-tember 26th, 1860.

[2]Also see 15 U. C. Chancery Report, p 701, and 17 U. C. Chancery Report, p. 163

1899, 1900; Cecil Swale, 1901, 1902; John Robinson, 1903, 1904, 1906, and John Armstrong in 1905. It would be like the play of "Hamlet," with Hamlet left out, if in writing the history of the municipal affairs of the township of Amabel the name of R. H. Murray, the present township clerk, was left out. As recorded above, he was the first assessor of the township, a position he held for twenty-one years. He was collector one year, and also received the appointment of township treasurer, but resigned on being offered the clerkship in 1885. This position he now holds. Mr. Murray was born in Sutherlandshire, Scotland, September 21st, 1840. He came with his parents to Canada in 1857, settling in Amabel that year. Mr. Murray's long association with the municipal affairs of the township has made him an invaluable officer. Allenford has been his place of residence for a number of years. There he conducts an agency and conveyancing business. Active and enthusiastic in all work he undertakes, and maintaining the goodwill of the community, it is the wish of all that he may be enabled to fulfil his many duties for years to come. The township of Amabel has not always been as fortunate in the trustworthiness and efficiency of its officers as in the case of the one just recorded. It is regrettable to have to record that the township has lost heavily by trusted officials. In 1890 the collector of taxes, who had filled this post for some years previous, was a defaulter to the extent of about $2,000. His estate yielded something, but as the costs of a lawsuit to collect the same were heavy, the net loss to the township was not far from the above-mentioned amount. In February, 1902, a fire of unaccountable origin consumed the house of the then township treasurer, and with it, so he claimed, about $2,500 of township funds. The township undertook to recover from the guarantee company, which had given a bond securing the municipality. A compromise was made between the corporation and the company by the latter paying $500 in full of all claims. The township lost in this instance, it is supposed, about the same as in the case of the collector of taxes.

While writing upon the municipal affairs of Amabel, the liberal action of the township in granting a bonus to the Stratford and Huron Railway Company must not be overlooked. A bonus of $40,000 was granted in November, 1878, but nine months later, when it was seen that more assistance was needed to complete the construction of the railway to Wiarton, an additional grant of $3,000 was made, the total being $43,000. Of this large sum Wiarton assumed $4,000 on its incorporation as a separate municipality. The Township Council failed unpardonably, in the first years after the debenture by-law came into operation, to provide a sinking fund to pay the debentures at maturity. It was 1885 before the nucleus of a sinking fund was made. The consequence of this neglect was that when the debentures fell due in 1898, there was only $21,200 on hand to meet them. Recourse was made to Parliament, which passed an Act[1] authorizing the issue of $21,800 worth of debentures to supply the deficiency in the sinking fund. The railway has proved of great benefit to the township, supplying it with five stations from which produce might be shipped. Large as was the bonus given, the township has been fully recouped therefor.

The first school in the peninsula was on concession B, Amabel, north of Elsinore, which was opened in 1863. In the succeeding year a second school was opened, this at Chesley Lake, and in the fall of 1865 a third, this latter at Allenford.

In the original survey of the township of Amabel two town plots were laid out, both near the northerly end of the township. Of these, Oliphant is near the westerly terminus of the "Diagonal" road (which road extends from near Owen Sound to Lake Huron in the vicinity of the Fishing Islands). The other town plot, Wiarton, is situated on the county line at the point where it touches Colpoy's Bay. This town has been successfully developed, and demands a chapter of this history to itself, so that here it will be no more than mentioned. "Oliphant" was named after Laurence Oliphant, who in 1854 was Superintendent-General of Indian Affairs. As related in Chapter I., he in that year negotiated with the Indians the surrender of the Saugeen Peninsula. This town plot has been a disappointment, never developing even into a village. Being close to the Fishing Islands, hopes were entertained as to its becoming a business centre; when these failed to materialize, after some thirty years of waiting, its numerous town lots were re-surveyed and made into park lots for farm purposes. The locality attracts summer visitors from Wiarton and other places, who have erected summer cottages in which they may enjoy the healthful breezes that blow over Lake Huron and the restful environment of the place. The post-office of Oliphant was established in 1874.

"Allenford" (named after James Allen, as previously stated),[2]

[1] 61 Vic. Chap 37.
[2] This point was known by the Indians as " Drift Wood Crossing "

was surveyed in 1867, and its post-office was established in 1868[1]
It is situated about half-way between Southampton and Owen Sound
on the North Gravel Road, and has a railway station. This little
burg has not made much progress of late years, and it is difficult to
assign a reason therefor. Its present population is about 250. The
Methodist congregation at Allenford erected their first church building in 1873, the Presbyterian theirs in 1875

Regarding the origin of the name "Hepworth," bestowed on the
largest village in the township, Mr. John M. McNabb, of Southampton, in a letter to one of the local papers, states that: "The original
owner of the land on which Hepworth stands belonged to a William
Plews, who proposed laying out a town plot on his property. Being
at a loss for a name, he asked the Rev. Mr. Green (a Methodist
clergyman) to suggest one. Mr Green at once said, 'Why not name
your town "Epworth" after the birthplace of John Wesley?' Mr.
Plews, being an Englishman, pronounced the name as if the initial
letter was an 'H.' Unaware of the error, the name stuck, hence
'Hepworth.'" This thriving village contains a population of six
or eight hundred, lying partly in the county of Grey and partly in
the county of Bruce. It commenced to take form about the middle
of the sixties. In 1866[2] a post-office was established there, which
received its supply of mail matter from Owen Sound. The nucleus
around which the village started was the hotel, a large log building,
erected by William Spencer. William Plews was also a hotel-keeper
in the early days His business was bought out by William Driffel,
who surveyed and offered for sale a number of lots that form part
of the town plot. Thomas Briggs was the first one to establish a
store at Hepworth, Mr. Driffel following his example shortly afterwards. The establishment of the post-office contributed to the
centring of business there and the place very soon began to rapidly
develop, being the distributing point of a section of good farming
country ·which surrounds it. The railway materially added to the
prosperity of the village, enabling a ready shipment to be made from
the·several saw-mills established there. The town really received its
chief impetus from the presumption that it was to be the centre of
an oil district. In 1890 a man who had had considerable experience
in the oil fields of Canada and Pennsylvania happened to visit Hep-

[1]This, however, was not the first post-office in Amabel, which was the
one established in 1865 at Elsinore, of which D McLeod was the first
postmaster

[2]Two years previous to Wiarton obtaining postal service.

worth, and expressed his firm opinion, after examining the surface indications, that there was an underlying oil-bearing strata of rock. William Driffel and William Beacock undertook to sink a well, but lacked in capital and proper appliances. The next step taken was to form a company. The first attempt, however, was unsuccessful. In 1897 Mr. E. P. Roe, principal of the public school, renewed the agitation to organize a company to bore for oil. Mr. Roe, having at one time resided at Petrolea, was satisfied from past experience that there were indications that a supply of oil existed underneath where the town lay. His enthusiasm was contagious, and a company was established with a capital of $2,000. This company drilled a well to the depth of 1,326 feet, when some of the tools were lost in the well; the company's funds at the same time were exhausted, and the well was therefore abandoned, although the indications of oil near at hand were plentiful. The next person to take up the matter was Mr. John Caldwell; he and Mr. Roe organized a new company with a capital of $4,500. The result was that on August 22nd, 1900, the drill opened a vein which has yielded gas in large quantities. This natural gas has been used to a large extent, both for heating and lighting purposes, but it has not been piped to other points for consumption. The Standard Oil Company of America took a great interest in the prospects of oil in this field, and it is said has secured leases to the extent of about 20,000 acres of land adjacent to Hepworth. It also sunk wells in this vicinity at different points, but the result has been the same everywhere; there is gas to be found, but no oil. So far there has been little return for the large expenditure and outlay of labor and capital made in the search for oil. Other names that might be mentioned in connection with Hepworth besides those already mentioned are: J. E. Murphy, C. H. Witthun, Robert Halls, J. E Campbell, Dr. Frank Campbell, James Vance and Edward Brigham. Hepworth was erected into a police village by county by-law, passed December 14th, 1899.

The following incident, which had some laughable features regarding it, involved a portion of the township of Amabel, and is but little known. A firm calling itself "The Lake Publishing Company," of Toronto, issued a circular worded as follows: "On or about the 1st July, 1892, the Lake Publishing Company will issue the initial number of *The Lake,* a magazine which will prove to be without a peer in Canada Without loss of time we propose

making the following unparalleled offer   To the first 3,000 sub-
scribers who send us $3 00 we will mail one copy of the magazine
for one year, and give them a warranty deed of a lot, 25 by 120 feet,
in Huron Park. . . Huron Park adjoins the town-plot of Oliphant, overlooking Lake Huron. This is one of the most delightful
locations along the shores of this charming lake, directly opposite
the well-known Fishing Islands of Lake Huron, with bass and other
fishing unexcelled on the great lakes. Remember, there are no blanks,
the magazine alone is worth the money, but this is our method to
save time in introducing it to the public A first-class publication
and a lot with a clear title for $3 00" How long the magazine was
published the author is unable to say. The company had about
twenty-nine acres of lot 48 in concession " D," divided into blocks
of the size mentioned. Some of the owners of these seemed to have
had exaggerated ideas of their value, as the author is aware of some
of them being mortgaged to the extent of $3,500.   To any one
acquainted with the value of land in that vicinity the whole affair
seems farcical.

The mills, run by power derived from the Sauble Falls, have been
operated by different parties since the first settlement of the township,
but never with very satisfactory results.   The McLean Brothers,
Hector, Lachlin and Hugh, possibly operated the mills for the
longest period of any of the proprietors. One interesting fact in
connection with their possession of this property was their purchase
of the little steamer, *Water Witch*, mentioned in the chapter on
" Paisley." This steamer, some 40 feet long and 8 feet wide, was
transported by the McLean Brothers, on two sleighs, in January,
1883, from the Saugeen River to Boat Lake. They used it for a
number of years in towing logs on Boat Lake, Pike River, and Lake
Sky This vessel, for many years the sole representative of steam
navigation for commercial purposes on the inland waters of Bruce,
now lies, or did until lately, a dismantled and rotting hulk, near
the exit of Boat Lake

Each new settlement has had its tragedy. Too often they are
unknown and unrecorded Mr. B. B. Miller, of Wiarton, has supplied the author with the particulars of one in which an Amabel
settler figured. It was in the fall of 1868 that George Fathergill
bought a farm in Amabel, near Boat Lake He came from the
vicinity of Whitby, and was, for a backwoods settler, very well off.
After a short stay on his farm he went to Owen Sound, presumably

to draw some money from the bank and purchase fall wheat for seed. Returning in a sail-boat to Wiarton, the crew and passengers of which consisted of Fathergill, George Brown the postmaster at Owen Sound, one John Robinson, of Owen Sound, lately arrived from New Orleans, and a man named Kennedy, the boat was seen to enter Colpoy's Bay in the evening. Next day the boat was found on White Cloud Island right side up, and in it Kennedy, lying dead. A dog was found on the island which had been in the boat; also a gun. None of the other three persons were ever heard of again A suspicion of foul play to get Fathergill's money was felt, but nothing has ever developed to clear up the mystery.

In a local history the origin of the names borne by certain places is of interest; to those already given in this chapter the following are added: Lake " Gould," named after George Gould, who conducted the survey of this part of the township. He afterwards held the office of county clerk for many years. Lake " Chesley " and Lake " Spry " each bear the name of a member of the surveying party under Mr. Gould " Elsinore " is a name given by Mr Sweetman, the post-office inspector, suggested by the historic spot in Denmark of this name being visited by some members of the Royal Family at the time the post-office was opened.

Visitors to Main Station Island have wondered and questioned as to who it was that erected the massive stone buildings, the ruins of which are to be seen there. This question has been thoroughly discussed in Chapter III., on " The Pioneers " Other municipalities in the county may find many things to boast of, but Amabel, in the possession of these ruins, has the proof that the exploiting of her natural resources attracted the first of the pioneers of Bruce.

CHAPTER XIII.

WIARTON.[1]

EXTRACT FROM THE REPORT OF COUNTY VALUATORS, 1901.

" We found the greatest increase here of any town or village in the county. A hum of industry, with their many large saw-mills, furniture, table and many other factories, being pushed to their utmost limit. Their beautiful harbor, the best on Lake Huron or Georgian Bay, affords admirable shipping facilities, and stimulated by the large tract of timber lands on the north, causes a hum of industry along the waterfront and is a general benefit to the town "

THE beauty of the site on which Wiarton is built places it in a unique position among the towns in the county of Bruce, none other of which can compare with it in picturesqueness The view from the hill at the south of Wiarton charms every visitor. At one's feet lies the busy town, with its numerous factories and mills; further on, at the docks, are to be seen crafts of all descriptions. Beyond, the view extends for miles down Colpoy's Bay, with White Cloud and Hay Islands in the distance. The cultivated fields on the Keppel side of the bay seem to set off the bold limestone cliffs, commencing almost at the spectator's left hand and extending as far as the eye can reach along the west shore Beauty of scenery is, however, only one of the natural advantages possessed by Wiarton. Its position at the south end of the peninsula resulted in its being for years the sole market town for all that stretch of country, and, dating from the entrance of the railway, the shipping point as well for all the peninsula could produce from its forests and fields. Large and predominating are now the interests of Wiarton on Colpoy's Bay, but at first no evidence was given that such was to be the case. Oxenden claims to have been the first place on the bay to receive settlers. Shortly afterwards another group of settlers took up land at or near where the post-office is which now bears the name of " Colpoy's Bay " These settlements date back to 1856, whereas

---

[1] " Wiarton " received its name, presumably, from the birthplace of Sir Edmund Walker Head. Governor-General at the time of its survey, who was born (see *Ency Brit*) at Wiarton Place, near Maidstone, Kent.

220

Wiarton town lots[1] were not offered for sale until 1868. In evidence of the total absence of settlement at Wiarton as late as 1866, the author gives an experience of Mr B. B. Miller[2] as related by him. In company with William McLaughlan, at that time tax collector in Amabel, Mr. Miller started on foot from " Colpoy's," going southward. When in the town-plot of Wiarton they missed the trail, owing to its being covered with fallen leaves, and were compelled to spend the night in the bush

The claim of James Lennox[3] to be first settler at Wiarton is un-disputed. The date of his arrival was November 16th, 1866. His first work was to build a log shanty, this being the first building erected for permanent habitation at Wiarton.

The absence of anything in the way of a wharf or facilities for shipping in the early days, resulted in the nucleus of the town being

[1]The original price of these lots was $6, subsequently raised to $10, and again to $40

[2]B B Miller is a man who has been identified with Wiarton from its inception until the present day. During these forty years of residence Mr. Miller has ever held a leading position. He was Wiarton's first post-master, the first Division Court clerk, the first Indian lands agent, the first police magistrate, the first mayor, and also was reeve when the municipality was a village.

Kircudbrightshire, Scotland, is Mr. Miller's birthplace There he was born, January 25th, 1836. When he was ten years of age his family emigrated to Canada and settled at first in Toronto Township, and later in Bentinck After finishing his course at school, Mr. Miller served as a clerk in a store at Durham Being desirous of seeing more of the world, he visited and spent a short time in the States Returning to Canada, he qualified himself as a schoolteacher, and subsequently taught for four years in Arran and Elderslie His next venture was that of storekeeping at Paisley This business he sold out in July, 1866, and opened a store at Oxenden. In 1867 he moved to Wiarton, and has been closely associated in every movement for the welfare and development of the town since then

[3]" On Friday, November 16th, 1902, the grim reaper claimed Wiarton's oldest resident, in the person of Mr. James Lennox, at the age of 87 years Mr. Lennox was born in Ireland in 1815, and came to America in 1822 with his parents, who settled in New Jersey. The political troubles of the day soon induced the subject of this sketch to again seek the protection of the British flag, and he emigrated to Canada, settling at Guelph for a time, then removing to Mount Forest, and finally, on November 16th, 1866, to Wiarton—just thirty-six years previous to the day of his death. Wiarton was practically a wilderness when Mr. Lennox arrived; all was bush or scrub, and he built the first house in the place, and founded what is to-day the most thriving town in the whole county He was a staunch Conservative all his life, and espoused the Loyalist cause in the troubles of '37 and '38. He was a quiet, highly-respected and law-loving citizen, and his demise is generally regretted He leaves an aged widow and two sons in Wiarton, in comfortable circumstances "
—Extract from the *Wiarton Canadian*

established on top of the hill, the business centre being at the corner where Gould Street is crossed by Division Street. There, in 1868, B. B. Miller built an hotel and opened the post-office, just established. There also John Hodgins and, some months later, David Dinsmore started storekeeping. After the wharves were constructed and mills had been erected below the hill, the places of business moved to Berford Street, and by 1879 Gould Street became what it is now, largely a residential street.

The first start Wiarton received was derived from a grant of $300, made by the Indian Department towards the building of a wharf. In 1868 a steamer owned at Collingwood, named the *Hero*, called once or twice a week. This service was improved upon in 1869, when the steamer *Champion*, Captain Monk, owned by John Hodgins, above mentioned, made daily trips to Owen Sound, thus connecting the little settlement with the world at large. It was not long after the dock was built that a storehouse followed close at hand, the owner being E. C Jones: this gave the neighboring farmers an opportunity to market their grain without travelling a long distance. Among the business men of Wiarton in the sixties, besides those already mentioned, should be named R. Greenlees, merchant, and J. Paterson, druggist, also Thomas Gilpin and Dr. A. Williams, who erected the first saw-mill. In a Directory of Ontario, that claimed to be revised to January, 1870, is to be found a description of Wiarton, somewhat as follows. "Population about 200, grain and lumber form the principal trade here. It has a mail four times a week" (brought from Owen Sound *via* Presqu' Isle, Big Bay and Oxenden). Other names of residents to be found in this Directory besides those previously mentioned in this chapter are, Miss Martha Gilpin, school-teacher, Rev. J. C. Collins and Rev. Geo Smith, ministers, both of the Bible Christian denomination. There were two hotels, kept by Joseph Crandon and Mrs. Currie.

A Directory of a later date, published in April, 1876, has the following items regarding Wiarton: "Population about 400. A steamboat makes daily trips to Owen Sound. A tri-weekly stage runs to Owen Sound carrying the mails, but after May 1st there is to be a daily stage. There is an office of the telegraph company and a grist mill lately been opened and run by W. H. Heberden." From the same authority we learn that there were two steam saw-mills, owned by John Ashcroft and A. Jones, respectively, also a planing mill run by F. Lickman and a tannery by D. G. Millar. There were four churches, of which the oldest was that of the Church of England, erected in 1871. This building was seated for 160, and cost about $600. Rev. T. S. Campbell was the minister in charge. The Bible Christians had a larger church, a frame building that cost about $1,400. The Congregationalists had a church erected in 1875, costing $900. The fourth church was a frame building erected by the Methodists in 1876, seated for 200, and costing $600.

The prospect of a railway reaching Wiarton caused the population to increase rapidly. An increase of population called for an increase of school accommodation With commendable enterprise, a commodious stone school-house was built in 1877 at a cost of $2,200. In the same year church buildings were erected by the Presbyterians and the Disciples; the latter edifice was of brick, the other was frame. These two buildings gave a total of six churches in a village which two years later, in 1879, only claimed to have a population of 752. Denominationalism was certainly a feature in Wiarton at that time. Before passing to another topic, it might be as well to state that in 1891 the two congregations, Presbyterians and Congregationalists, united and so formed a large body. Up to 1883 the Wiarton Presbyterians were included in the home mission work of the Presbyterian Church, but when the Rev. E. B. Millard was inducted as minister, June 25th of that year, the charge was erected to the status of a self-sustained congregation

Wiarton became an incorporated village by special Act of Parliament,[1] assented to 5th March, 1880 The reason a special Act of incorporation was necessary arose from the fact that there was not in the original town plot of Wiarton a population sufficient in number to comply with the requirements of the Municipal Act,[2] but the number could be made up by taking in that part of the village lying in the county of Grey. So the Act omitted from the area of the village Ranges 3, 4, 5 and 6 of park lots to the west of the town in the original survey, while it added thereto all now in the town plot east of the county line (Berford street), most of which was in the original survey of the township of Keppel. The population at the

[1] 43 Vic. Chap. 46.

[2] A population of over 750, within 500 acres, was what the " Municipal Act," R. S. O., 1877, gave as the requirements for the incorporation of a village.

time of incorporation was given as 752.[1] James Grier was appointed
by the Act of incorporation to be the returning officer to hold the
first nomination and election of a reeve and four councillors. The
Agricultural Hall was where the nomination was held, and there,
too, the village council held its first meeting on March 22nd, 1880.
The members of the first Council were: David Dinsmore, reeve; Hiram
Brown, James McKim, D. G. Miller and J. W. Jermyn, councillors;
Thomas D Galloway, clerk; Neil McMillan, treasurer. In the following December the wardens of Bruce and Grey met with the village
reeve, and it was decided that the county of Bruce should assume
the proportion of indebtedness that the Keppel part of Wiarton
owed the county of Grey. The amount was fixed at $400. The
County Council of Bruce in the following January confirmed this
by by-law (No 173), and the money was promptly paid over to the
county of Grey. On becoming a separate municipality the financial
claims of the two townships, in which the village had developed, for
debts incurred had to be provided for. In settling with the township of Keppel, Wiarton assumed one-eleventh of the $30,000 bonus
to the railway, and $1,410 of the $2,000 subsequent bonus, and $399
of Keppel's county rates; total about $4,500 The basis of settle-
ment with the township of Amabel was one-tenth of the railway
bonus of $40,000 and two-thirds of the similar bonus of $3,000,
making a total of $6,000 In addition to the amounts so assumed
from Keppel and Amabel, Wiarton had an indebtedness of over $2,000

---

[1] "To secure the special Act to incorporate the village, it was necessary
that $125 should be deposited with the Government, $100 of which the
Legislature held and $25 of which went to draw up the bill of incorpora-
tion The settlers never at any time had too much money, so in order
to raise the amount twenty-five persons went on a joint note for $5 each—
Messrs Adam Doupe, J. W Jermyn, J. J. Jermyn, James McNeill, Henry
Trout, Neil Langford, John Ashcroft, G Bingham, and others whose
names have not been learned. Messrs Doupe and Jermyn were instructed
to negotiate the loan, which necessitated their travelling on foot to Owen
Sound as no conveyance was available. They secured the money. Shortly
after this some farmers in the vicinity of the contemplated village
opposed the proposed incorporation and a public meeting was called, the
hat was passed around and $12 collected to support the opposition move-
ment, which failed to have any effect Messrs Bingham, Ashcroft and
J. W. Jermyn were appointed a deputation to proceed to Toronto to lobby
the bill through. They went via Own Sound, on the old narrow-gauge
railway The trip took one whole day The bill was given in charge of
Donald Sinclair, the then member of this riding for the local Legislature.
"When Wiarton threw off its swaddling clothes there was not a cent
in the treasury. The minutes of the first council meeting were written
on paper and with pen and ink purchased by Messrs. Millar and Jermyn,
each giving five cents! That's the way the village of Wiarton was
started off."—Extract from *Wiarton Canadian Souvenir.*

.for the new school-house, so that Wiarton on entering into existence as a separate municipality, did so with a debt of $13,000, a large financial burden for an infant municipality. But the inhabitants of Wiarton have never been backward in assuming such burdens if there, was a prospect of the betterment of the town thereby. This optimistic spirit has induced what many of Wiarton's people think the assuming of a burden of debt too large, considering the size of the place. Certainly it resulted in the town having to ask the Legislative Assembly in 1894 to pass an Act to consolidate the debt of the town and extend the payment over thirty years. This relief, so asked for, was obtained.[1] The preamble of the Act passed states the debenture debt to be, at that date, $43,199, with no sinking fund, and also a floating debt of $5,149. The lesson of the past was not taken to heart by the sanguine-spirited people of Wiarton, and long ere the next decade had passed the debenture debt of Wiarton had passed into six figures.[2] The chief cause of this increase of indebtedness was the financial assistance given by the town to the beet sugar refinery, of which more will be said later on.

The prospect of the railway reaching the village was one long kept dangling before the eyes of its inhabitants. The Stratford and Lake Huron Railway (originally chartered in 1855) lacked capital from the very first; then, after the construction of the railway began, for some reason the government withheld the bonus which was expected and calculated upon to help to build the road. Some townships, Carrick for instance, refused to grant a bonus. So the company had to ask those municipalities that had manifested a willingness to grant financial assistance for an additional bonus It was not until the Grand Trunk Railway leased the road, May, 1880, that it seemed assured that the railway would be completed. To comply with the time limit, and so obtain the promised bonuses, the track layers pushed on their work and reached Wiarton November 29th, 1881. Without loss of time a locomotive and some flat cars entered the village, crossing Frank street about 6 p.m. of that day, having on board J. C. Boyd, of Simcoe, Superintendent of Construction. The conductor was William Cook and the engineer Joshua Wilson. After success to the enterprise had been drunk in lager beer, the train departed south, and work on the line ceased for the season. At this time, and for a number of months, Chesley was the northern ter-

---

[1] 57 Vic. Chap. 86.

[2] On December 31st, 1905, the debenture indebtedness was $147,735.16.

9

minus of the line, the road not being opened for traffic to Wiarton until August 1st, 1882. This line of railway has proved one of the most profitable branches in the Grand Trunk Railway System. It has also done much to make Wiarton what it is, the commercial entrepôt for the peninsula.

That the newly opened railway might obtain its share of the lake traffic enlarged wharfage accommodation was needed. Pressure was brought to bear on the Dominion Government, with the result that a grant of $35,000 was made. This the village supplemented with $7,500 from the sale of debentures. Work on the new wharf was commenced in 1882, and completed in August of the following year. The new wharf had a frontage of 1,040 feet, a breadth of 18 to 25 feet, and extended into the water so as to give 18 to 25 feet depth of water along the front. It is said that the total cost was upward of $60,000. By how much the government supplemented its original grant the author cannot say. The increase of wharfage accommodation resulted in an increase of shipping, followed by Wiarton being erected into an Out-post of Customs, under the survey of the Collector at Stratford. This was done September 26th, 1882.

With such a large number of frame buildings it is surprising that Wiarton has not suffered severely from fires. Possibly the narrowest escape it had was on August 31st, 1881. The preceding summer had been very dry. The smoke of destructive bush fires was to be seen in every direction. Urged on by a strong wind the fires approached the village The air was filled with smoke so dense as to be almost suffocating. Nearer and nearer the flames came, until the villagers in self-preservation had to turn out and fight them. In this they were partially successful, but one house, that of E. C Jones, was burned down Fortunately the wind blew in such a direction that the saw and grist mills were not seriously imperilled, but much of the beautiful growth of timber below and on top of the cliff was burnt, a loss that will take many years to repair, as over considerable areas nearly all the soil was also burned away, and for lack of it the trees and verdure can never be the same.

As a measure conducive to the public health, as well as for fire protection, it was decided in 1887 to construct a system of waterworks for the town The system was installed shortly afterwards, and has been largely extended as the town enlarged and the need for pure water and adequate fire protection became more generally recognized. The plan decided upon provided for water being pumped direct from the bay into the mains, the engine automatically maintaining the requisite pressure. In 1904 further improvements were made in the system by the construction of a reservoir and by placing the pumps further down the bay, so as to be certain of obtaining pure water. The cost had been heavy, but the citizens have acted wisely in inaugurating a system which gives them abundance of that necessity of life, good water.

Wiarton's first newspaper was *The Echo*, published by George Bingham and Colin F. Campbell. Its initial number bears date of 4th July, 1879. The ownership of *The Echo* has changed hands several times during the vicissitudes and struggles a local newspaper encounters in its limited field. In 1885 S. W. Cross became the sole proprietor and successfully conducted the paper for ten years. At present *The Echo* is edited and published by A Logan. *The Encore* was the name of the next journal published at Wiarton. It had an existence of about three years, but failing to attain the success of *The Echo*, it ceased publication in October, 1892. About the same time as *The Encore* was issued a paper called *The News* was published by H. T. Butler; this journal also failed to obtain patronage sufficient to warrant the publication of it being continued. *The Wiarton Canadian* dates back to 1893. Its founder was A. Megraw, who for a number of years previous had met with good success as the publisher of the *Paisley Advocate*. The north riding of Bruce being largely Conservative in politics, and as the new paper advocated in an able manner Conservative principles, it met with success, and continues to flourish, W. J. Whitlock being the publisher at present.

For many years the sole banking business of Wiarton was conducted by G. W. Ames & Co., private bankers, first established in June, 1880. The need of a chartered bank being much felt, application was made to several of the large banking institutions of the country to establish a branch at Wiarton, but with no success until 1892, when the Union Bank opened a branch with E. W. Burinot as manager. Ten years later the Canadian Bank of Commerce also decided to open a branch and at the same time to advertise itself by erecting a handsome building. A central position on Berford Street was obtained, and a building erected that is an ornament to the town.

Owing to the continued growth of population an enlarged accommodation for the pupils attending the school was necessary, and the School Board in 1885 asked the village Council to raise $2,000 for this purpose. This the Council of that year refused to do   The clash of these representative bodies created quite a little excitement at the time. The Council of the following year was more amenable to the educational interests of the town than its predecessor, and raised the necessary amount. The public school building of Wiarton to-day, one of eight rooms, is certainly a very handsome structure, and a credit to the town. In 1891 Wiarton was set apart by the County Council as a high school district; this was after a very close contest with Paisley. The old public school building, an excellent stone structure and much enlarged, is now occupied as the high school. The following gentlemen composed the first Board of High School Trustees: D. G. Millar, R. M. Fisher, M.D., Rev. T. S. Campbell, J. Paterson, J. Walmsley and A. M. Tyson. The first head master of the high school was T. H. Farrell, succeeded October 1st, 1892, by Henry De La Mater.

In 1893 the inhabitants of Wiarton found they were numerous enough to take unto themselves the privileges and honor of a town. The preliminary proceedings were taken that year,[1] with the result that since the 1st January, 1894, Wiarton has been numbered among the towns of the province. In a footnote[2] are to be found the names of the heads of the municipality, whether as reeve or as mayor, from its first incorporation as a municipality to 1906.

At the time of the opening of the railway an issue of *The Echo* gives a paragraph of Wiarton's wants. Among them are the following: a village hall, a town bell, and mails to be carried by the railway. These have all been supplied. In December, 1888, the municipality bought the back part of lot 13, west of Berford and south of Division Streets, on which they erected a building to contain the fire-fighting apparatus, a tower for a bell, and a hall in which the village Council could meet. This building did service for the above purposes for a number of years. In 1899 the front part of the same lot, on which stood a building known as " The Robinson Hall," was

[1]The Lieutenant-Governor's proclamation of incorporation bears date 14th December, 1893. It came into effect on 1st January, 1894.

[2]*Reeves*—David Dinsmore, 1880, '81, '82; Hiram Brown, 1883; A. M. Tyson, 1884, '85; C. V. Parke, 1886, '87; Hiram Wigle, 1888, '89; B B Millar, 1890; D M Jermyn, 1891, '92; James Hunter, 1893, '94, '95; James Symon, 1896

Mayors—B .B Millar, 1894; D. M. Jermyn, 1895, '96; James Hunter, 1897 and 1905; Charles Reckin, 1898; S A. Perry, 1899; James Symon, 1900; G. Kastner, 1901; William Bernie, 1902; G. S. Sinclair, 1903, '04; S J Cameron, 1906

thrown on the market. The opportunity offered was seized, and for a very moderate sum the town bought the building, which is one exceedingly well suited for a town hall. An addition was built in which there is a handsome council chamber on the second storey, while underneath is a lock-up and fire hall. The present town bell was put into position in August, 1900. It cost something like $412, weighs 832 pounds, and hangs in a tower 75 feet high, adjoining the hall.

Among the important industries of Wiarton is that of the manufacture of furniture, several large factories being in constant operation. We have to look back to 1879 to find the pioneer firm of this industry, Messrs. Falk, Morlock & Wegenert, who in that year started Wiarton's first furniture factory. Another industry was started the same year, namely the "Wiarton Woollen Mill," William Turner being the owner of the same. In 1880 or 1881 the Vulcan Foundry, owned by George S. Sinclair, added another to the successful industries of the town.

The Dominion Fish Co. has its central packing plant located at Wiarton. Here are frozen and packed all the fish taken at some ten stations operated by the company, scattered around the Georgian Bay and the Manitoulin Island. As the stations have from two to three tugs each, engaged in setting and lifting nets, it can easily be credited that about 120,000 pounds of fish per week are received at Wiarton. A visit to this large establishment is most interesting.

"The Wiarton Beet Sugar Manufacturing Company, Limited"[1] was incorporated 21st October, 1896, with a capital of $150,000, increased to $500,000 by letters patent on 10th October, 1901. After the obtaining of a charter it took several years to thoroughly convince the public of the feasibility of the undertaking, to show that beets grown in the vicinity gave an exceptionally high percentage of sugar; that owing to the facilities for shipping by water the area from which beets could be shipped, with profit to the grower, was of great extent. These advantages decided many to take stock in the company. Of these a large number were farmers, who were asked to pay only 5 per cent. of amount of stock subscribed for in cash, the balance to be paid in beets. The Colonial Construction Company of Detroit undertook to erect and equip the factory. Ground for building operations was broken in October, 1901, and in the follow-

[1]The original charter was in the name of " The Owen Sound Sugar Manufacturing Company."

ing spring the walls were being built.   On June 5th, 1902, the corner-
stone was laid by James Mills, President of the Ontario Agricultural
College, Guelph.   The principal buildings erected are of stone, the
main building being four stories in height, two hundred and forty
feet long, and one hundred and twenty feet wide, sixty-six of this
being four stories in height, and fifty-four being of one and two
stories.   To the north of the main building is the sugar storage
warehouse, also of stone, one storey high, two hundred feet long by
seventy-five feet wide.   On the south side of the main building are
located the beet store-houses, having a capacity of six thousand tons.
Besides these huge structures, there is a cooper-house, an office, and
other necessary buildings.   There is also a wharf and a railway
switch, so that everything was provided for the economical handling
and receiving of supplies, and for the shipping of the finished product.   The factory was also fitted throughout with the best machinery
known to the trade.   A large acreage of beets was secured in 1902,
and great were the hopes for the success of the enterprise.   Unfortunately, the contract with the Colonial Construction Co. called upon
them to run the factory for the first season.   What was the result?
Because of the improper installing of the machinery, and because of
the manager not understanding the business, less than half of the
quantity of sugar was obtained from the beets that might have been
secured if he had been competent.   It is said that fully $50,000
worth of juice and beets was carried by the sewers into the bay.   At
the end of the first season the board of directors faced a loss of over
$63,000.   What was to be done?   The town, which had given at the
outset of the undertaking a bonus of $25,000, was now asked to grant
a loan of $25,000, which it did.   To supply needed capital, private
individuals entered into bonds for $110,000 in addition.   A new
superintendent was secured, and the season of 1903 was entered upon
with the hope that at last success was in sight, but alas! the enterprise seemed to have some fatality attached to it, and the season
ended as unfortunately as the previous one.   The bondmen were
called upon to make good the bonds entered upon.   January 12th,
1904, was the date fixed by the Union Bank to pay up.   To the credit
of these gentlemen, it is to be recorded that not one of them failed
to respond, although the amounts were large, $4,000, $9,000, $10,000
and $12,000 being paid by different individuals, the smallest amount
being $750.   It is questionable if any town of its size in the province
has ever received such a financial blow.   The loss amounted to about

$200,000, made up as follows: The town bonus $25,000, the town loan, $25,000, the bondsmen $110,000, and the balance in stock subscribed. The courts decided in 1905 that the farmers who had taken stock, 95 per cent. of which was to be paid in beets, must make up in cash what had not already been covered by cash and beets. This seems hard, as it was not their fault that they could not, owing to the closing of the factory, pay up according to the original agreement.

Unlike most localities in the county of Bruce, Wiarton has connected with it an Indian legend entitled "The Spirit Rock." An excellent recital of the old legend is to be found in the *Wiarton Canadian Souvenir,* which the author takes the liberty of transposing to these pages. It is as follows:

"Situated between Wiarton and Whicher's Point, the Spirit Rock can be seen quite distinctly from the bay. On the face of the cliff, standing out in bold relief, the crevices and stains have depicted a woman's face, above which there is a blasted pine There is a tradition in connection with the rock. A squaw, the daughter of a chief of one of the tribes whose hunting ground was in the immediate vicinity of Colpoy's Bay, of whom now only a few relics remain, was carried off by an Eastern tribe, who bore her miles away and condemned to a life of drudgery this daughter of a hated foe. The Eastern chieftain passed one day while she was singing a sad, plaintive song. The song, the youthfulness and attractiveness of the maiden, wakened in the chieftain's breast feelings of admiration and love. He released her from her bondage, and with simple rites the chief and maid were wed. The warriors of the tribe were angered at this union and plotted so effectively that dire disaster met the bride and her consort. Her warrior chief was stricken from her side, but she escaped and wandered back to her tribe, arriving weary and footsore, but only to be refused admittance into the band, as she by becoming the willing bride of their deadly foe had brought dishonor on herself.

> "For hours she stood upon that rocky height,
> Till night's dark curtain had shut out the light
> And hid the cruel rocks from sight.
> Then, with a cry like a lost soul in woe,
> She sprang to her death and her grave below,
> While moaning winds murmured a funeral strain,
> And sighing waves echoed a sad refrain."

Colpoy's Bay has had its share of marine casualties. Probably the one best remembered and spoken of is that of the loss of the *Jane Miller,* which occurred November 25th, 1881. The propeller *Jane Miller* (built in 1879, classed A 2 1-2 of 150 tons burden) was a Wiarton boat, owned by Captain A. Port. She left Big Bay for Wiarton at 8.30 p.m. on the above date, a heavy gale blowing at the time. Her cargo was a large one, and was stowed principally on the main deck, making her top-heavy. Her lights were seen when she was in the vicinity of Cameron's dock, but that was the last known of her. All on board perished, twenty-eight souls in all. Hardly any traces of her have been picked up and the spot where she foundered is unknown.

Another well-remembered fatality on the bay occurred 27th July, 1892. It was associated with a tornado that struck the town and bay on the evening of that day. The town suffered severely, every smoke stack but two being blown down. William Young's saw-mill was unroofed, the skating rink and some stables were demolished, and the large public bath and boat house, owned by Ralph Eby, with its contents, were destroyed. The loss of property would be as nothing if no lives had been lost. Just before the storm broke a sail-boat was seen a short distance down the bay. In the boat were George Stevens, of Chesley, his wife and two sisters, Mrs. L. Currie and daughter, of Wiarton, John Savage, of Chesley, a man named J. Lembke and an Indian. Seeing the storm coming the sail was lowered and the boat headed to the wind, but the instant the tornado struck it everyone on board found themselves in the water. The six whose names are first given in the above list were carried away and drowned; the other three clung on to the bow-sprit until gallantly rescued by John and Henry Dance and a young man named Wyburn, who put out in a small, leaky skiff. Braving the storm and the heavy sea, they reached the shipwrecked men in time to rescue them   The boat was too small to take any on board, but by holding on to the gunwale they were towed to shore, reaching it in a much exhausted condition.

It is said that the gentlemen who surveyed the town plot of Wiarton named many of the streets after themselves and their wives. Certainly the names of Frank Berford and George Gould, who were in the surveying party, are to be found in four of the streets of the town. Brown Street bears the name of a man who worked in the surveying party, and who subsequently settled a short distance south of the town on the county line   Gleason Street preserves the name of one of the first settlers on Colpoy's Bay. Beyond these six names the author cannot venture a suggestion.

Wiarton has made more rapid progress than any other village or town in the county of Bruce. True, it has had its setbacks, such as occurred when the Grand Trunk Railway opened the Owen Sound branch and made that point its principal northern terminus, and again when the sugar refinery failed. Still, it is the busiest town in the county, and the townspeople are hopeful and confident of continued and prolonged prosperity. We trust that these fond hopes may be fully realized.

CHAPTER XIV.

TOWNSHIP OF ALBEMARLE.[1]

EXTRACT FROM THE REPORT OF COUNTY VALUATORS, 1879.

" The east side of this township is rock, with only a few stony farms scattered through it, the west side is sand and swamp It has very little village property. The average price per acre is about $4."

EXTRACT FROM THE REPORT OF COUNTY VALUATORS, 1901.

" In Albemarle there is a small section of fair land at Mar, but rock and stone seems to crop up everywhere, and roads are bad. Large sections of these townships are less valuable now than twelve years ago, and the outlook is not bright The rate per acre is $3 25 "

AN examination of the map of Albemarle shows that two different lines of survey met at lot 10[2] on each of the concession lines. The southerly part of the township was surveyed for Charles Rankin by George Gould, in the latter part of the fall of 1855, after he had finished his share of the survey of the township of Amabel. The northern part of Albemarle was surveyed by the party of surveyors who surveyed the township of Eastnor. The only town plot laid out in the township was that of Adair, on Hope Bay, which contained 2,025 acres. A town, however, failed to develop there, so in response to a petition the County Council, in 1879, urged the Indian Land Department to have the town plot sold as farm lands This was acceded to, but not until the town and park lots had first been offered for sale at auction at Owen Sound in October, 1880. In 1887 only 191 acres of the whole town plot had been cleared, and in that year it was re-surveyed into farm lots.

The peninsula to the east of Albemarle geographically belongs to the township, but it has been set apart as an Indian reserve. It contains 15,586 acres, and is known as the Cape Croker Reserve. Particulars respecting it are to be found in Appendix C.

[1] " Albemarle " is the title of Lord Bury's family, the Earls of Albemarle. The Lord Bury referred to so frequently in this History became the seventh Earl of Albemarle.

[2] Mr. Andrew Weir, ex-reeve, says that his farm shows that lines of survey met at lot 15, but the maps do not indicate this

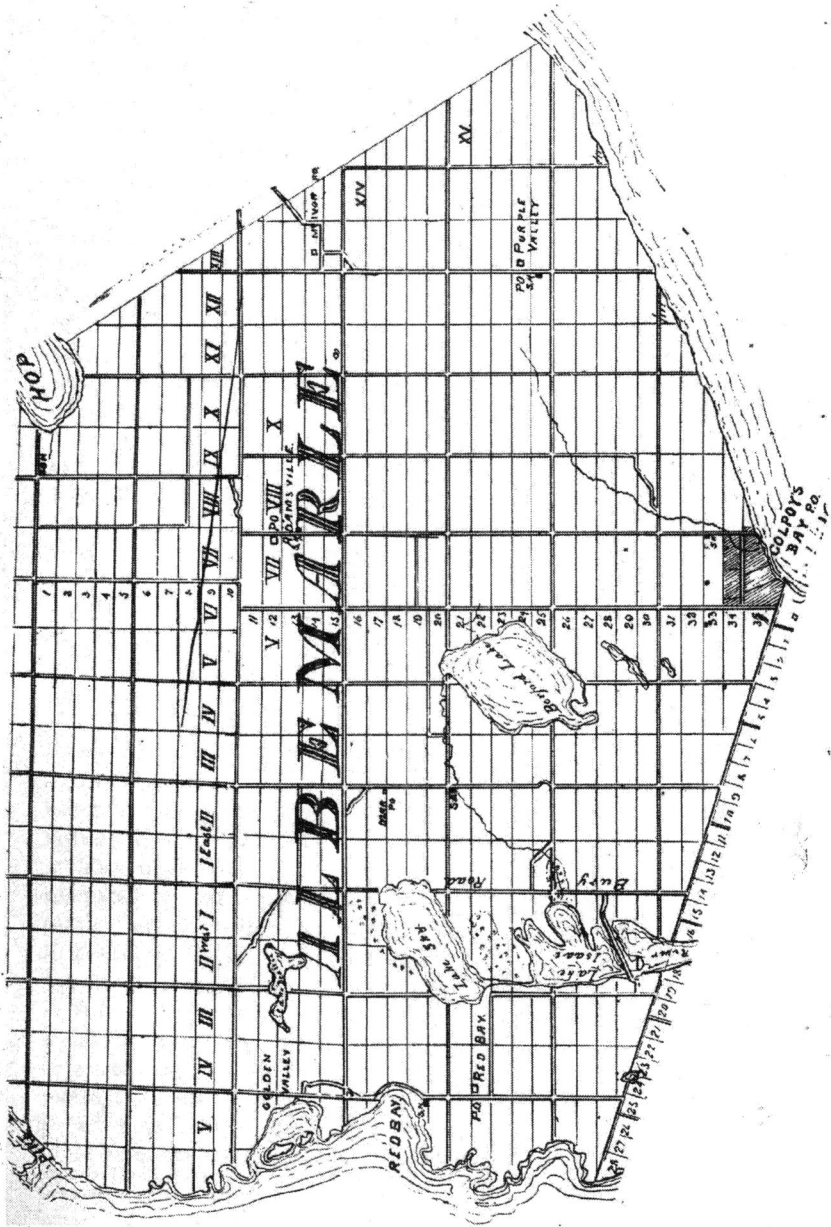

ALBEMARLE

HOP

GOLDEN VALLEY

REDBN

PO RED BAX

PO PURPLE VALLEY

COLPOY'S BAY PO.

ORMAVILLE

Lone Pine Bay

Lake Bay Road

Buty

McINTOR PR

In December, 1857, the first settlers in the township took up their lands. They were John Wood and Samuel Atkinson, who settled on lots 31 and 30, concession 8, E.B.R. In the month of May following they were joined by five families, who were brought over from Owen Sound by the steamer *Canadian*. These were Rev. Ludwick Kribs,[1] Henry Kribs, Caleb Spragge, Joseph Stringer and Ludwick Spragge. Of these the last-mentioned is the sole survivor. Late in the fall of 1857 Henry Kribs and Joseph Stringer went to Owen Sound in a sail-boat to obtain supplies for their families and others of the infant settlement. On their return trip they were caught in a storm too severe for their small craft to successfully encounter, and the unfortunate men found a grave in the cold waters of the Georgian Bay.

In the summer of 1858 Leonard Gleason commenced to build a saw-mill at Colpoy's Bay. He had only to move across from Oxenden, where he had previously resided, having been sent there a year or two previous by the Indian Department to show the Indians how to erect and run a saw-mill. The establishing of this first-mentioned saw-mill, followed shortly after by the erection of a saw and grist mill by Ludwick Kribs, had the effect of centring the trading of the settlement at the little village that now bears the name of Colpoy's Bay. A post-office was opened there in 1863, L. Kribs being the postmaster. At one time it was expected " Colpoy's " would become the town Wiarton now is. Seeing it had ten years of a start, these expectations seemed warranted, but such hopes have not been realized. The village has made no progress for many years, and being so near to the larger town at the northern terminus of the railway, there is little chance of further development.

The inflow of settlers into Albemarle has never been large when compared to that experienced by the more fertile townships to the south. As stated in a foregoing paragraph, Albemarle received its first settlers in 1857. Four years later, when the census of 1861 was taken, the population was only 54 souls all told. This number in 1871 had increased to 678. Since then the census returns exhibit a slow but constant increase, showing in 1901 a population of 1962, or almost three times that of 1871. The several localities which received the earliest settlers were; first, in the vicinity of " Colpoy's," next between the Amabel boundary and the centre of the

[1] In 1852, and for some subsequent years, Mr. Kribs acted as a missionary to the Indians at Colpoy's Bay, working under the auspices of the Congregational Church.

township in the vicinity of Mar, and, at a later date, near Purple Valley. The earliest road opened was that on the town line between Amabel and Albemarle, thence north through Mar to Eastnor; the full extent of this was done by the end of the sixties.[1] The road to Cape Croker reserve was also one early opened   The opening of other roads has been done gradually as required.

Albemarle was united for municipal purposes to the united townships of Arran and Amabel by a by-law of the United Counties Council, passed 29th December, 1857   This union lasted for three years, when Amabel and Albemarle were separated from Arran by a by-law passed September 26th, 1860   On June 18th, 1869, this latter union was dissolved and Albemarle and Eastnor were united into one municipality.   To the corporation of these two townships an addition was made June 21st, 1872, by uniting to it the townships of Lindsay and St. Edmunds   On June 8th, 1877, the three northerly townships were erected into a separate municipality, and for the first time Albemarle was free from a partnership in municipal affairs.

The first reeve of the united townships of Amabel and Albemarle was Ludwick Kribs.   To attend the meetings of the United Counties Council at Goderich he had to make the following roundabout journey   He first of all sailed to Collingwood and there took the Northern Railway to Toronto, thence by Grand Trunk and Buffalo and Lake Huron Railways to Goderich   He was allowed on the pay sheet for a mileage of between 200 and 300 miles   The necessity of travelling such a roundabout route speaks conclusively as to the impassable state of the roads throughout the county of Bruce in the early sixties.

On January 1st, 1870, Albemarle having been separated from Amabel, became the senior township of the northern townships on the Peninsula which formed the new municipality then created. The first reeve was Thomas H. Lee,[2] while the two offices of clerk and treasurer were filled by John Shackleton

When the time came (at the end of 1877) for the breaking of

[1]This road was largely opened out by the Government; Hiram Parker, of Southampton (subsequently the first settler at Golden Valley), was the contractor; William Bull was the inspector of the work

[2]The following are the names of those who have filled the office of reeve of Albemarle—Thos H Lee, 1870, '71, '72, '73; Ludwick Spragge, 1874, '75, '76 and '77, John Shackleton, 1878, '79; John H. Whicher, 1880, '81, '83, '84; Dr H. Wigle, 1882, John McIver, 1885, '86, part of 1888, '89 and 1895; Thomas Rydall, 1887 and part of 1888; Eph Cross, 1890, T S Cotton, 1891, '92; Andrew Weir, 1893, '94, '96, '97 and 1900; Thomas Crane, 1898, '99; William Chisholm, 1901, '02; John Pruder, 1903, '04; E Andrews, 1905, John Ashcroft, 1906

the municipal tie which united Eastnor, Lindsay and St. Edmunds with Albemarle, trouble arose over the finances and four years of litigation and arbitration followed, the costs of which ran up into the thousands.[1] The settlement was finally reached in July, 1881, at a joint meeting of the Councils of the two municipalities, held at the "Half-way House" (W Colwell's), when on motion of F. W. Stuart and R. Davidson, the united townships of Eastnor, Lindsay and St. Edmunds agreed to pay the township of Albemarle $300, in two payments (January 1st, 1883, and January 1st, 1884), with interest, in final settlement of claim. Each party to pay their costs of suit. This offer the Albemarle Council accepted and so closed this long and vexatious litigation, which might have been settled by the same method years before, and saved the large sums paid in law costs.

The report of the county valuators in 1879 enabled the people in the north to see that they had been too highly assessed by the County Council in the past; on this being pointed out, a committee was appointed, which reported that for five years the assessment of the northern townships had been too high, and recommended that 50 per cent of the indebtedness of each municipality on account of rates be remitted   (The amount of indebtedness of Albemarle on the 1st January previous was $2,781 67, showing arrears for about four years)   The remission of $1,292 72 of county rates proved a great relief to the finances of the municipality.

There are not many names in Albemarle of which the origin can be given. Mr John M McNabb, of Southampton, says that Cape Croker bears the name of John Wilson Croker, who was Secretary to the Admiralty; and Colpoy's Bay of Sir John Colpoy, an admiral in the British Navy, both names being bestowed by Capt Bayfield during his survey of Lake Huron and Georgian Bay. Prior to this the bay was called Sturgeon Bay. and is so named in a map now in the Department of Archives at Ottawa, prepared in 1792 for Lieut.-Governor Simcoe.

The prospects for the future of Albemarle can hardly be said to be as bright as those cherished by the more southerly townships; the extent of rocky land precludes the thought of it. The past has witnessed the lumberman gather in rich returns from her forests, and the cleared farms, where the land has been arable, have well

[1]The details of the suit are to be found in 45 and 46 U. C Queen's Bench Reports

repaid the labor expended thereon. This is attested by the numerous comfortable farm-houses to be seen throughout the township. One of these, it might be said in passing, is possibly the finest up-to-date farm-house in the whole county, namely, that of Mr. John McIver, and there a hospitality is extended by the owner and his good lady that accords with their big and handsome house. Mr. McIver's success has come from engaging largely in stock raising, and it is most probable that the future prosperity of Albemarle will be in carrying out this branch of farming.

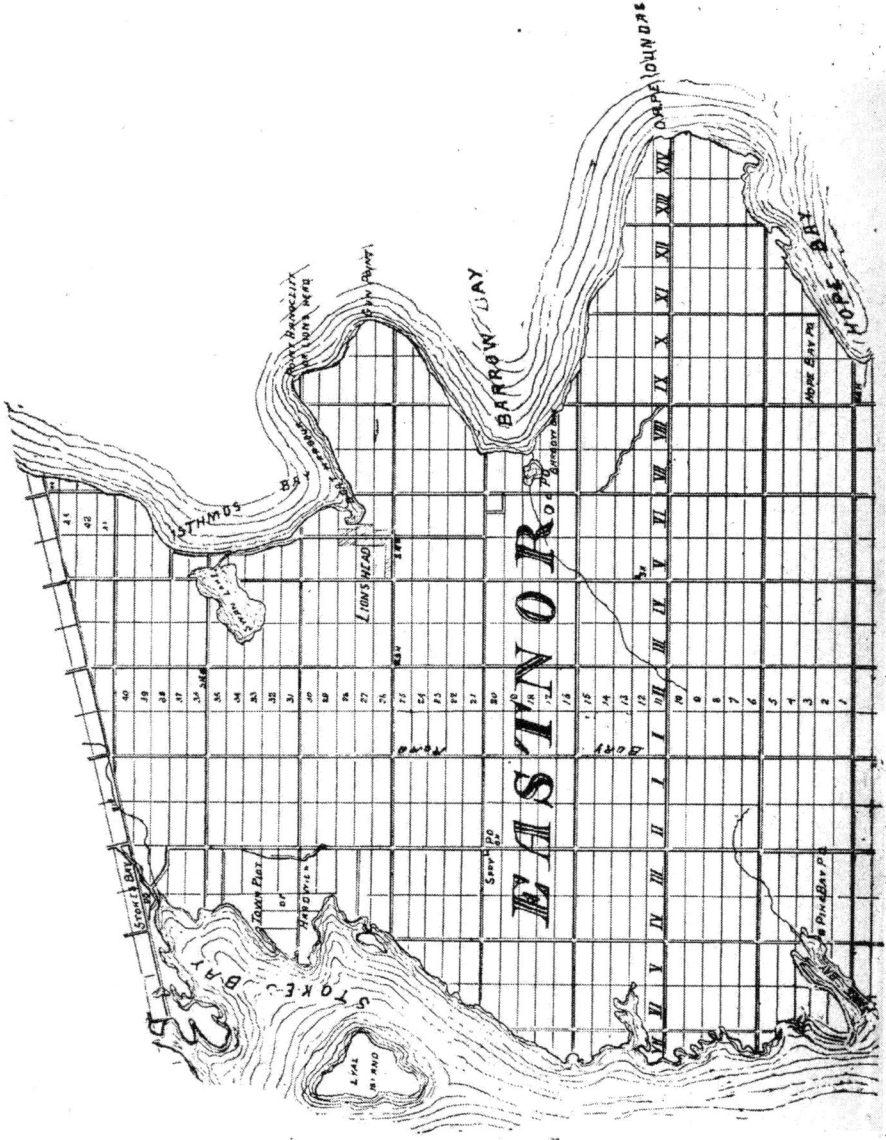

EASTNOR

BARROW BAY

ISTHMUS BAY

LIONS HEAD

STOKES BAY

HARDWICKE

TOWN PLOT

CAPE DUNDAS

Spry Rd

Barrow Rd

CHAPTER XV.

TOWNSHIP OF EASTNOR.[1]

EXTRACT FROM THE REPORT OF COUNTY VALUATORS, 1901.

" There is a great deal of good land in Eastnor, which shows decided improvement since the last valuation, and in the near future will compare favorably with any portion of the county, but a railroad is much needed, especially in regard to the shipment of stock and postal facilities We think we are within the mark in saying that fully one-third of Eastnor will be first-class land when the present drainage contracts are completed, and the balance of what is known as the Eastnor swamp is cleared up. The balance of the township, however, is very inferior, rock everywhere and timber gone, which leaves the lots (we cannot say land) valueless. This statement applies largely to the four northern townships. Fire and lumbermen have devastated these townships and have left behind a barren waste.''

EASTNOR possesses physical features peculiar to itself among the municipalities of the county. In it are to be seen as fine farms, buildings included, as are to be found in the highly favored southern townships of Bruce. At the same time in it are to be found large areas of rock, as bare of soil as can be seen in any part of the Peninsula Its bays, deeply indenting the coast line, result in the narrowest part of the county, excepting near the point of the Peninsula, being found within its boundaries (the township is less than five miles wide at the 35 side road), while in another part its extending peninsulas give to it a breadth excelled by only one other township. Although far north, yet it is less liable to summer frosts than townships further south, this is because of the large bodies of water on each side of it. Its large swamps, thought at one time to be a detriment to the township, are now in a large measure drained, and the finest land is that which was only lately a swamp

The first purchases of land in Eastnor were made in 1862, but settlers do not seem to have taken up their lands until 1869 or 1870. The first assessment roll of the township, that for 1871, is so interest-

---

[1] " This township was named in honor of John Somers Cocks, Earl of Somers, Viscount Eastnor of Eastnor Castle, county of Hereford, who was closely related to the wife of Sir Edward W. Head, the Governor-General in 1855, who chose the name of ' Eastnor ' for the township in compliment to his wife's relations.''—'' *Nothing but Names.*''

ing that extracts from it are here given. The roll contains eighteen names,[1] three of which seem to have been non-residents. Six of these ratepayers seem to have been alone on their clearings, while nine had families. The total number of inhabitants, as given in the roll, is fifty-one. Three ratepayers are entered as having clearings of five acres each. One, that of ten acres; the rest had no clearings. Each one hundred acres was assessed at the same amount, namely $100; as there were twenty-three lots taken up, the assessment roll shows a total of $2,300. This assessment was much increased in the roll of 1872, the amount there being $10,395, showing a marked advance. The development of the township is noticeable in the next record we shall quote, that of the county valuators, who in 1879 valued the real estate in Eastnor at $133,448.

They who may be named as the first settlers in Eastnor, when selecting their lands for settlement, seem to have favored the vicinity of Lion's Head; the wave of settlement moved thence south as far as the 20 side-line and adjacent lands, and thence westward to where Spry is now. Francis Waugh, near Hope Bay, and Joseph Eveleigh and Patrick Judge, at Barrow Bay, being exceptions.

Owing to the difficulty of access into the township by land, the roads being in a deplorable condition for many years, most of the traffic in the early days to points outside the township was by water. The following are the names of some of the steamboats that in the seventies or eighties visited Lion's Head and Barrow Bay. The *Okonra,* Captain Dunn, was one of the earliest vessels to be engaged on the route between Owen Sound, Wiarton and the Peninsula. She was succeeded about 1879 by the *Wiarton Belle,* and the latter boat by the *Comet,* and that by the *Annie Watt* and the ill-fated *Jane Miller.* For the accommodation of these and other vessels it was necessary that a wharf should be constructed at Lion's Head. Realizing this the township, in the summer of 1883, offered to pay what sum was necessary to place material on the ground sufficient to construct a dock 200 feet long, on condition that the government have the work performed. The government in that year sent a dredge to clear a channel, some 13 feet deep and 80 feet long, through a

---

[1]As it may interest some to know who these eighteen were, their names are here given, viz , Joseph Andrew, John Cale, Allen Erwin, David Harris, Thomas and Francis Hart, Francis and Michael Hagin, Thomas Harkness, Robert McCarter, George Moore, Jacob Schermahorn, Samuel Slack, L. Sherlock, Richard Tackaberry, Wm. Tunan, Joseph Waugh and Francis Waugh. As to which of the amove mentioned was Eastnor's first settler it is not known. George Moore and Richard Tackaberry each claimed it.

bar that extended across the entrance to the harbor. This improvement to navigation was supplemented by the construction of the pier.

On 18th June, 1869, the township of Eastnor was by by-law of the County Council united for municipal purposes to the township of Albemarle. To this union of municipalities there was a further addition made June 21st, 1872, when the County Council added thereto the townships of Lindsay and St. Edmunds. This large municipality of united townships began to dissolve when on June 8th, 1877, the three northern townships were by by-law separated from Albemarle, to become a separate municipality on the 1st January following, with Eastnor as the senior township.[1] These three townships remained united as one municipality until Lindsay and St. Edmunds, having developed and attained to the required qualifications within their own bounds, were set apart as a separate municipality, and since that date, January 1st, 1883, Eastnor has known nothing of a municipal partnership. The first township council consisted of Francis Waters, William Freeman, Jos. Waugh and James Elder, with David Scott, jun., as reeve,[2] C. W. W. Dalton[3] as township clerk, and Richard Tackaberry as township treasurer.

The earliest attempt to establish a manufacturing industry in the township was in 1874, when a saw-mill, built and run by Patrick Judge, was put in operation at Barrow Bay. Some three years later the same man had a grist-mill of one run of stones; this mill was more used for " chopping " than for flour. In 1879 a bonus of $1,600 was given by the townships to Robert Watt[4] to erect a grist and saw-mill at Lion's Head. This mill was completed and running in the month of July in the following year, and for years the hum of its machinery might be heard until in an unfortunate fire it was burned down in 1889. This mill has been replaced by an excellent

[1]The first municipal election was held at the schoolhouse for S S No 1, C W. W Dalton being returning officer.

[2]The following are the names of those who have been reeves of Eastnor from 1878 onwards: David Scott, 1878, '79, 1880; William Hale, 1881; Robert Watt, 1882, '84; Thomas Boyle, 1883; Alex. Chisholm, 1885, '86, 1892, '93 and '94; F. W. Stewart, 1887; R E. Moore, 1888, '89, 1890, '91; John H. Cook, 1895, '96, '98, '99, 1900, '01 and '05; Robert Bain, 1897; Thomas J. Bridge, 1902, '03 and '04; W B Moshier, 1906

[3]C. W. W. Dalton filled the office of township clerk until March, 1905, when he removed from Eastnor to the Niagara District

[4]Robert Watt subsequently became reeve of Eastnor, and later, while residing at Wiarton, he was elected a county councillor, and in 1903 warden of the county of Bruce In 1905 he retired from business, that of a saw-miller and lumberman, left Wiarton, and moved to Toronto

roller-process mill built by a joint stock company. In 1883 Messrs.
Judge and Inksetter built a steam saw-mill at Barrow Bay, and there,
in 1892, the Barrow Bay Lumber Company built a large, roller-
process grist-mill. A number of saw-mills have at various times
been put in operation throughout the township, some of which have
had to close down because of the growing scarcity of logs.

Before the village of Lion's Head had taken form, what was
known as Tackaberry's Corners (lot 20 and 21, concessions 4 and 5,
E B.R.) was looked upon as the "hub" of the township. Lion's
Head in 1875 consisted only of the post-office (opened in August of
that year, with F. W. Stewart as postmaster) and one store, the
only store in the township. An old settler furnished the author with
a list of prices he had there paid for necessaries of life. As these
backwoods prices contrast markedly with those of the present day,
they are here given as received: Axes, $2 50 each; coal-oil, 50c. a
gallon, salt, 5c. lb.; tobacco, $1 25 lb; tea, lowest price, 75c. per lb.;
pork, 19c. lb.; scythe stones, 37 1-2c. each

The village of Lion's Head takes its name from the resemblance
to a lion's head to be discerned on a rocky cliff lying about a mile
east of the harbor   At one time the resemblance was quite marked,
but the action of the elements is causing the likeness to fade away.
As noted in a previous paragraph, in 1875 the village consisted only
of a store and post-office. A visitor in the fall of 1879 states that
there was then in course of erection a number of dwelling-houses,
two hotels, a store, a grist-mill and a planing-mill, while there was
in operation a saw-mill, a pump factory, two stores and a blacksmith
shop, the stores being run by F. W. Stewart and George P. Webster,
while the population was estimated to be about 100. Another visitor
in 1882 estimates the population as 200, with two hotels, one a brick
building, and five stores. The spiritual needs of the residents at
Lion's Head and vicinity seemed to have been first attended to by
a Rev. Mr. Leggett, a Methodist minister. The Presbyterians seemed
to have been a little later in entering upon this field, but met with
strong support, and erected the first church edifice in the township.
The first minister of this denomination to labor in this field was the
Rev. W. M. Rogers; this was in 1879   He was followed by a Mr.
McKibbon, a student from one of the Presbyterian colleges, in the
summer of 1880, the services being held in the summer months in
the old Webster mill, and when the weather became unsuitable for
services there they were held in the house of Mr. Robert Watt, where
also was held the first tea-meeting in the settlement. A Mr. Marr,

another student, filled this field in the summer of 1881, and in the following year the Rev. Mr. McLennan was inducted as pastor of the congregation, which already had erected a church building 22 x 40 feet. This building was dedicated May 22nd, 1881. This congregation was advanced to the status of a self-sustaining congregation when the Rev. T. A. Nelson was inducted as its pastor January 10th, 1905. The Church of England had a representative stationed at Lion's Head in the person of the Rev. Mr. Hutchison in the fall of 1882. He was successful in stirring up his flock to proceed to the erection of a church edifice, the foundation stone of which was laid May 3rd, 1883. The building is 50 x 26 feet, built of frame on a stone foundation, and exhibits good taste in its architecture. Not far from this church edifice is to be seen the Eastnor township hall, a very neat structure, erected in 1897, and admirably fitted for public gatherings. It is claimed to be the best township hall in the county.

When the County Council in 1879 made a refund to the four northern townships of part of their arrears of county rates, on account of previous over-assessment during the five years preceding, the united townships of Eastnor, Lindsay and St Edmunds received a rebate of $438 76, which was a very welcome relief to an impoverished municipality.

Eastnor, although not a wealthy township, has from the first exhibited a broad-mindedness in the matter of public improvements that is commendable. The first step in this direction was the giving of a bonus of $1,600 towards the erecting of a grist-mill at Lion's Head. This was followed by an issue of debentures amounting to $6,000 to improve the roads. The three extensive drainage schemes within the township have also cost a large sum   In all, Eastnor has issued debentures to the amount of $34,000, all for public improvements, as shown in a footnote.[1] When the townships of Lindsay and St.

[1]LIST OF DEBENTURES ISSUED BY THE TOWNSHIP OF EASTNOR.

In the year 1879 To bonus a Grist Mill $1,600
            1880 For improving public roads   6,000
            1884-85 Judge Creek Drainage Scheme   7,200
            1896 Fern Creek Drainage Scheme   2,300
            1901 Judge Creek Drainage Scheme, 2nd issue ...   10,000
            1906 Judge Creek Drainage Scheme, 3rd issue..   2,800
            1906 Fern Creek Drainage Scheme, 2nd issue   1,200
            1906 Swan Lake Drainage Scheme   1,400
            1906 For Granolithic Sidewalks at Lion's Head   .   1,500
                                                                 _____
                                                                $34,000
In addition to the above the various school sections have issued debentures to erect schoolhouses

Edmunds separated from Eastnor they were, with the latter township, liable for the two first issues of debentures above-mentioned, amounting to $7,600. The arrangement arrived at at the time of separation was somewhat as follows, namely: Eastnor, as the senior township, was to assume this indebtedness, and Lindsay and St. Edmunds agreed to pay three-eighths of the required annual rate to Eastnor during the seventeen years the debentures had to run.

Of the several drainage schemes of the township, that known as the Judge Creek Scheme drains the land back of Barrow Bay, the Fern Creek Scheme the lands lying west of Lion's Head, and the Swan Lake Scheme lands lying north-west of Lion's Head. The lands to be benefited are expected to become in time the garden of the township The engineering difficulties met with in the Judge Creek drain consisted in the enlarging of the bed of the creek by blasting the rock, an undertaking of some magnitude. This was done by a contractor from Toronto. The almost dead level of the land in the Fern Creek district presented an engineering difficulty of another sort, it being difficult to obtain the necessary fall for a rapid flow of water.

Besides Lion's Head there are but three villages in Eastnor, Barrow Bay, Spry and Stokes Bay, the last-mentioned being the most flourishing of the three. John Shute has had part of lots 38 and 39, concession 3, W.B.R., surveyed and subdivided into the lots which comprise the village of Stokes Bay. Sanguine expectations are held as to the ultimate development of the village, as it has the trade of a good part of Lindsay and St. Edmunds, and also a good wharf, so that shipments can readily be made from there. The lighthouse on Lyal Island, at the entrance to Stokes Bay, has been a guide to mariners since 1885.

LINDSAY

CHAPTER XVI.

TOWNSHIP OF LINDSAY.[1]

EXTRACT FROM THE REPORT OF COUNTY VALUATORS, 1879

" Lindsay and St Edmunds It would be difficult to place any value on these townships, as we have not seen any land fit for cultivation, and not more than a dozen settlers, and one saw-mill in the whole of the two townships. The greater part of the land that was purchased in these townships was bought for the timber, and when that was taken off the land was abandoned We set it down at $1 50 per acre."

EXTRACT FROM THE REPORT OF COUNTY VALUATORS, 1901.

" Owing to the limited time at our disposal, we are unable to give complete reports of the townships of Lindsay and St Edmunds. These townships possess very little good land St Edmunds is largely a waste. The inhabitants of Dyer's Bay and Tobermory sections are at a great disadvantage, being so far removed from a line of railroad, and the roads leading to those places are in an almost impassable condition Land is so sparsely settled that it is utterly out of the power of the people of these townships to maintain the roads Their lines have not fallen to them in pleasant places, certainly not their concession lines."

THE first sale of lands in the township of Lindsay was made in the year 1870. Previous, however, to any sales of land the pioneer settler of Lindsay, Abraham West, had come into the township and located. The land he selected was lot 5, concession 2, W.B.R., and on that lot the first clearing in the township was made.   The first neighbor Mr. West had was William Clark, who settled on land but four lots south. The little settlement progressed but slowly in numbers; the census of 1871 gives the number of the inhabitants of the whole township as twenty. By 1879, however, the population had so grown as to warrant the establishing of a school section and the building of a school-house. The first Board of Trustees consisted of John Kelly, George Ceasor and Alexander McDonald. The school-house, built of logs, was at " McDonald's " (lot 4, con. 1, W.B.R.), and the first teacher who therein imparted instruction was a Miss Hurst, who was succeeded by Miss Christie Stringer.

[1] The name this township bears is said to have been given in honor of Earl Lindsay.

The roads in Lindsay could not at any time, by any stretch of the imagination, be called good; in fact, it has only been in very late years that it has been possible to drive safely a buggy on either of the two main roads which lead through the township. The west side main road of the Peninsula was opened through to Lindsay in the year 1870, and that from Lion's Head to Dyer's Bay in 1880. The following anecdote, related of one of the pioneers, will illustrate the hardships they endured from lack of roads passable by a team: One of the settlers went to Owen Sound and bought six bushels of potatoes, which he had taken to Lion's Head by boat, and then had to carry them on his back the rest of the way home, a distance of some nine miles. Another undertook to carry home a barrel of flour. He was not an especially strong man, so had the flour placed in two bags. One of these he would carry for a bit, and "while resting," as he called it, would go back for the other bag and carry that up to or beyond the first. This was repeated again and again until a number of miles were covered and home reached at last.

A number of Lindsay's early settlers were young men of Highland origin who came from the township of Huron. Prominent among them was Alexander McDonald, referred to more fully in a footnote.[1]

It was some ten years or more after the first settlers had located in Lindsay before they had the luxury of a post-office in their own township Previous to 1881 they were dependent upon the post-office at Mar, Lion's Head or Spry for their supply of mail matter. In the year just mentioned a post-office was established, known as "Stokes Bay,"[2] but at first located on lot 5, concession 2, W.B.R., Lindsay In the same year "Dyer's Bay "[3] post-office was established. This proved a great convenience to those settled in the eastern part of the township.

The municipal history of Lindsay is as follows: On the 1st

[1]Alexander McDonald settled in Lindsay in 1877 He was for many years reeve of the township and also county commissioner, which position he filled at the time of his death, which occurred in June, 1903. Mr. McDonald was an active Christian man and at the schoolhouse above mentioned he started a Sunday-school, of which he was superintendent until his death; he also, in the absence of a settled minister, conducted regularly a weekly prayer-meeting; through his efforts a church building was also erected When Mr McDonald first became reeve the township was largely in debt; under his judicious, cautious and economical guidance this debt was much reduced

[2]Wm. Lyons was first postmaster, he was succeeded by John Gibson, and he by John Shute, who held the office for twenty-three years.

[3]Thomas Tindall was first postmaster.

REV. WM. FRASER

p. 431

B. B. MILLER

p. 221

ALEX. MCDONALD

p. 252

JOHN DOUGLASS

p. 269

January, 1873, it became one of the townships in the municipality of the united townships of Albemarle, Eastnor, Lindsay and St. Edmunds. On the 1st January, 1878, the three northern townships were separated from Albemarle. On the 1st of January, 1883, Lindsay and St. Edmunds were erected into a separate municipality, which union continued to exist until the 1st January, 1903, when each of these two townships became separate municipalities. In a footnote[1] are given the names of the various parties who have filled the position of reeve for the united townships of Lindsay and St. Edmunds, and since the separation as reeve of Lindsay. The debenture debt of the three united townships at the date of the dissolution of the union amounted to $7,600. The two united townships of Lindsay and St. Edmunds, in settlement of the proportion of this indebtedness due by them, agreed to pay to Eastnor an annual payment of $257.22 until the debentures matured, some seventeen years later. The first Council of the united townships of Lindsay and St. Edmunds consisted of Donald McDonald, Alex. Patch, John Shute, councillors, and Peter McVicar, reeve. The joint office of clerk and treasurer was held by James Weatherhead, and Alex. Currie was the first collector.

The following are the names of some of the pioneers of Lindsay, in addition to those who are already mentioned: Kenneth Smith, Roderick McLennan, John Kelly, John Ceasor, Donald McLean, Andrew Clarke, James Finch, James Nixon, John McArthur, Sam Bestward, John Holmes, John Steip, John Witherspoon (postmaster at Miller Lake for many years), John Smith, James, William and Alex. Weatherhead, Alex. Currie (township treasurer for several years), Thomas Tyndall, William Matheson, James Watson, John Jackman, William McNair, John McDonald, John and James Shute and Norman Smith.

From the very first lumbering has been the main industry in Lindsay. Probably the first mill was that of Hiram Lymburner, at Gillies Lake, erected in 1880, and which he and his sons operated until 1905. Power was derived by widening and deepening the little creek flowing from the lake; this enlargement was increased from time to time as the demand for power made it necessary. The Messrs.

[1]The following are the names of the reeves of the township of Lindsay and St. Edmunds: Peter McVicar, 1883; J. Weatherhead, 1884, '86; James Shute, 1885; Alex. McDonald, 1887, '88, '89, 1890, '91, '92, '93, '94, '95, '96, '97, '98, '99, 1900; John Shute, 1901, '02. As reeve of Lindsay, Peter Alderson, 1903, '04, '05, '06.

Lymburner showed a good deal of enterprise in launching a small tug on Gillies Lake named the *Gertie,* used to tow rafts of logs to the mill, this little boat being the second steamer ever used on the inland waters of the county.

Lindsay is the only township in the county of Bruce in which mining for precious metals has been carried on. In the early nineties a Mr E. Clendening sank a shaft over 300 feet deep on lots 9 and 10, concession 4, E B.R The work was continued for two summers and one winter Ore is said to have been found which showed some silver, but not in sufficient quantities to pay for working it. Mr. Clendening later on did some prospecting on lot 5, concession 2, W.B.R , but with similar results. Those who were engaged in this prospecting supplied but little information to outsiders, so what is here given is but from hearsay.

The amount of land in Lindsay that might be classed as good farming land is not very large. A visitor to the township finds the principal settlement therein between the fourth concession west of the Bury Road and the fifth concession east of it, with a limit of about four miles in width north from the Eastnor boundary.

The following incident, the facts of which are given in the *Wiarton Canadian,* although not strictly speaking an historical item, yet deserves to be recorded as an instance of motherly love and devotion as manifested by one of the good wives of Lindsay. " Though rattlesnakes are reported to be fairly plentiful in Lindsay and St. Edmunds, fortunately accidents of a serious nature such as follow the bite of these reptiles have not been numerous, and settlers have become rather careless. On a warm day in August, 1902, a six-year-old son of Mr. Robt. Bartley, residing north of Dyer's Bay, playing about his home bare-footed and bare-legged to his knees, was so unfortunate as to step on a three-foot snake, which was lying basking in the sun The rude awakening aroused the temper of the reptile, and in a twinkling its fangs were buried in the child's leg. An angry snake strikes very quickly, and before the child got beyond reach the beast struck him in five different places. His screams brought his mother to the scene, and realizing the trouble and danger, instead of fainting or going into hysterics, she bravely sucked the wounds, tied a ligature tightly round the limb to stop the circulation of the blood, then hitched a horse and started on a fifteen-mile drive to Lion's Head with the boy. Before reaching medical aid at that village the child was nearly crazy from the pain caused by the ligature stopping the circulation in the limb, and his cries could be heard for a long distance. But the heroic woman held on and fortunately found Dr. Sloan at home. The wounds were cauterized and dressed, and fortunately little or no ill effects resulted from this exciting experience."

The origin of the following names in Lindsay are here given by the author on what he considers good authority: Lake Miller bears the name of B. B. Miller, first Indian Land Agent at Wiarton; Gillies Lake is called after John Gillies, M.P. for North Bruce in the seventies; Cabot Head is said to have been named by Governor Simcoe in honor of Cabot, the discoverer of Canada. The lighthouse at this point was established in 1896.

CHAPTER XVII.

TOWNSHIP OF ST. EDMUNDS.[1]

THE chapters in this volume which give the history of a township are in each instance prefaced by extracts from the report of the county valuators, with the solitary exception of St. Edmunds. For such information referring specially to St. Edmunds as is to be found in these extracts the reader is referred back to the preceding chapter, because the valuators in every report have joined Lindsay and St. Edmunds together, and it is impossible to separate the general remarks of the valuators and apply specially to Lindsay or St. Edmunds.

Although further north than Lindsay, St. Edmunds seems to have been but little behind it in receiving its pioneer settlers, it being in the summer of 1871 that Captain John Charles Earl[2] settled at what is known as " The Big Tub." In November of the same year Captain Earl had a companion come to share the loneliness of his pioneer life in the person of Abraham Davis, who settled at Dunk's Bay. These pioneers were joined at various intervals, in somewhat of the following order, by Captain Alexander Marks, Michael Belrose, Jacob Belrose, George and Neil Currie, Robert, John C. and James H. Hopkins, Thomas and George Bartman, Benjamin and Alexander Butchart, Donald McDonald (first postmaster at Tobermory) and Benjamin and William Young. Mr. Solomon Spears (to whom the

---

[1] This township is named after Bury St. Edmunds. There has been from the first a disagreement as to the spelling of the name; the Toronto Government officials giving "s" as the final letter, and the Indian Land Office, Ottawa, spelling it without The township, on its becoming incorporated, adopted the former method of spelling and calls itself " St. Edmunds."

[2] The perfect safety with which vessels could lie in the basin at Tobermory has made it a much frequented harbor of refuge. For the convenience of navigators, Captain Earl made a practice of hanging a lantern at the top of a high pole as a range light and so ensure safe navigation to vessels when making the harbor. He was remunerated for this service by various captains, they presenting him with useful house supplies, such as a bag of potatoes, flour, or some coal-oil, etc. In the course of a few years the Government acknowledged this service and paid him a salary of about $30 a year.

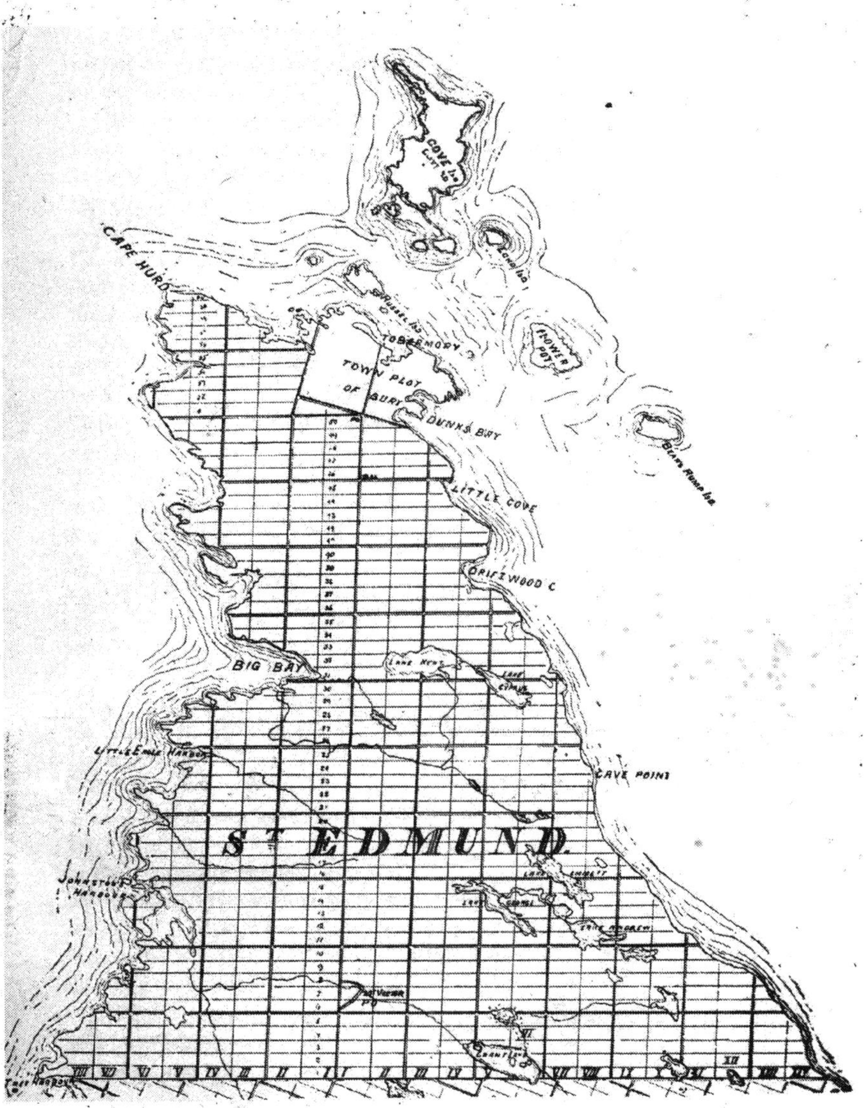
COVE Isd.
CAPE HURD
TOBERMORY
TOWN PLOT OF BURY
FLOWER POT
DUNKS BAY
LITTLE COVE
DRIFTWOOD C
BIG BAY
CAVE POINT
ST EDMUND
JOHNSTON'S HARBOUR

author is indebted for many of the facts connected with the history of St. Edmunds) settled in the township in March, 1883.

The lumbering resources of St. Edmunds have been exploited to an extent not equalled in any other township of the county. In 1872 Cockwell & Grant erected a large saw-mill and shingle-mill on the Crane River, at what is now called "McVicar's" This firm cut a road from Pine Tree Harbor through the woods for a distance of ten miles to a point at which they built their saw-mill; they also laid out a large sum in cleaning the river so that the produce of their mill might be floated down to the harbor. This mill and its limits were purchased in 1880 by Peter McVicar,[1] who built another mill in the following year as well as a wharf at Johnston's Harbor. In 1881 a mill was built at Tobermory by Messrs Maitland & Rixon. This mill was burnt down in March, 1883, but rebuilt in the same year by the same firm, who after running it six years moved it to Owen Sound. About 1892 the Southampton Lumber Company built a saw-mill at Pine Tree Harbor. In 1895 a mill was built at Tobermory by Richard Badstone (since purchased and run by Hector Currie) In 1900 another mill was erected by E. M. Meirs, and another in the following year by Messrs. Simpson & Culbert, which gave Tobermory three saw-mills in constant operation, adding materially to the trade of the village

The post-office at Tobermory was established in 1881, the mail being carried on foot from Stokes Bay Mr. Benjamin Butchart was the first mail-carrier St. Edmunds' first school was opened in 1883, Its first Board of Trustees were Michael Belrose, Donald McDonald and Jacob Belrose. The first teacher was a Miss Ella Conklin

As a separate municipality St. Edmunds has existed since the 1st of January, 1903. Its previous municipal relations are related in the preceding chapter, referring to the township of Lindsay. The first reeve of the municipality was Solomon Spears, who also filled the office in 1906, his successor for 1904 and 1905 being William Simpson. The clerk of the municipality was James Campbell and the treasurer John C. Hopkins.

The first public religious service in the township is said to have been conducted by a Presbyterian student, possibly a Mr. Peter McLean, who was the first to preach in Lindsay. The first regular .

[1]Peter. McVicar continued the running of this mill for twenty years, when, in 1901, he retired to spend his declining years at the town of Perth Mr. McVicar was the first reeve of Carrick, in 1856 and 1857, and also the first reeve of the united townships of Lindsay and St Edmunds in 1883.

stationed minister belonged to the Methodist Church, the Rev. Robert
Walker. Succeeding him was the Rev. Mr. Sparling. Under his
ministration a church was built at Tobermory Harbor. The next
minister was the Rev. W. D. Dainard, who was instrumental in the
building of a church at "The Settlement," a point on the Bury Road
some two and a half or three miles south of the harbor. There is
also a Baptist church at the town plot of Bury, but the author is not
able to give the year of its erection.

St. Edmunds being at the extreme north of the peninsula nearly
all the vessels passing into the Georgian Bay sail along its coast.
This has necessitated the erection of several lighthouses. The first
one to be erected was that at Cove Island.[1] This is a white, circular
stone building, built in 1859, which in addition to a powerful light
is also equipped with a fog horn to indicate the locality when fog
covers the water. The lighthouse at Tobermory was erected in
1885, and the one at Flower Pot Island in 1897.

In regard to the local names in St. Edmunds the following comprises all the information the author has been able to obtain: Lake
Kent on the maps, but locally called Lake Cameron, is named after
John Cameron, of Southampton, a man well known to the Indians
and fishermen throughout the Peninsula in the days before settlements were formed   Lake Cyprus received its name from the island
in the Mediterranean Sea, the name being given at the time that island
was ceded to Great Britain. Tobermory was named by the Highland
fishermen after a town in Mull. (In Bayfield's chart it is named
" Collins Harbor.") The three lakes on concessions 5, 6, 7 and 8,
east of the Bury Road, were intended to bear the names of the patron
saints of England, Scotland and Ireland. This was carried out to
the extent of St George and St. Andrew, but a young man named
Emmett Smith, working in the office of B. B. Miller, the Indian
Land Agent, persuaded Mr. Miller to let one of the lakes be called
after him, so as Lake Emmett it will probably be always known.
Bury town plot is named after Viscount Bury, Superintendent-
General of Indian Affairs in 1855.

The entrance of the telegraph and telephone wires into Tobermory
has brought what was the jumping-off place of the county into touch
with the rest of the world, and if the proposed railway ever reaches
there we shall look for great things in the township of St. Edmunds.

---

[1]After being in charge of Cove Island lighthouse for twenty-five years,
George Currie retired in the summer of 1903. He was succeeded by
Kenneth McLeod, of Tobermory.

FLOWER POT ISLAND, TOWNSHIP OF ST. EDMUNDS.   p. 261

There are extensive caves to be seen in St. Edmunds The lime-stone rock, so common throughout the peninsula, seemingly has here suffered from the erosion of water more than elsewhere. Possibly the largest of these caves is to be seen on Flower Pot Island, the extent of which is not known, as it has not been fully explored. The island takes its name, that of "Flower Pot," from a peculiar shaped rock standing about fifty feet in height. The illustration here given shows what a natural curiosity it is and how appropriate is the name.

CHAPTER XVIII.

TOWNSHIP OF ARRAN.[1]

EXTRACT FROM THE REPORT OF COUNTY VALUATORS, 1901.

" Stone is the chief drawback to this township, and while there has been a large quantity gathered into heaps and fences, yet there is a great work to be done in this respect still. There are some places it would cost more to clear the land of stones than it would be worth after the work was done   Arran is well watered generally, the swamp lands in the north half of the township are very difficult to drain, and in many places they are not so valuable as they were twelve years ago, as since that time the timber has been removed, and the land generally has not been improved   The Sauble is a poor source of drainage, having no banks and a slow current.   There is considerable wet land from Arran Lake north-eastward to the corner of the township, which it is doubtful if it will ever be of much value   The soil of Arran is fair, with the exception of about two thousand acres in the north-west corner, which is almost unproductive, it being so light   It comes in touch here with the north part of Saugeen Township, and is largely similar in quality.   Buildings and orchards compare favorably with any municipality in the county. The roads also are good.   The rate per acre is $31 11, of which amount the village property makes 90 cents per acre "

THE lands in the township of Arran were those classed as " school lands," and were opened for sale July 30th, 1852.[2]   This sale included all lots which were in the original survey of the township.   The lands included in " The Half Mile Strip," as noted in Chapter V., were offered for sale by the Indian Land Department,[3]

[1] The township of Arran is named after the Island of Arran, at the mouth of the Clyde, Scotland

[2] See Appendix J   The first whose name was entered as a purchaser was Mathew Latimer, for lots 3 and 4, concession 8th, date being September 29th, 1852.   Mr John M McNabb, in a published letter, stated: " That in the year 1852 the late Alex McNabb, Crown Land Agent for the county of Bruce, was in receipt of a communication from Mr. Ezra Jewett, a famous raiser of Merino sheep, in which letter Mr. Jewett stated that he and his friends residing in the Eastern States were anxious to acquire the whole township of Arran for the purpose of raising sheep on a large scale, provided they obtained it on reasonable terms.   The Government of the day refused to enter into any terms on account of the parties being Americans, and the scheme fell through."

[3] See Appendix I   The shape of these lots is unique within the county, they being in depth but half a mile, only four lots could be included from side-road to side-road if the lots were to approximate one hundred acres each.

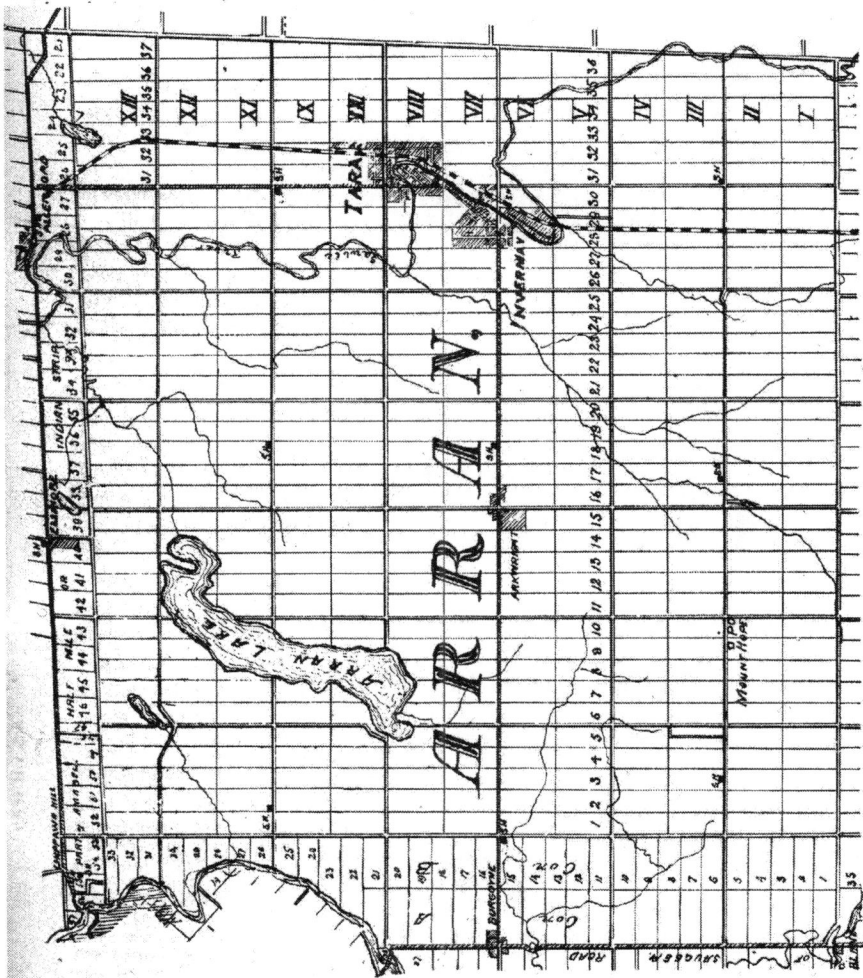

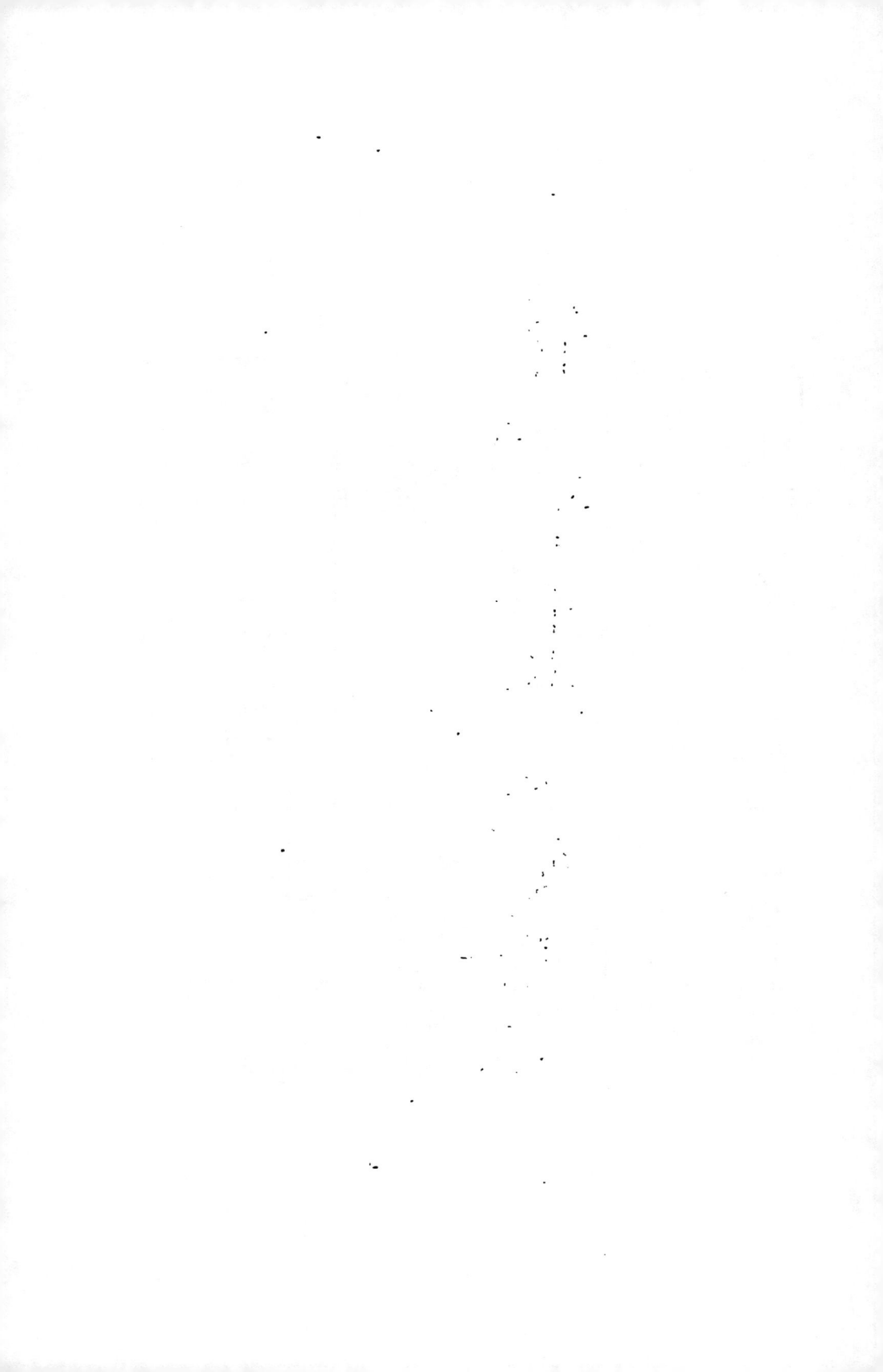

July 23rd, 1852 The survey of the township, both of Indian and school lands, was made in the year 1851; Charles Rankin had the contract from the Government of making these surveys, but the work was done by George Gould, afterwards County Clerk.

Arran's pioneer settler was Henry Boyle; his coming into Arran antedating by a year that of the surveyors. He took up the most northerly lot (No. 21) on concession A, where, when the necessity arose later on, from the large number of persons seeking lands, he opened a tavern

The author has met with much difficulty in fixing the order of priority of settlement of the pioneers of Arran. This has arisen because of a common practice which prevailed among them of returning to the settlements to earn some money, just as soon as they had done enough work on their bush lot to establish their squatter's claim thereto, which consisted in making a small "slashing" and building a bit of a shanty. During their absence other settlers came in, these remaining permanently and not finding on their entrance into the bush any one in the neighborhood, felt justified in claiming the title of being the first settlers This explanation is given in case the assertion be made that this narrative lacks in accuracy If such should be the case, the author can only say that every effort possible has been put forth to obtain information at first hands; then, when these sources of his information seemed to be contradictory, to try and blend the several narratives to the best of his ability into the account as here presented to the reader.

The author has received from David Chalmers, the first to settle in the eastern part of Arran, a letter giving an account of his experiences on entering the township in 1851. This letter, with some few omissions, is given in a footnote,[1] believing that the narrative will be appreciated.

[1]. . "In the month of May, 1851, three travellers left Owen Sound on a land hunt, intending to locate and settle as farmers in the township of Arran The party consisted of Mr David Butchart, a man of about forty years of age; Mr James Roch, an importation from Dundee, Scotland, and myself, a lad of about twenty years of age. All three of us were practically green at bush work; on starting we took the road carrying heavy loads of provisions and an axe each, and such a road ! But we were strong and of good courage and so floundered through mud and water for twelve miles : there were only three shanties with small clearings all the way. When at last we arrived at the house of Mr James Barber, 12th concession of Derby, on the boundary between Grey and Bruce, we were very tired and gladly accepted the hospitality of Mr. Barber for the night Enquiries were made as to our object in visiting him, and on being informed that we wanted land, he told us that we were somewhat premature in our visit, that the township of Arran was not yet surveyed

When the surveying party returned to Owen Sound after completing the survey of the township of Arran, which was in the fall of 1851, two of the staff, who had been impressed with the undeveloped possibilities of the township, decided to take up land therein in the vicinity of where water power might be developed. These two were George Gould and Richard Berford. Each sought out a companion to go with him, one who might prove helpful as a future neighbor. Mr. Gould found such a one in J. W. Linton, and Mr. Berford in John Hamilton No time was lost, for fear that someone else might pre-empt the lands they thought of taking up before their arrival, so

and that there would be no use coming to hunt for farms until midsummer However, we were anxious to see the land we came to seek, so in the morning we started on the old *blaze* of the county line. About one and a half miles north on that line we started to fell timber to clear a potato patch. We piled the brush, built a small shanty of small logs, bought five bushels of potatoes from Mr. Barber, and planted them among the logs. The crop turned out well I dug the crop up in the fall as Mr Butchart and Mr Roch did not turn up to assist These potatoes which I raised can safely be called the first crop raised in Arran.

" In the summer the survey of the township was proceeded with, and early in the fall I started to select a farm for myself. I went alone. On lot 25, concession 6, I found the surveyor's party, with whom I stayed all night This party was, I remember, in charge of Mr George Gould and Mr Richard Berford One of the party was my old fellow traveller, James Roch He asked me, as a friend, if I would do a little chopping for him between lots 29 and 30, concession 8, as he could not leave his work on the survey Of course, like a greeny, I consented and felled some timber to indicate that the lots were located, and thus gave up the chance of possessing two of the most valuable lots in Arran. Tara is now on lots 30 and 31 Roch never came near the property afterwards I left the camp in the morning and went north up side-line 25 and 26, then went east until I came to the Sauble again, on lot 27, concession 9, and made up my mind to locate on it, which I did, and it was my home from that time until 1874, when I removed to Manitoba with my family. In the fall of the year I got a friend to assist me to put up a shanty. We cut such poles as we could carry on our shoulders, put up the building and covered it with cedar clapboards I think I spent the happiest days of my life chopping down the big trees and allowing more sunlight in my little clearing I baked my saleratus-cakes, fried my pork, made my black-currant-leaf-tea, or bread-coffee and made my supper, as happy as a king. I would put on a big fire of beech or maple logs, stretch out on the floor and read till bed-time, and retire to my one-post bedstead, which had a heavy layer of hemlock brush for a mattress, and awake in the morning with sometimes two inches of " the beautiful " on my bedcover, the snow having drifted through the cracks of my clapboard roof. I was contented, hopeful for the future, and happy. For three years I kept bachelor's hall and never felt lonely. After getting fairly domiciled in my shanty on the banks of the Sauble, the question of grub for the winter's work presented itself, a most serious matter, as it necessitated my carrying it on my back from Mr. Robert Linn's in Derby, a distance of eleven miles, four miles of which were merely a surveyor's blaze. As I had bought a pig from Mr. Linn, I determined that my pork should carry itself I got my piggy along very well for seven miles, then it began to get tuckered out These seven miles of road had been chopped through the bush, but the remaining four miles were only blazed. How to get my

in less than a week from their return to Owen Sound the four whose names have been mentioned were on their way to locate their lots. Ladened as they were with necessary supplies, utensils and implements, the tramp through the woods of Derby Township was trying and wearisome. Their route was one indicated by the blaze made by a surveyor, which led them past the spot where the village of Kilsyth in after days developed. Reaching and crossing the Sauble River, Messrs. Berford and Hamilton, on coming to the eighth concession of Arran, decided to locate on the ground on which Tara now stands.

pig these four miles was a problem, but I had to face it I started with a very reluctant grunter, making my way through bush and over logs until I came to a small cedar swamp about one mile from my house. As in most cedar swamps, there was considerable windfall, and here piggy, being tired, came to a dead stop, but eventually I got it to my domicile Arrived there, I tried my hand in transforming pig into pork, but will not harrow your feelings by describing how I did it. Three or four days before Christmas snow fell to a depth of nearly four feet As I had not got any supply of flour for the winter, and the snow being so deep, I concluded to give up bachelor's hall for the winter, and having salted my pork in two white ash troughs and put it in the cellar, I started out for Mr Barber's and floundered through the snow, arriving there in the evening, tired and hungry

" Before one year was over I had neighbors In the second year of my bachelor life I had the good fortune to have a call from two land hunters, Mr Robert Douglass and his brother John Robert settled on the next farm to mine, and John settled next to his brother on lot 29, 9th concession John Douglass and I have worked many hard days together chopping and logging One day in chopping, the snow being very deep, we were felling a maple, he in front, I at the back. The tree had a bow and as it struck the ground it swung round and carried John with it, burying him in the snow I thought he was killed and set to work to release him from the tree I got him out unhurt, with damages consisting of torn suspenders and a demoralized shirt

" Before two years had elapsed all the land around me was taken up and Tara had begun to aspire to be called a village It is sad to think that most of the early settlers who came in after me and settled around me in the early days are sleeping in the Tara cemetery, and I, an old man of 74 years, am left to speak of the good comradeship and friendly feelings that existed among our early settlers What pleasure we all had in subduing the forest, what struggles we had for precedence of work at our logging bees, and the jolly time we had after the day's work was over with the dance and song, and the mirth would not slacken till the last drop of ' the crather ' gave out

" The Brinkman family are dead or have left. Willie Hall, of Hall's Corners, died two years ago (A fine neighbor.) James Broadfoot and Archie McRae, good friends of mine, are gone. Thomas Smith, a noble fellow, Archie Wilson and John Kennedy, my next neighbors, they too rest in the graveyard on the 30th side-line. There are many more of my old friends and neighbors who have departed this life, while quite a few have come west like myself. Hoping you may find these few reminiscences of the early days of Arran of some interest,

" Believe me,
" Yours truly,
" DAVID CHALMERS

" Rosewood, Man., 30th Oct , 1905 "

Messrs. Gould and Linton passed on to the next concession road, and at Invermay, as now known, they selected their lands. There a fair-sized shanty had been put up by the survey party during the previous summer, as their headquarters [1] For a few days each of the little party was busy making a small clearing, and then each helped the other in putting up a small shanty. When this was done Mr. Gould went on to Southampton to register the squatter's claim for each of the party at the Crown Land Agency, while Mr. Hamilton and Mr. Berford returned to Owen Sound to obtain supplies. On the journey back to their lots each ladened himself with a hundredweight of provisions, in addition to necessary implements, such as an axe, an adze, a cross-cut saw, and a 2-inch auger and chisel. Arriving back at their shanties, they made preparations to remain there all winter. Owing to the illness of his father, Mr Berford was forced to return to Owen Sound, leaving his companion alone in the forest, who for some thirteen days was without the sight of a human face or the sound of a human voice. It was the following spring before Messrs. Gould and Linton finally settled on their lots. Other settlers who came into Arran in 1851 were Archibald Roy, at Burgoyne,[2] Wm. Cunningham, J. T. Conaway[3] and his father—these all settled near Burgoyne. More in the centre of the township were Francis Hammel and Mathew McAulay, who located their farm lots that year. W. D. Marmion was another pioneer of '51. His son, born in 1852, was the first white child born in the township. In the spring of 1852 Charles Sang, Sr,[4] and his brother William took up lots 25, 26, 27

[1]Although falling to pieces from decay, this old log house was standing a few years ago, possibly it is yet Being the oldest building in Arran, it was of interest to those aware of the circumstances The old settlers remember how to any weary traveller its doors stood wide open, for the hospitality of the genial, warm-hearted George Gould was proverbial and has not been forgotten.

[2]When the post-office was opened, in 1853, at "West Arran," now Burgoyne, Archibald Roy received the appointment of postmaster. He also was the first township clerk of Arran. In later years he was postmaster at Port Elgin.

[3]J. T. Conaway, getting tired of roughing it in the bush, traded his farm for village property at Southampton, where he moved to and there spent the rest of his days, until his death, in 1898 The lot which his father took up was one which an Irishman claimed. The man had cut a few trees, did a little underbrushing, and planted some potatoes, but having run out of provision he was compelled to scrape up the seed potatoes for food Mr Conaway coming along, he sold out his claim to him.

[4]Charles Sang, Sr., was a man of exceptional intelligence, and one who commanded the respect of all who had the pleasure of his acquaintance. Mr. Sang was a native of Perthshire, Scotland, where he was born in the year 1821 He settled in Arran, as above stated, in the spring of 1852,

and 28, in concession B. Shortly afterward, during the summer of the same year, Donald McLachlan settled on lots 21 and 22 in concession B, and in the fall of the same year the north-west part of Arran received the following settlers: John McPhail, John Currie, Norman McLeod, John McKillop and Mathew Latimer, while earlier in the year John Douglass[1] took up land at Tara and William Hall settled and opened a tavern on the Owen Sound Road on the eleventh concession.

The opening of the Saugeen and Owen Sound Road through the centre of the township in 1852, as related in Chapter V, and that of the Elora and Saugeen Road along the west side of the township in 1854, made every part of Arran accessible to those seeking locations for settlement; the result was that Arran was settled rapidly.[2] Among these early settlers there may be mentioned: William, Henry and Copeland Trelford, John and Wm Kennedy, Wm Tippin, John B. Briggs, Henry Esplen, Sr., Joseph Briggs, William Nelson, Stephen McKechnie, James Roberts and William Hunt. The last mentioned, in 1853, was the first to settle in the south-west part of Arran.

The early settlers in Arran, like those in other portions of the county, had their full share of hardship, although they were not so badly off in the matter of roads as were many other localities. J. M. Monkman, township clerk, relates the following as his experience when he had to rough it as an early settler "I came to Arran in 1854, when only 15 years of age, and kept bachelor's hall for some

and was early made one of the Justices of the Peace for the county. The author is under considerable obligation to Mr. Sang for lucid and accurate description furnished by him of the settlement of the north-west part of Arran. Mr Sang departed this life November 17th, 1904, in his 84th year.

[1]John Douglass was born in Perthshire, Scotland, in 1833. He was nineteen years of age when his widowed mother and two brothers emigrated, coming to Canada They at once decided to try their fortunes in the backwoods and came to Arran via Owen Sound Mr Douglass says one of the first persons he met on entering the township, which was in July, 1852, was George Gould, busily engaged in carrying out his contract of opening the Owen Sound road Mr Douglass had his full share of hardships and privations of pioneer life He was elected to be the first reeve of Tara, and in 1889 had the further honor of being made warden of the county. He has been connected with the volunteer movement from the very first and his name is to be found in connection therewith in Chapter X Mr Douglass has retired from active life and is residing at Tara, enjoying the respect and esteem of his fellow citizens. In politics he is a Liberal. He is a Presbyterian and has always taken an active part in any good work. He has also filled the position of a Justice of the Peace for many years.

[2]A study of the figures in Appendix M shows the relative development of Arran compared to the other townships within the county up to 1857.

time. This was lonely indeed, as at times I did not see a living soul
for weeks, not even an Indian. The first fall I was in my shanty I
had to go to Southampton, some thirteen miles distant, to obtain a
supply of provisions. This entailed a walk through the woods by a
blazed path, a tramp over so-called roads, which were in reality but
one long-stretched-out mud-hole, while the crossing of creeks on mere
footsticks was quite a feat; it was a most fatiguing journey. At
Southampton all the flour I could get was some fifteen pounds, the
supply in the village having run out. This I carried back with me,
along with some pork just out of the pickle, for which I had to pay
a shilling a pound. Laden with the above, also sugar, tea and other
necessaries, which I carried on my back and shoulders or tucked in
my smock, I trudged back the weary miles to my shanty in the bush."

When in 1852 the inflow of settlers into Arran attained some
volume, Arran was part of the municipality known as " The United
Townships in the County of Bruce " No assessment was made or
taxes collected in Arran that year; the first levy of taxes was made
in 1853, when John Guest was the assessor in Arran for the above-
named municipality, and J. T. Conaway the collector. The total
amount of the levy for all purposes for that year was £55 6s. 9d.
When the dissolution of the municipal union of the townships took
place at the end of 1853, and new municipalities created,[1] Arran
became the senior township in the municipality of the united townships of Arran and Elderslie. Archibald Roy was the returning
officer, and the first municipal election was held at his house. The
first reeve was Richard Berford, and the councillors, Henry Esplen,
William Hunt, Thomas Woodsides and Edward Sparling. The township clerk was Archibald Roy In a footnote[2] there is given the
names of all the reeves of Arran down to 1906. The union of Arran
and Elderslie continued in force for only two years. Following the
dissolution of the union, during the year 1856 the township existed
as a separate municipality, but in 1857 the township of Amabel was
united to it for municipal purposes by by-law of the County Council;

[1] See Appendix F.
[2] The following are the names of the reeves of the township of Arran :
Richard Berford, 1854, William Barber, 1855, '56; William Riddell, 1857;
John M Lumsden, 1858, 1860, '63, '64, '65, '66, 1871, '72; James Monkman,
1859; Michael Babington, 1861, '62, 1873, '74; Andrew Freeborn, 1867, '68,
'69, 1870, '75, '76, '77, 1896; H. T. Potts, 1878, '79, 1880, '81, '82, '83,
'84, '85; John Hearst, 1886, '87, '88, '89; William Mackintosh, 1890, '91,
'92, '93, '94, '95, John Geddes, Jr., 1897, '98, '99; James Miller, 1900;
John Watson, 1901, '02; Richard Nicholson, 1903, '04, '05; Wm. Jacques,
1906.

to which union was added, in 1858, the township of Albemarle. These three townships continued as one municipal corporation until the close of 1860. Since then, commencing with January 1st, 1861, Arran has remained permanently a separate municipality. The separation of Albemarle and Amabel from Arran resulted in a prolonged lawsuit.[1] On the separation of these three townships into two municipalities, the two corporations executed an instrument whereby Amabel and Albemarle agreed to pay Arran an amount of indebtedness, mutually agreed upon as $2,832, as soon as the amount could be collected from the non-resident arrears of taxes in the hands of the county treasurer. The fixing of a particular fund to pay the debt was a mistake Therefrom a legal difficulty arose, it being discovered, subsequent to the signing of the agreement, that these non-resident taxes were largely charged on non-patented lands; as the law then stood, such lands were not liable to taxation; in fact, only some $250 was collected of $5,000 of these taxes standing in the books of the county treasurer. The suit was not finally settled until 1870.

The naming of the first post-offices in the township was in accordance with the custom which prevailed at the time of the settlement of Bruce, of giving the name of the township to its first post-office; so we find that in 1853 a post-office bearing the name of " Arran " was opened, George Gould being the postmaster. The name of this post-office was changed in 1859 to Invermay. Mr. Gould held the office of postmaster for only a very short time, and was succeeded by John Morton. " West Arran " post-office, now Burgoyne, was also opened in 1853, the first postmaster[2] being Archibald Roy, afterwards the postmaster at Port Elgin. " Arkwright," opened in 1857, was the next post-office in the township; its first postmaster was J. Faulkner.

Shortly after settlers first came into Arran there was formed the nucleus of three villages. Two of these were at the post-offices mentioned in the preceding paragraph. The third was Tara. Of these Tara is the only one which has developed into a place of importance. For a long time it was doubtful whether Tara or Invermay, situated only a mile apart, would take the lead. As Tara has a chapter to itself, we shall here speak only of Invermay. This latter village was

[1] See 45 U. C Queen's Bench Reports, page 133, also 17 Chancery Reports, page 163, and 15 Chancery Reports, page 701, for particulars of this noted lawsuit

[2] The old settlers say that J. T. Conaway was the first postmaster, while the official records give the name of Archibald Roy. The tenure of office of one of these men was possibly not for any length of time, which would explain the matter.

surveyed into village lots in 1855. The plan of this survey shows only four houses as there built, all of which were near the corner of the concession road and the street leading to Tara. The sale of village lots could not have been brisk, as it was not found necessary to register the plan until 1858. The building by Luke Gardner of a saw-mill in 1855 or '56 and of a grist-mill in 1857 helped to make Invermay a business centre. A directory of an early date gives details of the little village as it was in 1865, as follows· "It has a population of 250, contains two stores, two tanneries, one grist-mill and two saw-mills, two churches and two doctors, etc. Quite a business is done in this village, it being situated on the main travelled road." Of the churches mentioned one was a Methodist, built of brick, in 1861 It is now occupied by the Baptists. The other church edifice was Christ Church (Ch. of England). This was built about 1861. In 1877 it was replaced by a much handsomer structure, which cost $5,000. It was largely owing to the strenuous efforts of the late Rev. Rural Dean R. C. Cooper that this fine building was built. (He was also instrumental in the erection of the Church of the Redeemer at Elsinore, and of St Stephen's at Arran Lake) The first store at Invermay was opened by Wm Riddell about 1853, the first in the township The mills built by Luke Gardner, situated about half a mile south of Invermay post-office, bore the name of "Arran Vale Mills", after passing out of Mr. Gardner's hands they were run for a number of years by Syrian Cummer. A name long connected with Invermay is that of the late Abraham Neelands, who was postmaster, storekeeper and Division Court clerk there for many years, whose reputation as an upright man and a consistent Christian will long survive him [1]

---

[1] At the close of the sitting of the Seventh Division Court, held in Vandusen's Hall, Tara, July 5th, 1899, a very pleasing incident took place. It was the last time that the venerable and respected clerk, Mr. A. Neelands, would occupy that position, and Judge Klein, before dismissing the court, made a few interesting and appropriate remarks relative to the occasion, mentioning that Mr Neelands was appointed Division Court Bailiff at Owen Sound in 1847, which position he occupied for nearly five years, afterwards occupying the same position at Invermay, and was then appointed Clerk of the Seventh Division Court, which he has held for the past fifteen years. He went on to enumerate other positions held by Mr Neelands—treasurer of Arran for 34 years, postmaster at Invermay for 36 years, etc He stated that the relation of Judge with Mr Neelands had been most cordial and pleasant, no complaints had been presented against him, and the duties of his office had been performed ably and honestly. He was sorry to part with such an old official, and hoped he would be long spared to enjoy the rest which he deserved. Mr Neelands died February 24th, 1902, at the age of eighty-six.

A reference to Chapter IX. shows that in 1855 Arran's school population was returned as only 50, and no school buildings whatever. There must have been some error in regard to the number of the school population, as we find that six schools were opened in the following year. This number was added to from time to time until there were in 1863 eleven school buildings, a number which has not been further added to.

Arran has among its farmers two who have filled the position of warden of the county of Bruce, namely, H. T. Potts and Wm. Mackintosh. These two men, possessing the esteem of many, have also been nominated for Parliamentary honors. If space permitted, it would be interesting to local readers to have written of others in the township whose reputation has extended beyond its borders, or of some of the older families such as those that bear the name of Esplin, Wark, Morran, Morrow, Swinton, Monkman, etc., etc. Such a task might well be taken up by some local historian, and this suggestion, it is hoped, may before long be carried out.

CHAPTER XIX.

VILLAGE OF TARA.[1]

THE reader is referred back to the preceding chapter for particulars relating to its settlement by Tara's pioneer settlers, Richard Berford and John Hamilton. They, in the fall of 1851, came into the unbroken forest, which covered the township, and located on the farm lots afterward to be surveyed into a village.[2] It is not to be imagined that the village commenced to take form at once; the evolving of a business centre in a township not fully settled until some years later required time. The fact that Tara is situated about half way between Owen Sound and Southampton, on the road opened out in 1852, had much to do with the developing of a village there. Within two or three years after he had taken up his land, John Hamilton built a fair-sized building of hewed logs, where he furnished accommodation for the travelling public, which consisted of incoming settlers and land-seekers passing on into the backwoods of Arran and the adjoining townships It is said that in the first year after being opened it was no uncommon sight to see from ten to twenty teams drawn up before the door of this small hostelry, whose resources were taxed to the utmost to supply the demands made upon it For a number of years a strong rivalry existed between the village of Tara and Invermay, situated only a mile apart, as to which should take the first place in the process of development and become the business centre of the locality The result has been not so much a survival of the fittest in respect to location and natural advantages, for in these particulars there was little to choose between the two places. It has been more because of the enterprise shown by the people of Tara that it has developed at the expense of its neighbor. The survey of each of the villages was made about the same time. The par-

[1]The village bears the name of a town in the county of Meath, Ireland, a seat of royalty in ancient days Referred to by Moore in his poem, " The Harp that once through Tara's Halls "

[2]Richard Berford took up lots 31 and 32, and John Hamilton lots 29 and 30, concession 8, Arran.

274

ticulars of that of Tara as given in a footnote[1] are the dates given
on the plans as registered, but preliminary surveys had been made in
1854 by Richard Berford, assisted by his three brothers.

Mrs. St. L. Berford has been kind enough to supply the author
with many facts about the early days of Tara which have been made
use of in this chapter She says: " In the early summer of 1854 the
Berfords raised the first house (a log one) built in Tara; this was
for their father, John F. Berford.[2] This building was on the site
where now stands the British Hotel In the same year Richard and
St. Lawrence Berford built upon their respective properties. Others
also who had bought lots, or had them given to them on condition of
building, erected buildings that year." Among the first to open stores
at Tara were F. Armstrong, Donald Sutherland and H. Le Pan A
saw-mill was built in 1855 by H W. M Richards, which was the first
manufacturing industry known in the village. To this he, in 1857,
added a grist mill. The largest manufacturing industry in Tara, the
foundry and agricultural implement works of W. A. Gerolamy, was
founded in 1857. It was in that year that George Gerolamy and his
two brothers-in-law, John and James Toby, purchased some lots in
the village. After clearing the same they put up a modest workshop
and commenced the manufacture of fanning mills. In the course of
two or three years W. A. Gerolamy took over the business, which had
not attained to large proportions by any means. By energetic efforts
and pluck, combined with upright principles, he has had the satisfaction of seeing the business gradually grow to its present large dimensions He was the first maker in Canada to introduce perforated zinc
for sieves in fanning mills For this improvement he obtained a
patent. As a result, at the World's Fairs held at Philadelphia, Paris
and Chicago, he was awarded the highest prizes.

Among the earliest of Tara's industries was a steam saw-mill
owned by G. W. Drinkwater, a woollen mill operated by Thomas
Thompson, and a potash factory by Samuel Shoveller. Among the
early mechanics might be mentioned Peter Chesterfield, cabinet-maker,

[1]The survey of lots 31 and 32, concession 8, Arran, was made by Richard
Berford; date, May 17th, 1858.
The survey of lots 31 and 32, concession 9, Arran, was made by St
Lawrence Berford; date, November 10th, 1858
The survey of lot 30, concession 8, Arran, was made by John Hamilton;
date, March 24th, 1859.
The survey of lots part 29 and 30, concession 8, Arran, was made by
John M. Lumsden; date, November 22nd, 1860

[2]John Fitzwilliam Berford was a retired officer of the British Navy.
He only survived a few years after moving to Tara. His burial place is
on a knoll in the park lot that bears his name.

who is still living, and James W Allen and Moses Kellow, carpenters and builders Donald Urquhart, cooper (at one time editor of a Gaelic paper in Hamilton), was one who became known as a local scribe.

The first school teacher at Tara was J. R. Vandusen. For many years he retained the position of principal, and is remembered by numbers of those who in their youthful days attended the village school.

A post-office was not opened at Tara until 1862. D Sutherland was the first to receive the appointment of postmaster, which post he held for only a short time, his successor being John Toby. This post-office bore the name of " Eblana " during its first year, when it was changed to Tara.

As the village grew in population a desire was felt that it be separated from the township and assume municipal responsibilities. Henry Vandusen was appointed in 1880 to take the census, and so ascertain if the village contained a population sufficient to claim incorporation. The return showed that there were 806 inhabitants within the proposed boundaries. On this showing, the County Council passed the required by-law, to come into force January 1st, 1881. The first municipal election was held at the old Presbyterian Church, J. R. Vandusen being the returning officer The reeve[1] elected was John Douglass, and the gentleman composing the first Council were W. A. Gerolamy, John Dunn, W. Vandusen and Isaac Shannon. J. D. Toby was appointed village clerk, and J. H Vandusen, village treasurer. These two gentlemen have retained their offices ever since

The first meetings for religious services were conducted before any regular congregation had been organized, and were held in Gerolamy's workshop, and on some occasions in the pottery. Then, later, the school-house was used In time, congregations in connection, with the various Protestant denominations were formed, and church buildings were erected. The Presbyterians seem to have been the first to build. Their first edifice was of frame, put up in 1860, but was destroyed by a wind storm before ever a service had been held in it In the following year they built a more substantial building of brick The growth of the congregation in the following years necessitated a still larger edifice. This resulted in the building, in 1876,

---

[1]The following are the names of those who have been reeves of Tara, with the years in which they filled the office : John Douglass, 1881, '82, '83, '84, '85, '86, '87, '88, '89; William Campbell, 1890, '91, '95, '96; J. F. Smith, 1892, '93, '94, A Trelford, 1897, '98, '99; John Hamilton, 1900; F A Thomas, 1901, '02; J S. Colwell, 1903, '04; Isaac Colwell, 1905; Wm Collins, 1906

of the present commodious church. In the year 1861 the Methodists built a brick church half way between Tara and Invermay. This building they sold to the Baptists after the present handsome edifice in Tara had been built, the corner-stone of which was laid July 28th, 1875.

It was October 10th, 1881, when the first locomotive reached Tara. For some months it was the most northerly station to which freight was carried by the railway company. The sectional bonus to the railway of $5,000 given by Tara was a large one, considering the size of the village. At the same time it must be remembered that the railway has done a great deal for Tara, making it a point of shipment for the products of a considerable section of country.

In the summer of 1880, with the prospect of the village becoming incorporated, and also with the promise of the railway being opened in the immediate future, a newspaper was felt to be a pressing need. This was met by W. J. Whitlock (now of the *Wiarton Canadian*), who proceeded to publish *The Tara Leader,* continuing to do so until 1893, when the Rev. Thomas Hall purchased the paper. He sold out in 1897 to J. E. Hammond, who in 1899 disposed of it to its present publisher, H. A. Vandusen

Tara has not done much in the way of bonusing manufactures, its one venture not having been very successful. The bonus referred to was voted upon September 23rd, 1898, granting the sum of $4,000 to Messrs Biette & Co, to help them to go extensively into the manufactore of barrels, cheese boxes, etc. The business was shut down in 1901, and the village took possession of the property, but it has not been able to obtain therefrom repayment of the amount advanced.

J. M. Lumsden was for a number of years a prominent man in Tara, and one who during the years he sat in the County Council as reeve of Arran was held in high esteem. He removed to Galt in the seventies. Another prominent citizen of Tara who has moved away was Whitford Vandusen. Mr. Vandusen at one time taught school at Invermay. Then he commenced a mercantile business at Tara. Prospering, he opened a private bank, which business the Merchants Bank of Canada purchased when it opened an agency in the village in 1901. Mr. Vandusen now resides in Toronto.

At the present day Tara is an attractive little place. Its two steel bridges (built by the county), its granolithic sidewalks, its numerous places of business and its many comfortable-looking dwellings evidence a community possessing and enjoying a large share of prosperity and contentment.

CHAPTER XX.

TOWNSHIP OF BRANT.[1]

EXTRACT FROM THE REPORT OF COUNTY VALUATORS, 1901.

"This is the largest township in the county, being nearly 70,000 acres in extent. A large portion is very good land, but there is considerable poor and rough land. The Saugeen River enters the township at Hanover, running westerly to Walkerton, then in a northerly direction till it passes into Eldershe. The land on each side of the river for some distance is rough and generally light. There is some rather stiff clay around Malcolm. Land, however, is selling well in this township. The fact of the county town being within its limits no doubt enhances value of property in that district. Brant is well watered, has good roads, good buildings, and sufficient fuel and timber for years to come. The rate per acre is $36 94; of this sum the village property amounts to $2.58 per acre."

BRANT certainly is justified in claiming to be the premier township in the county of Bruce, possessing as it does the largest area, combined with the highest assessment, and, if Walkerton is included, it also has within its limits the greatest population of any township in the county. Its share of county rates is almost one-tenth of the annual levy of the whole county. The farms within its boundaries as a whole are not excelled by others in any part of the province. Indeed, one of its farms (that of the late Andrew Waechter) carried off the gold medal in 1891 as the best farm within the four counties of Huron, Perth, Wellington and Bruce.

The first lands in Brant opened for settlement were the "free grants," consisting of the first and second concessions north and south of the Durham Road. These were offered on the conditions to be found in Appendix E, in June, 1849. All the lots on these four concessions were taken up before the rest of the township, which consisted of "school lands," which were offered for sale on August 5th, 1851.[2] The price asked by the Government for school lands was

---

[1] Named after the celebrated Indian chief, Joseph Brant, or Thayendanegea

[2] See Appendix H. The first purchaser under this sale was Wm Mills, for lots 34 and 35, concession 3, S D R, on August 6th, 1851. The first patent was issued to John Eckford, on March 5th, 1852, for lot 1, concession 6.

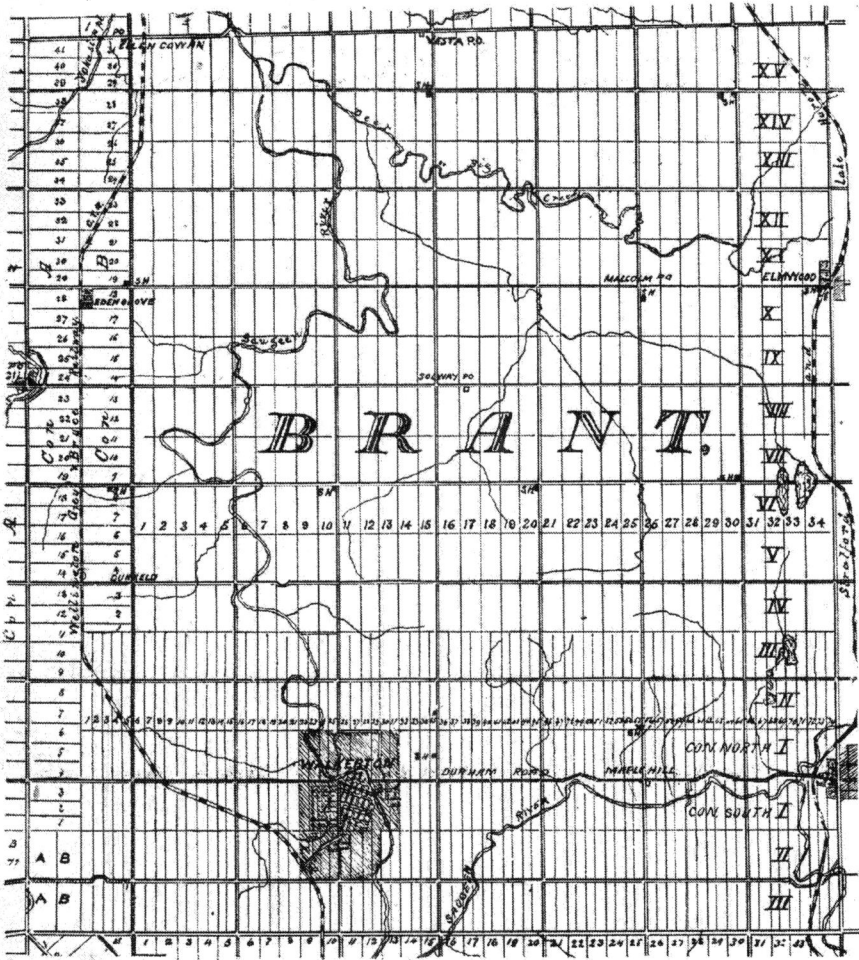

BRANT,

twelve shillings and sixpence ($2.50) per acre, a figure subsequently reduced to ten shillings. The reader is referred back to Chapter II. for information relating to the survey of the township and to Chapters III. and XXI. for information as to the very earliest of the pioneers who took up free grants lots. They certainly endured hardships unknown to those who went into the bush in 1853 and 1854, little as the author would minimize what the latter had to endure. In 1849 and 1850, of roads or bridges there were none; of saw and grist mills, as well as post-offices, none were nearer than Durham These disadvantages were much reduced in 1853, when the last large inflow of settlers to lands in Brant occurred. Of the early pioneers, not elsewhere named, was William Smith (now residing in Manitoba), who entered the town-ship of Brant in 1849, the first year of its settlement. Lot 21, con-cession 1, S D R., was the farm lot on which he settled. When having this lot allotted to him he at the same time secured the adjoining lot for his father, David Smith.[1] His neighbors were Alexander and Archibald Stewart, who had taken up lots on the north side of the Durham Road opposite. In the helpful spirit so characteristic of the backwoods, assistance was freely reciprocated by these men in the building of their log shanties The land-seeker of 1850, after pass-ing the Stewarts, in his westward march, in a short time came to the shanty and clearing of Joseph Bacon,[2] who had been accompanied into the bush by his brave wife, the first woman to become a permanent settler in the township. Their little shanty was one whose door was ever open to offer the open-handed hospitality of the backwoods to the tired traveller.

Among the early pioneers to be mentioned is Patrick Godfrey, who in the fall of 1849, settled on lots 13 and 14, concession 2, N.D.R.

[1] It was on May 23rd, 1850 (which was the day previous to the arrival of Joseph Walker—at the place afterward to bear his name), that David Smith and family settled on the farm lot adjoining Walkerton. There he resided for several years. David Smith was one of the first elders in the Presbyterian congregation organized in 1851. When the north part of the township was opened for settlement he took up a farm lot on the thirteenth concession, where he died, December, 1880, aged 78

[2] Joseph Bacon was a native of Essex, England, where he was born, February 3rd, 1795 In March, 1835, he emigrated to Canada and resided in the vicinity of Hamilton. On the opening of the Garafraxa Road he, settled in the township of Arthur When the free grants of the Durham Road were opened for settlement, he was one of the earliest to settle in Brant, taking up lot 14, on concession 1, N D R. He had the contract for cutting out the Elora Road through the township of Carrick Mr. Bacon was a man of marked religious principles. His death occurred December 22nd, 1882

By hard work he cleared these lots, and in time had one of the finest farms in the vicinity, retiring when age crept upon him to reside in Walkerton, where he died in 1903   Another pioneer of 1849 was Thomas Todd, who took up several lots just east of Walkerton. After clearing these and residing there for nearly thirty years, he moved to the Parry Sound District. His son, Archibald, now a retired farmer, is a resident of Walkerton.

The narrative of a tragic incident of the early days will not be out of place while writing of the first pioneers of the township. One James Wallace, who had settled on a lot on the south line near where the Walkerton Railway station is, was, in the winter of 1850, returning from Durham where he had gone to obtain supplies   After crossing the Saugeen at the jam, referred to in Chapter III., he walked along the north line to Mr McWhinney's and rested. As night drew on he started to cross to the Durham line, expecting to get as far as Mrs. Jasper's that night. There was no broken path through the snow, and he seemed to have missed the blaze on the trees. After night fell, his shouts were heard at the Jaspers' shanty. Some strangers, guests there that night, and the boys lighted cedar torches and went out in the darkness into the forest to find out the reason of the shouting. Starting in a wrong direction, as they found by the feebler sound, they returned and started again, when some foolish one suggested that the cries were not those of a human being, but those of a panther—in the woods at night, a very plausible theory, and one that was accepted by all but Mrs. Jasper. As soon as it was day she sent her boys out to try and find in the snow a trail or other evidence of who or what had uttered the cries. Charles Jasper found a trail, which he followed up, and before long found the body of poor James Wallace, frozen stiff, a victim to the dangers of life in the backwoods. One of Mrs Jasper's sons walked all the way to Owen Sound for a coroner, a Dr. Gordon. The verdict, of course, was in accordance with facts as here related   The body was buried in the bush not far from where it was found.

In Chapter V are to be found the facts relating to the opening up through the forest of the Durham Road in 1850, and in the following year of the road then called the Durham and Southampton Road, which road commenced between lots 15 and 16 of the Durham Road, and ran north to the fifth concession, thence west to the present Elora Road, which from that point was also opened that year to Paisley.[1] The opening of these roads enabled settlers to take up lands back of the free grants. Among the most prominent of those who did so was John Eckford[2] and William Chisholm. For some months these two families were the most northerly settlers in the township, being separated from their nearest neighbors by one or two miles of unbroken forest. The names of some of the other early settlers not elsewhere mentioned are as follows: William Mills, Richard Everett, Philip Geeson, Thomas Traynor, Sebastian, John and Andrew Kirstine, Leonard and William Dickison and John McNeil, on the south line; James and Samuel McWhinney, Robert Gowanlock, John Little, Joseph and John Harkley, John and Joseph Lamb, Abram, James, Andrew and William Rowand, John and Robert Bruce, James Bell, Anthony, James and Charles Myles, on the north line; Robert Horne, Robert Frame, William Morden, Adam Clement, George B. Lamont, James, Thomas and Andrew Wilson, William and Richard Guinn and those mentioned in Chapter III. and elsewhere, who took up farm lots on the Durham line. Besides these early settlers here mentioned, there were many others, some of whom have moved away and left but the recollection of a name. The first boy baby which came to brighten the home of a pioneer of Brant came to the log shanty of William ("King") Johnston in June, 1850. This addition to the settlement was christened Nathaniel. To Mr.

[1] In the original draft of Colonization Roads in the county of Bruce, the Elora Road was laid out to run along the boundary line between Brant and Greenock The order making the change, causing the road to follow the line east of concession "B," the author has been unable to discover The "jog" (as the detour was called), as above described, opening up the road a block still further to the east, is said to have been the result of influence brought to bear by a land speculator, who had purchased a block known as "Proudfoot's Block," consisting of lots 1 to 5, concessions 4 and 5

[2] John Eckford was by birth a Scotchman Educated for the ministry at Edinburgh University, he was for twenty-five years a clergyman of the United Presbyterian Church in Scotland. When in middle life he, with his family, emigrated, in the summer of 1851, to Canada. His objective point was some desirable spot in the backwoods. This he found in the woods of Brant, where he took up lots 1 and 2, concession 6, and lot 1, concession 7. His family remained for three months at Durham, while a log shanty was being built Mr. Eckford was ever ready to give his services in the conducting of public worship; there are but few Presbyterian congregations in this part of the county in which he has not preached His services were much appreciated and were in great demand to fill any temporary vacancy many a congregation would have been glad to have had him as its settled minister. In 1857 he was elected reeve, but resigned to accept the position of Local Superintendent of Schools, which office he held until it was abolished, in 1871. Mr Eckford also held the office of township treasurer from 1872 until his death, which occurred October 22nd, 1881, when he was in his eighty-second year.

and Mrs. Thomas Adair, four months later, came the first girl baby
born in the township, who, on attaining womanhood, was married to
Donald Sinclair, M.P.P., and survives the death of her esteemed
husband. The first medical man to render professional assistance to
the pioneers was Dr. William Bird, who resided near Hanover, on
lot 67, concession-1, S. D R.

In December, 1852, the settlers of Brant were the victims of a
false alarm, which at the time created quite a sensation. A rumor
in some manner spread from shanty to shanty through the woods that
there was likely to be a rising of the Indians, with the object of driving out the Whites. So alarmed was one of the settlers, J. G.
Breckenridge, a local preacher, that he packed up his effects and
cleared out, never to return. That Christmas Eve a large party of
friends were gathered in one of the homes toward Hanover, celebrating the season in a convivial manner. Hearing some unusual
shouting, the doors were opened to hear more distinctly, when the
cry came upon their ears, "The Indians have come, the Indians have
come!" In an instant all was confusion and consternation. The
women folk hastily gathered together a few things preparatory to a
hurried flight, while the men went out to investigate, which resulted
in their finding that the noise was but the loud shouting of a band
of drunken men, who, carrying a pail of whiskey, were going from
door to door wishing every one "A Merry Christmas." The falsity of
the rumor about the Indians was soon established, and the settlers
quieted down after a bad scare.

After the "free grant" lands were taken up, settlers coming into
the county seeking lands were largely influenced in their decision
where to settle by the consideration of accessibility. Brant at the
early period of its settlement was accessible only by way of the Durham Road. This fact, to a certain extent, deflected the tide of
settlers to other localities After the Elora as well as the Durham
Road was opened, Brant offered to the settler as desirable lands and
as equally accessible as any other of the inland townships in the
county; but even then Brant failed to receive a fair share of settlers,
because in some manner a report spread that the lands in Carrick
were more desirable than those in Brant So just as soon as the surveyors had completed the survey of Carrick, which was in 1852, a
rush set in to obtain a squatter's claim[1] to a farm lot in that township,

_____
[1]These lands in Carrick did not come into the market until the time
of the "Big Land Sale" in 1854   See Appendix K.

:and for a short time the lands in Brant were comparatively neglected. In 1853 the settlement of Brant from concession 4 north commenced in earnest, and by the end of 1854 it was completed. Prominent among those who entered Brant at this time were Richard and James Brocklebank.[1] The following narrative, related by Henry McNally, of his settling in Brant about this time, throws a light upon the conditions which existed at those years: Henry McNally, accompanied by his brother George, entered Brant, prospecting for farm lands, March 28th, 1853 They found that beyond the north line lay an unbroken forest that had been explored by few. Realizing the advantage it would be to them in making a selection of desirable land, to have some one who had at least tramped through that part of the township, they struck a bargain with "Stonemason" Horne, whom they met at his farm a little west of Hanover, to take them back into the bush. After a day or so spent in going along the blazed lines as left by the surveyors, they decided on lands situated on the sixth and seventh concessions After making the necessary slashing to establish a squatter's claim, they proceeded to Saugeen to register the same, and make their first payment of ten per cent, which was equal to $20 per lot. These lots were the first to be taken up on this concession line, but when they moved in twelve months later, there was only one lot left which had not been taken up. This they also secured. Mr. McNally says that Malcolm McLean, the postmaster at Walkerton, acted as a local deputy for the Crown Land Agent. He had a map of the township, on which he would write in pencil the name of any person wishing to secure a lot, then when word came from Mr McNabb that the necessary application and payment had

[1]James Brocklebank was born in September, 1828, at Malton, county of Peel He was engaged in farming in his native county until in 1853 he moved to Brant, where he took up several farm lots on the fifth concession, which he farmed successfully. He also, a number of years later, engaged in milling, having purchased a large interest in the Maple Hill Mills, but in this venture he lost money. Mr Brocklebank early took an interest in municipal politics. He held the position of deputy reeve of Brant for the years 1859, '60, '61, and of reeve of the township from 1862 to 1868, and from 1876 to 1879, and from 1897 to 1900, inclusive, making a total of fifteen years. Mr. Brocklebank was also warden of the county for the five years, 1864 to 1868, inclusive In politics Mr. Brocklebank was a Conservative. He unsuccessfully, in 1867, contested the riding of South Bruce with the Hon Edward Blake for the House of Assembly. In 1872 he again entered the field of politics, running for a seat in the House of Commons, but was defeated by R. M. Wells. Mr. Brocklebank was a consistent member of the Methodist Church, and was largely instrumental in the building of a frame church for that denomination, erected in the year 1869, on a corner of his farm. After an active life he entered into his rest, July 3rd, 1901, much regretted.

been made, the name would be written in ink. It is claimed that one- third of the inhabitants of Brant are of German birth or descent. It was about the time of which we are writing that they commenced to come into the township, taking up land pretty much in one locality, the easterly part of Brant These Germans were large from Mecklenburg and the north of Germany ; in religion, they were mostly Protestants. Excellent, thrifty settlers they proved to be. The following are the names of some of the earliest of these German settlers: —John Dierstein, Charles and Frederic Stade, John Wilkin, Martin Stadtlander, Michael and Gottlieb Schroeder, Henry Ruhl, John and Frederick Montag.

When the municipal union of all of the townships in the county was broken up,[1] the two townships of Brant and Carrick were formed into one municipality. This union lasted for the years 1854 and 1855, on the 1st January, 1856, each township became a separate municipal corporation. The first Council of the united municipality consisted of Joseph Walker, John Eckford, Nathaniel Lines, William Walker and James Benson Joseph Walker was chosen reeve,[2] and Archibald McVicar township clerk. The names of his successors in office are given in a footnote.[3] He was township treasurer as well,[4] but this latter position passed in 1857 to W. Willoughby, who held it for twelve years He was succeeded by J. G. Cooper and he by John Eckford, who died in office; his son James C Eckford then received the appointment and held the office of township treasurer from 1881 until the end of 1905 During his administration the finances of Brant have been in a most satisfactory state; the judicious manage-

[1]See Appendix F

[2]The following are the names, with the years of office, of those who have held the reeveship of Brant down to 1906 Joseph Walker, 1854, '55, '56, John Eckford, part of 1857; William Hall, part of 1857, '58; John Bruce, 1859, '60, '61, James Brocklebank, 1862, '63, '64, '65, '66, '67, '68, '76, '77, '78, and part of 1879, '97, '98, '99, 1900; J C. Eckford, 1869, '70; Johnston Smith, 1871; William Collins, 1872, '73, '74, '75; B Cannon, part of 1879; James Tolton, 1880, '81, '82, '83, '84, '85, '86, '87, '88, '89; Andrew Waechter, 1890, '91; Robert Long, 1892; William Little, 1893, '94, '96, George Sirrs, 1895; R Richardson, 1901; W H. Brocklebank, 1902; Alex Anderson, 1903, '04; Fred Frooke, 1905, '06.

[3]The following are the names of the succeeding township clerks to the year 1906 · Peter McVicar, William J. Scott, A. S Mackintosh, J. Jamieson, J G Cooper, D Sullivan, J. C Eckford, Thos. R. Todd, James S. Laurie, and J H Cannon

[4]There was a shortage of a large amount in his accounts, the particulars of which is needless to record

ment of its·" Reserve Fund "[1] has permitted the erection of several
expensive steel bridges, which have been built without any excessive
increase in taxes, or in the issue of debentures to pay for their construction. ·The only debentures which Brant has issued for construction of public works were for a scheme of drainage, affecting some
thirty-six farm lots near Johnston's Corners. The work was commenced in 1879, and completed two years later. To pay for this work,
debentures for $3,600 were issued in 1880, followed in the next year
by. an issue amounting to $1,500 Besides these debentures, Brant
has issued others in aid of railways. In 1878, the year that bonuses
were sought for the construction of the railway to Wiarton, Brant
gave a bonus towards it of $15,000 The railway company being
financially stranded, it came back for a further bonus the following
year. As there was no hope of the township as a whole undertaking
this additional financial burden, the ratepayers in the eastern part
of the township were asked to do so, and in response voted a sectional
bonus, amounting to $5,000. The necessary by-law for this carried,
and the debentures were issued in 1879.

Of the families which settled on the free grant lands in Brant
there were many who came from settlements where they had possessed and prized the privilege of attending church services It was
to be expected, then, that steps would be early taken by such to provide
that which, here in the bush, they missed so greatly. The result of
the efforts they put forth to meet this want was the building of the
first church edifice in the county. It was but a plain log house 20 feet
by 26 feet in size, but as it was the first of many churches afterwards
to be erected in the county, it will be but proper to give in detail the
particulars of its inception, even if the author may err in being somewhat prolix. Many of the facts here given are as related by Mr.
Thomas Adair, one of its founders. A meeting of the settlers was
held July 5th, 1851, at the house of Robert Frame (lot 45, concession
1, S.D.R.) to take steps toward erecting a building for public worship. Among those present were members of the Church of England,
Methodists, Presbyterian and one Congregationalist (Mr. Frame).
The first intention of the meeting was to arrange for a building to be

[1] This fund, amounting to about $4,500, originated in grants received
from the Government on account of the " Land Improvement Fund."
The Township Council of each year have abstained from encroaching on
this reserve, using it simply for the purpose of tiding the municipality
over times of heavy expenditure, spreading such over several years, and
this without resorting to the borrowing of money.

used as a union meeting house for all denominations. Mr. Adair said: "As far as I remember, the names of those in favor of a union meeting-house were the Messrs. Todd, two of the Wilsons and two of the Mordens. At first I favored the same; so did Robert Frame and Adam Clement. After a friendly discussion, George B. Lamont, who appeared well versed in church law, took the ground that this plan would not work, as the building and land would have to belong to some one denomination there represented. Mr. Lamont's resolution to this effect was agreed to by a majority. On a show of hands being taken, a large majority was found to be in favor of the building being built by the Presbyterians. Those belonging to other denominations then left the meeting. The next step was the appointing of a committee to collect subscriptions. The committee consisted of George B. Lamont, John Bruce and myself. After a canvass of the settlement from the county line to Johnston's Corners we were able to report £6 18s 6d subscribed, two bunches of shingle, and the land on which the building was to stand, given by Robert Frame. The logs were got out, and two weeks after the meeting a bee was held for the raising. The corner men were Joseph Lamont, James Rowand, John and Thomas Adair." The Rev. Dr. Torrance, in a letter, thus describes this place of worship: "On Sabbath preached in the new church of Brant, the first place of worship that has been raised in the township. The building is of logs, the spaces between which had not been chinked; there was no door, neither were there any windows; the boards were just laid down for the floor, and the seats were temporary. Not having been aware that the church was to be occupied on this occasion I was altogether unprepared with an opening sermon; but I prefaced Psalm cxxii at considerable length, and gave my remarks as direct a bearing as I could upon the circumstances of the congregation." It is to be noted that the building was not completed or fitted for worship directly after the walls were raised, and the Rev. Dr. Torrance's description is of the building in 1852. During the intervening period services were held in the house of George B. Lamont, close at hand It was there that the Rev. J. W. Barrie organized (September 14th, 1851) the congregation which was known as the "United Presbyterian Church, Durham Line, Brant." It was six years after this before this congregation had a settled minister— the late Rev R. C. Moffatt, D D. During these six years Brant was but a mission station, supplied by members of the Presbytery, students and whatever other supply was available, the Rev. John Eckford fre-

JOHN ECKFORD

p. 283

LT -COL A SPROAT

p 186

JAMES BROCKLEBANK

p. 285

JOSEPH WALKER

p 294

quently filling the pulpit. The congregation here described built a frame church in 1860 in Walkerton. Its further history is recorded in the chapter on Walkerton. The Rev. Mr. Moffatt, when he accepted the pastorate in 1857, stipulated that the congregation build him a small house as a dwelling. This was put at the west end of the church building, and was as modest in its dimensions as was the church, being only twenty feet by twenty-two feet. Rev. Mr. Moffatt had a large field in which to labor, and laid the foundation for the Presbyterian churches at West Brant, Hanover, Malcolm and West Bentinck. His stipend from all the various charges during several years was but $400 per annum. The first church at Malcolm was a building of logs erected late in the fifties. In 1873 this simple structure was replaced by a good-sized brick building, which was opened free of debt. Rev. Daniel Duff was the first pastor, and continued in charge until his death in the fall of 1899. His successor is the Rev. A. Leslie. The West Brant congregation above referred to worships in a substantial stone building erected in the summer of 1869, and opened for worship on the last Sabbath of that year. This congregation has for years been united to the one at Pinkerton, forming a joint charge. The author regrets not having the data to enable him to mention when the other congregations in the township were formed and churches erected.

The number of tavern licenses in Brant were more numerous in 1857 than forty years later. The license fee at the earlier date was only £3 It may interest some reader, whose memory goes back as far, to recall the names of the license-holders in that year. They were: James Waterson, William Ruminge, John Sherridan, Henry Halm, John Hopper, Peter McVicar, Thomas Bilkie, Hugh Bell, John Smith, Peter Grabbin, James Jones and James Gaffaney. This latter's tavern gave a name to the locality, which was known as " Gaffaney's Corners " (lot 4, concession A), where, besides the hotel, there was also a store which was kept by one William McDonald. Here a peculiar accident occurred in 1858 The proprietor of the store, after striking a match to light a candle, carelessly threw the yet blazing match behind him, where, even more carelessly, lay a powder keg with the lid off, and a small quantity of powder therein. As soon as the match lit on the powder there was an explosion that blew the front out of the store, and McDonald with it. Unfortunately, the damage and loss was not confined to the building and its contents, Mr. McDonald suffering total loss of sight as the result of the explosion.

11

Walkerton, for four years after it became the county town, continued to remain a part of the township of Brant. It was 1871 before the Act of incorporation was passed and the separation of the town from the township took place. The apportionment of financial obligations and assets was arranged by a Board of Arbitrators, consisting of Judge Kingsmill, James Brocklebank and W. H Ruby. The basis in most cases for division was in the proportion of $2 to $23. Over the Land Improvement Fund, payable by the Government, some difficulty arose   What was the final settlement of this point the author is unable to state

The fact of a railway skirting along both the east and west boundary of the township has led to the growth of villages adjacent to the railways, while the rest of the township at a distance from the railways has a village population only at Malcolm   Maple Hill, when the mills were erected, gave promise of developing into a village, but being so near both Walkerton and Hanover, it has given up the struggle   Dunkeld and Ellengowan, in the days before the railway was opened, when the Elora Road was one of the main arteries of communication within the county, also promised to be centres of trade for the inhabitants in the immediate vicinity   There again the railway blighted the bud before the flower blossomed, and trade strayed to Cargill and Eden Grove.

Cargill is on the boundary line of Brant and Greenock, and will be specially referred to in the chapter on the latter township   Its three handsome brick churches lie in Brant, as does also its railway station, which is connected by a long stretch of granolithic pavement with the village proper.

Eden Grove, or " Pinkerton Station," as styled in the railway time-tables, commenced its existence with the opening of the Wellington, Grey and Bruce Railway. Munn & Webster about that time built a saw and shingle mill, which gave employment to about ten hands. The post-office was established in 1875   Alex Shaw was first postmaster   Thomas Pinkerton was the next postmaster   He also kept a general store. and as a competitor in seeking the trade of that locality he had Thomas McKay   The Methodists here built a neat frame church at an early date, in which has worshipped an active congregation to this day. Eden Grove is the point on the railway used for shipment by Pinkerton, Glammis and all that section of country   Its nearness to Pinkerton and Cargill precludes the hope of much further expansion.

Elmwood received its name from a gigantic elm tree that once stood at the intersection of Main and Queen Streets. The post-office there was established in 1864; the duties of postmaster were under-taken by John Dirstein, to whom as much as to anyone belongs the credit of the founding of the village. By 1875 there were two stores there, one kept by John Reinhardt, the other by Schroeder & Watson In the same year the place boasted of two saw-mills owned by Johnson Smith and John Dirstein respectively. Shortly after the year last mentioned churches were built by the Methodists, the Mennonites, and German Evangelical congregations It was on August 27th, 1881, that the first locomotive reached Elmwood. This was the advent of assured prosperity to the village, which, situated, as it is, half way between Hanover and Chesley, is the shipping point for a large section of country.

Hanover, until 1903, lay partly in the township of Brant On action being taken to extend the boundaries of the village, but lately incorporated, so as to include in the corporation all on the Brant side of the village, the Brant people interested objected to this *nolens volens* course of action. In this the County Council supported them, but it was unavailing The village prevailed upon the Legislature to pass an Act[1] extending its boundaries so as to embrace 175 acres of land in Brant, on which resided 325 inhabitants, and a large number of buildings, among which were two furniture factories, a grist mill, a woollen mill, besides shops, stores and dwellings, which altogether had an assessed value of $95,650 It was to be expected that some of the ratepayers would feel sore over what was thought to be a proceeding somewhat arbitrary in its nature; but cooler thoughts have prevailed, and reflection shows that if advantages are derived from proximity to a town, it is only fair and proper to pay to the town a rightful tax.

In 1893 the Brant Board of Health took vigorous action in opposition to the proposed system of sewerage of the town of Walkerton being permitted to flow into the Saugeen River. Mr James Nesbitt, the secretary of the board, was very persistent and succeeded in having the Provincial Board of Health visit Walkerton and hear the evidence in support of the claim of the township, that the river would be dangerously polluted by the flow of sewage into it. The Elderslie Board of Health united with that of Brant in the action taken, but were unsuccessful in obtaining the injunction asked for.

[1] III Edw VII Chap 56

It would hardly be fair to Brant Township to close this chapter devoted to its history without referring to a remarkable natural curiosity it has to show to the visitor. What is known as "The Blue Spring" is situated not far from Maple Hill, a little up stream on the south side of the river, about a quarter of a mile back from and some sixty feet above it. The water of this spring possesses a slight mineral taste, yet is so highly saturated with mineral matter that the moss through which the overflow of the spring percolates becomes petrified, and large objects of wood sunk in the spring are encrusted as with stone the color of iron rust. The spring may be found by following up the rivulet flowing from it from the place where it empties into the Saugeen. The spring is situated in a clump of dense woods which have hardly been touched by man. The water rises in a large basin some fifty feet or more in diameter and of considerable depth. The water is as clear as possible, but in bulk, as seen in the basin it fills, it exhibits a markedly rich blue tint, hence its name. In many places in the basin are to be seen, sunk at various depths and at all angles to one another, trunks of trees covered with the stony deposit. When the sun's rays pierce through the tops of the surrounding trees and illumine the depths of the basin it glows as with the fire of a sapphire, in strong contrast to the dark shade of the surrounding forest, impressing the beholder with a never-to-be-forgotten sense of beauty. This spot has frequently been suggested as a site for a sanitarium. Some day, possibly, this suggestion may become an accomplished fact.

CHAPTER XXI.

WALKERTON.[1]

THE history of the town of Walkerton is so closely associated with that of the township of Brant, of which municipality it formed for many years a part, until by special Act of Parliament it was incorporated as a town,[2] that in writing of the town it is necessary to refer to the township also.

The first part of the township of Brant to be surveyed by the Crown for settlement was the tract consisting of the first and second concessions north and south of the Durham Road. The farm lots on these concessions were known as " free grants." (The third concessions were also surveyed at the same time, but the farms thereon were not " free grants.") This survey was made under the direction of an Order-in-Council dated 26th August, 1848, and was executed by A. P. Brough, P L.S. The farms in the " free grant" tract were open for location in the spring and summer of 1849, and immediately thereafter land was taken up in what now forms the town plot of Walkerton.

During his tour of prospecting for a " free grant" location, in the month of May, 1849, Thomas Adair[3] stood on the " Clay Banks " overlooking the present site of Walkerton, late one afternoon as the sun was declining in the west, viewing, as he has since expressed it, the most beautiful landscape he ever beheld. The valley beneath him contained many wild cherry and plum trees, then robed white with blossoms, and whose perfume ladened the air with rich sweetness. In every direction hill and vale were covered by an expanse of primeval forest, shining bright in its coat of verdure fresh from the hand of spring. The sun as it sank lightened up, or cast in deep shade, the masses of foliage, and projected long shadows over the flashing waters of the Saugeen, making a combination of sylvan

[1]The Indian name for this place is " Mah-sko-se-sing," meaning " A little marsh "

[2]Walkerton is probably unique as a municipality, inasmuch as it never was a village, but blossomed into being a full-fledged town at a bound

[3]See in Chapter III. where Mr. Adair and the other early pioneers are further mentioned.

293

loveliness so enchanting that Mr. Adair ever spoke of it with enthusiasm, while Kenneth Kemp, a staid, unimpassioned Scot, his sole companion, after silently contemplating the lovely prospect, vented his feelings by saying, " Eh mon, if Eden was anything like this, what a fool Adam was to eat the apple."[1]

The first settlers on any of the lands now included in the town of Walkerton were William Jasper and Edward Boulton, who took up farm lots just east of the river in June or July, 1849, and there erected the first house in what afterwards became the town of Walkerton, the site of this log shanty being in the gore formed by Bay and Mary Streets and the Durham Road That same summer or fall John Lundy and Moses Stewart settled west of the river To these were added, in the spring of 1850, Thomas Bilkie, whose name is still borne by the hill on the west of the town

Among the settlers who took up land in 1850 one of the most noted was Joseph Walker,[2] a man who will always be remembered in

---

[1]Another description of the primeval appearance of Walkerton is here given, being an extract from the Report of Survey made by A. P. Brough, P L S, of the Durham Road It is as follows :

" Township of Brant, lots 35-25 The line on this block proceeds over a waving surface, composed of a good clay soil, and containing heavy hardwood timber, a distance of 61 chains and 80 links, when it drops forty feet into the valley of the Saugeen River and crosses valuable flats of five chains in width When the Saugeen is met, the river is crossed obliquely, and at the crossing-point is intersected by an alluvial island standing six feet over the water, thus forming two channels in the river, the east one of which is shallow, with a rapid current, and is 185 feet in width The west channel is also rapid and is four feet in depth and 87 feet in width The island is crossed at its northern extremity, and is 177 feet in width, it will form a convenient resting-place for piers in erecting a bridge; the total distance across the river, including the island, is 449 feet, This is the second time in which the Saugeen River is crossed, and now the stream pursues a northerly direction and is no more met with by the Durham Road Above the crossing point the river is intersected by numerous small islands, and immediately below occur small rapids, and the river takes a sharp turn' nearly at right angles toward the west, having its east banks rising to an elevation of over one hundred feet and composed of a clay bluff, while its west bank is low. The line having crossed the river pursues its course over a nearly level surface composed of a sandy loam soil and producing large hardwood timber, crosses two small streams, but which run dry in summer, and meets the side road at lots 25, 26, at the distance of 1 chain 89 links from the Saugeen, on its north side Immediately at the side road, between lots 25, 26, the line crosses Silver Creek, which falls into the Saugeen close to the line Silver Creek is a rapid stream, with a shingle bottom from eight to twelve inches in depth and twenty-seven feet in width, and ought to afford a mill privilege "

[2]Joseph Walker, familiarly spoken of as " Old Joe," was by nationality an Irishman, and claimed, so it is said, the county of Tyrone as his birthplace Before arriving at the years of manhood he came to this country,

connection with the county town of Bruce, appropriately named after him. If any one can claim to have founded Walkerton it certainly is Joseph Walker. When he constructed a dam across the Saugeen and erected mills that cut lumber and ground flour in those early days for the scattered settlers, the certainty of a town developing at that spot was assured. Realizing this, Joseph Walker had the adjacent farm lots which stood in his own, or his son William's name, surveyed into a town plot. It was largely through his efforts that the infant settlement became a busy business centre. If any can claim to have struggled to make the settlement a town, it is Joseph Walker. During the prolonged contest for the county town, it was he who championed the cause of Walkerton, and that successfully; never despairing during that prolonged nine years' struggle, even when his cause seemed all but lost, manifesting throughout a buoyant courage, determination and versatility of resource that commanded the admiration even of his opponents

To take up land for the purpose of farming was not the object Joseph Walker had in view when he entered Bruce. His vocation had been that of a miller, and he came seeking for a mill site on the line of the Durham Road. In the spring of 1850 he left Durham, in the vicinity of which he had been residing, accompanied by three friends, John McLean, William McIntosh and Archibald Fraser, all thorough backwoodsmen They walked to Owen Sound, thence by the

and resided for a number of years in the vicinity of Cookstown, from whence he removed to the county of Grey. At the time he entered the county of Bruce he was a man of forty-nine years of age, stoutly and compactly built, rather below the average height, energetic, tenacious of purpose, and of an active, nervous temperament. Many of the old settlers speak warmly of him for the kindly acts extended to them in the early days, when nearly every one was in comparatively poor circumstances He was twice married—first to Jane Pinkerton, by whom he had four children, and on her death to a Mrs. Bailey, who kept the "White Horse" hotel near Durham. Besides the log-house first erected by him, he also built the stone house now occupied by R. E Truax, and also the one occupied by the late Judge Kingsmill, and the one on the corner of Colborne and Cayley Streets, now occupied by Mr. Alexander Menzies. He was the reeve of Brant for several terms, and was also Walkerton's first mayor. He was rather careless in his business methods, the result being that finding his means slipping through his fingers, he in 1870 gathered together what he had left to make a fresh start on the Manitoulin Island He purchased a mill privilege and erected a grist mill at Sheguindah village. He spent the last winter of his life at Walkerton, returning to the Manitoulin in the spring His end came in June, 1873, at the age of 72. Further biographical details are dispensed with, as his name and actions will appear in other parts of this History, especially in that relating to the contest for the county town. A large sized portrait of Mr. Walker fittingly hangs in the Walkerton Town Hall, enabling later generations to become acquainted with the lineaments of its founder.

"Gimby Trail" to the mouth of the Saugeen, and on to Kincardine. It was a long, round-about way to reach the spot on which he ultimately settled, and we can only offer a surmise for his doing so, which is, that he had learned of applications having been made for the near at hand mill privileges,[1] and so travelled the route he did hoping to find at, or near, Kincardine a suitable water power not taken up. Being unsuccessful at first, they journeyed eastward over the blazed path which then marked the Durham Road. Walker's companions found lands which suited them in Greenock, but he pushed on until the Saugeen was reached, and there decided to locate. The records of the Crown Lands Department show that on 15th July, 1851, Mr. George Jackson recommended that Joseph Walker be the locatee for the mill site and lands where the Saugeen crossed the Durham Road, which recommendation the Department confirmed July 26th of the same year.

It was in May, 1850, that Joseph Walker arrived at the locality with which his name is associated, and located upon lots 27 and 28, concession 1, N.D.R., and lot 29, concession 1, S.D.R., taken in his own name and that of his son William. Subsequently he obtained the assignment of the rights of other settlers, or purchased them, so that patents were issued to him or his son for ten of the twenty-eight farm lots which subsequently were included within the corporation of the town of Walkerton.

Those who first settled at or near what is now the town of Walkerton entered the county from the east, passing through Durham, where the Crown Lands agency for the "free grants" was located. From there, through the unbroken forest, they made their way by the surveyor's marks, as any claim to a road consisted of nothing but a blazed path. It was not until the fall of 1850 that the Durham Line in the township of Brant was chopped and logged and a bridge built over the Saugeen river at the site of the future county town, which bridge lasted until 1855, when it was rebuilt.

Joseph Walker after taking up his land proceeded to erect a log house As the conditions of settlement required that this should not be less than 18 x 24 feet, it is not difficult to picture the appearance of the first building erected by him in Walkerton. Its site was where Durham and Mill Streets now intersect. This house was not

---

[1] Mr. Archibald Todd, of Walkerton, says the mill privilege there was first applied for by one Anderson Foster, in 1849, but he threw up his claim before the application was granted

only a dwelling for Mr. Walker and his family, but was the hotel of the settlement for many a day, where the weary pioneer obtained rest and lodgings when on his way to the lands he had taken up in "the bush." Walker must have worked hard after settling on his lots, as we find that he was the first man in the township of Brant who, having complied with the conditions of settlement (which among them required that twelve acres of land on each lot should be cleared), obtained his patent from the Crown; this not for one lot only, but for four. The date of these patents is 17th December, 1851. Having obtained his patents, Walker proceeded to erect a saw-mill, which was completed in 1852. The construction of a dam to give the necessary motive power was no small engineering feat in those days in a small settlement where help was hard to be got and money none too plentiful. The initial dam at Walkerton was in two parts, one from each bank of the river, thrown across it to a wooded island in the centre of the stream. The present dam was constructed by S. & T. H. Noxon & Co., in the early seventies.

The village of Durham was the base of supplies for the first settlers who came into Brant. It was there they had to go for their mail matter, and also to have ground into flour the first grain grown on their small clearings, as well as to purchase their groceries and clothing. These inconveniences were partially overcome when in 1851 Messrs. Jardine & Valentine, having erected the building familiar to Walkertonians of the present day as "the old post-office," they there established the first mercantile business known to Walkerton. The building referred to was nearly opposite Joseph Walker's tavern. Between them a small stream of water flowed, which long since has disappeared. Shortly after the opening of Jardine & Valentine's store, John Shennan opened another, which was located on Willoughby's Hill, east of the river. In 1852 Shennan was appointed postmaster, the office being known as "Brant" It was the third post-office established within the county, the offices at Kincardine and Southampton having been established the preceding year. As Shennan was unacquainted with the duties of the office, he had Malcolm McLean, at that time engaged as a clerk with Jardine & Valentine, and who had experience in post-office duties, to open and send out the first mails from the office. Shennan after holding the office for about a year resigned, when Malcolm McLean received the appointment, dated 15th November, 1853, and has held it to this day, possibly the oldest postmaster in Canada. The name of the

post-office was changed to " Walkerton," September 24th, 1857. The
next to open places of business in Walkerton were John Bruce and
James Jamieson. The former claims to have built, in 1853, the first
frame building, and in 1859 the first brick building erected in the
town.

In 1853 the need of a grist mill was a want so seriously felt by
the settlers that an effort was made to have one built. Maple Hill.
was the site spoken of as the most promising   At a meeting held to
discuss the project, Joseph Walker was present and succeeded in
persuading the majority present to unite with him and erect the
mill at Walkerton. The farmers gave a very substantial support to
this undertaking by subscribing $1,600, which financial assistance
assured the building of the needed mill. The many difficulties arising from the transporting of the heavy machinery over the almost
impassable roads through the woods were overcome   Alex. McPhail
was engaged as the first miller, and in November, 1853, the mill was
set in operation [1]   As since then the hum of machinery has always
been heard in Walkerton, the evolution of its industries may as well
be referred to here as later on

The saw and grist mills which Mr. Walker's energy had secured
for Walkerton were for some years the only manufacturing industries
of the place. A tannery seems to have been the next industry established   Following these were an oatmeal mill, a planing mill and a
woollen factory   In 1864 James Blair opened a foundry and machine
shop on the site of the present town hall, and ran it successfully
until it fell a prey to the flames in May, 1871. The grist mill was
unfortunately burnt in the early part of 1864, and it was not until
January, 1870, that it was rebuilt and running again, being owned
at that time by Noxon, Saylor & Co   This mill was enlarged to six
run of stones by the Noxon brothers, who became sole owners afterwards   In April, 1877, it passed into the hands of David Moore.
Not finding it profitable, it remained idle for a while, during which
time the mill was burnt down.   Obtaining municipal assistance,
R. B. Clement rebuilt the mill in 1886. This time the mill was built
of brick and of four stories in height, and fitted with machinery for
the " roller process " of gristing   It is run at present by S. W. Vogan

[1]William McBride, of Elderslie, relates that in the winter of 1854-55
the head-race of Walker's mill became so blocked with anchor ice that
he could only run one pair of stones out of three, and that only at the
rate of a bushel and a half per hour. A grist he took at Christmas time
was not delivered until July.

& Son. The grist mill west of Silver Creek was used at first as a planing mill, but was changed into a grist mill and run by George Harrington, who having obtained a municipal bonus was thereby enabled to change the machinery in the mill and install the " roller process " The mill has been run for a number of years by John Lee.

Several industries which flourished at Walkerton for a time under the stimulus of a municipal bonus have disappeared. Among those may be mentioned the felt-boot factory, which was started in 1881 on receiving a bonus of $3,000 This business existed for about sixteen years under various proprietors, but at last had to be closed down. Another was the woollen mill. This received a bonus of $4,000, granted to Messrs. Kennedy & Bunson. On their failure, the business passed through several hands and ultimately was taken up by Rife & Co, who were induced to remove the machinery of this mill to Cargill in 1902. O G. Anderson received a bonus of $6,000 in 1887 to enable him to extend his furniture factory Mr Anderson in many ways is a remarkable man. His first attempt at manufacturing at Walkerton was in connection with a stave mill in 1877. This was developed and enlarged to a furniture factory, which at the time of his leaving Walkerton had 125 hands on the pay roll Mr. Anderson's reputation had extended to Woodstock, where the largest furniture factory in Canada existed This business had become financially embarrassed, and those interested in looking around for a suitable man to conduct it, robbed Walkerton of one of the most enterprising men who have resided in it. The whole plant of this concern was transferred to Woodstock, August, 1895 The town-felt the loss of this extensive industry in a marked degree, and an effort was made to start another industry of similar description This resulted in the formation of a company called the Walkerton Chair Factory Co, in the year 1896, which in the following year received a loan from the town of $6,000 This business was ultimately taken over by the Knechtel Furniture Co (of Hanover), and is carried on by it, they having assumed all the conditions in reference to the repayment of the loan If some industrial concerns moved away from Walkerton, others have moved to it, foremost of which is the American Rattan Co., late of Toronto, the move from that centre of manufactures being largely the result of the efforts of Mr. John R Shaw, a well-known Walkertonian residing at Toronto, This business is under the supervision of Mr. L. C. Benton, manager, and ships its artistic products to all parts of Canada, from Halifax to Victoria.

In 1902 three bonuses or loans were granted by the town to as many new industries. A $5,000 bonus was given to the Walkerton Hosiery Co., this company having taken over the machinery of D. Williams, who had conducted a similar business at Collingwood; $5,000 was loaned to Pett & Son to start a biscuit and confectionery factory, and $2,000 to the Canada Bobbin Co. This latter company had carried on business years before in Walkerton under the name of Kerr & Harcourt, but expecting to obtain lumber cheaper at Wiarton and Parry Sound had moved thither, but finding that labor could be more readily and cheaply had at Walkerton, decided to return. The business is now managed by Wm. M. Shaw. The business carried on by Messrs. Pett & Son did not prove successful, and the corporation became owners of the land and buildings under the mortgage. Possibly the most prominent industry in the history of Walkerton is that at present controlled by R. Truax & Co. This saw and planing mill is on the site of the saw-mill originally erected by Joseph Walker, and has under one firm or another been carried on continuously to the present day. It emerged from the mere saw-mill stage in January, 1871, when S. & T. H. Noxon & Co. procured the machinery to do all kinds of planed work. The ownership of this valuable property remained in their hands until about 1877, when it was purchased by David Moore, who carried on the business for a short time, then leased it, in December, 1878, to R Truax & Co. This firm ultimately purchased the plant and water privilege, and have extensively increased the business; employing a large number of men and keeping installed the latest machinery it has been enabled to obtain orders from the most prominent centres of our province. Mr. Alexander Menzies and Mr. James Watt, as manager and foreman, have been connected with this firm from the beginning, and assisted greatly in the development of the business. To Mr. Truax much credit is due for the success he has achieved.

As it might cumber this chapter with too great a mass of detail to refer in particular to all the manufacturing industries that have existed, or are in existence, at Walkerton, a brief mention of some of the most notable will close the subject. Among those which have been, might be mentioned the flax mill, also the oatmeal mill, run by George Shortt, the ruins of which are by no means unpicturesque. The manufacture of brick has been carried on at Walkerton for over forty years, the clay to be found there making durable bricks and tiles. The names connected with this industry are A. McVicar, W. Carter, E. Kilmer, Thomas Adamson and his son William, Louis Yaeck, and others. Hemlock bark being available in quantities, Walkerton had among its industries at an early date a tannery, the first tanner being Andrew Thompson. Of late years Thomas Pellow, Samuel Arscott and his sons, have carried on the industry in the three tanneries at present existing. The factory that is perhaps the most widely known of any which have carried on business in Walkerton is that for the manufacture of binder twine, established in 1900. The shares of this company are largely in the hands of farmers scattered throughout this and neighboring counties. James Tolton, a man who was prominent in the municipal and agricultural interests of Brant for many years, was selected by the shareholders to be the manager. This industry unfortunately met a competitor shortly after it commenced to manufacture twine in the American Binder Twine Trust, which, being determined to crush out all opposition, and having immense capital to do so, first captured the sisal market and then placed the price of the manufactured article at a lower figure than it is possible for the Walkerton factory to produce it, the directors of which have wisely decided to cease manufacturing at a loss.

The first survey into town lots of the various farm lots now within the limits of the corporation of Walkerton, was that known as " Bilkie's survey of part of lot 23, concession 1, S.D R.," the plan of which as registered bears date of 4th December, 1855. The next survey was made by Joseph and William Walker, of lots 24 to 31, concession 1, S.D.R., and of parts of lots 25 to 28, concession 1, N.D.R. The plan of this survey is dated 4th of February, 1857 The survey in both cases was made by E. H. Kertland, P.L.S.

That Walkerton did not seek to obtain a separate municipal existence earlier than it did is not easy of explanation, except upon the ground of the seeming incongruity of the county town being merely a village municipality; so as part of the township of Brant it remained for some years after it attained to the required number (750) of inhabitants necessary to entitle it to be incorporated as a village. Being comprised in the municipality of the united townships of Brant and Carrick, Walkerton was represented in 1854 and 1855 at the Council of the united counties of Huron and Bruce by Joseph Walker, its reeve, which office he held also in subsequent years for the township of Brant when it became a separate municipality.

The contest for the county town commenced with the first meeting of the provisional County Council of Bruce, held in March, 1857, a contest in which each village in the county contended. This struggle continued for nine years before being finally settled in favor of Walkerton. A bare recital of some of the facts of this contest is all that can here be related. The first vote taken in the provisional County Council, "To select a fit and proper place to recommend to the Governor-General as the one to be mentioned in his proclamation as the county town of Bruce," resulted in favor of Walkerton. The Governor-General, in accordance with this vote, proclaimed Walkerton the county town. This was on the 15th of June, 1857. This proclamation was, however, on petition, set aside by Act of Parliament on August 16th, 1858. After another struggle by Joseph Walker—for he almost single-handed fought the battle for Walkerton—the Governor-General again (8th November, 1860) proclaimed Walkerton as county town. This proclamation was also petitioned against, and Parliament, yielding to the petition, voided the proclamation 30th June, 1864. A decision was arrived at in 1865 which was confirmed and put beyond local influences, when Parliament passed an Act on the 15th September, 1865, declaring Walkerton to be the county town of Bruce. In the same year the county buildings were commenced, and completed toward the end of 1866. On the 1st day of January, 1867, Walkerton became in fact, what it had been *de jure,* the county town of the flourishing county of Bruce. At that time this ambitious little place had not population enough to enable it to claim incorporation as a village, nor did it have for some time after. The incongruity of the county town not being a separate municipality was overcome by special Act of Parliament (34 Vic., chap. 69) passed 15th February, 1871, which enabled Walkerton, without ever having been a village municipality, to assume the dignity of a town. The population of the town in the year of its incorporation was only 995. It rose to 2,604 in 1881, and to 3,061 in 1891, but fell in 1901 to 2,971. The rapid increase in population which marked the first decade of its municipal existence was the result, in a large measure, of the opening of railway communication with the outside world, resulting in an excellent grain market being established there.

The first school-house in Walkerton was a shanty-roofed building on the hill east of the river. It was opened as a school in 1852, the teacher being a Miss Nancy Wilson,[1] who taught for four years, and was succeeded in 1856 by Mr. Donald Reid, afterwards township clerk of Amabel, and he, in February, 1857, by Mr William Collins[2] The attendance of scholars during the first years after the school was opened was never large. Among the remarks entered in the visitor's book of the school in the year 1855, it is stated that at the time of the visit the attendance was "14," "14," "20," etc As the school population increased the need of more accommodation was felt, so after the building of the old Orange Hall on Orange Street was completed, it was used as a school-house until another move was made to a frame building erected purposely for a school on the corner of Jackson and Catharine Streets This in time gave way to the commodious brick buildings on Colborne and Victoria Streets, now in use, the first of which was built in 1875 and the second in 1888. Before passing on to other items of history, attention is drawn to a school-boy's composition, printed in a footnote,[3] that was preserved

[1] Miss Wilson, while teaching, married David Moore, of the Walkerton Grist Mills, but continued to teach until a successor was found qualified to impart instruction to the handful of scholars ·

[2] Mr. William Collins resided in Walkerton for many years after teaching school, filling many important positions He was born in the county of Antrim, Ireland, in the year 1833 When he was of the age of fifteen his father immigrated to Canada with his family, and settled in the township of Finch. William Collins was educated for a schoolteacher, and pursued this vocation for several years in the eastern part of the province From 1853 to 1856 he followed photography, at Owen Sound and other places. His position of schoolteacher he resigned on his receiving the appointment of Division Court Clerk in the year 1859, an office he held until his death. Of the many other public offices Mr Collins filled the following are some of them Reeve for eight years of the township of Brant, also reeve of the town of Walkerton, town treasurer, and County Master of the Orange Order for East Bruce. He married Miss Jamieson, of Walkerton, in 1858, and had a family of six sons and two daughters In politics he was a very strong Conservative and a hard fighter in an election contest His death, which occurred April 19th, 1901, was deeply lamented by a large circle of friends

[3] Copy of a composition by a schoolboy at the Walkerton Public School in 1858, on "Topographical Description of Walkerton"
"Walkerton, the county town of the county of Bruce, is beautifully situated on the river Saugeen, about seventeen miles west of Durham, and is also within twenty-eight miles of Lake Huron It is divided near the centre by the Saugeen, on which river is erected a good grist and saw mill, and there is also a beautiful bridge built over it Walkerton is surrounded, except on the south, by hills, on the top of one of which an Episcopal Church is in the course of erection, and from the church can be seen a fine picturesque view. It has water privilege capable of forcing any quantity of machinery. I should mention that a railroad is expected to come there, or near it, and if it does it will certainly be a place of some importance. It already contains a population of 175, a post office, five stores, four taverns, three shoemakers, two blacksmiths, two tailors, a tannery, two cabinet-makers, and several carpenters and joiners. It is situated in the midst of a very fertile and healthy country and promises fair to be a fine place "

by Mr. Collins. It tells us something of Walkerton as it was in the year 1858.

The Orange Hall, mentioned in the preceding paragraph, was the sole public building in the early years of Walkerton. It was used, as its name indicates, as a lodge room, and also used as a school. In this building also worship was conducted by the various Protestant denominations each Sunday, in the following rotation: the Church of England in the morning, the Presbyterians in the afternoon, and the Methodists in the evening. It was in this building that all public meetings, as well as the Division Courts, were held in those pioneer days.

With the incorporation of the town and the opening of the railway, the erection of a town hall became necessary. So in 1872[1] the site for a market-place and town hall was purchased, and the building of the latter proceeded with. It was only a frame building, 30 x 62, with a bell tower and a lean-to for the caretaker's residence. David Siebert was the builder. After lasting for a quarter of a century, it had to make way for the more pretentious and commodious civic building erected in 1897. It might be well to here give the names of those who have filled the mayor's chair from the incorporation of the town to date. They are as follows: In 1871, Joseph Walker; 1872, Paul Ross; 1873, 1874, James G. Cooper; 1875, Alex. Shaw, 1876, Alex. Sproat; 1877, 1878, Paul Ross; 1879, Malcolm McLean; 1880, 1881, H. P. O'Connor; 1882, David Moore; 1883, 1884, A. B. Klein; 1885, Andrew McLean; 1886, 1887, C. W. Stovel; 1888, 1889, Reuben E. Truax; 1890, 1891, 1906, David Robertson; 1892, 1893, William Richardson; 1894, 1895, Hugh Birss; 1896, John Standish; 1897, 1898, Alex. Menzies; 1899, 1900, M. Stalker, M.D.; 1901, S. H. McKay; 1902, C. W. Cryderman; 1903, S. W. Vogan; 1904, 1905, R. H. McKay.[2]

The incorporation of the town was followed in the succeeding year

[1] A by-law to raise $2,700 for the purchase of a market-place and erection of a town hall thereon was voted on and carried April 8th, 1872. $1,000 for the land, $1,500 for the building, and $200 for anticipated expenses.

[2] No time was lost after the bill incorporating the town was passed in electing a town council, the first meeting of which was held on 17th March, 1871, at Waterson's Hall. Its members were: Joseph Walker, mayor; William McVicar, reeve; councillors—Stephen Noxon, David Moore, Hugh W. Todd, Louis Wisser, William Shannon, James F. Davis, William Smith, Paul Ross, and Moses Stewart. The first officers were: W. L. Watt, town clerk; W. L. Watt, town treasurer; Thomas Burrell, town inspector; James Flett, assessor.

by the establishment of a high school. For lack of a proper building, the school had a migratory existence for some years. At first it was held in the Orange Hall, on Catherine Street (a building which originally was built by the New Connexion Methodists as their church). From this building the school was removed to a hall over the *Herald* office, on the south side of Durham Street. From thence it was removed to the town hall, and then again to the public school building, when that building was completed in 1876, where it occupied two rooms. This was the last move prior to taking possession, in February or March, 1879, of the present fine high school building. The first head-master in the high school was Arnoldus Miller, B A., who was succeeded by Dr. Morrison, M.A., in 1880, and he again in October, 1881, by Joseph Morgan, M.A., who still fills the position. In 1877 the Walkerton public school was constituted a county model school for the preliminary training of public school teachers, and for over a quarter of a century has, under the various head-masters, maintained an enviable record for efficiency.

The pioneer settlers manifested an honest pride in the products of their new farms, the virgin soil of which yielded magnificent returns, both as to quantity and quality, and they early organized an Agricultural Society. The first of the fall shows was held in 1854 or 1855, the indoor exhibits being shown in and about the store of Jardine & Valentine, while the live stock was scattered along the street and over the bridge. Annual exhibitions in this line finally developed into the Northern Exhibition, conducted under an incorporated company, liberally aided by the town, which issued $4,500 of debentures towards this object. The present buildings, at a cost of $4,555 were erected in 1877. For many years the Northern Exhibition ranked high among the fall exhibitions held in the province, but of late, owing to the number of township fairs, it has not been as successful as formerly.

In the early pioneer days it was difficult to supply the scattered settlers with regular religious services, and many hardships had the early pastors to endure as they tended to the spiritual needs of their respective flocks. The facts, as here given, regarding the various churches in Walkerton are much condensed, as to give more than the leading facts would extend the narrative to too great length. The various denominations are referred to in alphabetical order. The Baptist congregation was organized in 1879, and until their church was opened (November 4th, 1883) worshipped in the court house, the Rev. Henry Cocks being their first pastor. The Disciples of Christ used the town hall as a place of worship until the present church edifice was first used for worship, October 9th, 1881. The first Church of England services (and also the first of any denomination in Walkerton) were held in Joseph Walker's tavern. To conduct these the Rev. A H Mulholland, of Owen Sound, paid monthly visits to Walkerton, which at that time was an outlying station. Rev. T P Hodge succeeded him as a missionary in this parish The first settled minister was the Rev. T. E. Saunders, who took charge of the spiritual interests of this flock in 1859. In 1858 a church edifice was erected on land given by Thomas Todd, on Willoughby's Hill The construction extended as far as the roofing of the building, but it was never completed owing to the foundation being insecure. No services were ever held therein The present church, bearing the name of St Thomas, was erected about 1864-5, during the incumbency of the Rev E Softly. The ministers who have subsequently occupied this charge were the Rev John P. Curran, the Rev John Greenfield, the Rev. Wm Shortt, the Rev J. H Fatt, the Rev S F Robinson and the Rev T G A. Wright. The Evangelical Lutherans have from an early date been fairly numerous in Walkerton and vicinity, and they erected a neat church building on the gore formed by Colborne and Yonge Streets in 1885 Unfortunately they have not been able at all times to maintain a permanent pastorate. The Evangelical Association (German Methodist) held religious services in the council chamber of the county buildings for a number of years, when, increasing in strength, they built for themselves, in 1899, a brick church on the corner of Colborne and Prince Streets, which possibly was the only church building ever opened in Walkerton free of debt Methodism was first represented in Walkerton by the New Connexion Methodists Their first missionary was the Rev. Andrew Clark, who came to Walkerton in 1854. They erected a frame building for their church on Catherine Street, which subsequently has been used as the Orange Hall The Wesleyan Methodists sent their first missionary, the Rev. John Hutchinson, to Walkerton in 1860 They built for themselves a brick church on Catherine Street, which was opened October 23rd, 1870. This building afterwards was used as a public hall, bearing the name of "Rothwell's Hall" These two Methodist bodies were officially united September, 1874 In 1886 they purchased St. Paul's Church from the Presbyterian congregation, which building is still their place of worship. Presbyterianism was represented at an early date by the United Presbyterians and the Church of Scotland. The former had their first church erected in 1851 at Frame's Corners, two and a half miles east of the town, but moved in 1859 to a commodious frame church building built east of the river. This was used until the congregation erected the brick church on the corner of Cayley and Colborne Streets, built in 1875, at first called Free St. John's, but after the union with St Paul's congregation, in 1886, it was known as Knox Church. In this church was placed, in 1896, the first pipe organ known to Walkerton. The Rev. R. C. Moffat, D.D , was the pastor of this congregation until the union with St. Paul's. The congregation known as St. Paul's was originally formed in connection with the Church of Scotland. This was organized about 1869 by the Rev. M W McLean, who came from Paisley at intervals, holding service in Waterson's Hall at first, afterwards in the Court House. This congregation entered into their handsome church building in 1877, the Rev. Dr. Bell being their pastor at that time. The following are the reverend gentlemen who have had charge of the united Presbyterian congregation of Knox Church.[1] Rev. John James, D D., Rev. Donald Guthrie, Rev J S. Conning and the Rev Thomas Wilson The spiritual needs of our Roman Catholic brethren were at an early date attended to by a French priest, who held services in the house of one known as " protestant " John Smith The brick church they now occupy was erected in 1874, and the convent building adjoining was opened in 1879, the first resident priest being Father Keough, who came to Walkerton in 1872 and remained in charge of this parish until 1877.

The press first became an institution in Walkerton in 1861, when the *Bruce Herald* was established by W. T Cox, who sold it in 1863 to Wm. Brown, who conducted it until 1883 Since then it has been under the proprietorship of Messrs Kribs & Wesley, W Wesley, W. R Telford, and at present of L H McNamara[2] *The Walkerton Telescope* was established in December, 1869, by D W. Ross, and subsequently was conducted by Wallace Graham, Joseph Craig, D. C

---

[1] The Jubilee services of this congregation were held in September, 1901

[2] During the excitement attending the war in South Africa, there was issued a small daily sheet from the *Herald* office, bearing the title, *Daily War News* The issue of this commenced January 29th, 1900, and ceased May 7th following, owing to the excitement to some extent having diminished This has been the only attempt in the way of publishing a daily paper within the county.

Sullivan, T. H. Preston, J. B. Sheppard, A. Eby, J. B. Stephens, and at present by A. W. Robb. *Die Glocke,* published in the German language, was first issued by John Klein in February, 1870. The paper was sold by him to A. Eby and J. A. Rittinger. Subsequently it passed into the hands of J. A. Rittinger solely, who continued to publish it until June, 1903, when the plant was moved to Berlin. *The Times,* the latest addition to the newspapers of the town, conducted by W. Wesley, was first issued in September, 1905.

Like most inland towns lacking cheap and speedy freight communication with outside markets, Walkerton did not rank high as a local market until the Wellington, Grey and Bruce Railway had opened a station there. The local papers prior to that time published the market quotations of Port Elgin, Kincardine and Guelph, as well as the prices for grain that were offered by S. & T. H. Noxon & Co. at their flour mill. It may be of interest to compare the prices as given in the papers issued one week previous to grain buyers being able to make use of the railway for shipping purposes, and those of a week subsequent to that event, and note what a gain to the farmers resulted from the opening of the railway, the price of fall wheat at the various markets being that here given: At Walkerton $1 05, at Port Elgin $1.12, at Kincardine $1.15, and at Guelph $1.25 The following week the prices at Walkerton were at a level with those of Port Elgin and Kincardine. The first locomotive to reach the town of Walkerton did so November 30th, 1871, it being one used by the contractors in the construction of the road; nevertheless, it was the advent of the "Steam Horse," and was hailed with great joy and celebrated by a supper at Waterson's Hotel. The first train carrying freight from Walkerton left the station on the 10th February, 1872, and the railway was opened for passenger traffic August 5th following. The following extract from the *Bruce Herald* of January 26th, 1872, gives an idea of the change brought to Walkerton by the opening of the railway: "The sight of a number of teams on the streets with wheat, pork, etc., for sale is something new to Walkerton. There has probably been purchased within the last ten or twelve days on our streets more grain than there ever was since the place came into existence. Hitherto Walkerton has been so situated that, unless for home consumption, it offered little inducement as a market. The produce of this section went from it in all directions,—to Southampton,

OLD VIEW OF DURHAM STREET, WALKERTON, ABOUT 1878

Kincardine, Seaforth, and Guelph. The railway is about to change all this, and give the farmers a market at their doors."

The propect of Walkerton becoming a point where large quantities of grain would be offered for sale by the farmers, induced Thomas Adair, at that time engaged in grain buying at Southampton, to come to Walkerton to engage in the same business there; he and John Bruce seem to have been the first to purchase at Walkerton for export.

Walkerton has always had cause to regret that the railway station was placed at such a distance from the town, the reason therefor being largely, it is understood, because speculators held the lands in the vicinity of the Carrick Road at too high a figure. As soon as it was definitely known where the railway station was to be, the town took steps to have streets surveyed to it, which resulted in a great deal of discussion as to the position of such streets, but at last McGivern and Ridout Streets as they now are were laid out. The amount to pay for the right of way and construction of these streets was raised by debentures, the by-law for which was voted upon December 20th, 1871. The amount so raised was $1,500.[1] The first-mentioned street was named after W. McGiverin, the President of the W. G. & B. Railway, and the latter after the Chief Engineer, Thomas Ridout.[2]

The county town question having been settled, the agency of the Commercial Bank of Canada, which had been located in Southampton for some time, was moved in June, 1867, to Walkerton. Unfortunately, in October of the same year this bank failed. The inconvenience arising therefrom was overcome when, about a year later, the Merchants Bank established an agency at Walkerton. In January, 1877, the Canadian Bank of Commerce opened a branch there also, since which time the town has not lacked for banking facilities.

The loss by fire of the foundry in May, 1871, stirred up the people of the town to take steps to ward off similar disasters in the future, and they shortly afterwards purchased a hand fire engine from the town of Brantford; this reached Walkerton in August following. To pay for the engine and for the construction of

[1]The W. G. & B. Railway gave $1,250 to assist in construction of these streets.

[2]A. H. Ridout, agent of the Bank of Hamilton, Port Elgin, is a son of the above.

water tanks, debentures were issued December 26th, 1871, for
$2,000   Hand fire engines have but a limited power; this Walkerton
learnt to its sorrow when it experienced its heaviest loss by fire, an
event which is still remembered and spoken of as "the big fire,"
which occurred May 28th, 1877, starting early in the afternoon of
that day in a stable situated back of where the present postoffice
stands   Favored by a high wind, it spread with marvellous rapidity,
defying the modest fire-fighting appliances above referred to.   It
swept over a large part of the business section of the town, destroying
forty-two buildings   The losses were heavy, but most bravely the
sufferers set to work to rebuild, and eventually buildings of a finer
and more substantial character were erected to replace those destroyed.
With the construction of a fine system of waterworks in 1891,[1] at a
cost considerably exceeding $30,000 (the first estimated cost), a
repetition of such another conflagration is not to be dreaded; whilst,
in addition, the town enjoys the blessing of an abundant supply of
the purest drinking water   The establishment of the system of
waterworks was followed by a system of sewerage.   A large trunk
sewer[2] was laid on Durham and Jackson Streets in 1895, and subsequent years have seen the system extended until a large part of the
town is now supplied with this sanitary convenience.

    Walkerton, for a town of its size, is fortunate in possess-
ing a number of handsome public buildings   Those erected by
the municipality include a handsome town hall (erected 1897),
three large two-story brick school-houses, and an extensive Exhibition
Building   The government erected in 1890 a fine building for a
post-office, customs and inland revenue offices   The county buildings
(erected in 1866), while not as large or impressive as those at
Stratford or Woodstock, are convenient and provide ample accommodation   The House of Refuge (erected 1898) commands the attention of those who enter the town by the station road, being a building
of architectural good taste, as well as of commodious accommodation   The Bruce County General Hospital (erected in 1903) had
its origin in a bequest of the late W J Moore.   The amount
bequeathed has been increased by a grant of $2,000 from the town,
and one of $1,500 from the county, as well as by numerous private

---

[1]In August, 1877, as a result of " the big fire," a by-law was submitted
to the ratepayers to authorize the expenditure of $11,000 on a system of
waterworks, which failed to carry

[2]The county contributed $2,000 toward the cost of this sewer, the
Inspector of Prisons having ordered that a sewer from the gaol be laid.

subscriptions Further particulars are to be found in Chaptei VIII. regarding the founding of this institution.

A number of isolated minor facts relating to the history of and development of Walkerton may properly conclude this chapter

For a long time in the early day: a town-bell was a felt want At last someone was stirred up to take action, which resulted in a public meeting being held to discuss the matter, the upshot of which was the passing around of a subscription list, to which the town people readily responded to the extent of about $200. This fund was increased by receipts from "Sixpenny Readings," held in the court house, and from other sources, until the necessary amount, in the vicinity of $275, was raised. Alexander Sproat, M P , succeeded in obtaining from the government permission for the bell to be imported free of duty. When it reached the town in the summei of 1870 it was placed on a high derrick, erected in the court house grounds, and was rung, as required, by William Richardson, the caretaker, until removed in March, 1873, to the market square At present it hangs in the tower of the town hall.

The property which now comprises the public park known as "The Bend" was sold at sheriff's sale in May, 1874 The mayor was instructed to act for the town, and purchase it at a price not exceeding $400. This action of the Council in securing such a lovely spot for a public park will be gratefully commended by the future generations that use it as a recreation ground [1]

No provision had been made when the town was first surveyed for a cemetery. Burying grounds in connection with the several churches met this need for a time, but at best it could be but a temporary procedure This fact forced itself upon the citizens, who in 1877 commenced to take action in the matter. After much discussion as to the proper location for a cemetery, the present ground was secured and the first lots therein were offered for sale in July, 1879.

The Walkerton Public Library, or to call it by the name it bore at first, the Mechanics' Institute, was organized November 19th, 1875. After varying vicissitudes a free public reading room, in connection therewith was thrown open to the public The Town Council also installed it on the ground floor of the town hall when that building was opened in 1898

[1] Since the above was written it has been decided to allow the C.P.Ry. to build its station on "The Bend."

The first steps to organize a Board of Trade date back to February 14th, 1872, immediately after the opening of the railway for freight shipments. In January, 1878, it came under the general act of incorporation passed by the Dominion Government regarding Boards of Trade. It has on various occasions been of much benefit in advancing the interests of the town, as it is able to voice in a manner that carries weight the ideas of business men of the place. It was possibly owing to the influence of the Board of Trade that Walkerton was made a port of entry for customs on June 1st, 1878.

The wires of the Montreal Telegraph Company reached Walkerton in 1868. Sixteen years later those of the Bell Telephone Company followed, local service being established in 1884, and in 1886 the town enjoyed the privilege of service with other towns and cities. Arc electric lamps were introduced in October, 1886, for the lighting of the streets, churches and shops, and eight years after the incandescent system was established anad largely adopted for private residences.

Walkerton has taken an interest for many years in athletic sports. The oldest society it can boast which is extant under this heading is the curling club,[1] which was organized in February, 1870. The first skips appointed were John Bruce and Alexander Sproat. The old drill-shed was used every winter to curl in (being used, as well, as a skating rink). With the practice there acquired this club became prominent in this district, and in 1890 carried off the Ontario Silver Tankard, in competition with the best clubs in the province. The banner awarded them at that time, with the names of the successful players embroidered thereon, has for years hung in the office of the manager of the Bank of Commerce. Walkerton's Bowling Club in 1888 carried off the silver medal at a tournament held at Toronto, open to all clubs in the province. The cricket, baseball and lacrosse teams of Walkerton have in various years obtained a high record for their efficiency, to the great jubilation of the town.

[1]Before the curlers organized into a club they played many a friendly game on the ice covering the mill-pond The " stanes " were blocks of wood, turned, when possible, from a large knot. To these were attached iron handles manufactured by a local smith The " stanes " being clumsy to carry and being of no monetary value, were left on the ice after the close of each game during the curling season This was done once too often. A sudden thaw came on, followed by a freshet, and ice and " stanes " together went over the dam and disappeared down the river. This disaster could not damp the ardor of the lovers of the " roaring game," but had the effect of a club being formed, with the use of regulation stones in a rink

The first apology for sidewalks known to Walkerton consisted of plank platforms placed in front of each shop. By-and-bye, when the stumps were cut out, these were connected and extended, until the plank sidewalks on the various streets were over several miles in length. As long as lumber could be procured at a moderate price, such sidewalks answered well enough, but with increased prices for plank a change had to be made In 1891 the first granolithic walk was laid alongside the post-office. Each year since then has witnessed a further extension of this enduring and satisfactory kind of side-walk, until in 1905 over five miles of it have been laid, adding greatly to the appearance of the streets. The practice of removing all fences in front of residences, commenced in 1897. This, combined with the large number of shade trees[1] gives the citizens of Walkerton cause to boast of the beauty of the street of their town.

During the summer of 1906 the Canadian Pacific Railway announced its intention of constructing a branch line from the vicinity of Flesherton to Walkerton. This announcement was quickly followed by work being commenced. At the time of writing the closing pages of this work such progress has been made in the grad-ing of the road as to warrant the assurance that in 1907 Walkerton will possess all the advantages that may be had from the presence of competing lines of railway.

[1] To encourage the planting of shade trees, the town council passed a by-law (June 18th, 1877) offering to pay twenty-five cents, on certain conditions, for each tree so planted along the streets of the town

CHAPTER XXII.

TOWNSHIP OF BRUCE.[1]

EXTRACT FROM THE REPORT OF COUNTY VALUATORS, 1901.

" In this township there is a great deal of very good land and fine, well-kept farms, while the lake range and the south-east corner are very light and stony In fact, a greater portion of the former, as the figures will show, is almost without value Your valuators lost about $30,000 on the lake range One half of this amount was lost on the once prosperous village of Inverhuron, nothing of which now remains but drifting sand and a few small farm-houses of little value Formerly this range was valuable for its large quantity of cedar, which has now disappeared, leaving nothing but stone and sand of little value. There are some sections of this township of too stiff clay, which detracts somewhat from its value. A great deal of Bruce is badly watered, and some seasons parts of the township have to draw water for miles This is the only township south of Wiarton without a railway station. In order to make a fair comparison between Bruce and some of the other townships, it would be only fair to strike off the shore range of 6,386 acres, valued at $20,100, then the balance will give a rate of nearly $32 per acre. The rate per acre for this township, including village property, is $29.03. The village property amounts to only 58 cents per acre "

THE first surveyor to enter this township was A. Wilkinson, in 1847. His work covered a large area, extending not only beyond the township, but the county also, and was in part of a preliminary character by which to form a basis for subsequent surveys. When passing along the front of this township his survey was limited to the marking. at every mile and a quarter, each block of ten farm lots in the Lake Shore Range In 1851 A. P Brough commenced the survey of the township (as related in Chapter V.), but by the time his work had progressed to the 10th side-line he contracted a fatal illness and the work had to be stopped In the following year C. Miller, P.L S., completed the survey of the township

· The lands in the township of Bruce were among the " School Lands " opened for sale August 17th, 1854 [2] Prior to this a large

---

[1] James Bruce, 8th Earl of Elgin and Kincardine, was Governor-General of Canada from 1847 to 1854 Out of compliment to him this township, as well as the county, bears the name of Bruce

[2] See Appendix K

314

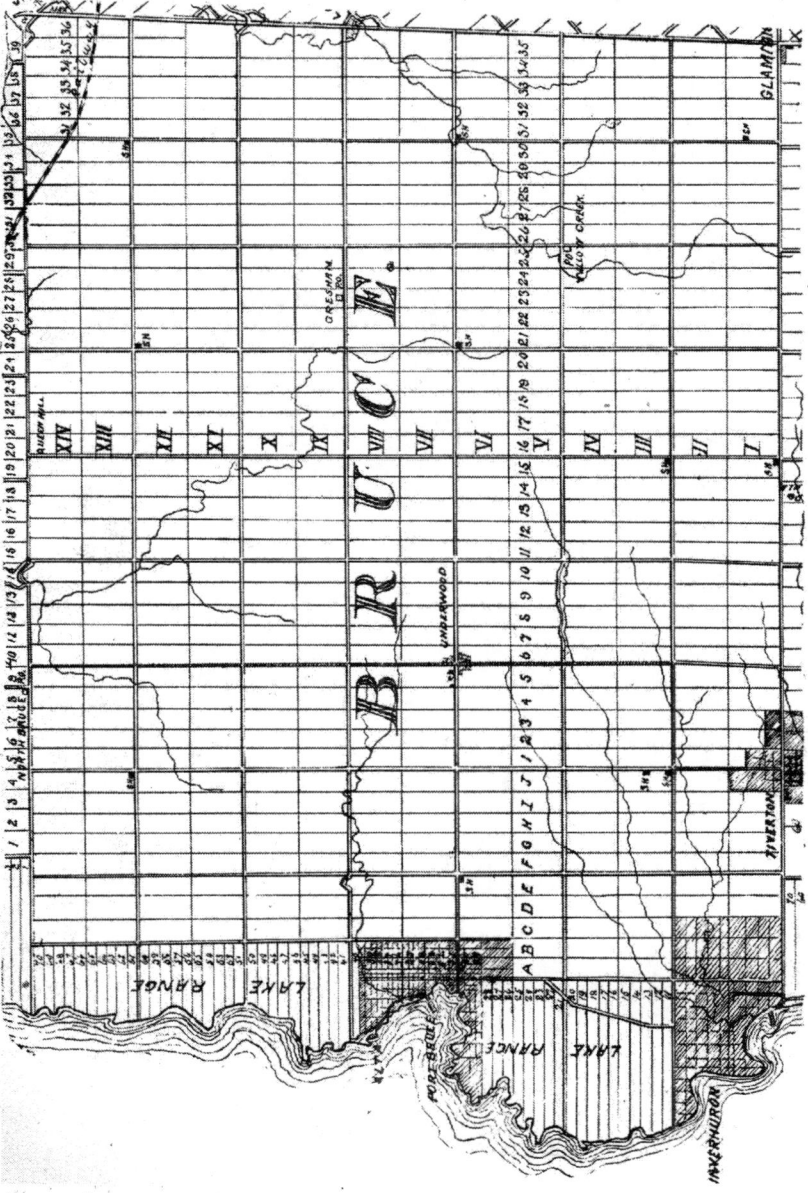

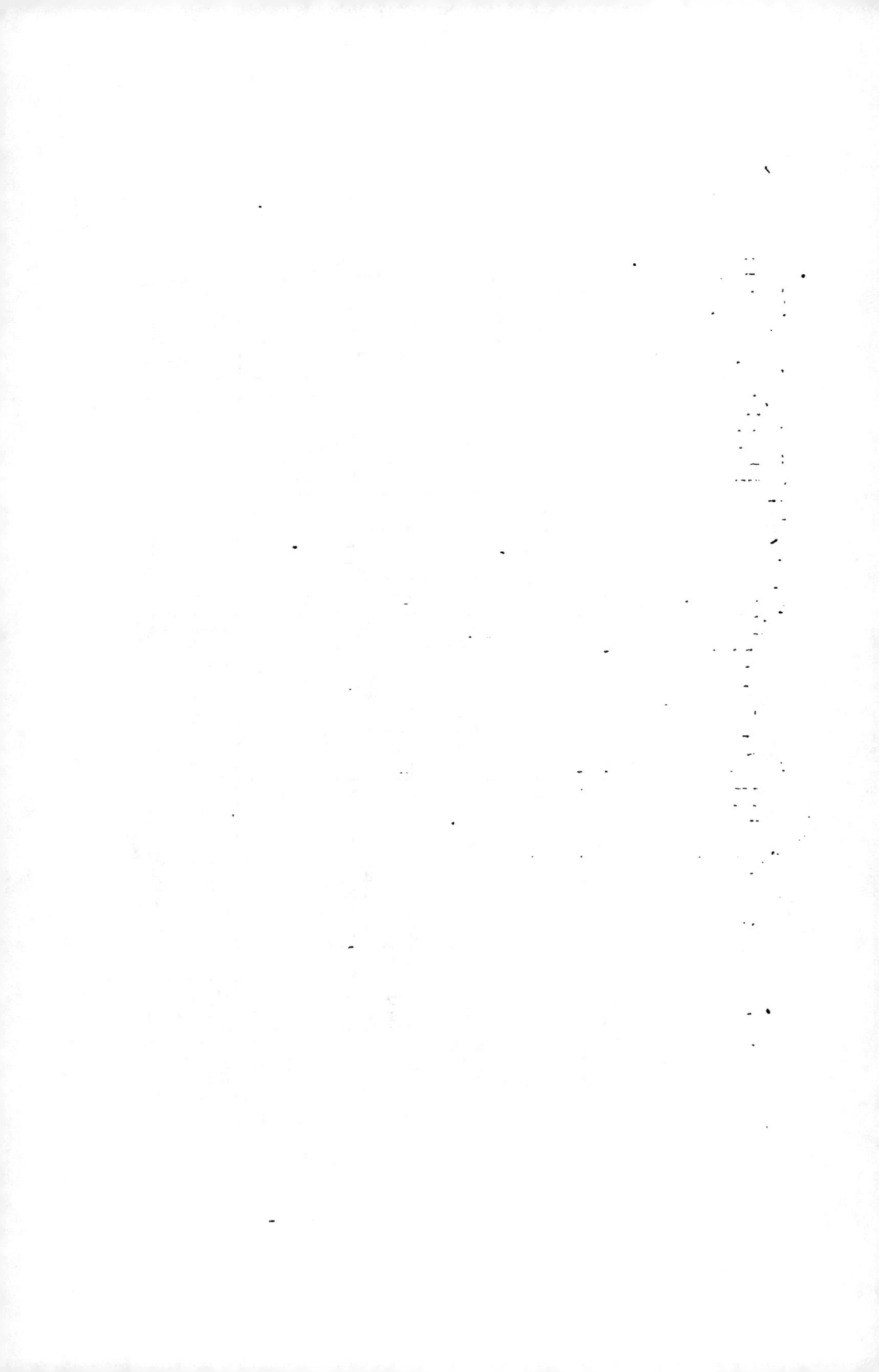

number of settlers had squatted on lands in various parts of the
township. The first of these squatters is said[1] to have been Timothy
Allan, who located on lot 2, concession 1, and Hugh and William
McManamy on the same concession nearer the lake; these settled on
their lots in the fall of 1850 or during the following winter. In May,
1851, the fourth settler in Bruce, Michael Green, took up lot "J"
on the second concession. After this, for the next three years the
stream of land-seekers looking for a desirable location developed in
volume until all the best lands in the township were squatted upon.
These land-seekers many a time realized that travelling in the backwoods of Bruce involved hardships; it meant that often they had to
sleep in the bush, roughing it as best they could, and that largely
they had to depend for food on what they carried with them. At the
same time, it should be remembered that the log shanties of the
settlers were, with proverbial hospitality, thrown open to travellers,
and their meagre fare generously shared. The following incidents
illustrate how open-handed this hospitality was: Michael Green,
above mentioned, tells of thirteen men who came to his shanty one
evening asking for something to eat and a night's lodging. Fortunately for his guests, he that day had brought home a half-barrel of
fresh fish; for their evening meal he cooked a pot of fish and two
large pots of potatoes. After they had eaten to their heart's content,
one old gentleman of their number placed a one-dollar bill on the
table, telling the rest to do likewise, resulting in thirteen one-dollar
bills being placed on the table. In three weeks the old gentleman
returned, accompanied by another gentleman, and asked for a night's
lodging. Michael told them they could get that on one condition,
namely, that they would not insist on him taking any remuneration
for their keep. Of course they complied. Before leaving in the
morning the old gentleman asked his host if he would be kind enough
to fetch them a fresh drink of water from the spring near-by He
went, but not with the best of grace, thinking they might do this act
themselves. They met him outside on his return, and, thanking him
for his hospitality, took their departure On entering his shanty
Michael noticed a cup turned face downward, and on lifting it found
two shining half-dollars; it then dawned upon him why he had been
sent for the water. Elsewhere, about the same time, six men seeking
for land came to a shanty and asked the good lady of the house if

[1]See " Historical Sketch " in *Belden's Atlas of County of Bruce*

they could get anything to eat , She told them to step in and they
could have the best in the house.   She cooked a large pot of potatoes,
but having no table and but few dishes, she pulled a large empty box
to the middle of the floor, emptied the contents of the potato pot on
the centre of it, placed a pinch of salt before each man, and explained
that she had no bread or meat, or any other food but potatoes and
salt to live on, her husband and sons being away earning money to·
pay for the first instalment on the land   After completing their
homely fare they departed, and that evening came to a small clearing
where they found potatoes planted   They made a fire and cooked
some of the potatoes under the ashes. at the same time wishing they
had some of the salt the good lady had given them for breakfast.
Such incidents illustrate the experiences of the early settlers.

In 1852 William Gunn[1] settled at Inverhuron   Mr Gunn for the
next fifteen years occupied a prominent place in the affairs of the
township   His choice of Inverhuron as an advantageous point at
which to settle arose from a conviction he cherished that a harbor of
refuge would be constructed at that point, and that it would become
one of the principal ports in the county   Mr Gunn was the first
postmaster of the post-office established there in 1854.   Inverhuron
was the second post-office in the township, the first, opened in 1853,
being at Sinclair's Corners, known as " Bruce " P O.   Peter Sinclair
was the officer in charge.   These two offices were on the Kincardine
and Southampton mail route, over which, twice each week, John
Urquhart (of the Boundary) tramped, carrying the mails on his
back.

In 1852 Archibald Sinclair[2] sold his farm in Kincardine town-

[1]See biographical sketch of Mr Gunn in Chapter VII

[2]It was in the summer of 1849 that Archibald Sinclair left his home,
near Martintown, Glengarry, to inspect the new lands then being opened
for settlement in the Huron district, his purpose being to provide farms
for his three sons, the eldest of which was then approaching manhood He
found lands to suit him in the township of Kincardine, in the Lake Range.
After taking the necessary steps to secure a title to the lands selected,·he
returned for his family   The start for their new home in the bush was
made in October, 1849, there being no railways in Ontario at that time,
The first part of their journey, as far as Hamilton, was made by steamboat, thence by waggon to Goderich   The story of their trip · from
Goderich to Kincardine is to be found in Chapter V , as related by Mr.
Sinclair's daughter, Mrs. John Reekie   When Bruce separated from Kincardine township and became, in 1856, a separate municipality, Archibald
Sinclair was elected as the first reeve, an honor he gave up before the
end of the first year He died May 11th, 1858, and was buried in Tiverton cemetery, where many others of the pioneers of Bruce are sleeping
their last sleep

ship, where he had settled three years previous, and moved into
Bruce, taking up land a mile and a quarter north of what we now
know as Tiverton, then marked only by a squatter's shanty and a
small clearing. The locality where Mr. Sinclair took up land still
bears the name of " Sinclair's Corners " There Mr. Sinclair built
a sawmill, and then a grist-mill, the first in the township. It was
owing to the fact of these mills being there situated, as well as to
friendly feelings felt for their owner, that David Gibson, the government engineer, when letting the contracts for cutting out the Saugeen
and Goderich road, had it take the jog it had at the second concession, instead of continuing it on the fifth side-road to the Kincardine
boundary.

Adam Burwash, who settled on the fifth concession, is to be mentioned as one of the very earliest pioneers of the township. Another
of those who entered Bruce in 1852, or earlier, was Allan McLean,
who settled on lot 12, concession 8.[1] When he put up his shanty he
was without a neighbor on that concession The author has been
favored with a full and detailed account of one of the settlers of
1853, Murdoch L Martin (which in an epitomized form is here given
in a foot-note[2]), the experiences of any one pioneer being the tale of
all to a greater or less extent is excuse enough for this lengthy sketch.

[1]Allan McLean was a native of the Island of Tiree, Scotland He
had been five years in Canada before settling in Bruce, in which township
he has filled a prominent place, as councillor, collector, and assessor

[2]Murdoch L Martin and his brother, in September, 1853, landed at
Inverhuron, then known as the Sauble. Starting off into the bush to find
land on which to settle, they walked along " the boundary," staying the
first night in the log shanty of a settler, where they were hospitably
entertained. In the morning, guided by one of the sons of this settler,
they walked on to the present site of Glammis As all the best lots
along the boundary line had been taken up, they passed into Greenock,
where his brother took up 200 acres, while Mr Martin located in Bruce
(lot 35, concession 5). The first thing he did was to erect a shanty—
12 x 14 feet was its dimensions—built of logs and roofed with basswood
scoops. As winter was drawing on and lacking a supply of provisions,
Mr. Martin went to Stratford to seek work under some contractor engaged
in the construction of the Buffalo and Lake Huron Railway The weather
that winter was very broken and work irregular, consequently no money
was saved When spring came, he returned to his shanty in the bush,
walking all the way from Stratford. When he reached Kincardine he
purchased as much flour as he could carry on his back, in addition to a
Dutch oven, in which to bake bread Reaching his lot, a small piece of
ground was cleared in which to plant potatoes. The next thing was to
obtain seed potatoes. After inquiry and search a few bushels were purchased from Archie McLean (who lived a few miles below Tiverton), and
a hoe was bought at Kincardine. The carrying of the seed potatoes
through the bush for twelve miles was no small undertaking, but it had
to be done. To earn money to purchase provisions for the coming winter

In 1854 there moved into Bruce Richard McGregor, with his family of eleven sons, and took, up 1,750 acres of land near the Greenock boundary on the fourth, fifth and sixth concessions and in the sixteenth concession of Greenock. They came from the county of Elgin. Being acquainted with Canadian modes of farming and being fairly well-to-do they made good progress in clearing up their land. They also built a sawmill, run by water-power derived from a creek which ran through one of their farms George, one of the

another journey to Stratford was made, and the summer spent in working for the railway contractors. This was the summer of 1854. When the time of the "Big Land Sale" drew near work had to be given up so as to attend the sale. The journey to Goderich was by stage, and the sixty miles beyond, to Southampton, was covered on foot. Regarding the sale, Mr Martin says : Mr. McNabb and Mr. Gunn were at the land office to receive the payments from the settlers The building itself was a small log shanty, with an open window, through which the money in payment for land was handed and a certificate of purchase given in return The crowd was so large that the supply of provisions in the village gave out; the second day nothing could be had but potatoes, fish and whiskey. Of the latter some partook too freely, which resulted in quarrels and fights The crowd never seemed to diminish, the place of those who had completed their business being taken by fresh arrivals

In the fall his sister and a neighbor, with his family, seven in all, arrived. As this party had not a roof to cover their heads Mr. Martin received them into his limited quarters. One end of the shanty was fitted out with bunks, one above another ; at the other end of the shanty a fireplace of stones was constructed, with a chimney built of splints of wood covered with clay. Having an abundance of wood, the shanty was kept warm all winter. The supply of flour, however, gave out, and owing to severe snow storms it was impossible to go for a fresh supply, so their fare was reduced to potatoes and turnips for a while. As soon as possible in the spring the winter's chopping was logged and burnt. On the land so cleared wheat of the Black Sea variety was sown, the ground being prepared with a hoe The crop being put in the ground, again and for the third summer the farm had to be left, so as to work elsewhere to obtain some ready money

Speaking of one occasion where some household effects were to be brought home, Mr. Martin says Our company consisted of a man, his three boys and myself. At Kincardine we came across a settler who offered to take on his ox-sleigh our boxes as far as his own place, some ten miles on our way When we reached there it was dark, so we were invited to remain all night We were all ravenously hungry and were delighted on entering the house to see abundant provisions in the shape of a pot full of potatoes on the table, flanked by a saucer of salt. These were speedily disposed of by the thirteen people that ranged themselves without loss of time around the table. The next day we proceeded on our journey, each ladened with all he could carry. Time was lost by missing their direction in the woods, and it was getting dark as they were passing through a swamp, walking single file Just then they heard a wild hoot, which in their inexperience they attributed to some wild beast Urged on by fear, they pressed forward with all haste so as to get out of the swamp; but again the hoot was heard, this time directly overhead., Terror gave speed to. their feet, and in a short time they reached a clearing, where, on relating their adventures to the dweller thereon, were heartily laughed at and informed that the cry they heard was but the hoot of an owl

sons, told the author that in the year of their arrival he drove the first yoke of oxen which had ever been driven over the boundary line. Angus, the last of the eleven sons, lately retired from farming and moved to Kincardine.

In September, 1854, the United Counties Council received a petition from John McLaren and others, praying that the township of Bruce be separated from the township of Kincardine and erected into a distinct municipality. The committee appointed to consider the petition reported as follows: " Upon inquiry we have ascertained that no natural impediments (other than such as might reasonably be expected in a new place) exist. Further, we are informed that although a number of squatters are upon lands of this township, yet not a single grant, patent, or other authority from government has been obtained for its settlement. Accompanying the petition we find an affidavit setting forth that the body of the petition is not in all respects similar to that upon which the signatures were obtained. Taking these matters into consideration, we cannot recommend that the prayer of the petition be granted." A similar petition, presented the following year by Hugh Matheson and others, met with a better reception, and the favor asked was granted; and on the 1st January, 1856, Bruce township became a separate municipality The first election for councillors was held at the house of James Kippen, Peter Sinclair being the returning officer. The following are the names of those then' elected Archibald Sinclair, Alex. McKinnon, Nath. Burwash, Richard McGregor and George Butchart. At that time the choice of a reeve was made by the council from among its members. Arch. Sinclair was the one chosen, but he, after retaining the reeveship for a few months, resigned. Dr. Hotchkin Haynes was elected to fill in the balance of the year. In a footnote[1] a list of the various reeves of the township up to 1906 is given. The offices of clerk and treasurer of the township were jointly held by Peter . Sinclair from the formation of the municipality until

[1]The following are the names of those who have been reeve of the township of Bruce, with year of office : Arch Sinclair, part 1856; Dr. H Haynes, part 1856, Alex. McKinnon, 1857; Thos Brown, 1858, Wm. Gunn, 1859, 1864; Donald McLellan, 1860, '61, '62, '63, '66, '67, '68, '76; John Scott, part 1865; John McEwen, part of 1865; J. H Coulthard, 1869, 1870, '71, '72, '73; E. J. Brown, 1874, '75, '77, '78, '79, 1880, '81, John Tolmie, 1882, '83, '84, '85, Geo Leeds, 1886, '87, '94, '95, '96, '97, '98; Dr Andrew MacKay, 1888, '89 and part of 1890; R. H. Curry, part of 1890; D. McNaughton, 1891, '92, '93; John McNellidge, 1899, 1900; Wm. Brown, 1901, '02; A. McLean, 1903, '04; James McEwen, 1905, '06.

12

his death in 1869. Hugh Murray[1] succeeded Mr Sinclair to the
position of clerk and treasurer, filling the various duties incumbent
upon him for a third of a century to the satisfaction of all concerned.
The offices left vacant on Mr. Murray's death were during the next
fifteen months filled by Mrs. Murray and her two sons, Clark and
Hugh Murray, Jr   In 1904 J. G. McKay was appointed clerk and
treasurer, which offices he continues to hold. The first assessor
appointed by the Council was Alex. G. Smith, and the first collector
was Alex McLaren. The first township auditors were David Cowan
and Malcolm McKinnon.

The " Famine Year," 1859, will be remembered in Bruce as long
as any who witnessed it survive. As the details connected with it,
particularly regarding this township, are given in full in Chapter VI.
and Appendix P, the reader is referred to them there.

The interests of the township of Bruce have been, and are, chiefly
of an agricultural character. As there exists no river in the township to furnish good and continuous water-power, manufactures have
not developed to any extent; consequently its villages have never
attained any considerable size   Kincardine, Port Elgin and Paisley
have all along attracted a good deal of the trade of the township;
this is shared by Tiverton (of which only one-half is in Bruce), and
by Glammis (lying partly in Bruce, Greenock and Kincardine);
Underwood, the only village wholly in the township, does not receive
the share of business given to some other villages in the county by
the surrounding townships—e g., such as Carrick gives to Mildmay,
Culross to Teeswater, or Huron to Ripley.

At the time the township was surveyed it was decided to lay out
a town-plot on lots 1 to 10, Lake Range, but it was 1856 before the
survey of Inverhuron was made. The possibilities for making a harbor of refuge there have not been developed. The money received
from government toward building a breakwater, extending from the

---

[1]Hugh Murray was born in Sutherlandshire, Scotland, in 1833. Having
received a good education, he engaged in business until he emigrated to
Canada in 1857. The following year he came to Bruce For about seven
years he taught school in the township In 1869 he received the appointment of township clerk and treasurer, and held the position until his
death, which occurred November 10th, 1902. He was made Division
Court Clerk about the same time as he received the municipal appointments, and some six years later was made postmaster at Underwood. Mr.
Murray held several other positions of public trust, showing how largely
he possessed the confidence of the community in which he dwelt.

point southward, was expended in building a pier. This enabled
steamers to call, which was a great thing for trade and travel in the
days before railways had entered the county, but it was not a harbor
of refuge, which, if built, would have fixed a town there. The little
village in its palmiest days had a population of about 200 A grist
mill and two or three sawmills found plenty to do in the sixties; a
decade later the sawmills were reduced to one, but three grain warehouses had been erected, and Inverhuron became quite a grain market, as much as 100,000 bushels of grain having been shipped in a
season from there by water Hemlock bark was also a large item
in the list of exports The fishermen who lived at Inverhuron were
prosperous, and the place boasted of a brick school-house The prosperity of the little village closed suddenly: on April 13th, 1882, the
three grain warehouses were burnt and 30,000 bushels of grain in
them. The fire is said to have been of incendiary origin. However
it arose, the fire killed Inverhuron, and to-day, as one gazes at its
mounds of white, shifting sand, it is hard to believe a flourishing
village ever existed there. On a map of the township of Bruce, some
three or four miles north of Inverhuron, there will be seen the two
town-plots of Port Bruce and Malta. These adjoin one another, and
together surround the expanse of water that bears the name of
"Baie de Dore"[1] This bay impresses a stranger who views it for the
first time, as possessing in a marked degree the shelter required in
a harbor of refuge; as such, however, the bay can be used to only a
limited extent, owing to the presence of extensive rocky shoals extending under the waters of the bay. The two town-plots mentioned
above were surveyed at the same time. In the year 1855 George
Butchart had the survey made of Port Bruce, and Capt A. Murray
McGregor that of Malta The first settler at Port Bruce was Duncan
Bannerman; he was also the first merchant. In the same line of
business there were Cowan & Brownlee, and Walter MacFarlane &
Co., John Lindsay ran a sawmill, and Wm. Turner and D. McCannell
kept hotels, and Geo. Bridges did a conveyancing business. The
total number of inhabitants was about 150 At Malta, Murray
McGregor's two brothers, John and Gregor, put up the first sawmill;
this, however, was burnt in the fall of 1858. The post-office, established in 1856, was in charge of W. Chisholm. George and John

---

[1]This spelling is said to be a corruption of what is claimed to be the
original French name—Baie du Dard; or, Bay of Darts—applicable, owing
to the large fields of reeds at the south end of the bay.

Foard were shipbuilders. In all there were about 125 inhabitants in Malta. These two adjoining villages seemed to be thriving and likely to develop into an important commercial centre, when, on July 4th, 1862, a conflagration wiped the two villages out of existence. Only one house was left   The inhabitants lost everything; not having the means to rebuild, there was no recovery from the blow, and the villages were not   The names are almost forgotten, and the locality where Port Bruce and Malta stood is now known as Baie de Dore

Underwood became a post-office in 1863. J. H. Coulthard was the first to hold the position of postmaster   He also had a pearl-ash factory and kept a store; from these the village appears to have developed.   An hotel, of course, was early there, the "Green Bush," kept by Charles McLean.   The addition of a sawmill in 1870, a grist mill in 1875, and also a cheese factory in the same year, and the building of two churches, with the location of the township hall there, helped to make Underwood the municipal, business and social centre of a large portion of the township.[1]   But the greatest impetus that Underwood received was from the wiping out of the competition exerted by Port Bruce and Malta.   The bulk of the trade which had gone to these villages previous to their destruction by fire naturally drifted to Underwood, as well as some of the population of the two defunct villages

Glammis[2] is situated at the junction of three townships, and while noticing it among the villages of the township of Bruce, the author is aware that it would have been as appropriate to include it in the chapter on Greenock or Kincardine townships.   It was in 1852 when the first settlers at Glammis[3] took up their farm lots   Their names were Allan Ross and Duncan Campbell.   At that time there was no

[1] Of the two churches above referred to, the first erected was a frame building built about 1869 by the united efforts of the Presbyterians and Baptists, who jointly worshipped there   The latter denomination ultimately sold its share in the building to the Presbyterians, who now own the edifice   The second church mentioned was built by the Methodists in 1876   It is a brick building and cost in the vicinity of $1,800

[2] "Glammis" is the spelling adopted by our Post Office authorities The inhabitants of the village prefer spelling it "Glamis," which agrees with the present spelling of "Glamis Castle," Forfarshire, Scotland. But there the word is pronounced as if spelled "Glams"   There seems to be no reason to doubt that the village is named after Glamis Castle, made famous in Shakespeare's "Macbeth."

[3] The author desires to acknowledge his indebtedness for many of the facts here given to an historical sketch of Glammis village, prepared by F H. Leslie, and published in 1900.

thought of a village developing there; but in time a Presbyterian congregation was formed in the locality, and there, in 1858, they erected a fine hewed log building as a church in which to worship. Then, in 1860, a post-office was opened, and the place had a name. James Crawford, the first merchant, became also the first postmaster. R. W. Harrison, in 1867, was the next to open a store, and he acted as postmaster for many years. The first sawmill is said to have been built by one John Fraser. This passed into the hands of M. J. McIntyre. It was ultimately purchased by Thos. Pickard, and the business, with a new mill, is now run by T. Pickard & Son The Presbyterian church remained unplastered for about five years after being erected, and was used until 1896, when it was replaced by the present handsome edifice. The Baptists built a modest building for a church in 1866, which was used until 1884, when a new church was built across the street. The Methodists in 1889 built the church they now occupy. This little village gives evidence of developing, and promises to continue the business centre for the immediate district surrounding it.

If the annals of the early school days in Bruce could be written by the pen of a "Ralph Connor," they would prove to be an interesting chapter in the experiences of a new settlement in the bush The author is pleased to acknowledge the kindness of the Rev N D McKinnon in supplying some recollections of his early school days spent in a Bruce school. As he remembers it, the school buildings at first were generally of logs. The furniture was the simplest possible, consisting of a long desk along each side of the room, with corresponding benches for the pupils to sit on. The walls adorned with but few maps. The blackboard, about 3 x 4 feet, on which, with a piece of carpenter's chalk, problems in mathematics were worked out. Instruction was to a large extent conveyed by a "tanning process." There was a teacher in S. S No 14 in the year 1864, well remembered because of his severity, who on one occasion punished a girl so unreasonably that her enraged father came to the school with the intent of dealing out summary justice to the teacher, had not the latter circumnavigated the area around the stove so nimbly that he could not be caught. As a last resort the father called his children out of the school, and other parents who had come to witness the teacher being thrashed, did likewise. For the remaining three months to the end of the year the regular attendance of scholars was one lonely boy, varied by the occasional appearance of three others toward the end of the term. But there were other teachers of a different type. One school in the township (S.S. No. 13) attained more than a local reputation for the interest manifested in higher education. A teacher in the person of Peter McTavish was secured for this school, a man of scholarly attainments, filled with an intense desire to impart instruction. That this enthusiasm was recognized is shown by the fact that grown-up men and women, from not only Bruce but Saugeen, came to satisfy their thirst at this fountain of knowledge. As a result of such a teacher, the honor-roll of men and women from this school who have, in their several ways, made a name for themselves in the battle of life will favorably compare with that of any other school in the county. Of these the following entered the ministry: the Rev. D. Finlay, Rev J M McLeod, Rev. Donald McGillivray (missionary to China), Rev. John McGillivray, Rev. Malcolm McGillivray, Rev. N. D. McKinnon, Rev. Albert Jones, Rev. Jacob Howe, and Dr. Margaret McKellar (medical missionary in India) Of teachers, those who have entered the profession from this school are the following A. H. Smith, James McKinnon, Charles Cameron, D. McKinnon, Mrs. P. McTavish, Mrs. J. Anderson, and others

The churches in which the people of the township worshipped are mostly mentioned elsewhere in this chapter, or in that on Tiverton. Of those not to be so found are two churches of the United Brethren in Christ, on the fifth concession. Originally there was but one congregation, but when the denomination at large divided on some point, this congregation followed suit, the seceders building for themselves a brick church not far from the site of the parent one

The Presbyterian church on the Saugeen boundary, known as that of the Queen's Hill, or North Bruce congregation, was built in 1866. Its first minister was the Rev. Wm Matheson, following him was the Rev. John Scott, D D, inducted April 28th, 1875. The minister at present in charge is the Rev. Hector McQuarrie. At first the congregation at North Bruce was united to one on the eighth concession at Gresham, known as the Centre Bruce congregation. This union was dissolved, North Bruce becoming united with St. Andrew's, Saugeen, and Centre Bruce with the Underwood congregation.

Of public works on which the municipality has spent money, the township of Bruce has but little to show, the drainage of the hem-

lock swamp on the fourth concession being about all. Debentures
for $800 were issued to pay for this work, which was carried out in
the late seventies.

The first settlers in Bruce township were largely natives of Scotland, or of Scotch parentage; their descendants of to-day evidence
by their general prosperity and by the honorable position they occupy
in the community at large that they are worthy descendants of the
sturdy, God-fearing Scotch settlers who, dreading not the hardships
of pioneer life in the bush, have been instrumental in making the
township of Bruce what it is to-day, one of the most prosperous in
the county.

CHAPTER XXIII.

VILLAGE OF TIVERTON.[1]

It was in the fall of 1850 that the primeval forest that covered the present site of Tiverton was entered by its first settler, Timothy Allan. The survey of the north part of Kincardine Township had just been completed, but that part of the township of Bruce in which Tiverton lies had not been commenced. For several years the work of clearing the bush went steadily on before the idea of a village at that spot was thought of. It was the fortune of the author, in the spring of 1857, to tramp along the "Boundary Line" from Inverhuron east to the fifteenth side-road, but he cannot recall of then seeing any evidence of the village that subsequently was developed. It was, however, in the same year that Norman McInnis there opened a store, and it is probably the year which Tiverton may claim as that when it commenced to take form; but it was 1860 before it became known by the name it now bears, that is, when "Tiverton" was given as the name of the post-office then opened. The one store was the most suitable place for the office, so naturally the postmastership was given to Norman McInnis, of whom it may be said in passing, he, as much as anyone else, deserves the honor of being called the founder of the village. He it was who opened the first store and also the first manufacturing industry of the place, which was a pot and pearl-ash factory, which he commenced to operate in September, 1860. The next industry added to this was a wool-carding mill run by A. McBain, which mill at a later date passed into the hands of James McLeod. About the end of the sixties a grist mill was added to the industries of the village, John McLeod being the miller. John

[1] The name of a town in Devonshire, England. It is said that Norman McInnis and the other petitioners, when applying for a post-office, suggested the name " St. Andrews " This the Department would not agree to, there being another post-office of that name. Of several names offered " Tiverton " was chosen, it being the name of the borough for which Lord Palmerston, the English Prime Minister, sat in Parliament, and this no doubt had something to do with the choice made

Dewar, also, about the same time, opened a store, the second in Tiverton. From this time, and for the next ten or twelve years Tiverton became somewhat of a market. The grain there purchased used to be delivered at one of the warehouses at Inverhuron; this business ceased with the burning of these warehouses in 1882, as they never were rebuilt. It was during these years the village attained to its highest notch as a business centre, and new industries were started, among which were a sawmill, a planing-mill and machine shop, but the largest and most prominent of them was John McDonald's tannery, which employed about twenty-five hands and had an output of about $20,000 worth of leather per annum.

In 1874 *The Watchman,* Tiverton's newspaper, was founded by Alfred Robinson, who, after publishing it for a few years, sold out to John Pollard, who conducted the paper until 1890; since that date three or four different publishers have supplied, through the columns of *The Watchman,* the village with its local and general news

The congregation now known as that of Knox Church, Tiverton, when first organized was called the congregation of South Bruce, and worshipped in a log building at Sinclair's Corners In 1860 a new frame church was built at Tiverton, and the first settled pastor, the Rev Alex. McKay, was that same year inducted into his first charge. The Rev. John Anderson[1] in 1870 commenced a long pastorate of a quarter of a century. He was followed in the pastorate, for the years 1895-97, by the Rev. J. Stevens, and he by the present incumbent, the Rev. K. McLennan, D.D. In 1868 Glammis was united with the Tiverton congregation; the union, however, was but temporary. On July 2nd, 1900, the corner-stone was laid of the handsome and commodious brick edifice in which this congregation now worships A good deal was made of the opportunity thus offered—and rightly so— to refer back to the early days of the congregation, and many outsiders were in attendance. The dedicatory services were held January 6th, 1901, the Rev. Principal Grant, of Queen's University, officiating.

The Baptist congregation was organized in 1855, under the zealous efforts of the Rev. Wm. Fraser, who used to walk from his farm at Lorne to Tiverton every Sunday, where he conducted services in

[1]On October 14th, 1904, the Rev Mr Anderson commemorated the fiftieth anniversary of his ordination A number of members of the Presbytery of Bruce were present to unite with his old congregation in offering congratulations

English and Gaelic The year 1857 was that in which the first church
was built; the present one was built in 1865.[1]

One week and a day after the corner-stone of Knox Church was
laid, the Methodists of Tiverton engaged in a similar ceremony.
This congregation, feeling that the day of frame buildings for church
edifices was past, have erected a commodious brick church.

Being somewhat out of the main current of the world's activities,
Tiverton in the early days had at times to depend upon local effort
to conduct its religious meetings In illustration of this, the writer
recalls an incident related to him at the time, which was somewhere
about 1862. The annual meeting of the Bible Society was announced
for a certain evening, at which an address was to be given by a travelling agent of the Society. The evening came, and with it a fair
number in attendance, but no agent of the Society. The roads were
heavy, so allowance was made for that. To hold the audience
together until the expected speaker arrived, the chairman announced,
" We will sing the 119th Psalm. (This, the reader will remember,
contains 176 verses.)   The tune, some familiar one such as " Bal-
erma," was raised, and bravely the audience started to sing, and sing
they did through thirty-two verses, when the flow of psalmody was
stopped by the arrival of the Bible Society agent.

The County Council of Bruce passed a by-law, December 5th,
1878, incorporating the village of Tiverton. According to the " Municipal Act," it was necessary that three months elapse before the
by-law could become operative; this was overlooked, and the election
of a reeve and councillors took place on the last Monday of December. To correct this oversight it was necessary to have the House of
Assembly pass an act, which it did (42 Vic. chap 43), to confirm the

_____

.[1]This little church has made a record that many a city church might
be proud of in the number of ministers it has sent out to preach the
Gospel. Among those who have thus gone forth might be mentioned:
Rev. A A. Cameron, of First Church, Ottawa ; Rev. J. P. McEwen (late
Superintendent of Home Missions); Rev. P. A. McEwen, B.A, York Mills ;
Rev. James McEwen, B.Th , Wiarton , Rev. J. R. Coutts, Field Secretary
of Brandon College ; Rev. Wm Holbin, White Lake ; Rev. P. C. Cameron,
B.A , Paris ; Rev. Duncan Menzies (deceased); Rev. C. J. Cameron, B.A.,
Field Secretary of McMaster University, Rev. Carey M. Cameron
(deceased); Rev. Archibald Reekie, Bolivia Mission ; Rev. Lach. McLean,
Michigan ; Ebenezer Cameron, B.A., student pastor at Reaboro ; Rev. W.
P. Reekie, B A., Sparta ; Rev. E. J. McEwen, Uxbridge ; Rev. T. T.
Shields, Adelaide Street, London ; Henry Lowick, student at Chicago ;
Rev. P. A. McDiarmid, B.A , Rochester ; Rev. Edgar Shields, Kincardine ;
Rev. P. H McEwen, Vancouver ; Rev. D. P. McLaurin ; Rev. Alex. Kippen
(deceased); and Rev. D S McEwen—about twenty-five in all.

by-law and also the election of reeve and councillors. Their names
were as follows: Reeve—John C. McEwen; councillors—John Mc-
Aulay, Joseph Robertson, John McLeod and G. B Lamont. The
first village officials were: Duncan Cameron, clerk; Norman McInnis,
treasurer; Donald Robertson, assessor, and George Dayton, collector. The names of the various reeves of Tiverton and their years
of office are as follows: John C McEwen, 1879, 1880, 1885, 1886,
1887, 1888, John McDonald, 1881, J. J. Fee, 1882, 1883, 1884;
John Pollard, 1889, 1890, John McKellar, 1891, 1892, 1893; M.
L. McKinnon, 1894, 1896, 1897, R. Ballantyne, 1895; Dr W J.
Chambers, 1898, 1900, 1901; D. A. McLaren, 1899; N. McClure,
1902, 1903; J. H. McKay, 1904, 1905, A. McKinnon, 1906.

In the fall of 1897 Tiverton suffered from an extensive fire, which
caused serious loss of property in the business portion of the village,
most of the principal shops being among the buildings then destroyed.
In view of this severe loss, the County Council refunded to the village
the amount of the county rates for that year. The buildings
destroyed have been replaced by handsome structures, and it is questionable if any village of its size in the county can show such up-to-
date shops as Tiverton.

The public school building is one of good size built of brick, and
cost about $3,500. The frame building previously used for school
purposes has been turned into a town. hall In this building the
author, in June, 1882, made the only political speech he ever
attempted. The circumstance is here mentioned only to illustrate
the political leanings of the electorate of Tiverton at that time. The
meeting referred to was in the interests of J. H Scott, the Conservative candidate for West Bruce. There was at that time only one Conservative elector residing in Tiverton, and he refused to act as chairman of the meeting to be held; so a Liberal, John McDonald, the
tanner, was asked and kindly consented to act as chairman at this
meeting held in the interests of the Conservative party. Mr McDonald did this, no doubt, much against his inclinations, but it was a
gracious act. The meeting did but little to change the politics of
Tiverton at that time, but other causes have been at work, and the
political parties are not now so one-sided. The one Conservative
vote of 1882 had been multiplied in 1904 by more than thirty fold.

The subdivision of farm lots into village lots by a registered plan
occurred in the following order and at the dates given. The first
was made in October, 1868, and was of the west half of lot 1, conces-

sion 12, Kincardine. This was followed, in September, 1870, by one of lot 60, concession " C," Kincardine, and in May, 1873, by one of lot 1, concession 1, Bruce, and in October, 1874, by one of lot "J," concession 1, Bruce. These, with other subdivisions of farm lots, were combined in 1879 into what is known as the "Corporation Plan," comprising the five hundred acres contained in the village proper.

It is a pleasure to note that the business founded by Norman McInnis in 1857, and which was the germ from which Tiverton developed, is still flourishing, although the respected founder has passed to his rest. Another store in the village is that of John McKellar, a man who has helped to make Tiverton a business place. His name is associated with cheese manufactories, as well as with the mercantile interests of the place. Another of the business firms of Tiverton is that of Ballantyne & Ord, both members of the firm being long identified with the making of the village.

At the time of its incorporation Tiverton claimed to have a population of 834 This must have been an error, for two years later, by the census of 1881, the population was only 545. Tiverton is the smallest municipality in the county, but this designation will be changed when that day comes when the projected electric railway reaches and makes a town of Tiverton.

Subsequent to the writing of the foregoing, Tiverton has suffered again by fire. On July 19th, 1906, the grist mill owned by McCracken Bros was burned. As there is a doubt about this industry being rebuilt in as complete a form as before the fire, the injury to the village can be appreciated.

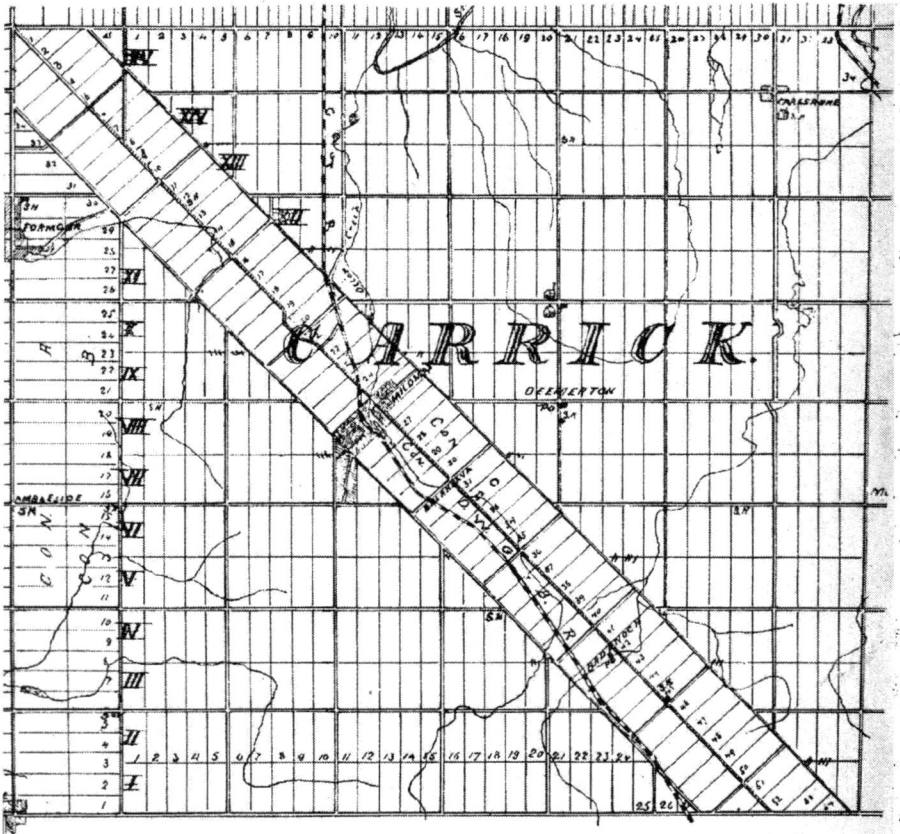

CARRICK.

CHAPTER XXIV.

TOWNSHIP OF CARRICK.[1]

EXTRACT FROM THE REPORT OF COUNTY VALUATORS, 1879

"This we found to be the best adapted township for stock and dairy farming of any in the county, on account of its numerous springs, and its soil, which is mostly loam mixed with limestone, which is better for grazing and root growing than stiff clay. There is a strip of very rough, gravelly land running through it, termed "The Forty Hills," which is very inferior land, but the balance of the township is mostly ordinary land. It has the best outbuildings of any township in the county, and has a large amount of village property Its average price per acre is $35 25 "

EXTRACT FROM THE REPORT OF COUNTY VALUATORS, 1901.

"There is a great deal of very good land in this township, and there is considerable quantity of the roughest land to be found in the county The latter applies to the south-western portion of the township, nevertheless the settlers seem to be very industrious and prosperous, even in the worst sections Land is selling readily and at good prices The township is well watered with spring creeks, and stiff clay is not to be found The facilities for making roads are good, gravel is abundant, and as a result good roads prevail Buildings and fences are good and farms well kept and clean Carrick has good railroad facilities, and is also close to the county town The Elora Road, running diagonally through the township, causes a number of gores in each concession The rate per acre is $39 13, of which the village property is $4 30 per acre '"

THE township of Carrick was settled with greater rapidity than possibly any other township in the county. There were several reasons for this. The lands, being Crown lands, were to be had at a lower price ($1.50) than School lands Then a rumor got abroad regarding the quality of the soil, to the effect that this township contained the choicest farm lands that were opened for sale in this district, a fact sufficient in itself to explain why settlers entered with a rush.

In 1850-51 A P Brough laid out the Elora Road from the north-west corner of Carrick down to the township of Maryborough, staking out the lots in Carrick on concessions " C " and " D " on each

---

[1] The title of Earl of Carrick was one borne by Robert the Bruce, and now by the eldest son of the Sovereign of Great Britain

side of the road; the rest of the township was surveyed in 1852 by
J. D. Daniel. Prior to survey several squatters had entered and
taken up lands in the northerly part of the township. Among these
were John Hogg,[1] Andrew Hutton, Louis Fournier and John Toran-
jeau. These men squatted on their lots in the summer of 1851.
Shortly after the survey was finished the rush to locate farm lots
commenced. Although the lands were not in the market, and were
not offered for sale until the "Big Land Sale," held in September,
1854[2] long before that date every lot in the township was squatted
upon.

Early in 1853 the inflow of settlers into Carrick commenced.
Prominent among those who took up land in the township in this
year were Wm. Dickison, Edward Hickling, Wm. Thomson, who settled in the north-eastern part of the township; Angus, Robert and
John McPhail, Samuel Clendening and his sons, Thomas, William
and Charles; Robert A. Morden, Abraham Johnston, Charles,
Thomas and Frederick Jasper, Alexander and Donald McKay, Robert Wills and Arthur Deacon, who settled nearer the centre of the
township. The first settlers to take up land in the vicinity of Mildmay were Robert Young, James Grey, Thomas Liscoe, Andrew

[1]As the first settler in Carrick, John Hogg deserves a short biographical
sketch John Hogg was a native of Edinburgh, Scotland In 1844 he came
with his parents, to Canada, being at that time fourteen years of age.
The family settled in the county of Renfrew. In 1850 John Hogg came to
Bruce After working in the vicinity of Walkerton he, in the following
year, squatted on land which, when the survey was made, proved to
be lots 18, on concessions 13 and 14, of that township, for which lots he
subsequently obtained a patent On entering the bush, of money he had
little, and his outfit consisted of little beyond an axe and a few necessary
cooking and eating utensils. His bed was but a pile of hemlock brush
spread out on the usual single-posted bedstead. (This backwoods bedstead
was always found in the corner of the shanty, the walls of which
supported three corners so that only one post was needed) The staple
article of his diet at first was potatoes After he had grown wheat he had
to take it to Durham to be ground. He relates that on one occasion, after
a long and tedious journey with a yoke of oxen, he reached Durham without
any money, so he could not go to the hotel for a meal By and by a bag
of his grist was filled up and he proceeded to relieve the pangs of hunger.
The process of baking was as follows : The top of the bag was thrown
down, exposing the flour, some water was poured into it and the two were
mixed into a batter, this was kneaded roughly into dough in the form of
a scone and placed upon the top of the stove used for heating the mill,
and baked, first on one side, then on the other. It required the digestion
of a backwoodsman to digest such an article of diet. Mr. Hogg took an
interest in the municipal matters of the township and was deputy reeve
in the years 1864 and 1865 He was prominently connected with the
Walkerton Presbyterian Church He was married in 1857 to Miss Bell,
who survived him. His end came on February 1st, 1902 "

[2]See Appendix K.

Dunbar and his son James, Joseph Young, Samuel Carr, Adam
Johnston, James Clark, James Butchart, John Reddon and his bro-
ther-in-law, John Campbell, Alex. McLaren and Thomas B. Taylor
These were followed by John, Peter and Thomas Shennan, who settled at Balaclava. The south-western part of the township shortly
afterwards received its pioneer settlers, among whom were Anthony
Wynn, Thomas McMichael, Henry McDermott, George, John and
Thomas Inglis, James and Adam Darling. It may be safely stated
that all of the foregoing entered the county by way of the Durham
Road, as the Elora Road was not chopped out until the summer of
1854, the work being done by Joseph Bacon, as mentioned in Chapter V.

Carrick is distinct among the townships of the county in having
a large percentage of its inhabitants claiming either German birth
or descent; in fact, in many portions of the township the German
element forms the majority of the population. The first body of
those of this nationality to settle in the county were those commonly
called " Pennsylvania Dutch," Mennonites in religion, who settled
in the township of Saugeen. Carrick received the next contingent,
who settled in 1853-54 in the vicinity of Formosa; these were largely
natives of the southerly part of Germany or from Alsace. Prominent
among them were Michael Fischer, Joseph and Michael Seitz, Andrew
Zettle, Philip Hauck, Anthony Schumacher, J.P. (commonly known
as " Baier Tony "), Michael Mosack and Charles Uhrich. This class
of settlers had resided long enough in "New Germany," Waterloo
County, to acquire a knowledge of Canadian ways of farming, and
as a class were well-to-do settlers. Others who about the same time
settled in the eastern part of the township were Matthias Bickel, P.
Binkle, Henry Evers, Peter and Jacob Eckel, John Bieman, John
and Matthias Stroder and Henry Dahmer. In the centre of the
township, in the vicinity of Deemerton, there settled Andrew,[1]
Anthony and Thomas Diemert, Peter and Joseph Emel, John and
Jacob Wiegand. The earliest German settlers in the vicinity of
Mildmay were George, Frederick and Joseph Weiler, Charles Weis-
hahn, Ernest, Frederick and Henry Zinn, August and Frederick
Kleist. It is to the credit of Carrick that its inhabitants of varied
races, different languages and diverse faiths have lived from the first
with an entire absence of feeling as to race or creed, markedly

[1]Andrew built the first tannery and Anthony the first sawmill at this
point.

attested all these years by the composite character of the Township Council and its officers.

The first assessment made in Carrick was in 1853. At this time Carrick formed part of the municipality of the United Townships in the county of Bruce Carrick's total assessment for that year was £373, and the amount of the municipal levy £2 9s 9d. The rapid development in wealth of the township from this year may be seen by an examination of Appendix M. In 1854 the union of all the townships in the county as one municipality was dissolved, and Brant and Carrick as united townships became a municipality.[1] Joseph Walker, of Brant, was the reeve of this municipality for the years 1854-55 In 1856 this last-mentioned union was dissolved, and Carrick commenced its separate municipal existence. The first meeting of the Township Council was held at Balaclava, at John Shennan's tavern, on January 21st, 1856. The council consisted of Michael Fischer, Seth Rogers, Wm. McVicar, Peter McVicar and A. Diemert, James Gorsline acting as clerk at this meeting, which elected Peter McVicar as reeve At the second meeting Edmund Savage was appointed to the joint office of clerk and treasurer, which position he held until June, 1872 In a footnote[2] are to be found the names of those who have held the position of reeve of Carrick from the year 1856 to 1906

The township of Carrick has certain natural advantages which have saved it from incurring large financial obligations necessitating the issuing of debentures Being in a great measure free of swamps

[1] An effort was made in 1854 to have Carrick erected into a separate municipality, as the following extract from the County Council Minutes of Report of Special Committee on the separation of union of the townships in Bruce, shows

" Petition of Thomas Liscoe and others praying that the township of Carrick be erected into a distinct municipality We cannot recommend that the prayer of this petition be complied with, inasmuch as the gross assessment of the township, upon which county taxes are applotted, is only £330, and calculating the county taxes for this year at 2d in the pound, the whole sum payable by this township would amount to only £2 15s We respectfully submit that it is quite unnecessary that a reeve should be sent here, at a cost of £12 or £14 to the county, for the purpose of guarding the interests of this township "

[2] List of reeves in the township of Carrick Peter McVicar, 1856, '57; Michael Fischer, 1858, '59, '60, '61, '62, '63, '64, '65, '66, '67, '73, '74, '75, '76, 1880, Ignatius Kormann, 1868, '69, '70, '71, '72, J Murphy, M.D.; 1877, '78, M. Campbell, 1879, Wm Dickison, 1881, '82, '83, '84, '85, '86, '87; John Henderson, 1888, '89, '90, '91; George Lobsinger, 1892; Aaron Moyer, 1893; C Liesemer, 1894, '95; James Darling, 1896; James Johnston, 1897, R E Clapp, M D, 1898, '99; L. Lintz, 1900, Moses Filsinger, 1901, '02, '03, '04; Conrad Schmidt, 1905, '06

it has no scheme of drainage to provide for, and, unlike the township of Brant, to the north, it has no large streams to bridge, with the involved necessity of expensive structures for that purpose The debentures issued by the township have been on account of the village of Mildmay, for the erection of a school building and to purchase a fire-engine, for which sectional assessments are made. The issue of debentures for the school building was $3,200, and for the fire-engine $4,000.

The settlement commenced by the three Shennan brothers at Balaclava seems to have been the first to have taken upon itself the form of a village. John Shennan's tavern there was the first in the township, and the first store in the township was there opened by his brother. For a number of years Balaclava was a thriving little village and was the hub of the township, the municipal nominations and most of the Council meetings being held there A Presbyterian congregation in connection with the Church of Scotland was there formed about 1861, which along with the congregation at Mount Forest formed a charge over which was settled the Rev. John Hay, a very gifted minister A post-office established there in 1856 bore the name of " Glenlyon," of which John Shennan was postmaster, his successor in office being William Hay. This office, after remaining open for about sixteen years, was closed in 1872 Balaclava at one time had a population of about 150, this would be about high-water mark in its best days The reason for the decay of Balaclava was that in the contest for the position of the railway station Mildmay had the good fortune to secure it, as referred to in the following paragraph

Mildmay commenced to take form as a village about 1867, when Samuel Merner had a survey made of part of lot 26, concession " C." For the first half-dozen years the place was called Mernersville, although the post-office, which was established in 1868, was known as Mildmay. The first postmaster was Donald McLean, who also was the first merchant of the place. The three water privileges on Otter Creek, in or about Mildmay, have all been used to advantage. The first industry to which water-power was applied was a sawmill erected by Samuel Carr, near the present railway station. A grist-mill is said to have been established by a man named Stewart late in the fifties; of this the author cannot affirm, but in 1867 there was a good grist-mill run by William Murray. The nucleus around which villages form in a new district is generally a blacksmith shop

and an hotel   The first of each of these in Mildmay was started
respectively by John Lenhardt and Charles Schiel.   Before the railway had reached the county of Bruce there were established at Mildmay a woollen factory by Edmund Berry, and a pottery by I. Bit-
schey, besides grist and sawmills.   Having these industries located,
and also having good water-power for further industries, the village
of Mildmay presented greater inducements to the railway company
for the fixing of their station at that point than could Balaclava, and
therefore obtained the coveted prize.   Since the opening of the railway Mildmay has made very rapid progress, so much so that it is
doubtful if there is another unincorporated village in the province of
its size and activity, certainly it can rightly claim to possess a larger
amount of trade than several of the incorporated villages within the
county.   It has its local newspaper, *The Mildmay Gazette*, established about 1893, a system of electric lighting and banking facilities, the Merchants Bank having established an agency there in 1900.
No village in the county is more loyally supported by the surrounding
country than is Mildmay, which fact seems to assure its continued
prosperity.

Next to Mildmay the most important village in the township of
Carrick is Formosa   Its situation is unique, being in a valley
through which runs Stoney Creek, supplying water-power to the mills.
In this valley there are places where low, rocky cliffs picturesquely
intrude themselves upon the line of the highway, to avoid which the
street has to forsake the usual straight line until the rocks are
past.   A settlement was formed at this point in 1854, but the village
did not take form until some years later.   John B. Kroetsch started
a sawmill here in the fifties, which was the first industry of the place;
some ten years later he added to this a grist-mill.   The first store
was kept by A. Schick, and the first hotel by John Kartes.   The
post-office was established there in 1862, the first postmaster being F.
X. Messner.   It is not too much to say that Messrs. Anthony and
F. X. Messner were the leading spirits of Formosa for about thirty
years as storekeepers and private bankers   In a footnote[1] is given

[1]The death of Mr Francis X Messner, which occurred March 10th,
1906, removes a prominent pioneer and philanthropist.   In 1862 he, with
his brother Anthony, settled in the locality of Formosa, then a dense
forest, and started several business enterprises, encouraging settlers and
helping them to establish the homes they are now enjoying   An earnest
promoter of Catholic education, he built two convents, one in Formosa
and another in Walkerton   His philanthrophy was not confined to Bruce;
he was ever ready to assist charities throughout Canada.   He was most

a biographical sketch of F. X. Messner which will enable the reader to see why he will be remembered in connection with Formosa as long as the present generation of the village are alive.

The inhabitants of Formosa are almost entirely of German or Alsatian birth or descent, and are members of the Roman Catholic Church. The church they have erected is by long odds the finest ecclesiastical building in the county. It is built of stone. Its dimentions are 160 by 60 feet, and its lofty spire, glistening in the sunlight, may be seen for miles around. During the erection of the building services were held in the old frame church erected some twenty years previously, the peculiar feature being that the new building was built around and about the old one, until at last but glimpses of it only could be had through the windows of the building which was being erected. This fine church was opened December 9th, 1883. The first church services at Formosa were held in the old log school-house, that stood on the site of the present school building. The first priest to be stationed at Formosa was the Rev. Father Stier. The Rev. Father Gehl is the priest at present in charge of the parish. After the church the next prominent building in the village is the convent, under the charge of the Sisters de Notre Dame. This building, the gift of A. and F. X. Messner, was opened by Bishop Farrel, October 20th, 1872. A boarding-school conducted by the sisters has been well patronized.

Some few years ago it was asserted that there were indications of the existence of coal oil at Formosa. An artesian well was sunk over a thousand feet deep, and at one time it was thought that they were on the point of striking oil, but only to be disappointed. Another well not far off was sunk with like result. A fine flow of water comes from these wells, which is all the unfortunate shareholders have to show for their expenditure. A German settlement without a brewery would be incomplete. This need was supplied to Formosa about 1869, when Andrew Rau built his brewery, which, under different owners, is still in operation. In a purely German settlement lager beer is partaken of as one of the ordinary and necessary things of life. How much this is so has been evidenced at For-

successful in business until an unfortunate enterprise caused him great losses and saddened the last few years of his life, owing to the fact that some of his friends were involved with him. Mr. Messner was a prominent Liberal, and on one occasion received the unanimous nomination in East Bruce for the House of Commons, an honor which he declined. He is survived by his widow. —*The Globe*, Toronto.

mosa in days now past, where every Sunday morning, after hearing
mass, the hotels were filled by the church-goers having a quiet mug of
beer before starting on their drive back to the farm; and, strange as
it may seem, the license inspectors did not think it advisable to enforce
the law there in regard to prohibited hours.

Another of the villages of Carrick is Carlsruhe, which derives its
name from the capital of the Grand Duchy of Baden, in Germany.
Its location is elevated and healthy, and its inhabitants are said to
be noted for their sociability. (*Deutsche Ausland und Gemuetlich-
keit.*) A post-office was opened there in 1864, Ignatius Korman
being the first postmaster and also the first merchant. His successor
was Ernst Seeber.[1] The Roman Catholic church in the village is one
of the foremost in the diocese. It is modelled after the cathedral at
Roermonde, in Holland, and is of the Romanesque style of architecture. It was built in 1873, at a cost of over $15,000. Its numerous
stained-glass windows are artistic and worthy of inspection. The
first resident priest was the Rev. Franz Rassaerts, M.I.H.S., a man
of scholastic attainments and large-heartedness. His death occurred
in October, 1886. The present incumbent, the Rev. J. E. Wey, P.L.,
possesses the affection and respect of his parishioners. There are in
the village both a public and a Roman Catholic separate school.
Carlsruhe, although not a populous village, has many of the luxuries
of larger places, such as electric lights, two daily mails, and is connected with the outer world by both telegraph and telephone.

Otter Creek, although not a large stream, has been made the most
of as a source of power. After driving the mills at Mildmay, it is
next used to furnish power to the Saugeen Valley Roller Mill, now
owned by Jacob Steinmiller & Son. This mill was originally built
in the seventies by Wm. H. Clendening and Wm. Brown. He failed
to make a success of it, and the mill passed into the hands of the
Merchants Bank, who sold it in 1886 to Mr. Steinmiller.[2] Under his
management the mill has obtained a wide-spread reputation for the
high grade of flour produced. It was awarded a bronze medal at the
World's Fair at Chicago in 1893. It also carried off the *Grand Prix*

[1] Mr. Seeber filled the office of postmaster from 1869 until 1906, excepting four years which he spent teaching school at Neustadt. During this
interim Albert Goetz held the office.

[2] Jacob Steinmiller came to this county from Germany, in 1867. His
experience as a miller extends over half a century. He claims to have,
in 1875, set up the first roller machinery in the province, the machinery
being imported from Vienna by Messrs. Snider, of St. Jacobs.

at the Paris Exposition of 1900, and a diploma at the International Exposition at Glasgow in 1901. This mill has a capacity of 125 to 150 barrels a day. A large proportion of the flour Mr Steinmiller grinds is exported Further down the stream, near where it empties into the Saugeen River, George Harrington in 1862 erected a grist-mill. This was run for about twenty-five years by different proprietors, when it unfortunately was burnt down, and has not been rebuilt.

One of the first congregations of any denomination to be organized in Carrick was that of the German Evangelical Association on the eleventh concession, which event occurred in 1855 The Rev D. Dippel was one of the pioneer ministers of this denomination in Carrick; through his efforts, and those of other workers, not only this church was established, but also one of the same denomination on the seventh concession, and another in Mildmay. The Lutheran church on the eleventh concession was early organized. It is claimed that this was the first Lutheran congregation formed in the county. The first minister was the Rev Mr Wunderlich.

The farmers of Carrick were heavy losers by the failure of F. X. Messner in 1897, and of the Carrick Banking Company in the following year, many having deposited their savings with these two firms. These losses have been more than made up during the subsequent years of prosperity, for the farmers of Carrick are thrifty and successful agriculturists. With such characteristics as these we may always expect to see Carrick among the premier townships of the county of Bruce.

CHAPTER XXV.

TOWNSHIP OF CULROSS.[1]

EXTRACT FROM THE REPORT OF COUNTY VALUATORS, 1901.

"We found the greater portion of this township first-class soil and well improved, good buildings, good fences, and in a good state of cultivation Land is selling at good prices, and is well adapted for all kinds of farming, being well watered and having first-class roads There is, however, a very rough strip of about two miles and a half along the western boundary, which reduces the average rate per acre very considerably, while being very hilly it grows fair crops Having Teeswater in the centre, with C P R connections, and having Wingham and Mildmay with the G T R, within easy reach of southern and eastern borders, the people of Culross enjoy a choice of markets, an advantage no other municipality in the county has got The north-west part of the township has been considerably improved since the last valuation, in clearing and draining low lands Some large drains were being constructed when your valuators were there last fall The rate per acre for this township is $32.90, of which the village property amounts to 79 cents per acre."

THE township of Culross, like its neighbors to the north, east and west, namely, the townships of Greenock, Carrick and Kinloss, was classed among those known as Crown lands. The survey of this township took place in 1852, and was made by G. McPhilips. Of all the townships comprised in the original county of Bruce, Culross was the latest in being settled This may be accounted for by the fact that no leading road entered it The lands in Culross were opened for sale at the time of the "big land sale,"[2] September, 1854. Settlers entered the township in this its first year of settlement, and were fairly numerous, considering they were only squatters. At this time it was part of the united townships of Greenock and Culross, and the amount of assessment for the year 1854 was £2,923. Among the early settlers were the following. Andrew Zettle, Alexander and Archibald McIntyre, Matthew Hadwin, Thomas Maloney, Charles Irwin, P. B. Brown, James Reid, Charles and James Turner, Michael Brennan,

---

[1] "Culross" is the name of a royal burgh and district in Perthshire, Scotland, and also is said to be the name of an estate of the Earl of Elgin, the Governor-General at the time the survey of this township was made

[2] See Appendix K.

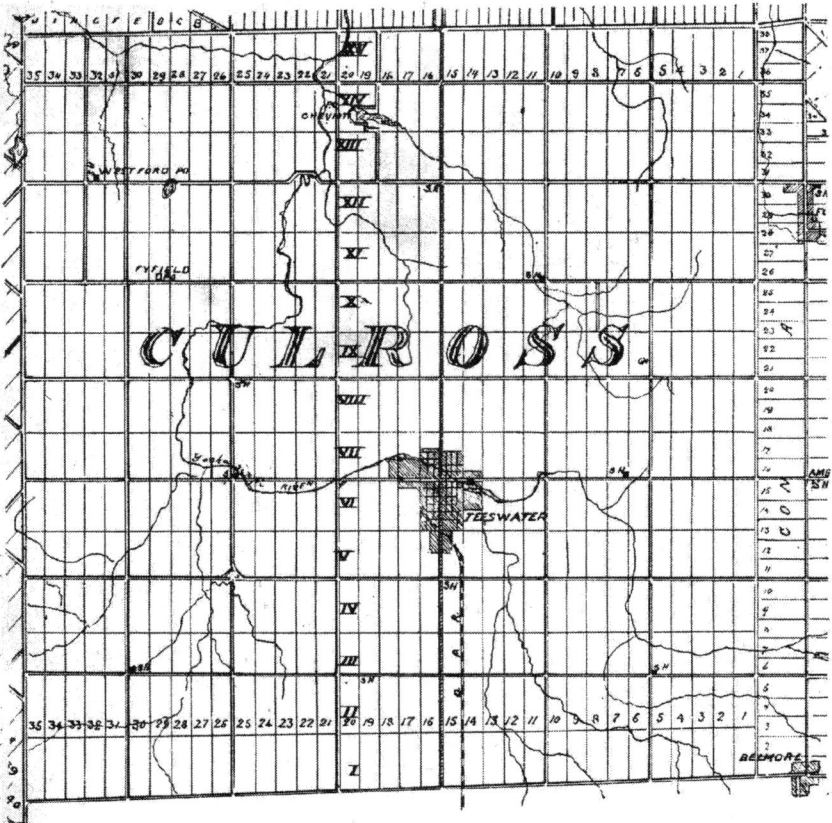

Dougal Campbell, H. Davis, Henry Haldenby, Anthony Shoemaker,
Wm. Roame, Alexander Forsyth, Ira Fulford, John McKague and
others whose names the author has not been able to obtain. As an
illustration of what the early settlers in Culross passed through, the
experience of James Reid is here given. Mr. Reid, being stirred up
by a request of the author for an account of his entrance and residence
in Culross, wrote a letter in March, 1902, which was published in the
Teeswater *News* Somewhat abridged, it is here given:

" I landed in Culross about the 13th of September, 1854. There
were very few shanties in the township, then an unbroken forest, and
I was guided by the surveyor's blaze The lots were all numbered
with a sharp iron on a short post put in the ground. I took up the
two lots that I am now on, on the 7th concession. Culross was mostly
settled with Scotch, Irish and English, the north-east corner with
Germans The " Big Land Sale " was held on the 27th Sept., 1854.
A lot of us left here' on Monday morning, the 25th, and got to
Southampton on Tuesday afternoon We found it a little place
with about two or three hundred of a population, three hotels, and
not much accommodation for such a mass of people; but the weather
was all that could be desired. A McNabb was the Crown Lands
Agent The office was a log building about 16 x 18 feet, with a
small window in the back, which was open to permit the buyers to
hand in their letters, with £7 10s. enclosed, along with the number
of their lots, concession and township £7 10s. was the first instalment. Owing to the crowd it was almost impossible to get to the
office window, so Mr McNabb got two men to carry in these letters
from the people The two men were John Shennan, from Balaclava,
Carrick, and Mr. M. McLean, the postmaster at Walkerton. The
crowding still continued so great that Mr McNabb saw a better
plan might be adopted, which was as follows: Two constables, whom
he had to keep order, told the people to all move back from the
office, then two hours would be given to each township at a time,
until all the county was attended to The work went on well and
was finished on Saturday afternoon. It took all the week for the
sale of the lots, except some inferior lands in the townships which
were sold in after years When the sale was over the people went to
their several townships to put up shanties to prepare for the winter, many of these being put up in October following The next
thing was to get something to live on all winter, and to get roads
opened through the forest. In those days flour and pork were very
high in price, owing to the Russian War. Flour was $10 per barrel
and pork $10 and $11 per hundred lbs Many of us in Culross

carried the first flour we used on our backs 16 or 17 miles, but when the snow came we got a man and oxen to bring what we needed. Then, for work through the winter, you would hear axes going and trees falling, everyone anxious to get the forest cut down and to hew out a home. The timber in those days was of no value. In the fall of 1855 we in Culross had no mail service nearer than Mr. Ritchie's, who kept the post office on the Durham line near Enniskillen, so a few of us met where Teeswater village is now and forwarded an application to the Postmaster-General for mail service, which we soon got, the post-office being named Teeswater after the river. Matthew Hadwin was the first postmaster. In the summer of '55 and '56 some of the settlers had a little crop and a few cattle. Lumber was much needed to put up buildings for what little crop there was and for the cattle The need was supplied by the late Peter B Brown, who had taken up lots 14 and 15 on the 6th concession, which forms a part of Teeswater village now. P. B. Brown was an enterprising man. The river crossed the front of h.s two lots, which gave him a fall of about 8 feet of water, so in the summer of 1855 he built a dam and in the fall he put up a sawmill. In the fall of 1856 he put up a grist mill, which was running in the winter of '56 and '57 The settlers were busy with chopping and logging bees, clearing up their farms and putting up log houses, log barns and also some frame buildings. We were a happy people in those days, and all went on well for years. Culross was, and is, famed as a grain-producing township. I have known a yield of fifty bushels of fall wheat per acre and weighing sixty-four lbs per bushel, and of thirty bushels of spring wheat per acre of sixty-two lbs. per bushel Being far from market it became quite a task in a stormy winter to get the grain marketed. Clinton, thirty-four miles distant, was the nearest railway station, and it took two days for one trip. Clinton was our market for years. The farmers became very anxious for a nearer market as the quantity of produce increased, so we were well pleased when in the winter of 1869 and '70 Messrs. Laidlaw, Baxter and Dickey came up from Toronto to Teeswater to agitate in a movement for the construction of a narrow gauge railway. Among other things these men made us farmers believe was that we would realize five or six dollars a cord for two foot wood in Toronto The Company got a bonus of $43,000 from Culross, although only three miles and three-quarters of the road lies within the township, and I think the road was in operation in the year '74, and it ran four or five years. The narrow gauge was not bad in summer, but in a stormy winter it was no good. The little horse was as nothing in a snow drift One winter it was put in the engine house about the end of January and stayed there until spring. As the narrow gauge could not do the work required, the Company tried to get another bonus to make the road one of standard broad gauge, but failed, and the road passed into the hands of the Canada Pacific Railway Company Culross and Teeswater have had very good railway accommodation ever since "

As complemental to the foregoing, another interesting narrative of one of the pioneers of Culross, relating his experiences on entering the bush, is here inserted It has been furnished by Archibald McIntyre, of that township:

" We, the McIntyre family, consisting of mother, we three brothers and three sisters, left Hinchinbrook, Lower Canada, in the spring of 1854, when the last of the Government Lands in the County of Bruce were to be opened up for sale We took our teams and waggon and some luggage with us, came up the St Lawrence, and landing in Hamilton off the steamer *Arabian,* thankful for having passed in safety through a severe storm on the way up. An older sister and her husband, who had come to Upper Canada some years previously, were settled in Oneida Township, twenty-five miles out of Hamilton. My oldest brother and myself left the family and stuff with them and started for the bush We tramped all the way, *via* Goderich, Kincardine, Greenock, and into Culross until we struck the Teeswater River As we liked the timber and soil there we went no further. From an uncle in Greenock we obtained axes, flour and tea, and set about underbrushing on the lots on either side of the 15 side-line, in order to establish a claim to those lots. We did not see the face of a soul after crossing the stream, to us then nameless, but afterwards called Teeswater We worked a week and underbrushed quite a piece of land We baked our scones on coals spread over with ashes I was cook, Alec was fisherman and fared weh, but as I never liked fish I had naught but tea with my scones. We slept peacefully on brush, disturbed by neither man nor beast, until the bright June mornings summoned our armed, winged enemies to begin their stinging attacks. It was beautiful weather, no rain all the time we were at work on our supposed claim. Sufficient underbrushing done, we trudged back to Oneida and worked among the farmers until near the end of September; then we made a final start with our team and folk for a home in Culross We came by way of the Garafraxa road to Durham and thence to my uncle's on the Durham line. From Durham to Walkerton we were in constant fear that our horses' limbs would be broken, the crossway road was so bad However, we got to Greenock in safety, and there we left our belongings until we should prepare a habitation on our lots for their occupancy. We were amazed at the rush of people looking for land at this time Every lot appeared to be taken When we got to what we thought were our lots, we found P B. Brown and a Mr. Ford had shanties put up on them We could have held on to the lots, having done the first work on them, but gave way in favor of Mr. Brown as he purposed putting up a grist mill, this being such a necessity in the settlement. We took up our stakes and went south to the second and third concessions and there took up the lots 21 and 22 on each concession. We built a good big shanty, and thither we brought our folks. As the horses would be of no use in the bush we sold them in Greenock and bought oxen Coming in we had to make our own road, cutting underbrush and small trees, and winding around large ones, avoiding marshes and getting around about hills Our ox team with waggon was the first that forded the Teeswater River at that point, and the only team in the neighborhood until springtime. Provisions were hard to get the first winter. Many a back load was carried miles through the wilderness of woods in those days. To buy boots for myself and Alec I walked to Goderich, a distance of 30 miles, as we could get them no nearer. There were wolves, but we did not see them Only once did we hear a howling pack of wolves in the settlement. That was one night the second winter we were in. Their yells were hideous, and many a shanty door was barricaded until their sound died away in the distance The Highlanders were prominent in the first settlement of Culross McKinnon, McKay, McKenzie, McDonald and many other representatives of the different clans were strongly in evidence; but many of them not being so famous with the axe in the forest as their ancestors were with the broadsword on the battlefield, they gave up and sold their claims to newcomers from the older counties. P B Brown's mill was erected as promised, grinding slowly, to be sure, but sufficient to supply local need Mr. Hadwin began in a small way to bring some commodities to the village for sale, making it our trade centre Among those who came to our neighborhood and purchased from the first settlers their claims were the Ballaghs, Colvins, McAllisters, McGregors, Caslick, Straths, Marshalls and Allisons, mostly all these bought small farms. It was thus that settlers came in throughout the township, making an excellent community, who observed the Sabbath and also held meetings for worship in private houses until churches and schools were built, the history of which institutions I must leave to an abler pen than mine. Notwithstanding the dangers of the felling of trees, great and small, there were not many accidents and very few fatalities in the township Marriages were numerous and every household seemed happy, thus laying a good foundation for the advancement and prosperity which Culross now enjoys "

When the union of the townships comprising the county of Bruce[1] was passed the townships of Greenock and Culross were united, for municipal purposes, to form one municipality. This union lasted for two years, George Cromar being reeve during both years. On January 1st, 1856, the union was dissolved, and the township of Culross from that date onward has existed as a separate municipality. The first Council of the township consisted of Peter B Brown as reeve, Wm McKenzie, Thomas Maloney, John Gilroy and Alexander Ross as councillors In a footnote[2] are given the names of those who have filled the office of reeve from 1856 to 1906. Robert Watson was elected clerk and treasurer. In a footnote[3] is a list of the names of his successors in these offices down to the present time The Township Council of Culross has always contained men of ability, and has ever been economical in the trend of its legislation. A marked exception to this characteristic was the submitting, in 1871, to the ratepayers for their vote a by-law granting a bonus of $43,000[4] to the Toronto, Grey and Bruce (narrow gauge) Railway This action was taken from a recognition of the great need of a local market for farm produce, and which could only be secured by the entrance of a railway into the township. This by-law carried. An effort was made on several occasions to have this large indebtedness assumed, in whole or in part, by the county, but on every occasion the County Council voted the proposition down. The township was relieved of part of this liability by the village of Teeswater when it was separated from the township on January 1st, 1875

[1] See Appendix F

[2] Names of the reeves of Culross Peter B Brown, 1856, '57, part of '58, '59; Wm. McKague, part 1858, Thomas Maloney, 1860, Alex McIntyre, 1861, '62, '63, '64, '66, '67, F. H Schoals, 1865, '68, '69, part of '70; A Gibson, part 1870; George McKibbon, 1871, '72, '73. '74; William Scott, 1875 to 1889; Jos Moir, 1890, '91, '92; Joseph Welwood, 1893, '94, '95, '96; Henry McKay, 1897, '98, '99, 1900, '01, '02; E C. Kuntz, 1903, '04; Jas. Donaldson, 1905, '06

[3] Robert Watson was elected clerk and treasurer, which offices he filled for three years, when John Logan received the appointment to both offices. In 1862 Thomas Fairbairn was made clerk, which office he filled until 1873, when it passed into the hands of John Marshall, who held it for the next thirteen years Since then the position has been held by R E Little, A. Gibson, George Wilson, and the present township clerk, Charles Button, who has held the office since 1891. The township treasurership was held by John Logan till 1872, then by Wm. Colvin till 1886, then by Samuel Kirkland until his death, in 1893 He was succeeded by Peter Clark, who also held the office until his death, in 1905. John Clark, his son, is now the holder of the office.

[4] $5,000 of this amount was a sectional bonus raised by that part of the township afterwards incorporated as the village of Teeswater

The only attempt made to develop a village within the township of Culross that succeeded was in the case of Teeswater. Other villages, such as Belmore and Formosa, are on the boundary of the township, and are not wholly in Culross Moscow (or Cheviot P.O) is different, being nearer the heart of the township. Here Paul Ross[1] tried to lay the foundations of a village, having a survey made in the same year, 1856, as Teeswater was surveyed. He early had a sawmill in operation, and in 1868 he had also a grist mill. A tannery, established by Wm. Clark, was one of the industries of the little burg. Mr. Ross made some money on gravel road contracts, and, wishing to live nearer the county town, he in 1869 disposed of his Moscow property to Andrew McLean, who succeeded to the title, " Emperor of Moscow," one that had been humorously bestowed on Mr. Ross. A farewell supper to Mr. Ross, on his leaving Moscow, was given on January 7th, 1870 The Moscow mills were destroyed by fire January 12th, 1880, and with that catastrophe the prospects of a town developing there faded away. The water power at this point is still available, and may some day be utilized to generate electric power.

The large area of lands in the township of Greenock, and to a less extent in Culross, that approach more or less the conditions of swamp lands, which condition would be changed if the Teeswater River were only deepened for a part of its course, has attracted attention for many years The first survey made to determine the best course to pursue was made in 1868, and is referred to in Chapter XXX. Nothing, however, seems to have been done until about 1902, when the matter again came up. Andrew McLean addressed the County Council, and tried, unsuccessfully, to get that body to take action. The member for South Bruce, R. E. Truax, Esq., about the same time obtained the promise of a grant towards the work from the Provincial Government. The municipal councils of the two townships interested decided to take action in so far as to find out the probable cost, and also benefit of deepening the river, so in the winter of 1902-03, when the river was frozen over, James Warren, C E , under the direction of the township councils, made the necessary surveys, and drew a profile of the bed of the river from Chepstowe to the eighth concession of Culross. That part of his report referring to the township of Culross is as follows:

" I have made an examination of the Teeswater River from the boundary of Greenock to the 8th concession of Culross, with the view

[1]Afterwards a mayor of Walkerton.

of having the river deepened, and beg to report as follows, viz.:—

"I find that the river runs very dead in a good part of the way, but from the 8th to the 10th concession the fall is enough to give a good current, there are no very great obstacles in the way of deepening the channel, as most of the bottom is mud, or muck, that can be easily removed.

"I would recommend that the channel be deepened 30 inches at the 8th concession bridge, and continued on as shewn on the profile, as prepared. I would have the channel 20 feet wide so as to include the river in low water, and that would also help to keep the channel clear better than if it was wider. The distance from the south boundary of Greenock to the 8th concession of Culross is 9 1-4 miles

"I would estimate the probable cost of the work at $4,390. The total acreage of the lots affected in whole or in part is 6,714 acres, of which I would place the value at $101,650, and the total benefit of the lands affected at $5,455, and the average cost of the work, counting the whole acreage of the lots affected in whole or in part, would be 65 1-2 cents per acre nearly.

"Taking the scheme as a whole in both the township of Greenock and Culross the work is quite feasible, and would be of great value to the township, as it would thus enable lands to be cultivated that cannot now be cleared up, owing to the river not giving sufficient drainage for surface water. When these lands are once cleared up, they will make excellent grass lands, and would also be good for roots When the land would become somewhat consolidated the land would yield good crops of grain."

The above report, although it showed that a most desirable improvement that would add wealth to the municipality was perfectly feasible, was not acted upon, and the Teeswater River flows on now as sluggishly as of yore.

Excepting in the rougher lands towards its westerly boundary, there is no township in the county that exhibits greater evidences of the prosperity of its farmers than does Culross. Some of its farmers have obtained a provincial reputation in their several specialties, such as Henry and Peter Arkell for their breed of sheep.

The author would have made this chapter on Culross longer if he could, but after many futile efforts to obtain further facts and data about the settlement and history of the township from those in the township who could supply the local coloring so necessary, he gave it up, and closes the chapter.

13

CHAPTER XXVI.

VILLAGE OF TEESWATER.[1]

THE present flourishing village of Teeswater commenced to take form in 1856, when the owners of farm lots Nos. 15 and 16, on each of the concessions 6 and 7, in the township of Culross, had a survey made of portions of their farm lots dividing them into village lots. The names of the owners of these farm lots so subdivided were Messrs. P. B. Brown, Alex. Gibson, Ira Fulford and Matthew Hadwin. In the preceding chapter it will be noted that two of these lots were first taken up in 1854 by Alexander and Archibald McIntyre, but who surrendered their squatter's claim, owing to the promise Mr. Brown gave of erecting a grist mill at that point. The first mill dam was erected by Mr. Brown in the summer of 1855, and in the fall of that year he had a sawmill started. In the course of a couple of years a grist mill also was built and running. The presence of these mills at this early date, with ample water-power, together with the establishing of a post-office,[2] give assurance that a village would develop at this point. In addition to the advantages just mentioned, the site of the village being almost in the centre of the township, made it the "hub" of the municipality, as well as an excellent distributing point. Like other villages in the backwoods with only a local trade, its growth for years was very slow. In 1861 all it contained, besides private dwellings, were two stores, two taverns and a grist and sawmill, with a weekly mail service. By 1866 the following industries had been added to the village: A foundry, founded by David Fairbairn, Jr., a tannery and a pearl ash factory.

The prospect of a railway coming to Teeswater gave an impetus to the growth of the village. In the strenuous contest throughout the county, in 1869, as to which railway was to receive the promised county bonus, Teeswater and the township of Culross at large fought

---

[1]The name of the village is derived from the name given to the river flowing through it But who named the stream, or when named, or why so called, the author has not been able authentically to find out, but it is said to have been given by one of the surveyors of the township who was born near the river Tees, in England

[2]The post-office was established September 1st, 1856, Mathew Hadwin being the first postmaster

hard for the Toronto, Grey and Bruce Railway, and, as may be imagined, the inhabitants were by no means satisfied when the Wellington, Grey and Bruce Railway Company obtained the majority of the votes cast throughout the county. Determined to have a railway, the question of granting the bonus to the Toronto, Grey and Bruce Company from the township and village was suggested and carried. The township as a whole, including at that time the village of Teeswater, gave a bonus of $38,000. In addition to this, that part of the township which afterwards became incorporated into the village of Teeswater gave a sectional bonus of $5,000, making a total of $43,000 received by the railway company.

There is no doubt that the railway has proved the making of the village of Teeswater, a fact which has justified the granting of such a large bonus. The initial step in the construction of the railway, which has had Teeswater as its western terminus for so many years, was the turning of the first sod at Weston, in October, 1869, by H.R.H. Prince Arthur. The payment of the bonus to this railway promised by the Government seemed to have been delayed somewhat, which prolonged the time of construction, so that it was November 16th, 1874, before the first passenger train reached Teeswater. This train brought up a large number of those who were interested in the road, who were warmly greeted on their arrival, and to whom a banquet was given that evening. The number of arrivals was so much in excess of the accommodation which could be furnished by the hotels in the village of Teeswater at that date, that although many of the citizens hospitably threw open their homes to the visitors, yet many of them slept that night on benches in the town hall.

Teeswater as a separate municipal corporation commenced its existence on the 1st January, 1875, the by-law authorizing this having been passed by the County Council on June 5th, 1874. The first Council consisted of the following members: Alexander Gibson, reeve; J. Fraser, T. Stephens, J. Ballagh and M. Hadwin, councillors. Wellington McVety was appointed village clerk, and Thomas McKague, village treasurer. In a footnote[1] are to be found the names of those who have filled the office of reeve from 1875 to 1906. The basis

[1]The names of the reeves of the village of Teeswater: A. Gibson, 1875, '76; Jas. Fraser, 1877, '79; T. Shannon, 1878; T. Stephens, 1880, '81, '83, '90, '91; T. Fairbairn, 1882, '86, '87, '88; W. R. Thompson, 1884, '85, '94, '95, '96; L. A. Brink, 1889, 1900, '01; John Campbell, 1892, '93; Dugald Stewart, 1897; W. G. Orr, 1898; D. Donaldson, 1899; S. R. Brill, 1902; Peter Purves, 1903; D. Ferguson, 1904, '05; W. J. Hardy, 1906.

of settlement between the township of Culross and the newly incorporated village of Teeswater, arrived at at the time of the separation, regarding the apportionment of assets and liabilities, was based upon the assessment roll of 1874 in the proportion of 31/34s. for the township, and 3/34s for the village. This resulted in the village receiving at that time from the township $120 of funds for the current year in the hands of the township treasurer, and $281 of sinking funds raised on account of the sectional bonus to the railway. On the other hand, the village undertook to pay, by way of sinking fund and interest on its share of the $38,000 railway bonus debentures annually, the sum of $103 for sinking fund, and $135 for interest, until the maturity of the debentures. The village also gave a debenture to the township for $1,300 for the township's share in the real estate known as Edmunds Square. Since the time of separation the village has undertaken extensive local improvements, which called for issues of debentures as follows: For water works, $9,000; for public park, $1,500; for granolithic sidewalks, $7,847; for additions and repairs to water works, $1,550, and Arscott loan, $2,000.

The town hall dates back to the days when it was the township hall of Culross, it having been erected before the village and township separated. The present fine school building is the third the village has possessed. The first was erected about 1858, and was also the first building of its kind in the township of Culross; its site was on lot 34, north of Elora Street, but the building has long ceased to be. It has been described as a square log building with a cottage roof. A description of the interior said: The teacher's desk occupied the north end of the school-room. Facing this were two rows of long desks with an aisle between; there were also aisles between the desks and the east and west walls. In these aisles were low benches, on which the smaller scholars sat. Peter Clark was the first teacher, a position he held for two and a half years. He was succeeded by a Mr. Gordon, who came from Whitby. The second school building was a fine stone structure that afforded accommodation for three departments. The cost of this building was about $2,000. The present school building was erected in 1878 at a cost of about $6,000. It is built of white brick and is of two stories in height, with a mansard roof, and has provision for four departments.

Another municipal asset, and one that shows wise prudence and forethought, is the system of water works installed for fire protection. It was in 1889 that this public utility was constructed, costing the town about $9,000. After being in use for sixteen years it was necessary (in 1905) to spend some $1,550 for repairs and improvements. The cost to the town has been more than made up indirectly by the reduced rates of fire insurance premiums, as well as in prevention of fire loss.

The public park, purchased by the town in 1896 at a cost of $1,500 is another possession that the village may contemplate with satisfaction. More and more the necessity of public grounds of this description is being felt, and future generations will be pleased to have this space for purposes of relaxation and amusement.

The first minister that is said to have held a public religious service at Teeswater was the Rev. A. Bradshaw, of the Episcopal Methodist Church, who was stationed, in 1855, at Kincardine. In 1856 the Rev. William Maidens was settled at Teeswater. He was the first minister of that denomination in the village. His early successors were the following, in the order named: Rev. J. Davey, Rev. J. M. Collins, and in 1860 Rev. J. H. Hilts, a man whom the author remembers with respect and appreciation. Mr. Hilts was a good example of a type of backwoods preacher of half a century ago. His Christian zeal, sound grasp of evangelical truth and forceful expression of the same, excused all defects arising from the lack of a college training.

The Wesleyan Methodists also entered this field at an early date. Their first settled minister was the Rev. Thomas Hadwin. He was stationed at Teeswater in 1856-1857, and was succeeded by the Rev. Ed. Sallows, and he by the Rev. William Sutton. The present Methodist Church at Teeswater was erected in 1879 at a cost of about $5,500.

As early as 1856 the Free Church Presbytery of London sent the Rev. John Scott to minister to the spiritual needs of the Presbyterians in the vicinity of Teeswater, following this up by sending other ministers. As a result a congregation was organized, which proceeded to erect a place of worship. All this was before the end of the "fifties." The Rev. Adam McKay was the first minister. His pastorate lasted from 1862 to 1870. In the last-mentioned year the congregation divided, part continued to worship in the old church, which then became known as Zion Church, with the Rev. Peter Currie as its minister. The seceding part of the original congregation worshipped for about a year and a half in the town hall, and then erected a church building that bore the name of Westminster Church.

The Rev. D. Wardrope was the pastor of this congregation from 1871 to 1886, and the Rev. James Malcolm from 1888 to 1905. During the ministry of the last-mentioned clergyman the two congregations became united. They now worship in the old church building, which at present bears the name of Knox Church. The Rev. D. Tait is at present the minister over the united congregation. The author is pleased to be able to insert here an account, which appeared in the Teeswater *News*, written by James Reid, that vividly tells of the early life of the Presbyterian congregation, and of other incidents of pioneer days, as follows· "Your correspondent came to Culross in September, 1854. In the summer of 1855 some twelve of us met at the corners of Samuel Wood's lots on the 8th concession, now owned by Mr. David McDonald, to consider about purchasing a plot of ground in which to bury our dead, and on which to erect a church in which to worship God. Those south of the river overruled those north of the river, and it was agreed to purchase two acres on the 4th concession from Mr Thomas Nicholson, for the sum of $40. This is the site of the present Teeswater cemetery. At the same meeting some one inquired if there was no one present who knew of any minister whom they knew who could be written to and asked to give us a sermon or two, as we were getting hungry, not having heard a sermon for nine or ten months. Alex. Graham, who lived on the 10th concession, where the Henderson family now lives, said he would write to Rev. John B. Mowat, of Niagara, who came in September of the same year, 1855, and preached in Mr. Gibson's shanty, that being the only place at the time where a meeting could be held. This was the first sermon preached in Teeswater by a Presbyterian minister After this Rev. John Ross, of Brucefield, preached a few times. These two men advised us not to put up the church on the 4th concession, but to put it where the village was likely to be In the spring of 1856 James Reid put up his first house, expecting his mother and brother from the province of Quebec, but as they did not come he lived on in his old shanty, and his house was used as a church during the summers of 1856 and 1857. The Presbytery of London, of which Rev. John Scott was moderator, sent up a preacher now and then during these years to keep us alive until better times came. Among those who visited us then were William Clark, who was an elder and catechist; Rev. Donald McLean, who was for a time stationed at Mount Forest, and Rev. John McMillan, of Fingal, who was afterwards also many years in Mount Forest. In October, 1857, the Pres-

bytery sent up Rev. Alex. Young and Mr. Sutherland, two powerful
preachers of the Gospel, and these two dispensed the sacrament of the
Lord's Supper for the first time in Culross. Mr. Young preached in
English in the house, and Mr. Sutherland in Gaelic in the barn.
This solemn feast was observed in the good old way—four days
preaching—on Thursday, Saturday, Sunday and Monday, the last
being a day for the giving of thanks. On Thursday it was found
necessary to have elders appointed for the Sabbath services, so the
ministers asked Mr. Gibson whom he would recommend. After some
consideration he named John McDonald and Hugh McDonald, both
from the 8th concession, and Hector McKay, the catechist, who lived
on the 4th concession, where Thomas Ross now lives. The last-named
preached in Gaelic to the people living in the region known as the
Alps. In those days there was a much clearer line between the church
and the world than there is at present. Many of us now ask, Where
is the church for which our forefathers died. The Sabbath at
present has become a day of business, pleasure and toil rather than a
day of worship. During the times of these communion services in the
early days James Reid, then a bachelor living in his shanty, made
the minister's dinner for them. Mrs. Gibson's shanty was the manse,
and she hung up a carpet across the room to make a bedroom for the
ministers. The shanty was covered with elm bark. One night a
severe rainstorm came up and Mr. Gibson had to put an umbrella
over the ministers to keep them dry. Compare that manse with the
present one. Little do the ministers of the present day know about
the difficulties of the pioneer church. Mr. and Mrs. Gibson were very
kind to all the ministers in those early days, and their house was
made the preacher's home. They probably did more for the church
in those early days than any other persons in Culross. The ground
on which Knox Church stands was a gift from him, and yet his name
appears in no place in the church records. In the winter of 1857-
1858 the Presbytery sent up Rev. John McKay to us. An uncle of
his, the Rev. A. McKay, of Lucknow, was also with us for three
months, and boarded with Mr. Reid. Before he left in the following
spring the contract of the first Presbyterian Church in Teeswater was
let to a man named Westover, who lived on the 12th concession of
Culross. The church was not completed until 1862. In that same
summer the congregation extended a call to Rev. Adam McKay, and
he was ordained and inducted into the charge. He was the first
regularly settled Presbyterian minister in Teeswater or Culross. Pre-

vious to this time, in the fall of 1856, Rev. John Scott, of London, preached in Mr. P. B. Brown's grist-mill, before the machinery was put in, and on the following Monday he baptized sixteen children."

The Church of England congregation worship in a brick edifice erected in 1875, the cost of which was about $2,300. The Baptists had their church built in 1876. The Roman Catholic Church was dedicated by the Bishop of Hamilton, September 15th, 1878. In the following July a bell, which had been imported from Baltimore, was hung in the steeple, and has rung out its calls to worship since. Rev. Father Corcoran has been in charge of this congregation for over a quarter of a century.

For many years one of the leading, if not the leading industry, of the village was the foundry and agricultural implement works of Messrs. Gillies & Martin. The business was established in 1869 by James Fraser. Shortly after commencing business Archibald Gillies was admitted into partnership. In April, 1878, Mr. Fraser retired, and his place in the firm was taken by James Martin The original firm had met a serious loss by fire, which occurred November 4th, 1877. The loss was estimated at the time to be about $20,000, but the buildings destroyed were soon rebuilt and in an enlarged form. In May, 1892, the firm extended its capacity by opening up a branch at Listowel, where they erected some fine buildings. The agricultural implements manufactured by this firm have a wide market throughout the Dominion.

The first medical men to settle at Teeswater are said to have been Dr. John F. Halstead and Dr. James Murphy. The stay of neither was of any length Dr John Gillies, one of the leading men of the village for over a third of a century, came to Teeswater in August, 1867. Having acquired a large practice he accumulated money and established a private bank, which was for years the sole financial institution of the village This business he disposed of to the Sovereign Bank not long before his death Dr Gillies was the village treasurer for many years His death occurred August 15th, 1905.

Another honorable citizen of Teeswater now passed away was W. R. Thomson. He commenced business there about the end of the seventies as a cooper. Possessing a keen business instinct and abundance of energy, he developed a large lumber manufacturing business, exporting largely to England of his products.

The name of S. R. Brill is one largely known in the dairy world, the creamery he established at Teeswater being one of the first, if not the first, in the county.

L. A. Brink, the present postmaster, has been prominently connected with Teeswater for the last thirty years, filling the office of reeve and county commissioner, and has been called upon to fill other responsible positions by his fellow-citizens. As a produce merchant he has done much to make Teeswater a good grain market.

The Teeswater *News*, the local paper of the village and township, was first issued in 1874, G. T. Hagyard being the publisher and editor. Since that date it has passed through the hands of Thomas Fairbairn, A. G. Stewart, A. Colwell, Alex. Butchart, and at present is under the editorship of A. D. McKenzie.

In the fall of 1901 an effort was made by those owning lands within the village, used solely for farming purposes (which amounted to 187 acres), to have the same detached from the village and attached to the township. R. E. Little and Charles Thomson supported the petition brought before the County Council. This body passed the required by-law, which, however, the arbitrators pointed out, was void, as the lands to be detached reduced the area of the village below that specified by statute.

Like many villages in this section of the province, Teeswater has felt the repressive effect of a railway monopoly, and hopes for a future when it may enjoy the privilege of competitive railways, and thereby bring an era of prosperity and progress to the village.

CHAPTER XXVII.

TOWNSHIP OF ELDERSLIE.[1]

EXTRACT FROM THE REPORT OF COUNTY VALUATORS, 1879.

" This township has a large amount of heavy clay land, with portions low and wet, also a considerable amount of swamp. A portion of the township is broken up by the Saugeen River. The largest amount of good land commences at the south-east corner and runs north-west until it strikes the township of Saugeen It is very well watered and has a large amount of mill property. Its average price is $28 33 ''

EXTRACT FROM THE REPORT OF COUNTY VALUATORS, 1901

" Elderslie is a fair average township, with very little, if any, waste land It is well watered; good buildings and orchards are the rule. There are three railway stations in the township, namely, Paisley, Chesley and Dobbinton. The large swamp in the centre of the township is being cleared up and it will not be long until it all becomes good grazing land There are a few stiff clay sections that take down the average somewhat, and we might say is the only serious drawback to the township. The Saugeen River breaks a portion of the township towards the south-west, as also does the Teeswater River The rate per acre for this township is $32.70; of this amount the village property is equal to 54 cents per acre.''

Elderslie received its first settlers on April 18th, 1851, when Simon Orchard and his family, after floating down the Saugeen River on a raft from Walkerton, landed where the village of Paisley now stands Three weeks later Samuel T Rowe, with his family, followed his old friend in the venturesome voyage down the Saugeen and settled alongside of him As the circumstances connected with the settlement of these two pioneers of the township are given pretty freely in Chapters V. and XXIX , the fact of their settlement at this early date is here only mentioned. The lands in the south-western part of the township were the first to receive their quota of settlers. This was owing to the facility of access afforded by the Saugeen River, which permitted them to float down its waters on rafts, thereby conveying them, their families and effects from the vicinity of either Hanover or Walkerton.

[1]Named after Scotland's patriot, Sir William Wallace, Knight of Elderslie.

362

ELDERSLIE,

The survey of this township was performed by G. McPhilips during the summer of 1851. Elderslie was classed among the school lands of the province, and was opened for sale on July 30th, 1852.[1] The first person who is entered in the books of the Crown Land Office as a purchaser of lands in Elderslie was John Fraser, for lot 34, concession A, the date being December 6th, 1852.

The first to follow Messrs. Orchard and Rowe in taking up lands in the township were David Lyons and Thomas Hembroff, who settled on the north branch of the Saugeen River at that point afterwards to be known as Lockerby. In a footnote[2] is given an account of their settlement, condensed from a narrative published in the **Paisley** *Advocate* in 1896. The house which Thomas Hembroff put up on lot 2, concession 7, is said to be still standing and to be in good condition, being the oldest house extant in the township of Elderslie. By the end of 1851 four log shanties had been built in Elderslie, but only the families of Orchard and Rowe spent the winter there. The next addition to the group of pioneer families settled in Elderslie was possibly made by the arrival of Henry Brown. The story of his settlement and also of the early days of Elderslie, appeared in the " Souvenir Number of the Chesley *Enterprise*," published at Christ-

[1]See Appendix J.

[2]David Lyons and Thomas Hembroff learned of the excellent prospects for settlers in Elderslie through a brother of the last named, who had been engaged with the survey party under Mr McPhilips. These two men lost no time after the survey was completed in selecting a point at which to settle. They were at that time residing at Chatsworth, in the neighboring county. One morning in October, 1851, saw them leaving home loaded with necessaries for a stay in the bush Travelling south they at length reached the north branch of the Saugeen River ; following it, partly on foot and partly by canoe, they arrived at the county line. Owing to the amount of driftwood met with in the river there they had to pursue the rest·of their journey altogether on foot, following the course of the river. Being satisfied with the location where the sixth concession crosses the north branch of the Saugeen River, they, after doing enough work to secure for themselves a squatter's claim, returned home, to return in the following month with necessary supplies. The families and effects of these men were brought into the bush in May of the following year. The first stage was by team from Chatsworth to Hanover. There a raft, 12 x 30 feet, was constructed, and on it the families and their belongings were placed. It took two days to complete the voyage. A shanty, about sixteen feet square, was put up that summer, in which both families lived About a year and a half later Mr. Lyons again placed his family on a raft and floated down to Southampton, where he engaged in saw-milling Unfortunately he was burned out, when he then returned to Elderslie The first shanty these men erected was utilized as a schoolhouse, the first in the township, the teacher being Mrs. Thomas Pearce, a sister of the present township clerk, J. C McIntyre

mas, 1902. By permission of the editor, an extract from **Henry Brown's** narrative is here given:

"In the early fall of 1852 the writer (Henry Brown) and a young man named Robert Cochrane walked from Durham to visit their old neighbors, Rowe and Orchard, and see the much praised new country. With Simon Orchard as pioneer guide we located lots 1, 2 and 3 on the 2nd and 3rd concessions, went home and returned in November to take possession. Having got our outfit to Walkerton (at that time containing two stores and a post-office), we made the usual raft and started down stream. That was 50 years ago, but the memory of that voyage still lives fresh in my mind. The river was very low; neither of us had ever been on a raft in our lives before or knew how to handle one. We got stuck on bars and fast on stones, and there was nothing for it but to jump into the water and pry the raft clear. Night found us about the 4th concession of Brant, soaked in ice cold water to the armpits. Our matches had got wet in our pockets, but luckily our powder was dry, so with the gun and some batting from a corner of a quilt we soon started a fire and dried ourselves, made a bed of brush and each of us rolled in a blanket We went to sleep and awakened in the morning with six inches of snow on top of us. Next day we had better luck, and struck Deer Rapids (so called by the surveyors from the number of deer seen standing in the water to protect themselves from the flies). By good chance we found the blaze and got to Rowe's at dark, two tired and hungry men. Next day, with the help of Rowe and Orchard, we raised our shanty, 12 by 14, floored it with split basswood, and roofed it with scoops. This, to the best of my knowledge, was the fifth shanty in Elderslie. Shortly after Cochrane went home and I stayed till midwinter and did my first chopping. Wolves were plentiful One night when getting in my wood a pack came hunting up the river. They killed a deer a few yards from the shanty and kept howling around all night. In the morning I went and looked at the place. Some bloody snow, a few tufts of hair, and scraps of bone was all that was left of the deer. On the whole it was a pleasant two months; with a few good books the solitude had no terrors for me

"In 1853 the Clements and others from Holland came and settled on the 10th and 11th concessions, and Mr. Green, Wm. McBride and the McCartneys from Esquesing settled on concessions 'A' and 'B,' south of Paisley The same year the Gillies family had located a large block on the 6th and 7th concessions, soon followed by the Taylors, Blues and other old neighbors from Argyleshire. On the 8th and 9th concessions the McDougalds, McNeils, Galbraiths, Munns,

Curries and a whole colony of natives of the island of Colousay settled clear down to the Elora road. Thus we see that the Scottish element figured largely in the early settlement of Elderslie. I have before me the collector's roll for the year 1854 (issued from Arran, to which we were attached), which unfortunately is the only one of the early records to be found. On it are 65 names and of these 26 have the prefix "Mac," 11 being McNeils, and many others spoke the Gaelic. The collector was an Arran man. There was no assessment, the names evidently being copied from the agent's book. No assessor could have found his way through Elderslie in the spring of that year. There was nothing but the surveyor's blaze to guide you, and if you lost that you were, too, as many a one found to his sorrow. The roll was made out in Halifax currency and the tax was 10 shillings and 6 pence (equal to $2.10) for every 200 acres, and $1.05 for every one hundred acres, every lot being the same value. This roll was returned to the treasurer of Arran on 23rd of June, 1856, with "not paid" marked against one-half of the names.

"In 1853 Mr. Rowe built a commodious tavern of hewed logs on the site where the Central Hotel now stands, which gave ample accommodation to the rapidly increasing travel, and Mr. Valentine had got his sawmill running, which enabled the settlers to erect better buildings In 1854 the great rush began. Early in the season the McBeaths arrived and located the lands on the east side of the river, which they still occupy. At the same time Mr. D. Porter arrived from Peterboro'. He took up eight lots, and on his return home started the great rush of Peterboro' men, the McDonalds, McGregors, Balfours, McLaggans, Lillicos, Fortunes and others, who settled on the 1st, 2d and 3rd concessions Mr. Porter's old friend, Andrew Dobbin, followed and took up 1,000 acres around where Dobbinton now stands The same year Thomas Orchard built the first store (now occupied by R. Scott, seedsman) and opened out a general stock of hardware, dry goods, groceries, etc That fall the great land sale at Southampton took place, and in the rush every lot was taken up. So great was the number of those who passed through Paisley to attend the land sale that in two days Mrs. Rowe cooked and served the carcass of an ox, while Mr Rowe attended to the liquid portion of the business. Two large sugar kettles, one with beef and the other with potatoes, were kept boiling all the time It was a great strain on the resources of the Paisley of that day, but as Rowe had a good stock of cattle and a field of potatoes it was simply a question of killing and digging By what device the liquid stock held out has always been a mooted question."

Prominent among those who settled in Elderslie in 1853, but

omitted in the list given by Henry Brown in the foregoing extract,
were Donald McIntyre, for four years reeve of the township, and
Alexander Elves, a member at one time of the Township Council, now
a resident of Paisley, and Hugh McDougald (lately removed to Owen
Sound), who took up land in Elderslie in 1853. At that time he
was but eighteen years of age. Sufficient work to establish his claim
to the lot was all he did at first His actual settlement dates from
1856 At the age of sixteen he worked for his uncle, Donald Currie,
in Saugeen. He relates that while there he on one occasion went to
Southampton for a supply of flour, which he purchased of James
Calder Shouldering his load, he followed the blazed path through
what is now the village of Port Elgin. Halting at "Lochboie"
McLean's tavern to rest he met Peter Smith, who noticed that the
load was too much for the lad, so good-heartedly he shouldered it
himself, in addition to his own similar load. Of the crop of wheat
Mr. McDougald grew in 1858 he sold enough at 50 cents a bushel to
pay that year's taxes, holding the rest until 1859 ("starvation year"),
when he obtained $2 a bushel for it. Mr. McDougald for seven years
held the position of deputy reeve of Elderslie. Another prominent
man was John McDonald, who, as councillor and reeve, sat in the
Township Council for nineteen years. It was in April, 1855 that he
took up his lot, No. 34, concession 7. His son William, publisher of
the Chesley *Enterprise,* has followed his father in obtaining municipal
honors, and was warden of the county in 1905. This list of early
settlers we close with an example of fortitude in enduring the hardships of clearing a farm in the backwoods. Neil Munn, in 1855,
moved with his wife and family from Esquesing to Elderslie. Upon
arriving at Paisley their trials began. There was no bridge over the
Saugeen, and they had to cross the river at Rae's, to take the round-
about way to their land on the 6th concession. One of the horses of
the team they had engaged to bring them and their effects up from
Erin village broke its leg at the "Hog's Back," while near the end of
their journey, yet their progress was very much delayed by the accident, and the final stage rendered very laborious. Mrs. Munn was
obliged to carry her young son all the way in her arms. From the
time of reaching their new home until 1860 Mr. and Mrs. Munn
steadily and patiently applied themselves to the duties of clearing
their farm and rearing the little family growing up around them,
but in that year a heavy stroke of affliction fell upon the household
when Mr. Munn was paralyzed by a tree falling upon his back while

working in the bush. He survived the accident for fourteen years, but was a bedfast cripple until he died in 1874. Mrs. Munn bravely and successfully shouldered the responsibility of carrying on the farm and supporting the family after the accident, battling with Christian fortitude against great odds until relieved by the assistance of her growing sons.

At the time the pioneer settlers of Elderslie entered that township there was no road nearer it than the Durham road, running east and west through the southerly part of Brant. In the summer of 1851 (as noted in Chapter V.) the Crown Lands officers asked for tenders to cut a road, which they called the Durham and Southampton Road, through to the boundary of Elderslie Very little more work to improve the roads was done until 1854, when the Bureau of Agriculture, which had assumed the duty of seeing after the construction of colonization roads, proposed a scheme, alluded to in Chapter V., which would give Elderslie the Elora Road and one along its southerly boundary. The Elora Road, as originally planned, entered the county at its south-east corner, and passed diagonally through Carrick to the corner where the four townships of Carrick, Culross, Brant and Greenock join, thence northerly along the boundary between the townships of Brant and Greenock, Elderslie and Saugeen. The surveyors who laid out Brant and Elderslie must have reported to the department the difficulties of constructing a road on the boundary of the townships near the point where the Teeswater and the Saugeen unite. These views being accepted by the department, J. H. Price, Commissioner of Crown Lands, wrote to George McPhilips while he was engaged in making the survey of Elderslie, under date of July 14th, 1851, as follows: " Previous to surveying the river, mark out a line for a road from the rear of Brant to the Saugeen River in Elderslie, in the general direction marked in red on the accompanying sketch, selecting the best site for bridges over the Mud River and River Saugeen, and making the necessary sinuosities to avoid hills and swamps. The line is not to be the boundary of the lots, but you will deduct the area of a road, one chain in width, from the contents of the lots it passes over." Almost simultaneously with this letter George Jackson, Crown Land Agent at Durham, advertised for tenders to cut a road through Brant a mile and a quarter east of the intended Elora Road, but in line with the road laid out by Mr. McPhilips as above. When the Bureau of Agriculture took up the construction of colonization roads, and possibly unaware of the surveyor's report, it announced the Elora Road as per original plan. It is but a fair inference to suppose that when David Gibson surveyed it he saw the reasonableness of accepting the road already cut out, which has since been known as the Elora Road.

The early municipal life of Elderslie is a blank until the year 1854 Prior to that year it was nominally a part of the municipality of the united townships in the county of Bruce, as referred to at length in Chapter IV. In 1854 Elderslie was united to Arran for municipal purposes.[1] It was in this year the first assessment of the township was made, which, as equalized by the County Council, amounted to £7,037 On September 20th, 1855, the United Counties Council passed a by-law dissolving the union of Elderslie to Arran, to come into effect on January 1st, 1856 Thomas Orchard was the returning officer at the first municipal election. The polling booth was at Rowe's tavern, Paisley. The names of those elected as councillors were: George Williscroft, Charles Ginty, John Gillies, Robert Falconer and S T. Rowe. These at their first meeting, as the law was then, elected S. T. Rowe as reeve. George C. Urquhart was appointed township clerk; Thomas Orchard, township treasurer; Donald McIntyre and John Henderson, auditors, and Hugh McDougald, and Samuel Scott, assessors. The total financial expenditure made by this Council for the year 1856 was only £107 14s 1 1-2d In a footnote[2] are to be found the names of the various reeves of Elderslie. An examination of Appendix M will enable the reader to see the relative standing and development of Elderslie with neighboring townships in their early days.

The Municipal Council of Elderslie has during half a century guided the affairs of the township with a wise hand. Among other matters, the drainage of the swamp in the centre of the township was recognized to be a necessity, so as early as 1877 debentures were issued for about $2,000 to prosecute this work. This was supplemented in 1883-84 by two other issues of debentures, one for $4,474 and the other for $2,100. When the Stratford and Lake Huron Railway asked.for a bonus, the Council submitted to the ratepayers a by-law authorizing the issue of debentures for $45,000 to aid the pro-

[1] See Appendix F

[2] Names of the various reeves of Elderslie: S T. Rowe, 1856; John Gillies, 1857 to 1873; Archibald Ewart, 1874, '75, '76; Henry Brown, 1877, '78, '85, '86, '87; George Thompson, 1879, '80, '81, '82, '83, '84; Donald McIntyre, 1888, '89, '90, '91; James Shouldice, 1892, '93, '94, '95, '96; John McDonald, 1897, '98; D N McIntyre, 1899, 1900; James Clements, 1901, '02; David McBeath, 1903, '04; George McKay, 1905, '06.

ject,[1] which was carried by a majority of 77. In 1875 the township gave a municipal centre to the township by the erection of a township hall on lot 15, concession 6, at a cost of nearly $2,000 The Township Council has been aided in its efficiency by its officials, who deserve to have their names remembered, for they have done their part faithfully in attending to the business of the township. Their names are given in a footnote.[2] Elderslie plumes itself on having paid off all debenture indebtedness, and also in that no licenses for the sale of liquor are issued within the township.

The first school in the township was opened in 1855 at Lockerby, and was taught by Miss McIntyre (afterwards Mrs. Thomas Pearce).[3] In 1856 Miss Falconer (afterwards Mrs. Thomas Fleming) taught a small school on lot 11, concession 5 The following year the Township Council took action in regard to schools that can best be described by an extract from the report of Local Superintendent McNaughton, for the year 1857, as follows: " The township of Elderslie has done admirably in the way of school buildings during the past year. Although the newest of three townships under my charge, it is now the first with regard to school-houses. This may be attributed in a great measure to the wisdom of the Township Council offering certain sums of money to each section, on condition that a schoolhouse be erected within the year. The result is there is not a single section without a schoolhouse." The staff of teachers in the different school sections in 1858 consisted of Miss Eliza Stewart, Paisley; Mr. Murray, Chesley; Archibald Ewart, S. S No. 6; Donald Gillies, S. S. No. 5; J. C. McIntyre, S. S No 4; Miss Jane Porter, S. S No. 2; Malcolm Munn, S. S. No. 10; James Saunders, S. S. No. 7.

Although to-day there is not within the township of Elderslie an unincorporated village of any pretensions, it has nourished and witnessed the swarming off of two of the busiest villages of the county,

---

[1] $10,000 of this was a sectional grant, levied on that part of the township afterwards incorporated as the village of Chesley.

[2] List of township treasurers and clerks from 1856· Township treasurers —Thos Orchard, 1856-'59; Dr. S. D Crawford, 1860, '61; M. McMillan, 1862-'65; Geo. C. Urquhart, 1866-'72; Wm. W. Hogg, 1873-1901; S. M. Ewart, 1902-1906. Township clerks—George C. Urquhart, 1856-'61, F. Featherstonhaugh, 1867; P. H Sinclair, 1868; Daniel Sinclair, 1869-'71; Ed. Saunders, 1872; S. Shannon, 1873-'76, D McKechnie, 1877-'92; J. C. McIntyre, 1893-1906

[3] Thomas Pearce was one of Mr. McPhilips' chainmen in the survey of the township. When married, in 1856, to Miss McIntyre, the young couple walked all the way to Southampton so that the ceremony might be performed by a Presbyterian clergyman

Chesley and Paisley. The development of these two villages sealed
the hopes and fate of two other places that were sanguine of becoming
in time the trade centres of their respective localities, namely, Lockerby and Scone. The settlement at Lockerby by Thomas Hembroff is
mentioned in the first part of the chapter. The water-power at this
point was early made use of, and a grist mill was in operation there
about 1856, within a short time of that at Paisley. A little earlier
than this a rumor spread that the Elora Road, about to be opened up,
was to be brought up the side line at lot 5 as far as the 6th concession, then to turn west to the township boundary,[1] passing through
Lockerby   At the time the grist mill was built George Jardine had
portions of adjoining farm lots surveyed into village lots. Plans of
this survey were scattered far and wide, and every effort made to
boom this town on paper into tangible being, even going as far as the
holding of a sale of lots at Hamilton. All Mr. Jardine's efforts were
fruitless, the Elora Road was cut so as to pass through Paisley,
and Lockerby never developed. In 1866 Jardine and Hembroff were
engaged in a lawsuit as to the ownership of the mill and adjacent
property. Jardine, thinking that if he were in possession of the mill
his claim would be more firmly established, one day in the fall of 1866
went to it when no one was about, pried open one end of a board and
sought to enter through the opening. In some way he failed to keep
the boards apart, and they coming together, he was caught like a
mouse in a trap, and, unable either to extricate himself or to make
himself heard, was held until death relieved him from his sufferings.
The water-power at Lockerby is now made use of by Donald McIntyre
to supply electric current for lighting purposes to Paisley.

Scone began to take form and put on the appearance of a village
before Chesley—ultimately its successful rival—was thought of. The
founder of the village, Thomas Bearman, came to Elderslie in 1854.
Being possessed of means, he purchased about seventeen hundred
acres of land in Elderslie and Sullivan, started a sawmill about 1856,
a grist mill some years later, and also a potash factory, and opened a
store   In 1858 a post-office, bearing the name of Scone, was opened.
Thomas Adair (who owned the most north-easterly lot in Brant), was
the first postmaster, but he soon left the locality, and the post-office
was moved to the house of Thomas Bearman, his successor. The little

[1]There may have been something in the rumor, as the engineer in
charge of opening the Elora Road purchased lots 16 and 17, concession
B, and lot 16, concession "A" (where the road would make the turn).
Presumably he bought on speculation

village flourished until, overtopped by the growth of Chesley, all hopes for its development vanished

One of the most noted men Elderslie has had was John Gillies, who for seventeen years was reeve of the township. His portrait, with a biographical sketch, are to be found in Chapter VI.

Owing to the large emigration to the North-West provinces, Elderslie has suffered marked loss in population. In 1881 the census returns showed Elderslie to have 3,273 inhabitants. The assessor's return for 1906 gives a population of 2,018, less than 62 per cent. of what it was a quarter of a century previous. This but illustrates what has been going on all through the county. The youth of its population is moving to the West to establish homes for themselves there.

CHAPTER XXVIII.

TOWN OF CHESLEY.[1]

THE greater part of the lands situated in the vicinity of what is now Chesley were taken up in 1854, but not settled upon until the following year. In the early spring of 1855 the brothers, John, Alexander and Peter McLaggan settled on lots 30 and 31 in the third concession, and the same summer John and Archibald McDonald on lots 29, 30 and 31 on the second concession of Elderslie. On these farm lots the major part of the town of Chesley now stands.

Very little progress had been made in the way of clearing the land when, in 1858, A. S Elliot[2] purchased lots 30 and 31 on the second concession from Archibald McDonald, and he with his sons began to make preparation to develop the water power of the river flowing by and to erect mills   In 1859 they had a sawmill started, and in 1860 a small grist mill was in operation.   In 1865 a few building lots of a quarter acre each, situated on each side of the side road, were sold on the easy terms of twenty dollars apiece, conditional upon immediate occupation, which condition secured the commencement of the village.   In 1866 the population of Chesley consisted of the following named and their families: A. S. Elliot, miller, J H. Elliot, storekeeper; John Cameron and William Ross,

[1] The name Chesley was given to the post-office without any regard to the wishes of the people of the locality being shown by the Post Office authorities. Solomon Chesley an erstwhile official in the Indian Office, is he whose name is preserved in the name of the village

[2] Adam Scott Elliot, the founder of Chesley, was a native of Howick, Scotland He was but nine years of age when his parents emigrated to Canada in 1816, along with their family, and settled in the county of Lanark In early manhood he engaged in farming and milling As early as 1843 he visited the county of Grey with the thought of settling there, but did not carry out the idea until 1856, when he purchased property in Sullivan township and built there a saw and grist mill.   In 1858 he purchased the land which forms part of the present site of the village of Chesley.   In 1868 he sold out his Chesley business to his son, John H., and moved to Williamsford, in the county of Grey.   In later years he returned to Chesley, where he passed away, July 3rd, 1899, in his ninety-second year.   He was married to Janet Halliday, and had a family of ten children Active and enterprising, he was a successful business man. In religion a staunch Presbyterian of the old school; kindly of heart, he did much good Chesley has every reason to be proud of the man who was its founder

storekeepers; John Dobbie, blacksmith; John Shea, shoemaker, and Martin Schruder. A census taken the following year gives the population as but sixty persons. The little village made but slow growth at first. A plan of the survey of village lots made in the summer of 1868 shows only ten houses on the west side of Main Street, three on the east side, and seven other houses scattered about, making twenty in all, besides the saw and grist mill. Such was the extent of development attained by Chesley ten years after its beginning. It was in 1868 that John H. Elliot[1] purchased his father's property at Chesley

[1] J. H. Elliot was born at Smith's Falls, Lanark County, in 1836. He moved, with his parents, to near Chatsworth, where they established what was known as Sullivan Mills, and in 1858 came with his father to Elderslie and laid the foundation of Chesley. They started a sawmill and gristmill, and Mr. J. H. Elliot soon became famed far and near as a first-class miller. He also started the first store in Chesley. When Mr. Elliot surveyed his lands into village lots he did not reserve every other one for himself, as a selfishly-inclined man would have done, but sold them at $20 each, and gave buyers as long as they chose to pay for them. The 30th side-road was at that time in an almost impassable condition, and to the improvement of this road Mr. Elliot devoted his attention, and to him more than to any other man is due the credit of transforming the forest road, through frog pond and boggy ground, into a highway which to-day is one of the leading roads of the county. At this time all goods had to be teamed from Paisley to Chesley, and as this gave the business men of the former town a decided advantage over Chesley merchants, the commercial life of this place was threatened. Mr. Elliot saw the crisis, and when the opportunity arose he threw his whole energy into the railway project and was a leader in the struggle to have the Lake Erie and Georgian Bay division of the G. T. R. constructed from Stratford to Wiarton. J. H. Elliot assisted a great many men in their business ventures, and there was scarcely a business man in the village, especially in the early days, who was not indebted to him for assistance rendered. Mr. Elliot not only encouraged others to erect buildings, but he built many himself. Two grist-mills, one of which is the present large mill, two sawmills, and scores of houses were built at his expense and under his personal supervision. He was one of the company that built the town hall, took shares in and strongly advocated the erection of the chair factory, and was a leading spirit among those who encouraged the locating of the furniture factory there. It would be impossible to give in detail the industries that he assisted in Chesley, suffice it to say that whatever was for the advancement of Chesley Mr. J. H. Elliot could always be counted on to give it his active support. His private interests were a secondary consideration where the welfare of the village was concerned. It is not surprising that one who had been such a public benefactor should hold a warm place in the hearts of the people. Before this village was incorporated he had been elected deputy reeve of Elderslie, and when Chesley was incorporated as a village, in 1879, he was elected by acclamation as the first reeve, at the elections in January of the following year. He occupied this position for eleven years, and before retiring was honored by his fellow county councillors by being chosen warden of Bruce County. Mr. Elliot carried on for eighteen years a private bank here, known as J. H. Elliot & Co. Nor was it only in material prosperity J. H. Elliot was anxious to see this village progress; everything that tended to the moral and religious life of the community had his active sympathy and support. Mr. Elliot's end came May 11th, 1901. He was

and proceeded to have a survey made of village lots. It was in the same year that a post-office was opened in the village with Mark McManus as postmaster. Up to this time all mail matter was obtained at Scone, and Sconeville was the name Chesley was known by.

A resident of Chesley writing about the village in the winter of 1870-1, said: " We have got one of the best oatmeal and flour mills in the county, owned by Mr. Elliot, a cabinet factory, a shingle factory, three first-class general stores, two blacksmith shops, two waggon shops, two first-class hotels, kept by Messrs. McGaw and Adams, two cooper shops, one shoe shop, a tannery, a limekiln, and last but not least a skilful and obliging physician in the person of Dr. George Cooke.[1] Nor are the intellectual wants of the people neglected, not by way of preaching, however, for sermons in Chesley are like angel's visits, few and far between, but by way of lectures under the auspices of the Chesley Literary Association." In October, 1875, another resident, in describing the village, after reporting the above-mentioned industries, increased somewhat in number, adds to the list a pottery, a brickyard, a sash and door factory, and a woollen mill operated by T. M. Chase. He mentions two churches—the Canada Presbyterian, with the Rev. John Bethune as pastor; the other a Baptist church, then without a pastor. " We have about five hundred inhabitants, but have no school-house," he adds, in closing.

survived by his widow and five daughters The funeral was large and representative, both town and country people being anxious to show the last mark of respect to one broad in sympathy and strong in faith, whose aim was to promote the glory of God and the good of man. The village council, on the occasion of Mr Elliot's decease, passed the following resolution · " Resolved, that this council feels impelled to express its profound regret at the death of Mr. John Halliday Elliot, who, in company with his father, laid down the foundation of this village, and to whose fostering care, perhaps more than to any other man, is due the credit of its present prosperity. We know that in its early struggle for existence he was the principal, if not the only, promoter of its business enterprises, and at every stage of its growth he was its most constant friend. He was at all times most anxious to render assistance to all proper schemes for promoting its welfare, and he has left us a noble example in the many sacrifices he made to improve the material condition as well as the mental and moral welfare of the residents of this village In him the business men have lost a wise and prudent adviser and the poor a generous friend." —*Chesley Enterprise.*

[1]Dr. Geo Cooke, a native of Cookstown, Simcoe County, settled in Chesley in 1866, and was for many years one of its prominent citizens. During the years 1887 and 1888 he was reeve of the village. Dr. Cooke continued the practice of medicine at Chesley for a third of a century, when, owing to failing health, he removed to Toronto. His end came in December, 1903

The village from the time mentioned in the last paragraph made rapid progress. The prospect of a railway being run through to the Georgian Bay gave a feeling of security to all efforts made to develop the place. It was on September 3rd, 1881, that the first locomotive reached Chesley. In a week from that date the first shipment of freight by rail was made. For some months after this Chesley was the most northerly station on the line, making it indeed a busy little place.

The prosperity and development mentioned in the previous paragraph led to the taking of steps necessary for the incorporation of the village. On a census being taken the population of the village was found to be nine hundred and five. On this being represented, along with a petition, to the County Council, it passed, December 12th, 1879, the necessary by-law of incorporation, and appointed D. M. Halliday as the returning officer for the election of a reeve and councillors, which was to be held at Kilbourn Hall. Just here a hitch occurred which had not been foreseen. The Municipal Act required that such election should take place on the first Monday in January occurring after the by-law had been three months in existence. This would throw the first municipal election over until 1881. To avoid this the aid of the Legislature was sought, which passed an Act[1] validating an election made on the last Monday of December, 1879. The following were the councillors then elected: J. H. Elliot, reeve; Jas Halliday, George Stanley, Dr. N B. Gillies and Alex. Ramage, councillors. In a footnote[2] are given the names of those who have filled the reeveship from 1880 to 1906. The first village clerk was John McBain. D. M. Halliday was appointed treasurer of the village,[3] an office he held until his death in 1904. His successor, William McDonald, still holds office. The first assessor was Geo. Husband, who was expected to perform the duties of that office for a yearly salary of ten dollars.

Chesley has been broad-minded and liberal in its willingness to assume financial obligations when the interests of the village at large were concerned. The first public indebtedness was assumed

[1] 43 Vic. Chap. 39.

[2] Names of the reeves of Chesley· J. H Elliot, 1880, '81, '82, '89 to 1896; H. A Bonnar, M.D, 1883; George Stanley, 1884, '85, '86; George Cooke, M.D., 1887, '88; J. M. Stewart, M.D, 1897, '98, '99, 1900, '01; W. A. Crow, D.D S, 1902, '03, '04; Conrad Krug, 1905, '06

[3] The salary fixed for both the clerk and treasurer was but $25 per annum.

in 1876, when the first school-house was built. To accomplish this
$1,650 was raised by the sale of debentures In 1878, when the first
bonus was asked for by the Stratford and Georgian Bay Railway,
Chesley, as part of the township of Elderslie, voted that $35,000 be
given as a bonus.[1] In 1879, when the railway came begging for a
second grant, Chesley in response assumed a sectional indebtedness
of $10,000. The next debt contracted was in 1888; this was for the
purchase of a steam fire-engine at a cost of $5,200. The decision to
erect the present school-house in 1897-8 called for the issue of
$15,000 worth of debentures.   In 1900, and in each year since,
debentures have been issued to pay for local improvements, such as
granolithic sidewalks and sewers The aggregate of debentures so
issued up to time of writing, six years in all, form a total of $31,441.
Large as is the debenture indebtedness of the municipality, the
villagers would not recall this expenditure, as it has been wisely and
prudently invested for the good of the public.

As mentioned in a previous paragraph, up to 1875 (and for a year
later, in fact) Chesley was without a school within its own limits.
The following facts regarding the cause of education in Chesley are,
by permission of the editor, extracted from *The Chesley Enterprise,*
souvenir number:

"The children of the earlier settlers studied and recited their
lessons in an old log school-house[2] situated on Donald McGregor's
farm on the second concession of Elderslie, and at least two Chesley
matrons have personal recollections of the early school life. When
the school became too small the classes were held in the old Presbyterian church on the second concession, the frame of which was
afterwards moved to Chesley, and formed the skeleton of the old
Methodist church.

"But Chesley's first, really, truly own school was built in 1876.
This is the old school-house[3] across the river, which still remains
although now used for other than educational purposes. The original
building consisted of but two rooms, and it was much later, when
these quarters became too small, that the addition on the north side
was built. This was until 1897 the hall of learning, and around it

[1] The total of the annual levies Chesley raised to pay its share of this
bonus aggregated nearly $6,000.
[2] A Mr. Murray, in 1858, seems to have been the first teacher of this
school
[3] This old building cost $1,650.   At least, that was the amount of the
debenture issued to pay for it.

HIGH SCHOOL
CHESLEY ONT.

(Courtesy of Chesley *Enterprise*)   p. 379

cluster the school-day associations of most of the present generation. Walter Bell, who taught in the pioneer school on " the Second," labored here also and ruled, not by the rod, but by moral suasion. W. M. Atton forced ideas into the young minds by the frequent application of the tawse. A. W. Robb, of the *Walkerton Telescope*, urged the children gently but surely along the thorny path of learning. Mr. Cullen succeeded him, but proved inefficient. D. F. Ritchie built up a reputation for the school that caused it to figure frequently at the top of the list in Bruce County. It was Mr. Ritchie who was principal when the school removed to its present commodious quarters, where there are nine class rooms, a teachers' room, a trustees' room and a large assembly hall. After teaching for two years in the new building Mr. Ritchie resigned his position to remove to Owen Sound, and R. D. McMurchy, who had been for four months teacher of the private high school, was appointed principal in his place, and the high school was merged in the continuation classes, which became a noted feature in the work of the school.[1] At first only two high school teachers were employed, but a third was subsequently added."

In 1903 an effort was made to have Chesley made a high school district, which was acceded to by the County Council, and the required by-law was passed in January, 1904. The Chesley school building[2] ranks as the most complete and up-to-date of any in the county. Within its walls are accommodated both the public and high schools. The present principal is James T. Luton, M.A., who is doing excellent work. Chesley of to-day has indeed right to be proud of its school.

The church life now centred in Chesley commenced to take form in the locality of which it is now the centre in the summer of 1859, when the Rev. Alex. Stewart, a Baptist minister stationed at Durham, preached in the house of Archibald McGregor. In September of that year a congregation was organized which formed part of a charge that comprised Durham and Hanover as well. Over this widely extended charge the Rev. Mr. Stewart ministered. Lacking a church building the congregation at Chesley held services in the school-

[1] R. C. Halliday, of the Chesley Public School, had the honor of being the first public school student to ever gain a scholarship in the Departmental Examinations, which he did in July, 1903 He stood fourth in the province.

[2] Erected in 1897, at a cost of about $15,000

house and in public halls until 1875, when a modest church edifice was erected, which is still in use.

Following close in point of time to the Baptists, the Presbyterians commenced to form the nucleus of a congregation afterwards to bear the name of the Geneva Presbyterian Church. The little body of worshippers met for worship in the log school-house which stood on lot 26, concession 3, of Elderslie. Every other Sunday from 1860 for a number of years the Rev. Geo. Bremner, the then lately ordained minister at Paisley, conducted the services. At times the village part of the congregation held services in Elliot's Hall. In 1872 a church was built in Chesley, and on October 20th, 1874, the Rev. John Bethune was inducted as minister of the congregation. He was succeeded in 1879 by the Rev. John Ferguson, who after a most successful pastorate passed to his reward in 1890. It was while Rev. Mr. Ferguson was the minister of Geneva Church that the present commodious church building was erected,[1] the opening of which took place January 11th, 1885, the Rev. Dr. Grant, Principal of Queen's University, officiating. The Rev. David Perrie was the next minister of the congregation. He resigned in 1894, and was followed in the pastorate by the Rev. E. A. MacKenzie (now filling a professor's chair in the Presbyterian College, Montreal), and he in 1900 by the Rev. J. J. Paterson. In 1904 the Rev. R Atkinson, the present minister, was inducted.

The Associate Presbyterian congregation was organized in 1873. At first it existed in connection with the United Presbyterian Church of the United States. The congregation consisted of two charges, one at Chesley, the other at Williamsford in Grey County. The Rev. Thos. Hannay, D.D., who resided at Williamsford, attended, as far as his health permitted, to the spiritual needs of the flock. In 1876 the Rev. Wm. Findley was inducted to the pastorate, which lasted for three years, during which the church and manse were built. Then came a long vacancy. In 1889 the congregation was transferred to the Associate Presbyterian Church of North America. The present pastor, the Rev. S. H McNeel, was inducted to this charge in July, 1890

The Methodists were late in the day in organizing a congregation at Chesley, the date being about 1875. The Rev. W. B. Danard was the first minister Services were held at first in Halliday's Hall.

[1]The old church was sold for $1,000 to the Church of England congregation

In 1876 the old frame church built by the Presbyterians on the second concession of Elderslie was purchased, taken down and re-erected in the village with the addition of a veneer of brick. This building being too small to accommodate the growing congregation, the present large and handsome edifice was built, the corner-stone of which was laid August 29th, 1898. The cost of this building was about $8,000.

The Church of England has not a large congregation at Chesley. At first it held services in Kilbourn's Hall. Then in 1884 it purchased from the Presbyterians their original church edifice. After worshipping there for twelve years, in 1896 steps were taken to build, and on August 4th of that year the corner-stone of the new church was laid. This congregation for a long time formed a joint charge with that at Hanover.

The settling of a number of German families at Chesley necessitated the forming of a congregation in connection with the German Evangelical Church, which in 1887 built the neat looking edifice in which they worship.

The press, as represented by *The Chesley Enterprise*, made its bow to the public in the early part of 1877, R. H Spedding being the original publisher. Since he ceased to be the proprietor of the paper it has passed through the hands of the following: J. B. Stephens, Wm. Kay, A. W. Robb, Adolph & McDonald, and is now edited and published by Wm. McDonald. When Adolph & McDonald dissolved partnership (1893) the latter continued to publish *The Enterprise,* and the former, John Adolph, started *The Free Press,* which existed for about five years In 1902 *The Enterprise* did itself credit by publishing a souvenir number, in which the story of Chesley, past and present, were ably told and delineated The author was courteously permitted by Mr. McDonald to make use of anything therein which might add to the interest and value of this history, which offer has been gratefully accepted.

The growth of Chesley has arisen in a large measure from its manufacturing industries. The first of these were the mills built in the fifties by A. S. Elliot The grist mill as it now stands was built by J. H. Elliot and Alex. Ramage in 1875. At that date it was the most complete mill of its kind in this district. Even to-day there are only two or three in the whole county to be compared with it. The Krug Bros' furniture factory is a large industry that adds greatly to the output of Chesley's manufactures. Commencing in a modest way during the eighties, the business has now a market extending over the Dominion. In 1884 Stevens Bros. started a planing mill that has continued to increase year by year. D. Stevens is the present proprietor.

The first banking institution to open business in Chesley was a private bank known as that of Hay Bros., J. McBain, manager, After being in business for a few years they were bought out in 1879 by J. H. Elliot & Co., this latter firm being composed of J. H. Elliot, D. M. Halliday and J. McBain. Continuing to do a profitable business for twenty years, the firm sold out to the Merchants Bank of Canada in 1899. The first chartered bank to commence business in Chesley was the Bank of Hamilton, which opened a branch there in November, 1889.

June 9th, 1888, is a date that will be remembered in the history of Chesley as that of the great fire. At the time it certainly looked like a crushing blow, but it has proved rather of the nature of a blessing, in that the burned-over tract has been rebuilt with a handsomer class of buildings than were there before. The stranger entering Chesley from the south and looking down the main street from the top of the hill is struck by the handsome appearance of the business part of the town. It is unfortunate that the back and side streets do not convey as favorable an impression. Streets only forty and fifty feet in width are not in conformity with modern ideas. These narrow streets are the result of private surveys of village lots, which were not conceived on a broad and generous plan. The private residences of Chesley are a marked feature of the town, impressing the visitor with a sense of the number of well-to-do people in this community.

For many years the good people of Chesley were ambitious to have their municipality numbered among the towns of the province. A census taken in the summer of 1906 revealed the fact that the required number of inhabitants dwelt within the bounds of the corporation. The preliminary proceedings were then completed, and the Lieut.-Governor issued a proclamation erecting the village into a town and dividing it into three wards. The proclamation came into effect on October 1st, 1906.

CHAPTER XXIX.

VILLAGE OF PAISLEY.[1]

In taking up the chapter on the history of Paisley the author does so with the consciousness that the chronicles of the village have been ably and well written by Ainsley Megraw. His work appeared in a special edition of the *Paisley Advocate,* February 20th, 1890. The press has written up various places in the county at different times, but no village or town has been so fortunate as Paisley in having its history written so fully, systematically and accurately. The writing of Paisley's history was a labor of love to Mr. Megraw Paisley is his native town, and there he had resided up to the time he compiled his narrative. He had, as it were, breathed in the history of the village, and was enabled to impart to his narrative the local coloring which it is vain for a stranger to try to imitate. Mr. Megraw had also taken great pains to be accurate in his facts. Realizing all this fully, the author wrote to Mr. Megraw, and also to Mr. D. McKenzie, the present publisher of the *Advocate,* requesting permission to use the material published, as above mentioned. From both gentlemen a ready and courteous compliance was given. Where in this chapter portions are taken *en bloc* from Mr. Megraw's narrative, credit will be given to the *Advocate.* In other cases where his account is mixed in with facts the author has obtained this may not be possible.

In Chapter V. reference is made to the settlement made at Paisley by its pioneer settlers, Simon Orchard and Samuel T. Rowe. Although in a measure repeating what was there said, the author feels that the story of the settlement prepared by Mr. Rowe, and which was published in the *Port Elgin Times,* should here appear, at least in part. Messrs. Orchard and Rowe were among the pioneer settlers who took up land in 1842 on the Garafraxa Road, in the townships of Egremont and Normanby. After the opening up of the free grants along the Durham Road, they learned of the superior quality of the soil in Brant, and Rowe decided to settle there and start a tavern at

[1]The village bears the name of a town in Renfrewshire, Scotland But why the name came to be bestowed the author has not been able to ascertain

the locality afterwards known as Gaffaney's Corners, but before he
reached the place the land had been taken up by another. Orchard
sold his farm in Egremont, while Rowe rented his on a ten-year lease.
During the winter of 1850-51 they teamed their effects to Walkerton,
ready for the opening of spring. About the middle of April, 1851,
Mr. Orchard brought his family to Walkerton. Learning of desirable
lands located down the river, he decided to try his fortune in that
direction. With the help of a hired man, he made a raft of cedar
logs. On this he placed his family and household effects and started,
unappalled by the dangers and difficulties that lay before them, on a
voyage down the Saugeen. Mr Orchard had some information about
the land and the appearance of the locality at the mouth of Mud
River, as it was then called. He said he had had a dream about it,
and if it were like what he saw in the dream he would stay there, and
he wanted to be there first. It turned out, so he found when he
arrived, to be just like what he dreamed about. Mr. Rowe was
delayed owing to the sickness and death of his son, and was unable
to start with Mr. Orchard. He was also further detained for a few
days at Walkerton, to be "corner man" at the putting up of a two-
story log house, owned by his cousin, Wm. Jasper. While there, on
the first day of May, a foot of snow fell, but by night the logs were
swept and the building raised. Mr. Rowe engaged William Walker,
W. Jasper, George Neeley and Alex. McIntyre to build two large rafts
and take him down the river They started on the 9th day of May, and
landed safely at the site of what was afterwards to be known as the
village of Paisley early that afternoon. The two pioneers were well
pleased with the look of the land. Mr. Orchard was satisfied with his
choice on the north side of the river, and so was Mr. Rowe with his on
the south side. Mr Rowe's hired men returned next day, leaving the
two families with one hired man alone in the forest, miles from the
nearest settler. Mr Orchard had already erected a good shanty of
poles. In three days after the arrival of Mr. Rowe and family the three
men and two women, with the help of oxen, put up a large shanty for
the newly arrived family. Mr. Orchard then cut logs for a new house.
At this time the party of surveyors under Mr. (afterward Senator) A.
Vidal, engaged in the survey of the township of Saugeen, happened to
come along, and helped to raise it. This building will be remembered as the store that Mr. Samuel Steel occupied for some time. The
winter of 1851-52 was a notably severe one Mr. Orchard had four
cows and Mr. Rowe fourteen head of cattle to winter that season, with

SIMON ORCHARD

p. 383

SAMUEL T. ROWE

p. 383

JOHN S. McDONALD

p. 421

CAPT. DUNCAN ROWAN

p. 436

nothing to feed them on but tree tops. The two settlers each hired a man to chop all winter. Mr. Rowe hired his man on the 12th of October. The first snow fell that night. For months it had an average depth of five feet, and was to be seen in the swamps in the following June; but the cattle got through well. When the ice began to break up on the river Mr. Orchard's four cows came down to the river for a drink, as usual. Standing on the rotten ice, it broke beneath them, and the cows were never seen again In the summer of 1852 Mr. Rowe, with the assistance of hired help, cut the logs and built what was known for years as Rowe's tavern. Its site was opposite the present Town Hall, and it stood projecting on the street at an angle thereto. Its measurements were thirty by twenty-four, with a lean-to for a kitchen, and another lean-to for a dining-room. The families of the two settlers were separated by the Teeswater River. To overcome this inconvenience one of the first things they undertook was to erect a foot-bridge over the stream. Unfortunately, the next spring freshet washed it away, and for a while they depended upon a dog, which was trained to swim across and carry small things from one shanty to the other.

In August, 1851, John Valentine sent two men to take possession of the mill site which he had applied for at the Crown Lands Office. One of the men, David Ross[1] by name, took ill and died during the following month Owing to scarcity of lumber in the settlement, some of the boards that formed the floor in the house of Mr Rowe had to be used for the coffin, while a carpenter, James Benson, had to be brought down the river from Walkerton to make it Two brothers of the deceased, who resided at Fergus, were able to be present at the funeral, which was the first in the township of Elderslie.

In the chapter on Elderslie is to be found the names of those who early took up land at or in the vicinity of Paisley. One who early became identified with the settlement was John Megraw. In 1851 he took up a farm lot in the township of Saugeen, but had the misfortune in the following spring to have his shanty burned down John Valentine, who was passing down the river to Southampton, happened to meet Mr. Megraw, and persuaded him to leave the farm and work at the building of his dam and sawmill at Paisley. In the fall of that year Mr. Megraw took up the farm lot on which the railway station at

[1]David Ross was an uncle of the Rev. J S Ross, D D , of the Canadian Methodist Church, late of Walkerton, and a brother of Wm Ross, town clerk of Fergus.

14

Paisley now stands, and in the month of October, 1851, installed his family in a little shanty he had there constructed. The Valentine sawmill was running in 1852, supplying settlers near at hand, and also for some distance down the river with lumber required for building purposes. It was the practice of the last mentioned to raft and float down the river the lumber they purchased.

Messrs. Rowe and Orchard, realizing the possibilities for the development of a town on the lands they had squatted upon, were desirous to secure a patent therefor from the Crown, and early paid into the hands of the Crown Lands Agent[1] the required amount. But the Department also seemed to have realized it would be desirable to have a town plot surveyed at the junction of the Saugeen and Teeswater Rivers; or quite probably there were those who were pulling the wires of political influence to obtain the lands and hold the same for speculative purposes. Whatever was the reason, the Crown patent remained year after year unissued, notwithstanding repeated visits of Mr. Rowe to the Crown Land Department at Quebec and Toronto. At last the Department decided to have a town plot there laid out, and in 1856 Francis Kerr, P.L.S., made the necessary survey.[2] The rights of Messrs Rowe and Orchard were respected, and patent after patent in their names, issued on September 17th, 1856, for village and park lots are to be found entered in the books of the Registry Office. A plan of this survey was lithographed and published, a copy of this, in the hands of the author, portrays the extent of development attained by the village in 1856-57. The plan shows but thirty-six buildings in all, scattered along Queen Street, and thence down Alma Street to Valentine's mill. In the plan are shown three sawmills, one grist mill, the school-house and Rowe's tavern, besides unnamed buildings. There is no bridge over the Saugeen, or Willow Creek, while the bridge over the Teeswater seems as if it extended from the high bank on the south side, nearly to Church Street. After leaving the river bank it most probably was a sort of causeway till higher ground was reached.

The name of Paisley was given to the village when the post-office was opened, February 1st, 1856. The first postmaster was Thomas

[1]Lands in Elderslie were opened for sale, July 30th, 1852. See Appendix J.

[2]The survey was made at the time of the Crimean War. This explains why there is commemorated in the nomenclature of the streets the battles, and the names of English and French generals in command in the Crimea. The survey included lands in both the townships of Elderslie and Greenock, with an acreage of 1,500 acres, consisting of 318½ acres of streets, 137½ mill sites and rivers, and 1,044 acres in town and park lots When incorporated the area of the village was reduced about one half.

Orchard. He also was the first merchant. At the time he opened out his stock of goods it was in a room in Rowe's tavern, but in 1854 he built the first store erected in the village, occupied subsequently for years by Robert Scott as a flour and feed store. As time wore on, "Tradesmen and others began to make their appearance in Paisley, and bit by bit the cluster of little shanties in the small patch of clearing began to widen out, and the whole to take on the appearance of a town. Speaking of tradesmen, Mr. Thomas Irving was in those days an essential part of the community, and when difficulties of a mechanical nature arose, invariably his aid was sought. His little workhouse on the bank overlooking Stark's mill was a veritable curiosity shop. It was a foundry and a watchmaker's shop; everything from a broken-down printing press to an old gun or a sick watch, was benefited by his treatment. Long will the memory of his quaint sayings remain, with the younger people especially " (*Paisley Advocate*). The hum of industry early pervaded the village The grist mill built by John Valentine in 1855 was in operation in 1856 The mill privilege, now known as the Fisher Mill property, was purchased from S. T Rowe in 1859, and developed by Mr. David D. Hanna and milling actively carried on. Industries of various descriptions also commenced to develop, such as sash and door factories, owned by Joseph Christie and the Sinclair Brothers. A tannery was started by James Bone, a blacksmith shop by Joseph Donald, a foundry by James Bradley, who sold out in 1870 to Laidlaw & Robinson; a brickyard, by Wm. Anstead. Various other trades and professions also began to be represented, so that by the time ten years or so had passed Paisley presented all the appearance of a thriving little village. It was in 1859 that the author paid his first visit to Paisley, to be present at the opening of St. Andrew's Church. Willie Bain, a youth of his own age, showed him over the place. The impressions which he can now recall refer principally to the *soirée* at the church; the stores of Thomas Orchard and Richard Dick, which seemed small; Valentine's mill; the scattered appearance of the buildings, and Sergison's hotel, where he put up. The fire in the wide brick fireplace in the bar-room, piled high with four-foot logs, gave out a most welcome warmth after a long sleigh ride from Kincardine. One looks in vain for such a cheery wood fire in the now almost deforested county of Bruce.

The narrative of the schools must be given in Mr Megraw's own words: " At a public meeting held on the 5th of September, 1856, steps were taken for the organization of a school under the provisions of the Upper Canada Consolidated School Act. At this meeting Thomas Orchard, William McBride and John A. Murdoch were elected trustees, and after a little sparring as to the school site, they decided that the building which they purposed erecting should be built on the centre of lot 11, concession A, and that it be of flatted logs twenty by twenty-four feet inside. Tenders were called for the job, and it was let to John McDonald for $120. Miss Stewart was offered the position of teacher at £50 per annum, on condition that she provide herself with a legal certificate, which offer she accepted. The first levy made to cover school purposes was that of £84. Miss Stewart's teaching in the public school began in January, 1857, and she taught two years. She was succeeded by Duff McDonald, who only taught a week or so in the beginning of 1859, and then came Daniel Duff (afterwards the Rev. Mr. Duff, of Malcolm), who taught for one year and nine months, viz., 1859 and part of 1860. Fleming May put in the balance of that year and the next.

" With the beginning of 1862 came Mr. James Saunders, who was engaged to teach the school for that year for £87. In the beginning of 1863 part of School Section No 8, Greenock, was added to the Paisley section, and Mr. Saunders' salary was increased to $380, owing to the extra labor put upon him in teaching and keeping in order the big boys from the gore of Greenock. The interior of that old school is now quite distinct in our memory. It sat about twenty feet or so to the east of the " Old Brick," which is still standing near the station yard The door was in the east end, facing the road The teacher's desk was in the opposite end To the left of this desk three long pine desks with benches in rear, ran the full length of the school, with the exception of about two feet at each end to enable the boys to get behind. To the right, in the south-west corner, was a map case, with all the maps in creation attached to rollers encased in a handsome stained and varnished case, which was attached to the wall by large wooden pins fixed in auger holes in about the sixth or seventh log above the floor From this frame were a lot of strings with little wooden knots on the end, and by a skilful and mysterious manipulation of these Mr. Saunders could bring out any map he wanted—Ireland, Scotland or the Fiji Islands—and we little folks thought he was a regular wizard. About twelve or fourteen desks about eight or nine feet long, arranged one behind the other, filled up the balance of the space on the right. On the last of these all the big fellows with whiskers sat.

This left a space down the centre about eight feet wide from end to end, and in the centre of this the classes stood. Towards the end of its term the old school began to get demoralized. A big hole in the floor corresponded with another in the foundation, and by a subterranean passage the boys occasionally made surreptitious expeditions to the outer world. One time the boys took a craze for firing off gunpowder, and any little tube, whether wood, iron or brass, that could be got was used for shooting. One charge was fixed in a chink of the school, the muzzle pointing inward, when a boy was detailed off to ask out, and when outside fire off the shot The gunner on that occasion, if we remember right, is now Rev J Hay, pastor of the Presbyterian Church at Renfrew. This old log school is now (1890) a stable on Mr. Elijah Welsford's farm.

"In June, 1866, the contract was let for building a new brick school. In July, 1867, a very rainy Monday, it was opened. Soon an assistant teacher, Miss Lucy McLellan, was put in the school, and she was succeeded in 1868 by Miss McIntosh, who taught for five years. Mr. Saunders was principal until July, 1869, when he was succeeded by Mr. T. J. Bell. Mr. Saunders was kind-hearted and frank with his pupils, and the writer will never forget him. True, he had a little whip with a handle about eleven inches long, and a leather lace for a lash about eighteen inches long, with a knot on the end, but it was wielded with mercy, for

> " ' He was kind, and if severe in aught,
> The love he bore to learning was in fault '

"With Mr Bell's advent, we remember, began the work of logging and cleaning up the ground lying between the school and where the present railway station is, for a cricket field. Mr. Bell himself was a finished cricketer. The boys took kindly to the game, and under his coaching, with practice morning, noon and night, two years served to develop a team of youngsters that could do Walkerton men up in an innings. About the time that Mr. Bell took the school the Education Department had issued a limit table, and for the first time a fair attempt was made to observe it, but when we consider that the old style in vogue before that was to teach reading and spelling as the main things, and advance from form to form as the pupils became proficient in these, independent of how much or how little they knew of other studies, we can easily see how unpopular a movement for grading would be to one who was in the Fifth Book and could not do short division, perhaps not know the multiplication table up to twelve times. There was, however, a general turning back and a considerable amount of howling, but as more stress was put on arithmetic and other studies that, according to the limit table, they were most behind in, the matter began to adjust itself.

" The temptation is strong to devote a few paragraphs to the boys of the ' Old Brick ' who wielded the cricket bat in summer time and did battle with the shinnies when winter came. There were the McBride boys, the Shaws, Malcolm and Dan; the Scotts, the Vances, the McDonalds, the Mahers, the Stodders, Jack Reid, Jim Fitzpatrick, Jack Urquhart, George Nicol, Will McCalder, Bob McGavin, and who not? There was Jack McCool,[1] too, a raw boy from the Emerald Isle, who had a hard road to hoe when he first came to the school, but, full of pluck from top to bottom, he fought (not metaphorically, but literally) his way into the heart of his quondam persecutors. Mr. Bell taught until the end of 1872. During his time the attendance had increased to such an extent that the trustees had to grapple with the question of more school accommodation. Accordingly, early in January, 1872, the trustees decided to call a meeting of the ratepayers to take into consideration the selection of a site for a new school, and as a result of that meeting the present site was selected, the old site to be sold for what the trustees could make it bring. Mr. B. Mills was appointed to draw out the plan, and in June the contract was let to Sinclair & Blackburn for $4,600. With a new school the Board seemed to think that everything else should be new as well, and proceeded to obtain a new staff. Thus Mr. Bell, who had conducted the school with signal success for three years and a half, was allowed, like Moses, to have a glimpse of the promised land (the new school-house), but was not allowed to enter therein. There was engaged for the new school J. C. Elliot, principal; Anson G. Anderson and Miss Maggie Adair, assistants. The principal was very lame, and he had an old horse called Paddy, which drew him around. In fact, the impression was general that they were two old plugs together, so next year the Board dispensed with the service of one, and were deprived of the services of the other Next year an improvement was made by securing Mr. Hugh McKellar as principal, and the first assistant that year is now the Rev. Dr. McTavish, of Toronto. Mr. McKellar was a very successful teacher, and a very superior man. He taught during 1874, 1875 and 1876, after which Mr. Donald McIntyre came and put

[1]The present Inspector of Public Schools in East Bruce

in a year. Mr. McKee taught in 1878 and 1879; Mr. Ming taught in 1880. During the winter of 1881 he was taken ill. After a month or so of sick leave absence he returned and resumed work, but died shortly afterwards from bleeding of the lungs. His place was taken by Mr. John McBride, who finished out the year 1881. Mr. R. Munro taught during 1882, 1883, 1884, 1885 and 1886, and Mr. John Keith from 1885 to 1892. There have also been many very excellent teachers among the assistants, both male and female.

"During the summer of 1888 it was found necessary to build an addition to the schoolhouse, by which all the rooms in the old building were made considerably larger and more convenient, and two new rooms were added."—*Paisley Advocate*.

Following Mr. Keith, the principals have been G. F. Morrison, John Taylor, W. I. Chisholm, J. E. Hodgson, E. W. Dickenson, and, in 1905-06, R. T. Fuller. The last-mentioned has six assistants; five of the teaching staff attend to the regular public school work, and the two others to the continuation classes.

The opening of the post-office in 1856 was concurrent with the establishing of the mail route between Elora and Southampton. The service was tri-weekly, and the first mail carrier was one John Lyons. Just how long the tri-weekly service lasted the author cannot say, but some time in the sixties it became a daily one. This improved communication was followed in 1869 by the entrance of the Montreal Telegraph Company, which established an office in that year in the village.

The route followed by travel and commerce for twenty years after its settlement, between Paisley and the wide world beyond, was during the season of navigation principally by way of Southampton, thence by steamboat to Goderich. After navigation closed there was nothing for it but to drive a distance of about eighty miles to Guelph to reach the railway there. Enduring such disadvantages for so long a time, it is easy to imagine with what pleasure the villagers viewed the construction of the railway, and how heartily they cheered when the first locomotive came in on June 7th, 1872. The road was opened for freight and passengers on August 28th following.

With railway communication established, the village grew as never before. Instead of witnessing the passing along its main street of strings of sleighs conveying grain to be marketed at Southampton, Paisley now could offer as good a market, with the added advantage of a shorter haul; and, as farmers purchase their supplies as a rule where they sell their produce, every tradesman and merchant prospered in consequence. As can readily be supposed, the population increased, and this led to steps being taken to have the village incorporated. A census showed that there was 1,038 inhabitants in the village, being in excess of the required number. On a petition for incorporation being presented to the County Council, a by-law was passed, June 7th, 1873, incorporating the village and directing that the municipal election be held at Graham's Hotel, and that Edward Saunders be the returning officer. At the election held January 5th, 1874, the following were the successful candidates: James Saunders, reeve;[1] Duncan Fisher, Alex. Colborne, Wm. M. Smith and Robert Porteous, councillors. The Council appointed Edward Saunders to the joint offices of clerk and treasurer. The village was divided into two polling subdivisions in 1876. The first election under this arrangement took place at the following municipal election It was in the fall of 1876 that the present Town Hall was built. The Village Council held its first meeting therein on March 20th, 1877. December 15th, 1887, witnessed the installing in the village of an excellent system of waterworks for fire protection, the cost of which was $6,500. This has had the effect of reducing the premiums on fire insurance to a marked extent. Prior to this the town was without any means to fight a serious fire, and met with some heavy losses in consequence, such as J A Murdoch's woollen mill in 1871 and Stark's mill in 1884 In a footnote[2] are given a list of debentures issued by the village since the time of its incorporation.

[1]The following are the names of those who have been elected reeves of the village down to 1906 · James Saunders, 1874, '75, '76, '77, '78, '79, '80, '82, I E Fenton, 1881; D. J. Bain, 1883, '84, '85, '89, '90; R. Porteous, 1886, '87, '88, S McArton, M.D., 1891, '92, '93, '94, '95; Archibald Fisher, 1896, 1901; W. H McFarlane, 1897; S J. Robb, 1898, 1899, 1900, Wm. Rusk, 1902; W. W Hogg, 1903; James H. Steele, 1904, '05; I Shoemaker, 1906
The following are those who have filled the municipal offices of village clerk and treasurer : As clerk—E Saunders, D James Bain, S Shannon, J Claxton, Neil MacKechnie and J C. Gibson. As treasurer—E. Saunders, Dr P McLaren, and George Chambers.

[2]List of debentures issued by the village of Paisley · $2,050, for schools, April 14th, 1885; $5,500, for waterworks, December 15th, 1887; $1,800, for schools, June 13th, 1888 ; $1,000, for waterworks, December 15th, 1888; $14,000, loan to Carpet Factory, July 8th, 1901; and the following for granolithic sidewalks $2,400 in 1903, $1,940 and $1,882 in 1904, and $1,060 in 1905.
The cost of the public school building erected in 1872 was paid for by a debenture amounting to $5,000, issued by the township of Elderslie, but provided for by the Paisley School Section, and is properly to be included among the debenture issue of Paisley

The first minister to hold a public religious service in Paisley was the Rev. James Hutchinson; this was in 1853. The place where the service was held was Rowe's tavern. The first church erected in Paisley was St. Andrew's, built by the Presbyterian congregation in connection with the Church of Scotland. The church was opened in the winter of 1859. The Presbyterians in the settlement had services held by representatives of both the " Auld Kirk " and the " Free " before a congregation of either church was organized. The date when St. Andrew's congregation was organized the author cannot give, but in 1856 the Rev Kenneth McLennan was inducted as its minister, the first settled minister in the village. Here we would let Mr. Megraw speak: " Rev. Mr. McLennan was a man of robust constitution, and with a readiness to adapt himself to circumstances, and make the most of his surroundings. Mr. McLennan was well suited to the arduous task which he set himself to perform. In Valentine's mill services were held while the little white church was being erected on the hill, and while he preached the gospel on Sundays, he was ready through the week to lend a hand in the building. This church and its location gave the name to our present Church Street, and in the olden days no more harmonious flock could well be found than that which wended its way every Sunday up to this little church door. With it some of the writer's earliest memories are associated. Among Mr. McLennan's flock there were none who were stauncher friends than the gore of Greenock contingent, consisting of James Mair, the Brockie family, the Lambs, the Davies, Ledgerwoods, and Messrs. Leask and Megraw. George Brockie led the Psalms and took an active part in the work of the congregation. There was also a considerable part of the congregation from Gillies' Hill. At a soirée held in the old log schoolhouse Mr. McLennan, in the course of a humorous speech, had the misfortune to give expression to some remarks that gave mortal offence to the Highland part of the congregation. The words used paid a high compliment to their love of music, but reflected rather seriously upon both their valor and their industry, and as a result some thirty of them left the congregation, and most of these drifted into the Baptist denomination, then in considerable strength in West Arran. Mr. McLennan left early in the sixties, and the congregation got along with supplies for a few years until Mr. McLean, a divinity student from Kingston, preached for a summer, and was given a call when he completed his studies. This was about 1866. During his pastorate the congregation made good progress, and a good feeling existed. He left in 1871, and was succeeded by Rev. Mr. Gordon in 1873. Then the question of union forced itself on the attention, and a section of the congregation held out against. The unionists had to take themselves off to Knox Church, and the remnant being unable to support a minister, an interval of about eight years ensued, broken only by occasional spells of service, and during a great part of this time certain properties were in litigation. In 1884 Rev. Mr. Duncan resuscitated the congregation, collected funds for the building of a handsome new church on the bank of the Saugeen, at the corner of Water and Albert streets, and accepted a call as its pastor. Loss of health compelled him to give up the charge in 1888, and he was succeeded by Rev. John Gillies, who remained as pastor until 1891. Efforts made to maintain the entity of the congregation failed, and gradually the members united to Knox Church.

"The first stage of the history of Knox Church in Paisley was that of St. Andrew's as well, viz., visits from Mr McNaughton, of Southampton, and others Mr. McNaughton preached in Mr. Rowe's tavern in 1855 His pulpit was a little washstand, and his hearers sat around on whiskey barrels, beer kegs and whatever else they could find handy. Mr. McMorran led the psalmody, and as the strains of 'Old Hundred,' 'Martyrdom,' and other old, familiar tunes floated out upon the air and died away among the tall, waving trees, there were some of the listeners whose thoughts, no doubt, were carried away to former days among heathery hills. Mr. McMullen, a student from Knox Church, and Mr. McDonald, of Seaforth, were the next who preached to them, and these services were held in the old log schoolhouse. Mr. Blount preached in the summer of 1858; he was afterwards drowned on his way to the Old Country. The date of organization cannot be fastened on, but it occurred in the old log schoolhouse, most likely in 1858, possibly in '57. Dr. Scott, of London, dispensed the sacrament. Mr. Bremner came in 1859, was ordained in 1860, and the first entry in the sessions books is by his hand in February of that year, the minute showing previous organization. The elders, at their first meeting of session with a placed minister as moderator, were John Ewing, Malcolm Campbell and John Rusk, and to these at the next meeting in May, 1860, were added James Rankin, William McBride and Donald McIntyre, Sr. The first church which the congregation erected was of frame, that was moved away to make room for the present structure, which was built in 1875. The old frame is now standing on the corner of Queen and Alma Streets, as a dwelling, and as it has sometimes sheltered two or three families at once, it has been somewhat irreverently called 'The Ark.'

"Mr. Bremner remained from 1860 to 1870; Mr. Straith, from May, 1871, to October, 1882; Mr. Greig, from December, 1883, to October, 1886, and the present pastor, Rev. J. Johnston, has been in charge since February 1888, and has the honor of being the senior minister of the place, the occupants of the pulpits of all the other churches in town having come since that date."—*Paisley Advocate.*

The Methodist Church furnished the first minister to preach at Paisley, but it was not the first to be supplied with a regular pastor. It was in 1857 that the Rev. James A. Iveson came to the village as the first minister of the Wesleyan Methodist Church. He remained there during that and the following year as well. During 1859, 1860 and 1861 the congregation was united with that at Southampton, and ministerial services were supplied from there. The Rev George Jacques was settled at Paisley in 1862, and since then there has been a continuous succession of pastors in the usual itinerary of the church. At first, church services were held in the old log school-house. In 1875 (following the union of the various Methodist bodies) Paisley ceased to be a mission, and became a self-sustaining circuit. The New Connexion Methodists established a mission at Paisley, 1861, the Rev. Thomas Fox being the minister in charge. He was succeeded by the Rev. Joseph Rawson the following year, and he again by the Rev. S. F. Depew; the mission was closed in 1870.

The first Church of England service held in the village was in 1855, the Rev. J. P. Hodge officiating. In 1859 a congregation was organized, when Bishop Cronyn preached, the St. Andrew's congregation having given the use of their church for this service. A pretty brick church was built in 1864, known as the Church of the Ascension, largely through the efforts of the Rev. R. S. Cooper, the cost of which was about $1,500.

The Baptists at first held services in Sergison's Hall, which was conducted by the Rev. Neil Sinclair. In 1862 a church was built on the Elora Road; the locality being found unsuitable, in 1869 a brick church was erected in the village, and some twenty years later a manse.

The fact that four streams meet at or in the vicinity of Paisley made the question of bridges one of importance from the date when the two lone families of settlers experienced the inconveniences arising from being separated by the waters of the Teeswater River. The first bridge over this stream was built by Simon Orchard, in 1851. Rae's bridge over the Saugeen River was in course of construction at the time the settlers were going to Southampton to attend the "big land sale" in 1854. The Goldie Street bridge was built, Simon Orchard being the contractor, in 1859. All of these bridges have been replaced by fine steel structures built in the following mentioned years. The present two-span steel bridge over the Teeswater was opened for traffic in the first week of January, 1895; Rae's bridge in 1893, and the Goldie Street bridge in 1891. Before the first bridge over the Saugeen was built scows were used to transport the traffic. These were also used in times of freshet.[1] Freshets of almost annual occurrence have at times wrought considerable damage to property in Paisley It is said that after the freshet of 1870 nearly every house north of the Teeswater had its foundation raised, so that inconvenience from this source might be avoided at next high flood.

The Saugeen has not been looked upon as a navigable stream, but it remained for a citizen of Paisley to prove the contrary. In the summer of 1879 D Hanna built a flat-bottomed steamer, which he named the *Waterwitch* Its dimensions were: Length, 40 feet, with a beam of 8 feet. The engine used was one of only six horsepower. Nevertheless it was powerful enough to give the craft a good headway against the pretty strong current. During Fall Exhibition week of that year Mr. Hanna did a rushing excursion business, as everybody wanted a cruise on the little steamer. In 1880 and again in the following year the *Waterwitch* steamed up the river to Walkerton, taking thirteen hours to go up the river, but returning in four hours. In 1883 Messrs. McLean Brothers, of the Sauble Falls Mills, purchased the vessel, and conveyed it on sleighs to Boat Lake. Its further history is given in Chapter XII.

Wonder has sometimes been expressed that Paisley, with the Saugeen River flowing through it ready to be harnessed and give out its potential powers, has not developed manufacturing industries to a greater extent than has been The Teeswater has two dams across it at Paisley. Why one across the Saugeen has not been constructed is not for the author to say.

Paisley made a mistake in the only loan it has made toward the

[1]An account of Wm. Sergison was presented to the County Council, June, 1869, for ferrying travellers and passengers across the river flats at Paisley during the spring freshets of that year, for a period of six days and nights

encouraging and establishing of manufactures in the village. In 1902 a loan of $14,000 was made to George A. Burrows to help him to build a carpet factory. The factory was built and run for a while, but closed down long before the first instalment toward the repayment of the loan was due.

The press has been represented in the village since February 17th, 1865, the date of the first issue of the *Paisley Advocate* The first publisher was Richard Goldie. He retained possession of the paper for four years, selling out to James M. Bishop. In August, 1872, the paper passed into the hands of John A Murdoch, an able writer, who published the paper until the fall of 1876. For a very short time it was in the hands of Mr. E. Saunders, who passed it over to M. A. Clark, and he to John Collie, and the latter to James R Aitcheson. On the 1st of May, 1885, Ainsley Megraw purchased the paper, and proved himself to be a well-qualified journalist. He continued as the editor and publisher for about eight years. The *Advocate* is now issued by D. McKenzie, who maintains a standard worthy of emulating by publishers of local newspapers.

The Canadian Bank of Commerce opened a branch at Paisley in 1875. The amount of business secured did not warrant the bank in continuing the agency, which was closed in 1877. This want of success is said to have arisen from faults in the manner of the agent. Following the closing of the chartered bank, Robert Porteous opened a private bank. For some years Edward Saunders was in partnership with him in this business, which was continued until Mr. Porteous' death in 1896. The Western Bank of Canada established a branch at Paisley in October, 1886, with C. L. Rennie as agent. He was succeeded by F. Biette, and he by the present popular agent, S M. Hutcheson.

Ever since September, 1861, Dr. P. McLaren has been a resident of Paisley, and has practised his profession there for a far longer period than any other one who has sought to cure the ills and sicknesses of the community. The first doctor to reside in Paisley was Dr. Crawford. His daughter, Miss Isabelle Valancey Crawford, achieved a merited reputation as an authoress in Canadian literature. Of other medical men long resident in Paisley the names of Dr. John Baird and Dr. S. McArton will come to the memory of the older residents.

The legal profession has never been largely represented at Paisley. In the early days of the county, conveyancers who undertook to draw out deeds, agreements, etc., were found in every village and hamlet, Paisley being no exception. The work done by these conveyancers cut seriously into the business of the regular legal practitioners. George W. Malloch, who came to Paisley in 1865, was for many years the only lawyer in the village. His practice there extended over some twenty-eight years Hector Cowan, since 1885, when he settled in Paisley, has possessed the leading legal practice of the place.

Space will not permit the author to refer to all of those who have done their part in the development of Paisley, while some who deserve an extended notice are but briefly referred to. John Valentine, James Stark and Duncan Fisher are names that should be remembered in this connection, for the industries they carried on have helped to make Paisley what it is to-day, a village that possesses as much wealth for its size as any to be found in the county of Bruce.

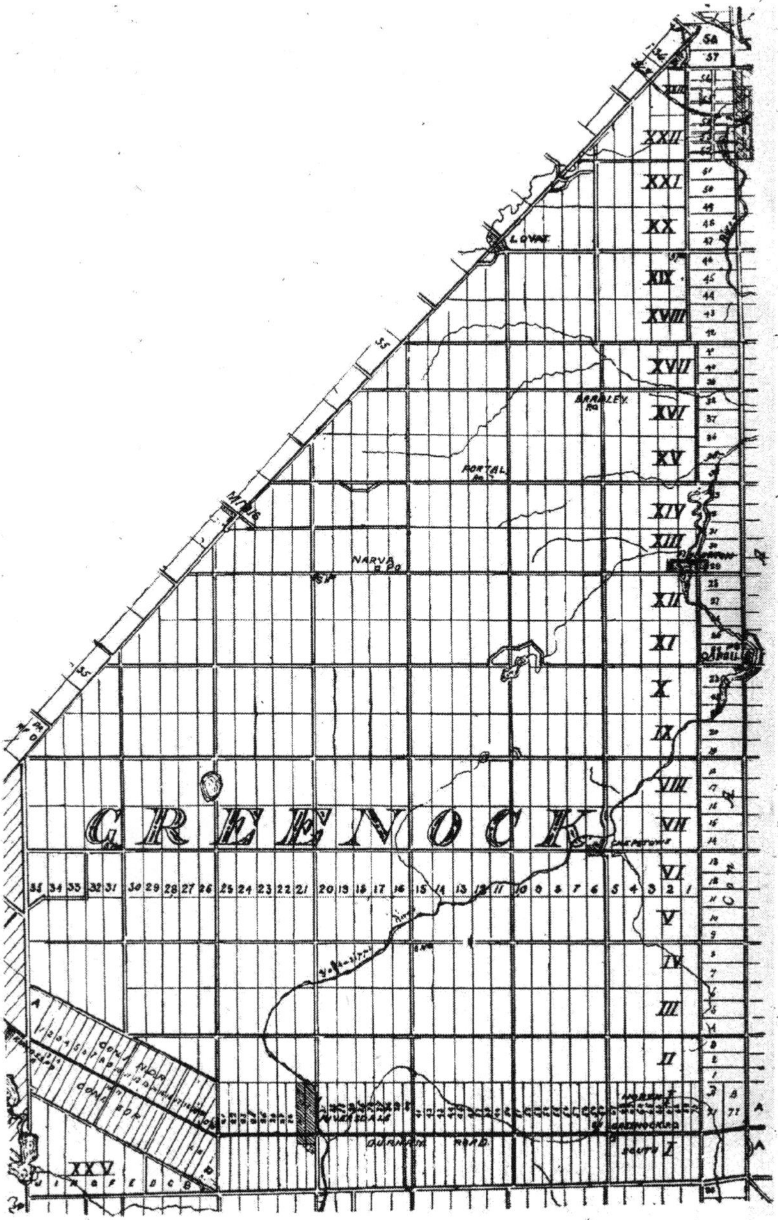
GREENOCK
LOVAT
NARVA
PORTAL
BRADLEY
DURHAM ROAD
XXV
XXII
XXI
XX
XIX
XVIII
XVII
XVI
XV
XIV
XIII
XII
XI
X
IX
VIII
VII
VI
V
IV
III
II
35 34 33 32 31 30 29 28 27 26 25 24 23 22 21 20 19 18 17 16 15 14 13 12 11 10 9 8 7 6 5 4 3 2 1

CHAPTER XXX.

TOWNSHIP OF GREENOCK.[1]

EXTRACT FROM THE REPORT OF COUNTY VALUATORS, 1879.

" Greenock township has more inferior land than any other south of the peninsula. The Mud River having hardly any banks around it for a long distance is flooded in the spring to the depth of three or four feet. It has a far larger amount of swamp than any other in the county, and when the pine is taken off it will not be of any value. There is a portion of good land around Chepstowe, and the most of the gore is first-class land It has a large amount of mill property. Its average price is $22 60 per acre ''

EXTRACT FROM THE REPORT OF COUNTY VALUATORS, 1901.

" Greenock is a gore township and very few roads are open through from east to west, none being open between the Durham Road and the 10th concession, on account of what is known as the Greenock swamp. A portion of this swamp has been reclaimed since the last valuation, but still there is a great deal to do in the same line The 6th concession was being opened through the swamp when your valuators were there, which will be a great convenience, especially to the settlers in the western part of the township, and also to those of the eastern part of Kincardine township. There are portions of Greenock as good as can be found in the county, but a very considerable portion is swamp, and a great deal of the northern part is stiff clay, in fact, so stiff that it affects its value considerably The rate per acre, including village property, is $25 66, of which amount the village property is $2 39 per acre.''

GREENOCK Township has the appearance geographically of being the core around which were laid out most of the other townships of the original county of Bruce. In reality the reverse was the procedure, Greenock being the last township south of the peninsula to be surveyed. After the boundaries of the other townships placed along the borders of the county were settled, there remained a large section in the centre of the county. This formed the township of Greenock, the survey of which was made in 1852 by R. Walsh, P.L S.[2]

[1]The name is that of a seaport town on the Clyde in Scotland.

[2]Mr Walsh commenced his survey at the blind line at the back of the first concession, N D.R., and proceeded north. On reaching the apex at the north of the township he thought his contract completed, and was preparing to leave when, remembering the strip of land forming a gore in the south-west of the township, now the twenty-fifth concession, he took his staff there and made the survey of it ; this was late in the fall, after the snow was on the ground.

401

In Chapter II. are to be found particulars of the survey of the Durham Road through this township, and also the reason why in Greenock only, the free grant lots are confined to one concession on each side of the Durham Road

Greenock, excepting the " free grants," was included among the Crown lands which were opened for sale at the time of the " big land sale," September 27th, 1854.[1] The price at which these lands were offered by the Crown was 7s 6d. per acre. The first settlers to take up land in the township were Joseph Chartrand and John Caskanette, French-Canadians, who had been on the staff of A. P. Brough, P.L.S., when he surveyed the Durham Road. Anticipating the development of a town at the point where the Teeswater River is crossed by the Durham Road, they took up the lots on which the village of Riversdale now stands, and brought in their families in the spring of 1850. Along with them came other families from the same part of Lower Canada in which they had resided. The offer of free grant farm lots in Greenock was held back at first by the Crown Lands Department.[2] Whether this was on account of uncertainty as to future action in regard to extending the free grants in Greenock, as elsewhere, to four concessions in width, or whether the difficulty and expense of cutting a road through the swamp seemed too formidable at the time, the author cannot say; either surmise is quite supposable On the withdrawal of this restriction in April, 1851, the desirable lots along the Durham line were quickly taken up. The names of those who took up these lots are given in Chapter V. Before the lands in Greenock were open for sale numerous squatters had settled in the township. Especially was this the case along concession A, and in the " Gore " of the township Among these early settlers were Lewis Lamb, James Mair, James Ledgerwood, John Megraw, David, John, George and William Brockie, John Shennan, John and Dennis Phelan and Edward Boulton.[3] The mill site secured by John Valentine in 1851 puts his name in the forefront of any list of settlers in the northern

[1]See Appendix K

[2]Extract from letter sent to George Jackson, Crown Lands Agent, Durham, by the Department of Crown Lands, August 15th, 1850 : Re Township of Greenock—" As the survey is not fully completed and as there is no intentions of opening the road through the township at present, it is desirable that no locations should be made thereon this season ''

[3]Edward Boulton seems to have belonged to a class of backwoodsmen, by no means uncommon, whose restless enterprise kept them always in the front of the wave of settlement He was one of the first settlers in Walkerton, also of Greenock, and again in Amabel. He was residing at or near Meaford when his death occurred some few years ago

part of Greenock. The last-named settlers came into the township either *via* Owen Sound or Durham. There were others who came in *via* the Bruce and Kincardine boundary line, among whom were Allan Ross and Duncan Campbell in 1852, and later the Camerons and others. Among the leading families who early settled in Greenock were the McKees and the Pinkertons (the name of the latter is perpetuated by the pretty little village of that name). Among those who located lands in Greenock at this time, in addition to others elsewhere mentioned, were the following: William Clark, Richard Garland, George Leask, John M. Wells, George and James Cromar, James Donnelly and Alex. Symon.

To chop down the trees, log, burn and clear up a farm in Greenock meant much and long-continued hard work, many privations and hardships, and demanded, as everywhere in the backwoods, indomitable pluck and an amount of perseverance that might be classed as heroic. The later settlers of Greenock possessed advantages over the pioneers of 1849 and 1850, for some attempt had been made before they settled to open leading highways, such as the Elora and Durham Roads;[1] so that they had some show of access to saw and grist mills already built and in operation, as well as to stores and post-offices at Walkerton and other villages. The first post-office opened in the township still bears the name of Greenock, for here, as elsewhere in the county at that time, on the first post-office established in a township the name of it was bestowed. This office was opened October 9th, 1852. J. B. Ritchie[2] was the first postmaster. The next office opened was at Riversdale, in 1853 or 1854, George Cromar being the postmaster.

At first the municipal existence of Greenock was merged in that of the "United Townships in the County of Bruce." The first year an assessment was made was 1851, the total of which amounted to £1,902 [3] This seemed to have fixed the assessment for the following year, which was for the same amount. In 1853 the assessment stood at 3,571, and the first taxes were paid in that year, amounting to the very modest sum of £33 17s. 2 1-2d. When the

---

[1] In Chapter V. are to be found particulars, giving names of contractors, etc, who opened these roads

[2] See Chapter V for an account, from the pen of Mr J B Ritchie, of this office and the mail service thereto.

[3] In Appendix M is to be found a statement of amount of assessment as equalized, for the first seven years of the township's existence, showing the progress of development in these years

union of all of the townships of the county was dissolved,[1] Greenock and Culross were united for municipal purposes. The first municipal election was held in January, 1854, at George Cromar's house. J. B. Ritchie was the returning officer. He had to go to Lorne to receive from the old reeve of the united townships, the Rev. Wm. Fraser, the election papers and be sworn in. The first reeve was George Cromar, who at a later date was the first warden of the county of Bruce. After filling the office of reeve for four years, he resigned it to accept the office of county treasurer. His successor in the reeveship[2] was John Valentine, who held the position for six years. In a footnote[3] are given the names of all the reeves of Greenock from the first up to 1906.

The offices of clerk and treasurer of the united townships of Greenock and Culross were held respectively by Archibald Fraser and John McGregor. When Greenock became a separate municipality the two offices of clerk and treasurer were held by James Cromar. As township clerk he acted until the end of 1868. William Clark succeeded him, and remained in office until 1881. The subsequent holders of the clerkship have been John Millar, J. W. McNab and J. J. Donnelly. The township has had as its treasurers, James Cromar (1856 to 1858), Hugh Montgomery (1859-60), William Clark[4] (1861 to 1905), and M. M. Schurter, the present treasurer.

[1]See Appendix F.

[2]John Valentine was a native of Montrose, Scotland, where he was born in 1817. He came to Walkerton in 1851 and opened a store in partnership with George Jardine. Securing a mill privilege on the Teeswater River, at Paisley, he built a saw-mill there in 1852 and a grist-mill in 1855 or '56. His family resided at Southampton at first, but from 1855 they lived at Paisley. Mr. Valentine's property was largely in Greenock, and he filled the office of reeve of the township for six years. Mr. Valentine held a prominent place in the County Council, which in 1859 elected him warden of the county. His public life bore a clean record, while as a man he was highly esteemed. His death occurred August 12th, 1872.

[3]Reeves of the township of Greenock: George Cromar, 1854, '55, '56, '57; John Valentine, 1858, '59, '60, '61, '62, '65; Robert Pinkerton, 1863, '64, '66, '67, '69, '70, '71; James Mair, 1868, '72, '73; J. Millar, 1874; William Bradley, 1875, '76, '77, '78, '79, '80, '81, '82, '83, part of 1891 part of 1892; W. W. Reed, 1884; Henry Cargill, 1885, '86, '87; John Coumans, 1888, '89, '90, part of '91; Lewis Lamb, part of 1892; A. Symons, 1893, '94, '95; John McKee, 1896, '99, 1900, '01; J. J. Donnelly, 1897, '98; James Daniels, 1902; John Meagher, 1903, '04; F. Fullerton, 1905; M. McNab, part of 1906; S. Hawthorne, part of 1906.

[4]William Clark, on March 20th, 1905, relinquished his official connection with the township of Greenock, after serving it for twelve years as township clerk, and forty-four years as township treasurer. During this long term of service no complaint was ever made as to the manner in which he performed his duties, which was efficiency itself.

Mr. Clark is a native of Edinburgh, Scotland, where he was born in

The first public work of importance undertaken by the Township Council was in connection with the rebuilding of the bridge at Riversdale. The contract for this work was let to William McVicar, for which he received $2,413, the work being done during the summer of 1863. To pay for this, debentures for $3,250 were issued. These, although bearing 6 per cent. interest, were sold at a discount of 15 per cent. As a help to pay the interest on these debentures, and also to raise a sinking fund, the Council established a toll-gate[1] at the bridge, at which a man of the name of Mahon was installed as keeper. A good deal of opposition arose as a result of a toll being charged for crossing the bridge, and to test the authority for doing so Paul Ross laid a charge before J. B. Ritchie, J.P., against Mahon for obstructing the Queen's highway, with the result that he was committed to jail at Goderich The matter was settled at last by the County Council, in December, 1864, assuming the payment of the debentures issued by the Township Council, on condition that the toll-gate be removed.

The big swamp in the centre of Greenock was looked upon for a long time after settlement began as a drawback to the development of the township, and from an agricultural point of view justly so, but from an industrial standpoint Greenock swamp has been a mine of wealth The Teeswater River, flowing the full length of the township from south to north (the damming up of which by a natural formation of the ground resulted in the big swamp being formed, as related farther on), has furnished power required to manufacture into lumber the pine that grew so abundantly in the swamp. The first mill on the Teeswater was that built by John Valentine in 1852 at Paisley. In a year or so after this John Shennan had a mill built at Pinkerton, which he sold to David Pinkerton Then, at Chepstow John Phelan had a mill, and again at Riversdale there was a steam saw and grist mill, run by George Cromar, in 1857.

The foundation was laid of the village of Cargill, the busiest manu-

1834. After serving for some time in the audit office of the North British Railway, he emigrated to Canada with his parents in 1852 He attended the '' Big '' land sale in September, 1854, at Southampton, and purchased lots 3 and 4, concession 10, township of Greenock. He married, on February 28th, 1856, Miss Sarah Griffin, of U. E Loyalist stock, from Nova Scotia As soon as the season permitted, they entered upon backwoods life, on their uncleared farm, where they resided for nearly half a century. Lately they moved into the village of Cargill, and in their new residence there they had the pleasure of celebrating their golden wedding.

[1]This was the only toll-gate ever established in the county of Bruce as far as the author is aware of

facturing centre in Greenock, in the late fifties. The land on and in the vicinity of the village was taken up by five brothers of the name of McNeil—William, James, Donald, Charles and Malcolm, who purchased some ten farm lots. When coming into the county they first resided at Riversdale. From there, in the spring of 1856, they rafted down the river to the locality where their farms were a quantity of timber they had prepared for the frame of a mill, and shortly after commenced the construction of a dam. At this stage they were persuaded to sell their mill privilege, and whatever they had done towards the building of a mill, to George Elphick, who previously had been working as a miller at Pinkerton for his father-in-law, David Pinkerton. The dam was soon completed, and the grist mill set in operation. But it was not till a later date that a village commenced to gather about the mill.

In October, 1871, the Commissioner of Crown Lands sold at the Court House at Walkerton the lands contained in the Greenock and Culross swamps, 8,417 acres in all. The attendance at the sale was large; but the purchasing was confined to the following: Charles Mickle, Sr., Henry Cargill, J. F. Wilson, T. W. McMurray, G. B. Ferguson, William Edgar and O. Phelps. The average price obtained for these lands was $4.66 per acre. Charles Mickle, Sr., secured limits of some 1,700 acres in extent at the sale, and in addition purchased 2,400 acres more from private parties, and also purchased the mill privilege from George Elphick. Erecting a sawmill at this point, he commenced the manufacture of lumber for shipment, the railway having been completed and a station, named " Mickles "[1] (now Cargill), located at a convenient distance from the mill. At the sale of the timber limits above mentioned Henry Cargill was a large buyer. In addition to purchases then made, he secured, at a liberal advance from some other purchasers, enough of these lands to bring his total acreage up to one-half of that sold. Six of the original purchasers, Mr. Cargill being one of them, held the property jointly for about a year, when the others sold out their respective holdings to Mr. Cargill. After this, in January, 1879, Charles Mickle, Sr., sold his mill property and some 4,100 acres of timbered lands to Mr. Cargill. This last purchase gave Mr. Cargill practically all the lands in the Greenock swamp. The beginning of Mr. Cargill's identification with the manufacturing industries of Greenock was when he leased, in

---

[1]The village which then commenced to grow was called " Yokassippi," a corruption of the Indian name of the river.

1872, from Messrs. Toohey and Coumans their mill at Chepstow; but with the purchase of the Mickle mill property the development by him of the wealth that lay in the swamp commenced. Canals parallel with concession and side-roads were dug, by which to float the timber from where it had been cut to the mill. These canals have also drained the swamp, turning miles of it into good dry farm land, and making possible the opening of roads through it. To the water-power sawmill Mr. Cargill added a large steam sawmill, a steam planing mill and grist mill. The thriving village of Cargill preserves the name of its founder, and its prosperity tells the tale of the broad-minded business efforts of Henry Cargill,[1] and continued by W. D. Cargill, his son. A " captain of industry " is a title that was fittingly bestowed on the founder of this extensive business. The rapid increase of the population of Cargill village, owing to the establishment of fresh industries and the enlargement of old ones, led the various religious denominations having congregations there to take steps toward the building of churches. This determination seems to have been reached at one and the same time by the Church of England, the Methodists and the Presbyterians, and during the summer of 1902 three handsome brick church edifices were erected for these three bodies.[2] No unincorporated village of the same population in the

[1] In a footnote in Chapter VIII. a short biographical sketch of Mr. Cargill is to be found. The following extract from a local paper shows a side of his character worthy of being remembered. " H. C.," writing in the *Kincardine Review*, has the following . " On the day of Henry Cargill's funeral I was talking to a prominent Liberal about him. ' No one ever heard me say an ill word against Henry Cargill,' he said, ' and I would have no peace in my family if I did And I'll tell you why. Many years ago a little girl was walking into Walkerton with a market-basket. Mr. Cargill drove up and offered her a ride. Nearing the corner of the road leading into Walkerton he inquired how far it was into town She said it was two miles and a half. He drove her to the store, turned around and drove back He had gone five miles out of his way to give a ride to a little girl with a market-basket. She's my wife now and wouldn't let me say a word against Henry Cargill if I felt inclined, which I never did.'

" Last spring I met him in Ottawa, and he asked me to go with him to Booth's sawmills. Accompanied by W H. Bennett, M P., and T. I. Thompson, M.P., we went to the great mills, where a thousand men and the most approved machinery turn every part of a log worth saving to some account. Mr Cargill was engrossed with the work going on. He talked with the laborers, inquired about every feature that was new to him, and when he came away, in his quiet, deliberate way, said " Boys, if I only owned this mill—and I would rather own it than the Canadian Pacific Railway—instead of having a seat over in that house across the river, I'd have an armchair here, where I could sit down and smell the lumber." He said it so sententiously that no one could doubt he meant it.' "

[2] These churches, although spoken of as being in Cargill, are really in the township of Brant, and not in Greenock.

county equals Cargill in appearance. What with granolithic sidewalks, electric street lighting and handsome residences, the villagers
have reason to be proud of their place of residence.

The village of Pinkerton may claim priority over any other in
the township as to the year when it began to take form as a business
centre. It is prettily situated, and if the decision to make it the
county town, referred to in Chapter VI., had been adhered to, there
is no doubt but that a beautiful, busy town would have developed
there The land forming the site of the village was squatted on about
1853 by John Shennan.[1] As early as possible he took steps toward
the erection of a saw and grist mill. Before completing the same he
sold out his rights and improvements to David Pinkerton, who had
the sawmill in operation about 1854, and the grist mills some three
or four years later, following which, in the course of a few years, a
carding and fulling mill was added to the industries of the place.
Thomas Pinkerton was for a number of years the leading man of the
village, its several mills having passed into his hands The Presbyterian congregation at Pinkerton is united to that in West Brant,
forming one charge; the church at Pinkerton is a frame building, and
was erected in 1874. The Church of England also have a congregation there, which erected in 1878 a church edifice, a roughcast
building, that has accommodation for about 250 worshippers.

Riversdale was surveyed into village lots in 1855, at the instance
of Joseph C. Chartrand, George Cromar and James Bennie; but it
may date its commencement from the time a post-office was established there in 1854 George Cromar was the foremost man in the
little village at that time, and continued as such until his death, which
occurred in the summer of 1861. In 1857 he built a steam saw and
grist mill, then the usual supply of blacksmith shops and hotels
appeared one after another. A Division Court also had its office
there. In 1860 James Millar and Anthony Mason rented the mills
from Mr. Cromar, and after his death purchased them from the
executors of the estate. These mills have had an unfortunate experience from fire, having been burned down some five or six times. The
Presbyterian congregation at Riversdale was formed about 1857, the
Rev. Walter Inglis being the first minister. The present church
building of this congregation was dedicated in October, 1880. There
is also at Riversdale a Roman Catholic church, but for many years
there has been no resident priest there

[1]Walkerton's first postmaster, and after leaving Greenock, the founder
of Balaclava, in Carrick

The village of Chepstow came into being because of the water-power developed there, locally known as " Phelan's dam," and where a saw-mill was built by John Phelan. There is a story about how the village received its name, which is here given for what it is worth, without vouching for its truth or accuracy. " Mr. Phelan and the early settlers in the neighborhood, who were nearly all Irish (although now more than half are of German descent), petitioned the Post-office Department for a post-office, which was to bear the name of ' Emmett,' in memory of the Irish patriot, who was hanged for rebellion in 1803. ' And what do you think,' said Mr. Phelan, ' some blackguard in the Department who knew Irish history, changed the name to Chepstow, which was the residence of Earl Strongbow, the first English invader of Ireland!' " Mr Phelan never forgave the Government for this outrage In 1857 a frame church was built by the Roman Catholic congregation, which bore the name of St. John's In 1903-04 a very fine church edifice was erected to take the place of the old one, and was dedicated by Bishop Dowling, of Hamilton, October 2nd, 1904. The proximity of the flourishing village of Cargill precludes much further development at Chepstow

From the day when the surveying party engaged in laying out the Durham Road tried to find a place where a road could be made across the Greenock swamp, covered as it was with a rank, tangled growth of vegetation, and that offered no better footing than spongy knolls of grass and moss standing in pools of water, down to a comparatively late date, the Greenock swamp has seemed a section of the county lying beyond the powers of the settlers to reclaim and transform into agricultural lands, and it was left to be exploited by the lumberman, who found therein timber of all descriptions that has been most profitable to cut and market. The initial movement towards finding out what was necessary to be done if the swamp was to be drained began in 1868. As the result of a memorial from the County Council in August of that year the Commissioner of Public Works directed Robert Gilmour, C E., of Paisley to examine the swamp and see what were its possibilities, and see what had to be done to develop them. Mr. Gilmour reported to the following effect: " At lot 14, concession 5 of the township of Greenock, the Teeswater is crossed by an escarp-ment of limestone rock, which comes up within three feet of the summer level of the river. To break through this barrier (which appears to be the natural dam which has mainly contributed to the formation of the swamp), an extensive excavation for some distance would be required " Mr Gilmour proposed a plan of digging ɔ canal from above this natural dam to a small creek that empties into the Teeswater near Pinkerton, and also another canal from the swamp, to the Penetangore River. No action seems to have resulted from Mr. Gilmour's report. In 1883 Mr. McCallum, Chief of the Public Works Department of the Province of Ontario, inspected the Teeswater River, with a view of getting the swamp drained, but nothing more was done   In 1887, as a result of a largely signed petition, the County Council voted a sum of money for the removal of Phelan's dam at Chepstow, as many held it to be the cause of the waters of the Teeswater being dammed back to such an extent. The removal of the dam in the following year did not affect, to any extent, the flooded lands. On February 2nd, 1903, a meeting was held in the village of Riversdale to consider the subject of having the swamp drained. This meeting urged upon the municipal councils of Greenock and Culross to take steps towards the object sought. Mr. James Warren, C.E., was engaged to make a survey of the river. His report, in part, to the Township Council of Greenock is as follows:

EXTRACT FROM REPORT OF JAMES WARREN, C.E.

WALKERTON, April 2nd, 1903.
John Meagher, Esq., Reeve of the Township of Greenock:

"Sir,—At your request I made an examination of the Teeswater River from Chepstow to the townline of Culross, with the view of ascertaining the probable cost of deepening the river, so as to get better drainage for the lands now affected by the water of the river.

"I find a good fall from lot 15, con. 5, to Chepstow, which will give that part of the river a good current; from lot 16 to the south boundary there is little difference in the level, only enough to give the water a fair flow. The chief obstructions are from lot 15 to Phelan's Dam at Chepstow. This part or section will be the hardest cutting, as it is gravel. From lot 15 to the boundary of Culross the bottom is soft and can be easily removed.

"In the section from Thompson's Bridge to Culross boundary, I would recommend a channel 20 feet wide, and to the depths shown on the profile, and from Thompson's Bridge to the old site of Phelan's Dam the channel should be 25 feet wide. In many places south of Thompson's Bridge the river would clear itself if the outlet was cleared away.

"The estimate of the probable cost from Phelan's Dam to Thompson's Bridge of clearing out the outlet I would place at $6,018 30, which is the hardest section on the work, as the cutting is deeper and harder to take out.

" From Thompson's Bridge to the south boundary of the township, I would estimate the cost at $2,041.50, being a total of $8,059.80.

" Counting the farm lots benefited in whole or part, the acreage is 16,559 acres, which I would value at $185,150, according to the annexed schedule, which shows the value set on each lot, also the benefit derived.

" The total benefit derived I would place at $18,975, or at an average of 84 cents per acre, and the cost of construction I would place at 50 cents per acre on the whole of the lots affected by the drainage of the river.

" Taking the lots as a whole, it is quite feasible and would be of great value to the township, as it would enable the lands to be cleared and cultivated, which at present cannot be done, and when these lands are cleared they will be excellent grazing lands, and after a short time, when the soil would be somewhat consolidated, would yield good crops of grain and roots.

" I have prepared a profile of the bottom of the river from Chepstow to the boundary of Culross, a total distance of 8.910 miles. I was fortunate enough to be able to take the measurements on the ice, which was more accurately done than could be done on the land at any other time.

" If the whole work cannot be gone on with, I would strongly recommend that that portion between Thompson's Bridge and Phelan's Dam to be done, as that would give a good outlet to that part of the river south of Thompson's Bridge."

About the same time the Ontario Government was approached by R. E. Truax, M.P.P., and a grant of $7,000 was obtained for the dredging of the river, which was a little more than half of the expected entire cost. This grant was to be made available only when the balance of the amount required for the work had been provided by the county and the two townships interested. The County Council was willing to aid in the work, and its members so expressed themselves, adding that they thought that Greenock and Culross, the two interested townships, should assume the larger share of the financial obligations This the two township councils would not do. The matter, therefore, has remained in *status quo.*

For fully half a century after the first settler had entered Greenock no east and west road through the township had been opened in that stretch of territory lying between the Durham line and the 12th concession, on account of the impassable swamp. As the effect of the drains or canals cut in the swamp by Henry Cargill in his lumbering operations, as related in a preceding paragraph, the time came when there arose the possibility of constructing a highway through the swamp In 1899 the township voted $500 to open the 6th and 10th concession roads, this was supplemented by a grant of equal amount by the County Council and the Provincial Government, a donation of $500 was made by Henry Cargill to help this needed undertaking The work was commenced in 1900 and completed in 1901.

For a number of years in the centre of the county there dwelt a group of men of marked intellectuality, of whom the leaders were William Bradley and William Bowes, of Greenock, and Henry Brown, of Elderslie. They have all passed away, Mr. Bradley dying in 1892, Mr Brown in 1903, and Mr. Bowes, the last, in 1906. Robert Munro, the editor of the Port Elgin *Times,* on the death of the last-mentioned of the group, wrote as follows:

"By the death of Mr. Wm. Bowes (June 17th, 1906) one of the most remarkable of the early settlers of Bruce has been taken away. Born in Scotland, he came to Canada when a young man, and at once attracted attention by his wide fund of information, acquaintance with the best literature, and intelligent interest in scientific and social problems In the days of George Brown the letters of Mr. Bowes on the labor question, ethical topics, and on various subjects of interest, were frequently found in the *Globe,* and he contributed many an excellent article to the local press He had a keen incisive style, with a fine command of words, but his subjects were too abtruse for the mass of readers to get hold of He was liberal in his views on theological, political and literary topics. As a conversationalist he excelled, and delighted to cross swords with men like Alexander Shaw, Judge Kingsmill, Henry Cargill, James Innes, ex-M P., and even George Brown himself Of the death of Mr. Bowes we may say, 'There goes the last of the Romans,' the last of a band of men of whom ' Bowes, Brown and Bradley ' were the well-known types. He lived in Greenock till a few years ago, when he came to spend his last days with his daughter. Mrs Handbidge, of Arran. The funeral took place at Pinkerton The editor of *The Times* knew Mr Bowes at first hand for twenty-four years, and has nothing 'but kindly recollections of his great ability, almost daring humor, and intellectual honesty in dealing with the problems that attract' thinking men "

With this appreciative encomium of one of the prominent men of Greenock, whom the local press playfully called the " Philosopher of Greenock Swamp," the author would bring this chapter, on possibly the most unique of the townships in the county of Bruce to a close.

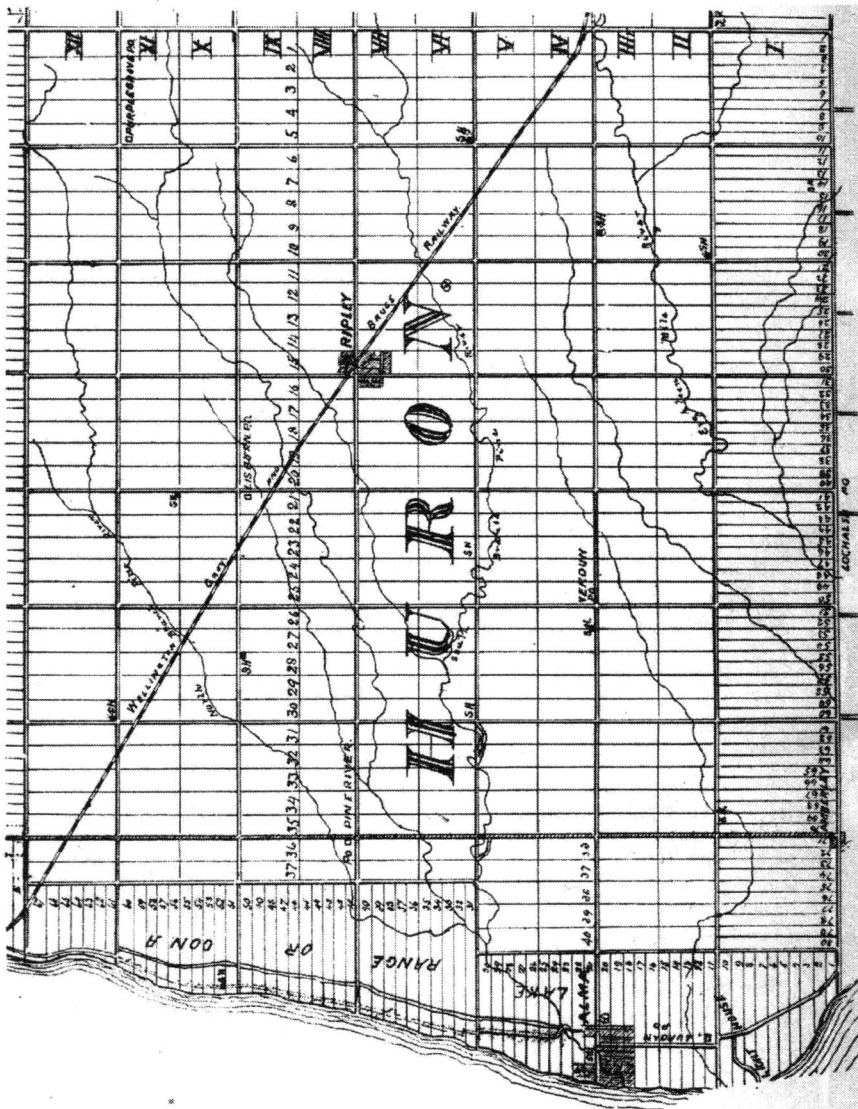

CHAPTER XXXI.

TOWNSHIP OF HURON.[1]

EXTRACT FROM THE REPORT OF COUNTY VALUATORS, 1901.

" This township possesses a very large proportion of first-class land, and farm property is changing hands readily at good figures. The reputation of Huron stands high as an agricultural district; goods roads, good fences and level land, little or no stone, it is fast becoming an ideal township. The chief drawbacks are scarcity of wood and water, although a large number have overcome the latter want by drilling deep wells and pumping by wind power There are two light streaks across the township, the quality of which is very poor, which our figures will bear out. The Lake Range affects this township somewhat, but not to any very great extent, as the good land comes much closer to the lake shore than in the townships to the north The rate per acre for Huron, including the village of Ripley, is $37.31, Ripley making a sum equal to $2 25 of this amount per acre.''

IN the second chapter of this history is related an account of the entrance of the first surveyor into the township of Huron, A. P. Wilkinson, P.L.S., in the year 1847. The survey made by him was confined to the first concession of the Lake Range, or concession A, as it is sometimes called. The remaining portion of the township, lying back of this range and north of the first concession, was surveyed in the summer of 1851 by E R. Jones, P L.S.[2]

The lands in the township of Huron were among those known as School Lands, and were among those offered for sale[3] July 30th, 1852. A number of squatters had entered the township prior to the date of this sale. The names of several of these are mentioned as among the very earliest pioneers of the county in the second chapter of this book. The author has had an opportunity of examining the field notes of the survey of this township made by E. R. Jones, and has placed in a footnote what he has found relating to settlers at

---

[1] It is but fitting that Huron, the name of the noble lake, the shore of which forms the western boundary of the county of Bruce, should be conferred upon one of its townships.

[2] The report of E. R. Jones of the survey of the township sums up the area as follows : Lands, exclusive of roads, 58,484 acres ; lands included in road allowances, 1,392 acres. Total, 59,876 acres.

[3] See Appendix J.

that time in the township of Huron. The extract[1] is long, and the author's excuse for inserting it is because it is perfectly authoritative as to the names of the actual first settlers on the Lake Range and their date of settlement. The point made clear by these field notes of the surveyors is that the settlement of the township was at first confined almost exclusively to the Lake Shore Range. It is not difficult to arrive at the reason why this should have been so, which was its accessibility in summer by water and in winter on the ice   Then the smooth, wide beach provided a highway on which one could travel north or south with but little difficulty. One settlement,

[1] EARLY SETTLERS OF HURON TOWNSHIP

Lot	Name of Settler.	Date of Settlement	Buildings	Clearings.
1 to 15	No remarks about these lots			
16	Thomas Barnes	Oct., 1849	.	No remarks.
17	Elishu Barnes .	Oct , 1849	...	12 acres cleared.
19	David Walden	May 28, 1849	.	24 ac. pt. improved.
20	Peter Wanamaker	May 10, 1849	.	24 " "
21	Robt. Jardine	. Nov , 1850	.	4 acres cleared.
22, 23	Jas Keys (dead) wife, Ann Keys		{ Small log house and barn . . . }	} 24 ac on each lot.
24, 25	Wm Blair	May, 1849	Frame barn on 25	...About same clearance.
26-28	No remarks			
29	Margt Donnelly	May, 1849	. . .	20 ac cleared.
30	Jas. Donnelly . .	May, 1849	...	20 " "
31-35	No remarks.			
36	Louis Bellemore .	June, 1849	...	13 " "
37, 38	Vacant .			
39	Hugh Cameron	Sept , 1850		10 " "
40 42	Vacant.			
43, 44	John Emmerton	Nov , 1849	..	12 " "
45	Joseph Barker	Sept , 1849		7 " " { Clearings
46	C R Barker .	Sept., 1849	. .	7 " " { join.
47, 48	Louis Lizzars	Oct , 1848 ..		12 " "
49, 50	Alex St. Germain	. .	" not to be noticed "	.8 and 13 acres cleared.
51	Joseph Veyett .. .		" "	13 ac. cleared.
52	Joseph Ayotte	. . ...	" "	13 " "
53, 54	Abraham Holmes	May 4, 1849	. .	18 " "
55	Edward Sharman	July, 1851		8 " "
56	Levi Vaughan ..	Nov., 1850		7½ " " on south side
57	Edward Creeck	April, 1851		3 acres cleared.
58	John Inglis ..	Jan , 1851		4½ " "
59	James Cook	April, 1850		2½ pt. cleared.
60, 61	Eric McKenzie	—— 1850	.	6 acres cleared
62	Vacant			
63	James Sloane ..	May, 1849 .		10 " "
64	James Donnelly	. March, 1850	Log house .	..12 " " .
65	John Smith .	May 1, 1851	"	7 " "
66	Wm Harper	July 20, 1850	.	4 " "
67	— Devaline .	May, 1850	Log house	. 10 " "

The only other clearings in the township mentioned in these field notes are the following . On lots 20, 21 28 (Charles Richter), 29 (Fred Goesel), and 31 on Concession 12, and lots 40 and 41 (Malcolm McRae) on Concession 1.

however, was made as early as October, 1849, back in the township, these brave pioneers being Malcolm McRae and his son "Big" Duncan, Alex McRae and his two sons, "Red" Duncan and Donald-Buie, Finlay McLellan and their families. The land they took up was on the first concession five miles back from the lake. Of all the pioneers of Huron, Louis Bellemore is credited with being the earliest, he having in the year 1848 settled on lot 19, Lake Range, at the mouth of the Pine River. Here he had a tavern patronized by land-seekers, they being about the only species of travellers that ventured into the wilds of the county at that time. Bellemore sold out his squatter's rights to David Walden in the following year, when he moved north to lot 36, where he again opened a tavern, referred to in Chapter III. Among other of the earliest settlers on the lake shore might be mentioned the name of James Keys, who had squatted on lots 22 and 23. He was the first to fall a victim to the perils attending pioneer life in the settlement. His death came about in this wise: In August, 1851, he was engaged in taking a raft laden with supplies to Penetangore, his sole companion being his step-daughter, afterwards Mrs. Henry Teskey. He fell into the water, and although quickly pulled out, he could not be resuscitated. His widow sold the squatter's rights to John Hunter. There was also one Joseph Lindsay who met with the sad fate that has overtaken many a backwoodsman, being killed by the fall of a tree which he was engaged in felling. In the Pine River cemetery, on a tombstone more than half covered with drifting sand, there can yet be made out the words, "Joseph Lindsay—1853." His widow sold out her rights as a squatter in 1853 to Thomas Welsh.

The vicinity of the mouth of Pine River is said to have been, before man had marred it, one of the most beautiful spots to be found along the lake shore. The river's banks were timbered almost to the water's edge. To the north of the river was a grove of red pines that grew as if planted in an open park. What to-day is drifting sands was at that time covered with a carpet of vegetable mould studded with pine needles and patches of green moss, soft and enjoyable to walk upon. A sleigh track was cut through the woods of Ashfield in the winter of 1849-50 and the lake shore road through Huron was cut out in 1853, a substantial timber bridge at the same time being placed across Pine River. Thomas Blair was the contractor for the work done in this last-mentioned year. What a lovely drive it was along that road. On one hand, as seen through the

15

openings in the evergreens, was the seemingly limitless expanse of the waters of Lake Huron beating with rhythmical flow on the hard, sandy beach. On the other hand was the dark verdure of the evergreens, through which the road had been cut, and which filled the air with a resinous perfume mixed at times with that of a Balm of Gilead tree. In addition to this there was always that cool, exhilarating freshness of the breeze that had passed over the miles and miles of waters of Lake Huron. In some places deep sand made the road heavy, but this provided an excuse to slow up and be satiated with the beauty nature had so freely supplied. This road lost much of the travel which at one time passed over it when the Goderich road, extending north from Amberley, was opened.

As is elsewhere pointed out, the settlers who first peopled the county of Bruce were, as a whole, of numerous and varied vocations, and in regard to nationality they were pretty thoroughly mixed up. This heterogeneity served a good purpose in the making of the county. Huron Township received at one time, in the fall of 1852, a large group of settlers, sufficient if so allocated to have taken up every lot on three concessions, who differed in every respect from the foregoing. This was the Lewis settlement It consisted of one hundred and nine families who took up land in the centre of the township. These were all from the Island of Lewis, and had been evicted from their croftings by their landlord, Sir James ·Matheson. Laboring under the disadvantage of being able to speak English but imperfectly —Gaelic being their mother tongue, many, indeed, could speak no other—and whose calling was that of sailors or fishermen, they were utterly ignorant of how to set to work to clear up a bush farm, and lacked also the necessary experience how to work it after it had been cleared In addition to this, being settled close together they had consequently no opportunity to study the object lesson which a native Canadian backwoodsman in his daily task of chopping, logging and ploughing would have set before them Is it any wonder, then, when all these circumstances are considered, that the progress of the Lewis settlement was at the first slow.

The author has been favored by Mr. Angus Martyn, of Ripley, a son of one of the Highlanders from Lewis, with a short account of the movement which brought this large number of families to settle in Huron. The following is Mr. Martyn's account: " The Highlanders from Lewis, Rosshire, Scotland, who settled in Huron emigrated to this country in 1851. Two shiploads left Stornoway,

in Lewis, in that year. They were nine weeks and four days in crossing the Atlantic. They came on sailing vessels and landed at Quebec
on the 4th August, 1851. They then went by boat to Port St Francis,
where the party of emigrants divided, the majority going to the
county of Compton, Lower Canada, and the remainder went on the
same boat to Montreal, from there by another boat to Hamilton,
touching at Toronto. From August to December they remained in
Hamilton, the men working on the Great Western Railway, which
was then in course of construction. Smallpox broke out among them
in Hamilton and carried off many. In December they scattered,
going to Guelph, Stratford, Galt and Goderich All met in Goderich
in the summer of 1852. Some more emigrants from Lewis came to
Canada in 1852 and joined the others at Goderich in the fall of
that year, when all moved to Huron Township in the county of
Bruce. There were one hundred and nine families in all. The
names of the heads of the families are given in a footnote[1] A

[1] Names of the heads of families who settled on the 8th concession of
Huron : Roderick McDonald, John McDonald, Donald McDonald, (Yarrie)
John Martyn, Donald Martyn, Malcolm McDonald, John McDonald, Allan
McLay, Murdoch McLennan, Roderick McLennan, John McDonald, Malcolm
McDonald, Angus Murray, Donald McDonald, Murdoch McLean, John
McLeod, Charles McDonald, Donald Matheson, Donald McLeod, Murdoch·
Matheson, John McDonald, Malcolm McLennan, Sr , Malcolm McLennan,
Jr., Donald McLennan   (The McLennans came from Cape Breton.)
    Names of the heads of families who settled on the 7th concession of
Huron : Donald Smith, Angus Smith, Malcolm McLean, William McDonald,.
Christina Smith (widow), Murdoch McLeod (Shepherd), Malcolm McIver, .
Angus McIver, Angus McDonald, Donald McDonald (Councillor), John
McIver, James McIver, Donald McDonald, Allan McDonald, Donald
McDonald, Norman McLean, John McLean, Angus McDonald, Alexander
McDonald, Donald McDonald, Allan McLay, Angus McDonald, and John
McDonald (Keeper), and Angus Graham
    Names of the heads of families who settled on the 9th and 10th
concessions : Malcolm Campbell, Malcolm Smith, William Smith, Murdoch
McLeod, John McLeod, Malcolm McIver (Elder), William McLeod (10),
Donald McLeod, Malcolm McIver, Angus McFarlane (10), Kenneth Mc-
Donald, Alexander McKenzie (10).
    Names of the heads of families who settled on the 11th concession :
Donald McGregor, John McGregor, and Murdoch McGregor.
    Names of the heads of families who settled on the 5th concession :
Angus McDonald, John McDonald (Dorrie), Angus McKay, John McKay,
Angus McDonald, Murdoch McFarlane, Donald McLeod, Edward McLeod,
Malcolm McLeod, Donald McIver, Angus McArthur, Murdoch Martin, and
John McDonald.
    Names of the heads of families who settled on the 6th concession :
John McKay, Malcolm McKay, John McKay, Norman McKay, Angus
McKay, Murdoch McKay, Duncan McLeod, Malcolm McLeod, John Murray,
Donald McLeod, John McLeod (Elder), Donald McGregor, Malcolm Mc-
Gregor, Donald McLeod, John McArthur, Neil McArthur, Murdoch Mc-
Ritchie (from Cape Breton), John McLean, Malcolm McDonald, Angus

process of evicting by the proprietor of the island of Lewis was the cause of the emigration of this large number from one locality To smooth over the heartlessness of eviction the proprietor of the island offered a free passage to any part of Canada to any one who was willing to emigrate, and at the same time offered to purchase their horses, cattle and sheep if they could not otherwise get sale for them. The men among the passengers were all fishermen, as accustomed to the sea as the crews of the vessels on which they crossed the Atlantic, and so during a severe storm were able to render valuable aid in weathering the gale. One of the ships lost two of her masts during this storm and to ease her fifty tons of pig iron were cast overboard. During the first year of the settlement in Huron these hardy pioneers had to get their supplies, flour, etc., in Goderich, from which place they brought them on their backs, along the lake shore to the foot of the eighth concession, and thence home through the bush "

If these Highlanders came into the bush lacking in the knowledge possessed by an experienced backwoodsman, they were not lacking in physical strength and powers of endurance. It is related of one, who having purchased a hundredweight of flour at Kincardine, proceeded to carry it on his back the long fourteen miles to his shanty. He could have carried it in a bag, but on a barrel being offered him as a present, he placed the flour therein, and solely that he might have the barrel for use at home, shouldered it with the enclosed flour. Awkward as this was to carry he reached home in due time. When asked if he were tired after such exertion, he said, " Heugh no, but she'll be a little pit sore about the back."

After the group of names already mentioned of men who are to be classed as the earliest of the pioneers of Huron, there are many who settled there at a date early enough to enable them to experience a full share of the hardships of backwoods life, early enough to have the call made on them to put forth all the strength of their manhood to maintain their families and at the same time hew out for them a home out of the tangled woods which covered the township. Of this second group there was John and Archibald

McDonald, Murdoch McLeod, John McLeod, Angus McKay (Og), and John McKay.
Names of the heads of families who settled on the 4th concession of the township of Huron : Norman Smith, Murdoch McDonald, Donald McDonald (Sly), Malcolm Smith, Duncan McLennan and his five sons, Donald, Neil, John, Sr , Alexander and John, Jr , and John McLeod and son John.

Campbell, with their sister (now Mrs Joseph Barker of Kincardine), Cowan Keyes, Thomas Welsh, William Welsh,[1] J. W. Gamble, John Hunter, Thomas Henry, Alex. McCosh, and Archibald McDonald. All of these resided on the Lake Range. Of those who settled back from the lake, a few names only can be here mentioned. There were the Stanley and Collins families in the north-east part of the township; Thomas Wilson and Robert Montgomery, who filled municipal offices at different times, Ninian Hyslop, and John S. McDonald The last-mentioned settled on his lot in 1855, with no more of this world's possessions than the ordinary settler. Being a man of energy and ability, he soon came to the front, and, from being a township councillor, became reeve of the township, then warden of the county, and then represented the riding of Centre Bruce in Parliament from 1894 to 1898. Mr McDonald had his own share of the hardships of the early days. In speaking of them, he said:—[2]"We used a wecht in cleaning our first grain. This wecht was made from sheepskins, with the wool removed The skin was tacked on to a wooden rim, and was formed something like the end of a drum. We used this implement as a scoop to lift the wheat from the bin, and allowed the grain to fall from the wecht to a sheet laid on the ground, the wind cleaning the chaff from the wheat as the latter fell One day when we were about out of flour there was no wind to clean the grain; about dusk, however, the wind came up and I kept on cleaning, in the way I have described, by the light of the moon until two o'clock in the morning I did this after having threshed with a flail all day Before daylight I was off with the grist, so prepared, to the Harris' Mill, beyond Dungannon, twenty miles away All the settlers from about here took grists to this mill The grist was usually carried on a jumper, and sometimes it would not consist of more than three bags of wheat. The journey there was made in one day, and the wheat was ground in the mill while the owner spent the night in the tavern near by, the return journey being made the following day. This tavern was a log cabin, and in going to bed upstairs we had to climb a

---

[1]The author desires to express his thanks to Mr Welsh for a number of facts regarding the settlement of Huron township, which he has incorporated in this chapter, and to recommend to all who can do so the preservation of a series of letters on " The Settlement and the Woods of Our County," written by Mr. Welsh, which appeared in the *Kincardine Review* in the spring of 1904.

[2]Extract from the *Kincardine Review.*

ladder. The roof was just a little above our heads, and in the
morning the ceiling was coated with frost from the air breathed by
the men; our cowhide boots, in which we had tramped through
slush and water in going to the mill, and which had been thoroughly
soaked on our arrival, were frozen as stiff as bricks, so that we
could not get them on until after thawing them out by the side of the
stove."

There were many Highland Scotch settled in Huron other than
those from Lewis. The combination resulted in the number of
" Mac's " being in such excess, that nicknames had to be used to
designate the individual—such as little, big, red, black, long,
short, and other adjectives. It is said that in school section No. 5
the John McDonalds had to be separately designated by a letter of
the alphabet, as John A., John B , and so on, until John U. closed
the list. The Donald McDonalds were as numerous, and were
similarly treated, requiring all letters from " A " to " U " to distinguish one Donald from another

" Pine River " was the name of the first post-office established
in Huron   J W. Gamble was the first postmaster. This office
was not located where the present " Pine River " office is, but on the
lake shore, near the mouth of the river, and was opened in 1853.
The mails were delivered by the Goderich and Kincardine mail
carrier, who passed to and fro each way thrice a week on horseback.
The author remembers on one occasion in the fifties travelling for
company's sake with the mail carrier, each on horseback, and both
mere lads It was a warm summer morning as they left Pine River
for Kincardine, and the cool waters of the lake looked so tempting
that the despatch required in the conveyance of Her Majesty's mail
was forgotten for half an hour, while the two lads frolicked in the
water.

The first sawmill in Huron is said to have been built in 1855 at
Pine River by William Blair, and was run by his two sons, Thomas
and George. The mill and water privileges were purchased some
five years later by John Hicks, who had previously filled the position
of head miller for William Sutton at Kincardine. Mr. Hicks on
coming into possession added a grist mill to the plant These
mills were successfully run until a freshet, which occurred in 1868,
destroyed both dam and mills.

In 1856 Capt. Henry C. Gamble, an Irish gentleman of some
means, came to Pine River on a visit to his brother, J. W. Gamble.

The locality struck his fancy, and he decided to remain and do his
utmost to develop into a business centre the town plot at the mouth.
of the river, surveyed in 1855, which consisted of parts of lots 18
to 22 of the Lake Range. The survey was known as the Alma town
plot. Capt Gamble obtained a transfer of the rights to the east
half of lots 16 and 17 adjoining the Alma survey, and here he
proceeded to erect a saw and grist mill The government shortly
after commenced the erection of the lighthouse[1] at Pine Point. The
combination of this work with Capt. Gamble's efforts made quite a
stir for some time in the neighborhood of "The Point." Shortly
after the opening of the Goderich Road the Pine River post-office
was moved to its present more central locality. The loss of the office
was followed by the forwarding of a petition asking for a post-office
at "The Point," which was granted, and in 1860 Lurgan post-office
was there opened, but subsequently moved further north. The name
is that of a town in the north of Ireland, said to be the native place
of Capt Gamble. The attempt to develop a town at Alma or Lurgan
proved to be a complete failure. After the sinking of a large amount
Capt. Gamble gave up the attempt and returned to the Old Country

When the municipality of the united townships in the county of
Bruce was dissolved,[2] at the end of 1853, and six municipalities
formed out of it, the township of Huron was found to have a sufficiently large population and an aggregate assessment large enough
to be able to assume the responsibility of separate municipal existence,
unlike most of the other townships in the county, which had to unite
in partnerships of twos and threes The affairs of the young municipality in 1854, the first year of its existence, were in the hands of
a Township Council composed of William Blair, Robt. Huston,
William Wilson and Samuel Wright, over which John Hunter, as
reeve, presided; J. W Gamble acted as clerk and John Campbell as
treasurer. In a footnote[3] there is given the names of all who have
had the honor of the reeveship conferred upon them. In the year

[1]The Point Clark, or Pine Point, lighthouse commenced to show its
light in 1859 It is a circular stone building, 87 feet high The height of
the light above high-water is 93 feet, and is visible for fifteen miles.
The light is what is known as a revolving one, and shows a white light
every thirty seconds

[2]See Appendix F.

[3]Names of the reeves of the township of Huron from 1854 to 1906
inclusive : John Hunter, 1854. '63, Ninian Hyslop, 1855, Malcolm McLennan, 1856, '57; John Good, 1858, '59, '67; Robt Johnston, 1860, '62, '64,
'65, '66, '68, '69, '70, '77, John McLay, 1861; John Stewart, 1871, '72, '73,
'74; Thomas Yemen, 1875, '76; David Henderson, 1878, '79, '80, '81, '82,

1855 there appears in the minutes of the United Counties Council, January session, in the " Report on the Validity of the Election of Councillors," the following *re* " Certificate of the township clerk of Huron to the effect that Ninian Hyslop was duly elected town reeve. We find no evidence that the oath of qualification has been taken, nor is there any reason why this oath should be omitted." On the report being presented to the County Council the following motion to enable Mr. Hyslop to take his seat was carried, " That the affidavit of the clerk of the township of Huron to the effect that there were no parties rated in the township of Huron to a sufficient amount (£100) to enable them to take the oath of qualification is satisfactory."[1] The above incident is recorded to show the impoverished circumstances of the first settlers in the township. In a wealthy community such as now resides in Huron, it seems incredible that there was a time in the history of the township when there was not one ratepayer who had enough of worldly goods to be assessed for four hundred dollars

The post-office at Ripley was established in 1856 at lot 4, concession 8, township of Huron The first postmaster was M MacLennan,[2] He had the office for two years, and was succeeded by Thomas Harris, the office being then located at his house on lot 2, concession 8, Kinloss John Brown was the next postmaster, and the office was moved to lot 12, concession 7, Huron The next move of the post-office was

'83, John Ballantyne, 1884, '85, '86, '87; John S McDonald, 1888, '89, '90, '91, Robert Thompson, 1892, '93, '94, '95, '96, Richard Robertson, 1897, '98, '99, 1900, '02; G H Humphreys, 1901, James Brown, 1903, '04, '05, '06

[1]Mr Joseph Barker, who succeeded Mr. Gamble, in 1855, to the office of township clerk, wrote to the author in regard to this incident as follows : " The council-elect for 1855 were all fresh men, and the clerk, J W Gamble, felt sore and refused to give Ninian Hyslop the certificate required to enable him to take his seat , because of such refusal the Council bounced Mr. Gamble and appointed the writer as clerk, and requested me to go with the reeve-elect to Goderich and explain the reason why Mr Hyslop could not get his certificate from Mr Gamble. The Counties Council, after hearing my statement, decided, by resolution, that Mr. Hyslop might take his seat on my giving certificate, which was done.''

[2]Malcolm MacLennan was long connected with the township of Huron. He was reeve of the township in 1856, '57, was a member of the Township Council for two other years, and filled the office of township clerk for ten years He came, in July, 1852, from Cape Breton, with his father, to Goderich In the following year they took up land on the 8th concession of Huron It was not until January, 1856, he settled on this lot, having followed school-teaching in the interim He was the third person who filled the position of teacher of the Kincardine Public School—this was in 1854 Mr MacLennan some years ago moved to Algoma, where he still resides. A post-office there bears his name

a permanent one. Donald McDonald, the next postmaster, resided on lot 15, concession 7, and there the village bearing the name of the post-office developed. The successor in office to Mr McDonald was Paul D. McInnes. On the death of the latter the office was given to his widow. "Ripley"[1] was the name conferred upon this post-office in 1856, and was retained until 1874, the year Paul D. McInnes was appointed postmaster. He, wishing to have a name somewhat consonant with the native land of the majority of the population, agitated for a change of name, which was granted, and "Dingwall" became the name of the post-office. But as the railway station was called Ripley, and as this name had been associated for so, many years with the post-office, it was found necessary to revert to the old name and in 1880 the post-office again bore the name of Ripley, which it has retained. When the railway company made Ripley a station, business soon focussed there. The year 1874, which witnessed the opening of the railway, also witnessed the erection of a number of buildings at Ripley. In the following year a visitor reported the village as having both a grist and a sawmill, six stores and a Presbyterian church Shortly after this the town hall was built, and also three grain storehouses required by grain buyers, whose efforts made Ripley a good grain market. As the village developed the desire was felt by the inhabitants to have complete control over local improvements. To obtain this the County Council was petitioned to create Ripley into a police village, which was granted. The first Board of Trustees were elected in January, 1898. For years the banking of the village, and largely of the township, was done with a firm of private bankers, S. T. Jackson & Co This business was purchased in 1903 by the Bank of Hamilton, who retained Mr. Jackson as its agent. In 1904 the Trader's Bank, on the outlook for a good opening for an agency, selected Ripley and opened an office there, thus giving the village banking accommodation not possessed by many places of larger size A printing press for job work was started in the village by H. P. Chapman about 1889 In 1892 he commenced the issue of a newspaper called *The Enquirer*, which name was changed some two years later to that of *The Ripley Express*, a newspaper that still flourishes.

The two Presbyterian churches at Ripley had as a common origin the first efforts to hold religious services when the settlement was but young. In 1855 a catechist labored in Huron holding services

[1] "Ripley" is the name of a town in Derbyshire, England.

in the Gaelic language These were held in private houses or barns, according to circumstances. In time the catechists were succeeded by students and probationers, and efforts were then made to organize a congregation and erect a church. These efforts were so successful that in 1858 a church was built on lot 14 on the 6th concession. It was built of hewed logs, and was supposed to seat four hundred persons. The congregation which worshipped there was one in a union charge, the other congregation being in the township of Ashfield. It was some years before a minister was regularly settled over these two congregations, the first being the Rev. Alexander Grant. The total stipend paid him was but $700, half of which was paid by each congregation. Services were held in each church on alternate Sundays. As the congregations grew it was decided to make of each a separate charge. This was in 1875. Rev. Mr. Grant continued with the Ashfield congregation, leaving the Huron congregation to seek a new minister. In trying to decide who this should be a split in the congregation occurred The majority decided to build a church at Ripley. This they did, erecting a frame building (subsequently veneered with brick) calculated to seat about four hundred and fifty worshippers. This congregation was known as that of Knox Church, while the old church and congregation bore the name of the Huron Church. The Rev. Adam McKay was the minister called to Knox Church. His successors have been the Rev. Alexander Sutherland, the Rev. C Sinclair, the Rev. F J Maxwell, and the Rev. W. A. Bremner. The Huron church called the Rev. A. F. McQueen, who remained in charge until 1893. The Rev. R. McLeod is his successor. This congregation in 1886 built a new church in Ripley, a commodious building of brick, with a seating capacity for five hundred, the cost being about $4,500. Before the congregation deserted their old church, services used to be held at Ripley, in the town hall, on Sunday afternoons, in the English language. Services in both Gaelic and English are still conducted in Huron church. In Knox Church only English is used.

The sturdy type of settlers who cleared and settled the township of Huron have been succeeded by a generation who well maintain the standard of their forbears. Those of them who have sought a wider field of action have as a rule been successful, and have made for themselves a name, while they who remain on the old homesteads may be depended upon to keep their native township in the front rank of the municipalities of the county of Bruce

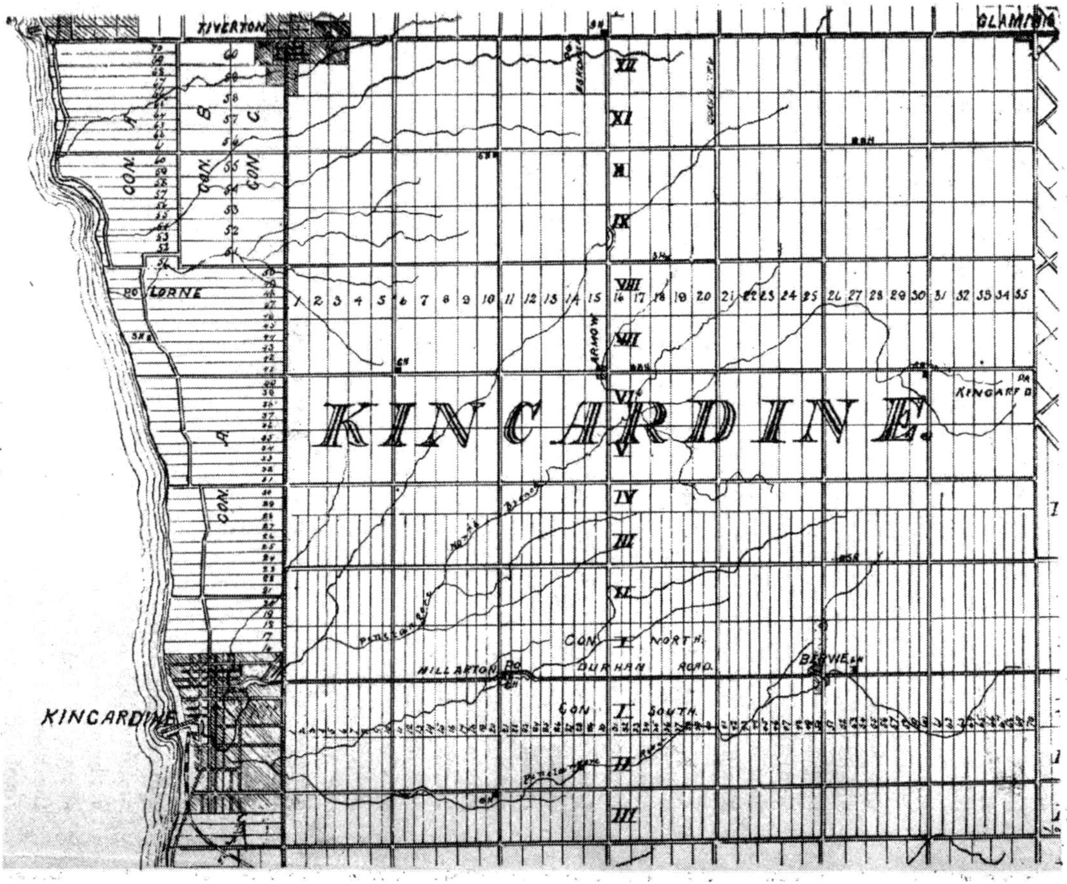

KINCARDINE

BRANT

TIVERTON

KINGARF B

CON B

BERVIE

CON. I NORTH

DURHAM ROAD

CON. I SOUTH

MILLARTON

CON C

CON B

LORNE

CON A

CON

CON F

KINCARDINE

XII XI X IX VIII VII VI V IV III

1 2 3 4 5 6 7 8 9 10 11 12 13 14 15 16 17 18 19 20 21 22 23 24 25 26 27 28 29 30 31 32 33 34 35

CHAPTER XXXII.

TOWNSHIP OF KINCARDINE.[1]

EXTRACT FROM THE REPORT OF COUNTY VALUATORS, 1901.

" This township has a very considerable portion of rough land, broken by creeks that are very injurious, rendering agricultural pursuits difficult, many farms with scarcely a level field upon them These remarks apply to that portion of the township south of the 6th concession There is considerable light, sandy land in this township. Two strips cross from north to south and average from one and a half to two miles in width. There is also considerable light and stony land on the Lake Range. In buildings this township has not kept pace with adjoining municipalities, excepting the northern portion, which will compare very favorably with other parts of the county. The rate per acre for Kincardine township is $32 45 The rate per acre of village property in this township is about 34 cents. ''

THE survey of Kincardine Township was not made, like that of most of the townships in the county, as a whole and at one time, but in three sections and in different years   As related in Chapter II, in 1847 Alex. Wilkinson, P.L.S, surveyed the Lake Range lots, and in 1848-49 A. P Brough, P.L.S, laid out the Durham Road and three concessions to the north and south of it. Then followed, in 1850, the survey of the remaining portion of the township, which included concessions four to twelve. This last survey was made by J. W. Bridgland, P.L.S., under circumstances mentioned in Chapter V. The lands in Kincardine were among those set apart as school lands, the price of which at first was fixed by the Crown at 12s. 6d., but subsequently reduced to 10s. In Appendix H is given a copy of the advertisement offering the lands in the township for sale,[2] which were among the first in the county offered for sale.

[1] " Kincardine '' is one of the titles of the Governor-General of Canada in office at the time the survey of the " Queen's Bush '' was made, viz, the Earl of Elgin and Kincardine.

In the outline map of the proposed townships in the " Queen's Bush '' referred to in Chapter II the name first written as that of this township was " Lambert,'' while the name " Kincardine '' appears on that now known as " Wallace,'' in the county of Perth These two names there show as being crossed out and the present names written in with lead-pencil.

[2] The entries in the books of the Crown Land Department show that the first sale was made on August 19th, 1851, to Sam Splan, of lot 26, concession 3, S D R

429

For the first ten years of its history Kincardine was the leading township in the county of Bruce. This was brought about by the comparative readiness of access thereto by water, giving it not only the earliest of the pioneer settlers, but also the largest number of them. That it was the senior township in the pioneer days is borne out by the corporate name by which the municipality of the county was then known, namely, "The United Townships of Kincardine and the remaining townships within the county of Bruce." Leading, therefore, as Kincardine did, in settlement and also in municipal matters, the author has, in the writing of this History, been led to record, in Chapters III , IV. and V., relating to the history of the county at large, many early events especially associated with Kincardine, and the reader of these pages of the township's history is asked to recall what is written relating to it in the above-mentioned chapters; and as until January 1st, 1858, the village of Penetangore was unincorporated and formed part of the township of Kincardine, the history of the village at first was that of the township, so that the chapter following this, on the town of Kincardine, must also be consulted to obtain a complete historical narrative of the township.

The first settlers to enter the township, as well as the first in the county,·were Allan Cameron and Wm Withers, who in the spring of 1848 settled at the mouth of the Penetangore River, months before the town-plot of Kincardine was surveyed During the following summer and fall, Donald, Alexander and John McCaskill, James and Alexander Munroe and some others settled on the Lake Range and on the North Line. At the same time the Durham Line received its first settlers in the persons of John C. Digman and Major William Daniel.

There was a steady inflow of settlers into Kincardine in 1849, who squatted on lands not yet offered for sale. Along the lake shore farm lots were taken up by George and Alex Ross, George and Alex. Murray, James, Duncan, Robert and John Rowan, Malcolm, John and Murdoch McLeod and Archibald Sinclair. About this time also the "free grant" lots received many settlers—so many, in fact, that only a few names can be here mentioned, such as George Ryckman, Samuel Taylor, William Fanning, Robert Stewart, John Sellery, William Millar, Robert Brown, Thomas Harris, John Hays, Nicol McIntyre, William (Dalhousie) Miller and W. L. Armstrong, all residing on the south side of the Durham Road. On the north side there was Jacob Latschaw, John Mosely, William G. Cuyler, John

Hicks, William and Henry Daniel, Patrick and Daniel Kehoe, Frank Bone, Andrew Horne, Samuel McCloskey, Samuel Colwell and Samuel McLellan. The North and South Lines each similarly received a contingent of settlers, among them being Archibald Robinson, John McCullough, John Evans, Andrew Gardiner and Robt., Alex., Donald and Kenneth McKenzie, who settled on concession 2, N.D.R., and George and John Morrison, William Withers, S. Clements, Robert, George and Andrew Atcheson, S. Shelton, the Emmersons and Touchbournes who took up land on concession 2, S.D R. As the township from concession 4 north was not surveyed until 1850, settlers did not penetrate into the centre of the township before that date. The first to do so is said to have been Harvey Wilson, who squatted on lot 17, concession 7. After the lands in Kincardine were offered for sale in 1851 its settlement was rapid. A large portion of the settlers who came in then were Highland Scotch, either by birth or descent. Among the many fine types of settlers and citizens of this stock who helped in the making of Kincardine Township, the author would prominently place the Rev. William Fraser. Active in municipal matters, he was elected to fill the office of reeve on three occasions; he was also local superintendent of public schools for the western district of the county for six years. His enterprising spirit led him to erect the first mills in the township outside of the village. Mr. Fraser's influence and example was wholesome and tended to setting high the standard of citizenship Mrs. John Reekie, of Margaret, Man., has supplied the author with some facts regarding the Rev William Fraser, which he is pleased to insert here. They are as follows:

"In the summer of 1850 the Rev. W. Fraser, Baptist minister, resigned his charge at Breadalbane, Glengarry, being desirous of procuring land for his boys. With this end in view he travelled through a good part of the Western States, as well as sections of Canada, but finally located at Kincardine, as in his estimation it was the most promising of all places he had seen He first settled on a farm adjoining the town, but afterwards moved to what is now known as Lorne, where he built both a saw and a grist mill, the former in 1851 and the latter in 1854. In those early days religious privileges were very few, so Mr. Fraser opened his own house for church service, preaching every Sunday two sermons, one in Gaelic and one in English; the service usually lasted three hours These services were held first in his own home at Kincardine, afterwards

at Mr. Rowan's at Stoney Island, then at his own house at Lorne,
at Mr John Patterson's near Tiverton, at the first school house at
Tiverton, and finally in the church built in that village. Mr. Fraser
walked five miles and a half to Tiverton every Sunday, preached
three hours and then walked back again This he did for years, all
without fee or reward save the blessing of the Master, whose he was
and whom he served. Mr Fraser was for some time the only one
nearer than Goderich that was authorized to perform the marriage
ceremony.[1] Sometimes he had to travel several miles on foot for
this purpose, and considered himself amply recompensed when a
couple of dollars were pressed into his hand by the happy bride-
groom Good old man, he rests from his labors and has his reward.
He sleeps in Tiverton cemetery with many of his flock about him.
His chief monument is the congregation he was so instrumental in
gathering together "[2]

While referring to the Highland Scotch settlers, so numerous and
influential in Kincardine, the memory of the author reverts back to
a long list of prominent men who had the prefix "Mac" to their
surname   McLeod, McDonald, McKenzie, McKay, McKinnon,
McLean, McLennan and others, and he feels at a loss whom to par-
ticularize. There was Murdoch (Elder) McLennan and Donald his
namesake on the same concession, J. P. McIntyre, for seven years
reeve; Murdoch McLeod, also a reeve, and later township treasurer
for years. There are the McDougald brothers on "the tenth"—
Malcolm, Allan, John, Donald, Charles and Neil, sons of Donald
McDougald   The McEwens on "the boundary," who have sent
several of their sons into the ministry; and many others, as well as
those mentioned who were not "Macs," the Campbells, Mathesons,
Frasers and Rowans, men who have done their part faithfully.
Besides the Highland Scotch, the township had among its original
settlers many fine men of Lowland Scotch, English, and North of
Ireland origin   Of Lowland Scotch lineage there was William Millar,
who gave his name to a post-office on the Durham Road, and who
was reeve or deputy reeve of the township for over a dozen years; his
namesake also at Bervie, the owner of one of the finest farms in the
township, William and John Reckie, the founders of Armow, and

[1]James Millar, who had charge of Mr Sutton's mill from 1854-'56, says
that one day a young man and woman came in with a small grist. Leaving
it to be ground, they started afoot and walked the four miles of rough
road to the Rev. Mr. Fraser's, were married, came back for the grist, and
then off to their shanty in the bush A marked contrast to the extended
honeymoon trips of the present day.

[2]The Rev Wm Fraser was a native of Invernesshire, where he was
born in 1800. His death occurred August 30th, 1883.

Forbes Robertson. While as representative of those of English birth there might be mentioned William and George Daniel, William Withers, Samuel Avery and John Sellery, men who did yeoman service in the development of the township. It is in the vicinity of Bervie that we find the largest number of North of Ireland men, and the fine farms they hewed out of the bush speak volumes as to their worth as settlers.

As in all backwoods settlements, the roads, so-called, in pioneer days followed a blaze made by an axe on the trees. Settlers landing at Kincardine and seeking to reach the Durham line left the town-plot by way of Russell Street. Major William Daniel relates the following recollections in regard to this entrance to the township: "I remember when Frank Bone moved in, he had a sleigh-load of furniture, provisions, a stove, besides various boxes and bags. The blaze led down the hill past the English church There were no roads or bridges; it was a case of climb mounds and slide down hollows. Mr. Bone found it so rough that he was afraid to drive his horses down the hill, so after unhitching them he let the sleigh go down alone. Before reaching the bottom it capsized and scattered the load broadcast." Of his own experience Major Daniel says: "The first load I hauled in was by sleigh in winter time. I had to drive the horses through the rivers, as the ice was not strong enough to bear them. It was late in the day when we reached my shanty, and wet as the horses were I had to picket them to the trees all night without anything to eat." Of a slightly later date the Major says: "At Lot 19 on the Durham Road there is a hill, at the foot of it the road was crossed by a small stream. The oxen, by constantly slipping down, had at this point cut the road into a slough that was about three feet deep and thirty feet in length. Coming down this hill ox-sleighs would shoot out of sight in the mud and water. Sometimes the drivers would be unfortunate enough to tumble into the mud, and on passing my place, some rods farther on, presented a sorry sight."

The promise of the Government to open up the Durham Road was carried out, as far as Kincardine was concerned, in the summer of 1851, George Jackson, the Crown land agent, reporting under date of July 12th of that year that the Durham line was opened, cleared and causewayed.[1] The reader of to-day should not be carried away with the thought that the work reported as finished furnished easy access to the back country, or enabled travel to be made with

[1] The cost of this work, extending a little over nine miles, was £215

comfort. Grading was not called for in the road contracts[1] nor even
were the larger stumps of trees removed, and the path twisted and
turned about these stumps. The black mould of the woods, that
formed the surface of the road, retained moisture and was readily
transformed into mud. There were no side ditches to drain off the
water, so it remained until by the absorption of the soil and the evap-
oration caused by the heat of the sun the mud dried up, as it sometimes did, about the middle of the summer. The author has not
the data giving the year of the opening of the " base line," but is of
the opinion that it was not opened until 1853-54, under the supervision of David Gibson, Superintendent of Colonization Roads, as
mentioned in Chapter V. The traffic to the north from Kincardine
village was by the old lake shore road. This pursued a sinuous way
along the beach as far as McCaskill's Bay, where it mounted the high
bank and continued north along it as far as Stoney Island, where it
came down to the beach. After passing the few houses there it
entered the small timber, through which, at a short distance from the
lake, the roadway was cut, continuing therein until Inverhuron was
reached, the only clearing passed being John McRae's. This was a
pleasant road to travel over on a bright, sunny summer day. The
smell of the woods, the cool, fresh air of the lake, the dry, soft soil,
made walking enjoyable, while the song of birds and the murmur of
the waves lapping on the pebbly beach near-by combined to give one,
during a walk along this part of the road, the consciousness that it
was happiness to live and enjoy these charms of nature. The present
Lake Shore Road, a continuation of the main street of the town of
Kincardine, was opened about the year 1858 by consent of the owners
of the various farms through which it is laid out. Prior to that, a
foot-path along the fences existed, which was used by pedestrians.
Some delay occurred in obtaining from all the proprietors a gift of the
right-of-way, but, as far as the author recollects, no compensation was
allowed to any of them for the land surrendered.

The municipal life of each local municipality has received some
notice in this History. To do the same in respect to Kincardine
Township means that some of the facts given in Chapter IV. and elsewhere must be repeated, but to do justice to the history of the township the narrative of its municipal life must be related, even if some
repetitions occur. The occasion for such repetitions is the unique

[1]See a footnote in Chapter V. for requirements of contracts for opening
up the Durham Road. The names of the contractors are to be found in
a second footnote in the same chapter

position Kincardine occupied as the mother municipality of the county as it was originally constituted. From it, by a process similar to that to be witnessed in an apiary, the several townships swarmed off from the parent hive to exist in future as separate municipalities. Kincardine, as the name of a municipality, dates back to January 1st, 1852. As stated elsewhere, the full title of the municipality was, " The United Townships of Kincardine and the Remaining Townships in the County of Bruce." This union of eleven townships existed during 1852 and 1853.[1] On January 1st, 1854, a general shake-up of the municipal units within the county took place,[2] the townships of Bruce and Kinloss alone remaining united for municipal purposes with Kincardine. After the lapse of one year Kinloss retired from this union, while Bruce remained united to Kincardine until January 1st, 1856, since which date Kincardine has existed as a separate municipality. Nevertheless the township has lost in territory since then, through the incorporation of Kincardine village (January 1st, 1858), and of Tiverton village in 1879. In a footnote[3] are to be found the names of the various reeves who presided over the Council Board from 1852 to 1906.

Besides Kincardine and Tiverton the township had at one time another village of which great hopes were entertained, namely, Stoney Island, or Port Head. Owing to the shelter afforded to vessels by the small stony island, and the possibility of constructing a breakwater and harbor on a projecting reef, Captain Duncan Rowan, who owned the land in the vicinity, sought there to develop a town. With this object in view he, in the summer of 1856, had lots 32, 33 and 34 on the Lake Range surveyed into village lots. Ere this date, at the island a wharf had been built which faced the mainland; alongside it was a storehouse used for the purpose of storing freight delivered by the steamer *Ploughboy* on its regular trips. John McLeod had a store on the beach; William and James Baird built a good-sized steam sawmill on the hill, and a post-office,

---

[1]The names of the members of the Township Council and of its officers, amount of taxes levied, etc , are recorded in Chapter IV

[2]See Appendix F

[3]Names of the reeves of the township of Kincardine : William Rastall, 1852, '54, part of 1857; Rev Wm Fraser, 1853, part of 1858, part of 1859; Malcolm McPherson, 1855; David McKendrick, 1856, part of 1857; Archibald Leitch, part of 1858; Wm. Millar, part of 1859, 1860 to 1870; Thomas Blair, 1871, '72; John Corbett, 1873 to 1880, and 1886; M McKinnon, 1881, '82; Wm Reekie, 1883, '84, '85; Thomas Bradley, M D , 1887, '89, '90, '91, '92; L T. Bland, 1888, '93, '94, '95, '96; Leonard Shewfelt, 1897, '98; Robert Johnston, 1899, 1900; F Colwell, 1901, '02, '03, '04; John Evans, 1905, '06

called Port Head, was opened in 1857. For a time the prospects of the little burg were bright, but in the fall of 1857 an unusually severe storm carried away the wharf and storehouse with its contents. This catastrophe proved a death-blow to Port Head. The mill was closed down in 1858, Mr. McLeod moved his store, building and stock, to Kincardine, and rapidly the village faded away. Captain Rowan lost heavily by this venture.[1]

As the settlers along the Durham line saw Cowan Keyes carrying Her Majesty's mail, slung over his shoulder, on his wearisome tramps to and fro between Penetangore and Durham, they quickly arrived at the conclusion that with very little extra cost to the Province there might be opened, for their convenience, a post-office somewhere between Kincardine and Greenock. This the Department acquiesced in, and in 1853 a post-office named Bervie[2] was opened on lot 53, concession 1, S D.R., of which Nicol McIntyre was appointed post-master, an office he held until his death nearly fifty years later. The post-office, of course, gave a name to the locality, and it seemed but natural that a village should there spring up Both the 50th and 60th side-road corners put forth efforts to have the village. At the last-mentioned corner John McKinney had a tavern, and near-by, through his efforts, a Presbyterian church[3] was erected. At the other

[1] Captain Duncan Rowan was a native of Argyleshire, Scotland, where he was born in October, 1822. He inherited an instinct for sailing from his father, who claimed to have piloted the first steamboat that steamed on the Clyde Captain Rowan, along with his brother, John, settled at Stoney Island in February, 1849, as is narrated in Chapter III. In the following year he forsook farming to take command of a small schooner, the "Mary Ann," which he sailed during the seasons of 1850, '51. Following that, he commanded the schooner "Emily," 1852-'55; the steamer "Ploughboy" in 1856, '57; the "Islander," 1858, '59, the "Kaloolah" in 1860, the "Valley City" in 1861, '62; then the "Bruce," the "Silver Spray," and the "Horton." He closed his career as a sailor in 1871 and retired to his farm Ultimately he moved to Kincardine, where he died, July 20th, 1903 In 1852 he married Miss McLean She sailed with him on the lake for years Her manner, so quiet, retiring and ladylike, would not lead a stranger to suspect that she possessed a knowledge of seaman-ship and of skill as a wheelsman which was exceptional and unexpected in a woman and which in emergencies proved of great service. On the occasion of the collision of the "Silver Spray" with another steamer in the St. Clair River, Captain Rowan was instrumental in rescuing thirty-nine persons, who but for his efforts would have been drowned Between Captain Rowan and the author there existed a warm, appreciative friendship, extending over nearly half a century, the memory of which the latter will ever cherish The hearty Highland welcome and honest handshake he extended to his friends was characteristic of the man—a man known to all travellers who came to the county of Bruce before the day of railroads.

[2] Named after a sea-coast town in Kincardineshire, Scotland.

[3] The Rev. Walter Inglis held services there The building was of frame, about 30 x 50 feet, placed broadside to the road, from which two doorways gave entrance A few marble gravestones in what was the graveyard are all that now marks the spot

corner a store and a sawmill were to be found, and gradually at this point the village of Bervie developed, the school-house, the Church of England, the Methodist church and the Orange Hall being the earliest public buildings erected. At one time Bervie had two sawmills, a planing mill and a grist mill, but it is not as well off to-day in the matter of industries It has three handsome churches and is the centre of trade for a large section of the farming community. One of its merchants, William Henderson, has been in business there for over thirty years. Its physician, Dr. Thomas Bradley, had been a resident of Bervie since 1861.

The little village of Armow, in the centre of the township, had as its founder William Reekie, who in 1854 there built a saw and grist mill. In September, 1857, a post-office was opened bearing the name of Reekie, with Joseph Shier as postmaster In 1868 he resigned the position, and the office was closed. In the following year the post-office was reopened under the name of Armow, with Caleb Bennet as postmaster. About the same time the first store at this point was opened by Alex. Gardner As the town hall is at Armow it is quite proper to call it the hub of the township.

A portion of the township bears the nickname "Egypt" Mrs. John Reekie gives the origin of the name as follows· "That part of the tenth concession that lies east of the 20th side-line was named 'Egypt' through a Mr. Bell, who was perhaps the first pathmaster appointed in that section of the township. He was such a hard taskmaster that he was called 'Pharaoh,' and the section over which he presided was named 'Egypt.' He was ever after known as 'the King of Egypt.' That part of the 'Tenth' between the 20th and the 15th side-roads was known as the 'Wilderness and Red Sea,' as it was rough and swampy. West of the 15th side-road it was called 'Canaan,'." "Pope" George Daniel gives a different account of the origin of "Egypt," as follows: "In 1859, Starvation Year, I was in the Township Council. Corn had been purchased to meet the needs of the settlers for food, the Council met to distribute the corn, which we arranged should be divided, an equal portion going to each polling subdivision. The southern part of the township was well settled, the northern part was not. The result was that the man living in the north received seven bushels to the southern man's three. As a result corn was none too plentiful in the south, but there was plenty in the north—'there was corn in Egypt.' That is how the name originated" Some old settlers say that the name was common as

early as 1853, if so, Mrs. Reekie's account seems to be the probable
one.

The first public school in the county was opened in 1851 at Kincardine, while it was still a part of the township. For some years
the increase in the number of schools was slow, there being in 1855
but four schools in the township; three of these were built of logs,
and one only, that in the village, was of frame. The school population in that year was but 540. With a large increase of population
in the following years came the demand for more schools In 1863
there were nine schools, and in 1870 the number had increased to
fourteen, the same number as is within the township to-day. As may
be said generally of the public schools in the county, the schools in
Kincardine have done good work, e g , school section No. 5, on the
seventh concession, claims to have had, in about thirty years, eighteen
of its pupils enter the teaching profession, pressing on, two of these
entered the ministry, and two others the practice of medicine; which
certainly is a good record for a country school. Among the many
prominent sons of the township who received their primary education
in its public schools, the two following might be mentioned: The Rt.
Rev Isaac O. Stringer, Bishop of Selkirk, and Lieut -Col. Hugh
Clark, M P.P. Of the first-mentioned it may be said that the con-
secrated, self-sacrificing life and work of this faithful missionary
and his wife[1] among the Esquimaux in the regions within the Arctic
Circle is something that has brought honor to the cause so dear to his
heart, as well as to his native county, and which his church has wisely
recognized in conferring upon him a diocese which affords opportunities for the further exercise of that selfsame spirit of Christian
service which he has shown in the past. The author regrets that he
is compelled to omit, as too numerous to be mentioned, the other sons
of the township who have come to the front in life's struggle among
surroundings far away from the scenes of their boyhood. How many
there are, may be imagined by a comparison of the several census
returns as given in Appendix L. There the fact is revealed that of all
the townships in the county, Kincardine alone had a smaller population in 1901 than it had in 1861, and 1,651 less than in 1881. " Where
has the population gone?" is but a natural question. Ask the Western
States and our own Western Provinces. There, in numerous prominent positions, as well as on ranches, farms and mines, are to be found
the " Old Boys " of Kincardine Township, with a warm, warm place
in their hearts for the place of their birth.

[1]Also a native of the county of Bruce

CHAPTER XXXIII.

TOWN OF KINCARDINE.[1]

In proceeding to the narrative of Kincardine's history, it is with the great advantage of a description of the place as it appeared fresh from nature's hand, which gives the reader an opportunity of comparing the town as it is at the present time with its pristine aspect, and, if pensively inclined, to contemplate what has been wrought during a half century to make or mar The description of Kincardine above referred to is A. P. Brough's report to the Commissioner ·of Crown Lands of the survey of the town plot, which was made in 1849, and which, with some slight omissions, is here given at length:

" The town of Penetangore embraces a tract of land 110 chains in length, with an average width of 93 chains, and contains about 1,023 acres divided into building and park lots. It is situated on Lake Huron at the western terminus of the Durham Road, on a river of the same name, which here empties itself into Lake Huron. The name Penetangore is a corruption of the Indian name Na-Benem-tan-gaugh, signifying ' the river with the sand on one side,'[2]

[1] The reader will please consult a footnote at the opening of Chapter XXXII. as to the origin of the name " Kincardine " Kincardine at first was known as Penetangore, which name was bestowed at the time of its survey into a town plot, being derived from the river of that name that there finds its way into the lake. The settlement which was early formed there came to be' known by the name of the township, and Kincardine being a word that fitted more easily an English tongue than did the long Indian word of Penetangore, it gradually grew into common use and was chosen to designate the post-office when it was established in 1851. Both names were in current use until the settlement was incorporated as a village in 1858. An interchangeable use of the two names was common and will also be found in this History. Penetangore was retained as the name of the port by the Customs Department until, by Order-in-Council, 8th October, 1875, " Kincardine, late Penetangore," was constituted a Port of Entry and a Warehousing Port

[2] In the Geological Report of work done in this part of the province in 1848, the Penetangore River is referred to as the " Big Pine River," and further says : " The epithet ' Big,' however, is probably intended to qualify the wood rather than the water ; the surface is thickly grown over with pine of large size " The mouth of the river at that time was situated about 100 yards south of where the railway station is now. On one side was the clay bluff and on the other a sand dune, hence the Indian name.

The lake at Penetangore is bordered by a sandy beach about three chains in width and which is skirted by a bank from 4 to 10 feet in height, on the top of which a narrow strip of table land three to four chains in width occurs, and along which Saugeen and Goderich Streets run, there then occurs a higher bank of from 60 to 80 feet elevation over the lake, and which appears to have formed the original and permanent boundary to the waters of Lake Huron. Having ascended this bank, the country presents a level surface, constituting a table land of a dry, sandy loam soil and admirably adapted for building on. It is almost entirely free from swamp, and the whole included space may be considered as entirely available for the purposes for which it was intended; both from its elevated situation, the dryness of its soil and the purity of the water, it may be regarded as an exceedingly healthy situation for a town and free from ague and other diseases that new towns in this climate are often subject to

"The river Penetangore is exceedingly serpentine in its course and runs through a broad valley composed of rich flats, dry for the most part, and which lie at a depth of 50 to 60 feet below the natural surface of the adjoining table land. There are numerous springs of pure water issuing from the high banks over the valley, and the whole tract is intersected at several points by small streams. The river is composed of two main branches which unite at Victoria Street; they are of nearly similar capacities, about 70 feet in width with an average depth above the point of junction of 3 feet. During very dry summer weather the water in these channels becomes very low, but at all other seasons of the year they contain an abundant supply of water. From the present sawmill at 'Huron Terrace' down to the reserve for basin there is an average depth of 8 feet and a width of 64 feet; from there to the mouth it is shallow and may be considered useless for any purposes of navigation. The mouth itself is very narrow and generally contains only one foot of water, and when strong westerly winds blow, the shifting of the sands causes it to fill up and the water seeks some other outlet into the lake To meet this defect I have proposed to make a new cut at the large bend in the river at the end of Saugeen Street, where there is 8 to 10 feet of water. The river at this point approaches within 4 1-2 chains of the lake, the expense of the cut would be trifling, and by carrying out two paralled piers into the lake to about 18 feet of water, I conceive that all impediments from the shifting of the sands would be avoided and a safe, easy access to the town accomplished.

"On the inside I have made a reserve for a small basin of 5 1-2 acres in extent, should the importance of the place justify the outlay for the construction of it The ground is composed of low flats, and

is situated at the foot of Russell Street on Huron Terrace, and as
the river in its natural state is very narrow, such a basin is absolutely necessary to accommodate any considerable amount of trade;
and as the country in the rear of Penetangore is a noble tract for
agricultural purposes, it may be expected that at no distant day
Penetangore will become an important shipping port for agricultural produce.

"The timber within the town reserve consists of beech, maple,
elm and hemlock chiefly, and a few oak are met with on the north
side of the town, but there is no pine of any consequence with the
exception of a narrow belt of small red pine on the margin of the
beach, that must prove of much advantage to the first settlers, but
is of no importance as an article of trade.

"There are three mill-sites laid off within the town reserve, the
lowest on the river being the present sawmill lately erected by Mr.
Withers. It is a substantial, well-framed building, and was in full
operation during the last summer and fall; and Mr. Withers informed me that it was his intention to build a grist mill during
the current season, so as to have it in operation by the summer of
1851. Mr. Withers proposes to have 7 1-2 feet of head water to
supply his mills, and by allowing him to raise his dam so as to obtain
that head there will be no impediment caused by back water to the
efficient working of the other mills, situated the one on lot No. 4
on Park Street, and the other on park lot No. 2 on Wellington
Avenue; the former mill site had an elevation of 13 1-4 feet above
the bed of the flume at the sawmill owned by Mr. Withers, and the
mill site on lot No. 2 Wellington Avenue, has an elevation of 11 1-2
feet above the same point.

"I have reserved park lot No. 9 on the east side of Park Street,
five acres in extent, as a public burial ground for the use of the town.
I had no directions in my instructions to do so, but the matter was
so pleasing to the settlers and is in itself of so much importance,
that I should hope the Department will give the sanction to it.

"I have made no reserve for churches or school-houses, as I
consider that any of the building lots would suffice for that purpose, and parties wishing to erect churches, by applying to the
Department will have no difficulty, I conceive, in procuring suitable
sites, either gratis or at a moderate purchase

"The river Penetangore is so winding in its course that most
of the streets have to cross it, and in selecting the positions of the
several streets I was guided by the principle of making them cross
the river at the most favorable points for erecting bridges, hence the
width of the blocks extending from street to street are not of uniform
dimensions, by reason of which the size of the building lots on some

of the streets are half an acre, while in others, as Victoria and Princess Streets, they are only quarter acres, but half-acre building lots are the prevailing size, and in the case of broken lots some are much larger.

"There are two market-places laid off at opposite extremities of the town, containing three and a half acres each; they are located upon dry, level ground, and are surrounded with handsome building lots of half-acre size. The Durham market is supposed to accommodate all the settlers of the township who occupy the north side of the Durham Road, while Elgin market is intended for the south concession, Kincardine Avenue, on which it is situated, being a continuation of the south concession line. I may observe in general of the park lots, that they vary in size from 5 to 21 acres, are composed of a good sandy loam soil, and are well adapted for cultivation, and would be suited to growing of fruit and vegetables. On the north side of Durham Street I laid off a range of one and two-acre building lots, my reason for doing so being to embrace the whole of lake lot No. 11, through the centre of which Durham Street runs. By this means there are none of the lake lots interfered with; those occupied by the town are entire lots and no portions of the adjoining lots are encroached on.

"For further information I would beg to refer to you the field notes and plan, where all details are fully set forth.

"All of which is respectfully submitted.

"I have the honor to be, sir,

"Your very obedient servant,

"ALLEN PARK BROUGH, P.L.S.

"TORONTO, MAY, 1850."

In Chapter III is to be found the narrative of the settlement made at Kincardine in 1848. It is there recorded because this was the pioneer settlement of the county. The reader is asked to overlook any repetition of facts there mentioned, it being unavoidable in order to present a connected recital of events in the history of the town.

The undisputed distinction of being the first settlers at Kincardine belongs to Allan Cameron and William Withers. Shortly after the opening of navigation in the spring of 1848[1] these two men and their effects were landed at the mouth of the Penetangore River from the schooner owned and sailed by Captain A. Murray MacGregor. Close to the spot where they landed they built a log house, in which Mr. Cameron kept hotel, and at a later date John Keyworth kept store.

[1] The exact date is said to have been March 5th, 1848.

Some few settlers whose names are mentioned in Chapter III. joined them that summer. For the first year or so the settlement was confined to the flats in the neighborhood of the harbor and beach. It was there that the first two stores were opened. Withers' sawmill was where Mr. Macpherson's orchard is. Patrick Downie's hotel occupied the site where stands the brick building of the Rightmeyer Salt Works, and Francis Walker's hotel stood where the storehouse of the same works is at present.

The reader will bear in mind that the appearance of the town has changed most markedly in the vicinity of the harbor. The present basin has been excavated from a flat tract of land, originally well wooded. The course of the river has also been changed. Instead of flowing straight out into the lake, as at present, it took a sharp bend to the south at a point near the inward end of the south pier, and pursuing a southerly course parallel to the beach for about three hundred yards, and entered the lake opposite the present railway engine house, the river along this distance being separated from the lake by a sand dune some twenty feet' high, which sustained a stunted growth of evergreens. This sand dune, which barred a shorter outlet from the river, was cut through at the instance of Francis Walker. The exact year when this was done the author has been unable to fix. In 1856, the year he arrived at Kincardine, he had no difficulty in stepping across the small stream which flowed through the cutting which had been made. This he could not do when he reached the original mouth of the river, the flow of water there being too deep. That fall and winter contractors were at work driving piles for the two piers; between these the spring freshet of 1857 poured its waters, enlarging the channel, which since then has been the outlet of the river into the lake.

To engage in lumbering seems to have been Mr. Withers'[1] object in coming into the bush, so he proceeded to erect a dam and sawmill, which was in operation the following year. The spot where it was built is fully referred to in the chapter on "The Pioneers," and further particulars are given elsewhere in this chapter.

In 1849 two stores were opened at Kincardine. The names of these two enterprising merchants were John Riach (pronounced Ray

[1] Wm. Withers was a native of Portsmouth, England, and had resided in the county of Oxford prior to coming to Bruce. During the later years of his residence at Kincardine he filled the position of Inland Revenue Officer. In 1881 he moved to the State of Oregon, residing at Astoria, where he died in 1883, aged 81.

by the settlers) and William Rastall. Which took precedence as to the time of commencing business is hardly worth discussing, though each has partisans to sustain their claim to this honor. John Riach had in earlier life been a commercial traveller for a Glasgow firm on the Continent. Coming to Canada, he tried his hand at farming, somewhere near Goderich. Not succeeding thereat, he purchased a small stock of goods and came to Penetangore, with the intention of developing a trade there, and "grow up with the place." Building a small board shanty, near where the railway station is now, he there kept store for some time. His wife was the eldest daughter of Thomas Harris, a prominent man in the early settlement of Kincardine Township, who built for the accommodation of his son-in-law's business the frame building on the west side of the market square, still standing, and known for years as the British American Hotel [1] William Rastall, prior to his settlement at Kincardine, had carried on a trade with the Indians at Saugeen, as related in Chapter III. During the first twenty years of the history of Bruce no one filled a more prominent position, or was more generally esteemed, than William Rastall, and it is with pleasure that particulars of his life, obtained largely from his son Herbert and his brother Richard, are given in the accompanying footnote.[2]

[1]After Riach went out of business this stand was occupied by James Legear, on his leaving it (about 1854, '55) the building for forty years was used as a hotel, the first tenant being Thomas Kennard, who was succeeded by George Smith

[2]William Rastall was born in Edinburgh, Scotland, December 16th, 1827 When he was but six years of age his father, Dr Samuel Rastall, emigrated to Canada and settled at Goderich At the age of fourteen he went to Saugeen, under an engagement with Hugh Johnston, at that time engaged in trading with the Indians Later on, when he was only about seventeen years of age, William Rastall engaged in the same business on his own account at Saugeen ; subsequently, in 1849 he commenced a general mercantile business at Penetangore, his first shop being a "lean-to" at the side of Allan Cameron's tavern. Later on he removed to a log house he had built on the south side of the Market Square, where the planing mill now stands This gave place to a block of frame buildings which he was occupying when he sold out his stock and mercantile interests to Joseph Cooke in 1856. After that, for a number of years, he conducted a conveyancing and insurance business In 1880 he removed to Orangeville, where, in company with his son-in-law, J. H Brownell, he published the *Orangeville Advertiser*, which they conducted for several years, when Mr Rastall removed to Detroit, where he died, October 18th, 1890 Mr Rastall married, in 1850, Miss Mary I. Cameron, eldest daughter of Allan Cameron She survives her husband and resides with her son Herbert in Detroit Mr Rastall was the first reeve of the "United Townships within the County of Bruce" In 1854 he was reeve of the united townships of Kincardine, Bruce and Kinloss When, in 1858, Kincardine village became a municipality, he was the first reeve of it, but resigned during the year. He was reeve of the village for the years

The inflow of settlers into Bruce in the early fifties was steady and continuous Very many of these looked to Kincardine as the base from which supplies were to be obtained The natural result of supply and demand seeking to adjust themselves resulted in storekeepers being more plentiful at Kincardine in those days than they are to-day, over half a century later. The first to follow Messrs Riach and Rastall in storekeeping was David MacKendrick, who in 1851 opened a small store situated near where the river entered the lake at that time. Shortly afterward he built a large log house on the west side of Queen Street, north of the Market Square. This was followed by the erection of a frame building, which is still standing, in which he conducted his business until he finally sold out and retired from business. David MacKendrick was appointed postmaster at the time the office at Kincardine was opened in 1851. Public life he sought not, and it must, in a measure, have been somewhat against his will that he filled the position of reeve for the township of Kincardine in the years 1856-57. Old settlers have a kindly remembrance of David McKendrick. They knew that he scorned anything that had the least appearance of being dishonorable, and so forgave an unfortunate excitability of temper which gave rise to incidents that used to be recounted with a kindly smile at the time, to record which might create, in the mind of those who knew him not, a wrong impression of a character which was sound at the core.

Penetangore, as originally surveyed, had as its northerly limit the range of lots lying on the north side of Durham Street. All of that part of the town now known as Williamsburg has been added by a subdivision of lots 12 to 15 of the Lake Range in the township of Kincardine. The name Williamsburg was given by William Sutton, who had these farm lots surveyed into town lots.[1]

Francis Walker (familiarly spoken of as " Paddy Walker ") is a name not to be overlooked in any relation of Kincardine's early days.   He drove from Goderich on the ice, in the spring of 1850,

1859, '60, '61, '66, '67, '68 and '69 In politics he was a Reformer, and in 1867, at the first general election held after Confederation, he ran for the Dominion House of Commons, but was defeated by his opponent, Francis Hurdon.

[1] This survey was made by John Denison, P L S , in June, 1855, and June, 1856. The Crown patent for lots 12 and 13, Lake Range, was issued to William Sutton ; for lot 14 to his nephew, Richard Sutton, and for lot 15 to John Monilaus One George Moffat squatted on the lots afterwards held by William Sutton, and in 1849 he offered to sell his claim for $8 to Robert Rowan, who declined the offer. William Sutton probably purchased from George Moffat his squatter's claim.

passing the insignificant settlement at Kincardine town plot without noticing it, and had proceeded as far as Stoney Island, when hearing the sound of Capt. Rowan's axe, as he worked at underbrushing, he looked him up, and was directed back to the settlement that he had failed to notice in passing There Mr. Walker resided continuously until the day of his death a quarter of a century later.

The need of a grist mill was a want keenly felt by the settlers who raised the first harvests of grain in the county of Bruce. William Sutton[1] decided to supply this need, and proceeded to construct a dam across the north branch of the Penetangore,[2] and to erect a mill at what still is known as "Sutton's Hollow." The mill was of logs, and of modest dimensions. The required pair of mill stones were in due time landed on the beach, but before they were removed a storm sprang up. The loose sand on which the stones lay was quickly washed from beneath them by the heavy surf, or else transformed thereby into the nature of quicksand, and the stones were "drowned," to use the expressive phrase of an old settler, as he described their disappearance. This serious disaster was productive of delay, but did not diminish the efforts of Mr. Sutton, who purchased another pair of stones, and in 1852 had the first grist mill in the county in operation Settlers who before had taken their grists to Durham or Port Albert were now able to dispense with such long journeys Being, however, the only mill in the county, many a pioneer found he had a long and weary distance to cover before he could get his grist to "Sutton's Mill." It is related of such that while waiting for their grists to be finished they would light a hot fire on one of the large boulders near by, and when this was sufficiently heated, on it they would bake a cake, made from their newly ground flour and water crudely mixed. Unleavened and

---

[1] Wm. Sutton was born in Yorkshire, 29th February, 1828, and at an early age he learnt the business of a saddler. He came to Kincardine in 1850 His enterprising, energetic character gave him a prominent position in the settlement, a prominence retained during the forty-three years of his residence in the county. He was reeve of Kincardine from 1862 to 1865, and took a notable part in the settlement of the county town question. On the separation of Huron and Bruce he received the appointment of sheriff of the latter county, which office he held until 1892 In 1873 he became interested in lumbering in British Columbia and made money, but lost heavily through agents in Australia, to whom he had shipped the produce of his mills In 1893 he formed a new company, called "The Sutton Lumber and Trading Co.," of Euculet, B C., which he was conducting at the time of his death, which occurred March 10th, 1896, at Victoria, B C. In 1852 he married Sarah, daughter of John Keyworth. His widow (who died in 1905) and six children survived him.

[2] This dam was utilized to support the superstructure of a bridge, largely used by those who came into town by way of the Durham Road.

unseasoned such a cake certainly was, but to a hungry backwoodsman, tasting the initial harvest of his bush farm, it was delicious. Mr. Sutton, after running this mill for several years, built, in 1854, a much larger frame one, and in a few years later one of still greater capacity, which he continued to operate as long as he was in the milling business.

The dam built by William Withers, on what is shown in the map of the town as Mill Block No. 1, was washed away by a freshet. As he never had obtained any title from the Crown to the property, he took the frame of his mill to pieces and set it up again on his farm on the south line, where he had water-power. John Keyworth came out from England in 1851, and on August 22nd of that year applied to the Crown for this Mill Block. He also at the same time contracted for the erection of a good-sized frame mill building. On his return from England the next year, where he had gone to fetch his family, he found that the contractor had so botched his job of framing that the building could not be put together or erected. Feeling disappointed, Mr. Keyworth gave up the idea of milling, and confined himself to keeping store, continuing thereat until his death, in March, 1861.

In the winter of 1853-54 Malcolm MacPherson[1] came to Kincardine, and made arrangements to build both a grist and a sawmill and the necessary dam to obtain water-power Mr. MacPherson was for many years the proprietor of this mill, which is still operated, but it has passed through several hands since Mr. MacPherson disposed of it. It is now run by steam power, the water in the river for years past being insufficient to supply constant power throughout the year.

[1]Malcolm MacPherson was born in Perthshire, Scotland, June 1st, 1806, and came to Canada in 1815, when his parents immigrated to this country. The family settled where Perth is now, and Mr MacPherson's father felled the first tree cut on its site Mr MacPherson learned the trade of carpenter and joiner, and in his early days built many of the houses in Perth. He also, for eight years, was surveyor for the united counties of Lanark and Renfrew In February, 1854, he moved his family to Kincardine. He brought his family in a covered sleigh in which there was placed a small stove. At Arthur the stable in which all his effects were placed for the night was burned and he lost everything but the clothes in which he and the members of the family stood in. Arriving at Kincardine he, by strenuous efforts, succeeded in overcoming his loss. In the running of the mill he was assisted by his son John. Mr. MacPherson was married in 1832 to Elizabeth MacPherson, of Ernesttown, a daughter of a U. E. Loyalist. They had a family of eleven children. For about sixty years Mr MacPherson was an elder of the Presbyterian Church. He was mainly instrumental in the forming of a congregation in Kincardine in connection with the Church of Scotland In politics he was a prominent Reformer. His death occurred November 23rd, 1893

William Macklem (for many years a resident of Kincardine) settled there in the winter of 1849-50, and about 1853-54 built an oatmeal mill on the north branch of the river, north of Russell Street. This, with the mills operated by William Sutton and Malcolm Macpherson, fully supplied the needs of the farmers.

The work of cutting the standing timber on the streets in the town, as well as logging and burning it, was no small undertaking to the handful of settlers. For some time progress was slow. James Henry, who arrived at Kincardine August 18th, 1851, related how he assisted to fell some large trees then standing on Queen Street opposite his property at the head of Harbor Street. Mr. Henry was the first pathmaster appointed for the village. Many a log heap had to be disposed of before there was a roadway in the centre of the leading streets, and it was as late as the summer of 1856 before the Market Square was logged and burnt. The author remembers how, in the same year, in the Williamsburg part of Queen Street, and also on Broadway, the presence of stumps made the wagon track a devious one. Harbor Street was not in the original survey of the town, but the necessity for a convenient approach to the harbor being early felt, the want was supplied by the opening of this street, the gift of James Henry, Martin Craig, William Rastall and Francis Walker.[1] The hill on Harbor Street situated east of Huron Terrace was full of springs. Before a passable road at this point could be secured it was necessary to cover these over with a quantity of brush, on which was placed logs to make a causeway.

The appearance of the little village in 1856, as remembered by the author as he looked upon Kincardine for the first time, was somewhat as follows: From Princess Street to the lake was all cleared, but there was standing timber in several parts of the town where now there are numbers of dwellings; e.g., there was then a good sugar bush along South Street towards the High School, and a fine clump of giant hemlocks stood where the Water Tower now stands. The buildings were very much scattered, and stumps of trees were everywhere. Queen Street north of Williamsburg had not at that time been opened out. There existed only a footpath through the trees and clearings leading to Stoney Island. The wagon road along the beach was that used for travel not only to Stoney Island, but by those going further north. Archibald Campbell had a storehouse on the beach at the foot

[1] Harbor Street was assumed by the village, May 8th, 1861, and $500 spent in planking the roadway over the loose sand at the western end.

PETER ROBERTSON

p 450

WILLIAM SUTTON

p 446

WILLIAM RASTALL

p 444

D A MacCRIMMON, M D.

p. 484

of Lambton Street. When the *Ploughboy* arrived on her regular trips, a large scow owned by Mr. Campbell was rowed out to her, that is, if the weather was fine. In the scow freight and passengers were placed and brought ashore. If there was any " sea " on the lake, the *Ploughboy* passed on to Stoney Island, and at the wharf there landed Kincardine passengers and freight. The bridges over the river in the year mentioned were such as the primitive engineering skill of the settlers could erect. That on Huron Terrace Street had an open log abutment on each side of the river. On these were laid heavy stringers across the stream. On Queen Street the superstructure of the bridge was supported by Macpherson's dam, and the same method was in use at Sutton's dam. Russell Street was the thoroughfare at first for the traffic from the Durham line After Sutton's dam was erected, with the bridge as a superstructure thereon, Broadway was the most travelled. The uncertainty for several years where the centre of business was to be, resulted in the shops and taverns being spread over the town plot. There were two or three shops on the south side, one at the old mouth of the river, one on Huron Terrace Street, and another on Queen Street. On the north side shops were to be seen on Huron Terrace Street, Lambton, Durham and Queen Streets, on the Market Square, and in Sutton's Hollow. Of taverns there was Nelson Ross' on Broadway. The Union Hotel, kept by Tom Splann, and afterwards by John Barnes, stood on the site of the present Methodist Church. On the other side of the Market Square Thomas Kennard kept the British American. On the Beach, John Rowan and Francis Walker kept hotels, and on the south side William Anderson. At that time the town bell was such a one as is now in use on farms in the county. This bell was hung in front of Barnes' Hotel. The standard time was obtained by a mark on a stump placed there for the purpose by a surveyor. As this was " sun time," it of course varied, about twenty minutes too fast or too slow, during the course of the year.

During the first quarter of a century of its existence Kincardine was the chief centre of trade for a large section of territory, extending back as far as the Elora Road, and even further east if the sleighing was good. As a natural result merchants of all descriptions of goods established themselves there in numbers too great, it would almost seem, for the place. The following are the names of those who, although not the very first (these having been previously referred to), still may rightfully be classed among the early merchants of the town The names are given in the order of priority of settlement: James

16

Legear, David Gairdner, P. & N. McInnes, Joseph Cooke, Peter Robertson,[1] F. & W. H. Hurdon, and John McLeod. These were all engaged in business at Kincardine in the fifties. Cameron & Brownlee also were leading merchants. This firm commenced business in 1860. P. & N. McInnes, in addition to carrying on a large general store, established about 1857, works for the manufacture of pearl ash, enabling impoverished settlers to obtain by the sale of wood ashes, collected wherever a log heap had been burnt, a fresh source of income.

Possibly the first factory started in town other than saw or grist mills was one for the manufacture of furniture; this was in 1856. The building was situated on Broadway, just west of Queen Street. This business originated with George A. Dezeng. Several years earlier than this, business enterprise was shown by George Browne, who built a brewery on Park Street, near Macklem's Mill. In 1858 or 1859 another brewery was built on Queen Street North. The proprietors were Messrs. Huether & Schoenau. Their product was lager beer, a beverage at that time almost solely confined to Germans. That nationality were not numerous in the vicinity. It, therefore, lacked sufficient patronage to be successful, so after a trial of some half dozen years the plant was moved to Neustadt. A distillery operated by Messrs. Henry & Walker was another of the early enterprises in the place. The building stood where the lighthouse is now. This, too, was closed after an existence of a few years. No doubt the large quantity of whiskey that was smuggled from the United States in those days had something to do with its abbreviated existence.

In Chapter IX. is recorded the particulars respecting the establish-

[1]Peter Robertson was the son of a clergyman of the United Presbyterian Church, Scotland, and was born, August 2nd, 1811, at Kilmaurs, Ayrshire. His schooldays were spent at the Kilmarnock High School. On leaving home he was apprenticed to his uncle, a cloth draper, at Glasgow. He came to Canada in 1833 and was in the employ of James and Alex. Morris, of Brockville, until he commenced business for himself at Belleville, in 1836. The stirring times of the Rebellion of 1837 and '38 soon followed. Being suspected of being a rebel, Mr. Robertson was arrested and imprisoned in the fort at Kingston. When brought to trial the jury brought in " No Bill " against him. After this he was unintentionally mixed up in the burning of the steamer " Sir Robert Peel " by the rebels, being a passenger on the boat at the time. In 1856 he came to Kincardine and carried on a mercantile business until 1877, when he retired. His death occurred May 11th, 1885. Mr. Robertson was a man of marked intellectuality as well as of integrity, and passed away esteemed and respected by all who knew him. He married Sarah, daughter of John Ross, of Brockville, and had a family of four daughters and two sons, the only surviving ones being Mrs. Alex. Shaw and Norman Robertson, county treasurer, both of Walkerton.

ment of the first school in the county. This, Kincardine's first school, was opened in the summer of 1851. The building, a rented frame one, was situated on the river flats near where it flowed into the lake. Mrs. Jane Nairn, as teacher there, presided over 66 scholars, composed of 31 boys and 35 girls. During the first half dozen years the premises occupied for school purposes were many, until at last a permanent building was secured in 1855 or 1856. The first move the school made was to a small frame building on the east side of Queen Street opposite Harbor Street. After a short stay there, it occupied a log building on the opposite side of the street. The school next found a home in a log building standing where is now the residence of Mr. John Gentles. Its stay there was short, and its next location was on Russell Street, just west of the English Church Finally, the school moved into permanent quarters, a frame building erected purposely for a school, situated on Victoria Street, in rear of the present Central School building, which fine and commodious brick building was erected in 1872. The early teachers in the school during the period above indicated were Mrs. Jane Nairn, John Campbell, Malcolm McLennan and Thomas Scott. The public school at Kincardine has had one headmaster, whose long continuance in the office deserves to be recorded. F. C. Powell became principal in September, 1877, and for almost a quarter of a century he labored faithfully to maintain a high standard of education in all its departments. The Model School, established at the time he took the principalship, has also been a source of credit to this old servant of the public.

The first step taken to establish a County Grammar School at Kincardine was to obtain the consent and authority of the Council of the united counties of Huron and Bruce This was obtained at the December session, 1859. At the session held in January of the following year the Council appointed the members of the Board of Trustees. As it was to be a County Grammar School, the trustees were not all residents of Kincardine The following are the names of those appointed: M McKendrick, Alex. Shaw, Rev. Walter Inglis and Rev. Isaac Middleton, of Kincardine; Wm Gunn, of Inverhuron, and Rev. K. McLennan, of Paisley. The Board fixed the fee for tuition at $2 per quarter. In the month of July a union was brought about of the Grammar and Common School Boards, which union has continued down to the present. De W. H. Martyn, M D, was appointed secretary of the United Board in 1862, an office he held almost continuously until his death, July 19th, 1903. The first to fill the position of headmaster was Albert Andrews. His duties commenced with the fall term, 1860. The following are the names of those who have filled the same position down to the present day: J. H. Thom, July, 1867; Duncan Morrison, 1868; Benjamin Freer, 1869, June, 1871; J. Thomson, part 1871, 1872; J. E. Burgess, 1873 to 1876; Ben Freer, 1877 to 1887; Neil Robertson, 1888-89. S. W. Perry, the present headmaster, has held that position since January, 1890, to the complete satisfaction of all interested in Kincardine High School. Further facts referring to this school are to be found in Chapter IX. The list is a long one of those who have received a part of their higher education at the Kincardine Grammar and High School, and in that list are to be found names of many who have pushed their way on to the very front rank of their various professions and callings in life.

The first public religious service held at Kincardine is said to have been conducted by the Rev. Mr. Cox, a minister of the Episcopal Methodist Church, in 1849. The place of meeting was in a log house on Queen Street, nearly opposite the Queen's Hotel. In 1851 the first congregation[1] in connection with any denomination was organized, this initial step in the religious interest of the place being taken by the Wesleyan Methodist Church. The congregation then organized commenced with a membership of forty. Its first pastor was the Rev. Thomas Crews (1851-52). His successors in the pastorate during the early days were the Rev. A. A. Smith (1853), Rev. Wm. Creighton (1854), Rev. S. E. Mandsley (1855), Rev. Andrew Edwards (1856-58), Rev. J. F. Latimer (1859-60), and Rev. D. Connolly (1861-63). As far as the author has been able to trace, services were held at first in the public school-house until, in 1856, a neat brick church was built,[2] the opening services of which were held on Sunday, March 1st, 1857. The author was present at that and many ensuing services As the congregation assembled for the afternoon meeting the weather was warm, springlike and balmy, but on leaving the church when the service was concluded they encountered a blinding blizzard. The snow which fell then and subsequently did not leave until the end of April. For some time after the building was in use the seating accommodation consisted of rough two-inch planks, supported by blocks of cordwood of the necessary height. There was

[1]This was also the first congregation to be organized within the county outside of the Indian Missions.

[2]Now occupied as a dwelling by R. Rinker.

but one aisle, that up the centre of the church. On one side of this the women folks sat, on the other the men. The gable of this building was blown in by a high wind on March 3rd, 1862. It was never rebuilt, the roof being adapted to the new form of the walls when the repairs were made. In April, 1876, the contract for the present handsome edifice was let, the tender being $13,199. The actual cost of the building when completed was considerably in excess of the contract-price. In addition to this, the cost of land and fittings are to be added when considering the outlay of this congregation at this time.

The Episcopal Methodists were formed into a congregation in 1852, but did not have a settled pastor until 1854, the Rev. J. M. Collins being their first minister. At an early date services were held in a frame building, built for a lodge-room by the Good Templars. This was in a lane just north of Broadway, within a stone-throw of the site on which in 1877 was erected their large brick church. When in 1883 the union of this body with the Methodist Church of Canada took place, this building was deserted, the two amalgamated congregations worshipping together. Ultimately this building was sold for the building material it contained.

In 1850 the first Presbyterian service was held in Kincardine. The place where it was conducted was the bar-room of Pat Downie's hotel, the Rev. A. Mackid, of Goderich, officiating. This section of country, peopled as it was by a population of whom the majority were Presbyterians, was for several years under the supervision of the Home Mission Committee of the several Presbyterian bodies In January, 1852, the Free Church Presbytery, of London, deputed Rev. John Ross to visit Kincardine, to prepare the way for A. Currie, a catechist, who labored for some months in this field. Besides the Rev. John Ross, the Rev. John Fraser also labored here as a missionary in 1852-53. In 1854 steps were taken to build a Presbyterian Church, which was of frame, and the size thirty feet by fifty feet. Hugh Matheson was the contractor. To enable the undertaking to be successfully financed, George Murray, of "the lake shore," went to Zorra to solicit subscriptions for its erection Prior to the construction of this building, services were held in the log school building which stood on the site of John Gentles' residence. The church was built in 1855, but remained unplastered until late in the fall of 1856. While the plaster was still moist a hard frost occurred, which had the effect of taking the temper out of the mortar. On the next occasion for

holding church service, the heat from the stove speedily thawed the
plaster, and during service (which was the first the author attended in
Kincardine) portions of the ceiling kept dropping upon the heads of the
congregation, or fell with a thud on the open spaces of the floor. The
minister never halted the services, but the congregation had its eyes
turned heavenward on that occasion in a way which might betoken a
spiritual turn of mind, if one did not know that they were watching
where the next drop of plaster was to occur and seeing if they were in
a safe position About the time the church was built the congregation
was organized, bearing the name of Knox Church. At the time of the
induction of its first minister, Knox Church had sixty members on its
roll This induction, that of the Rev. John Stewart, took place
August 3rd, 1859. Owing to his resigning, the charge became vacant
in June, 1863, and for the next three years Knox Church had no
settled minister Nevertheless the congregation grew, and the church
edifice had to be enlarged in 1866 In August of that year its second
pastor, the Rev John Fraser, was inducted. His pastorate lasted
until January, 1878 On July 11th of the last-mentioned year the
present pastor, the Rev. J L Murray, D.D., was inducted. His
pastorate has been a most successful and happy one, the semi-jubilee
of which was celebrated in 1903, a pleasing feature of which was the
presentation to him and Mrs Murray of a cabinet of solid silver
tableware In 1875 steps were taken toward the building of the present commodious church edifice Its present state of completeness was
not reached at once On July 10th, 1876, the first services were held
therein, the congregation worshipping in the basement, and from then
on until September 7th, 1879, when the building proper, having been
completed, it was duly dedicated In 1889 the tower was finished,
and in 1894 the large pipe organ was installed.

Kincardine at one time had three Presbyterian churches, the
"Free," known as Knox Church, as above narrated; the "United
Presbyterian," and the "Church of Scotland." "West Church" was
the name of the congregation in which the "U. P.'s" worshipped.
This congregation was organized May 26th, 1857, with forty-five
members In 1859 a church building[1] was erected at the corner of
Durham and Huron Terrace Streets The Rev. Walter Inglis, at that
time of Riversdale, was called to this charge, and inducted April
27th, 1859. Mr. Inglis was the pastor of this congregation for ten
years For two years after he left, hopes were entertained of continu-

[1]This building is now occupied as a dwelling by Wm. Welsh

ing this as a separate charge. These hopes never materialized, and on April 25th, 1871, West Church congregation united with that of Knox Church.

St Andrew's Church, in connection with the Church of Scotland, was the first congregation in Kincardine that had a church building erected before organization, the building having been erected somewhere about 1862. The explanation of this is, Mr Malcolm Mac-Pherson, its leading elder, was a most enthusiastic member of the "Auld Kirk," and his time, means and enthusiasm resulted in the building of the church. The first pastor of this congregation was the Rev. Donald F. Maclean, in 1862. His successor was the Rev. Alex. Dawson, who came in 1863 In 1867 the Rev. John Ferguson became the pastor in charge In 1872 he was succeeded by the Rev. William Anderson The last minister of this church was the Rev. J. B. Hamilton, who was ordained and inducted to the pastorate April 27th, 1880. After his-resignation in January, 1884, the prospect of maintaining this as a separate congregation seemed small, and one by one its members united with Knox Church, so that after an existence of over twenty years the congregation of St. Andrew's ceased to be. The building was sold in 1885 to the Dominion Government, to be used as an armory for the company of volunteers at Kincardine

Church of England services in the early days were held in private houses. The author remembers attending one held at the home of John Keyworth. On that occasion that gentleman read the morning church service, and then a sermon selected out of the works of some divine. Later, the Rev. Isaac Middleton, who was the first settled minister, held church services for some time in the Orange Hall, until the present church building was erected and opened for services, which was on July 6th, 1862.

The Baptists had a strong man to take the initiative in forming a congregation of that denomination at Kincardine, in the person of the Rev. Wm. Fraser, who settled at Kincardine in 1850. His efforts resulted in the erecting of a neat log church. The building, small in size, was cruciform in shape. For a number of years this congregation were without a pastor. In 1876, through the efforts of the Rev. Alex. Grant it was resuscitated, and a large frame church was erected on Princess Street, which subsequently was moved to its present position on Queen Street. Of the many excellent and earnest men who have ministered to this charge the author specially recalls the Rev. H. Ware, now entered into his rest, a man of rare consecration and simplicity.

It is a far call from the old-time church buildings in existence half a century ago at Kincardine, to its commodious, modern and well-equipped churches of to-day. In looking back, memory recalls some features that may be considered interesting to record In these churches of the early settlement the seats, as has already been noted, were but rough planks, supported by equally rough wooden blocks The light for evening services—a truly "dim religious light"—was supplied by tallow candles, two or three only on each side wall, placed in tin sconces. These might be snuffed when required by the finger and thumb of some man sitting near-by. In time candles were replaced by old-time argand oil lamps with reflectors, lent by some of the merchants.[1] Then came coal oil lamps, the churches by this time being prosperous enough to provide their own lamps, which in time were fitted in expensive fixtures, and finally electric lighting, which now supplies all the light needed at evening services In the days of the early settlement the singing was led by a precentor [2] It was not long before a choir was formed to aid him in leading the singing. Then followed the organ, at first a modest reed instrument, and finally the pipe organ.

In Knox Church there has always been service in the two languages, English and Gaelic. At communion seasons—when held during the summer—the Gaelic congregation met and held their service in the open air. The author recollects one such service, held back of the present site of A. Malcolm's furniture factory. The pulpit, over which was built a shelter of rough boards, faced the east, Stretching out in front of it was the table, possibly forty or fifty feet in length, covered with a snowy white cloth, while rough planks placed alongside the table supplied the seats. The congregation sat on the green grass The amphitheatre-like formation of the ground enabled each one in the audience to clearly see and hear the preacher. The hot summer sun was pouring down on all, and as a protection from its rays numerous umbrellas were spread open. A

---

[1]The author remembers how Paul D. McInnes would bring to Knox Church four lamps, as above described, from the store of P. & N. McInnes, if the service was to be conducted by a Free Church minister, while he would bring from his father's store the needed lamps if the preacher belonged to the "U. P.'s," for before Knox Church had a settled pastor and before either of the other Presbyterian bodies had built itself a church home, the officers of Knox Church, when they had no service of their own, generously allowed the other Presbyterian bodies to hold service in their church.

[2]Wm. Millar, of Millarton, was considered the best precentor to be found in any of the churches in the settlement.

sight not to be met with in Bruce to-day was the number of Highland women, whose head covering was a white mutch, and over whose shoulders was spread a white kerchief neatly crossed and pinned over the bosom. The Psalms of David were used solely in the service of praise, the words being lined by the precentor, who chanted the next line to be sung on the last note used. The tunes, nearly all in the minor key, sweet and plaintive, would draw as spectators those who understood not the language used in the singing, who came after their own shorter church services had terminated. The author would, if he could, give some idea of the forceful address spoken at the "fencing of the table." The standard so set for those who would "worthily partake" being so high that in many cases none would presume to be seated at the table on the first invitation. At the second, wherein there would be more reference to God's grace and Christ's merits, some godly elders would come forward and be seated, followed on the third invitation by the body of the communicants, numerous enough to possibly fill a second or third table. At these Gaelic services were many strangers, some even from Zorra, who, as well as others, attended a series of communion services which commenced at Ashfield, succeeded by others held at Lucknow, Ripley, Kincardine and Tiverton. Each of these communion services covered a period of five days—Thursday being held as a fast day; Friday was known as the "Question Day" (in Gaelic, "la na Ceist"); Saturday as preparation day; then on Sunday the sacrament was dispensed; on Monday thanksgiving services were held. Of these five days the Question Day services were the most unique. After the assembly on that day had been opened by the usual services of prayer and praise, the minister conducting the same would request any who had any difficult religious question on which they required enlightenment to propound it to the meeting. On this being responded to, it might be found that the question was regarding the meaning of some obscure passage of Scripture.[1] "The men" ("na daoine," in Gaelic), for so the leaders of religious life were called, would one after another express their opinion. When the time to close the meeting had come, the minister would "sift" ("n'criathair," in Gaelic) or summarize what had been said, so that those assembled might remember it. It is said that the peculiar features of Question Day are rapidly disappearing, as "the men"—brought up in a school

[1] Especially such as tended to show what are the marks of sincerity in religious profession.

now almost passed away—have dropped off one by one. Among the most prominent of the " the men " were Kenneth Campbell, of Ashfield; Malcolm McLennan, of Huron, James Gordon and Donald McPherson, of Kinloss; Hector McKay, of Culross, and George Ross, of Kincardine.

The topic of church life in Kincardine is a feature which has been dwelt upon pretty fully in this chapter, but the author cannot close it without alluding to the Literary Society which for a number of years existed in connection with Knox Church. This Society proved attractive to students attending the High School. Under the wise guidance of the Rev Dr Murray, A. H. Smith (now of Moosomin, Sask.) and others, the young people were led to form and cherish ideals which, striven after, developed character, and resulted in after life in prominent positions being attained by them in their chosen professions. Of these, the names only of those who entered the ministry are here given. They are as follows: Rev. Messrs. A. G. McLeod, Robert Johnston, D.D , R. J Macpherson, Hector McKay, J A. Stewart, John M. and Ferguson Miller, Hugh Finlay, and John Matheson, of the Presbyterian Church, and the Rev. Thomas F. Whealen and the Right Rev I. O. Stringer, Bishop of Selkirk, of the Church of England

The author has been favored by Mrs. Wm. Rastall, of Detroit, with the perusal of an original document relating to the history of Kincardine, being the " Census of the Village of Penetangore," taken by Wm. Withers and R. G. Fowler, in October, 1857, to see if the population was sufficient to warrant the making application for incorporation as a village. The census contains 837 names This being more than sufficient, the village became a separate municipality on January 1st, 1858, under the name of the village of Kincardine, and dropped forever its dual name of Penetangore. The first reeve was William Rastall. In a footnote[1] the names of the various reeves of the village and town are given until 1896, the last year reeves sat at the County Council. The first town clerk was Joseph Barker. Of those since then who have filled the office of clerk of the municipality down to the present, it is questionable if any have been as near the

[1]Names of the various reeves of Kincardine town from 1858 to 1896, inclusive Wm Rastall, part 1858, '59, '60, '61, '66, '67, '68, '69; C R. Barker, part of 1858 and 1882; Wm Sutton, 1862, '63, '64, '65; Robert Baird, 1870, '71, '72, '73, '74, '75, '76, '77, '78, '79; T C Rooklidge, 1880; Alex Gordon, 1881; R T Walker, 1883, 1890; A Malcolm, 1884, '85, '86; De W H Martyn, 1887, '88, '89, J H Scott, 1891, '92, '93, '94, '95, '96.

standard of a model officer as the present town clerk, J. H. Scougall. As the population grew in numbers the time at length came when Kincardine might claim a higher municipal status. The date of this was the 1st of January, 1875, when Kincardine first entered into the ranks of the towns of the province. In a footnote[1] the names of those who have been mayors of Kincardine are given, and also their years of office.

It was not long after the incorporation of the village before a town hall was built. It was a fair-sized, two-storey, frame building, which stood on the site of the present town hall. The author has not been able to fix with certainty the year in which it was built, but remembers events of 1862 in connection with the building. The present town hall was completed in December, 1872. In it are the usual accommodations asked for in a municipal building, including a fire hall.

The need of a system of waterworks was felt for years before the town possessed them. They were urged both on sanitary grounds and also for fire protection. When they were established it was by private enterprise, Messrs. Moffatt, Hodgins and Clark being the principals in the Kincardine Waterworks Company, which commenced August 1st, 1890, to supply the town with pure water from the lake. The intake pipe extends out into the lake for 150 yards. The stand-pipe, which is 110 feet in height, stands back of Knox Church. Into this water is pumped, and gravitates through the system of water mains and connections. There are about four miles of water mains in the town. For four years the town paid annually to the Waterworks Company the sum of $2,100 for fire protection, for water required in watering the streets, and for water service at the school and town hall, when (as the town had the option of purchasing the plant) it was at length decided to go in for municipal ownership. The town obtained possession of the plant in September, 1894, the purchase price being $40,000. Further additions were made to the plant, which brought its cost up to $45,000.

Another form of municipal ownership that Kincardine has embarked in is electric lighting. In the late eighties an electric light

[1]Names of the various mayors of Kincardine: James Brown, 1875; W. P. Brown, 1876, '77, '78; Jas. A. MacPherson, 1879, 1880, '81, '82, 1891, '92, '96, '97, '98; Robert Baird, 1883, '84, '85, '86, '89, 1890; Edward Leslie, 1887, '88; Joseph Barker, 1893; John Tolmie, 1894, '95; De W. H. Martyn, 1899; Geo. R. MacKendrick, 1900, '01; W. J. Henry, 1902; John Ruttell, 1903; A. Malcolm, 1904; J. C. Cook, 1905; W. G. Temple, 1906.

plant was established in Kincardine. This passed into the hands of George Swan and Samuel Henry, who sold it to the municipality in 1894 for $10,000. The total cost to the town for the electric plant up to the end of 1904 was $15,792. Of these two businesses operated by the municipality, it is understood the waterworks are the most profitable.

The debentures issued by the town form a long list. Some of them have been for well-advised objects, such as those referred to in the preceding paragraphs, and for bridges and local improvements. Other issues of debentures, such as that known as the " Steel Horse Collar Bonus " and the " Stove Foundry Bonus," have failed to benefit the town to the extent hoped for. Another large expenditure, which will have to be met by an issue of debentures, is a system of sewerage, which at the time of writing is being discussed, and must ultimately be constructed before the town can be as healthful as it should be.

In Chapter V. there is related the first effort made to obtain a harbor at Kincardine, which was at as early a date as 1853. That effort proving abortive, the attention of the Government was directed to the necessity which existed for a harbor of refuge at this point. Recognizing the strength of the arguments adduced, and in response thereto, an attempt was made in 1855 to build a breakwater, constructed of cribs of timber filled with stone. Underestimating the power of the storms which sweep over Lake Huron, the breakwater was too weakly constructed, and lasted only a few months, when it was washed away. The remains of it were found by Government Engineer Grey a short distance north-west of the end of the present pier. After the destruction of the breakwater, the Department of Public Works in 1856 commenced the construction of two parallel piers at the mouth of the river, between which it discharged itself into the lake. These piers were one hundred feet apart. The north pier was 540 feet in length, and the south pier 190 feet. These works sufficed for some years. At the time of the passing of the County Gravel Roads By-law, Kincardine obtained a substantial grant towards the improvement of its harbor. Between the county and the village $23,000 was spent on the harbor in the years 1866 and 1867. During those years the dredging of the basin was commenced, and the north pier was extended to 757 feet, and the south pier to 495 feet. The Government also gave a grant of $4,500 to assist in this work. In 1872 there was commenced the work of dredging the harbor to its present extent of about four acres, and to a depth of 12 feet. This extensive work

VIEW OF KINCARDINE HARBOR IN 1878

was not completed until 1877. Further work in the way of dredging and repairs has been done nearly every year since. At present the north pier is 1,470 feet in length, and of a uniform width of 30 feet. The south pier is 840 feet in length. The east side of the harbor basin has a water frontage of 463 feet, the south side one of 253 feet, and the west side one of 440 feet. Over $200,000 has been spent on the Kincardine harbor, but owing to the entrance being narrow and the river always bringing down sediment, which is deposited in the basin, the harbor has never been worth the large amount spent upon it. The Government had the light near the pierhead established in 1874, and in 1881 the main lighthouse shed its guiding rays over the lake for the first time. William Kay was keeper of this lighthouse for many years. At present it is in charge of Thomas McGaw, Jr. As an additional aid to navigation, a steam foghorn is located at the waterworks pumping-house, which is 1,375 feet north of the entrance to the harbor.

Possessing a harbor, Kincardine before the advent of the railway was the best grain market in the county, and every winter its numerous warehouses were filled with the produce of the farms of all the townships lying back from the lake. Long processions of farmers' sleighs ladened with grain were a familiar sight on its street at that time. Some days as much as ten thousand bushels of grain would be purchased. The chief grain buyers were Robert Baird, Robert Walker, Francis Hurdon, Ross Robertson and Arch. Campbell. In the spring, when a schooner arrived to carry away to Buffalo, Toronto or Montreal a cargo of the grain which filled the warehouses, the town witnessed a busy sight. To save demurrage every effort possible was made to speedily laden the vessels. Men were paid 25 cents an hour (and were expected to earn it) shovelling grain into two-bushel bags. As soon as filled these were piled on wagons, teamed away to scows[1] to be transported to the vessel lying at anchor in deep water, quickly hoisted upon the deck, the bag strings were cut, and the golden grain poured into the vessel's hold. All work was rushed so as to get the vessels quickly away. Sometimes a squall or a gale would come before the vessel was laden, and she would have to slip her anchor and get well off shore. Sometimes this could not be done, and the vessel was driven upon the beach, to the great loss of her owners and also of the shippers of grain. After the railway was opened the above-mentioned

[1]When the piers were extended into deep enough water the vessels lay alongside the pier and were ladened there.

advantage which Kincardine possessed as a grain market was neutralized, and grain was not marketed there as of yore. Merchants and others, thinking that there was not competition enough among the grain buyers, sought to establish it, so they and others in 1899 organized " The Farmers' Elevator and Shipping Company." Unfortunately, the company made no money, and in 1905 were forced into liquidation. The object sought of improving the market was, however, attained. The warehouse used by the company was purchased by W J. Henry, who is endeavoring to maintain Kincardine's reputation as a good grain market.

Kincardine was very much interested in the various railway schemes that agitated the county at large in 1869, and it was a bitter pill to swallow, when the Wellington, Grey and Bruce Railway scheme carried, as related in Chapter VII., leaving Kincardine without any railway and with the prospect of being deprived of the trade which had been flowing into it for so many years, and see it go to build up towns elsewhere. However, before the railway was opened to Southampton the prospect brightened. Two bills passed the Legislature in 1871, authorizing the construction of separate lines of railway to Kincardine, namely, the Wellington, Grey and Bruce Railway, by a branch line from Listowel, and the London, Huron and Bruce Railway. The first of these received a bonus from the village of $8,000, and was completed to Kincardine in the fall of 1873.[1] The London, Huron and Bruce Railway never came nearer to Kincardine than Wingham, nevertheless the town gave it a bonus of $3,000. This road was opened in January, 1876.

On the discovery, in 1868, that large deposits of salt existed at less than a thousand feet beneath the surface at Kincardine, steps were taken to bring this necessity of life into the market. It was the Kincardine Salt Prospecting and Manufacturing Company (of which James Brown was president, and James A. MacPherson secretary-treasurer), which obtained the bonus offered by the County Council for sinking an artesian well and obtaining salt. Another company was formed, in which Walkerton capital was largely represented. This was known as the Bruce Salt Company. The method at first used to evaporate the brine pumped from the wells was not an economical one, the brine being boiled in potash kettles set in rows and bricked in, each row being called a "block." The consumption

---

[1] This branch was operated by the contractors until taken over by the railway company, December, 1874

of wood was enormous. As cordwood was not to be had at the low price of former days, the process was found to be too costly. Flat pans 75 to 100 feet in length and 20 to 25 feet in breadth were then tried, with better results. The two companies named not finding much profit in the manufacture of salt, after a few years' trial, closed down their works. About this time, early in the seventies, two American capitalists became interested in the salt industry, and each commenced to erect an extensive plant at Kincardine. That built by William Gray is said to have cost $75,000; that built by L. Rightmeyer was not quite so expensive. These firms shipped salt in bulk to Chicago.[1] The American tariff, however, was against them, and the Canadian market too small to permit the business to be profitably conducted, so about 1876 Mr. Gray closed down his plant. Mr. Rightmeyer continued the struggle for about fifteen years longer, and unfortunately lost the best part of his fortune in his efforts. After remaining idle for about ten years, the Gray Salt Block was purchased by the Ontario People's Salt Manufacturing Company, in 1885. This company has been run in connection with the Dominion Grange, and this connection has insured it a constant patronage. Its manager is John Tolmie, M.P. As some readers may be interested to know some facts connected with this establishment, they are given in a footnote.[2]

The fishing industry was established at Kincardine late in the fifties. By 1866 it had so developed that six boats sailed each morning from Kincardine harbor to lift and set their nets many miles out in the lake. Among those early engaged in this industry were Thomas McGaw, Alex. Gordon, Robert and Alex. Donnelly, Kenneth and Duncan McKenzie, Samuel Splan, also John, Peter and Thomas (Jr.) McGaw. They who follow the calling of a fisherman on Lake Huron experience many dangers and much hardship, and, after all, there is no very large returns for all their vicissitudes.[3] Kincardine fishermen have been fortunate in meeting with so few fatalities. During nearly

[1] In 1875 the product of salt at Kincardine amounted to 137,000 barrels, of which there was exported the equivalent of 90,000 barrels.

[2] Size of main building, 250 x 90 feet; size of addition, 110 x 70 feet. The well is 989 feet deep. The evaporating pans are " V " shaped, 12 x 100 feet and 7 feet deep, made of boiler iron and lined with sawed stone and heated with live steam pipes passing through the brine. The salt as precipitated by the brine is removed by an endless chain rake and deposited in bins. There is also an open flat evaporating pan, 100 x 28 feet, raked by hand.

[3] That a record may be preserved, the weight of some large fish, as mentioned in the local press, is here given. In July, 1875, Samuel Splan caught a salmon-trout weighing 74 lbs., and Charles Splan, in August, 1883, a whitefish that weighed 19½ lbs.

half a century only two have lost their lives while pursuing their calling. These were Elliott Hunter and a man named McIntosh, their
overladened boat being swamped in a gale while returning from the
Fishing Islands in 1882. Thomas McGaw, above-mentioned, has
earned a well-deserved reputation as a builder of fishing boats. One
built by him, called *The Belle,* and sailed by his son Peter, carried
off for three years in succession the cup offered at the Goderich
regatta for the fishermen's yacht race. Having been won three times
by the same boat, the trophy remains in the proud possession of Peter
McGaw. Another of Mr. McGaw's boats, the *Water Lily,* has been
very successful in carrying off prizes at various regattas.

In a former part of this chapter is mentioned the inception of
some of the industries of the town. For a list of those in existence in
1866 the author turns to an old " Directory of the County of Bruce,"
published by J W. Rooklidge (an old Kincardine boy, who has passed
away). We there learn that in that year Kincardine had three grist
mills, three sawmills, two tanneries, two woollen mills, two pearl ash
factories, two foundries—certainly a fine record for so early a date.
Ira J. Fisher is probably the man who has been the longest actively
engaged in manufacturing in Kincardine. He came to Kincardine in
1860, and built a foundry on Victoria Street, taking off his first heat
in October, 1861. Since then he has had his share of the vicissitudes
of life, but in them all has proved himself to be a good and worthy
citizen. John Watson (another man of worth) founded in 1858 the
present extensive furniture factory conducted by the Andrew Malcolm
Company. It was but a small concern at first, employing but few
hands, and which used horse-power to drive the machinery. One of
his employees was Elijah Miller, who for several years also carried on
a furniture factory. Messrs. Combe & Watson are another offshoot.
Their large factory on the harbor flats catches the eye of all who arrive
in town by either rail or water. The Hunter Bridge and Boiler Company, established in the early eighties, employs a number of hands,
and helps to make the town known at outside points. Pork packing
has long been one of the industries of the town. Started originally by
Wm. Rastall, it has been continued by T. C. Rooklidge and Robert
Madden, and flourishes to-day under the management of Henry Cole-
man, whose cured bacon has more than a local reputation. One of the
most unsuccessful ventures that Kincardine ever entered into was that
known as the Gundy Stove Foundry, which was bonused by the town

to the extent of $7,000. The town has never been recouped for this generous bonus, as the foundry was run for only a few years.

The press became a power in Kincardine when on the 4th of August, 1857, the first number of *The Western Canadian Commonwealth* was issued. The publisher was John McLay,.afterwards Registrar of Deeds for the county. At the time of his coming to Kincardine he was a young man of about 25 years of age The press, type and all the equipments of a printing office he brought with him from Glasgow, Scotland. Mr. McLay was a spicy writer, and in consequence made for himself some bitter enemies. When he received the office of registrar the paper passed into the hands of Joseph Lang, who changed its name to that of the *Bruce Review*. He was burned out October 29th, 1870, when he disposed of the paper. Up till then its politics were those of the Liberal party. The purchaser was C. Cliffe. From the time he took hold of the *Review* it has been an upholder of the Conservative party. T. C. Bartholomew was the next owner of the paper. He about the end of the seventies sold out to Mortimer Brothers, who changed the name of the paper to *The Kincardine Standard.*. In March, 1882, Andrew Denholm purchased the paper. After publishing the paper for about four years, Mr. Denholm sold out, and it passed once more into the hands of its former publisher, Joseph Lang, who changed the name to the *Kincardine Review*. Since 1891 Hugh Clark, M.P P., has been the editor and publisher of the paper, assisted part of the time by his brother, Charles Clark.

The Bruce Reporter was first issued 7th of December, 1866, by Albert Andrews, a resident of some years' standing as headmaster of the Grammar School. The ownership of the paper passed in the early seventies to Messrs. Crabbe & Brownell, then to J. H. Brownell, who sold the paper to W. M. Dack in 1879. Mr. Dack continued to publish the *Reporter* until the spring of 1901, when he received the appointment of Registrar of Deeds for the county. J S Gadd then became the publisher, and continued as such until the paper passed into the hands of. its present proprietor and editor, J. J Hunter, in 1905.

The author, in bringing this chapter to a close, regrets that he cannot write as fully as he would like to regarding some of the men who for years have been among the prominent citizens of Kincardine. There is Robert Baird, the present postmaster, who for over half a century has been a leader in the town, as reeve, mayor, warden of the county, Conservative candidate in two political campaigns, and a leading grain merchant. His predecessor in the position of postmaster,

Mathew Mackendrick, unpretentious in manner, but faithful almost to a fault in the performance of his duties. Then among those not to be forgotten is Dr. S. S. Secord, who has practised his profession in the county since 1857, who deserves to be remembered with Dr. McClure, of the "Bonnie Brier Bush." Another, and possibly the oldest settler in the town, is Joseph Barker, who, with his good wife, have ever been found on the side that maketh for righteousness. Also James A. MacPherson, who was elected mayor of the town on nine occasions. A list of town worthies must include the name of Rev. J. L. Murray, D.D , for nearly thirty years pastor of Knox Church. But the list must be curtailed, for the town has not lacked in men good and true, who have aided in its development, and in making the town what it is—one of the pleasantest towns in which to live in Ontario

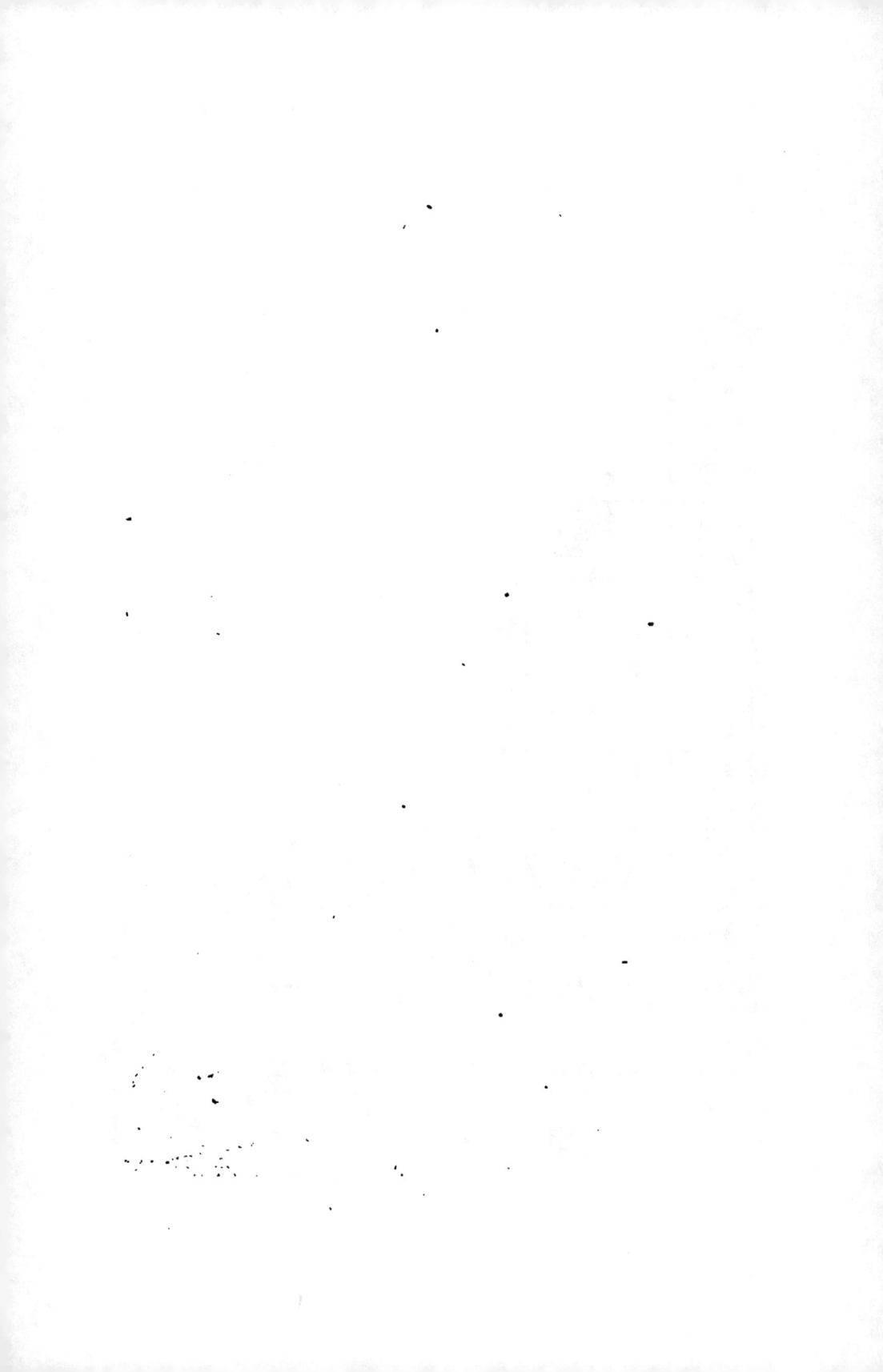

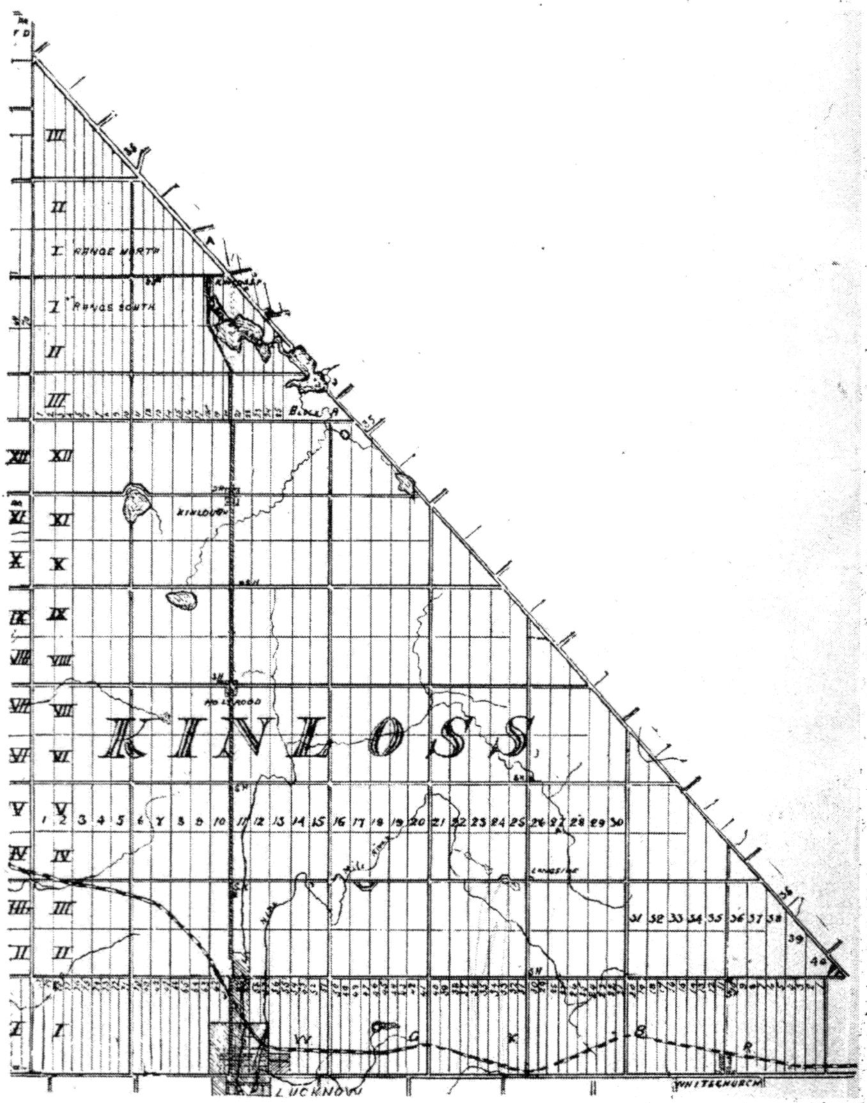
KINLOSS
RANGE NORTH
RANGE SOUTH
KINLOUGH
HOLYROOD
LANGSIDE
LUCKNOW
WHITECHURCH
W G B R

CHAPTER XXXIV.

TOWNSHIP OF KINLOSS.[1]

EXTRACT FROM THE REPORT OF COUNTY VALUATORS, 1901.

"This township runs largely to extremes, some portions being extra good, while other portions are very hilly and swampy. Interspersed with small lakes and being well watered, it is well calculated for mixed farming. No scarcity of timber in this township and the roads are excellent, gravel being plentiful Portions of Kinloss are greatly improved since the last valuation The rate per acre is $31.15, including village property, which equals $1.78 per acre for the whole township."

As pointed out in Chapter II. the first lands within the county surveyed into farm lots were those on the first concession of Kinloss. This survey was made in 1847 by Alex. Wilkinson, P.L.S. Two years later, in 1849, the Durham Road and the adjacent "Free Grant" lots were surveyed by A. P. Brough, P.L S.[2] Three years after this, in 1852, the residue of the township was surveyed by E R. Jones, P.L.S.

The "Free Grant" lands were opened for settlement in June, 1849, and Ranges Three, North, and South, of the Durham Road, were offered for sale at the same time. The remaining portion of the township came into the market at the "big" land sale,[3] held September 27th, 1854. The price at which the lots on the first concession were sold—it being classed as School lands—was ten shillings ($2 00) per acre. Concessions 2 to 12 are Crown lands, and the price at which they were sold was seven shillings and six pence ($1.50) per acre.

The first settlers in the township settled on the "Free Grants" in 1850. Among them were Joel Eli Stauffer, John and Wm. Shelton, Thomas Hodgins and Mankin Meredith These pioneers of the township deserve credit for having located on lands that were far

---

[1]The township derives its name from one of the titles of Lord Elgin, the Governor-General at the time the township was surveyed Among his many titles was that of Baron Bruce, of Kinloss

[2]Mr. Brough, in his report, gives the Indian names of the two lakes near the Black Horse, now called Silver Lakes ; translated, the names are Otter and Mud Turtle Lake respectively, for the north and south lake

[3]See Appendix K.

from a base of supplies, Kincardine being the nearest point at which purchases of provisions and other needed articles could be made. During the summer and fall of 1851 most of the settlers were able to earn a little money by working at the government job of opening the Durham Road, either as contractors[1] or as axemen. This public work was indeed a fortunate thing for these early settlers, as it performed the double purposes of providing them with a road and also with supplying them with much-needed cash. A tedious delay occurred in opening the other main roads in Kinloss. The tenth side-road from Lucknow to the Black Horse was opened, under the direction of David Gibson, P.L.S., by the Bureau of Agriculture in 1858,[2] which also in 1859-60 opened the county boundary line between Bruce and Huron The lack of roads in the early days had a decided retarding effect upon the development of the township. The first to take up land and settle in the southern part of the township are said to have been Norman Nicholson, Duncan and Alexander McKenzie, Martin McInnes, John McDonald, R Gollan, William, David and James Henderson, Wm. Bryce, Peter Reid, James, John, Thomas and David Falconer, Wm. and J. Tiffin, Andrew McManus. All of these and others also had squatted on their lots before they were opened for sale The year of the "big" land sale witnessed a great inflow of settlers, who took up the choicest of the remaining lots. Among those who came there about this time may be mentioned Alex. Graham, Thomas Harris,[3] Robert Purves,[4] S. A. Ferrie, Patrick, John and Peter Corrigan.

[1]Particulars of the Kinloss, Durham Road contracts, let July 11th, 1851 :
Samuel Colwell, to chop out road in front of lots 1 to 4, at rate of £22 per mile and 10s. per rod for causewaying
J Eli Stauffer, to chop out road in front of lots 5 to 8, at rate of £22 per mile, and 12s 6d per rod for causewaying
John Smith, to chop out road in front of lots 9 to 12, at rate of £24 per mile, and 8s 9d per rod for causewaying
Mankin Meredith, to chop out road in front of lots 13 to town line, at rate of £24 per mile
The total amount of all these contracts was £155 2s 6d On completion of the work payment was made October 28th and December 13th, 1851

[2]In 1854 the United Counties Council gave a grant of £50 to open this road, an offer having been received from Thos. Hodgins and others to give a roadway through their lands to avoid Silver Lake. The expenditure of this grant seems to have been the extent of work done on this road prior to letting of the Government contracts in 1858

[3]Thomas Harris' name appears elsewhere in this History in connection with the settlement of Kincardine and also with Ripley post-office. He was for some time the only Justice of the Peace in Kinloss.

[4]Robert Purves was one of the prominent men of Bruce for many years. A native of Berwickshire, he came to Canada in 1850, at the age of eighteen, and settled in the township of Wawanosh. In 1854 he took

In 1852 Kinloss, in common with the other townships in the
county was united to the township of Kincardine for municipal purposes At the session of the United Council held June, 1854, a
petition from the ratepayers of Kinloss was presented asking that
that township be made a separate municipality. The report of the
special committee appointed to consider the petition is here given,
as being a reliable statement showing the development of the township at that date. It is as follows: " Our committee cannot recommend that the prayer of the petition of Mankin Meredith and others
be granted. The assessment of this township is the least of any in
the counties, save one, it being only £1,170, and the expense of a
reeve sent from said township would be equal to two pence farthing
in the pound on the gross assessment for the year 1853, upon which
assessment your Council are now obliged to base their taxations for
the purpose of raising funds which may be available up to 1855.
Further, that we had no reliable document before us upon which to
arrive at a satisfactory conclusion that this township has the number
of names on its assessment roll which are requisite to enable it to
obtain a set-off." At the September session following, the question
of municipal separation came up again, and on the casting vote of
the warden the prayer of the petition was granted and the necessary
by-law passed The by-law appointed Wm. Shelton as returning
officer, and directed that " the election be holden at the house of
Wm. Meredith on the sixth concession." The Council elected were:
Boyer Paul, Murdoch McKenzie, Murdoch McDonald, Thomas Harris
and Wm. Shelton. This Council elected Boyer Paul[1] as reeve,[2] and

up the farm lots in the first concession of Kinloss, on which he lived during
the remainder of his life. In 1865 Mr Purves was elected reeve of
Kinloss, an office held, excepting during the year 1868, until the end of
1883.   After a retirement from municipal honors, he again, during the
years 1893, '94, '95, was elected as the chief officer of the township.
The County Council also elected him as warden of the county three times
in succession, for the years 1880, '81, '82. The repeated municipal honors
bestowed on Mr. Purves emphasized the appreciation in which he was
held as a man of sound judgment and prudence. His death occurred July
20th, 1902.

[1]Boyer Paul had negro blood in his veins. On his presenting his certificate of election as reeve of Kinloss at the first meeting of the United
Counties Council at Goderich, some members took objection to his taking
his seat at the council on account of his color, holding that he was non-
eligible, and expressed curiosity to know if the majority of the electors
in Kinloss were colored. After some discussion he was allowed to take
his seat

[2]List giving the names of the reeves of the township of Kinloss, from
1855 to 1900 : Boyer Paul, 1855; John Purvis, 1856 to 1863; Malcolm Camp-

appointed as its clerk Wm. Herndon. He held the office for only
one year, when he was succeeded in the clerkship by Peter Reid,[1] who
faithfully performed his duties for forty-four years, namely, from
1856 to 1899 inclusive. The office of the township treasurer was
held during the first nine years of the municipality by the following:
Thomas Hodgins, 1856; Peter Reid, 1857; Murdoch McKenzie,
1858-62, and John McRae for part of 1863. On the 19th October,
1863, Peter Corrigan was appointed the township treasurer, and has
held the office ever since to the satisfaction of all.

The lot of the pioneers of Kinloss had certain features which
added to the usual hardships that faced a backwoods settler. Being
located far back in the bush they had to make long journeys to obtain
the most ordinary necessaries. Then the almost total absence of
water privileges large enough to drive a good grist mill was a drawback, so that until the grist mill at Lucknow was running in 1859,
a trip to Walkerton, Kincardine or Dungannon was necessary whenever a few bags of wheat had to be ground. Sawmills were in operation in Kinloss as early as 1854 The first one built was erected by
J. Eli Stauffer at the "Black Horse." It was at this point in the
township that the first effort was made to develop a village, which
began to form around the post-office, known as "Kinloss," which
was opened in 1853-4, with Thomas Hodgins as the postmaster. To
him also belongs the credit of having opened the first store there.
About the same time, in 1854-5, a tavern was opened by Wm. Shelton.
This was called the "Black Horse," a name that was extended until
it became that by which the village was and has continued to be
known The first school in the township was also opened at this point.
The house put up for its use was, as were most of those at this time,
only a log one The earliest public religious services in the township
were held here, the first of which was conducted by the Rev. Thomas
Hadwin, a Methodist minister, at the house of Mr. Thomas Hodgins.
After the school-house was built these services were held in it, and
then, at a later date, in the Orange Hall. About 1857, Presbyterian
church services were held, the Rev. Walter Inglis, of Riversdale,

bell, part 1864, 1868; Chester Chapman, part of 1864; Robert Purves, 1865,
'66, '67, '69, 1870 to 1883, 1893; James Grant, 1884 to 1891; George
McIntosh, 1892; Alex Nicholson, 1896; J Johnston, 1897, '98; G. Moffatt,
1899; Frank Henry, 1900 to 1904; Dan. McDonald, 1905, '06.

[1]Peter Reid was a native of Glasgow, where he was born in 1819.
He settled in Kinloss in 1854, where he followed farming. His family had
the pleasure of celebrating the golden wedding of Mr and Mrs. Reid
two years before his death, which occurred in 1900.

officiating. He succeeded in forming the nucleus of the congregation now known as that of North Kinloss. His successor was the Rev. A. G. Forbes. In 1874 a brick church was built by the united efforts of the Presbyterians and the Methodists, still in use by the latter denomination. The Silver Lakes, situated close to the Black Horse, have attracted to them for a number of years parties of campers-out and picnickers from Lucknow, Kincardine and Walkerton. Certainly as long as the groves on their banks are preserved these parties are likely to seek recreation at this delightfully picturesque spot.

Kinlough, two miles and a half south of Kinloss P, O, is the larger village of the two. It began to take form in 1857, when John Scott opened a store there. Shortly afterwards Simon Corrigan helped to centralize business there by starting a sawmill and also an hotel. On a post-office being established in 1864 he was appointed postmaster. The village at present boasts of a handsome school-house, lately erected, and three churches, a Presbyterian, a Methodist and a Church of England.

Holyrood is situated two miles and a half south of Kinlough. Its post-office was opened August 1st, 1856, William McKenzie being the first to have charge of it. Here a large sawmill was built in 1864 and successfully operated for many years. The Roman Catholic congregation at this place was organized about 1870. They built a neat frame church, in which services are now conducted by the priest from Teeswater.

The township of Kinloss has been singularly free of indebtedness. The only debentures issued by the municipality were for drainage purposes, in 1882. They amounted to only $1,946, and were paid in ten years.

At the time (1871) the railways were seeking bonuses to construct lines through the southern part of the county to Kincardine, the people of Kinloss were urged to give a bonus by each of the two railway companies, namely, the narrow gauge from Teeswater or the wide gauge from Listowel, which ultimately was constructed. A meeting was held (July, 1871) at the Black Horse at which a resolution was passed asking the Township Council to submit a by-law to grant a bonus of $15,000 to the road from Teeswater. This the Township Council refused to do. Ultimately the township assumed its share (according to equalized assessment) of the $51,000 sectional bonus given to the Southern Extension Railroad by the townships of Huron, Kincardine and Kinloss. When Lucknow became separated from Kinloss in 1874 it assumed an annual payment of $130 as its share of the obligation of the township. .

This chapter may fittingly be closed by relating the history of the South Kinloss Presbyterian Church, as given to the author by its pastor, the Rev. F. A. MacLennan:

"Early in the fifties this district was thickly settled by immigrants, mostly from the north of Scotland, Nova Scotia and Prince Edward Island, nearly all of whom were Gaelic-speaking Presbyterians

"In 1856 they built a log church on the east side of the gravel road, about half a mile north of the present church building. About that time the congregation held its first communion services in the bush close to the log church, two ministerial members of the Presbytery of London officiating. The late Mr Hugh Rutherford, of St. Helens (who had been ordained in Scotland before coming to Canada), was the only elder present to officiate on the occasion. It seems that there was not an ordained Free Church elder in the whole district from Goderich to Culross at that date but himself. The late Mr. John Gordon, of St Helens, was the only English-speaking communicant present on Sabbath. For his benefit an English table was served The fact that the collection taken during the five days of the services amounted to $50, all coppers, not a single silver coin, shows that the attendance would average 1,000 at least

"Until 1863 the congregation worshipped in the church regularly, receiving such supplies as the Presbytery could send them. At that time the large church standing in the cemetery, and which is still occupied, was built The late Rev. John Fraser, of Thamesford, formally opened it for public worship. Every alternate Sunday the Rev. Adam McKay, of Teeswater, held service in this church until, in 1867, the Rev. John McNabb was ordained and inducted to this charge. Soon after the following were ordained elders and formed the first Kirk-Session, viz, Messrs Murdo Mackenzie, Peter Milne, Robert Young, James Gordon, Thomas Falconer and Donald MacPherson. Mr. McNabb resigned the charge in 1869 and was succeeded by the Rev. Duncan Cameron in 1872 Mr. Cameron resigned in 1881, and was succeeded by the Rev. Alexander MacKenzie in 1882. Mr. MacKenzie resigned in 1887, and was succeeded by the present pastor, the Rev F. A. MacLennan, translated from the Presbytery of Glengarry in May, 1882. Services from the very first have been held in this congregation in both English and Gaelic. Gaelic, the language of the congregation fifty years ago, is approaching the vanishing point. Still it dies hard."

CHAPTER XXXV.

VILLAGE OF LUCKNOW.[1]

THE present thriving village of Lucknow owes its origin to an offer made by the government of a grant of two hundred acres of land to any one who would erect a mill on the Nine-Mile River near the spot where it crossed the Woolwich and Huron Road, which road forms the boundary line between Kinloss and Wawanosh This offer was closed with by J. Eli Stauffer, a German from Waterloo County, mentioned in the preceding chapter as one of the first settlers on the Durham Road in the township of Kinloss It was in 1856-57 that Mr. Stauffer erected the dam and sawmill. The latter could hardly be called a first-class mill, but it supplied a much-felt need of the adjoining townships in Huron and Bruce. One of the first to settle near the mill was Ralph Miller, who in April, 1858, purchased a small parcel of land from Mr. Stauffer, on which he built a log tavern, that went by the name of the "Balaclava House." James Somerville,[2] who deservedly is entitled to be called the founder of the village, was probably living there at the time the agreement for this sale was drawn out, as his name appears thereon as witness to the signatures. During the summer of 1858 Mr. Somerville, having purchased from Mr. Stauffer the mill and his right to the land, had the south halves of lots 57, 58, 59 and 60 on the first concession of Kinloss surveyed into village lots The date of the

---

[1] The village of Lucknow bears the name of the city in India around which so much interest centred in the days of the Indian Mutiny, which was fresh in the minds of all at the time of the survey of the village A number of its streets are named after prominent generals in the Indian Army.

[2] James Somerville was born at Dunfermline, Scotland, in 1825, and came to Canada in 1841, with his parents, who settled at Dundas He there learned the trade of a millwright In 1851 he moved to Wawanosh and built a sawmill, between what is now Belfast and St. Helens Mr. Somerville, in 1858, secured Mr Stauffer's mill and right to the land From that date he continued to be associated with Lucknow until his death, which occurred September 19th, 1898 In 1872 he was the Reform candidate for the House of Commons for North Huron, but was defeated In 1882 he again was a candidate, this time for West Bruce, and was successful Mr. Somerville also sat in the township councils of Wawanosh and Kinloss

registering of this plan is September 21st, 1858.[1] This plan shows
both a saw and a grist mill, the latter built, in all probability, that
summer by Mr. Somerville. On September 1st, 1858, the village
lots were offered at auction, and the ceremony of naming the place
was celebrated by a salute of twenty-one—we cannot say guns—but
of explosions of that number of charges of gunpowder, placed in
large auger-holes bored in good-sized trees standing in the village
plot. The survey of the village lots on the Ashfield and Wawanosh
side of the village[2] was not made until the early spring of 1861.

The first merchant in Lucknow was Malcolm Campbell, who commenced business in 1859. He was also the first postmaster, the post-
office being established shortly after he came to the village. Other
merchants, foreseeing the possibilities of development at this point,
opened up business shortly after Mr. Campbell had done so. Half
a dozen years after the post-office was established the following were
carrying on business as merchants at Lucknow: In addition to Malcolm Campbell there was Walter Armstrong, Bingham & Little, Alex.
Murray, Charles Secord and John Treleaven. The grist and saw-
mills were then being operated by Walter Treleaven and Messrs. Lees
& Douglas ran a wool-carding mill. The population was then (1866)
placed at 430. The village received quite an impetus in the same
year from the construction of the gravel road northward through the
township of Kinloss, which had the effect of bringing to Lucknow
much of the trade of the township that had previously gone to Kincardine. The next forward step of note made by the village was the
result of the opening of the railway in 1873. No doubt the business
men of the village have complained loudly and deeply at the poor
service that the railway has given them at times; but it should be
borne in mind that it is the railway that has made Lucknow a grain
market, and the shipping point for the produce of the farms situated
for miles north and south of the village. It also has given the shipping facilities which induced manufacturers to there establish factories In fact, it is the railway which has made Lucknow the flourishing village of to-day.

[1]It seems strange that the Crown patent was not secured before the
survey was made. It was April 2nd, 1862, before the patent for the south
halves of 57 and 58 was issued to M. C. Cameron, and March 23rd, 1863,
when the patent for the south halves of 59 and 60 was issued to James
Somerville

[2]It was in October, 1854, that the lands in Ashfield and Wawanosh, now
in the village of Lucknow, were settled upon by Daniel Webster and James
Henderson respectively

The initial step taken with a view to Lucknow becoming a separate municipality was made in December, 1863, when, on petition of James Somerville and twenty-three others, the United Counties Council erected it into a police village.

The incorporation of the village of Lucknow was an event that created a commotion unusual in the ordinary routine of procedure as laid down in the Municipal Act for the incorporation of villages This arose from the fact of the village being located partly in the county of Bruce and partly in the county of Huron. The convenience of the inhabitants would perhaps have been secured to a greater extent by being united to Huron, as the county town would then be but twenty-two miles distant. But Bruce had an interest in retaining the village as part of the territory of the county. The arguments used on this side were: That the majority of the inhabitants and three-fifths of the area of the village were on the Bruce side of the county line; that the bulk of the business of the village came from, and would continue to come from, the Bruce side, and this as the result of gravel roads constructed at the cost of the county at large; and, lastly, that the large railway bonus paid by Bruce would, if the separation take place, be for the benefit of a village in another county This last argument, especially, made the Bruce County Council strongly oppose loss of territory at this point. But politics had possibly the largest share in influencing the decision finally reached. The member for South Bruce (R. M. Wells) had received at election times strong support at Lucknow, and he was unwilling to submit to the loss of so many votes as the placing of it in another electoral division involved, and so his influence, though unapparent, was felt in the contest. With so many interests at work, no wonder that a year passed before a settlement was arrived at. The history of the proceedings was, so far as the author has been able to trace, as follows: "At a meeting of the ratepayers of the village held in the spring of 1873, a motion was unanimously passed that the necessary steps be taken to have the village incorporated and annexed to the county of Huron. Messrs. R. Graham and R. Clendening were appointed delegates to bring the matter before the Huron County Council, and Messrs. James Somerville and Robert Hunter were to act in the same capacity before the Bruce County Council. The prayer of the petition was acceded to by each of these bodies, and both councils on the same day (June 7th, 1873) passed a by-law incorporating the village of Lucknow and annexing it to the county

which it represented. When it became apparent that a deadlock
was likely to ensue on account of this dual annexation, and the question would have to be decided by the Governor-in-Council, the Bruce
County Council appointed the warden (Robert Baird) and Robert
Purves as delegates to go to Toronto in the interests of the county.
The first Village Council (elected in January, 1874) at an early meeting passed a motion to memorialize the Lieut.-Governor to have the
village annexed to Huron County. Meanwhile the people of the
townships of Huron and Kinloss, who did their trading at Lucknow,
gave emphatic expression to the business men of the village of their
opinion, that it would be an unjust act to have Lucknow, which had
been largely built up by their trade, severed from their common
county and united to another. These pronounced expressions of
opinion produced an effect, and many in the village were prepared to
accede to the wishes of their customers; prominent among those
willing to do so were Malcolm Campbell, Robert Graham and Dr.
MacCrimmon. On the other hand an equal number held out that to
be united to the county of Huron was for the interests of the village.
The leaders of this party were James Somerville, Thomas Lawrence
and J. Treleaven. Each of the parties sent largely signed petitions
to the Lieut.-Governor presenting their views for his consideration.
Excitement in the village ran high; in fact, so many bitter feelings
were engendered at this time, as the result of the hotly fought controversy, that years passed before they were smoothed away. Finally
a meeting was called of the ratepayers, in hope of an agreement being
reached. After each side had presented its side of the question, a
vote was taken, which gave a majority of one in favor of the village
being annexed to Bruce. This vote was challenged on the ground
that one who was not a qualified ratepayer had voted for Bruce. In
April, 1874, at the suggestion of the authorities at Toronto, so it is
said, another vote was taken, which resulted in a majority of two
being obtained for union with the county of Huron. Notwithstanding this final vote, the Lieut.-Governor, on June 11th, 1874, issued
a proclamation annexing the incorporated village of Lucknow to the
county of Bruce. A week prior to the issuing of the proclamation,
a telegraph message announcing the decision arrived at was received
by the warden, and read to the Bruce County Council, then in session;
when it was moved that the reeve from Lucknow do now take his seat
at the Council board. Up to this date (June 4th, 1874) Lucknow
was unrepresented at the County Council of either county. In Jan-

uary, 1875, the respective wardens of Huron and Bruce met with the
reeve of Lucknow, and after consultation agreed that the proportionate share of the liabilities of the county of Huron chargeable to
Lucknow was twelve hundred dollars. This the county of Bruce
assumed, and payment was made in two instalments.

The first Village Council (elected January, 1874) was composed
of M. Campbell, reeve; and Thomas Lawrence, Charles Mooney,
Alex. McIntyre and Walter Treleaven, councillors. The joint offices
of clerk and treasurer were conferred upon George T. Burgess. In
a footnote[1] are given the names of the reeves and officers of the
municipality from its organization until 1906.

The building first used as a town hall was properly known as the
Temperance Hall. The land on which it stood was given by James
Somerville, at an early date, to a temperance society that they might
erect a hall thereon. This they did in or about 1862. The present
town hall was built in 1885,[2] at a cost of $4,500. It contains a fire-
hall and a lock-up on the ground floor. Over these, in the second
storey, is a commodious hall, suitable for public meetings and enter-
tainments. Unfortunately, the plan of this structure was defective
in respect to the roof, which, after the building was completed, had
to be given additional support in a way that has marred the appearance of the auditorium. In the present year (1906) an arrangement
was made with Andrew Carnegie, the millionaire, famous for his
gifts to public libraries, who has donated $7,500 for a public library
building. The building to be erected will be 50 x 80 feet in size. To
all intents and purposes it will be the town hall of the future, as in
addition to giving accommodation for a public library it will provide
an auditorium and a board-room The latter will be used by the
Village Council to meet in. The village, for its part in the agreement with Mr. Carnegie, undertakes to furnish the site and to make
an annual grant of $750 toward the maintenance of the library and
hall.

[1]List of reeves of the village of Lucknow, with years of office . M.
Campbell, 1874, '75, '76, '77; D A MacCrimmon, M D, 1878; George Kerr,
1879, '80, '81, '82; D Campbell, 1883, '84, '85; J. S. Tennant, M D, 1886,
'87; R Graham, 1888; James Bryan, 1889, '90, '91, '92, '93, James Lyons,
1894, '95, 96; J. G Murdoch, 1897, '98, '99; William Taylor, 1900,
William Allan, 1901, '02, '04, '05, A. D Davidson, 1903, J G Anderson,
1906.
List of village treasurers G. T. Burgess, D E Cameron, George A
Siddall, and John Murchison, at present in office.
List of village clerks . G. T. Burgess, W. H. Smith, Brown Mallough,
Hugh Morrison, and P. A. Malcolmson, at present in office

[2]The formal opening was on May 24th, 1886

The first public school building known to the village was a modest frame building 24 x 30 feet, erected in 1862. The pupils in attendance there were at first wholly from Kinloss. Three or four years later a union school section was formed by the adding of parts of the townships of Ashfield and Wawanosh. The first to teach in the new building was a Mr. Middleton.[1] In 1865-6 the teacher was D. A. MacCrimmon (now Dr. MacCrimmon, of Ripley). He was succeeded by James Warren, P.L.S. (of Walkerton), Angus McCharles (a prominent son of Huron Township, lately deceased), Charles Cliff (of the *Wingham Advocate*) and others. The last principal in the old school-house and the first in the new was C. Priest. He was succeeded by P. M. McEachern (now the Presbyterian minister at Glammis). D. D. Yule succeeded him, and continued as the principal of the school for seventeen years. Mr. Joseph Stalker, who entered upon his duties in 1902, is the present principal of the school. The commodious eight-room school-house now in use was built in 1878. The erection of this building necessitated the issue of the first debentures sold by the village In a footnote[2] these are to be found included in a list of all debentures issued by the village corporation.

Lucknow has on different occasions suffered severely by fire, which destroyed important sections in the business part of the village. The first of these serious losses occurred in 1864 Some time in the seventies a good hand fire-engine was purchased by the village. Ten years later, when a proposition was made to invest in a steam fire-engine, public opinion decided that the wisest thing to do would be to instal permanent waterworks for fire protection. This was done in 1890. Since then at the pump-house steam is kept up all the time The numerous hydrants are favorably located, giving an assurance of a bountiful supply of water if a fire should break out The result of this has been a marked reduction in insurance rates.

[1] Before the erection of the school building, school was held in a building on Campbell Street, previously used as a tannery.

[2] LIST OF DEBENTURES ISSUED BY THE VILLAGE OF LUCKNOW.

In 1878, for school building and furnishing, $10,113.
In 1885, for town hall, $4,500.
In 1890, for waterworks, $10,000.
In 1890, for Cliffe & Forester loan, $5,000
In 1902, for granolithic sidewalks, $7,100
In 1905, for granolithic sidewalks, $3,785.
In addition to the above, the village annually, from 1875 to 1890, inclusive, paid the sum of $130 as its share of the debentures given by the county as a bonus to the Southern Extension Railway.

The earliest public religious services held in the vicinity of Lucknow were conducted by a Presbyterian elder of the name of Campbell, who resided in Ashfield. This was at a time prior to that when roads had been cut through the forest, so the elder and his flock had of necessity to find 'their way to and from the place of meeting by the blaze on the trees. The Wesleyan Methodists organized a congregation at Lucknow in 1862, of which the Rev. David Ryan was the first minister. He was succeeded by the Rev. E. W. Fraser, and he by the Rev. Wm. Tucker. The New Connexion Methodists were organized into a congregation in 1865, the Rev. John Walker being the minister. The present handsome church edifice on the corner of Campbell and Havelock Streets, erected in 1885, in which the Methodist congregation worships, was preceded by a much less pretentious building of rough-cast, which did service as a place of worship for a number of years. Although Lucknow has always had a large Scotch element in its population, it was some time before a Presbyterian congregation was formed within the village, the "big" church (or South Kinloss congregation), just outside the village, being where the Presbyterians attended services. Sometimes, however, the minister at the "big church" held evening services in the village. About the time (1869) that the Rev. J. McNabb resigned the pastorate of the South Kinloss congregation, steps were taken by the Presbyterian residents of the village to there erect a church building. The result of these efforts was a good-sized frame edifice, known as Knox Church. Soon after the settlement of the Rev. Mr. Cameron at South Kinloss some of the leading members from the village separated from the congregation   Not obtaining what they wanted from the Presbytery of Huron, they applied to the Church of Scotland in Canada, and were erected into a congregation that bore the name of St. Andrew's, Lucknow, which built for itself a neat stone church.[1] The Rev. I. B Taylor was the first minister, but he resigned after a pastorate of seven or eight years, and was succeeded by the Rev. John McNabb in 1882. In 1886 the Rev Mr. Cameron, who continued his ministry in Knox Church, Lucknow, after resigning (in 1881) the South Kinloss part of his charge, and Mr. McNabb both resigned in order to afford the two congregations in the village the opportunity of uniting, which they did in September, 1886. In

---

[1]After the union of the two Presbyterian congregations in the village the building was sold to the Baptists   At present it is owned and occupied by the Roman Catholic congregation

17

1887 the united congregation called the Rev. Angus McKay, and in 1888-9 built the present large and substantial brick church. On Mr. McKay's resignation in 1904 the present pastor, the Rev. D. T. L. McKerroll, entered upon the pastorate of this large congregation The Church of England at Lucknow is known as St. Peter's, and was erected in 1878

It was in the first week of January, 1874, that *The Lucknow Sentinel* published its initial issue   Since then, week by week, this chronicle of the local events of village and country has been issued. The first proprietors were Messrs. Bowers and Hunt. In a short time the paper passed into the hands of D. B. Boyd, who conducted it for two or three years   On his death his widow continued to publish it until her marriage to James Bryan   For nearly three decades Mr Bryan filled the editorial chair of the *Sentinel,* until he sold his interest in the paper to Mr Albert McGregor, in October, 1906.

Ever since the railway has been in operation Lucknow has been a good market where the farmer could sell his grain and other farm produce. J G Smith was one of the first to be prominent as a grain buyer after the advent of the railway. Prior to that event merchants purchased grain, pork and other produce largely " for trade." To dispose of their purchases they had to team them to Goderich for shipment.

The author, lacking that intimate and personal acquaintance with the citizens of Lucknow, past and present, which might enable him to refer to them individually in these pages, must touch but lightly on such a topic. For a number of years the village possessed among its citizens a trio of medical doctors that stood out prominently   Dr. D. A. MacCrimmon, as chief of the Caledonia Society, is, referred to elsewhere. Dr. J. H. Garnier, noted as an ornithologist, possessed a collection of stuffed birds which numbered over twenty thousand, and Dr. J. S. Tennant, councillor and reeve of the village, and Conservative candidate for South Bruce, whose sudden death, September 12th, 1902, was so deeply lamented. Another old and worthy citizen, the local bard, is Robert Graham. What old curler is there in this part of the province but knows J. B. Hunter and the rinks of keen curlers that stood by him on the ice playing the " roaring game," one of the sports for which Lucknow has made a name for itself

If there is anything which more than another has bestowed on the village of Lucknow an almost continental fame it is the Lucknow

Caledonian Society. It is an acknowledged truism the world over, that the Scot, wherever his lot may be cast, cherishes with enthusiasm everything of a national character, its language, history, poetry, songs, pastimes, sports, and also the national costume. There are few sections, if any, in the province more thickly settled with Scotchmen, or those of Scottish descent, than the townships in the vicinity of Lucknow. These conditions existing, it only required a few leading spirits to inaugurate and maintain an organization the aim of which would be to develop and perpetuate everything characteristic of Scottish sentiment, life and practice Who was the first to suggest the formation of the Lucknow Caledonia Society the author cannot say.[1] The society, however, was enthusiastically inaugurated during the winter of 1874-5. Provision was made in the constitution for extending help to Scotchmen in need or to their families, also for the development of national sentiment by the holding of Scotch concerts, banquets and balls, and for what became the most prominent feature in the history of the society, the holding of annual gatherings for athletic sports. It was the success that attended these gatherings, celebrated on the second Wednesday in September in each year for twenty years, that gave the society a widely extended fame, and caused Lucknow to be appreciatively spoken of in many a far distant group of Scotia's sons. That these gatherings were so successful and so largely attended may be attributed, primarily, to the enthusiastic Scottish element of the adjoining district and to the untiring efforts of the officers to provide attractive features.[2] Then the management at all the gatherings was excellent, and everything promised in the programmes was carried out. With all this there was accorded a hearty, liberal support by the people of the village to the efforts of the society. Among those connected with the Society at its inception

[1]The records of the society have unfortunately suffered loss from fire on two occasions The author is indebted for the facts of the society to Chief MacCrimmon and his successor, Chief Alex MacPherson, and John Murchison, late financial secretary of the society.

[2]The Lucknow Caledonian Society was instrumental in inducing the following to visit America and be present at their gatherings : Donald Dinnie, the leading athlete of Scotland, also Geo. Davidson, another famous athlete ; the champion Scottish piper, Wm. McLennan, was another who left Scotland on a visit at the solicitation of the Society Duncan C. Ross, a noted athlete from the United States, was an annual competitor in the sports for several years. In 1881 one of the attractions was Piper Joseph Hendry, late of the 78th Highlanders, the sound of whose pipes were the first assurance the besieged in Lucknow (India) had of the nearness of the troops sent for their relief at the time of the Mutiny.

were the following: Donald A. MacCrimmon, M.D ,[1] Alex. McPherson, Capt. John McPherson, Alex. McIntyre, Wm. McIntosh, Allan McDonald, A. D. and A. K. Cameron, Alex. Currie, Dougal McKinnon, Malcolm Campbell, James Findlater, and others. Among other active members who joined the society at a later date might be mentioned John Murchison, D E. Cameron, George E. Kerr and D. D. Yule. The society held the first of its athletic gatherings in September, 1875. The place where held, both in this and the following year, was at Hugh McKay's grounds. From 1877 to 1880 the Agricultural Society's park was used for this purpose. After that all the gatherings were held at Lorne Park, a property purchased by the society. This park has an area of six acres, and is situated in the south-west corner of the village It is admirably adapted for the objects the society had in view when purchasing it On its south side there is a gradual slope rising to a considerable height, affording ample seating accommodation for thousands of spectators. To add to this the society erected on the west and north sides of the park large grand stands, on which some four thousand persons could be seated. The sward, on which the contests of strength and skill came off, perfectly level and of ample size, lay before the uninterrupted view of all these spectators. On the grounds there were also two platforms, on one of which the dancing for prizes came off; the other was occupied by bands of musicians and pipers, who enlivened the proceedings and filled up all intervals with music. In the park the society also built the Caledonian Hall, a large frame structure of octagonal shape. Of its eight sides each was sixty feet long. This building, erected in 1883, was unfortunately destroyed by fire in 1900. The first athletic gathering, as above-mentioned, was held in 1875. About $300 was then offered in prizes The attendance thereat was so encouraging that in the following year the management felt warranted in increasing the amount offered in prizes by $100. As the gathering in each succeeding year proved to be a greater

[1]Dr MacCrimmon was chief of the society from its formation until he left Lucknow, in 1890, excepting one year, when he was absent in Europe taking a post-graduate course. The doctor is a native of Glengarry, Ontario, where he was born in 1838. His first association with Lucknow was as the teacher of the public school, which position he held in 1865 and 1866. He resigned to take up the study of medicine. On obtaining his degree he commenced to practice in Lucknow, remaining there until 1890, when he moved to Underwood After a sojourn there of five years he took up his residence at Ripley, where he at present resides. There is no doubt but that the success of the Caledonia Society of Lucknow was largely due to the enthusiasm, energy and personality of Dr. MacCrimmon.

success than the preceding one, the prizes offered gradually increased in value until in 1883 and 1884 the handsome sum of $1,300 was offered. The attendance at the games increased from hundreds to thousands, until high water mark was reached in 1882, when fully twelve thousand persons attended the games. Such a large attendance could only be secured by the co-operation of the railway company, which in 1878 offered fares at excursion rates; then, as the demand for transport increased, furnished special trains. These would arrive filled to overflowing with enthusiastic Scots, of whom might be quoted the sentiment that headed each annual programme of sports, which was:

> '' Oh, Canada, I lo'e ye weel,
>   Altho' nae son o' thine ;
> Within thy wide domain there beats
>   Nae truer heart than mine
> But when a day like this com's roun'
>   Auld Scotia has her claims ,
> The thistle aye com's uppermost,
>   I'll gang to see the games.''

The main features of the sports were distinctly in accord with the name and objects of the society. Prizes were given to the best performer on the bagpipes, to the best dancer of reels, strathspeys, the Highland fling and sword dance, also to the best dressed man and boy in Highland costume. In feats of strength and skill the prizes offered covered a wide field familiar to all Scottish athletes. Then there was an archery contest for ladies and also a quoiting tournament   The various contests were eagerly watched and the winners were loudly cheered. The excitement reached its climax over the tug-of-war between teams chosen from the men of Bruce and Huron Counties   This was generally the last event on the programme The men are selected with care by each captain. As the muscular fellows that compose each team strip for the event their supporters are loud in prophesying victory for their county. Then when, each team in place and grasping the rope, the word " go " is given, the "tug" commences. Among the spectators the excitement is intense, some of them being so carried away by it that it is with difficulty they are prevented from seizing the rope to help their side to victory. The handkerchief that marks the centre of the rope quivers over the centre line. Each team, encouraged by the cheers of its friends, strains every muscle. Maybe a foot slips, a slight advantage for the other side is thus obtained. Encouraged thereby yet one more effort is put forth, and amid the shouts of thousands a " draw " is made, and their opponents are pulled across the line.

It seems a pity that these annual sports have for the last ten years been given up, but from various causes the Caledonia Society has not the strength it once possessed. Some of its most interested and active members. have left the village; many others have become members of " The Sons of Scotland." Weakened as it has thus been, the feature of the annual games has been dropped, let us hope but for a time.

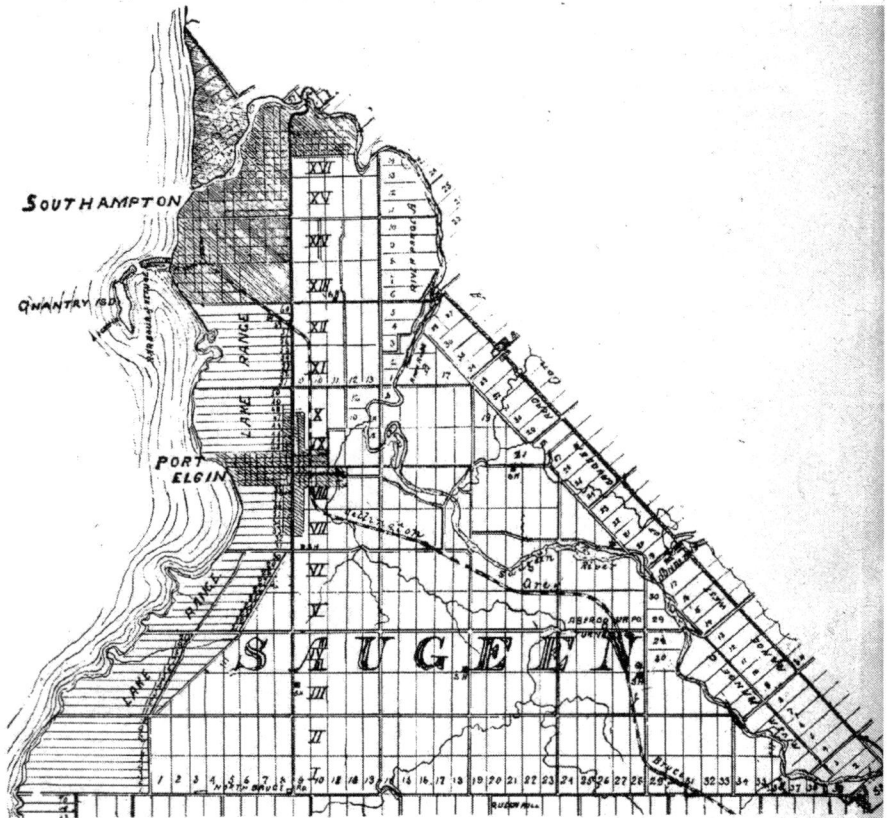

SOUTHAMPTON

CHANTRY ISD

PORT ELGIN

SAUGEEN

CHAPTER XXXVI.

TOWNSHIP OF SAUGEEN.[1]

EXTRACT FROM THE REPORT OF COUNTY VALUATORS, 1901.

" This township, in proportion to its acreage, has more inferior land, we think, than any township south of the peninsula. The shore range, while much better than that of Bruce, is far below the average This range, together with the thousands of acres of drift sand in the north, and cut as the township is through its whole length by Mill Creek, the Saugeen River, and the railroad, combine to pull down the average value very much. However, there are a number of very fine farms in Saugeen that will compare favorably with any in the county. There are some sections of very stiff clay, and the land is very rough along the banks of the Saugeen River The rate per acre for this township is $28 66. There is no village property in Saugeen ''

MEN with keen eyes to perceive latent possibilities and who purposed settling in the Queen's Bush petitioned, as early as 1847, the government to have a survey made of the lands at the mouth of the Saugeen River and open the same for settlement. The locality was visited by Alex. Wilkinson, P L S.,[2] in the fall of that year, but no lands were surveyed at that time. The survey of Saugeen Township into farm lots was conducted by A. Vidal, P.L.S.[3] His commission to do this work was dated January 13th, 1851. Gathering his party of men and necessary supplies, he left Sarnia by boat and reached the mouth of the Saugeen River on April 18th following. Securing canoes the party proceeded up the river to near the point where they were to commence work. Mr. Vidal's instructions were: Commencing at the north-west corner of the township of Brant, to carry the Elora Road, as originally projected, through to some place near the mouth of the Saugeen River, and then survey the township into farm lots. The starting point was reached April 22nd, and work, immediately commenced. The line thus laid was the base for the

[1]" Saugeen '' is the corrupted form of an Indian word meaning the entrance or mouth of the river.
[2]See Chapter II.
[3]Afterwards elevated to the Senate of the Dominion

survey of the rest of the township,[1] which was completed August 22nd, 1851.

In seeking to name the first settlers in Saugeen, the reader is asked to remember that at the first, and for some subsequent years, the present town of Southampton and the village of Port Elgin formed an integral part of the township. This it is necessary to bear in mind, as it was at these points the first settlements in Saugeen were made. It was in June, 1848, that Capt. John Spence and William Kennedy settled at Southampton, as is narrated in Chapter III During the following year these pioneers were joined by James Orr and George Butchart. It was in the fall of 1849 that settlement was made at Port Elgin, the first settler being Lachlin (Loch Buie) McLean, who after a season spent at the Fishing Islands, landed at Port Elgin Bay and built a small log shanty in which he spent the first winter alone, and which as a tavern was at a later date known to all the settlers in Saugeen In 1850 the first party of land-seekers entered the township These were Peter Smith, Dugald Bell and Donald McIntosh. As their home was in the county of Grey, on the Garafraxa Road, they in all probability descended the river on a raft or scow and made their way to the township in this manner. Satisfied with the prospects, they returned to make arrangements to settle in the following spring. The next party of prospectors were William[2] and David Kennedy. From their home near Guelph they, in January, 1851, drove to Owen Sound, then guided by an Indian they walked to Southampton and thence into the interior of the township. Thoroughly pleased with the outlook for settlement, they retraced their steps, to return in April following. David Kennedy, in his book entitled " Incidents of Pioneer Days,"[3] describes the wearisome journey over the Garafraxa and Durham Roads to Hanover in March, 1851 The building of a large scow there (the lumber for which they cut with a whip-saw out of a large pine tree they had felled), then the tedious delay owing to high water in the Saugeen,

[1] A peculiarity about the survey of Saugeen is the " Marine allowance " along the edge of the river in this township, a feature not found elsewhere on the river Saugeen.

[2] William Kennedy was for thirty years a resident if Saugeen. He then moved to the township of Derby, residing there for ten years, when he retired from farming and resided at Tara, where he died, July 31st, 1903. For twenty-five years he was an elder of the Presbyterian Church at Burgoyne and latterly at Tara also

[3] A perusal of this little book is earnestly recommended to any one interested in the pioneer days of the county of Bruce.

the final start of the party of twelve in number, the narrow escapes from shipwreck, and at length, on reaching Saugeen Township, the gladsome welcome given them by the earliest settler, Alexander Wallace and James D. Cathay, the latter a teacher and missionary at the Indian village. As far as the author has been able to ascertain, Alexander Wallace is entitled to the credit of being the first settler in what is now the township of Saugeen While the snow was still on the ground, in the spring of 1851, Mr Wallace left Owen Sound for "the bush," drawing after him a toboggan on which was piled his household effects, his brave wife, ladened with bundles, accompanying him. Reaching the Indian village Mrs. Wallace remained as the guest of Mrs. Cathay, while her husband sought a desirable spot on which to locate. Having found one to his liking, he proceeded to erect a log shanty. It is related of Mrs Wallace, that becoming anxious to assist her husband, she left her hospitable quarters and sought her husband's shanty, the walls only of which were erected. As neither door, window or roof had been made, she entered her new home by climbing over the top of the log wall. From that time she remained with her husband roughing it in the bush,[1] and nobly doing her part in making a home in the wilderness.

The following are the names of some of the pioneers of Saugeen who settled in the township in 1851: Alexander and John Wallace, William and David Kennedy, Thomas Burgess, Philip Strowger, John and Jacob Atkinson, William Gowanlock, James Rowand, Silas Fuller, Peter, Thomas and John Smith, William, Joseph and John Stirton, Archibald Armstrong, Thomas Turner, Neil Bell, John King, Archibald Pollock and Robert Craig.

The majority of those above-mentioned found their way to their new homes in the bush by way of the river Saugeen, either on rafts or roughly constructed scows. To persons unaccustomed to handling such unwieldy crafts mishaps were a common occurrence. Some were shipwrecked on sunken snags, others had a portion of their cargo swept off into the turbulent waters by low-hanging branches of trees that bent over the stream So dangerous to inexperienced sailors was the navigation that it was with feelings of thankfulness the passengers reached their destination and stepped ashore. Hardly any of these voyagers but could relate a tale of hairbreadth escapes during the course of their passage down the Saugeen.

[1]This estimable and much esteemed woman passed away, February 12th, 1906, having survived her husband some thirteen years

The number of incoming settlers increased in the following years. Among those who entered the township in 1852-3 the following may be mentioned: "Donald Currie, Dugald Bell, Robert Leeder, Iden Goble, James Stewart, Clement Seiffert, Henry and Adam Hilker, John Stafford, John and Angus McPhee, Donald, Archibald and Angus Galbraith. These years also marked the beginning of a flow into the township of settlers of German nationality from Waterloo County, men who as a rule were pretty well-to-do. So satisfied were these first-comers in regard to the prospects of the settlement that a proposition was made to Mr. McNabb, the Crown Land Agent, to settle the rest of the township with Germans from the locality they came from. This proposition was not, however, entertained. Notwithstanding, the flow of German settlers continued. Prominent among them were Benjamin Shantz, Samuel Bricker, W. H. Ruby, John Goble, Peter Wagner and John Zant.

The following incident of the early settlers is worthy of being recorded. It is an extract from the *Paisley Advocate*. Late in December, 1851, two travellers seeking to cross the Saugeen were obligingly ferried across in a canoe by two of Mr. Gowanlock's daughters. On returning, the river, which had all morning been running snow, slush and ice, became so blocked thereby that the two young women found that it was impossible to force the canoe across the river. They certainly were in a perilous position, as no rope or pole could be got that would reach them from the shore. Sometimes the canoe with its surrounding of slush would remain immovable, then breaking loose would start swiftly down the river, and all the while little or no progress was made shoreward. It was bitterly cold, and only by incessant attempts at paddling could the young women keep themselves from freezing. It was not until about dusk that they were rescued from their dangerous situation, and then it was accomplished by felling a small tree into the river, which by the greatest good fortune they were able to grasp in passing. One of these young ladies afterwards became the wife of James Rowand, the member for West Bruce for the years 1887 to 1895.

The lands in Saugeen were among those classed as "School Lands," and as such were opened for sale[1] July 30th, 1852, at the price of ten shillings ($2.00) per acre. Pioneers who had located themselves on farm lots prior to this date were known as squatters,

[1]See Appendix J.

and they had, on the appearance of the notice offering the lands in the township for sale, to take immediate steps to have recognized their "squatter's rights" to the lots on which they were living.

Saugeen is the smallest township in Bruce. Nevertheless, in the early years of settlement up to 1856, owing to the rapid inflow of industrious settlers, it occupied a second or third place in regard to the amount of its equalized assessment among the townships in the county.[1] It was this fact that led the United Counties Council, when it dissolved the union of townships within the county of Bruce,[2] to make it a separate municipality, instead of uniting it with some other township, as was done in the case of all the other townships, Huron excepted. The first municipal election was held in January, 1854. The one polling place was at Belcher's tavern at Southampton, and the returning officer was Alex. McNabb. The members of Council then elected were Messrs. James Calder, John Valentine, Thomas Turner, Alexander McNabb and John Smith. The first meeting of the Township Council was held at the house of James D. Cathay, on January 16th, 1854, the first business of which was the election of a reeve, which honor was unanimously conferred on Alexander McNabb, and James D. Cathay was appointed township clerk In a footnote[3] the names of the various reeves of the township from the first to the time of writing are given, also of the township clerks and treasurers.

In Chapter VI. are narrated the measures taken to relieve the destitution that existed throughout the county in 1859 ("Starvation Year"). Saugeen Township shared in the common calamity, but to

[1]See Appendix M

[2]See Appendix F.

[3]Reeves of the township of Saugeen from 1854 to 1906, inclusive: Alex McNabb, 1854, '56, '57; Robert Reid, 1855; Donald Currie, 1858; Thomas Brown, 1859, '60, '61; William H. Ruby, 1862, '63; James Rowand, 1864, '67, '68, '69, '70; John Wallace, 1865, '66; Henry Hilker, 1871, '72, '73; N. Cassidy, 1874, '75, '76; John Peirson, 1877 to 1888; P. Cummings, 1889 to 1894; A. R Hutchison, 1895, '96; M. Cook, 1897, '98; Alex. McKinnon, 1899, 1900; Alex. McCannel, 1901, '02; Robert Smyth, 1903 to 1906.

Names of the township clerks of Saugeen from 1854 to 1906 : James D. Cathay, 1854, Dr. H. Haynes, 1855; John Eastwood, 1856, '57, '58 and 1871 to 1876; Archibald Roy, 1859 to 1867; John C Currie, 1868, '69, '70; R. B Fleming, 1877 to 1904, Fred. W. Elliott, 1905, '06.

Names of the township treasurers of Saugeen : In 1854 and 1855 the author has reason to believe that the township clerk was also township treasurer, but has not been able to obtain conclusive evidence. John Eastwood, 1856, '57, '58; Archibald Roy, 1859 to 1869; W. H. Ruby, 1870 to his death, August 9th, 1892; N. E. Leeder, Sr., part of 1892 to 1906

its credit be it noted that it and the village of Southampton were the only municipalities within the county that declined to accept aid from the County Destitution Fund. The Township Council, at a meeting held April 14th, 1859, decided to use whatever funds were in the township treasury, and also whatever more that might be obtained by the sale of Non-Resident Loan Fund Debentures to purchase seed grain, which was to be sold to any resident of the township, for which an approved joint note, payable in October following, would be accepted. . Councillors Joseph Schell and John Stafford were appointed a committee to receive and distribute the grain thus purchased.

The first expenditure made by the government towards opening roads in Saugeen was in 1852, when that part of the Elora Road which lies north of Burgoyne was opened as part of the Saugeen and Sydenham Road, the contract of which was let by Mr. McNabb, Crown Land Agent After the appointment of David Gibson as Superintendent of Colonization Roads in September, 1853, contracts were let for making a good " Winter Road "[1] on what are known as the Elora and Goderich Roads. The principal contractor for work on the Elora Road was James Campbell, who was paid £270. On the Goderich Road the largest contracts were let to Joseph Gilbert and James Turner, who received respectively £250 and £180. The work in these several contracts was performed in 1854. Very little, if any, work was done under government direction in 1855 in Saugeen, but in 1856 Joseph Gilbert received a contract for work on the Elora Road that amounted to £1,020, which outlay was made in the endeavor to make of it a "summer road." The County Gravel Road By-law, passed in 1865, provided liberally for the township of Saugeen, both the Elora and Goderich Roads being gravelled, giving the east and west sides of the township excellent roads.

. Saugeen and Brant are the two townships in the county that are the most burdened with the expense of constructing and maintaining large bridges. The Saugeen River is a noble and deservedly admired stream, but when its course lies through the full length of a township, as in Saugeen, and bridges have to be stretched across its waters and over good-sized tributaries as well, a large outlay is demanded, first to build the bridges and then an annual charge to keep them in

[1]In a foot-note in Chapter V., referring to Mr. Gibson's work, the specifications of a " winter road " are to be found.

repair. The township of Saugeen, the town of Southampton and the villages of Port Elgin and Paisley have reason to congratulate themselves upon the relief from this financial burden that has come from the county. In some instances this has come because of the liberal, broad-minded views held by members of the County Council. In other cases this has been because of statutory compulsion, as in the case of Stirton's bridge.[1] Upon the boundaries of these four minor municipalities above mentioned or within their limits, the county is responsible for sixteen bridges, about two-thirds of these being expensive structures, e.g., McCalder's bridge, the cost of which was over $9,000. Notwithstanding the help received from the county, Saugeen has eleven bridges over 75 feet in length to maintain, the names and length of which are given in a footnote.[2]

Saugeen, although the smallest township in the county Bruce, has been by no means the one of the least influence. At an early date in the history of the county it was of sufficient importance to be one of the first two townships to be created into a separate municipality. On two occasions have its reeves been elected to the wardenship of the county, in the persons of John Peirson and P Cummings. From the ranks of its yeomanry, in the person of James Rowand, it has furnished the member for North Bruce to sit in the House of Commons, and in the person of Lieut.-Col. J. W. S. Biggar a representative to the House of Assembly at Toronto The settlers who took up land in Saugeen were of good stock, and their descendants may be relied upon to maintain, as they of the past have done, the good name and reputation of the township.

[1]The oft-repeated refusal of the County Council to assume this bridge, which is 334 feet in length, led the member for North Bruce (C. M Bowman), at the suggestion of some of his constituents, to seek to have the Municipal Act amended so that counties be compelled to assume all bridges over 300 feet in length that are required for general traffic The House of Assembly passed the Amendment (see 3 Edw. VII Chap 18, Sec. 132) and Stirton's Bridge became a county bridge.

[2]List of some of the bridges in Saugeen, with their length · Over Mill Creek—McRae's (235 feet), Schwass' (231 feet), Zant's (174 feet), Keetle's (115 feet), Murkar's (114 feet), McEwen's (81 feet); over Snake Creek—Bell's (275 feet), Goldberg's (189 feet), Stewart's (119 feet), Gowanlock's (77 feet); over Beaver Creek, (115 feet)

CHAPTER XXXVII.

VILLAGE OF PORT ELGIN.[1]

As mentioned in the preceding Chapter, the first person to settle in the bush that covered the present site of Port Elgin village was Lachlan ("Loch Buie") McLean. The summer of 1849 had seen him engaged at the Fishing Islands. After the work of the season there was over, he found his way to Port Elgin Bay. The supply of provisions he had was small; nevertheless he made up his mind to settle there for the winter at least. On land lying just north of Market Street he built a shanty, in which he kept a tavern for several years. His patrons consisted principally of the settlers in Saugeen, Bruce and Elderslie, and of land-seekers going into these townships. The amount of travel past "Loch Buie's" was by no means inconsiderable before the erection of Burgess' (now McCalder's) bridge, as the route taken by travellers going to the townships above named from Southampton was along the lake shore as far as the bay at Port Elgin; there it struck inland. At "Loch Buie's" the heavy loads of flour or other supplies the settler had carried on his back thus far were set down, and rest and refreshments were sought.

George Butchart, one of the very earliest of the pioneers of Bruce, came to the county with the idea of engaging in lumbering operations on the Saugeen. Perceiving how much more easily a dam could be erected across Mill Creek than the wide Saugeen River, not to mention the difference in cost, he in the spring of 1852 commenced the erection of a dam and saw-mill on Mill Creek, at a point now within the village limits This mill he operated for a couple of years, to the great convenience of immediate settlers, until 1854, when he sold the water privilege and sawmill to Benjamin Shantz and moved to Baie de Dore. Mr. Shantz, on becoming possessed of the property, commenced the erection of a grist mill, which was completed in 1855.

There is always a reason why for the originating and developing, or not doing so, of an industrial and trading centre in new settlements.

[1]The name borne by the village is supposed to have been given in honor of the Earl of Elgin, Governor-General at the time the village began to take form.

CAPT. JOHN SPENCE   p. 508

LT.-COL. A. E. BELCHER   p. 512

HENRY HILKER   p. 497

THOMAS ADAIR   p. 513

This in some cases is none too apparent, as is shown in Appendix N, where there is given the names of a number of places in this county which at first promised well, but failed to develop In the case of Port Elgin, however, we see a village that rapidly developed, although handicapped by close proximity to another village which possessed the advantage of an earlier start, and which also was expected to be made the county town; and yet for several decades the younger village was the most prosperous of the two. This is largely attributable to the men who founded or afterwards lived in the village of Port Elgin. Its founders were Henry Hilker,[1] Samuel Bricker,[2] Clement Sieffert, Benjamin Shantz,[3] Martin Hoover and John Stafford. The presence of a mill and a tavern located at cross-roads possibly formed the nucleus for the village, and the above-mentioned energetic, resolute men supplied the necessary enterprise which evolved from a settlement in the bush the thriving village of Port Elgin It was in 1852, 1853 and 1854 that the above-mentioned men settled on the farm lots which afterwards they had surveyed into village lots.[4] Prior to the survey portions of the farm lots had been sold for building purposes, but only to a limited extent. Confirming this, the author has been told by Mr. J. C. Kennedy that when he came to Port Elgin, in September, 1855, the village then consisted of but seven houses, of which two were taverns kept by John Stafford and H. Hilker. The author has been fortunate in receiving from A H. R. Kennedy a letter, giving interesting particulars regarding the early settlement of Port Elgin The

[1] Henry Hilker was born near Heidelburg, Germany, in 1824. When ten years of age he went, with his father, to Jamaica Their stay there lasted only until 1837, when they came to Canada and settled at Preston. In the fall of 1852 Mr Hilker came to Bruce. After taking up land, part of which is now in Port Elgin village, he returned to Waterloo. In the following spring he brought his family with him to his bush farm. From then until his death (which occurred January 2nd, 1900) Mr Hilker was constantly engaged in enterprises which helped to make Port Elgin all that it is to-day As a member of the firm of Ruby & Hilker, merchants and grain buyers, his name became widely known throughout the county. The Commercial Block, built by him, and in which the firm carried on business, has few to equal it in appearance outside of our cities Mr. Hilker held the reeveship of Saugeen for three years, and that of the village for seven years For many years he was a member of the United Brethren Church, but latterly he united with the Presbyterian Church

[2] E. N. Brower was the original squatter on lot 9, concession 8, township of Saugeen (now part of the village plot). His rights were purchased by Samuel Bricker.

[3] George Butchart was the original squatter on lot 41, lake range, township Saugeen (now part of the village plot). His rights were purchased by Benjamin Shantz

[4] The date of the plan of the survey is March 2nd, 1857.

letter was accompanied by a map, showing the corners at the crossing
of the eighth concession road by the Goderich and Saugeen Road, now
the corner of Mill and Goderich Streets, Port Elgin.   On the north-
east corner of lot 40, Lake Range (now block 47) stood John Stafford's tavern   Across the road, on the north-west corner of lot 9, concession 8 (now block 1) was E. N. Brower's shanty, and on the south-
east corner of lot 41, Lake Range (now block 68), was the log house
in which Mr. Kennedy kept store   In his letter he says:

" I was the first store-keeper in the township of Saugeen, having
opened a store in what is now the village of Port Elgin on May 27th,
1854.   At that time the village contained only three houses, a tavern
unfinished log-house that I bought for a store, that had been built
by a Mr. Butchart, who had sold out to Benjamin Shantz before I
went to Saugeen   I bought the house and 1-4 acre of land on the
corner from Benjamin Shantz.   After opening my store the people
got me to petition the Post Office Department to establish a post-
office   The petition was granted, and I was appointed postmaster.
The post-office was named Normanton[1] on account of it, at that time,
being considered one of the most northern post-offices in Canada.
The nearest date I can find as to when the Normanton P.O. commenced business is about the 16th December, 1854.   At that time
there was no waggon road through Port Elgin; the mails were
brought on foot by a man of the name of John Urquhart, who once
a week carried the mail from Kincardine to Southampton."

After conducting the business above-mentioned until April, 1855,
Mr. Kennedy disposed of it to Messrs. Lehnen & Ruby.[2]   Mechanics
and others also in increasing numbers were led at an early date to
settle at Port Elgin.   By united effort they had the satisfaction of
witnessing the surrounding walls of forest trees being pushed further

[1]This office at first was known as " Normanton," a name it bore until
April 1st, 1874, when the post-office authorities consented to change it to
Port Elgin   A H. R. Kennedy continued to act as postmaster for about
a year, when he was succeeded by John J. Lehnen, who held
the position until 1864.   Archibald Roy was the next postmaster.   On his
death, in 1868, his widow was appointed his successor in office, which
position Mrs. Roy has retained until the present day.

[2]J. J. Lehnen only remained in the firm for a few years, after which
he sold his interest to H Hilker, when the name of the firm became Ruby
& Hilker.   On Mr. Ruby's death (August 9th, 1892) the business was
continued under the present name of Hilker & Co., by Henry E. Hilker.
It is satisfactory to think that the first mercantile business started in the
village is, after half a century, still flourishing.   The next merchants to
commence business in Port Elgin were George Craig and Edward Gordon

back, roads opened, houses built, and trade and commerce increase. These last-mentioned features received a marked impetus by the construction of a pier, built in 1857-58, by private enterprise, which permitted the landing of passengers and goods. Prior to this, when the steamboat entered the bay on its way to and from Goderich a large scow (built by George Fenwick) was rowed out until it lay alongside the steamer. By it all passengers and freight found their way to land. The pier helped to a great extent to build up the export trade of the village. Grain buyers appeared in the persons of Martin Hoover and Samuel Bricker, who built, at the harbor, grain storehouses About the time the pier was built the government undertook the construction of a small breakwater, the initial step toward the making of a harbor

Among the early settlers of Port Elgin alive to-day and a resident of the village, is J. C. Kennedy September, 1855, is the date when he first set foot there. After he had succeeded in erecting a house and shop he commenced business at his trade as a wagonmaker, which he carried on successfully during many years until he retired. In May, 1856, James Muir, another of the pioneer artisans of Port Elgin, took up his abode in the village, and since then has been one of its active citizens. Andrew Hood was Port Elgin's first blacksmith, but unfortunately he met an untimely end. He, with his family and brother, had been enjoying a sail on the lake, Returning therefrom, and after having entered the bay, by some mishap the boat capsized and all were drowned.

Of industries that developed about the time referred to there might be mentioned the steam sawmill built in 1856 by Samuel Bricker The boiler for this was floated down the Saugeen. To successfully navigate such an unwieldy craft pieces of timber were secured to its sides at the water line, forming a rough sort of a deck on which to stand. They also served as outriggers to prevent the boiler from rolling over.[1] A foundry was commenced in a small way by Alex McLauchlan in 1859. The extent of the plant can be judged from the fact that horse-power was used to drive the air-blast required when smelting. A few years later, when his brother Robert became a partner in the business, a ten horse-power engine was installed Brickmaking was started by Barthold Smith in 1860. A woollen mill was another industry of the village, inaugurated in the early sixties by

[1] The incident, clipped from the *Paisley Advocate*, given in a footnote in Chapter V., about floating a boiler down the Saugeen, doubtless referred to this exploit, although the *Advocate* fixes it earlier and says that the boiler was for a mill at Southampton

Messrs. Buschlin & Eby. They who subsequently carried on this industry have been Betzner & Sons, McCarthay & Wilson, Lewis McCarthy and M. G. Barber.

A description of Port Elgin in 1866 is to be found in a Directory published early in the following year. The population is therein stated to be about 630. In addition, the following particulars are given. There were five churches in the village belonging to the following denominations, namely: Methodist, Mennonites, United Brethren, Presbyterian and the Church of the New Jerusalem, two schools, a commodious Town Hall, four stores, three hotels, a job printing office, a brewery, two tanneries, a woollen factory, a foundry, two sawmills, a grist mill, a pottery, besides a goodly number of the smaller handicrafts, and one physician, Dr. Robert Douglass.[1]

During the half dozen years or so subsequent to the last-mentioned date the growth of the village was not rapid. This is shown by a comparison of the amount of assessments. In 1868 the assessed value of village property was $31,120. Five years later, in 1873, it was but $92,000. The following disconnected incidents belong to this period. Port Elgin, with other lake ports, came in for its share of harbor grants from the county, which spent in 1867-68 some $3,600 on works in the harbor.[2] Some time about the year 1869 Port Elgin was first connected with the outer world by electric telegraph. In the same year[3] a sectional tax was levied by the township of Saugeen on the property in the village. " To raise the sum of $350 to defray the expense of fencing ground and erecting a suitable building within the limits of the village for agricultural and other exhibitions." Not much could be done with this small amount, yet from such humble beginnings has sprung the highly successful North Bruce Riding Exhibition of to-day. Another event of this period in the history of Port Elgin was the establishing in 1869 of a local newspaper, *The Free Press*. The enterprising publisher was H. J. Benner. For seventeen years this paper experienced the usual vicissitudes of country journalism, till, in 1886, it and *The Busy Times* were merged into one under the name of *The Port Elgin Times,* now *The Times. The Busy Times* made its first appearance in the last week of December, 1877. W. S. Johnston (now of Toronto) was the proprietor and

[1]The first medical man to settle at Port Elgin was Dr. Hill, who came about 1856

[2]Port Elgin Harbor Works in 1867 and 1868 are described as consisting of a landing pier extending 264 feet out into the lake and of a breakwater 509 feet in length.

[3]See By-law No 36 of County of Bruce, passed December 9th, 1869.

editor. In 1888 Robert Munro purchased *The Times,* and has conducted it ever since most successfully.

The opening of the railway for traffic in 1873 resulted in bringing to Port Elgin an augmented volume of trade. The population increased and attained to a number that authorized an effort being made to have the village incorporated. On a census being taken that year, the population was found to be 941. The County Council thereupon passed, on June 7th, 1873, a by-law incorporating the village of Port Elgin, also directed that the first municipal election " be held in the old school-house on the south side of Mill Street," and that John Eastwood be the returning officer. The election, which was held the following January, resulted in the return of H. Hilker as reeve,[1] and D. O. Bricker, James Muir, Martin Hoover and John McIntosh as councillors. Following the separation from the township of Saugeen an adjustment of assets and liabilities of the two municipalities had to be arranged. In this matter Henry Hilker and James Muir acted for the village, and Neil Cassidy and John Peirson for the township. The decision arrived at was that the village assume, as its share of the liabilities of the township, the sum of $535.30.

The decade following the opening of the railway may properly be looked upon as the most prosperous period in the first half century of Port Elgin. Not only did it become incorporated, but business was conducted on a scale larger than previously known. Farmers found it to be a satisfactory market at which to sell their various descriptions of produce, while its reputation as a grain market was widespread. The most prominent and energetic of Port Elgin's business men of this period was D. O. Bricker,[2] although others there were deserving of mention who also developed large commercial and industrial enter-

[1]The following are the names of those who have been reeves of the village of Port Elgin, with the years in which they held office, viz.: H. Hilker, 1874, '75, '77, '78, '79, '80, '82 ; A. C. Sinclair, M.D., 1876; D. J. Izzard, 1881, 1891; W. S. Johnston, 1883 to 1890; R. Munro, 1892, '93; J. A. Chapman, 1894, '95, '96; J. R. Paterson, M.D., 1897; H. E. Hilker, 1898, '99; John George, 1900; D. Geddes, 1901 to 1906.

[2]Dilman Oberholt Bricker was born, in the year 1840, in the county of Waterloo, of Pennsylvania Dutch parents of the Mennonite faith. His father, Samuel Bricker, with his family, settled in Port Elgin in March, 1854. D. O. Bricker was at an early age engaged in business for himself. His energy and enterprise not only brought him to the front, but the village also. For years he conducted his varied business enterprises successfully. To carry these on conveniently he built the Arlington Block, which provided the largest premises occupied by any firm in the county. Suffering heavy losses in grain, Mr. Bricker, in the fall of 1880, became bankrupt. To retrieve his fortunes Mr. Bricker went to Winnipeg and was again successful. After twenty years there his health gave way and he returned to Port Elgin, where he spent the last two years of his life. His death occurred April 17th, 1904.

prises, such as Zinkan, Cress & Co. Their tannery, manufacturing for the shipping trade, employed a large number of workmen, and was one of the leading industries of the village. The promise the village gave of further growth induced the Bank of Hamilton to open a branch there in 1873. For thirty-three years this was the sole chartered bank in Port Elgin, although a private bank (Allen, McMahon & Co, afterwards H. A. Allen) carried on business for about fifteen years of this period, until it closed its doors in 1894. In the summer of 1906 the Metropolitan Bank opened an agency in the village, supplying it with abundant banking facilities and incidentally showing the increased business importance of Port Elgin.

After the incorporation of the village, the need was felt of a suitable town hall. The matter was taken up in 1875 by the Village Council, which at one of its first meetings passed a by-law to raise a loan of $3,000 for this purpose. The site, at a cost of $900, was purchased from Edward Gordon, and the contract was let to J. McLachlan for $2,460, and in August following the corner-stone of the building was laid   The sum raised as above mentioned, being insufficient to complete the building, more money had to be raised. To do this, in 1877 the Legislative Assembly was applied to, which, in response to a petition, passed an Act[1] authorizing the sale by the corporation of certain public squares and reserves on the following mentioned conditions · " The proceeds of every such sale by the said corporation . . . shall be held and applied by it, in fully finishing and completing the town hall   .   and in aiding the Board of School Trustees .   . in purchasing a site and erecting such school buildings as the said Board may require to have built." The new town hall was opened March 7th, 1877, with a concert and a ball.

The harbor at Port Elgin, like all others on the eastern shores of Lake Huron, has cost a large sum   The initial work, as before stated, was commenced in 1857-58. In 1872 Alex. Sproat, the member for North Bruce, stated in the House of Commons that the expenditure up to then on this harbor was in excess of $30,000, of which but a small proportion had been paid by the government. The departmental report for the year ending June 30th, 1899, states that the expenditure by it up to then amounted to $80,652. Since then further large sums have been expended, so that it is safe to say that the cost of making the harbor what it is to-day is greatly in excess of $100,000. Mariners may say that its entrance is none too easy under certain

[1] 40 Vic Chap 36

conditions of wind and weather, but, once in, vessels have all the protection needed Port Elgin harbor is an excellent one for a vessel to winter in, there being no danger from spring freshets, as is the case where the harbor is placed at the mouth of a river.

The village of Port Elgin has ever been liberal and public-spirited in granting bonuses and loans to encourage the establishment of industries in its midst, and also in providing means for useful and needed public improvements, as the following list of issues of debentures shows Prior to 1885 the total issue amounted to $16,000. The following list up to that year is probably correct; after that year it is so:

```
In 1875 Debentures issued for $3,000 for town hall.
 "  1875      "         "      5,000 for school purposes
 "  1879      "         "      3,000 for bonus to grist mill(Grey & McChesney)
 "  1880      "         "      5,000 for harbor improvements
 "  1885      "         "      1,000 for bonus to foundry.
 "  1887      "         "      5,000 for loan to grist mill (Geo A McKay).
 "  1888      "         "      5,000 for loan to button factory
 "  1890      "         "      4,000 to build High School
 "  1890      "         "      4,200 to build Public School
```

In 1897 the unpaid debenture debt and interest amounted to $13,127.06. There existed at the same time a floating debt of the village and the two School Boards which amounted to $3,992 39, making a total indebtedness at that time of $17,119.45 This being found burdensome and oppressive, application was made to Parliament to consolidate the debt and extend the payment of the same over twenty years The application was granted and an Act[1] passed authorizing the issue of debentures to the extent of $17,000 for the said purpose. Since then the further issue of debentures has been

```
In 1902 Debentures for $ 4,000 as bonus to brush factory.
 "  1903      "        "   10,000 as bonus ($3,000) and loan ($7,000) to Do-
                              minion Harness Co.
 "  1903      "        "    4,530 for construction of granolithic sidewalks,
                              "Local improvements."
 "  1904      "        "    5,800 for construction of granolithic sidewalks,
                              "Local improvements "
 "  1905 ⎫ By-laws passed, ⎧ 7,000 to Wm. McVicar, bonus to sawmill and
         ⎪                  ⎪        spur line of railway to harbor
 "  1906 ⎬ Debentures yet  ⎨ 30,000 for system of waterworks.
         ⎪                  ⎪ 10,000 loan to the Stevens, Hepner Company brush
 "  1906 ⎭ to be issued    ⎩        factory.
```

Prior to the vote being taken, in June, 1906, on the last two mentioned items, the then debenture debt of the village was stated to be $34,005.49, exclusive of local improvement debentures.

It will be noted what a large amount has been voted by the rate-

[1] 60 Vic. Chap 76

payers in the endeavor to build the village up as a manufacturing centre. Success has unfortunately not attended all these efforts. At picsent the leading industry of Port Elgin is probably the brush factory. This was established in 1883 by John Hepner (previously a resident of Napanee) and six business men of the village. Two years later, in February, 1885, the works were destroyed by fire. A stock company was then formed under the name of the Port Elgin Brush Co., Limited, and the works rebuilt. T. I. Thompson was president of this company, and B. B. Boyd manager. Ten years later the company went into liquidation. In June, 1896, the plant was purchased by H. H Stevens, John Hepner and E. H. Schiedel, who carried on the business under the name of Stevens, Hepner & Co. In 1901 the last-mentioned gentleman retired from the firm In that same year new buildings were erected and the capacity of the plant doubled. Five years later, in the spring of 1906, the firm made a proposition to the village, offering to erect an addition to their factory of 180x36 feet, of three stories and basement, and to double their capacity for production, provided the village would install a system of waterworks (affording fire protection), and guarantee a loan of $10,000 for ten years. The proposition was accepted by the village, and the required by-law was passed by a large majority. The business is at present carried on under the name of The Stevens, Hepner Co., Limited.

Another manufacturing plant that promises to add materially to the business of the village is the Wm. McVicar & Sons sawmill, at the harbor A bonus of $7,000 to this firm was voted upon and carried, September 16th, 1905, in consideration of which the firm undertook to erect a large sawmill, and also to purchase the right-of-way for a spur line of railway from the Grand Trunk Railway station to the harbor, to grade the same and supply the required railway ties, the Grand Trunk Railway Company at the same time offering to supply the rails and lay the track W. McVicar & Sons also agreed to furnish a locomotive and engine-house. At the time of writing considerable work has been done, and the line is almost completed.[1]

A bonus and loan totalling $10,000 was granted to the Dominion Harness Company, in 1903. This company has not, as originally

[1]At the time the railway to Southampton was surveyed the intention was to have the railway enter Port Elgin on the lake shore side, and the station in proximity to the harbor. Considerable and mistaken opposition to this proposal was met with from property holders in the eastern part of the village, under the impression the centre of business would be moved to the vicinity of the proposed station Unfortunately the views of these men carried, and it is only now, after many efforts, that the railway will reach the harbor

started, been a successful venture. In 1906 the company was reorganized under the name of the Dominion Pressed Steel Company, to manufacture shovels and similar goods. John George is the president of this company, and F. Miehle is the manager. High hopes are held that this firm may prove a success and the village derive benefit from the assistance rendered.

The first school building of the village stood on the site of the present High School A Miss Agnes Lawrence was the first teacher. Her father, Alexander Lawrence, was the next who endeavored to lead' the youth of the village in the paths of learning. The school buildings and furnishings at first were none too elaborate. These conditions improved, however, as the years rolled by In 1875 a good brick school-house was erected, and in 1890 a further advance was made when the present handsome school premises became the home of the village Public School. The High School was opened in the fall of 1889. For the first fifteen years J. T. Lillie, B.A., filled the position of headmaster, and did so in a manner that brought credit both to the school and to himself. On his resigning, Mr. J. Campbell Clark was appointed his successor In addition to the schools belonging to the regular educational system of the province, there existed an Academy, connected with the United Brethren Church, during the years 1880, 1881 and 1882, the principals of which were the Rev. A. B Sherk and D. B Sherk.

Public religious services were in the very early days held in a building erected for the common use of all denominations The Presbyterians were the first to be organized into a congregation The following extract from the Annual Report for 1894 of this congregation is so complete that it is worthy of permanent preservation, and a large extract therefrom is here given: " While yet the settlers were few in number and were separated from one another by the primitive forest, the Presbytery of London, realizing that many of them belonged to Presbyterian families, sent in one and another of their ministers to let the people feel that the church had not lost sight of them, and was interested in their welfare. Among the first to come (in 1854) was the Rev. John Scott, then of St. Andrew's, London (afterwards Rev. Dr. Scott, of North Bruce), who, having come early in his ministerial life to preach and dispense ordinances, and by the way to gather together the scattered few and lay the foundations of Presbyterianism in the district, spent the last ten years of his ministry among some of the very people for whom he had many years before done something to supply with the means of grace, and keep .them in connection with the church of their fathers. The reverend doctor tells how that in the early fifties he more than once or twice, by appointment of Presbytery, visited this northern country and preached at Southampton, Port Elgin, Dunblane, Paisley and North Bruce. One of the first services held within the bounds .of what afterwards became the Port Elgin congregation was conducted· by him in the house of Mr. John Smith, on the 6th concession of Saugeen. In those days so dense was the· bush that the minister failed to find Mr. Peter Smith's, although it was only about a mile and a half from his brother's at the riverside, on what is now the McGillivray farm. The Rev. W. Ball, then of Woodstock, visited the district in 1854, and dispensed ordinances at various places. The first ordained minister was the Rev. James H. McNaughton, who was settled over the congregation of Southampton from 1855 to 1859, and who had a number of preaching stations, Port Elgin among the rest,. which were supplied more or less regularly by him for several years; without their being united to form a pastoral charge. About the time of Mr McNaughton's resignation Mr. Alexander Fraser was appointed as missionary at Port Elgin, where he labored with so much acceptance that he was called as pastor, and ordained and inducted on the 22nd of October, 1861. In July, 1862, we find a communion roll of 53 members; but as eleven of these had been added since Mr. Fraser's settlement, the membership at that time must have been about 42. The first church, which was built in 1860, was soon found to be so inconveniently situated (the village having grown in a different direction from that which was originally expected) that it was never fully completed; and in 1870, although the membership was not by any means large or wealthy, yet, animated with commendable zeal, and realizing that a conveniently situated church was necessary to the advancement, if not of the very existence, of Presbyterianism here, the erection of the present church building was determined upon and a substantial and comfortable brick church with basement was erected. Early in 1871 the basement was opened for worship. The church had not been erected much more than a year, when the Rev Mr. Fraser, who had faithfully and amid not a few hardships ministered to the people for about eleven years, tendered his resignation, which was accepted early in 1872. After a vacancy of about eighteen months, during which a union had been consummated with Dunblane, the Rev. D. C McKay, M.A., was called and settled as pastor of the united charge. Scarcely had he entered upon his ministry when he was stricken down, and died on September 21st, 1873, after a short pastorate of only five weeks. Eighteen months again elapsed before the settlement of the Rev. James Gourlay, M.A., was effected. Meanwhile the church building had been completed and finished at a cost of about $4,000, besides a further expenditure for the bell, and was opened on September 27th, 1874, by Rev. A. Topp, D D , of Knox Church, Toronto " This building was enlarged in 1889 at a cost of $1,300, and extensively renovated in 1901. The pastorate of the Rev. Mr Gourlay, which extended over twenty years, was terminated by his resignation in July, 1895. The Rev. A. H. Drumm was the next to minister to the spiritual needs of the congregation. He was followed by the Rev. A. Mahaffy, who was inducted in January, 1900, to this charge, which he continues to minister to. The congregation held jubilee services on July 9th, 1905.

Other denominations were not long in following the example set by the Presbyterians, and proceeded to organize as congregations, the United Brethren being the next to do so. In 1866 there were five churches in the village, the three others not above mentioned being the Methodist, the Mennonites and the Church of the New Jerusalem. In a few years the congregation last mentioned ceased to be, but the number of denominations in the place remained the same, as the Baptists formed themselves into a congregation Subsequently, some time in the seventies, congregations belonging to the Church of England and the German Evangelical Church were formed. The above-mentioned number of religious denominations in this locality has of late years been increased by a congregation of Latter Day Saints (Mormons), whose church is just beyond the southerly boundary of the village.

The attractions that Port Elgin offers as a summer resort are yearly becoming more and more appreciated The splendid beach, the bracing breezes that blow from off Lake Huron, and the mineral spring and baths 'are attracting each season an increased number of visitors.

The efforts put forth by the people of Port Elgin to hold annual gatherings of the pioneers of the county are worthy of the fullest commendation. The first of these was held July, 1899, and is referred to in Chapter VIII. Since then these gatherings have been held annually, and are one of the events of the summer at Port Elgin

At the time of writing the village is possessed, as not before for years, with a sense of its possibilities. That it may have the courage to press on and attain is certainly the desire of its well-wishers

CHAPTER XXXVIII

TOWN OF SOUTHAMPTON.[1]

For a number of years in its early days the village was known by the names of Saugeen or Southampton, one as commonly used as the other. The former was that used by the Post-office and Custom House Departments, as well as by the public generally, while as Southampton it was known by the Crown Lands Department, besides being the name of the village mentioned in the special Act passed for its incorporation. It took many years[2] before unanimity was reached as to the name to be used when speaking of the village.

The idea of laying out a town plot at the mouth of the Saugeen River was early thought of by the heads of the Crown Lands Department. Even before a plan for the division of the county into townships had been settled upon the decision to have such a survey made was arrived at. This is indicated by a letter on record among the correspondence of the Department, dated October 1st, 1847, addressed to R. Lynn, P.L.S., directing him to survey a town plot at the mouth of the Saugeen River. Why he did not immediately proceed to carry out these instructions the author cannot say. Four years passed, and it was the summer of 1851 before he made the survey.

The first settlement made at Southampton was in 1848 by Capt. John Spence and William Kennedy, the particulars of which are to be found in Chapter III.[3] These two pioneers were before long joined by James Orr and George Butchart. At first they were all

[1]At the time the name Southampton was bestowed upon the prospective town it did not seem appropriate, as it was then the most northern lake port in the province. Possibly the name was bestowed in the hopes that in its development the town might rival in importance its famous English namesake

[2]It was 1889 or 1890 before the name of the post-office was changed from Saugeen to Southampton, and 1895 when, as a port of entry, Saugeen was changed to Southampton

[3]In addition to the biographical incidents relating to Captain John Spence given in Chapter III, it might be stated that he was a skilful, brave seaman, traits of character he markedly exhibited in the rescue of the crew of a large American vessel from a watery grave under most dangerous circumstances The American Government recognized this heroic act by presenting Capt Spence with a very fine gold watch.

engaged in carrying on a fishing business, Spence and Kennedy having
purchased of the Niagara Fishing Company its plant and rights at
the Fishing Islands. This did not prove a successful venture, and in
a few years was dropped. Capt. Spence took to sailing, being in command of a vessel called the *Sea Gull.* Wm. Kennedy, left to
engage in a search for Sir John Franklin, James Orr opened a tavern
in the village, and George Butchart took up land and started a sawmill at Port Elgin, as related in the next preceding chapter. Among
the earliest settlers who came in after the above-mentioned were
Alex. McDonald, John McLean, Jos Gilbert, Peter Brown, John
Cooke, Jas. Lambert, Thos. Lee, Robert Reid, Richard Hill and James
Calder. The last three mentioned were storekeepers In August,
1851, Crown Land Agent Alexander McNabb[1] and his son, John M.
McNabb, arrived at Southampton His stay that year lasted until
the beginning of December. In May of the following year he brought
his family to the village to take up their permanent residence there.
Among others that settled in the village in those early days, at a
slightly subsequent date, might be mentioned John C Coulson, John
Belcher, John Peck, J. M. Kelly and John Ewing

The winter of 1851-52 opened with sad forebodings for the handful of settlers at Southampton—some dozen or more families—who
depended for their supply of the absolute necessaries of life upon
what was brought from time to time to the village by sailing vessels
from Goderich. As the winter drew on, the supplies were found to be
running low. The settlement was relying upon Capt. Alex. McDonald, in command of the *Saucy Jack,* to bring in, before navigation
closed, what flour and other provisions would be required. Unfortunately he delayed his time of sailing too long. His vessel was caught
in a gale, and it, with all on board, perished. It was a black outlook
for the settlers, some of whom made their way to the older settlements, there to remain for the winter.[2] For those who stayed at the
village supplies sufficient to maintain existence were by some means
brought through the deep snow and a roadless forest from Owen
Sound. Nevertheless, it was a winter of many privations.

A graphic description of Southampton in 1852 is given in a letter
written by Mr. Andrew Crawford, a student missionary, sent by the

[1]A biographical sketch of Mr McNabb is given in a footnote in
Chapter V.

[2]Mr. Kennedy, in " Pioneer Days," p. 72, *seq*, gives a graphic account of
their tramp through the snow to Owen Sound

Presbytery of London, to minister to the spiritual needs of the people
in this locality. An extract from the letter which bears date May
25th, 1852, is here given:

" Our village (Southampton) is quite a new place; it only rose
into existence last summer, and already it numbers about thirty
houses. Though but a village at present, Southampton is laid out for
a large town, and judging from its situation and other advantages
connected with it, this contemplated design may be speedily realized.
Many town and park lots have already been taken up, and some excellent frame houses are being erected thereon. The streets are regular
and wide; some of them have been opened. Several large reserves
have been laid off for churches, schools, market buildings, court-house,
a cemetery and other public institutions. There are already three well-
filled stores, and even now the inhabitants have the privilege of weekly
mail, despatch and arrival. At present a few inconveniences arising
from the situation and circumstances of the place are, of course, to
be expected and experienced."

A post-office, known as Saugeen, was opened in the village in
1851. The first postmaster was Robert Reid. He held this office
until 1857, when Thomas Lee[1] received the appointment and retained
the position until his death in 1901.   On January 26th, 1855, the
present system of post-office money orders was instituted. Of the 160
offices in Canada at that time authorized to issue such orders, Saugeen
was the only one in the county of Bruce. There is no doubt this
privilege was on account of the presence of the Crown Land Office in
the village. Two years after the establishing of a post-office the government made Saugeen a port of entry for the collection of customs.
John McLean was the first officer in charge. That an idea may be
obtained of the business done at this port in the early days, the following figures from the returns of 1855 are given: Exports, $629.20;
imports, $6,614.02; amount of duties collected in 1855, $843.58. It
is said that a great deal of whiskey used to be smuggled in at this
point from the United States, and tales are told of the devices to
get the officer out of the way while the goods were being landed.

---

[1] Thomas Lee settled in Southampton in the spring of 1851. In partnership
with his father-in-law, Thomas Godfrey, he built the first bridge over the Saugeen
River, on the line of the Elora Road. The bridge was known as Burgess' bridge
and crossed the river in the vicinity of what is now known as McCalder's bridge.
Besides holding the office of postmaster he was engaged for some years as a for-
warder, commission merchant and insurance agent. For many years he was one of
the wardens in the Church of England congregation, and was the village treasurer
for twenty-six years. His death took place February 20th, 1901.

An agency of the Bank of Upper Canada was established at Southampton as early as 1854, Alexander McNabb being the agent. The large payments made on account of land purchases doubtless accounted for the presence of a chartered bank in what at that time was only a small backwoods village On the failure of the Bank of Upper Canada, the Commercial Bank of Canada opened an agency in Southampton, of which Alex. Proudfoot was agent. His successor was Alex. Sproat. Mr. Sproat was also county treasurer, and when it became necessary for him to remove to Walkerton when it became the county town, he succeeded in taking the agency with him. From that time (June, 1867) until the Bank of Hamilton in 1898 opened an agency in Southampton, the village was without a chartered bank.

At the time the provisional County Council commenced to thresh out the county town question (this was in 1857), the village of Southampton considered itself as possibly the premier village of the county because of having resident there the Crown Lands Office and a bank over and above all that Kincardine, its strongest rival, could boast of, except, possibly, in the matter of population, in which Kincardine slightly excelled. Into the fight for the county town Southampton, therefore, entered, with strong hopes of capturing the coveted prize. In addition it had assurances made by government officers that it was certain to be the county town. To strengthen its claims for the coveted honor, incorporation was sought As the required population did not reside within the proposed limits of the village, this could not be obtained in the manner laid down by statute, so Parliament was asked to pass an Act of incorporation,[1] which was done, July 24th, 1858. The record of the county town contest is given in Chapter VI. There is related how that on two occasions an effort was made to make Southampton the county town of the north half of a divided county. Both of these attempts came to naught, as well as those to make it the county town of the county as a whole.

The election of the first Village Council occurred shortly after incorporation, in the summer of 1858. In a footnote[2] the names are

[1]22 Vic. Chap 42.

[2]Reeves of the village of Southampton: James Calder, part of 1858; Thomas Webster, part of 1859; J. T Conaway, part of 1859, '60, '62, '63, '71, '72, '78, '79; John Eastwood, 1861; Thomas Adair, 1864 to 1868, 1873 to 1877; Alex. Sinclair, 1869, '70; W. S Scott, M.D , 1880 to 1883, 1888 to 1892; George E. Smith, 1884 to 1887, '93; A. E. Belcher, 1894, '95, part of '96, '98; C. M. Bowman, part of 1896, '97; William McGregor, 1899 to 1902, '04; N. B Zinkan, 1903.   List of mayors of the town of Southampton : A. E. Belcher, 1905, '06.

given of all those who held the honorable position of reeve during the years the municipality ranked as a village. In 1904 the necessary steps were taken to have Southampton raised to the status of a town. A census revealed a population of over 2,400 (but this was at the height of the season of summer visitors), so after the required notice had been given, the Lieutenant-Governor issued a proclamation that Southampton be erected into a town, which proclamation came into effect on Monday, December 26th, 1904. At the election that followed in 1905, A E Belcher[1] was elected the first mayor of the town, an honor conferred upon him again in 1906.

A month after the village was incorporated action was taken to have a town hall. A lot on the west side of Albert Street was secured, on which a building was erected which was used in a twofold capacity, the ground floor being fitted up for school purposes, and the second story as the town hall. This building still exists, and is known as the Masonic Hall The building now used as a town hall was built in 1862, by private subscriptions, as a drill shed for the Rifle Company organized in the previous year. When the headquarters of this company were removed to Port Elgin the village acquired the building for the purpose of being used as a town hall. It was opened as such by a concert and ball, December 27th, 1873.

In 1855 that part of the town plot lying north of the river was surveyed into village lots. The trouble that arose with the Indians about this survey is referred to in Chapter I

The author has in his possesion a map of the village of Southampton, dated July 30th, 1857, which outlines the village as it was at that date There are over 130 houses marked in this plan. At that time the business portion of the village seems to have been north of High .

---

[1]Lieut -Col. Alexander Emerson Belcher was born January 30th, 1844, at Toronto, and came, with his parents, to Southampton in 1852, where he received his education at the public school. Possessing a liking for military matters, he, when only fifteen years of age, raised a company of boys, which he drilled At the time of the Trent affair he joined the Southampton Rifle Company. In 1866 he went with it to Goderich, at the time of the Fenian Raid In 1868 he attended the Military School and obtained a first-class certificate In 1895 he was made Honorary Lieut-Colonel of Militia. From 1872 to 1888 he was engaged as a commercial traveller for wholesale houses doing business at Toronto In 1891 he returned to Southampton, where he has resided since He has taken an active part in politics, working in the interests of the Conservative party. Being likewise active in the Orange Society, he has held office in the four Grand Lodges of the Order He was first elected to the village council when only twenty-one years of age, and has been reeve of the village during three years, and was elected its first mayor Enthusiastic in regard to the history of the county, he has been president of the Historical Society from the beginning He is also a vice-president of the Bruce Pioneer Society.

Street, on Huron and Grosvenor Streets. On the east side of Huron Street, commencing close to the river, was the Crown Lands Office. A little south of this was the Bank of Upper Canada, and still farther south was the office of the Crown timber agent. In all, there are six shops shown on the plan, two hotels and five warehouses. These last were located near the mouth of the river. Of manufacturing establishments there is shown to be a planing mill (located on the beach near where the mineral water spring is now), a steam sawmill (on the river's edge, east of where the creek from the Little Lake enters it), and a saw and grist mill at the Indian Rapids. No wharf or pier is shown on this plan; but the author has been informed that the owner's of the warehouses had each a landing wharf constructed at the owner's expense and known by his name, as Reid's Wharf, Calder's Wharf, Belcher's Wharf, etc. A little later than this, in 1858, the government built a breakwater north of the river, and at a later date constructed piers on each side of the river. The government report made in 1898-99 shows that the total amounts spent on these works at the mouth of the river amounted to $32,757. Since then there has been a very large expenditure for dredging and deepening the channel In the sixties a pier was built that extended out into the lake from the beach, at a point a little south of the present pumping station, the remains of which, though under water, are still to be traced. This pier bore the name of the Bogus Dock

When speaking of the harbor at Southampton the extensive works at Chantry Island are first thought of. In the winter of 1870-71 the contracts for these were let, being for a pier that was to extend from the island towards the shore, and for one from the shore outwards, an opening, forming the entrance to this harbor of refuge being left between these two piers The contract for the first 500 feet from the. island was let to a contractor of the name of Brown; the next 2,200 feet was let to a syndicate composed of Robert Baird, Robert Reid, Robert Walker and Thomas Adair. Andrew Lindsay had the contract for the pier extending from the shore. A large part of this contract he sub-let to Thomas Adair.[1] •The total amount spent on this harbor

[1]Thomas Adair, of whom the author wishes to refer with the kindest memories and as one who was enthusiastic in obtaining material for this History, was born December 24th, 1826, a short distance north of Glasgow, Scotland He, with his father and the rest of the family, in August, 1844, emigrated to Canada, and settled in the township of Dummer, County of Peterboro'. After several years of hard work, some of the time in the lumber shanties, he managed to secure a little ready money. Having heard glowing accounts of the Queen's Bush, he, in the spring

18

of refuge by the government closely approximates the large sum of $300,000. Owing to the difficulty of entering under certain conditions of wind and weather, it is not of the service that was anticipated.

The lighthouse at Chantry Island, a circular stone structure, that exhibits its light at a height 94 feet above high water mark, has been sending out its warning and guiding rays over a radius of fifteen miles, since 1859, to the mariners sailing on Lake Huron. Duncan McG. Lambert was the first lighthouse-keeper. On his death the post was given to his son, W. McG. Lambert. On several occasions members of this family have heroically rescued shipwrecked mariners whose vessels have been lost on the shoals surrounding Chantry Island. On September 19th, 1879, in one of these gallant efforts, one of the sons, Ross Lambert, and another of the crew lost their lives through the capsizing of the boat in which they had gone to an attempted rescue.

The Government Meteorological Department is closely associated with the navigation of our Great Lakes, and it will be in place here to mention that one of the large observatories of this department has been stationed at Southampton since 1871. Mrs. and Miss Stewart, in charge, telegraph thrice daily their reports to the department at Toronto

The early settlers were not long before they had a school started in the village; 1852 was the year when it was opened, it being the second

of 1849, came to see what the free grants were like   In Chapters III. and XXI an account is given of his entry and settlement in the township of Brant   He sold his farm there in 1853 and took up land in the township of Saugeen, near Dunblane   After three years' work on his two lots he sold them and bought lot 34, concession 15, in the township of Brant. This he traded for one in Arran   In 1857 he came to Southampton and worked for James Calder, merchant   In 1861 he built a storehouse, and for the next twelve years was engaged in buying grain.   From 1871 to 1877 he was engaged on large contracts on the Southampton Harbor piers, along with Andrew Lindsay and others.   These contracts proved remunerative, yielding a handsome profit   He left Southampton in 1880, and after a residence of a year at London he moved to Toronto, where he resided until his death, which occurred on Christmas Day, 1901.   For ten years Mr. Adair filled the reeve's chair in the village council   He took a very active part in the railway bonus campaign of 1869.   He was one of the volunteers who went to the front in 1866, and was in charge of the teamsters that accompanied the Red River expedition, in 1870, as related in Chapter X   Mr Adair's gifts as a singer were well known throughout the county, and he was often called upon to sing at concerts and church socials.   In religion he was a Presbyterian and helped in the organization of the U P Church of Brant.   He was twice married—his first wife was a Miss Inglis, of Brant   To them were born ten children. His second wife was Miss Margaret Graham, who survived him.   Of this union three children were born   In politics Mr Adair was an enthusiastic Liberal.   His remains were brought to Southampton for interment.

or third in the county. The first teacher[1] was Nathaniel Squires. He was succeeded by Miss Gooding, of Goderich, and she by James D. McVittie. The school at first met in the log building erected as a Presbyterian Church, which stood in the south-west corner of High and Albert Streets. It was afterwards held in the New Connexion Methodist Church, and after that in what is now the Masonic Hall. The present school building was erected in 1880 at a cost of over $5,000.

The first medical man in Southampton was Dr A Walker, then came Dr. H. Haynes, but he in a short time moved to the township of Bruce, and was its reeve for part of 1856. The next who ministered to the ailments of the community was Dr. W. S. Scott,[2] who came in 1855, and made Southampton his home during the rest of his life.

The history of the church life of Southampton is not without interest. Owing to the fact of there being a mission at the Indian reserve, as mentioned in Chapter III., the Methodists were on the ground from the very first, and the minister at the reserve held services for the early settlers. The Wesleyan and New Connexion Methodists both organized congregations in the village in 1854. The Rev. George Jacques, William Richardson and Stephen Brownell were the first ministers of the Wesleyan Church. The Rev. S. B. Gundy, William Tindall and Rev. B. Hammersley were the first ministers of the New Connexion congregation. The church buildings erected for each of the congregations were of no great size, only about 20x30 feet After the union of these two churches a neat brick building was erected, that had a seating capacity for about 200. The congregation grew markedly, and a larger church has long been needed. On September 12th, 1906, the corner-stone was laid of a church building that is expected to cost about $12,000. About half of this sum has been contributed

[1]The author is indebted to Mr J McNabb's sketch of the History of the County of Bruce for the name of the first teacher He also desires to acknowledge the assistance he has received from the frequent historical items Mr McNabb has contributed to the public press from time to time Mr. McNabb's knowledge and memory of the events of the early days and early settlers is without an equal within the county of Bruce

[2]Dr. W. S. Scott was intimately associated with Southampton for forty-five years. He was a native of the township of Esquesing, where he was born in 1825. After completing his studies, he commenced the practice of medicine at Southampton, in 1855. His kindly, cheerful manner made him popular as a doctor throughout the adjoining townships, in which he possessed an extensive practice. In politics he was a Conservative, and on different occasions was made president of the North Bruce Conservative Association. His death occurred October 18th, 1900. Having been long associated with the Bruce Volunteers, he was given a military funeral under the charge of the officers of the 32nd Bruce Infantry

by C. M Bowman, M.P.P., and appropriately the ceremony of laying the corner-stone was performed by Mrs. Bowman.

No item in connection with the early history of Southampton 'has been related in the public press more frequently or with more detail than the starting of the Presbyterian congregation there. As it is desirable to collect and preserve these facts in a permanent form, the author here gives them in full. The Rev. J. B. Duncan, the first Presbyterian minister to visit Southampton, arrived there August 5th, 1851, in company with his uncle, Alex. McNabb, the Crown Lands Agent, having journeyed from Goderich in a sailboat. His first public service in the village was held in a house that stood on the site afterwards occupied by the Busby House. Mr. Duncan's sojourn in the village was short, but yet sufficiently long to stir the people up to apply to the Free Church Presbytery of London to be erected into a mission station, which request that body, on October 8th, 1851, agreed to, and resolved to send a missionary. On March 12th, 1852, the Presbytery arranged to send Mr. Archibald Crawford, a theological student, who arrived at Southampton, May 7th following. In a letter written by Mr. Crawford shortly after his arrival, he has the following to say regarding his mission:

" I was particularly pleased, upon landing, to find that the Presbyterians of this place had erected a neat and commodious place of worship, which was receiving the last touches of the tools of the mechanic on the day of our arrival On the Sabbath, the 16th inst , it was opened for worship and dedicated to the service of our God and Maker. I was kindly assisted on that occasion by the Rev. Mr. Hutchison, Methodist missionary to a company of Chippawa Indians, residing about three miles from this place, and by the Rev. Mr. Kribs, of the Congregational Church mission, Colpoy's Bay. The attendance was highly gratifying, and the collection, too. I rejoice to say that the church has been opened almost free of debt. Last Sabbath we had two diets, which were well attended, on which also our regular collection gave evidence of the liberality of the people. On the morning of that day we opened a Sabbath School,[1] when several teachers and twenty-four children commenced their interesting labors. I am happy to say that Alex. McNabb, Esq., who has done much for this place, has kindly undertaken the superintendence of the school. To-morrow evening I propose opening a Bible Class, where I hope to meet several young people I have managed to give a service

[1] This was the first Presbyterian Sunday-school established in the county, and probably the first within it of any denomination

every third Sabbath at a station in the country. Though there are no horses or means of conveyance here, yet I was glad to notice some in church who walked through the bush eight and ten miles."

The church building that Mr. Crawford mentions was built of logs, and stood on lot 8, south of High Street, near where the present post-office is. Its doors and windows were donated by Mr. Alex. McNabb, and were brought from Toronto. Friends in Toronto also contributed to the cost of erecting this building. In 1863 the lot was sold, and the building torn down. Services were then held in the Town Hall on Albert Street. After the union with the United Presbyterian congregation services were held in the building erected by them, which was on Clarendon Street, overlooking the river. In 1887 this building was moved to its present site on Albert Street. Mr. Crawford's stay at Southampton extended over the summer of 1852. In the following summer the Rev. John Scott (afterwards of London and North Bruce) ministered to this flock. In the year 1854 the Rev. James H. McNaughton was inducted into the pastorate of the congregation. He remained for some four years. After he left, the congregation was pastorless for four years until, in December, 1862, the Rev. Andrew Tolmie was inducted. His pastorate extended over thirty-five years. In 1898 the Rev. W. T. Ellison was ordained minister of this charge. His successor is the Rev. R. T Cockburn, the present minister of the congregation At one time there was a United Presbyterian congregation in Southampton. Its sole minister was the Rev. D. Waters, and his ministry was during the years 1861, '62 and '63. Patrick J. Hamilton gave to this congregation a lot on Clarendon Street as a church site. The church built thereon was erected free of debt; but Southampton at that time was not large enough for two Presbyterian congregations, and Mr. Waters resigned The union of the two congregations and the transference of the church property was not accomplished without some hard feelings, which are now, we hope, forgotten.

The Rev. A. H. R. Mulholland, of Owen Sound, is said to have been the first to hold Church of England services in Southampton. About 1856 the Rev J. P. Hodge was settled over the congregation that had there become organized. He only remained a year or so. After a vacancy, the Rev. J P. Curran was placed in charge of this parish. Under his efforts a church, a frame building, known as St. Paul's was built. In later years this has given place to the tasteful brick edifice in which this congregation worship.

The first attempt of the press to make itself known within the county was at Southampton, when, in 1856, *The Pioneer* made its bow to the public. Its existence was, however, of but short duration. David Culbert was the publisher, and he may justly be termed the pioneer printer of the county. In 1859 he sold out to D. McMillan, who published a newspaper known as *The Morning Star,* but this, too, faded away after an ephemeral existence. F. H. Lynch Staunton, in 1862, commenced to publish *The Bruce Vindicator.* This paper lasted until 1864, when it, too, ceased to be. After this about twenty years passed, and the village was without a newspaper of its own. Job printing was carried on during part of this time by David Culbert, who at last,·in 1888, commenced the publication of *The Pioneer* (No. 2). This was two years after *The Beacon* had been successfully launched. There was no room for two papers in the village, and Mr. Culbert's venture collapsed. William Graham was the founder of *The Beacon,* which is now published by Ernest E Short.

The first manufacturing industry that Southampton possessed was · a steam sawmill, started in 1853. It is that mentioned in a previous paragraph, where a plan of the village as it was in 1857 is spoken of. Messrs. Lines & Hamilton were the owners. This mill was burnt down. When rebuilt it was operated as a steam grist mill and distillery by William Brady. The mill privilege at the Indian Rapids was taken up by Messrs. Lines & Hamilton in 1852 or '53, and transferred by them in 1854 to Messrs. Dalton & McNabb, of Toronto, who, in.the following year, commenced the construction of a mill race. They also erected and partially enclosed a building intended for a grist mill. In 1856 they sold their rights to the mill privilege and the improvements to John Denny, who in that year cut a road through the bush to the village and moved his, family in. . By the spring of 1857 Mr. Denny had the grist mill in operation. In 1859 the sawmill was completed, and in 1865 the woollen mill was running. The head of water at first was not obtained by a dam thrown across the river, as at present, but by one that from the headgates ascended the river about mid-stream, to a sufficient distance to obtain the required head. Mr. Denny continued to operate these mills for many years, after which he retired to Toronto. This water privilege · was purchased in 1897 by the Saugeen Electric Light and Power Company, and the power developed furnishes electric current for lighting purposes to the town of Southampton and the village of Port Elgin.

The opening paragraphs of this chapter refer to fishing as the initial industry of Southampton. For many years it was also the most prominent, employing many men and a large amount of capital. The importance of this industry is apparent by a return made in 1885, which gives the number of men employed as 70, manning 18 boats, in which and their outfit some $30,000 of capital was invested. The day of the sailing fishboat is passing away, and steam tugs are replacing them. The latest statistics that are available to the author are for the year 1899. There were then engaged in the fishing business of this port five steam fishing tugs and five sailing fishboats. The tugs averaged about 40 tons measurement, and carried crews of five or six men. The outfit of each of these tugs in the way of nets, etc., was worth about $4,000. The outfit of a sailing fishboat was worth from $500 and upwards. The names of the Southampton fishermen indicate that many are of Scotch descent, such as McAulay, McLeod, McKenzie, Murray, Graham, and Logie, while others have names such as Dobson, Chambers, Foster, etc., which show that the Scotch do not have a monopoly of this occupation, involving so many hardships and so many ups and downs of fortune.

A large tannery was built in 1880 by Messrs. Bowman & Zinkan at the outlet of the Little Lake. The village gave the firm in the way of a bonus the site, comprising about six and one-half acres. To enable the corporation to do this a special Act of Parliament was passed.[1] For twenty years this business was the chief manufacturing industry of the village. On July 31st, 1900, a fire broke out and destroyed the greater part of the works, throwing over one hundred men out of employment, and causing a loss that exceeded $100,000. As the tannery was not rebuilt, its destruction was a serious blow to the village, but was not such a crushing blow at that time as it would have been ten years earlier, owing to the establishment in the meantime of the large furniture factories established by the Knechtel family, known as the Knechtel Furniture Company, the S. M Knechtel Chair Company, and the S Knechtel Wood Turning Company, some of which firms have been in operation in the town since 1895.

The loss by fire mentioned in the last paragraph was not the first time the village suffered seriously in that manner. Early in the morning of November 4th, 1886, a fire broke out which proved to be the most disastrous the village ever experienced. It started in the

[1]45 Vic. Chap. 42.

house of J. M. Kelly. The wind being high, it soon spread to the Busby House on the corner of Grosvenor and High Streets. From there it extended eastward, and this so rapidly that in four hours everything for two blocks along High Street was burnt to the ground. Over fifty buildings were consumed, and over thirty families rendered homeless. The loss was estimated at over $60,000, with but a small amount of insurance. Subscriptions for the relief of the sufferers were taken up that amounted to over $8,000, both municipalities and private individuals subscribing liberally. The County Council also remitted the county rates payable by the village 'that year.

There is no doubt that many people were disappointed in the growth and development of Southampton. Many settled there, expecting that in a short time it would become quite a good-sized town. Why the place was held back has been 'attributed to the following reasons: First, the village lots are too large for close settlement, so the people at first were too scattered. Then the lots were largely bought up by speculators, who held them for high prices. Such as these manifested no willingness to put forth effort for the common weal, but each for self, waiting for others to improve their property, that they thereby might receive indirect profit. People came to the village expecting to settle there, but were frozen out by ridiculous prices asked for property. Another reason was that until 1866 the village had hardly any back country to build it up by its trade. A glance at the map shows Southampton to be at the apex of a triangle. These reasons, in part, also account for the development of Port Elgin. The lots there were only one-fifth of an acre in extent, and purchasers had to settle on them. Then the older settlers at Port Elgin came largely from one district, and there existed a community of interest among them. Then the township of Bruce and a great part of Saugeen geographically were tributary to Port Elgin rather than to Southampton. Nevertheless there was no necessity for the second village, and there would not have been one if the result of speculative greed could have been clearly foreseen.

That Southampton might have some back country which could be depended upon to do its trading there, the people of the village, some time in the early sixties, petitioned the government to erect a bridge over the Saugeen River, that thereby the settlers in the townships of Amabel and the north part of Arran might be enabled to reach Southampton. The petition was acquiesced in, and a grant of $4,000 was made. With this grant the bridge known as Denny's bridge was built in 1865. The Southampton tradespeople, however, learned in time that Amabel people crossing at Denny's bridge found the distance to Port Elgin so very little more than Southampton that they were often tempted to go there. This started the agitation to have a bridge built nearer the mouth of the river. At last, in 1889, the present bridge was built, the county contributing $2,000 towards its erection. This bridge, some 430 feet long, is the longest in the county.

. Southampton seemed to take on a new lease of life about ten years ago, and this with a vigor that has been maintained. New blood was circulating, fresh ideas were received in an optimistic spirit, trade increased, handsome residences were erected, granolithic sidewalks laid, an expensive system of waterworks established, a park secured, and the village became a town. This is gratifying to record, but the most satisfactory point is the hopeful feeling possessed by the townspeople This became very apparent in August, 1906, when, although the debenture debt of the town was known to be $59,729, four by-laws were passed by an almost unanimous vote, granting substantial aid toward the establishing or enlarging of manufacturing industries. It is this spirit which has enabled the town to assume as its motto, " Progressive Southampton."

In bringing this volume to a close the author does so with a realization that one topic connected with the County of Bruce has not received the notice it deserves A chapter should have been devoted to Lake Huron, its navigators, its fisheries and fishermen. The story of dire disasters and shipwreck, of heroic efforts to rescue endangered lives, as well as the tales and legends connected with the lake, deserve to be recorded. The author does not feel capable of doing justice to the subject, having for the last twenty years resided at Walkerton, an inland town. He is conscious of having lost touch with those whose daily life is on the bosom of Lake Huron, not to mention missing the inspiration received from gazing on the broad expense of its waters and daily drinking in a sense of its grandeur and beauty. That these last-mentioned features might not be altogether overlooked in this volume, the author would bring his labors to a close by quoting some beautiful lines written by the late Thomas McQueen, and published half a century ago in *The Huron Signal*·

OUR OWN BROAD LAKE

We cannot boast of high, green hills,
  Of proud, bold cliffs where eagles gather,
Of moorland glen and mountain rills,
  That echo to the red-bell'd heather
We cannot boast of mouldering towers,
  Where ivy clasps the hoary turret;
Of chivalry in ladies' bowers,
  Of warlike fame and knight who won it,—
But had we Minstrel's Harp to wake,
We well might boast our own broad lake

And we have streams that run as clear,
  O'er shelvy rocks and pebbles rushing;
And meads as green, and nymphs as dear,
  In rosy beauty sweetly blushing.
And we have trees as tall as towers,
  And older than the feudal mansion;
And banks besprent with gorgeous flowers,
  And glens and woods with fire-flies glancing,—
But prouder, loftier boast we make,
The beauties of our own broad lake.

The lochs and lakes of other lands,
  Like gems, may grace a landscape painting,
Or where the lordly castle stands,
  May lend a charm where charms are wanting.
But ours is deep, and broad, and wide,
  With steamships thro' its waves careering,
And far upon its ample tide
  The bark its devious course is steering,
Whilst hoarse and loud the billows break
On islands on our own broad lake!

Immense, bright lake! I trace in thee
  An emblem of the mighty ocean,
And in thy restless waves I see
  Nature's eternal law of motion;
And fancy sees the Huron Chief
  Of the dim past kneel to implore thee—
With Indian awe he seeks relief,
  In pouring homage out before thee;
And I, too, feel my reverence wake,
As gazing on our own broad lake!

I cannot feel as I have felt,
    When life with hope and fire was teeming,
Nor kneel as I have often knelt,
    At beauty's shrine, devoutly dreaming
Some younger hand must strike the strings
    To tell of Huron's awful grandeur,
Her smooth and moonlight slumberings, ˙
    Her tempest voice loud as thunder ;
Some loftier lyre than mine must wake,
To sing our own broad gleaming lake !

APPENDICES.

INDIAN TREATY RELATING TO THE SURRENDER OF THE SAUGEEN PENINSULA.

We, the Chiefs, Sachems and Principal Men of the Indian Tribes resident at Saugeen, Owen Sound, confiding in the wisdom and protecting care of our Great Mother across the Big Lake, and believing that our Good Father, His Excellency the Earl of Elgin and Kincardine, Governor-General of Canada, is anxiously desirous to promote those interests which will most largely conduce to the welfare of His red children, have now, being in full Council assembled, in presence of the Superintendent General of Indian Affairs, and of the young men of both tribes, agreed that it will be highly desirable for us to make a full and complete surrender unto the Crown of that Peninsula known as the Saugeen and Owen Sound Indian Reserve, subject to certain restrictions and reservations to be hereinafter set forth We have therefore set our marks to this document, after having heard the same read to us, and do hereby surrender the whole of the above named tract of country, bounded on the south by a straight line drawn from the Indian village of Saugeen to the Indian village of Nawash, in continuation of the northern limits of the narrow strip recently surrendered by us to the Crown,[1] and bounded on the north-east and west by Georgian Bay and Lake Huron, with the following reservations, to wit : 1st. For the benefit of the Saugeen Indians we reserve all that block of land bounded on the west by a straight line running due north from the River Saugeen, at the spot where it is entered by a ravine, immediately to the west of the village, and over which a bridge has recently been constructed, to the shore of Lake Huron ; on the south by the aforesaid northern limit of the lately surrendered strip ; on the east by a line drawn from a spot upon the coast at a distance of about (9½) nine miles and a half from the western boundary aforesaid, and running parallel thereto until it touches the aforementioned northern limits of the recently surrendered strip ; and we wish it to be clearly understood that we wish the Peninsula at the mouth of the Saugeen River to the west of the western boundary aforesaid to be laid out in townpark lots and sold for our benefit without delay ; and we also wish it to be understood that our surrender includes

Known as the " Half Mile Strip '

that parcel of land which is in continuation of the strip recently surrendered to the Saugeen River

We do also reserve to ourselves that tract of land called Chief's Point, bounded on the east by a line drawn from a spot half a mile up the Sable River, and continued in a northerly direction to the bay, and upon all other sides by the lake.

2nd We reserve for the benefit of the Owen Sound Indians all that tract bounded on the south by the northern limit of the continuation of the strip recently surrendered ; on the north-west by a line drawn from the north-easterly angle of the aforesaid strip (as it was surrendered in 1851, in a north-easterly direction); on the south-east by the sound extending to the southern limit of the Caughnawaga Settlement ; on the north by a line two miles in length and forming the said southern limit. And we also reserve to ourselves all that tract of land called Cape Crocker, bounded on three sides by Georgian Bay, on the south-west side by a line drawn from the bottom of Nochemowenaing Bay to the mouth of Sucker River, and we include in the aforesaid surrender the parcel of land contained in the continuation to Owen's Sound of the recently surrendered strip aforesaid

3rd We do reserve for the benefit of the Colpoy's Bay Indians, in the presence and with the concurrence of John Beattie, who represents the tribe at this Council, a block of land containing 6,000 acres, and including their village, and bounded on the north by Colpoy's Bay.

All which reserves we hereby retain to ourselves and our children in perpetuity, and it is agreed that the interest of the principal sum arising out of the sale of our lands be regularly paid to them so long as there are Indians left to represent our tribe without diminution at half-yearly periods.

And we hereby request the sanction of our Great Father the Governor-General to this surrender, which we consider highly conducive to our general interests

Done in Council, at Saugeen, this thirteenth day of October, 1854

It is understood that no islands are included in this surrender.

	JOHN (totem) KADUHOEKWUN, [L.S.]
Signed and sealed .	ALEX (totem) MADWAYOSH, [L.S.]
L OLIPHANT,	JOHN (totem) MANEDSWAB, [L.S.]
Supt. Genl. Indian Affairs	JNO THOS. (totem) WAHBUHDICK, [L.S.]
PETER JACOBS,	PETER (totem) JONES, [L.S.]
Missionary	DAVID SAWYER, [L.S.]
	JOHN (totem) JOHNSTON, [L.S.]
	JOHN H. BEATY, [L.S.]
Witnesses	THOMAS (totem) PABAHMOSH, [L.S.]
JAS. ROSS, *M.P P.*,	JOHN (totem) MADWASHEMIND, [L S.]
C. RANKIN, *P.L S ,*	JOHN AUNJEGAHBOWH, [L.S.]
A. MCNABB,	JAMES NEWASH, [L.S.]
Crown Land Agent.	THOMAS (totem) WAHBUHDICK, [L.S.]
	CHARLES KEESHICK. [L.S.]

APPENDIX B.

COPY OF A REPORT OF A COMMITTEE OF THE HONORABLE THE EXECUTIVE COUNCIL, APPROVED BY HIS EXCELLENCY THE GOVERNOR-GENERAL ON THE 27TH SEPTEMBER, 1855

On a memorandum dated 12th instant, from the Superintendent General of Indian Affairs, submitting certain proposed changes, as shown in two certain plans, in the shape of the Indian reserves in the tract commonly called the Saugeen Peninsula, lately surrendered to the Crown, both changes having been assented to by the Indians in Council, and recommending

1st. That the reserve known as the Saugeen Reserve, now bounded on the west by a straight line running due north from the River Saugeen at the spot where it is entered by a ravine immediately to the west of the village, be bounded instead by the Indian path called the Copway Road, which takes a north-westerly direction, as shown by the red line in the plan. This change will give the Saugeen Indians a small increase of frontage on Lake Huron, and will not interfere with the town plot now laid out on the tongue of land contained between that lake and the River Saugeen

2nd. That the south-western boundary of the Cape Crocker Reserve, now formed by a line drawn from the bottom of Nochemowenaing Bay to the mouth of Sucker River, start instead from the south shore of Hope Bay, at a small point about a mile from its head, and strike Lake Huron two miles south of Sucker River, as shown by the plan. This change would cut off from the Indians one mile of frontage on Hope Bay, giving them in compensation two miles extra frontage on the Georgian Bay. The head of Hope Bay has been recommended by Mr. Dennis, the surveyor of the tract, as the site for a town, and the present position of the south-western boundary of the reserve would render it impossible to carry out his suggestion

The Committee recommend that the proposed changes be effected.

Certified

WM H. LEE,
C E C

APPENDIX C.

STATEMENT RELATING TO THE INDIANS ON RESERVES IN THE COUNTY OF BRUCE.

(Taken from Government Reports for the year ending June 30th, 1900.)

	Cape Croker Band.	Saugeen Band	Total.
Number of acres in Reserve	15,586	9,020	
" " " at Chief's Point		1,280	
Number of acres in Hunting Reserve in Township St Edmunds	2,000	1,800	
	17,586	12,100	29,686
Indian Fund—Capital Account	$396,634 55	$311,346 08	$707,980 63
Interest on above for year	14,652 29	12,002 86	26,655 15
" distributed to Band	9,724 59	6,780 47	16,505 06
Amount of pensions	433 75	371 00	804 75
Population by creeds—			
Methodists	241	256	
Roman Catholics	130	30	
Anglican	17	2	
Congregationalists		80	
	388	308	756
Acres of land cultivated or in pasture	1,500	1,020	2,520
" " fenced	600	850	1,450
Value of implements and vehicles	$5,000 00	$3,700 00	$8,700 00
" live stock	8,000 00	3,300 00	11,300 00
" real and personal property	75,500 00	114,752 00	190,252 00
" earnings	15,150 00	19,562 00	34,712 00
Number of Schools and Teachers	3	3	6
Total salaries paid to School Teachers	$900 00	$873 00	$1,773 00
Indian Agents (salary $500 each)	John McIver	J Scoffield	
Indian Chiefs	W. B. McGregor	Thos. Solomon Mandowoab	
" Chiefs' salaries	$200 00	$150 00	
" Secretaries.	Frederick Lamora diere	Henry Ritchie	
" Secretaries' salaries	$250 00	$93 75	
" Physicians' "	500 00	400 00	

Acreage of unsold lands in the Saugeen Peninsula, the proceeds of which, when sold, will increase the Indian Capital Account : Albemarle, 714 acres ; Amabel, 268 acres ; Eastnor, 1,048 acres ; Lindsay, 3,772 acres ; St. Edmunds, 4,267 acres ; Bury townplot, 807 acres ; Harwicke townplot, 1,111 acres , Oliphant townplot, 40 acres ; Southampton, 22 acres ; Wiarton, 25 acres ; Saugeen Fishing Islands, 880 acres ; Cape Hurd Islands, 7,720 acres

APPENDIX D.

COPY OF ORDER-IN-COUNCIL *RE* DURHAM ROAD AND FREE GRANTS.

August 26th, 1848.

IN COUNCIL ·—

His Excellency the Governor-General was pleased to direct the attention of the Executive Council to the subject of colonization settlement of the vacant lands of the Crown in Upper Canada.

By order of His Excellency, and in conformity with the opinion of the Council expressed in various deliberations in the presence of His Excellency, and as further connected with the same subject to a report of the Commissioner of Crown Lands proposing locations for colonization and settlement, His Excellency was pleased to state that proceedings had been taken in the several Departments for the purpose of commencing operations under the proposed plan, and His Excellency was pleased, for the purpose of giving the necessary authority for carrying out the purposes of the Government regarding colonization and settlement in the Wellington District, by and with advice of the Executive Council, to adopt the following order :

It is ordered by the Governor-General, by and with the advice and consent of the Executive Council—

That the tract of Crown Lands in the Huron, Wellington and Simcoe Districts bounded on the south by the Canada Company's lands, on the west by Lake Huron, on the north by the Simcoe District, and on the east by the townships of Maryborough, Peel and Garafraxa, be a locality for disposal and settlement on the plan adopted at the Owen Sound Settlement

It is further ordered that a road be laid out to commence in the unsurveyed lands of the Crown at a point as near the south-east corner of the township of Melancthon as convenient to be carried through Melancthon, Artemesia, Proton and Holland, so as to join the Garafraxa Road as near to the village of Sydenham as possible, and that upon the said Road being explored and laid down to the width of one chain, that two tiers of lots of fifty acres each be laid out on each side of the road.

It is further ordered that a road be laid out through the said tract of the width of one chain to commence on Hurontario Street, to be carried through the southern part of Nottawasaga and through the townships of Osprey, Artemesia and Glenelg to the Owen Sound Road, then across that road through the townships of Bentinck, Brant, Greenock and Kincardine to the mouth of the Penetangore River, on Lake Huron, and that a double line of lots, to contain fifty acres each, be laid out on each side of the said road, and that side lines or roads of the same width be allowed for at convenient distances to connect the front with the roads to be laid out in the rear of these lots.

It is further ordered that a parallel line of road be run on each side of the said two roads above named, of the width of one chain, but the said additional roads are not to be cleared at the expense of the Government

It is further ordered that the two main roads above mentioned be cleared of timber without eradicating the stumps of the trees any further than may, in some cases, be necessary to make the road passable, and that cheap causeways be laid over the swamps and bridges of cheap construction over the streams, so as to make the said roads passable for wheel carriages

It is further ordered that settlers being subjects of the Queen, males, and not under the age of eighteen years, be assigned each a lot of fifty acres. They are to be placed on their respective lots by the agent, and are to have a free grant of the same lots on clearing on the same respectively to the extent of twelve acres, within four years from the first day of January next after their taking possession of the said lots.

The said settlers are to be composed of persons who have the means of maintaining themselves until they can procure a maintenance by cultivating their lots

Upon the abandonment of any lot by a settler, the same is to be open for sale or grant to another.

The settlers receiving grants are to have the privilege of purchasing, in addition to their grants, so as to make up in the whole two hundred acres.

Settlers on parts of the tract not intersected by roads, and not included in the fifty-acre lots laid out for grant, are to have the privilege of purchasing to the extent of two hundred acres each

As it is desirable that there should be straight boundaries in the rear to the lots lying upon the road, and as by reason of deviations caused by the nature of the ground, in seeking a good line of road it may not be practicable to have the road in all cases run in a straight line. The agent should be instructed by the Commissioner of Crown Lands to locate upon lots which, by reason of the deviations aforesaid, shall contain more than fifty acres, persons who are prepared to purchase and pay for the surplus, and in case lots shall by such deviations be made to contain less than fifty acres, and parties shall not be willing to accept the lesser quantity in full of their grants, to locate upon such lots persons who shall be willing and prepared to purchase the surplus over and above fifty acres in two or more lots

It is further ordered, that so soon as it may be practicable, townships be surveyed and established on each side of the lines of road to be laid out, and that in the meantime and in anticipation of such establishment, the agent be instructed to locate persons on the lots laid out and surveyed

It is further ordered that the names of the locatees, with the numbers or designation of their lots, and also the names of the purchasers, be entered in a book to be kept by the agent, and also that a book in the like form be kept in the office of the Commissioner of Crown Lands, to be filled up from monthly returns to be made by the agent, so that the one book may be a duplicate of the other, and that alterations in locations or sales be noticed in each.

It is further ordered that the expenses of surveys, of agency, of clearing and making the aforesaid roads, be paid and charged by the Commissioner of Crown Lands in a separate account, and repaid to him by warrants issued from time to time in his favor.

It is further ordered that the agent be instructed to select a place for his residence, at some convenient place within the said tract where there shall be a site for a town or village, and in the neighborhood of water power, and that he shall erect a dwelling-house and make a clearing of twenty acres at the expense of Government, according to such instructions as has been conveyed to him or as shall be conveyed to him in that behalf by the Commissioner of Crown Lands.

It is further ordered that such portions of the above order as contains information for settlers and purchasers be published by the Commissioner of Crown Lands in such newspapers as he may select

APPENDIX E.

COPY OF HAND-BILLS ANNOUNCING THE OPENING OF THE FREE GRANT LANDS FOR SETTLEMENT.

AGENCY FOR THE SETTLEMENT OF THE CROWN LANDS IN THE WELLINGTON AND HURON DISTRICTS

24th August, 1848

The undersigned agent, appointed by His Excellency the Governor-General for the settlement of the Crown Lands in the townships of Glenelg, Bentinck, Brant, Greenock and Kincardine, in the county of Waterloo, hereby gives notice to all persons willing and having means of locating therein, that his office is temporarily fixed at or near " *Hunter's,*" *on the Garafraxa Road,* where he will receive the application of the settlers, every day of the week between the hours of nine and five o'clock, from the 15th day of September next.

Fifty acres of land will be given to any settler eighteen years old and a subject of Her Majesty, who will present himself, provided with a certificate of probity and sobriety, signed by known and respectable persons and having the means of providing for himself until the produce of his land is sufficient to maintain him. The bearer of that certificate shall mention to the agent (who will keep a registry thereof) his name, age, condition, trade or profession, whether he is married, and, if so, the name and age of his wife, how many children he has, the name and age of each of them, where he is from, whether he has somewhere any property, and in what township he wishes to settle

The conditions of the Location Tickets are To take possession within a month after the date of the ticket, and put in a state of cultivation at least twelve acres of the land in the course of four years ; to build a house and to reside on the lot until the conditions of settlement are duly fulfilled, after which accomplishment only shall the settlers have the right of obtaining a title of property. Families comprising several settlers entitled to lands, preferring to reside on a single lot, will be exempted from the obligation of building and of residence (except upon the lot on which they reside), provided the required clearing of the land is made on each lot. The non-accomplishment of these conditions will cause the immediate loss of the assigned lot of land, which will be sold or given to another

Leave will be granted to those who shall have obtained a lot gratis to purchase three other lots on the road (150 acres), at eight shillings per acre for ready money, so as to complete their two hundred acres in all.

The land intended to be settled is of the very best description and is well timbered and watered.

The roads will be opened on a breadth of 66 feet, and the land on each side will be divided in lots of 50 acres, each to be gratuitously given.

Beside the principal road, there will be others (one on each side of the principal road) marked out on the whole extent of the territory, and on which free locations of 50 acres will be made. But as the Government only intend to meet the expenses of survey on those additional roads the grantees will have to open the road in front of their location.

The most direct route to reach the agency on the Garafraxa Road is by way of Guelph and Elora, in the Wellington District.

GEORGE JACKSON,
Crown Lands Agent.

APPENDIX F.

BY-LAW   To dissolve the Union of Townships comprised within the County of Bruce, and form the same into separate Municipalities.

WHEREAS all the townships within the County of Bruce, one of the United Counties of Huron and Bruce, are at present formed into one Municipality, having the Township of Kincardine as the Senior Township ; and whereas the same is found to be very injurious and inconvenient for the inhabitants of these Townships ; and whereas since the same has been formed into one Municipality, the population within it has greatly increased, entitling the Union to be subdivided into separate Municipalities ; and whereas in terms of numerous petitions from the inhabitants, freeholders and householders of many of the said Townships, signed by at least two-thirds of the same, it is set forth that there are at least one-hundred names of resident freeholders on last year's Collector's Roll, and in others there are over fifty and less than one hundred names of resident freeholders on their respective Collector's Rolls for last year, and that from their position with regard to streams and other natural obstructions, it is very inconvenient to be united to the Township of Kincardine for Municipal purposes ; and whereas, it is expedient by one general By-law to dissolve the present Union of Townships comprised within the County of Bruce, and form them into separate Municipalities.

1. Be it therefore enacted by the Municipal Council of the United Counties of Huron and Bruce by virtue of the powers vested in them by the *Upper Canada Municipal Corporation Acts*, and it is hereby enacted by the authority of the same, that from and after the first day of January, in the year of our Lord one thousand eight hundred and fifty-four, the union of Townships comprised within the County of Bruce shall be dissolved, and the aftermentioned Townships shall be separated from the said Union, and shall from and after that date form separate and distinct Municipalities

2 And be it enacted, that the Township of Huron shall form one Municipality, and that William Gamble, Merchant, shall be the returning officer to hold the first election, the election to be holden at the School House, Pine River, Lake Shore Road

3 And be it enacted, that the Townships of Brant and Carrick, be united for municipal purposes and form one municipality, the Township of Brant to be the senior Township, and that John Eckford be the returning officer to hold the first election, the election to be holden at Mr. Joseph Walker's Tavern, in the Township of Brant

4 And be it enacted, that the Townships of Greenock and Culross be united for Municipal purposes, and form one Municipality, the Township of Greenock to be the senior Township, and that John B Ritchie be the returning officer to hold the first election, the election to be holden at George Cromar s house, No. 30, North Range, Durham Road

5 And be it enacted, that the Townships of Arran and Elderslie be united for Municipal purposes, and form one Municipality, the Township of Arran to be the senior Township, and that Archibald Roy be the returning officer to hold the first election, the election to be holden at the said Archibald Roy's house in the Township of Arran

6 And be it enacted, that the Township of Saugeen be a separate Municipality, and that Alexander McNabb be returning officer to hold the first election, the election to be holden at Belcher's Tavern, Village of Southampton, in the Township of Saugeen

7. And be it enacted, that the Townships of Bruce and Kinloss remain joined to the Township of Kincardine

WILLIAM CHALK,
Warden, Huron and Bruce.

Passed 21st Sept , 1853

D H. RITCHIE, *County Clerk*

APPENDIX G.

REGARDING THE APPOINTMENT OF A LOCAL CROWN LAND AGENT. COPY OF ORDER-IN-COUNCIL PASSED 29TH APRIL, 1851.

"On the Communication of the Honorable the Commissioner of Crown Lands, dated 28th April instant, respecting the appointment of a local Agent for the sale of Crown and School lands in the County of Bruce, who should reside in the Town of Southampton, and which communication is as follows, namely : ' The Commissioner of Crown Lands respectfully suggests to His Excellency the Governor-General in Council, the necessity of appointing a local Agent for the sale of Crown and School lands in the County of Bruce, to reside at the Town of Southampton, at the mouth of the River Saugeen. To this part of the Province public attention has been very generally directed as affording a large field for the settlement of the emigrants and for the rising families of the farmers living in the more populous parts of the Province, and hundreds of persons have gone and settled themselves even before the surveyors have been able to divide the lands into farm lots. Much difficulty is expected to arise unless these lands are offered for sale and settlement at an early day. It would therefore be very desirable at once to appoint a resident agent there, whose duties would be to sell the Crown and School lands in that County, to superintend the making of the two roads already ordered to be opened, and to issue timber licenses on the north shore of Lake Huron and Superior. The undersigned would suggest that Mr. Alex. McNabb be appointed to such agency. Mr. McNabb at present holds the position of Head Book Keeper in the Department of Crown Lands, and is a very efficient officer.'

"The Committee respectfully advise that the proposed agency be established and that should such be your Excellency's pleasure, Mr. McNabb be the Agent, on the conditions specified, and the Committee further advise that the several suggestions of the Commissioner be approved and acted on."

"WILLIAM H. LEE."

APPENDIX H.

CROWN LANDS DEPARTMENT.

Toronto, June 27th, 1851.

Notice is hereby given, that certain Lands (appropriated for School purposes under the Statute 12 Vic. Chap 200) in the Townships of Brant and Kincardine, and in the Villages of Penetangore and Southampton, in the County of Bruce, will be open for sale, upon application to Alexander McNabb, Esquire, on and after the fifth August next

Lists of lots and information as to the terms and conditions of Sale can be obtained at the Office of the Commissioner of Crown Lands ·

The Globe, the *Guelph Advertiser* and the *Huron Signal* will insert the above once a week until the day of Sale

Appearing in *Can. Gazette,* July 19th, 1851, and immediate subsequent issues.

APPENDIX I.

INDIAN DEPARTMENT.

Quebec, July 23rd, 1852.

Public notice is hereby given, that the strip of land situate North of the Townships of Arran and Derby, in the Counties of Grey and Bruce, and extending nearly from Sydenham to Saugeen, having recently been surrendered by the Chippawa Indians of Saugeen and Owen Sound, to Her Majesty the Queen in trust, to be sold for their benefit, and having been surveyed and laid out into Farm Lots, for the purpose of settlement, is now open for sale, excepting Lots, Nos 28, 29, 30, 31, and 32, subject to the condition of a road (now projected) being constructed through the whole length of the tract of such width and in such direction as may be hereafter determined upon Intending purchasers will, on application to John McLean, Esquire, of Guelph, the authorized Agent for the Indian Department, be informed of the price per acre, and terms of payment.

By Command,

R. BRUCE,
Superintendent General

APPENDIX J.

COPY OF ADVERTISEMENT APPEARING IN *THE CANADA GAZETTE,* JULY 31ST, 1852, OFFERING SCHOOL LANDS FOR SALE IN THE COUNTY OF BRUCE.

CROWN LANDS DEPARTMENT.

Quebec, 30th July, 1852.

Notice is hereby given, that the School Lands in the Counties of Bruce, Grey and Huron, are now open for sale to actual settlers on the following terms, viz.: The price to be ten shillings per acre, payable in Ten Annual Instalments, with interest ; the first instalment to be paid upon receiving authority to enter upon the land Actual occupation to be immediate and continuous;[1] the land to be cleared at the rate of five acres annually for every hundred acres during the first five years ; a dwelling-house, at least 18 by 26, to be erected ; the timber to be reserved until the land has been paid for in full and patented, and to be subject to any general timber duty thereafter ; a License of occupation, not assignable without permission to be granted ; the sale and the license of occupation to become null and void in case of neglect or violation of any of the conditions ; the settler to be entitled to obtain a Patent upon complying with all the conditions ; not more than two hundred acres to be sold to any one person on these terms.

First published in *The Canada Gazette*, July 31st, 1852.

All papers in the province to copy for one month.

APPENDIX K.

COPY OF NOTICE APPEARING IN *THE CANADA GAZETTE* OF AUGUST 17TH, 1854, SLIGHTLY ABRIDGED.

CROWN LANDS DEPARTMENT.

Quebec, 17th August, 1854.

Notice is hereby given that the undermentioned lands (set apart for school purposes under Statute 12, Vic. Chap. 200) in the County of Bruce, U. C., will be open for sale to actual settlers, upon application to Alex. McNabb, Esquire, at Southampton, in the Township of Saugeen, on and after the twenty-seventh of next month, on the following terms, viz.: The price to be Ten shillings per acre, payable in Ten equal annual Instalments, with interest : the first instalment to be paid upon receiving authority to enter upon the land. Actual occupation to be immediate and continuous : the land to be cleared at the rate of two acres annually for each hundred acres, during the first five years ; a dwelling house, at least sixteen feet by eighteen, to be erected : the timber to be reserved until the land has been paid for in full and patented, and to be subject to any general timber duty thereafter ; a License of occupation not assignable without permission will be granted : the sale and License of occupation to become null and void in case of neglect or violation of any of the conditions : the settler to be entitled to obtain a Patent upon complying with all the conditions, not more than two hundred acres to be

[1] The following resolution of the United Counties Council, passed June 24th, 1854, makes evident that the conditions mentioned in above advertisement were not in all cases successfully enforced : " That these Counties, in a financial point of view, are suffering serious loss in consequence of parties having got possession of a large portion of the most valuable lands in the County of Bruce, and by means of misstatements, insincere promises to the Crown Lands Agent, and other unfair means, have contrived to evade this wise condition imposed by Statute, namely, *actual and continuous settlement*, and thereby retarding the progress of improvement and its consequent increase of population and industry, which alone is the true source of individual and popular wealth. For this cause, and with a view to the prosperity of these Counties and its consequent most desirable increase of revenue, it is most judicious that the Warden be required to petition (at as early a period as may be) the Governor and Council, praying that such measures may be adopted as will make sure the practical performance of the evident good intentions of the Legislature as displayed in the 5th section of the Act 16 Vic., Chap. 159."

sold to any one person on these terms (What here follows regarding description of lands is condensed from notice as printed)

Township of Bruce—Lake Range, Lots 11-70 and rest of Township surveyed in Concessions.

Township of Kinloss—1 Concession, Lots 1 to 80.

Also : The undermentioned *Crown Lands*. Subject to the same conditions of Actual settlement and terms of payment, at 7s 6d per acre

Township of Carrick—All farm lots therein

Township of Culross—All farm lots therein

Township of Greenock—Lots on second Concession and all North of same.

Township of Kinloss—Lots on 2nd Concession to 12th Concession inclusive, and on Range 3 North and Range 3 South of the Durham Road

---

APPENDIX L

Population of the County of Bruce according to the Census taken in the following years ·

	1850[1]	1852	1861	1871	1881	1891	1901
Townships—							
Albemarle .		...	54	678	1,505	1 819	1,962
Amabel .			182	1,805	3,046	3,890	3,587
Arran ...		149	2,551	3,780	3,512	2,913	2,562
Brant		621	3,125	5,994	5,423	4,929	4,349
Bruce		-100	2,250	3,764	4,236	3,793	3,109
Carrick . .		.	3,163	5,005	5,909	5,503	5,023
Culross . .		..	2,266	3,839	3,807	3,345	2,955
Eastnor		..	.	(b)	1,364 •	1,484	1,830
Eldershe		14	1,774	3,699	3,273	3,047	2,458
Greenock ...		244	1,847	2,981	3,751	3,389	3,085
Huron ...	114	236	2,429	4,079	5,175	4,125	3,539
Kincardine	262	1,149	2,906	4,097	4,506	3,618	2,855
Kinloss		47	1,842	3,430	3,628	2,903	2,355
Lindsay . .		.	.	20	(d)	550	751
St. Edmund					(d)	287	623
Saugeen		277	1,520	2,579	2,090	1,813	1,581
Villages—							
Chesley ..		...	.	.	893	1,437	1,734
Lucknow .					1,162	1,285	1,111
Paisley			.	.	1,154	1,328	1,086
Port Elgin .			...	.	1,400	1,059	1,313
Southampton ...		....	609	858	1,141	1,437	1,636
Tara ...		..			561	695	625
Teeswater .		.	.		861	1,128	930
Tiverton .		.			545	550	470
Towns—							
Kincardine		....	981	1,907	2,876	2,631	2,077
Walkerton .		(a)	(a)	(a)(c)	2,604	3,061	2,971
Wiarton ...					796	1,984	2,443
	376	2,837	27,499	48,515	65,218	64,603	59,020

(a) Included in Brant. (b) Included in Albemarle (c) 995 on Assessment Roll
(d) Included with Eastnor.

[1] From the Assessment Roll, which is incomplete, as Brant and Saugeen are omitted.

APPENDIX M.

Equalized Assessment of the different Townships in the County of Bruce in each of the years from 1851 to 1857 inclusive. Showing the relative development of each during the first years after settlement :

	1851	1852	1853	1854	1855	1856	1857
Kincardine	£13,138	£22,992	£22,727	£37,273	£55,909	£59,027	£83,264
Bruce	61	61	3,792	14,487	14,487	48,385	67,176
Kinloss	375	375	1,170	7,998	9,597	34,050	33,436
Huron	1,051	1,051	7,674	16,248	48,746	57,715	58,261
Brant	5,665	7,554	9,322	17,667	35,335	70,907	79,762
Carrick	Nil.	Nil.	373	9,783	29,350	45,633	59,525
Greenock	1,902	1,902	3,571	8,236	24,708	36,673	44,015
Culross	Nil.	Nil.	Nil.	2,923	8,771	36,787	43,572
Saugeen	2,148	2,864	8,333	34,504	51,756	45,136	63,847
Arran	Nil.	Nil.	4,499	24,351	48,702	55,726	54,833
Elderslie	Nil	Nil.	Nil.	7,037	21,111	44,306	55,775
Total	£24,342	£36,801	£61,461	£180,510	£348,475	£534,348	£643,466

APPENDIX N.

List of places in the County of Bruce which have been before known by various designations, nick-names or otherwise, during their history. These several names may be found in this work.

Present Names	Other names by which the place has been known.
Aberdour	Pipe Clay
Allenford	Drift Wood Crossing
Armow	Reekie's Mills
Balaklava	Glenlyon.
Baie de Dore	Malta and Port Bruce
Burgoyne	West Arran P. O
Cargill	Yokassippi.
Cargill Station	Mickles.
Chesley	Sconeville
Deemerton	Beaford.
Eden Grove	Pinkerton Station.
Greenock P. O	Enniskillen.
Hanover	Buck's Crossing, or Buck's Bridge.
Inverhuron	Sauble town-plot, Little Sauble River.
Invermay	Arran P O.
Kincardine	Penetangore.
Kinloss	Black Horse.
Lurgan	Pine Point
Mildmay	Mernersville.

Present Names	Other names by which the place has been known
North Bruce	The Devil's Elbow.
Paisley	Mud River.
Pine River P. O.	Starvation.
Port Elgin	Normanton.
Ripley	Dingwall.
Riversdale	Mud River.
Southampton	Saugeen. The Mouth.
Stoney Island	Port Head.
Tara	Eblena.
Tobermory	Bury. The Tub. Collins' Harbour.
Vesta	Springvale.
Walkerton	Brant. Rouge's Hollow.
Wiarton	Colpoys.

Names of places in the County of Bruce which were expected to develop into towns, but instead of doing so have faded away :

Adair Town-plot	Township of Albemarle.
Alma	" Huron.
Balaklava	" Carrick.
Greenock Town-plot	" Brant and Greenock.
Hardwick Town-plot	" Eastnor.
Inverhuron	" Bruce.
Lockerby	" Elderslie.
Malta	" Bruce.
Moscow	" Culross.
Oliphant	" Amabel.
Port Bruce	" Bruce.
Port Head, or Stoney Island	" Kincardine.
Scone	" Elderslie.

APPENDIX O.

LAND IMPROVEMENT FUND.

HOW THE GOVERNMENT BROKE FAITH WITH THE SETTLERS.

At a meeting of the special committee appointed by the Legislature, held 2nd December, 1869, to inquire into the merits of the petitions from residents of Bruce, respecting the claims for the continuance of money for local improvement from the Land Improvement Fund, Crown Lands Agent, Alex. McNabb, gave the following evidence :

I was Crown Lands Agent for the County of Bruce from 1851. The county began to settle up in 1854, and it continued settling up rapidly for the subsequent five or six years. The lands, excepting three townships, were school lands—the school lands were not the best lands. We had

several applications from settlers to purchase In the petitions presented
to the House he recognized the hands of many of the original purchasers;
although some of them came in lately and some are assignees of the
original purchasers Messrs Gillies, Brown, Adair, Eckford, Rae and Rowe
were original purchasers.

Mr Blake having read the evidence given by Mr. Adair, Mr. McNabb
referred back to his original instructions. He said when he first went up
he told Mr Price, the commissioner, that roads were essential before they
could open up the country and facilitate settlement. The difficulty arose
how money for that purpose was to be obtained. The question was fully
considered and at length it was decided that a tax or fee of 30s. should
be raised upon every 200 acres sold, and 20s upon every 100 acres in the
township of Brant. A sum of £1,500 was advanced, to be repaid from the
fee fund, and he was instructed to enter into conjunction with Mr. Jackson,
who was then agent in Grey. He took charge of that portion of the road
from the Durham Road to the village of Paisley. He then took charge of
the balance of the road to the Saugeen River. This forms part of the
Elora Road Another road was opened with the assistance of Mr. Jackson.
In August, 1852, he received instructions to stay all sales. In September,
1852, he received instructions to open sales in certain townships The only
further instructions he received were in 1857, to keep the returns of each
township separate under Crown, Clergy, and School Reserves. The roads
referred to were completed at an expenditure of £1,800—an additional
£300 having been sanctioned by Mr. Rolfe, the commissioner who succeeded Mr. Price. Mr. McNabb had received a private letter from Mr.
M Cameron in 1852, which had been mislaid. It was private, but he
thought it was intended to inform the settlers It referred to the passage
of a Land Act and contained an intimation that the price of land would
be reduced and to allow a payment of 2s. 6d. out of purchase money for
the purpose of creating a fund to effect improvements. He knew of the
passage of the Act in 1853 and was aware of the clause with reference to
the Improvement Fund. Beyond the letter referred to he had had no
intimation from the Government In his own mind he considered that the
money would go towards opening up new roads and repairing those
already constructed Shortly after Mr. David Gibson, Government Superintendent of Colonization Roads, came to the county with reference to the
opening up of roads

Mr Richards objected to this evidence, but if the committee intended
to allow everything to be given in evidence he should say no more.

Mr. McNabb had frequent conversations with Mr. Gibson, who led him
to believe that the road would be opened up through the county and paid
for through that fund

Mr. McNabb, in selling lands, alluded to this whenever the subject
came up, which it frequently did He then explained the object of the
fund—that in consequence of the Land Act of the Legislature of 1853, the
Government had power to appropriate towards opening roads in the county
one-fourth of the proceeds of the purchase of school lands and one-fifth of
the crown lands He did not tell them that the government would
appropriate it, but that the Government had power to appropriate it. Subsequently Mr. McNabb said that he had told settlers that they would have

the benefit of that fund—that is, that the county would have the benefit of it. He did state to them that although the price of the land was 10s. it was virtually only 7s 6d, because there would be 2s 6d. expended in roads and bridges which they would otherwise have to pay themselves. That was his own honest belief, and in proof Mr. Gibson was sent up to complete the roads. The subject of the backwardness of the roads was constantly mentioned as an obstacle to settlement by intending settlers When this occurred he always referred to the Act of Parliament, and to Mr Gibson being in the county laying out the roads He thought the opening of the roads facilitated settlement He did not know that his statements had any such influence It may have had such influence, but he could not say. He mentioned it to show that the settlers would have good roads Some settlers came to him and went away without settling; but it was a subject of complaint He had complained of it himself He had sold to Mr. Adair, but did not recollect the conversation he had with him. Mr. Adair's evidence was read to Mr McNabb, who said he had no doubt it was true if Mr Adair said so, but he had no recollection He had had thousands of sales, and it was impossible to recollect the conversation he had with all of the applicants He did not remember any of the conversation, but such was his respect for Mr Sinclair and the others who had given evidence, that he could not question them All intending purchasers seemed much interested in the fund He always led them to believe that one-fourth or one-fifth of the proceeds was the amount to be returned, and Mr Gibson frequently had conversations in the same strain He was quite satisfied in his own mind that the settlers would get the benefit of this money, and he spoke of it as strongly as he felt himself He had thrown his lot in among them and felt a common interest. The opinion generally prevailed among the settlers that they would have this fourth or fifth There was no doubt entertained whatever. The bulk of the settlement of the county did not, in his opinion, take place upon the strength of his assurance. He could not have had conversations with so many people. He was also agent of the bank. It was all one office The same conversations were held there when people came to pay their deposits He felt that when the clause was omitted in the Act of 1859 it was a breach of faith He thought the Government had been pledged, and that was also the impression of the settlers The settlers never gave up the hope that justice would be done them by the restoration of the fund He remembered an election address signed by Malcolm Cameron in 1854 referring to the fact of their having obtained a Land Act which reduced the price of land to 10s, and gave a fourth to public improvements. He could give no other information about the other counties. He considered the Land Act of 1853 to be a general Act for the province.

REPORT OF THE COMMITTEE

The following report of the Land Improvement Fund Committee was presented to the House :

The Committee have held many meetings and examined numerous witnesses and papers, and carefully considered the matters referred to them, and they find unanimously .

1. That on the 7th of July, 1852, the Government of the day passed an Order in Council in the following words: Upon the memorandum submitted by the Commissioner of Crown Lands relative to the School Fund in the counties of Grey and Bruce, the Committee of Council recommend that the reduction in price from 12s. 6d. to 10s. an acre, as suggested, be approved, and that the regulations laid down in said report be approved, and further, that a measure be submitted to Parliament to authorize the expenditure of a sum equal to 2s. 6d. per acre of the purchase money on the improvement of the roads and harbors within the said counties, and the Committee further recommend that not more than 200 acres be sold to any one individual except upon special recommendation of the Commissioner of Crown Lands, approved by His Excellency in Council.

2. That by the Land Act of 1853 it was enacted that it should be lawful for the Governor in Council to reserve out of the proceeds of the School Lands in any county a sum not exceeding one-fourth of such proceeds as a fund for public improvements within the county, to be expended under the direction of the Governor in Council, and also to reserve out of the proceeds of unappropriated Crown Lands in any county a sum not exceeding one-fifth as a fund for public improvements within the county to be expended under the direction of the Governor in Council.

3. That at this period there were large tracts of Crown and School Lands in various counties settled; and it was the policy of the country to encourage the settlement thereof as much as possible.

4. That one of the greatest obstacles to settlement was the want of roads and bridges, and it was in order to induce the speedy settlement of the country by providing means for the construction of such works that the said Order and Act were passed.

5. That shortly after the passing of the said Act large numbers of persons purchased and settled on the vacant Crown and School lands, and within a very few years they were well settled, four-fifths of the School lands having been settled in 1853, 1854 and 1855.

6. That the general belief and opinion of the settlers was, that they would be entitled to have one-fourth of the price of School lands, and one-fifth of the price of Crown lands, expended within the municipalities, on the construction of roads and bridges.

7. That this belief and opinion was entertained by several of the Crown Land Agents who sold the lands.

8. That several of such agents stated to the intending settlers, that if they became settlers, one-fourth of the price of School lands, and one-fifth of the price of Crown lands, would be expended as aforesaid, and that thus the price of their lands was practically less than the stated price by these amounts, which would otherwise have to be raised by local taxation for the same purposes.

9. That large numbers of settlers purchased on the understanding with the agents stated in the preceding paragraph, especially in the county of Bruce, where the population increased from 2,837 in 1852, to 27,494 in 1861.

10. That the Government of the day, in an Order in Council, dated on the 27th February, A.D. 1855, referred to the Improvement Fund as being established by the Land Act of 1853, and ordered certain expenditure

thereon, and in another Order in Council, dated on the 27th of March, A.D. 1855, further assumed the existence and availability of the Fund.

11. That on the 11th December, 1855, the Government of the day, in an Order in Council, referred to the said Fund in the words following . " The Minister of Agriculture also brings under your Excellency's notice that numerous applications have been made for aid from the Improvement Fund, created by the 14th section of the Land Act, 16th Vic. Chap 159, which authorizes one-fourth of the proceeds of the sale of School lands, and one-fifth of those of Crown lands, to be expended in the several counties in which the sales are affected.

" That none of this Fund has as yet been set apart from the sales hitherto made, although an Order in Council has been passed for the expenditure of £25,000 thereon That it appears requisite that the Crown Lands Department should be directed to apprise the Inspector General of the amount at the credit of each county for proceeds of sale of both Crown and School lands so that the proportions accruing to the Improvement Fund may be set apart by the Receiver General for that purpose. Out of the Improvement Fund referred to he recommends that the following sums be appropriated to the objects hereafter stated, viz (Stating several applications)."

12. That on the 28th day of July, A.D. 1856, the Government of the day passed an Order in Council in the following words In reference to the Fund for Public Improvement formed under the 14th Section of the Act 16 Vic Chap. 59, the Committee recommend that the funds derived from the sale of lands in each particular township or other municipality, and applicable to the purposes of the Fund, and not already apportioned, be applied to the making, maintaining, altering or improving the roads or bridges in each of those townships or other municipalities respectively, and be for this purpose distributed and disposed of, by and through the Municipal Council of each such township or other municipality, each such Council to report to the Bureau of Agriculture the manner of expenditure of all such moneys, on the 1st days of January and July in each year, and at any intermediate time within ten days after having been called upon so to do by that Department.

13. That on several occasions during the years 1857, 1858, 1859 and 1860, the Government of the day, by Orders in Council, appropriated to purposes of local improvement moneys arising out of the Improvement Fund

14. That books were opened in the Crown Lands Department, labelled " Road Improvement Fund," with a heading to each page in the words, " Statements of the amount available for public improvements on sales of Crown lands, under 16 Vic Chap 159, Sec. 14, in each township in the county of ———," in which books the accounts of the fund were kept

15. That on the 6th March, A.D. 1861, the Government of the day made an Order in Council in the following words : " On the recommendation of the Honorable the Commissioner of Crown Lands, the Committee advise that the Order in Council of 7th December, 1855, authorizing the payment of the Improvement Fund created by the Land Act, 16 Vic Chap. 159, be rescinded " But no order has been made rescinding that of 28th July, 1856.

16 That no part of the Improvement Fund accruing since the 6th March, 1861, has been applied to the purposes of the Fund.

17. That large sums of money have, since 6th March, 1861, been received by the Government of the late Province of Canada from sales of Crown and School Lands, made between the date of the passing of the Land Act and the 6th March, 1861.

18. That further large sums have been received on account of such sales by the Government of Ontario, and further large sums remain due on account of such sales.

19. That large sums have been expended and large debts incurred by the various municipalities for the construction of roads and which would otherwise have been in whole or part conducted by means of the Improvement Fund.

20. The Committee beg leave, lastly, to report that they abstain from stating any opinion or making any recommendation, because they understood the order of reference to confine them to the ascertainment of the facts for the information of the Legislature.

That an idea be had of the amount derived from the Land Improvement Fund, the following figures are given, showing amounts available to various municipalities for the period from 31st December, 1859, to 6th March, 1861:

	Crown Lands.	School Lands.
Kincardine Township	$57 54	$1,829 20
Arran Township		2,624 81
Brant Township	21 76	2,499 79
Bruce Township		1,227 31
Carrick Township	901 73	
Culross Township	1,303 03	
Elderslie Township		1,385 51
Greenock Township	834 97	
Huron Township		1,764 75
Kinloss Township	901 81	277 31
Saugeen Township		1,159 02
Penetangore Town		63 57
Southampton Town	10 08	163 27
Paisley Town	171 14	217 74
Inverhuron Town		213 50
	$4,202 06	$13,425 78
		4,202 06
Total, less 6 per cent. of School Lands		$17,627 84

The loss to the several municipalities arising from the action of the Government in withholding payments, was the amount due to each from collections made from March 6th, 1861, to July 1st, 1867. Payments were made to the various municipalities of the principal and interest, compounded at 5 per cent., under 45 Vic. Chap. 3-49 Vic. Chap. 6. and 54 Vic. Chap. 9. In 1886 $31,889.69 was so paid to municipalities in Bruce on account of interest.

APPENDIX P.

REPORT OF COMMITTEE ON THE DESTITUTION EXISTING IN THE COUNTY OF BRUCE IN 1859.

The Committee on the destitution existing in the County of Bruce, consisting of Messrs. Fraser, Gillies, Brown, Gunn, and Brocklebank, having duly considered the lamentable state of the county, and having consulted the Crown Land Agent and others, beg most respectfully to report :

That they find that the deficiency in breadstuffs in this county prevail to a most serious and alarming extent

That this deficiency arises directly from causes beyond human control.

That your Committee have too good reason to believe that a very large portion of the prevailing destitution requires immediate relief, and that, in many cases, no time can with safety be lost.

Your Committee are of opinion that the most desirable and feasible mode of relieving this distress, will be, by passing By-laws in the suffering Townships, authorizing the issue of Debentures payable in five years, unless the Government is willing to advance the whole sum from the Improvement Fund without the issue of Debentures, in the following proportion, namely   Bruce, £1,000 ; Kincardine, £1,000; Huron, £1,000 ; Elderslie, £600 ; Kinloss, £500 ; Carrick, £500 ; Culross, £500 , Greenock, £500 ; Southampton, £500 ; Kincardine Village, £500 ; Saugeen, £500 ; Arran, £500 , and Brant, £500 ; mortgaging the Improvement Fund for the final payment of such Debentures. That such sum of money so raised shall be expended in opening up leading lines of roads in the respective municipalities, such work to be given out in small contracts to the needy and destitute, and to be paid for only in grain or flour, to be purchased by the municipalities, stored up in convenient localities, and distributed under their jurisdiction

That the principal leading roads through the several municipalities calculated to benefit the greatest number, be opened and improved.

Your Committee strongly recommend that this Council do petition Government in reference to this matter, authorizing the Provisional Warden to proceed to Toronto forthwith, in order to lay before Government and Parliament, if necessary, the state of affairs in this county, and to endeavor to obtain a sum of money in advance of whichever scheme may be adopted by Government for the relief of immediate distress, such sum, if received, to be handed over to the suffering Townships in proportion to the sums set down after each. Your Committee further beg to recommend that each Reeve shall, in his own Township, inculcate the absolute necessity of strict moderation and prudent management on the part of the people, as well in regard to unnecessary indulgences, as in reference to their general habit of living

All of which is respectfully submitted.

WILLIAM GUNN,
Chairman.

Committee Room, 5th Feb , 1859.
19

APPENDIX .Q.

NAMES AND RESIDENCE OF THE WARDENS OF THE COUNTY OF BRUCE, DOWN TO 1906.

Name	Year or Years of Office	Residence.
George Cromar	1857	Greenock.
John Purvis	1858, 1861	Kinloss.
John Valentine	1859	Greenock
John Bruce	1860	Brant.
J. T. Conaway	1862	Southampton.
John Gillies	1863, 1869, 1870, '71, '72	Elderslie.
James Brocklebank	1864, '65, '66, '67, '68	Brant
Robert Baird	1873, '74, '75, '76, '77, '78, '79	Kincardine town.
Robert Purves	1880, '81, '82	Kinloss
James Tolton	1883	Brant.
John Pierson	1884	Saugeen.
H T. Potts	1885	Arran
W S. Johnston	1886	Port Elgin
William Dickison	1887	Carrick
William Scott	1888	Culross
John Douglass	1889	Tara
James Gaunt	1890	Kinloss
J S McDonald	1891	Huron.
Thomas Bradley, M.D.	1892	Kincardine Township.
James Bryan	1893	Lucknow.
J H. Scott	1894	Kincardine town.
Wm. MacKintosh	1895	Arran
J H Elliot	1896	Chesley.
James Shouldice	1897	Elderslie.
L T Bland	1898	Kincardine Township
D M. Jermyn	1899	Wiarton.
P. Cummings	1900	Saugeen.
Benj. Cannon	1901	Brant.
J. J Donnelly	1902	Greenock.
Robert Watt	1903	Wiarton.
John McCharles	1904	Huron.
Wm McDonald	1905	Chesley.
A. W. Robb	1906	Walkerton

APPENDIX R.

RESULT OF VOTING ON THE SEVERAL OCCASIONS WHEN THE TEMPERANCE QUESTION HAS BEEN SUBMITTED TO THE ELECTORS OF BRUCE

	Voters on each Side	Majority	Total No of Votes Polled	Total No. Voters.
1877, Sept. 18.				
Dunkin Act		. . .	6,352	.. ...
For the Act . . .	3,747	1,142		... .
Against Act .	2,605	.		.. .
1879, Jan. 21.				
To repeal Dunkin Act.	.	......	1,679	
For the Act . ..	167	..		
Against Act	1,512	1,345	.	.
1884, Oct. 30.				
Scott Act .	.	.	7,690	..
For the Act	4,499	1,321		... .
Against Act .. .	3,178	....	. ....	. .
1888, March 2.				
Scott Act . . .	. ..		8,738	. .
For the Act.	3,673	..		....
Against Act .	5,065	1,392		...
1894, Jan. 1.				
Provincial Prohibition				
Plebiscite ..	..		10,033	15,848
For	6,884	3,735	.	.. ..
Against .	3,149	....	...	.. ..
1898, Sept. 29				
Dominion Prohibition				
Plebiscite	...	. .	7,559	16,423
For . .	4,862	2,165	. ..	
Against	2,697	.	..	
1902, Dec. 4				
Provincial Referendum				
in favor of putting				
in force the "Liquor				
Act of 1902" (prac-				
tically Prohibition)	. .	......	8,902	. . .
For . .	6,357	3,812	.	
Against . .	2,545	. .	...	.

APPENDIX S.

The following list contains the names of all members of the Independent Companies, (the Companies of which the 32nd Bruce Battalion was composed upon its organization on the 14th September, 1866), to whom has been awarded the Canadian General Service Medal for services rendered in the suppression of the Fenian Raid of 1866.

The 32nd Battalion was not called out on active service in 1870 and no medal, therefore, has been awarded for that year.

George Simpson.
Malcolm McGillivray
John A. Darling
Joseph Blakeway.
Samuel Nowry.
John Nowry.
Martin Schroeder.
Robert Dewstow.
Alex McDowell
Thomas Bailey
William S Scott
Angus Munn
Thomas Burgess
Alex. McNabb
Donald Currie.
Richard Tranter
Josiah Tranter.
William Tranter
John McTaggart
John Pierson.
James Johns
Donald Robertson.
James Scott.
Thomas Fortune.
Alex. E Belcher.
Chris F. Forest.
Chris Parker.
John Robertson.
John Johns
John Fortune.
Wm. J. McMenemy.
Chris R. Barker.
John Boal
James Burns.
Richard Collins.

William Fanning
Francis Graham
John Guest.
Robert Hunter.
William Johnston.
John H Kean.
James McCue.
Thomas McCue
Thomas McGinnis.
Wm. M. McKibbin.
*Samuel McLean.
Peter McPherson
Malcolm Ross
Francis Sellery.
John Sellery.
Henry Stanley.
Thomas Wilson
Joseph Harrison
George Green.
William Boyd.
William Brown.
Henry Collins
Robert Donnelly.
John R Kay.
Alex. Wright
Edward Colwell.
Daniel Gossell.
John Miller.
John King.
William Thompson.
John C. Byers.
George Elliott.
David Shanks.
John J Walker.
Thomas Levins.

William Hall.
Henry Hall.
Levi Walker.
Robert Arnill
James Bartley.
Edward Bowles.
Edward Collins
Edmund Collins.
Thomas Collins.
James Daniel.
William Daniel.
William C. Davie.
Gideon Doupe.
James Fair.
James Hay.
William Hunter.
Robert Irving
John Jolliffe.
Thomas Kidd
John Magill
John Merritt.
John D. Merryfield.
John Millar
William Mitchell.
Vincent Mosser.
Murdock Mackenzie.
Alex. McLean.
David Ogg.
John Parker.
William Sparrow.
Hugh Steele.
Samuel Steele.
William Tully.
Elijah Welsford.
James D. Wilkie.

Lachlan Boyd.	Henry R Collins	Thomas Morrison
David Kay.	Matthew Darling.	Pascho Saunders.
Jasper Lillie	Richard Kidd	Hugh Campbell
Alex Moffat.	Mounty Mick.	Cyrus Barnum
John Robinson	Andrew Millar.	Peter Larose.
Thomas Foster.	Duncan Mackenzie	William H Daniel.
Thomas Atchison.	Samuel B Osborne.	James Millar.
John Brown.	James G. Cooper.	John P. Quinn

Among other residents in the County who received Fenian Raid medals for service in other corps than the 32nd Battalion are : Thomas Dixon, H. P. O'Connor (deceased), David Traill, John Henderson, W. A. McLean (deceased), W. A. Green (deceased), and Norman Robertson

The following list contains the names of all members of the 32nd Regiment who have been awarded the Colonial Auxiliary Forces officers' Decoration or Long Service Medal respectively, and whose decorations or medals have been engraved '' 32nd Reg't.''

There are, probably, others who have been awarded the distinction, who counted time served in the 32nd Regiment towards the necessary qualifying of twenty years, but whose last service was performed in some other corps.

C A. F. OFFICERS' DECORATION.

Lieut.-Colonel J. H. Scott.
Surgeon-Major De W. H Martyn.
P. M. and Hon.-Major J. Henderson
Captain J. Douglas
Lieut C. A. Richards

C. A. F. LONG SERVICE MEDAL.

P M and Hon.-Major A. B. Klein
Q M and Hon.-Major D Robertson
Captain T Mitchell
Q M. Sergeant J. A. Hogg.
Bandmaster D. Fisher.
Sergeant C Hurford.
Sergeant H D Wettlaufer.
Private D. Bell.

APPENDIX T.

LIST OF DEBENTURES ISSUED AT VARIOUS TIMES BY THE COUNTY OF BRUCE

Date of Issue	Object of Debentures Issued.	Amount	Total.
1859—Feb. 1.	Relief—1st issue	$17,200	
1859—June 2.	Relief—2nd issue	16,800	
	Total for relief of destitution .		$34,000
1859—July 19.	County buildings—1st issue ...	$24,000	
1866—June 28.	County buildings—2nd issue .. .	20,000	
	Total for county buildings....		$44,000
1865—Oct. 5	Gravel roads—1st issue	$220,000	
1867—Dec 2	Gravel roads—2nd issue	20,000	
1868—June 27	Gravel roads—3rd issue . .	20,000	
1869—June 8.	Gravel roads—4th issue	20,000	
	Total for gravel roads ,.... .		$280,000
1869—Dec 7	Bonus to Wellington, Grey & Bruce Railway		$250,000
1872—Jan 10	Bonus to Southern Extension Railway[1] .		51,000
1885—Jan 11.	To meet debentures maturing . ..		20,000
1898—Oct 17	To erect and furnish House of Refuge . .		20,000
1903—Oct 11.	To rebuild McCalder's bridge		10,000
			$709,000

[1] These debentures were only guaranteed by the county, being paid by a sectional levy on the municipalities of Huron and Kincardine townships and Lucknow and Tiverton villages.

APPENDIX U.

COUNTY COUNCIL DIVISIONS OF THE COUNTY OF BRUCE
REPORT OF COMMISSIONERS

To His Honor the Lieutenant Governor in Council :

We the undersigned Commissioners appointed under " The County Council Act, 1896," by the Lieutenant Governor in Council, to divide the County of Bruce into County Council Divisions, report that having duly heard and considered all the evidence adduced before us, and having had due regard to the provisions of the said Act, we have divided the said County into nine County Council Divisions for the purposes of the said Act, as follows :

1 The First County Council Division to consist of the Townships of Albemarle, Eastnor, Lindsay, Bury St. Edmunds, and polling sub-division number five of the township of Amabel and the town of Wiarton

2. The Second Division to consist of the Township of Amabel, except polling sub-division number five, the Township of Arran and the Village of Tara

3. The Third Division to consist of the Township of Elderslie, polling sub-division number five of the Township of Greenock, and the Villages of Chesley and Paisley.

4 The Fourth Division to consist of the Township of Brant and the Town of Walkerton.

5. The Fifth Division to consist of the Townships of Carrick and polling sub-division number six of the Township of Culross

6. The Sixth Division to consist of the Township of Culross, except polling sub-division number six, and the Township of Greenock, except polling sub-division number five, and of the village of Teeswater

7. The Seventh Division to consist of the Townships of Huron and Kinloss and the Village of Lucknow

8 The Eighth Division to consist of the Town of Kincardine, the Township of Kincardine and the Village of Tiverton.

9 The Ninth Division to consist of the Townships of Bruce and Saugeen and the Villages of Port Elgin and Southampton

All of which is respectfully submitted.

Dated at the Town of Walkerton, in the said County of Bruce, the first day of July, A.D. 1896.

S. J. JONES,
JOHN CREASOR,
Commissioners.

APPENDIX V.

COPY OF THE ADVERTISEMENT OF THE LAND SALE AT OWEN SOUND, SEPTEMBER 2ND, 1856.

INDIAN LANDS SALE AT OWEN SOUND.

At Sydenham (Owen Sound), on Tuesday, the 2nd September next, and following days, at 10 o'clock a m., will be sold at public auction about 144,800 acres of Wild Land, consisting of the Townships of Keppel and Amabel, and the Town Plot of Southampton on the North side of the Saugeen River, being composed of the Southerly portion of the Saugeen Peninsula, adjoining the Townships of Arran and Derby.

The farm lands wil be put up to sale in lots or parcels of nearly 100 acres without any conditions of settlement duty excepting those fronting on the line of road laid out from Sydenham to the Fishing Islands, and the new line of road from Sydenham to Saugeen on these the Department will impose a condition that the purchaser shall, within one year after the date of purchase, cut and remove all the Timber from the centre of the road to the depth of ninety feet.

The valuable property within the Township of Amabel known' as the Falls or Mill Privilege, situated on the River Au Sable, comprising an area of 1,100 acres, will be sold in one block.

The Town and Park Lots in Saugeen will also be put up to sale at the same time

The terms will be one-third of the whole purchase price in cash at the time of sale, and the balance to be paid in six equal annual instalments, with interest at 6 per cent per annum.

The Department reserves to itself the power to attach to any lot, at the time of sale, the obligation on the part of the purchaser to pay for any improvements which may have been made on such lot by squatters. The fact that such improvements had been made before the date of this advertisement must be proved to the satisfaction of the Department before the 15th August next.

An Agent or person to conduct the sale will be in attendance at Owen Sound from and after the 20th August for the purpose of affording to intending purchasers such information as may be required.

R. T. PENNEFATHER,
Superintendent General.

Indian Department, Toronto, 18th July, 1856.

INDEX.

Somerville, James, 475.
Southampton, Town of : Surveys, 7,
16, 508 ; first settlers, 27, 508,
509 ; as it was in 1852, 510 ; incorporated, 84, 511 ; town hall,
512 ; harbor, 513 ; school, 515 ;
Presbyterian Church, 516 ; Methodist Church, 515 ; Church of England, 517 ; Newspapers, 518 ; industries, 518, 519 ; fishermen, 519 ;
development, why delayed, 520 ;
bridges, 521 ; big fire, 519 ; becomes a town, 512.
Spence, Captain John, 27, 56, 490,
508.
Sproat, Alex : Mayor of Walkerton,
304 ; as lieut.-colonel, 186, 190,
192 ; county treasurer, 100, 117,
135 ; banker, 511 ; as M.P., 105,
112, 311.
"Starvation Year," 85 seq., 494, 545.
Stauffer, J. Eli, 48, 467, 470, 472, 475.
Steinmiller & Son, Jacob, 342.
Stewart, Dr. J. M., 154, 377.
Stoney Island, 435 ; great storm
wrecks storehouses, 436.
Stringer, Rt. Rev. I. O., Bishop of
Selkirk, 438.
St. Edmunds, Township of : Surveys,
16, 74 ; first settlers, 256 ; lumber-
ing, 259 ; first school, 259 ; a sep-
arate municipality, 259.
Surveys : Amabel, 16, 74 ; Albe-
marle, 16, 74 ; Arran, 16, 50 ;
Brant, 15, 48 ; Bruce, 16, 50 ; Car-
rick, 16, 58, 336 ; Culross, 16, 58 ;
Eastnor, 16, 74 ; Elderslie, 16, 50 ;
Greenock, 16, 58 ; Huron, 11, 16,
50 ; Kincardine, 15, 48 ; Kinloss,
11, 16, 58 ; Lindsay, 16, 74 ; Sau-
geen, 16, 50 ; St. Edmunds, 16, 74 ;
Half Mile Strip, 12 ; Fishing
Islands, 16 ; Durham Road, 13 ;
Elora Road, 15, 48, 335 ; geological,
20 ; by A. Wilkinson, 11 ; by A. P.
Brough, 13, 18, 50, 335 ; by Charles
Rankin, 7, 12, 50 ; Adair, 234 ;
Alma, 423 ; Chesley, 375, 382 ;
Inverhuron, 322 ; Invermay, 271,
272 ; Kincardine (town), 15, 445 ;
Lucknow, 475, 476 ; Malta, 323 ;
Oliphant, 215 ; Paisley, 16 ; Port
Bruce, 323 ; Port Elgin, 497 ; Port
Head, 435 ; Riversdale, 408 ;
Stokes Bay, 248 ; Southampton, 7,
16 ; Tara, 275 ; Teeswater, 354 ;
Tiverton, 331, 332 ; Walkerton,
301, 132 ; Wiarton, 16.
Sutton, William : First mill, 62 ;
sheriff, 105 ; dismissed, 138 ; sur-

veys, 445 ; biographical sketch,
446 ; grist mill, 446.

Tara, Village of : As Eblana, 276 ;
surveys, 275 ; becomes incorporated, 125, 276 ; churches, 276 ;
Leader, 277.
Teeswater River, 14 ; to deepen, 352.
Teeswater, Village of : Postoffice,
348 ; surveyed, 354 ; earliest settlers, 354 ; incorporated, 355 ;
debentures, 356 ; schools, 356 ;
churches, 357 ; News, 361.
Thomson W. R., 360.
Timber dues, 200 ; licenses cancelled,
201.
Tiverton, Village of : Baptist Church,
329, 330 ; Presbyterian Church,
329 ; incorporated, 330 ; reeves,
331 ; first settlers, 331, 332 ; survey, 331.
Tolmic, John, 139, 141, 158.
Tolton, James, 15, 141, 546.
Traill, David, 549.
Treaties, Indian, 3, 5, 6, 69, 525, 527.
Truax, R. E., 136, 137, 139, 148, 154,
157, 300, 411.

Underwood, Village of, 324.
Urquhart, John, mail carrier, 318,
498.

Valentine, John, 45, 62, 91, 179, 297,
385, 386, 387, 402 ; sketch of, 404,
405, 546.
Valuation of the county, 123, 136,
151.
Vanstone, Richard, 134.
Volunteers : N. W. Rebellion, ordered
out, 132 ; first company, 180 ;
other companies, 179, 181 ; at
Goderich, 184 ; 32nd Battalion
formed, 186 ; colors presented,
187 ; General Luard reports, 189 ;
commanding officers of 32nd, 192 ;
Red River Expedition, 188 ; Fenian
Raid, 1866, 183 ; recipients of
medals, 548 ; county grants, 185,
189.

Walden, David, 30, 417.
Walker, Francis (Paddy), elected
reeve, 43, 52, 445.
Walker, Joseph, 294 ; erects dam
and saw mill, 297 ; grist mill, 298.
Walkerton, Town of : Becomes a
town, 14, 302 ; first settlers, 294 ;
first survey, 301 ; post-office called
Brant, 297 ; first store, 297 ; industries, 299 ; binder twine com-

CPSIA information can be obtained
at www.ICGtesting.com
Printed in the USA
LVHW04s2320250418
574947LV00003B/17/P

9 781362 745105